Study Guide

for use with

Economics

Sixth Edition

David Colander
Middlebury College

Prepared by
David Colander
Middlebury College

Douglas Copeland
Johnson County Community College

Jenifer Gamber

Boston   Burr Ridge, IL   Dubuque, IA   Madison, WI   New York   San Francisco   St. Louis
Bangkok   Bogotá   Caracas   Kuala Lumpur   Lisbon   London   Madrid   Mexico City
Milan   Montreal   New Delhi   Santiago   Seoul   Singapore   Sydney   Taipei   Toronto

Study Guide for use with
ECONOMICS
David Colander

Published by McGraw-Hill/Irwin, an imprint of The McGraw-Hill Companies, Inc., 1221 Avenue of the Americas, New York, NY 10020. Copyright © 2006 by The McGraw-Hill Companies, Inc. All rights reserved.

1 2 3 4 5 6 7 8 9 0 PTS/PTS 0 9 8 7 6 5

ISBN 0-07-302686-7

www.mhhe.com

The McGraw-Hill Companies

Contents

Preface

We wrote this study guide to help you do well in your economics courses. We know that even using a great book such as the Colander textbook, studying is not all fun. The reality is: most studying is hard work and a study guide won t change that. Your text and lectures will give you the foundation for doing well. So the first advice we will give you is:

1. Read the textbook.
2. Attend class.

We cannot emphasize that enough. Working through the study guide will not replace the text or lectures; this study guide is designed to help you retain the knowledge from the text and classroom by practicing the tools of economics. It is not an alternative to the book and class; it is **in addition to them**.

Having said that, we should point out that buying this guide isn t enough. You have to *use* it. Really, if it sits on your desk, or even under your pillow, it won t do you any good. Osmosis only works with plants. This study guide should be well worn by the end of the semester   dog-eared pages, scribbles beneath questions, some pages even torn out. It should look used.

WHAT CAN YOU EXPECT FROM THIS BOOK?

This study guide concentrates on the terminology and models in your text. It does not expand upon the material in the textbook; it reinforces it. It primarily serves to give you a good foundation to understanding principles of economics. Your professor has chosen this study guide for you, suggesting that your economics exams are going to focus on this kind of foundational understanding. You should be sure of this: if your professor is going to give you mainly essay exams, or complex questions about applying the foundations (such as the more difficult end-of-chapter questions in your textbook) this study guide will not be enough to ace that exam.

To get an idea of what your exams will be like, ask your professor to take a look at these questions and tell the class whether they are representative of the type of questions that will be on the exam. And if they will differ, how.

HOW SHOULD YOU USE THIS STUDY GUIDE?

As we stated above, this book works best if you have attended class and read the book. Ideally, you were awake during class and took notes, you have read the textbook chapters more than once, and have worked through some of the questions at the end of the chapter. (So, we re optimists.)

Just in case the material in the book isn t fresh in your mind, before turning to this study guide it is a good idea to refresh your memory about the material in the text. To do so:

1. Read through the margin comments in the text; they highlight the main concepts in each chapter.
2. Turn to the last few pages of the chapter and reread the chapter summary.
3. Look through the key terms, making sure they are familiar. (O.K., we re not only optimists, we re wild optimists.)

Even if you do not do the above, working though the questions in the study guide will help to tell you whether you really do know the material in the textbook chapters.

STRUCTURE OF THE STUDY GUIDE

This study guide has two main components: (1) a chapter-by-chapter review and (2) pretests based upon groups of chapters.

Chapter-by-chapter review
Each chapter has eight elements:

1. A chapter at a glance: A brief exposition and discussion of the learning objectives for the chapter.
2. Short-answer questions keyed to the learning objectives.
3. A test of matching the terms to their defini-

tions.
4.   Problems and applications.
5.   A brain teaser.
6.   Multiple choice questions.
7.   Potential essay questions
8.   Answers to all questions.

Each chapter presents the sections in the order that we believe are most beneficial to you. Here is how we suggest you use them:

Chapter at a Glance: These should jog your memory about the text and lecture. If you don t remember ever seeing the material before, you should go back and reread the textbook chapter. The numbers in parentheses following each learning objective refer to the page in the text that covers that objective. Remember, reading a chapter when you are thinking about a fantasy date is almost the same as not having read the chapter at all.

Short-Answer Questions: The short-answer questions will tell you if you are familiar with the learning objectives. Try to answer each within the space below each question. Don t just read the questions and assume you can write an answer. Actually writing an answer will reveal your weaknesses. If you can answer them all perfectly, great. But, quite honestly, we don t expect you to be able to answer them all perfectly. We only expect you to be able to sketch out an answer.

Of course, some other questions are important to know. For example, if there is a question about the economic decision rule and you don t remember that it excludes past costs and benefits, you need more studying. So the rule is: Know the central ideas of the chapter; be less concerned about the specific presentation of those central ideas.

After you have sketched out all your answers, check them with those at the end of the chapter and review those that you didn t get right. Since each question is based upon a specific learning objective in the text, for those you didn t get right, you may want to return to the textbook to review the material covering that learning objective.

Match the Terms and Concepts to Their Definitions: Since the definitions are listed, you should get most of these right. The best way to match these is to read the definition first, and then find the term on the left that it defines. If you are not sure of the matching term, circle that definition and move on to the next one. At the end, return to the remaining definitions and look at the remaining terms to complete the matches. After completing this part, check your answers with those in the back of the chapter and figure out what percent you got right. If that percent is below the grade you want to get on your exam, try to see why you missed the ones you did and review those terms and concepts in the textbook.

Problems and Applications: Now it s time to take on any problems in the chapter. These problems are generally more difficult than the short-answer questions. These problems focus on numerical and graphical aspects of the chapter.

Working through problems is perhaps one of the best ways to practice your understanding of economic principles. Even if you are expecting a multiple choice exam, working through these problems will give you a good handle on using the concepts in each chapter.

If you expect a multiple choice exam with no problems, you can work through these fairly quickly, making sure you understand the concepts being tested. If you will have a test with problems and exercises, make sure you can answer each of these questions accurately.

Work out the answers to all the problems in the space provided before checking them against the answers in the back of the chapter. Where our answers differ from yours, check to find out why. The answers refer to specific pages in the textbook so you can review the text again too.

Most of the problems are objective and have only one answer. A few are interpretative and have many answers. We recognize that some questions can be answered in different ways than we did. If you cannot reconcile your answer with ours, check with your professor. Once you are at this stage worrying about different interpretations   you re ahead of most students and, most likely, prepared for the exam.

A Brain Teaser: This section consists of one problem that is generally one step up in the level of difficulty from the Problems and Applications exercises or is a critical thought question. It is designed to provide a challenge to those students who have studied the way we have suggested.

Multiple Choice Questions: The next exercise in each chapter is the multiple choice test. It serves to test the breadth of your knowledge of the text material. Multiple choice questions are not the final arbiters of your understanding. They are, instead, a way of determining whether you have read the book and generally understood the material.

Take this test after having worked through the other questions. Give the answer that most closely corresponds to the answer presented in your text. If you can answer these questions you should be ready for the multiple choice part of your exam.

Work through all the questions in the test before grading yourself. Looking up the answer before you try to answer the questions is a poor way to study. For a multiple choice exam, the percent you answer correctly will be a good predictor of how well you will do on the test.

You can foul up on multiple choice questions in two ways   you can know too little and you can know too much. The answer to knowing too little is obvious: Study more   that is, read the chapters more carefully (and maybe more often). The answer to knowing too much is more complicated. Our suggestions for students who know too much is not to ask themselves   What is the answer?   but instead to ask   What is the answer the person writing the question wants?   Since, with these multiple choice questions, the writer of many of the questions is the textbook author, ask yourself: What answer would the textbook author want me to give?   Answering the questions in this way will stop you from going too deeply into them and trying to see nuances that aren t supposed to be there.

For the most part questions in this study guide are meant to be straightforward. There may be deeper levels at which other answers could be relevant, but searching for those deeper answers will generally get you in trouble and not be worth the cost.

If you are having difficulty answering a multiple choice question, make your best guess. Once you are familiar with the material, even if you don t know the answer to a question you can generally make a reasonable guess. What point do you think the writer of the question wanted to make with the question? Figuring out that point and then thinking of incorrect answers may be a way for you to eliminate wrong answers and then choose among the remaining options.

Notice that the answers at the end of the chapter are not just the lettered answers. We have provided an explanation for each answer   why the right one is right and why some of the other choices are wrong. If you miss a question, read that rationale carefully. If you are not convinced, or do not follow the reasoning, go to the page in the text referred to in the answer and reread the material. If you are still not convinced, see the caveat on the next page.

Potential Essay Questions: These questions provide yet another opportunity to test your understanding of what you have learned. Answering these questions will be especially helpful if you expect these types of questions on the exams. We have only sketched the beginning of an answer to these. This beginning should give you a good sense of the direction to go in your answer, but be aware that on an exam a more complete answer will be required.

Questions on Appendixes: In the chapters we have included a number of questions on the text appendixes. To separate these questions from the others, the letter A precedes the question number. They are for students who have been assigned the appendixes. If you have not been assigned them (and you have not read them on your own out of your great interest in economics) you can skip these.

Answers to All Questions: The answers to all questions appear at the end of each chapter. They begin on a new page so that you can tear out the answers and more easily check your answers against ours. We cannot emphasize enough that the best way to study is to answer the questions yourself first, and then check out our answers. Just looking at the questions and our answers may tell you what the answers are but will not give you the chance to see where your knowledge of the material is weak.

Pretests

Most class exams cover more than one chapter. To prepare you for such an exam, we provide multiple choice pretests for groups of chapters. These pretests consist of 20-40 multiple choice questions from the selected group of chapters. These questions are identical to earlier questions so if you have done the work, you should do well on these. We suggest you complete the entire exam before grading yourself.

We also suggest taking these under test conditions. Specifically,

Use a set time period to complete the exam.
Sit at a hard chair at a desk with good lighting.

Each answer will tell you the chapter on which the question is based, so if you did not cover one of the chapters in the text for your class, don t worry if you get that question wrong. If you get a number of questions wrong from the chapters your class has covered, worry.

There is another way to use these pretests that we hesitate to mention, but we re realists so we will. That way is to forget doing the chapter-by-chapter work and simply take the pretests. Go back and review the material you get wrong.

However you use the pretests, if it turns out that you consistently miss questions from the same chapter, return to your notes from the lecture and reread your textbook chapters.

A FINAL WORD OF ADVICE

That s about it. If you use it, this study guide can help you do better on the exam by giving you the opportunity to use the terms and models of economics. However, we reiterate one last time: The best way to do well in a course is to attend every class and read every chapter in the text as well as work through the chapters in this study guide. Start early and work consistently. Do not do all your studying the night before the exam.

THANKS AND A CAVEAT

We and our friends went through this book more times than we want to remember. All the authors proofed the entire book, as did our good friends, Pam Bodenhorn and Helen Reiff. We also had some superb students, Ted Iobst, Jamie Hand, Ellie Buechner, James Butcher, Amanda Brickell, Magdalena Bokiej, Kunihado Suzuto, Ryan Tomberg, Jeff Murphey, Alexandria Widas, Brad Hutchinson, Xin Lin, Liz Rice, Chris Wearn, and Daniela Simova, go through it. (Our sincere thanks go to them for doing so.) Despite our best efforts, there is always a chance that there s a correct answer other than the one the book tells you is the correct answer, or even that the answer the book gives is wrong. If you find a mistake, and it is a small problem about a number or an obvious mistake, assume the error is typographical. If that is not the case, and you still think another answer is the correct one, write up an alternative rationale and e-mail Professor Colander the question and the alternative rationale. Professor Colander s e-mail is:

colander@middlebury.edu.

When he gets it he will send you a note either thanking you immensely for finding another example of his fallibility, or explaining why we disagree with you. If you re the first one to have pointed out an error he will also send you a copy of an honors companion for economics just what you always wanted, right?

David Colander
Douglas Copeland
Jenifer Gamber

ECONOMICS AND ECONOMIC REASONING

CHAPTER AT A GLANCE

This review is based upon the learning objectives that open the chapter.

1a. Economics is the study of how human beings coordinate their wants and desires, given the decision-making mechanisms, social customs, and political realities of the society. (4)

1b. Three central coordination problems any economy must solve are: (5)
- What, and how much, to produce.
- How to produce it.
- For whom to produce it.

Most economic coordination problems involve scarcity.

2. If the marginal benefits of doing something exceed the marginal costs, do it. If the marginal costs of doing something exceed the marginal benefits, don't do it. This is known as the economic decision rule. (6)

You really need to think in terms of the marginal, or "extra" benefits (MB) and marginal, or "extra" costs (MC) of a course of action. Also, ignore sunk costs.

Economic decision rule:

If MB>MC → <u>Do more of it</u> because "it's worth it."

If MB<MC→ <u>Do less of it</u> because "it's not worth it."

NOTE: The symbol "→" means "implies" or "logically follows."

3. Opportunity cost is the basis of cost/benefit reasoning; it is the benefit forgone, or the cost of the next-best alternative to the activity you've chosen. That cost should be less than the benefit of what you've chosen. (8)

Opportunity cost → "What must be given up in order to get something else." Opportunity costs are often "hidden." You need to take into consideration <u>all</u> opportunity costs when making a decision.

4. Economic reality is controlled by economic forces, social forces, and political forces. (9-11)

What happens in a society can be seen as the reaction and interaction of these 3 forces.

- *Economic forces: The market forces of demand, supply, and prices, etc.*

- *Social and cultural forces: Social and cultural forces can prevent economic forces from becoming market forces.*

- *Political and legal forces: Political and legal forces affect decisions too.*

5. Microeconomics considers economic reasoning from the viewpoint of individuals and builds up; macroeconomics considers economic reasoning from the aggregate and builds down. (14)

Microeconomics (micro) → concerned with some particular segment of the economy. Macroeconomics (macro) → concerned with the entire economy.

6a. <u>Positive economics</u> is the study of what is, and how the economy works. (16)

Deals with "what is" (objective analysis).

6b. <u>Normative economics</u> is the study of what the goals of the economy should be. (16)

Deals with "what ought to be" (subjective).

6c. The <u>art of economics</u> is the application of the knowledge learned in positive economics to the achievement of the goals determined in normative economics. (16)

The art of economics is sometimes referred to as "policy economics."

"Good" policy tries to be objective. It tries to weigh all the benefits and costs associated with all policy options and chooses that option in which the benefits outweigh the costs to the greatest degree.

● SHORT-ANSWER QUESTIONS

1. What are the three central problems that every economy must solve?

2. What is scarcity? What are two elements that comprise scarcity? How do they affect relative scarcity?

3. State the economic decision rule.

4. Define opportunity cost.

5. What is the importance of opportunity cost to economic reasoning?

6. What is an economic force? What are the forces that can keep an economic force from becoming a market force?

7. How does microeconomics differ from macro-economics? Give an example of a macroeconomic issue and a microeconomic issue.

8. Define positive economics, normative economics, and the art of economics. How do they relate to one another?

MATCHING THE TERMS
Match the terms to their definitions

____ 1. art of economics

____ 2. economic decision rule

____ 3. economic forces

____ 4. economic model

____ 5. economic policies

____ 6. economic principle

____ 7. economics

____ 8. efficiency

____ 9. invisible hand

____ 10. invisible hand theory

____ 11. macroeconomics

____ 12. marginal benefit

____ 13. marginal cost

____ 14. market force

____ 15. microeconomics

____ 16. normative economics

____ 17. opportunity cost

____ 18. positive economics

____ 19. scarcity

____ 20. sunk costs

a. Additional benefit above what you've already derived.

b. Additional cost above what you've already incurred.

c. If benefits exceed costs, do it. If costs exceed benefits, don't.

d. The study of individual choice, and how that choice is influenced by economic forces.

e. Necessary reactions to scarcity.

f. The benefit forgone, or the cost, of the next-best alternative to the activity you've chosen.

g. The study of what is, and how the economy works.

h. The insight that a market economy, through the price mechanism, will allocate resources efficiently.

i. The study of the economy as a whole, which includes inflation, unemployment, business cycles, and growth.

j. The study of how human beings coordinate their wants.

k. Goods available are too few to satisfy individuals' desires.

l. The application of the knowledge learned in positive economics to the achievement of the goals determined in normative economics.

m. An economic force that is given relatively free rein by society to work through the market.

n. The price mechanism.

o. A framework that places the generalized insights of theory in a more specific contextual setting.

p. A commonly-held economic insight stated as a law or general assumption.

q. Achieving a goal as cheaply as possible.

r. Actions taken by government to influence economic actions.

s. Study of what the goals of the economy should be.

t. Costs that have already been incurred and cannot be recovered.

● PROBLEMS AND APPLICATIONS

1. State what happens to scarcity for each good in the following situations:

   a. New storage technology allows college dining services to keep peaches from rotting for a longer time. (Good: peaches).

   b. More students desire to live in single-sex dormitories. No new single-sex dormitories are established. (Good: single-sex dormitory rooms).

2. State as best you can:
   a. The opportunity cost of going out on a date tonight with the date you made last Wednesday.

   b. The opportunity cost of breaking the date for tonight you made last Wednesday.

   c. The opportunity cost of working through this study guide.

   d. The opportunity cost of buying this study guide.

3. Assume you have purchased a $15,000 car. The salesperson has offered you a maintenance contract covering all major repairs for the next 3 years, with some exclusions, for $750.

   a. What is the sunk cost of purchasing the maintenance contract? Should this sunk cost be considered when deciding to purchase a maintenance contract?

   b. What is the opportunity cost of purchasing that maintenance contract?

   c. What information would you need to make a decision based on the economic decision rule?

   d. Based upon that information how would you make your decision?

4. State for each of the following whether it is an example of political forces, social forces, or economic forces at work:

   a. Warm weather arrives and more people take Sunday afternoon drives. As a result, the price of gasoline rises.

   b. In some states, liquor cannot be sold before noon on Sunday.

   c. Minors cannot purchase cigarettes.

   d. Many parents will send money to their children in college without the expectation of being repaid.

● A BRAIN TEASER

1. Suppose you are a producer of hand-crafted picture frames. The going market price for your frames is $250 a piece. No matter how many frames you sell your revenue per unit (equal to the selling price per unit) is constant at $250 per frame. However, your per unit costs of producing each additional picture frame are not constant. Suppose the following table summarizes your costs of producing picture frames. Use cost/benefit analysis to determine the most economical (profit maximizing) number of frames to produce given the price per unit and the accompanying cost schedule shown. What are your total profits per week?

# of Frames	Price	Total Cost
0	$250	$0
1	$250	$25
2	$250	$75
3	$250	$150
4	$250	$300
5	$250	$560

● MULTIPLE CHOICE

Circle the one best answer for each of the following questions:

1. Economic reasoning:
   a. provides a framework with which to approach questions.
   b. provides correct answers to just about every question.
   c. is only used by economists.
   d. should only be applied to economic business matters.

2. Scarcity could be reduced if:
   a. individuals work less and want fewer consumption goods.
   b. individuals work more and want fewer consumption goods.
   c. world population grows and world production remains the same.
   d. innovation comes to a halt.

3. In the textbook, the author focuses on coordination rather than scarcity as the central point of the definition of economics because:
   a. economics is not really about scarcity.
   b. scarcity involves coercion, and the author doesn't like coercion.
   c. the author wants to emphasize that the quantity of goods and services depends upon human action and the ability to coordinate that human action.
   d. the concept "scarcity" does not fit within the institutional structure of the economy.

4. In the U.S. economy, who is in charge of organizing and coordinating overall economic activities?
   a. Government.
   b. Corporations.
   c. No one.
   d. Consumers.

5. You bought stock A for $10 and stock B for $50. The price of each is currently $20. Assuming no tax issues, which should you sell if you need money?
   a. Stock A.
   b. Stock B.
   c. The price at which you bought it doesn't matter.
   d. You should sell an equal amount of both.

6. In deciding whether to go to lectures in the middle of the semester, you should:
   a. include tuition as part of the cost of that decision.
   b. not include tuition as part of the cost of that decision.
   c. include a portion of tuition as part of the cost of that decision.
   d. only include tuition if you paid it rather than your parents.

7. In making economic decisions you should consider:
   a. marginal costs and marginal benefits.
   b. marginal costs and average benefits.
   c. average costs and average benefits.
   d. total costs and total benefits, including past costs and benefits.

8. In arriving at a decision, a good economist would say that:
   a. one should consider only total costs and total benefits.
   b. one should consider only marginal costs and marginal benefits.
   c. after one has considered marginal costs and benefits, one should integrate the social and moral implications and reconsider those costs and benefits.
   d. after considering the marginal costs and benefits, one should make the decision on social and moral grounds.

9. In making decisions economists primarily use:
    a. monetary costs.
    b. opportunity costs.
    c. benefit costs.
    d. dollar costs.

10. The opportunity cost of reading Chapter 1 of a 34-chapter text:
    a. is about 1/34 of the price you paid for the book because the chapter is about 1/34 of the book.
    b. is zero since you have already paid for the book
    c. has nothing to do with the price you paid for the book.
    d. is 1/34 the price of the book plus 1/34 the price of tuition for the course.

11. Rationing devices that our society uses include:
    a. the invisible hand only.
    b. the invisible hand and social forces only.
    c. the invisible hand and political forces only.
    d. the invisible hand, the social forces, and political forces.

12. If at Female College there are significantly more females than males (and there are not a significant number of gays), economic forces:
    a. will be pushing for females to pay on dates.
    b. will be pushing for males to pay on dates.
    c. will be pushing for neither to pay on dates.
    d. are irrelevant to this issue. Everyone knows that the males always should pay.

13. Individuals are prohibited from practicing medicine without a license. This is an example of:
    a. the invisible hand.
    b. social forces.
    c. political forces.
    d. market forces.

14. Which of the following is most likely an example of a microeconomic topic?
    a. The effect of a flood in the Midwest on the price of bottled water.
    b. How a government policy will affect inflation.
    c. The relationship between unemployment and inflation.
    d. Why an economy goes into a recession.

15. Which of the following is most strongly an example of a macroeconomic topic?
    a. The effect of a frost on the Florida orange crop.
    b. Wages of cross-country truckers.
    c. How the unemployment and inflation rates are related.
    d. How income is distributed in the United States.

16. The statement, "The distribution of income should be left to the market," is:
    a. a positive statement.
    b. a normative statement.
    c. an art-of-economics statement.
    d. an objective statement.

17. "Given certain conditions, the market achieves efficient results" is an example of:
    a. a positive statement.
    b. a normative statement.
    c. an art of economics statement.
    d. a subjective statement.

● POTENTIAL ESSAY QUESTIONS

You may also see essay questions similar to the "Problems & Applications" and "Brain Teasers" exercises.

1. Respond to the following statement: "Theories are of no use to me because they are not very practical. All I need are the facts because they speak for themselves."

2. The United States is one of the wealthiest nations on earth, yet our fundamental economic problem is scarcity. How can this be?

3. Does economics help teach us how to approach problems, or does it give us a set of answers to problems?

━━━━━ ANSWERS ━━━━━

SHORT-ANSWER QUESTIONS

1. The three central problems that every economy must solve are (1) what and how much to produce, (2) how to produce it, and (3) for whom to produce it. (5)

2. Scarcity occurs when there are not enough goods available to satisfy individuals' desires. Scarcity has two elements, our wants and our means of fulfilling those wants. Since each of these two elements can change, relative scarcity can also change. If we can reduce our wants, scarcity will fall. Likewise if we can increase our efforts to produce more goods or if technological changes allow people to produce more using the same resources, scarcity will fall. (5)

3. If the marginal benefits of doing something exceed the marginal costs, do it. If the marginal costs of doing something exceed the marginal benefits, don't do it. (6)

4. Opportunity cost is the benefit forgone by undertaking an activity. Indeed, it is the benefit forgone of the next best alternative to the activity you have chosen. Otherwise stated, it is what must be given up in order to get something else. (8-9)

5. Opportunity cost is the basis of cost/benefit economic reasoning. It takes into account benefits of all other options, and converts these alternative benefits into costs of the decision you're now making. In economic reasoning, opportunity cost will be less than the benefit of what you have chosen. (8-9)

6. An economic force is the necessary reaction to scarcity. All scarce goods must be rationed in some way. If an economic force is allowed to work through the market, that economic force becomes a market force. The invisible hand is the price mechanism, the rise and fall of prices that guides our actions in a market. Social and political forces can keep economic forces from becoming market forces. (9-10)

7. Microeconomics is the study of how individual choice is influenced by economic forces. Microeconomics focuses on a particular segment of the economy, like how a specific market price is determined and the quantity sold. Macroeconomics is the study of the economy as a whole. It considers the problems of inflation, unemployment, business cycles, and growth. (14)

8. Positive economics is the study of what is and how the economy works. Normative economics is the study of what the goals of the economy should be. The art of economics is the application of the knowledge learned in positive economics to the achievement of the goals one has determined in normative economics. (16)

━━━━━ ANSWERS ━━━━━

MATCHING

1-l; 2-c; 3-e; 4-o; 5-r; 6-p; 7-j; 8-q; 9-n; 10-h; 11-i; 12-a; 13-b; 14-m; 15-d; 16-s; 17-f; 18-g; 19-k; 20-t.

━━━━━ ANSWERS ━━━━━

PROBLEMS AND APPLICATIONS

1. a. Scarcity will fall because fewer peaches will rot. (5)
    b. Scarcity of single-sex dorm rooms will rise since the number of students desiring single-sex dorm rooms has risen, but the number available has not. (5)

2. a. The opportunity cost of going out on a date tonight that I made last Wednesday is the benefit forgone of the best alternative. If my best alternative was to study for an economics exam, it would be the increase in my exam grade that I would have otherwise gotten had I studied. Many answers are possible. (8-9)
    b. The opportunity cost of breaking the date for tonight that I made last Wednesday is the benefit forgone of going out on that date. It would be all the fun I would have had on that date. Other answers are possible. (8-9)

c. The opportunity cost of working through this study guide is the benefit forgone of the next-best alternative to studying. It could be the increase in the grade I would have received by studying for another exam, or the money I could have earned if I were working at the library. Many answers are possible. (8-9)

d. The opportunity cost of buying this study guide is the benefit forgone of spending that money on the next-best alternative. Perhaps it is the enjoyment forgone of eating two pizzas. Other answers are possible. (8-9)

3. a. The sunk cost of purchasing the maintenance contract is the $15,000 cost of the car because it is a cost that has already been incurred and cannot be recovered. Sunk costs should always be ignored when making a current decision because only marginal costs are relevant to the current decision. (8-9)

b. The opportunity cost of purchasing the maintenance contract is the benefit I could receive by spending that $750 on something else, such as a moon roof. (8-9)

c. I would need to know the benefit of the maintenance contract to assess whether the cost of $750 is worthwhile. (6-7)

d. For me the benefit of the maintenance contract is the expected cost of future repairs that would be covered and the peace of mind of knowing that future repairs are covered by the contract. The cost is the opportunity cost of using the $750 in another way. Notice that the cost of a decision includes opportunity costs only; it does not count sunk costs because they are not relevant. If the benefit exceeds the cost, do it. If the cost exceeds the benefit, do not do it. (6-7)

4. a. This is an example of an economic force. (9)

b. This is an example of political forces. Some states have laws, called blue laws, against selling liquor on Sundays altogether or selling it before noon. (9-11)

c. This is an example of a political force. This is a federal law. (9-11)

d. This is an example of a social force. (9-11)

ANSWERS

A BRAIN TEASER

1. The most economical (profit-maximizing) quantity of frames to produce is 4 frames. This is because the marginal benefit of producing frames (the revenue per unit equal to the price per unit of $250) exceeds the marginal (extra) cost of producing frames through the first 4 frames produced. The 5th frame should not be produced because the marginal benefit (the price received) is less than the marginal (extra) cost of production. You would be adding more to your costs than to your revenues and thereby reducing your profits. Your profit would total $700 per week if you produce 4 frames. (6-7)

Price (P) Marginal (Q)Benefit	Total Cost (TC)	Marginal Cost	Total Revenue (TR=PQ)	Profit TR−TC
0 $250	$0	—	$0	$0
1 $250	$25	$25	$250	$225
2 $250	$75	$50	$500	$425
3 $250	$150	$75	$750	$600
4 $250	$300	$150	$1000	$700
5 $250	$560	$260	$1250	$690

ANSWERS

MULTIPLE CHOICE

1. a   As discussed on pages 5 and 6, the textbook author clearly believes that economic reasoning applies to just about everything. This eliminates c and d. He also carefully points out that it is not the only reasoning that can be used; hence b does not fit. So the correct answer must be a.

2. b   On page 5 of the textbook, the author states that the problem of scarcity depends upon our wants and our means of fulfilling those wants. An implication of this is that scarcity could be reduced if individuals worked more and wanted less.

3. c   On page 5 of the textbook the author emphasizes the human action reason for focusing on coordination. He explicitly points out that scarcity is important, but

that the concept of coordination is broader.

4. c As discussed on page 9, the invisible hand of the market coordinates the activities and is a composite of many individuals rather than just any one individual. If you were tempted to say b, corporations, your instincts are right, but the "overall" eliminated that as a possible answer.

5. c As is discussed on page 6 of the book, in making economic decisions you consider that only costs from this point on are relevant; historical costs are sunk costs and therefore have no relevance. Since the prices of the stocks are currently the same, it doesn't matter which you sell.

6. b As discussed on page 6, in economic decisions, you only look at costs from this point on; sunk costs are sunk costs, so tuition can be forgotten. Economic decisions focus on forward-looking marginal costs and marginal benefits.

7. a The economic decision rule is "If marginal benefits exceed marginal costs, do it." As is discussed on page 6 of the text, the relevant benefits and relevant costs to be considered are indeed *marginal* (additional) costs and *marginal* benefits. The answer d is definitely ruled out by the qualifying phrase referring to past benefits and costs. Thus, only a is correct.

8. c As the textbook points out on page 6, economists use a framework of costs and benefits initially, but then later they add the social and moral implications to their conclusions. Adding these can change the estimates of costs and benefits, and in doing so can change the result of economic analysis, so there is an integration between the two. (This was a hard question that required careful reading of the text to answer correctly.)

9. b As discussed on page 8 of the text, opportunity costs include measures of nonmonetary costs. The other answers either do not include all the costs that an economist would consider, or are simply two words put together. The opportunity costs include the benefit forgone by undertaking an activity and should always be included in measuring marginal costs.

10. c As discussed on pages 8-9, the correct answer is that it has nothing to do with the price you paid since that is a sunk cost that has already been paid, so a and d are wrong. The opportunity cost is not zero, however, since there are costs of reading the book. The primary opportunity cost of reading the book is the value of the time you're spending on it, which is determined by what you could be doing with that time otherwise.

11. d As discussed on page 9 of the text, all of these are rationing devices. The invisible hand works through the market and thus is focused on in economics. However the others also play a role in determining what people want, either through legal means or through social control.

12. a As discussed on page 9 of the text, if there are significantly more of one gender than another, dates with that group must be rationed out among the other group. Economic forces will be pushing for the group in excess quantity supplied (in this case women) to pay. Economic forces may be pushing in that direction even though historical forces may push us in the opposite direction. Thus, even if males pay because of social forces, economic forces will be pushing for females to pay.

13. c As discussed on pages 9 and 10, laws are political forces.

14. a As discussed on page 14, macroeconomics is concerned with inflation, unemployment, business cycles and growth. Microeconomics is the study of individuals and individual markets.

15. c As discussed on page 14, macroeconomics is concerned with inflation, unemployment, business cycles and growth. Microeconomics is the study of individuals and individual markets. The distribution of income is a micro topic because it is concerned with the distribution of income among individuals.

16. b As discussed on pages 16 and 17, this could be either a normative or an art-of-economics statement, depending on whether there is an implicit "given the way the real-world economy operates." This qualifier is not there, so "normative" is the preferable answer. After all, normative economics deals with what *should* be.

17. a As discussed on page 16 this is a positive statement. It is a statement about *what is,* not about what should be.

ANSWERS

POTENTIAL ESSAY QUESTIONS

The following are annotated answers. They indicate the general idea behind the answer.

1. Theories are practical because they are generalizations based on real world observations or facts. They enable us to predict and to explain real-world economic behavior. Because they are generalizations, they enable us to avoid unnecessary details or facts. The drawback, however, is that because they are generalizations, at times there will be exceptions to the prediction we would generally expect to observe.

    Facts, on the other hand, do not always speak for themselves. One can often be overwhelmed by a large set of data or facts. Not until one systematically arranges, interprets and generalizes upon facts, tying them together, and distilling out a theory (general statement) related to those facts, do they take on any real meaning. In short, theory and facts are inseparable in the scientific process because theory gives meaning to facts and facts check the validity of theory.

2. The United States is still faced with scarcity because we are unable to have as much as we would like to have. Our resources (as vast as they are) are still scarce relative to the amount of goods and services we would like to have (indeed, our wants appear to be unlimited).

3. Economics is a methodology, or an approach to how we think about the world. It does not come to us equipped with a whole set of solutions to complex real-world problems. However, it may help shed some light on the complexities of real–world issues and thus help us to find solutions.

TRADE, TRADEOFFS, AND GOVERNMENT POLICY

CHAPTER AT A GLANCE

This review is based upon the learning objectives that open the chapter.

1. The production possibilities curve shows the trade-off (or opportunity cost) between two things. (23-26)

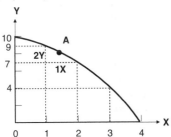

The slope tells you the opportunity cost of good X in terms of good Y. In this particular graph you have to give up 2 Y to get 1 X when you're around point A.

2. In general, the production possibility curve is bowed outward, meaning that in order to get more and more of something, we must give up ever-increasing quantities of something else. The outward bow of the production possibility curve is the result of comparative advantage. (27)

> *Some resources are better suited for the production of certain goods than they are for the production of other goods. The outward bow of the production possibility curve reflects that when more and more of a good is produced, we must use resources whose comparative advantage is in the production of the other good.*

3. The principle of increasing marginal opportunity cost states that opportunity costs increase the more you concentrate on the activity. In order to get more of something, one must give up ever-increasing quantities of something else. (28)

The following production possibility curve and table demonstrate the principle of increasing marginal opportunity cost.

Production Possibility Curve

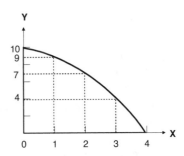

Production Possibility Table

X	Y	Opportunity cost of X (amount of Y which must be forgone)
0	10	1
1	9	2
2	7	3
3	4	4
4	0	

Note: As you get more of X you have to give up larger amounts of Y.

4. Countries can consume more if they specialize in those goods for which they have a comparative advantage and trade. (31-34)

Country A can produce 30Y or 10X, or any combination thereof, while Country B can produce 20Y or 30X or any combination thereof. Since country A has a comparative advantage in Y, it should produce 30Y and Country B should produce 30X. If they divide the goods equally, each can consume 15 units of each good, or point C in the graph on the next page. Each can consume beyond its individual production possibilities.

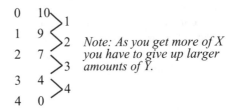

Constructing a production possibility curve that shows the combination of goods these two countries can produce together is useful. You can draw this curve by connecting three points: if both produce good X, if both produce good Y, and if each specializes in the good in which it has a comparative advantage. This is done below.

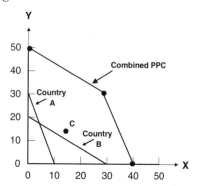

5. Outsourcing is a response to the forces of the law of one price. (35-37)

The law of one price states that wages of workers in one country will equal the wages of equal workers in countries with similar institutions. If wages differ sufficiently, companies will relocate jobs to the low-wage country until parity is reestablished.

Remember: all jobs cannot be outsourced. Every country has, by definition, a comparative advantage in the production of some good if the other country has a comparative advantage in the production of another good..

6. Six roles of government in a market economy are: (39-42)

- Provide a stable set of institutions and rules.
  The government specifies "the rules of the game."

- Promote effective and workable competition.

  Know the different consequences associated with competition vs. monopoly power.

- Correct for externalities.
  Government attempts to restrict the production and consumption of negative externalities, while promoting the production and consumption of positive externalities.

- Ensure economic stability and growth.
  Government tries to ensure: Full employment, Low inflation, Economic growth (which increases the standard of living)

- Provide for public goods.
  Government provides public goods by collecting taxes from everyone to try to eliminate the free-rider problem.

- Adjust for undesired market results.
  Sometimes the market result is not what society wants. For example, an unequal distribution of income may be undesirable. Government can adjust for these failures, but when correcting for these failures, it may make matters even worse. These are called "government failures."

7. Ongoing trade requires rules and the codification of methods of trade. Government's perform this role for domestic trade. However, there is no central world government to perform this role for international trade. Voluntary organizations have developed to fill some of these roles. (42-44)

Free trade agreements regulate international trade, but lack the ability to enforce those regulations.

See also, Appendix A: "Graphish: The Language of Graphs."

● SHORT-ANSWER QUESTIONS

1. Design a grade production possibility curve for studying economics and English, and show how it demonstrates the concept of opportunity cost.

2. State the principle of increasing marginal opportunity cost.

3. What would the production possibility curve look like if opportunity cost were constant?

4. What happens to the production possibility curve when people specialize and trade? Why do specialization and trade make individuals better off?

5. State the law of one price. How is it related to outsourcing?

6. What are the six roles of government?

7. Should government always intervene when markets fail?

8. Why are trade agreements important in the international market?

9. Why are production possibility models important?

MATCHING THE TERMS
Match the terms to their definitions

___ 1. comparative advantage

___ 2. demerit good

___ 3. externality

___ 4. free rider

___ 5. government failure

___ 6. laissez-faire

___ 7. law of one price

___ 8. merit good

___ 9. principle of increasing marginal opportunity cost

___ 10. outsourcing

___ 11. productive efficiency

___ 12. production possibility curve

___ 13. production possibility table

___ 14. progressive tax

___ 15. public good

___ 16. regressive tax

a. A curve measuring the maximum combination of outputs that can be obtained from a given number of inputs.

b. A good that if supplied to one person must be supplied to all and whose consumption by one individual does not prevent its consumption by another individual.

c. A good or activity that government believes is good for you even though you may not choose to engage in the activity or consume the good.

d. A situation where the government intervenes and makes things worse.

e. A person who participates in something for free because others have paid for it.

f. A tax whose rates decrease as a person's income increases.

g. A tax whose rates increase as a person's income increases.

h. Achieving as much output as possible from a given amount of inputs or resources.

i. An economic policy of leaving coordination of individuals' actions to the market.

j. Good or activity that society believes is bad for people even though they choose to use the good or engage in the activity.

k. In order to get more of something, one must give up ever-increasing quantities of something else.

l. Table that lists a choice's opportunity cost by summarizing alternative outputs that can be achieved with your inputs.

m. The advantage that attaches to a resource when that resource is better suited to the production of one good than to the production of another good.

n. The effect of a decision on a third party not taken into account by the decision maker.

o. The relocation to foreign countries of production once done in the United States.

p. Wages of (equal) workers in one country will not differ significantly from wages in another institutionally similar country.

PROBLEMS AND APPLICATIONS

1. Suppose a restaurant has the following production possibility table:

Resources devoted to pizza in % of total	Output of pizza in pies per week	Resources devoted to spaghetti in % of total	Output of spaghetti in bowls per week
100	50	0	0
80	40	20	10
60	30	40	17
40	20	60	22
20	10	80	25
0	0	100	27

a. Plot the restaurant's production possibility curve. Put output of pizza in pies on the horizontal axis.

b. What happens to the opportunity cost of making spaghetti as the number of bowls of spaghetti made increases?

c. What would happen to the production possibility curve if the restaurant found a way to toss and cook pizzas faster?

d. What would happen to the production possibility curve if the restaurant bought new stoves and ovens that cooked both pizzas and spaghetti faster?

2. Suppose Ecoland has the following production possibility table:

% resources devoted to production of guns	Number of guns	% resources devoted to production of butter	Pounds of butter
100	50	0	0
80	40	20	5
60	30	40	10
40	20	60	15
20	10	80	20
0	0	100	25

a. Plot the production possibility curve for the production of guns and butter. Put the number of guns on the horizontal axis.

b. What is the per unit opportunity cost of increasing the production of guns from 20 to 30? From 40 to 50?

c. What happens to the opportunity cost of producing guns as the production of guns increases?

d. What is the per unit opportunity cost of increasing the production of butter from 10 to 15? From 20 to 25?

e. What happens to the opportunity cost of producing butter as the production of butter increases?

f. Given this production possibility curve, is producing 26 guns and 13 pounds of butter possible?

g. Is producing 34 guns and 7 pounds of butter possible? Is it efficient?

3. Using the following production possibility tables and using production possibility curves, show how the United States and Japan would be better off specializing in the production of either food or machinery and then trading rather than producing both food and machinery themselves and not trading.

| United States Production per year | | Japan Production per year | |
Food (tons)	Machinery (1000 units)	Food (tons)	Machinery (1000 units)
10	0	12.5	0
8	5	10.0	1
6	10	7.5	2
4	15	5.0	3
2	20	2.5	4
0	25	0.0	5

4. Assume that France can produce wine for 25 euros per bottle and can produce butter for 5 euros per pound. Assume that Italy can produce wine for 16,000 euros per bottle and butter for 10,000 euros per pound.

a. In terms of pounds of butter, what is the opportunity cost of producing wine in each country?

b. Who has the comparative advantage in producing butter?

c. To obtain the greatest combined production possibilities, which country should specialize in wine and which should specialize in butter?

d. What is likely to happen to each country's consumption possibilities if each specializes in the good for which it has a comparative advantage and then trades?

⬤ A BRAIN TEASER

1. Consider the production possibilities for an entire nation. Within any national economy there are only two general kinds of products that can be produced–consumer products and capital products. Consumer products (e.g., food, clothes, medical services, etc.) satisfy our wants directly when we use them and while we consume them. Capital products (e.g., machines and other plant and equipment) satisfy our wants indirectly and in the future because they increase our productivity and help us produce even more products over time. Answer the following questions based on the production possibilities of consumer and capital products for a national economy shown in the following graph.

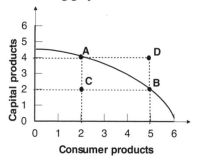

a. Does production possibility A or B provide the greatest amount of current consumption? Why?

b. What is the opportunity cost of moving from point B to point A?

c. Consider the choice of currently producing a relatively large amount of consumer products shown at point B (which means, given limited resources, relatively few capital products can be produced), compared to producing a relatively large amount of capital products now, shown at point A (which means relatively few consumer products can be produced). Which of these two points (or combinations of consumer and capital goods production) do you think will increase the production possibilities (shift the curve to the right) the most over time, giving rise to the greatest rate of economic growth? Why? *(Hint: Whenever workers have more capital, such as factories and machinery, to work with, they become more productive.)*

● MULTIPLE CHOICE

Circle the one best answer for each of the following questions:

1. If the opportunity cost of good X in terms of good Y is 2Y, so you'll have to give up 2Y to get one X, the production possibility curve would look like:

a. a.
b. b.
c. c.
d a, b and c.

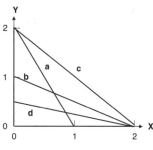

2. If the opportunity cost of good X in terms of good Y is 2Y, so you'll have to give up 2Y to get one X, the production possibility curve would look like:

a. a.
b. b.
c. c.
d d.

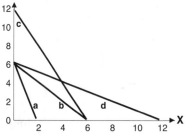

3. If the opportunity cost of good X in terms of good Y is 2Y, so you'll have to give up 2Y to get one X, the production possibility curve could look like:

a. A only.
b. B only.
c. C only.
d. A, B or C.

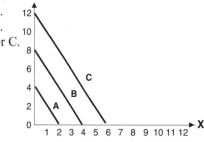

4. If the opportunity cost is constant for all combinations, the production possibility curve will look like:

a. a.
b. b.
c. c.
d d.

5. If the principle of increasing marginal opportunity cost applies at all points, using the graph for question 4, the production possibility curve looks like:

a. a.
b. b.
c. c.
d d.

6. Given the accompanying production possibility curve, when you're moving from point C to point B the opportunity cost of butter in terms of guns is:
    a. 1/3.
    b. 1.
    c. 2.
    d. 3/2.

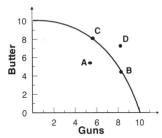

7. In the graph for question 6, in the range of points between A and B there is:
    a. a high opportunity cost of guns in terms of butter.
    b. a low opportunity cost of guns in terms of butter.
    c. no opportunity cost of guns in terms of butter.
    d. a high monetary cost of guns in terms of butter.

8. In the accompanying production possibility diagram, point A would be:

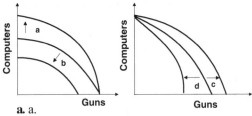

    a. an efficient point.
    b. a superefficient point.
    c. an inefficient point.
    d. a non-attainable point.

9. The efficiency of producing computers is increasing each year. Which of the four arrows would demonstrate the appropriate shifting of the production possibility curve?

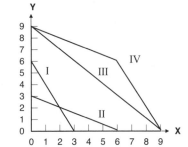

    a. a.
    b. b.
    c. c.
    d. d.

10. Say that methods of production are tied to particular income distributions, so that choosing one method will help some people but hurt others and that the society's income distribution is one of its goals. Say also that method A produces significantly more total output than method B. In this case:
    a. method A is more efficient than method B.
    b. method B is more efficient than method A.
    c. if method A produces more and gives more to the poor people, method A is more efficient.
    d. one can't say whether A or B is more efficient.

11. If the United States and Japan have production possibility curves as shown in the diagram below, at what point would their consumption posibilities most likely be after trade?
    a. A.
    b. B.
    c. C.
    d. D.

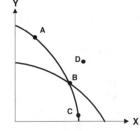

12. If countries A and B have production possibility curves A and B respectively, country A has a comparative advantage in the production of:
    a. no good.
    b. both goods.
    c. good X only.
    d. good Y only.

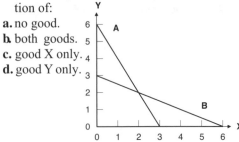

13. If countries X and Y have production possibility curves I and II respectively, which curve represents their combined production possibilities if they specialize and trade?
    a. I
    b. II
    c. III
    d. IV

14. Suppose country A can produce either 100 cars or 50 tractors, or any combination thereof, while country B can produce either 200 cars or 50 tractors, or any combination thereof, and both countries consume both goods. Which of the following combination of goods can be produced only if the countries specialize and trade:
   a. 300 cars, 0 tractors.
   b. 0 cars, 100 tractors.
   c. 200 cars, 50 tractors.
   d. 300 cars, 100 tractors.

15. Outsourcing in the United States is evidence that:
   a. the United States does not have any comparative advantages.
   b. the U.S. dollar is valued too low.
   c. the law of one price doesn't hold.
   d. the law of one price is affecting global production.

16. Because of international competition and the ease with which technology is transferable among many nations with similar institutional structures, we can expect the wages for workers with similar skills to:
   a. increase in developing countries faster than they increase in developed nations.
   b. decrease in developing countries while they increase in developed nations.
   c. increase in developed countries while they decrease in developing nations.
   d. decrease in both developed and developing countries.

17. When government attempts to adjust for the effect of decisions on third parties not taken into account by the decision makers, the government is attempting to:
   a. provide for a stable set of institutions and rules.
   b. promote effective and workable competition.
   c. provide for public goods and services.
   d. correct for externalities.

18. The ability of individuals or firms currently in business to prevent others from entering the same kind of business is:
   a. comparative advantage.
   b. market failure.
   c. monopoly power.
   d. externality.

19. In the international market, government agreements tend to be related to:
   a. provisions of public goods.
   b. free trade.
   c. environmental issues.
   d. redistribution of income.

20. A progressive income tax is:
   a. a tax whose rates increase as a person's income increases.
   b. a tax whose rates decrease as a person's income increases.
   c. a tax whose rates are constant at all income levels, no mater what a taxpayer's total annual income.
   d. not used in the United States.

21. A good whose consumption by one individual does not prevent its consumption by another individual has a characteristic of:
   a. a public good.
   b. a private good.
   c. a macroeconomic good.
   d. a demerit good.

22. When trade is allowed between two countries, the slope of the combined production possibility curve is determined by the country with:
   a. the highest output.
   b. the lowest output.
   c. the highest opportunity cost.
   d. the lowest opportunity cost.

23. Economic theory says government should:
   a. follow a policy of laissez-faire.
   b. get intricately involved in the economy.
   c. not get involved in the economy.
   d. base government intervention upon costs and benefits.

A1. In the graph below, point A represents:

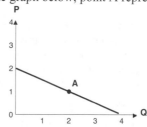

   a. a price of 1 and a quantity of 2.
   b. a price of 2 and a quantity of 2.
   c. a price of 2 and a quantity of 1.
   d. a price of 1 and a quantity of 1.

A2. The slope of the line in the graph below is

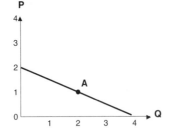

    a. 1/2.
    b. 2.
    c. minus 1/2.
    d. minus 2.

A3. At the maximum and minimum points of a nonlinear curve, the value of the slope is equal to

    a. 1.
    b. zero.
    c. minus 1.
    d. indeterminate.

A4. Which of the four lines in the graphs below has the largest slope?

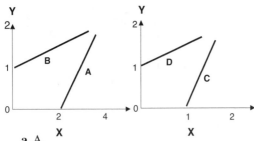

    a. A.
    b. B.
    c. C.
    d. A and C.

A5. Which of the following equations represents the line depicted in the graph to question A2?

    a. $P = 2 - .5Q$.
    b. $P = 2 - 2Q$.
    c. $Q = 4 - 2P$.
    d. $Q = 2 - .5P$.

A6. Suppose the demand curve is represented by $P = -2Q + 8$. Which of the following equations represents a *shift to the right* in that demand curve, with no change in slope?

    a. $P = -Q + 8$.
    b. $P = -2Q + 10$.
    c. $P = -2Q + 6$.
    d. $P = -4Q + 8$.

● POTENTIAL ESSAY QUESTIONS

You may also see essay questions similar to the "Problems & Applications" and "Brain Teasers" exercises.

1. Your study partner tells you that because wages are higher in the United States than in many other countries, eventually all U.S. jobs will be outsourced. How do you respond?

2. Discuss the six roles of government in a market economy. According to economic theory, to what extent should government intervene in our economy?

3. There has always been much political debate between "conservatives" and "liberals" in this country, as well as in other countries, over what constitutes the "appropriate" role for government to play in correcting for the problems of a market-oriented, capitalist economy.

    a. Is this controversy ever likely to go away? Why or why not?

    b. Could greater reliance upon positive economic analysis of "what is" as opposed to normative economic analysis of "what ought to be" help reduce some of this controversy?

ANSWERS

SHORT-ANSWER QUESTIONS

1. The production possibility curve below shows the highest combination of grades you can get with 20 hours of studying economics and English. The grade received in economics is on the vertical axis and the grade received in English is on the horizontal axis. The graph tells us the opportunity cost of spending any combination of 20 hours on economics and English. For example, the opportunity cost of increasing your grade in economics by 6 points is decreasing your English grade by 4 points (a 2/3-point reduction in English grade for each one-point improvement in economics grade). (24-26)

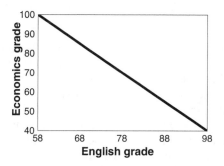

2. The principle of increasing marginal opportunity cost states that in order to get more of something, one must give up ever-increasing quantities of something else. (28)

3. Such a production possibility curve would be a straight line connecting the maximum number of units of each product that could be produced if all inputs were devoted to one or the other good. (27)

4. The production possibility curve shifts out with trade. By concentrating on those activities for which one has a comparative advantage and trading those goods for goods for which others have a comparative advantage, individuals can end up with a combination of goods to consume that would not be attainable without trade. (31-34)

5. The law of one price is that wages of workers in one country will not differ significantly from the wages of equal workers in another institutionally similar country. Outsourcing is the result of differing wages among countries. As the high-wage country outsources jobs to lower-wage countries, wages will tend to equalize. So, outsourcing is the result of the law of one price in action. (40-41)

6. Six roles of government are (1) provide a stable set of institutions and rules, (2) promote effective and workable competition, (3) correct for externalities, (4) provide public goods, (5) ensure economic stability and growth, and (6) adjust for undesirable market results. (39)

7. The fact that a market has failed does not mean that government intervention will improve the situation; it may make things worse. (42)

8. Ongoing trade requires rules and methods of trade. The international market has no central government to set rules and methods for trade. Governments enter into voluntary trade agreements to fulfill some of these roles. (42-44)

9. Production possibility models are important because they structure the discourse of debate about regulating the market. (44)

ANSWERS

MATCHING

1-m; 2-j; 3-n; 4-e; 5-d; 6-i; 7-p; 8-c; 9-k; 10-o; 11-h; 12-a; 13-l; 14-g; 15-b; 16-f.

ANSWERS

PROBLEMS AND APPLICATIONS

1. a. The restaurant's production possibility curve is shown below. (23-26)

    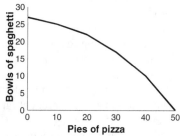

   b. The opportunity cost of spaghetti increases because the number of pizza pies that must be given up to make an additional bowl of spaghetti increases as the number of bowls of spaghetti produced increases. (25)

c. If the restaurant found a way to toss and cook pizzas faster, the production possibility curve would rotate out along the pizza axis as shown below. (29)

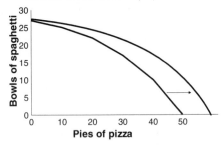

d The production possibility curve would shift out to the right as shown in the figure below. (29)

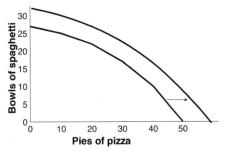

2. a. The production possibility curve is a straight line as shown below. (26-28)

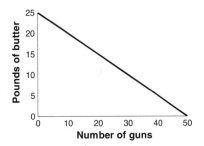

b. The opportunity cost of increasing the production of guns from 20 to 30 is 0.5 pounds of butter per gun. The opportunity cost of increasing the production of guns from 40 to 50 is also 0.5 pounds of butter per gun. (25-26)

c. The opportunity cost of producing guns stays the same as the production of guns increases. (25-26)

d The opportunity cost of increasing the production of butter from 10 to 15 is 2 guns per pound of butter. The opportunity cost of increasing the production of butter from 20 to 25 is also 2 guns per pound of butter. (25-26)

e. The opportunity cost of producing butter stays the same as the production of butter increases. (25-26)

f. Producing 26 guns and 13 lbs of butter is not attainable given this production possibility curve. We can produce 20 guns and 15 lbs of butter. To produce six more guns, Ecoland must give up 3 lbs of butter. Ecoland can produce only 26 guns and 12 lbs of butter. (25-26)

g. Ecoland can produce 34 guns and 7 pounds of butter. To see this, begin at 30 guns and 10 pounds of butter. To produce 4 more guns, 2 pounds of butter must be given up. Ecoland can produce 34 guns and 8 pounds of butter, which is more than 34 guns and 7 pounds of butter. 34 guns and 7 pounds of butter is an inefficient point of production. (25-26)

3. The production possibility of producing food and machinery for both Japan and the United States is shown in the graph below. The United States has a comparative advantage in the production of machinery. It must give up only 0.4 tons of food for each additional thousand units of machinery produced. Japan must give up 2.5 tons of food for each additional thousand units of machinery produced. If they specialize and trade, they could attain the combined production possibility curve shown below.

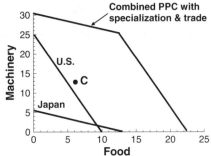

To draw the combined production possibility curve, connect these three points: (1) a point along the food axis when both produce food (22.5 units), (2) a point along the machinery axis when both produce machines (30 units), (3) a point where each produces only that good for which it has a comparative advantage (food = 12.5, machinery = 25). If each country specializes in their comparative advantage and equally divides that production they will each consume 6.25 units of food and 12.5 units of machinery (point C in the graph)—more than either could have consumed if they produced just for themselves. (31-34)

4. a. In France, the opportunity cost of producing wine is 5 pounds of butter. In Italy, the opportunity cost of producing wine is 1.6 pounds of butter. Calculate this by finding how much butter must be forgone for each bottle of wine in each country. (25-26)
   b. France has the comparative advantage in producing butter because it can produce butter at a lower opportunity cost. (25-26)
   c. To obtain the greatest combined production possibilities Italy should specialize in producing only wine and France should specialize in producing only butter. (25-27)
   d. Each country's consumption possibilities increase. (32-34)

ANSWERS

A BRAIN TEASER

1. a. Production possibility B. Why? Because consumer products provide for *current* satisfaction, and at B we are getting a relatively larger amount of consumer products. (24-28)
   b. 3 units of consumer products. (24-28)
   c. Point A. Producing a relatively larger amount of capital products now means workers will have more plant and equipment to work with in the future. This will increase workers' productivity and the nation's production possibilities over time. Producing more capital is an ingredient for economic growth (greater production possibilities over time). (24-28)

ANSWERS

MULTIPLE CHOICE

1. a   As discussed on page 24, the production possibility curve tells how much of one good you must give up to get more of the other good; here you must give up 2Y to get one X, making a the correct answer.

2. c   As discussed on pages 24-26, the production possibility curve tells how much of

one good you must give up to get more of another good. Opportunity cost is a ratio; it determines the slope, not the position, of the production possibility curve. Thus, the correct answer is c because the 12 to 6 trade-off reduces to a 2 to 1 trade-off.

3. d   As discussed on pages 24-26, the production possibility curve tells how much of one good you must give up to get more of the other good. Opportunity cost is a ratio; it determines the slope, not the position, of the ppc curve. Since all have the same correct slope, all three are correct, so d is the right answer.

4. b   As discussed on page 27 of the book, if the opportunity costs are constant, the PPC is a straight line, so b must be the answer.

5. c   As discussed on page 28 of the book, with increasing marginal opportunity costs, as you produce more and more of a good, you will have to give up more and more of the other good to do so. This means that the slope of the ppc must be bowed outward, so c is the correct answer. (See Figure 2-2, page 26 for an in-depth discussion.)

6. d   As discussed on pages 24-26, the slope of the PPC measures the trade-off of one good for the other. Since moving from point C to B means giving up 3 guns for 2 pounds of butter, the correct answer is 3/2 or d.

7. b   As discussed on page 27, the flatter the slope, the higher the opportunity cost of the good measured on the vertical axis; alternatively, the flatter the slope the lower the opportunity cost of the good measured on the horizontal axis. In the AB range the slope is flat so guns have a low opportunity cost in terms of butter; one need give up only one pound of butter to get four guns.

8. c   As discussed on page 29 (See Figure 2-3), point A is an inefficient point because it is inside the PPC.

9. a   As discussed on page 29 (See Figure 2-3), technological change that improves the efficiency of producing a good shifts the PPC out for that good, but not for the other good. So a is the correct answer.

10. d   The answer is "You can't say," as discussed on page 29. The term "efficiency" involves *achieving a goal as cheaply as possible.* Without specifying one's goal, one cannot say what method is more efficient. The concept of efficiency generally presumes that the goal includes preferring more to less, so if any method is more productive, it will be method A. But because there are distributional effects that involve making additional judgments, the correct answer is d. Some students may have been tempted to choose c because their goals involve more equity, but that is their particular judgment, and not all people may agree. Thus c would be incorrect, leaving d as the correct answer.

11. d   As discussed in Figure 2-7 on page 33, with trade, both countries can attain consumption possibilities outside their production possibility curves. The only point not already attainable by either country is D.

12. d   Country A must give up 2Y to produce an additional X while Country B must give up only 1/2 Y to produce an additional X. Therefore, Country A has a comparative advantage in good Y and Country B has a comparative advantage in good X. (See page 27.)

13. d   To construct the combined production possibilities with specialization and trade, sum the production if each country produced the same good (these are the axis intercepts). Connect these points with that point that represents the combination of goods if each country specialized in that good for which it has a comparative advantage. (See pages 32-34, especially Figure 2-7 on page 33.)

14. c   The greatest gains are when each country specializes in the good for which it has the lowest opportunity cost. If Country A specializes in tractors, producing 50 tractors, and Country B specializes in cars and produces 200 cars, production of 200 cars and 50 tractors is possible. The combination of 300 cars and 100 tractors is unattainable even with specialization and trade. The other combinations are possible without trade. (See pages 32-34, especially Figure 2-7.)

15. d   The law of one price is that workers in one country are paid the same as equal workers in other countries with similar institutional structures. If this isn't true, the forces of this law will lead to outsourcing. The United States continues to have comparative advantages. The U.S. dollar is likely too high to equalize wages across nations. (See pages 36-37.)

16. a   According to the law of one price, wages of (equal) workers in one country will not differ significantly from the wages of workers in another institutionally similar country. It is unlikely that wages will fall, but if the law of one price holds then wages in developing countries will rise faster than wages in developed nations rise. (See pages 36-37.)

17. d   Economists call the effect of a decision on a third party not taken into account by the decision maker an externality. Government sometimes attempts to adjust for these effects. (See page 40.)

18. c   Monopoly power is the ability of individuals or firms currently in business to prevent others from entering their businesses. Monopoly power gives existing firms or individuals the ability to raise their prices. (See page 40.)

19. b   At the international level there are few successful attempts to redistribute income, to provide a public good, or to deal with environmental issues. (See pages 42-44).

20. a   Option b is the definition of a regressive tax. Option c is the definition of a proportional tax. Progressive taxes are used in the United States. This leaves option a as the answer which is the definition of a progressive tax. (See page 42)

21. a   A public good is a good that if supplied to one person must be supplied to all and whose consumption by one individual does not prevent its consumption by another individual. (See page 41.)

22. d   This is the principle of lowest cost rules. It is by producing where costs are lowest that countries can achieve gains from trade. (See page 34.)

23. d   Government should get involved in our economy only if the benefits outweigh the costs. See page 42.

A1. a   As discussed in Appendix A, pages 49 and 50, a point represents the corresponding numbers on the horizontal and vertical number lines.

A2. c   As discussed on pages 50 and 51 of Appendix A, the slope of a line is defined as rise over run. Since the rise is -2 and the run is 4, the slope of the above line is minus 1/2.

A3. b   As discussed on pages 51 and 52 of Appendix A, at the maximum and minimum points of a nonlinear curve the slope is zero.

A4. c   As discussed in Appendix A, pages 51 and 52, the slope is defined as rise over run. Line C has the largest rise for a given run so c is the answer. Even though, visually, line A seems to have the same slope as line C, it has a different coordinate system. Line A has a slope of 1 whereas line B has a slope of 1/4. Always be careful about checking coordinate systems when visually interpreting a graph.

A5. a   To construct the equation, use the form $y = mx + b$ where m is the slope and b is the y-axis intercept. The y-axis intercept is 2 and the slope is -rise/run $= -2/4 = -.5$. Plugging in these values we get $y = -.5x + 2$. Since P is on the y-axis and Q is on the x axis, this can also be written as $P = 2 - .5Q$. See pages 53-54.

A6. b   A change in the intercept represents a shift in the curve. A higher intercept is a shift to the right. See pages 53-54.

ANSWERS

POTENTIAL ESSAY QUESTIONS

The following are annotated answers. They indicate the general idea behind the answer.

1.   I would remind my study partner that the jobs that are being outsourced tend to be in the manufacturing industry. The U.S. does have a comparative advantage in creativity and innovation and jobs in industries such as advertising and marketing are being insourced to the United States. In addition, I would remind my partner that the very definition of comparative advantage means that if one country has a comparative advantage in one good, the other country has a comparative advantage in the other good.

2.   Six roles of government are (1) provide a stable set of institutions and rules, (2) promote effective and workable competition, (3) correct for externalities, (4) provide public goods, (5) ensure economic stability and growth, and (6) adjust for undesired market results. Economic theory tells us that the government should intervene in our economy only if the benefits outweigh the costs. However, equally reasonable people are likely to weigh the benefits and costs of government involvement differently.

3.   **a.**   Although there is no debate over the existence of market failures, there is much debate over the extent to which they exist. Controversy often begins with equally reasonable and well–intentioned people assessing the extent of the problem differently. (For example, consider the controversy surrounding the extent of ozone damage.) If a consensus is reached, then the same equally reasonable, equally well intentioned people will likely measure the benefits and costs associated with government involvement differently. This gives rise to debate concerning the appropriate extent of government involvement.

   b.   There will likely always be some degree of inefficiency in measuring the benefits and the costs associated with any problem and of any government involvement. However, greater reliance upon positive economic analysis, because it is "objective" and deals with "what is," should help everyone to avoid emotion and to see more clearly the benefits and costs associated with government action. However, as was stated in the first chapter, "the art of economics is the application of the knowledge learned in positive economics to the achievement of the goals determined in normative economics. In the art of economics, it is difficult to be objective but it is important to try."

THE EVOLVING U.S. ECONOMY IN PERSPECTIVE

● CHAPTER AT A GLANCE

This review is based upon the learning objectives that open the chapter.

1. A <u>market economy</u> is an economic system based on private property and the market. It gives private property rights to individuals, and relies on market forces to coordinate economic activity. (59)

    A market economy is characterized by:
    (I) mainly private ownership of resources
    (II) a market system that solves the What? How? and For whom? problems.

    A market economy's solutions to the central economic problems are:
    *   *What to produce: what businesses believe people want, and what is profitable.*
    *   *How to produce: businesses decide how to produce efficiently, guided by their desire to make a profit.*
    *   *For whom to produce: distribution according to individuals' ability and/or inherited wealth.*

2. <u>Capitalism</u> is an economic system based on the market in which the ownership of the means of production resides with a small group of individuals called capitalists. (60-61)

    <u>Socialism</u> is, in theory, an economic system that tries to organize society in the same way that most families are organized—all people should contribute what they can, and get what they need. (60-61)

    Soviet-style socialism's solutions to the three central economic problems are:
    *   *What to produce: what central planners believe is socially beneficial.*
    *   *How to produce: central planners decide, based on what they think is good for the country.*
    *   *For whom to produce: central planners distribute goods based on what they determine are individuals' needs.*

    All economic systems are dynamic and evolve over time so the meaning of terms referring to economic systems is evolving. Ours has evolved from feudalism, mercantilism, and capitalism.

3. Businesses, households, and government interact in a market economy. (64)

    For a bird's-eye view of the U.S. economy, see Figure 3-1 (sometimes called the "circular flow of income model"). Be able to draw and explain it.

    Note: there are 3 basic economic institutions:

    *   *Businesses:*
        a. Supply goods in a goods market.
        b. Demand factors in a factor market.
        c. Pay taxes and receive benefits from government.

    *   *Households:*
        a. Supply factors.
        b. Demand goods.
        c. Pay taxes and receive benefits from government.

    *   *Government:*
        a. Demands goods.
        b. Demands factors.
        c. Collects taxes and provides services.

    It will be important to remember who does the demanding and the supplying in goods and factor (resource) markets.

4. The advantages and disadvantages of the three forms of business are shown in a table on page 67.

Know the advantages and disadvantages of the three forms of business:
- *Sole Proprietorship*
- *Partnership*
- *Corporation*

E-commerce is changing the nature of trade relationships among businesses and consumers.

5. Although, in principle, ultimate power resides with the people and households (consumer sovereignty), in practice the representatives of the people–firms and government–are sometimes removed from the people and, in the short run, are only indirectly monitored by the people. (70)

   Also note: Economics focuses on households' role as the suppliers of labor.

   - *Do we control business and government, or do they control us?*
   - *The distribution of income (rich vs. poor) determines the "for whom" question. If you're rich you get more.*
   - *Social forces affect what business and government do or don't do.*

6. Two general roles of government are: (70-72)

   - *As an actor:* Collects taxes and spends money.
   - *As referee:* Sets the rules governing relations between households and businesses.

7. Globalization increases the number of competitors for firms. More competition creates greater specialization and increased productivity. This leads to lower costs and prices. (75)

   Globalization results in a greater quantity, quality, and variety of products at lower prices. However, it hurts those businesses and workers who cannot compete. But, globalization creates new jobs. On balance, over time, the benefits of trade outweigh the costs for a nation as a whole. Many of the benefits of trade for the U.S. have already been consumed, while many of the costs have yet to be fully realized.

   The wages and standards of living in developing nations will likely catch up to those in the U.S. and Western Europe. This is known as <u>convergence</u>.

   The discussion often centers on the timing of these benefits and costs.

   See also, Appendix A: "The History of Economic Systems."

SHORT-ANSWER QUESTIONS

1. What is a market economy? How does it solve the three central economic problems?

2. What is socialism? In practice, how have socialist economies addressed the three central economic problems?

3. Draw a diagram of the U.S. economy showing the three groups that comprise the U.S. economy. What is the role of each group in the economy?

4. Your friend wants to buy a coin-operated laundromat. Her brother has offered to be a partner in the operation and put up half the money to buy the business. They have come to you for advice about what form of business to create. Of course you oblige, letting them know the three possibilities and the advantages and disadvantages of each.

5. What is consumer sovereignty? Why is much of the economic decision-making done by business and government even though households have the ultimate power?

6. Briefly distinguish between the two general roles of government.

7. How does globalization increase competition and lower costs?

8. Why is convergence more likely to happen now than to 30 years ago? What are two ways wages are expected to eventually converge?

A1. Why did feudalism evolve into mercantilism?

A2. Why did mercantilism evolve into capitalism?

A3. Explain what is meant by the statement that capitalism has evolved into welfare capitalism.

MATCHING THE TERMS
Match the terms to their definitions

___ 1. consumer sovereignty	**a.**	Businesses with two or more owners.
___ 2. corporations	**b.**	Principle that the consumer's wishes rule what's produced.
___ 3. entrepreneurship	**c.**	Corporations with substantial operations on both production and sales in more than one country.
___ 4. e-commerce	**d.**	Businesses that have only one owner.
___ 5. global corporation	**e.**	The stockholder's liability is limited to the amount that stockholder has invested in the company.
___ 6. market economy	**f.**	Buying and selling over the Internet.
___ 7. limited liability	**g.**	What's left over from total revenue after all appropriate costs have been subtracted.
___ 8. partnership	**h.**	The ability to organize and get something done.
___ 9. profit	**i.**	Businesses that are treated as a person, and are legally owned by their shareholders who are not liable for the actions of the corporate "person."
___ 10. sole proprietorship	**j.**	An economic system based on individuals' goodwill toward others, not on their own self-interest, in which society decides what, how, and for whom to produce.
___ 11. socialism	**k.**	An economic system based on private property and the market, in which individuals decide how, what, and for whom to produce.
___ 12. stock	**l.**	An organization committed to getting countries to agree not to impose new trade restrictions.
___ 13. World Trade Organization (WTO)	**m.**	Certificates of ownership of a corporation.

● PROBLEMS AND APPLICATIONS

1. Fill in the blanks with the appropriate economic institution (households, businesses, or government).
    a. In the goods market, _____ and _____ buy goods and services from _____.

    b. In the goods market, _____ sell goods and services to _____ and _____.

    c. In the factor market, _____ and _____ buy (or employ) the resources owned by _____.

    d. In the factor market, _____ supply labor and other factors of production to _____ and _____.

    e. _____ redistributes income.

    f. _____ provides services to the public with tax revenue.

2. For each of the following, state for which form or forms of business it is an advantage: Sole proprietorships, partnerships, corporations.

    a. Minimum bureaucratic hassle.

    b. Ability to share work and risks.

    c. Direct control by owner.

    d. Relatively easy (but not the easiest) to form.

    e. Limited individual liability.

    f. Greatest ability to get funds.

3. For each of the following, state for which form or forms of business it is a disadvantage: Sole proprietorships, partnerships, corporations.

   a. Unlimited personal liability.

   b. Possible double taxation of income.

   c. Limited ability to get funds

   d. Legal hassle to organize.

4. a. State one positive and one negative effect globalization has on firms.

   b. State one positive and one negative effect that globalization has on a nation.

   c. Do the benefits of globalization for a nation outweigh the costs, or do the costs outweigh the benefits?

A BRAIN TEASER

1. Why have some politicians who wish to significantly reduce federal government spending find it difficult to achieve that reduction in practice?

MULTIPLE CHOICE

Circle the one best answer for each of the following questions:

1. For a market to exist, you have to have:
   a. a capitalist economy.
   b. private property rights.
   c. no government intervention.
   d. externalities.

2. In theory, socialism is an economic system:
   a. that tries to organize society in the same ways as most families organize, striving to see that individuals get what they need.
   b. based on central planning and government ownership of the means of production.
   c. based on private property rights.
   d. based on markets.

3. Soviet-style socialism is an economic system:
   a. that tries to organize society in the same ways as most families organize, striving to see that individuals get what they need.
   b. based on central planning and government ownership of the means of production.
   c. based on private property rights.
   d. based on markets.

4. In a market economy, the "what to produce" decision in practice is most often made directly by:
   a. consumers.
   b. the market.
   c. government.
   d. firms.

5. In Soviet-style socialism, the "what to produce" decision in practice was most often made by:
   a. consumers.
   b. the market.
   c. government.
   d. firms.

6. In the factor market:
   a. businesses supply goods and services to households and government.
   b. government provides income support to households unable to supply factors of production to businesses.
   c. households supply labor and other factors of production to businesses.
   d. households purchase goods and services from businesses.

7. The ability to organize and get something done generally goes under the term:
   a. the corporate approach.
   b. entrepreneurship.
   c. efficiency.
   d. consumer sovereignty.

8. In terms of numbers, the largest percentage of businesses are:
   a. partnerships.
   b. sole proprietorships.
   c. corporations.
   d. nonprofit companies.

9. The largest percentage of business receipts are by:
   a. partnerships.
   b. sole proprietorships.
   c. corporations.
   d. nonprofit companies.

10. A sole proprietorship has the advantage of:
    a. raising funds by selling stocks or bonds.
    b. limited personal liability.
    c. minimum bureaucratic hassle.
    d. sharing work and risks.

11. All of the following are reasons why e-commerce and the Internet increase competition *except*:
    a. they increase the size of the marketplace in which goods are sold.
    b. they increase the value of companies who can establish brand name first.
    c. they reduce the cost of obtaining information.
    d. they reduce the importance of geographical location.

12. The largest percentage of federal government expenditures is on:
    a. education.
    b. health and medical care.
    c. infrastructure.
    d. income security.

13. The largest percentage of state and local expenditures is on:
    a. education.
    b. health and medical care.
    c. highways.
    d. income security.

14. All of the following are examples of government's role as referee *except*:
    a. setting limitations on when someone can be fired.
    b. collecting Social Security taxes from workers' paychecks.
    c. setting minimum safety regulations for the workplace.
    d. disallowing two competitors to meet to fix prices of their products.

15. Global corporations:
    a. offer enormous benefits to countries but rarely any problems.
    b. are easy for governments to control.
    c. reduce competition in countries.
    d. have substantial operations on both the production and the sales sides in more than one country.

16. Globalization:
    a. is decreasing in importance.
    b. increases competition.
    c. reduces the need to specialize.
    d. reduces productivity.

17. A more integrated global economy:
    a. gives rise to lower standards of living for most nations.
    b. tends to provide for a greater quantity and wider variety of higher quality products at lower costs.
    c. tends to reduce competition by making corporations subject to laws in more than one country.
    d. tends to reduce the ability of the most efficient firms to prosper.

18. Globalization has increased the likelihood of convergence because:
    a. people will no longer accept differences in wages and will protest.
    b. the forces of the law of one price are stronger with globalization.
    c. people now trade with a greater nuber of currencies.
    d. it has increased the probability that countries will impose trade barriers.

A1. In feudalism the most important force was:
   a. the price mechanism.
   b. cultural force.
   c. legal force.
   d. anarchy.

A2. In mercantilism, the guiding force is:
   a. the price mechanism.
   b. legal force.
   c. cultural force.
   d. anarchy.

A3. Mercantilism evolved into capitalism because:
   a. government investments did not pan out.
   b. the Industrial Revolution undermined the craft guilds' mercantilist method of production.
   c. the guilds wanted more freedom.
   d. serfs wanted more freedom.

A4. Marx saw the strongest tension between:
   a. rich capitalists and poor capitalists.
   b. capitalists and government.
   c. capitalists and the proletariat.
   d. government and the proletariat.

A5. State socialism is an economic system in which:
   a. business sees to it that people work for their own good until they can be relied upon to do that on their own.
   b. business sees to it that people work for the common good until they can be relied upon to do that on their own.
   c. government sees to it that people work for their own good until they can be relied upon to do so on their own.
   d. government sees to it that people work for the common good until they can be relied upon to do so on their own.

● POTENTIAL ESSAY QUESTIONS

You may also see essay questions similar to the "Problems & Applications" and "Brain Teasers" exercises.

1.   Contrast the market economy and the Soviet-style socialist economy in addressing the three fundamental economic problems.

2.   Uglies is a brand of boxer shorts sold on the Internet. Their claim to fame is that the front of the shorts doesn't match the back. Their marketing ploy is the boxer-short-of-the-month club. Suppose you were the one who came up with the idea for Uglies and wanted to start the business. What form of business would you select and why? (Thinking about where the funds to start the business will come from, who will make the shorts, and how the shorts will be sold will help you answer this question.)

3.   Discuss the pros and cons of globalization for nations.

ANSWERS

SHORT-ANSWER QUESTIONS

1. A market economy is an economic system based on private property and the market. It gives private property rights to individuals, and relies on market forces to coordinate economic activity. In a market economy businesses produce what they believe people want and think they can make a profit supplying. Businesses decide how to produce efficiently, guided by their desire to make a profit. Goods are distributed according to individuals' ability and/or inherited wealth. (59)

2. Socialism is an economic system that tries to organize society in the same way as do most families—all people should contribute what they can, and get what they need. Soviet-style socialist economies produce what central planners believe is socially beneficial. Central planners also decide how to produce, based (one hopes) on what they think is good for the country. Central planners distribute goods based on what they determine are individuals' needs. (60-61)

3. As seen in the diagram below, the three groups that comprise the U.S. economy are households, businesses, and government. Households supply factors of production to businesses in exchange for money; businesses produce goods and services and sell them to households and government in exchange for money. The government taxes businesses and households, buys goods and services from businesses and labor services from households, and provides goods and services to each of them. (64)

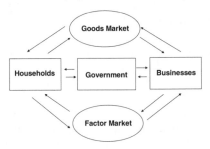

4. I would advise each of them to think hard about their situation. There are three main possibilities: sole proprietorship, partnership and a corporation. Each form of business has its disadvantages and advantages. If your friend wants to minimize bureaucratic hassle and be her own boss, the best form of business would be a sole proprietorship. However, she would be personally liable for all losses and might have difficulty obtaining additional funds should that be necessary. If her brother has some skills to offer the new business and is willing to share in the cost of purchasing the company, she might want to form a partnership with him. Beware, though: Both partners are liable for any losses regardless of whose fault it is. I would ask her if she trusts her brother's decision-making abilities.

   As a partnership they still might have problems getting additional funds. What about becoming a corporation? Her liability would be limited to her initial investment, her ability to get funds is greater, and she can shed personal income and gain added expenses to limit taxation. However, a corporation is a legal hassle to organize, may involve possible double taxation of income, and if she plans to hire many employees she may face difficulty monitoring the business once she becomes less involved. I would tell her she needs to weigh the costs and benefits of each option and choose the one that best suits her needs. (66-67)

5. Consumer sovereignty is the notion that the consumer's wishes rule what's produced. It means that if businesses wish to make a profit, they will need to produce what households want. That is not to say that businesses don't affect the desires of consumers through advertising. However, in practice, business and government do much of the economic decision-making even though households retain the ultimate power. This is because people have delegated much of that power to institutions and representatives–firms and the government–that are sometimes removed from the people. In the short run, households only indirectly control government and business. (69-70)

6. Two general roles of government are as actor and as referee. As an actor, government collects taxes and spends money. As a referee, government sets the rules governing relations between households and businesses. (70-72)

7. Globalization increases competition by providing more competitors to domestic firms at all levels of production and by creating a larger market so that firms can specialize more easily. Globalization reduces costs of production in two ways. First, it allows companies to specialize in smaller portions of the production process, which increases competition and lowers costs at all levels of the production process. Second, it allows companies to locate parts of the production process in those countries that have a comparative advantage in that portion of the production process. (75)

8. One reason why convergence is likely to happen is that more countries, such as China and India, have adopted market-based economies and have therefore become more competitive. Convergence will occur through the rising of wages in developing countries relative to wages in the United States, a decline in the value of the dollar, or a combination of the two. (76-77)

A1. Feudalism evolved into mercantilism as the development of money allowed trade to grow, undermining the traditional base of feudalism. Politics rather than social forces came to control the central economic decisions. (84-86)

A2. Mercantilism evolved into capitalism because the Industrial Revolution shifted the economic power base away from craftsmen toward industrialists and toward an understanding that markets could coordinate the economy without the active involvement of the government. (86-87)

A3. Capitalism has evolved into welfare capitalism. That is, the human abuses marked by early capitalist developments led to a criticism of the market economic system. Political forces have changed government's role in the market, making government a key player in determining distribution and in making the what, how, and for whom decisions. This characterizes the U.S. economy today. (87)

ANSWERS

MATCHING

1-b; 2-i; 3-h; 4-f; 5-c; 6-k; 7-e; 8-a; 9-g; 10-d; 11-j; 12-m; 13-l.

ANSWERS

PROBLEMS AND APPLICATIONS

1. a. In the goods market, **households** and **government** buy goods and services from **businesses**. (64)
    b. In the goods market, **businesses** sell goods and services to **households** and **government**. (64)
    c. In the factor market, **businesses** and **government** buy (or employ) the resources owned by **households**. (64)
    d. In the factor market, **households** supply labor and other factors of production to **businesses** and **government**. (64)
    e. **Government** redistributes income. (64)
    f. **Government** provides services to the public with tax revenue. (64)

2. a. Sole proprietorship. No special bureaucratic forms are required to start one. (66-67)
    b. Partnership. The owners have another to work with and risks are shared. (66-67)
    c. Sole proprietorship. This is a firm of one person who controls the business. (66-67)
    d. Partnership. This is easy to form relative to the easiest (sole proprietorship) and the hardest (corporation). (66-67)
    e. Corporation. The individual liability is limited by individual investment. (66-67)
    f. Corporation. Because it can issue stock and has limited liability, it has more access to financial capital. (66-67)

3. a. Sole proprietorship and partnership. (66-67)
    b. Corporation. (66-67)
    c. Sole proprietorship and partnership. (66-67)
    d. Corporation. (66-67)

4. a. Globalization increases the size of the gain to the firm that is a winner, but makes it harder to win, or to even stay in business. (75)
    b. A positive effect of globalization for a nation is increased competition. Greater competition results in greater quantity and a wider variety of higher quality products at lower prices. This ultimately means a higher average absolute standard of living for the nation as a whole. However,

globalization may result in some temporary loss of jobs or business failures as a result of the more intense global competition. (73-75)

   c. The benefits of globalization outweigh the costs for a nation over time. This is why so many nations are more aggressively pursuing greater participation in the global economy. However, much of the discussion centers on the timing of these benefits and costs. (72-75)

ANSWERS

A BRAIN TEASER

1. A significant reduction in federal government spending would require cuts in income security (like social security), national defense, and other major components of federal government expenditures that are politically popular. Many people applaud attempts to reduce government spending as long as there are no cuts in programs they support. (70-72)

ANSWERS

MULTIPLE CHOICE

1. b   As discussed on page 59, markets require private property rights because these give people the framework within which they can trade and markets rely on trading. Markets also require government, but government and private property rights are not the same thing, which rules out a and c. And d is a throwaway answer.

2. a   As discussed on page 60, a is the correct answer. If the question had said "Soviet-style socialism," b would have been an acceptable answer, but Soviet-style socialism was a response to real-world implementation problems, not part of the theory of socialism.

3. b   As discussed on page 61, b is the correct answer. If the question had said simply "socialism" a would have been an acceptable answer. But given that it said Soviet-style socialism, b is the preferable answer.

4. d   Under a market economy, firms decide what to produce based on what they think will sell. See page 65.

5. c   As discussed on page 61, under Soviet-style socialism, central planners decide what to produce based upon what they believe society needs.

6. c   In Figure 3-1 households supply labor and other factors of production while businesses demand these inputs into the production process. See page 64.

7. b   Entrepreneurship is the ability to organize and get something done. See page 65.

8. b   Most businesses are sole proprietorships. See Figure 3-2 on page 66.

9. c   Corporations account for most business receipts (revenues). See page 66.

10. c   Corporations have the advantages of options a and b. Partnerships have the advantage of option d. See page 67.

11. b   While it is true that e-commerce and the Internet can increase the value of companies that establish their brand names first, this characteristic decreases competition once that name brand is established. See pages 67-69.

12. d   The largest component of federal government spending is income security. See Figure 3-4 on page 72.

13. a   Most state and local government spending is on education. See Figure 3-3 on page 71.

14. b   Collecting Social Security taxes to fund the Social Security system is government as an actor. Government as referee refers to laws regulating interaction between households and businesses. See pages 71-72.

15. d   Option d is the definition of global corporations. They often create problems. Governments often find it difficult to control them and they increase competition, not decrease it. See pages 73-75.

16. b   Globalization is increasing in importance. It also increases specialization, productivity, and competition. See pages 72-77.

17. b   A more integrated global economy, or globalization, increases standards of living

for most nations because it increases competition. Greater competition gives rise to a greater quantity and wider variety of higher quality products at lower costs. It is the most inefficient firms that find it difficult to prosper. See pages 75-78.

18. b According to the law of one price, wage differentials and therefore standards of living for *similar* workers around the globe will become more equal. Global competition increases the likelihood of this convergence because factors of production can move to those countries with lower wages and input prices. See pages 78-79.

A1. b As discussed on pages 84-85, in feudalism tradition reigned.

A2. b As discussed on pages 84-85, in mercantilism government directed the economy.

A3. b Mercantilism evolved into capitalism because of the changes brought about by the Industrial Revolution. See pages 85-86.

A4. c See pages 87-89. To the degree that government was controlled by capitalists, d would be a correct answer, but it is not as good an answer as c, which represents the primary conflict. Remember, you are choosing the answer that best reflects the discussion in the text.

A5. d The author defines state socialism as option d. Socialists saw state socialism as a transition stage to pure socialism. See page 88.

ANSWERS

POTENTIAL ESSAY QUESTIONS

The following are annotated answers. They indicate the general idea behind the answer.

1. Both economic systems have to address the three central economic problems. (1) What to produce? In a market economy, firms produce what they believe people want and what will make them a profit. In socialism, central planners decide what is produced. (2) How to produce? In a market economy, firms decide how to produce efficiently, guided by their desire to make a profit. In socialism, central planners decide how to produce. (3) For whom to produce? In a market economy, distribution is decided according to ability and inherited wealth. In socialism, distribution is according to individuals' needs (as determined by central planners).

2. The answer to this question will vary from person to person and will depend on personal finances, how much risk one is able and willing to undertake, how much responsibility one wants to take on, and whether or not you want to share in any profits. Given limited financial resources, I'd find a partner I can trust who has the funds needed to launch a web site, hire a firm to carry out transactions, and build inventory. With a partnership I can share the work and the risks of the venture. Since the liability associated with selling boxer shorts is not too great, unlimited liability with a partnership is not a problem. I would not choose a corporation because establishing one is a legal hassle requiring even more money. I would not choose a sole proprietorship because I don't have the funds to start the company on my own.

3. Globalization benefits nations by providing a greater quantity and wider variety of higher quality products to consumers at lower prices. The greater competition in the nation as a result of globalization ensures this. This translates into a higher *average* absolute standard of living for the nation. The costs of globalization are borne by those businesses and their workers who cannot compete in the global economy. However, new jobs are created in those industries for which the country has or creates a comparative advantage.

   The challenge for all countries is to equip displaced workers with the skills necessary to absorb the new jobs that are created. The key is to enhance worker productivity through investment in education, training, technology, and infrastructure because it is differences in productivity that support differences in wages and standards of living internationally. Nevertheless, over time, the benefits of globalization outweigh the costs for a nation. This helps to explain why virtually all countries pursue greater involvement in international trade.

SUPPLY AND DEMAND

● CHAPTER AT A GLANCE

This review is based upon the learning objectives that open the chapter.

1. The <u>law of demand</u> states that the quantity of a good demanded is <u>inversely related</u> to the good's price. When price goes up, quantity demanded goes down. When price goes down, quantity demanded goes up. (91)

   Law of Demand (Inverse Relationship):
   arrows move in $\uparrow P \rightarrow \downarrow Q_d$
   opposite directions $\downarrow P \rightarrow \uparrow Q_d$

   Law of Demand expressed as a <u>downward-sloping curve</u>:

   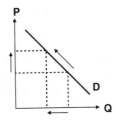

   To derive a demand curve from a demand table, plot each point on the demand table on a graph and connect the points.

   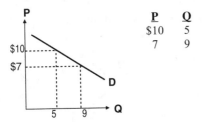

P	Q
$10	5
7	9

2a. The law of demand is based on opportunity cost and individuals' ability to substitute. If the price of a good rises, the opportunity cost of purchasing that good will also rise and consumers will substitute a good with a lower opportunity cost. (91)

   As the P of beef ↑s, we buy less beef and more chicken.

2b. The law of supply, like the law of demand, is based on opportunity cost and the individual firm's ability to substitute. Suppliers will substitute toward goods for which they receive higher relative prices. (97-98)

   If the P of wheat ↑s, farmers grow more wheat and less corn.

3. Changes in quantity demanded are shown by movements along a demand curve. Shifts in demand are shown by a shift of the entire demand curve. (92) *(Note: "Δ" means "change.")*

   Don't get this confused on the exam!

   ΔQ_d *is caused <u>only</u> by a* Δ *in the P of the good itself.*

   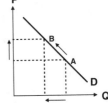

   $\Delta P \rightarrow \Delta Q_d \rightarrow$ *movement along a given D curve.*

   $\uparrow P \rightarrow \downarrow Q_d$*: movement along a curve (e.g. from point A to point B).*

   ΔD *is caused only by* Δ*s in the shift factors of D (<u>not</u> a* Δ *in the P of the good itself!)* <u>Δ *in shift factors of D*$\rightarrow \Delta D \rightarrow$ *shift of a D curve*</u>

   Know what can cause an increase and decrease in demand:
   $\uparrow D \rightarrow$ <u>*Rightward Shift*</u> $\downarrow D \rightarrow$ <u>*Leftward Shift*</u>

   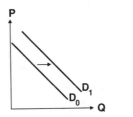 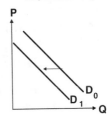

4. The <u>law of supply</u> states that the quantity of a good supplied is <u>directly</u> related to the good's price. When price goes up, quantity supplied goes up. When price goes down, quantity supplied goes down. (97-98)

Law of Supply (Direct Relationship):
arrows move in $\uparrow P \rightarrow \uparrow Q_s$
same direction $\downarrow P \rightarrow \downarrow Q_s$

Law of Supply expressed as an <u>upward-sloping curve</u>:

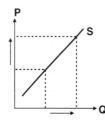

To derive a supply curve from a supply table, plot each point on the supply table on a graph and connect the points.

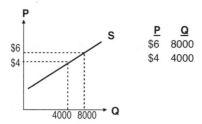

P	Q
$6	8000
$4	4000

5. Just as with demand, it is important to distinguish between a change in supply (due to a change in shift factors and reflected as a shift of the entire supply curve) and a change in the quantity supplied (due to a change in price and reflected as a movement along a supply curve). (98-100)
   Don't get this confused on the exam!

ΔQ_s *is caused <u>only</u> by a Δ in the P of the good itself.*

$\Delta P \rightarrow \Delta Q_s \rightarrow$ *movement along a given S curve.*

$\uparrow P \rightarrow \uparrow Q_s$: *movement along a curve (e.g. from point A to point B).*

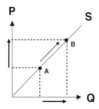

ΔS *is caused only by Δs in the shift factors of S (<u>not</u> a Δ in the P of the good itself!)*

<u>*Δ in shift factors of S $\rightarrow \Delta S \rightarrow$ shift of a S curve*</u>

Know what can cause an increase and decrease in supply:
$\uparrow S \rightarrow$ <u>*Rightward Shift*</u> $\downarrow S \rightarrow$ <u>*Leftward Shift*</u>

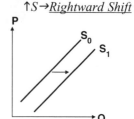 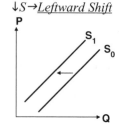

6. Equilibrium is where quantity supplied equals quantity demanded: (102-105)

   • If quantity demanded is greater than quantity supplied (excess demand), prices tend to rise;
   • If quantity supplied is greater than quantity demanded (excess supply), prices tend to fall.
   • When quantity demanded equals quantity supplied, prices have no tendency to change.

   <u>*Know this!*</u>
   • If $Q_d > Q_s \rightarrow$ Shortage$\rightarrow P$ will $\uparrow$.
   • If $Q_s > Q_d \rightarrow$ Surplus$\rightarrow P$ will $\downarrow$.
   • If $Q_s = Q_d \rightarrow$Equilibrium$\rightarrow$no tendency for P to change (because there is neither a surplus nor a shortage).

Shortage	**Surplus**	**Equilibrium**
($Q_d > Q_s$)	($Q_s > Q_d$)	($Q_s = Q_d$)
P is below equilibrium	P is above equilibrium	

7. Demand and supply curves enable us to determine the equilibrium price and quantity. In addition, changes (shifts) in demand and supply curves enable us to predict the effect on the equilibrium price and quantity in a market. (106-107)

Anything other than price that affects demand or supply will shift the curves.

Know how a change in demand or supply affects the equilibrium price and quantity!

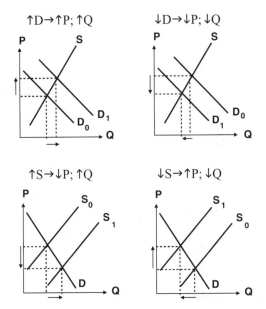

8. Simple supply and demand analysis holds other things constant. Sometimes supply and demand are interconnected, making it impossible to hold other things constant. When there is interdependence between supply and demand, a movement along one curve can cause the other curve to shift. Thus, supply and demand analysis used alone is not enough to determine where the equilibrium will be. (107-108)

When the "other things are constant" assumption is not realistic, feedback or ripple effects can become relevant. The degree of interdependence differs among various sets of issues. That is why there is a separate micro and macro analysis–microeconomics and macroeconomics.

The fallacy of composition is the false assumption that what is true for a part will also be true for the whole. This means that what is true in microeconomics may not be true in macroeconomics.

● SHORT-ANSWER QUESTIONS

1. What is the law of demand?

2. Draw a demand curve from the following
    demand table.

    Demand Table
Q	P
50	1
40	2
30	3
20	4

3. Demonstrate graphically a shift in demand and
    on another graph demonstrate movement
    along the demand curve.

4. State the law of supply.

5. What does the law of supply say that most
    individuals would do with the quantity of
    labor they supply employers if their wage
    increased? Explain the importance of substitu-
    tion in this decision.

6. Draw a supply curve from the following
    supply table.

    Supply Table
Q	P
20	1
30	2
40	3
50	4

7. Demonstrate graphically the effect of a new
    technology that reduces the cost of producing
    Linkin Park CDs on the supply of Linkin Park
    CDs.

8. Demonstrate graphically the effect of a rise in
    the price of Linkin Park CDs on the quantity
    supplied.

9. What are three things to note about supply
    and demand that help to explain how they
    interact to bring about equilibrium in a
    market?

10. Demonstrate graphically what happens to the
    equilibrium price and quantity of M&Ms if
    they suddenly become more popular.

11. Demonstrate graphically what happens to the equilibrium price and quantity of oranges if a frost destroys 50 percent of the orange crop.

12. What is the fallacy of composition and how is it related to why economists separate micro from macro economics?

MATCHING THE TERMS
Match the terms to their definitions

___ **1.** demand

___ **2.** demand curve

___ **3.** equilibrium

___ **4.** equilibrium price

___ **5.** equilibrium quantity

___ **6.** excess demand

___ **7.** excess supply

___ **8.** fallacy of composition

___ **9.** law of demand

___ **10.** law of supply

___ **11.** market demand curve

___ **12.** movement along a demand curve

___ **13.** movement along a supply curve

___ **14.** quantity demanded

___ **15.** quantity supplied

___ **16.** shift in demand

___ **17.** shift in supply

___ **18.** supply

___ **19.** supply curve

a. A specific amount that will be demanded per unit of time at a specific price, other things constant.

b. Curve that tells how much of a good will be bought at various prices.

c. The effect of a change in a shift factor on the supply curve.

d. Curve that tells how much of a good will be offered for sale at various prices.

e. The graphic representation of the effect of a change in price on the quantity supplied.

f. Quantity demanded rises as price falls, other things constant.

g. Quantity supplied rises as price rises, other things constant.

h. A schedule of quantities of a good that will be bought per unit of time at various prices, other things constant.

i. Quantity supplied is greater than quantity demanded.

j. A concept in which opposing dynamic forces cancel each other out.

k. The effect of a change in a shift factor on the demand curve.

l. The price toward which the invisible hand (economic forces) drives the market.

m. The horizontal sum of all individual demand curves.

n. Amount bought and sold at the equilibrium price.

o. Quantity demanded is greater than quantity supplied.

p. The graphic representation of the effect of a change in price on the quantity demanded.

q. A specific amount that will be offered for sale per unit of time at a specific price.

r. A schedule of quantities a seller is willing to sell per unit of time at various prices, other things constant.

s. The false assumption that what is true for a part will also be true for the whole.

● PROBLEMS AND APPLICATIONS

1. Draw two linear curves on the same graph from the following table, one relating P with Q_1 and the other relating P with Q_2.

P	Q_1	Q_2
$30	60	100
35	70	90
40	80	80
45	90	70

a. Label the curve that is most likely a demand curve. Explain your choice.

b. Label the curve that is most likely a supply curve. Explain your choice.

c. What is the equilibrium price and quantity? Choose points above and below that price and explain why each is not the equilibrium price.

2. Correct the following statements, if needed, so that the terms "demand," "quantity demanded," "supply," and "quantity supplied" are used correctly.

a. As the price of pizza increases, consumers demand less pizza.

b. Whenever the price of bicycles increases, the supply of bicycles increases.

c. The price of electricity is cheaper in the northwestern part of the United States and therefore the demand for electricity is greater in the northwest.

d. An increase in the incomes of car buyers will increase the quantity demanded for cars.

e. An increase in the quantity demanded of lobsters means consumers are willing and able to buy more lobsters at any given price.

f. A decrease in the supply of frog legs means suppliers will provide fewer frog legs at any given price.

3. You are given the following individual demand tables for compact discs.

Price	Juan	Philippe	Ramone
$7	3	20	50
$10	2	10	40
$13	1	7	32
$16	0	5	26
$19	0	3	20
$22	0	0	14

a. Determine the market demand table.

b. Graph the individual and market demand curves.

c. If the current market price is $13, what is the total market quantity demanded? What happens to total market quantity demanded if the price rises to $19 a disc?

d. Say that a new popular Usher compact disc hits the market that increases demand for compact discs by 25%. Show with a demand table what happens to the individual and market demand curves. Demonstrate graphically what happens to market demand.

4. The following table depicts the market supply and demand for oranges in the United States (in thousands of bushels).

Price per bushel	Quantity supplied	Quantity demanded
$15	7000	2000
$14	5500	3000
$13	4000	4000
$12	2500	5000
$11	1000	6000

    a. Graph the market supply and demand for oranges.

    b. What is the equilibrium price and quantity of oranges in the market? Why?

    c. Suppose the price is $14. Would we observe a surplus (excess supply) or a shortage (excess demand)? If so, by how much? What could be expected to happen to the price over time? Why?

    d. Suppose the price is $12. Would we observe a surplus or a shortage? If so, by how much? What could be expected to happen to the price over time? Why?

5. Draw a hypothetical demand and supply curve for cyber cafes — coffee houses with computers hooked up to the Internet with access to daily newspapers (among other things) at each table. Show how demand or supply is affected by the following:

    a. A technological breakthrough lowers the cost of computers.

    b. Consumers' income rises.

    c. A per-hour fee is charged to coffee houses to use the Internet.

    d. The price of newspapers in print rises.

    e. Possible suppliers expect cyber cafes to become more popular.

6. Use supply and demand curves to help you determine the impact that each of the following events has on the market for surfboards in Southern California.

    a. Southern California experiences unusually high temperatures, sending an unusually large number of people to its beaches.

    b. Large sharks are reported feeding near the beaches of Southern California.

c. Due to the large profits earned by surf-board producers there is a significant increase in the number of producers of surfboards.

d. There is a significant increase in the price of epoxy paint used to coat surfboards.

7. Use supply and demand curves to help you determine the impact that each of the following events has on the market for beef.

a. New genetic engineering technology enables ranchers to raise healthier, heavier cattle, significantly reducing costs.

b. The CBS program "60 Minutes" reports on the unsanitary conditions in poultry processing plants that may increase the chances of consumers getting sick by eating chicken.

c. In addition to developing new genetic engineering technology, highly credible new research results report that abundant consumption of fatty red meats actually prolongs average life expectancy.

d. Consumers expect the price of beef to fall in the near future.

● A BRAIN TEASER

1. The invention of a self-milking cow machine allows cows to milk themselves. Not only does this reduce the need for higher-cost human assistance in milking, but it also allows the cow to milk herself three times a day instead of two, leading to both a healthier cow and increased milk production.

a. Show the effect of this innovation on the equilibrium quantity and price of milk.

b. Show the likely effect on equilibrium price and quantity of apple juice (a substitute for milk).

● MULTIPLE CHOICE

Circle the one best answer for each of the following questions:

1. The law of demand states:
   a. quantity demanded increases as price falls, other things constant.
   b. more of a good will be demanded the higher its price, other things constant.
   c. people always want more.
   d. you can't always get what you want at the price you want.

2. There are many more substitutes for good A than for good B.
   a. The demand curve for good B will likely shift out further.
   b. The demand curve for good B will likely be flatter.
   c. You can't say anything about the likely relative flatness of the demand curves.
   d. The demand curve for good A will likely be flatter.

3. If the weather gets very hot, what will most likely happen?
   a. The supply of air conditioners will increase.
   b. Quantity of air conditioners demanded will increase.
   c. Demand for air conditioners will increase.
   d. The quality of air conditioners demanded will increase.

4. If the price of air conditioners falls, there will be:
   a. an increase in demand for air conditioners.
   b. an increase in the quantity of air conditioners demanded.
   c. an increase in the quantity of air conditioners supplied.
   d. a shift out of the demand for air conditioners.

5. An increase in demand:
   a. is reflected as a rightward (outward) shift of the demand curve.
   b. is caused by a decrease in price.
   c. means demanders are buying less at any price
   d. shifts the demand curve to the left (inward).

6. The demand curve will likely shift outward to the right if:
   a. society's income falls.
   b. the price of a substitute good falls.
   c. the price of the good is expected to rise in the near future.
   d. the good goes out of style.

7. The difference between the quantity demanded and demand is:
   a. the quantity demanded is associated with a whole set of prices, whereas demand is associated with a particular price.
   b. the quantity demanded is associated with a particular price, whereas demand is associated with a whole set of prices.

c. the quantity demanded is the whole demand curve, whereas demand is a particular point along a demand curve.
d. a change in the quantity demanded is reflected graphically as a shift of the demand curve, whereas a change in demand is reflected as movement along a given demand curve.

8. If there is a flood, what will most likely happen in the market for bottled water?
   a. Demand will increase.
   b. Demand will fall.
   c. Supply will increase.
   d. Supply will decrease.

9. The movement in the graph below from point A to point B represents:

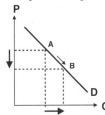

   a. an increase in demand.
   b. an increase in the quantity demanded.
   c. an increase in the quantity supplied.
   d. an increase in supply.

10. Using the standard axes, the demand curve associated with the following demand table is:

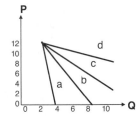

Demand Table	
P	**Q**
7	5
9	4
11	3

   a. a
   b. b
   c. c
   d. d

11. To derive a market demand curve from two individual demand curves:
   a. one adds the two demand curves horizontally.
   b. one adds the two demand curves vertically.
   c. one subtracts one demand curve from the other demand curve.
   d. one adds the demand curves both horizontally and vertically.

12. The market demand curve will always:
  a. be unrelated to the individual demand curves and slope.
  b. be steeper than the individual demand curves that make it up.
  c. have the same slope as the individual demand curves that make it up.
  d. be flatter than the individual demand curves that make it up.

13. The law of supply states that:
  a. quantity supplied increases as price increases, other things constant.
  b. quantity supplied decreases as price increases, other things constant.
  c. more of a good will be supplied the higher its price, other things changing proportionately.
  d. less of a good will be supplied the higher its price, other things changing proportionately.

14. In the graph below, the arrow refers to:

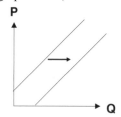

  a. a shift in demand.
  b. a shift in supply.
  c. a change in the quantity demanded.
  d. a change in the quantity supplied.

15. If there is an improvement in technology one would expect:
  a. a movement along the supply curve.
  b. a shift upward (or to the left) of the supply curve.
  c. a shift downward (or to the right) of the supply curve.
  d. a movement down along the supply curve.

16. You're the supplier of a good and suddenly a number of your long-lost friends call you to buy your product. Your good is most likely:
  a. in excess supply.
  b. in excess demand.
  c. in equilibrium.
  d. in both excess supply and demand.

17. At which point on the graph below will you expect the strongest downward pressure on prices?

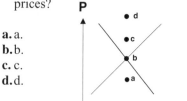

  a. a.
  b. b.
  c. c.
  d. d.

18. If at some price the quantity supplied exceeds the quantity demanded, then:
  a. a surplus (excess supply) exists and the price will fall over time as sellers competitively bid down the price.
  b. a shortage (excess demand) exists and the price will rise over time as buyers competitively bid up the price.
  c. the price is below equilibrium.
  d. equilibrium will be reestablished as the demand curve shifts to the left.

19. If the price of a good:
  a. rises, it is a response to a surplus (excess supply).
  b. falls, it is a response to a shortage (excess demand).
  c. is below equilibrium, then a shortage will be observed.
  d. is below equilibrium, then a surplus will be observed.

20. If the demand for a good increases, you will expect price to:
  a. fall and quantity to rise.
  b. rise and quantity to rise.
  c. fall and quantity to fall.
  d. rise and quantity to fall.

21. If the supply of a good decreases, you will expect price to:
  a. fall and quantity to rise.
  b. rise and quantity to rise.
  c. fall and quantity to fall.
  d. rise and quantity to fall.

22. Consider the market for bikinis. If bikinis suddenly become more fashionable, you will expect:
  a. a temporary shortage of bikinis that will be eliminated over time as the market price of

bikinis rises and a greater quantity is bought and sold.

b. a temporary shortage of bikinis that will be eliminated over time as the market price of bikinis rises and a smaller quantity is bought and sold.

c. a temporary surplus of bikinis that will be eliminated over time as the market price of bikinis falls and a smaller quantity is bought and sold.

d. a temporary surplus of bikinis that will be eliminated over time as the market price of bikinis rises and a greater quantity is bought and sold.

23. Compared to last year, fewer oranges are being purchased and the selling price has decreased. This could have been caused by:
   a. an increase in demand.
   b. an increase in supply.
   c. a decrease in demand.
   d. a decrease in supply.

24. If demand and supply both increase, this will cause:
   a. an increase in the equilibrium quantity, but an uncertain effect on the equilibrium price.
   b. an increase in the equilibrium price, but an uncertain effect on the equilibrium quantity.
   c. an increase in the equilibrium price and quantity.
   d. a decrease in the equilibrium price and quantity.

25. An increase in demand for a good will cause:
   a. excess demand (a shortage) before price changes.
   b. movement down along the demand curve as price changes.
   c. movement down along the supply curve as price changes.
   d. a higher price and a smaller quantity traded in the market.

26. The fallacy of composition is:
   a. the false assumption that what is false for a part will also be false for the whole.
   b. the false assumption that what is true for a part will also be true for the whole.
   c. the false assumption that what is false for a whole will also be false for the part.
   d. the false assumption that what is true for a whole will also be true for the part.

● POTENTIAL ESSAY QUESTIONS

You may also see essay questions similar to the "Problems & Applications" and "Brain Teaser" exercises.

1. Many university campuses sell parking permits to their students allowing them to park on campus in designated areas. Although most students complain about the relatively high cost of these parking permits, what annoys many students even more is that after having paid for their permits, vacant parking spaces in the designated lots are very difficult to find during much of the day. Many end up having to park off campus anyway, where permits are not required. Assuming the university is unable to build new parking facilities on campus due to insufficient funds, what recommendation might you make to remedy the problem of students with permits being unable to find places to park on campus?

2. Discuss how changes in demand or supply impact a market equilibrium price and quantity.

ANSWERS

SHORT-ANSWER QUESTIONS

1. The law of demand states that the quantity of a good demanded is inversely related to the good's price. When price goes up, quantity demanded goes down, other things constant. (91)

2. To derive a demand curve from a demand table, you plot each point on the demand table on a graph and connect the points. This is shown on the graph below. (94-95)

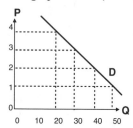

3. A shift in demand is shown by a shift of the entire demand curve resulting from a change in a shift factor of demand as shown in the graph below on the left (which illustrates an increase in demand because it is a rightward shift). A movement along a demand curve is shown on the right as a movement from point A to point B due to a price decrease. (92 and Figure 4-2 on page 94)

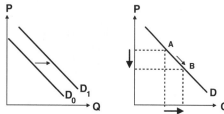

4. The law of supply states that the quantity supplied rises as price rises. Or alternatively: quantity supplied falls as price falls. (97-98)

5. The law of supply states that quantity supplied rises as price rises; quantity supplied falls as price falls. According to this law, most individuals would choose to supply a greater quantity of labor hours if their wage increased. They will substitute work for leisure. (See Figure 4-5 on page 98.)

6. To derive a supply curve from a supply table, you plot each point on the supply table on a graph and connect the points. This is shown on the graph in the next column. (100-101)

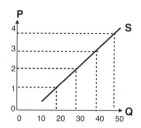

7. A new technology that reduces the cost of producing Linkin Park CDs will shift the entire supply curve to the right from S_0 to S_1, as shown in the graph below. (99-100)

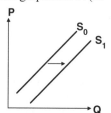

8. A rise in the price of Linkin Park CDs from P_0 to P_1 results in a movement up along a supply curve and the quantity of Linkin Park CDs supplied will rise from Q_0 to Q_1 as shown in the graph below. (99-100)

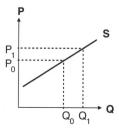

9. The first thing to note is that when quantity demanded is greater than quantity supplied, prices tend to rise and when quantity supplied is greater than quantity demanded, prices tend to fall. Each case is demonstrated in the graph below. Price tends away from P_1 and P_2 and toward P_0.

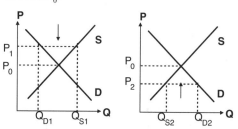

The second thing to note is that the larger the difference between quantity supplied and quantity demanded, the greater the pressure on prices to rise (if there is excess demand; a shortage) or fall (if there is excess supply; a surplus). This is demonstrated in the graph below. At P_2, the pressure for prices to fall toward P_0 is greater than the pressure at P_1 because excess supply (surplus) is greater at P_2 compared to excess supply at P_1.

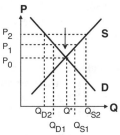

The third thing to note is that when quantity demanded equals quantity supplied, the market is in equilibrium. This is shown graphically at the point of intersection between the demand and supply curves. (102-105)

10. Increasing popularity of M&Ms means that at every price, more M&Ms are demanded. The demand curve shifts out to the right from D_0 to D_1, and both equilibrium price and quantity rise to P_1 and Q_1 respectively. (106-107)

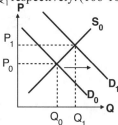

11. A frost damaging oranges means that at every price, suppliers will supply fewer oranges. The supply curve shifts in to the left from S_0 to S_1, and equilibrium price rises to P_1, and quantity traded falls to Q_1. (106-107)

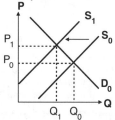

12. The fallacy of composition is the false assumption that what is true for a part will also be true for the whole. In micro, economists isolate an individual person's or firm's behavior and consider its effects, while the many side effects are kept in the background. In macro, those

side effects become too large and can no longer be held constant. These side effects are what account for the interdependence of supply and demand. Macro, thus, is not simply a summation of all micro results; it would be a fallacy of composition to take the sum of each individual's (micro) actions and say that this will be the aggregate (macro) result. (108)

ANSWERS

MATCHING

1-h; 2-b; 3-j; 4-l; 5-n; 6-o; 7-i; 8-s; 9-f; 10-g; 11-m; 12-p; 13-e; 14-a; 15-q; 16-k; 17-c; 18-r; 19-d.

ANSWERS

PROBLEMS AND APPLICATIONS

1. The linear curves are shown on the right. (See Figure 4-8 on page 98)

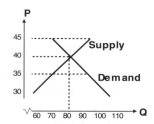

   a. As shown in the graph, the downward sloping curve is a demand curve. We deduce this from the law of demand: quantity demanded rises (falls) as the price decreases (increases). (91)
   b. As shown in the graph, the upward sloping curve is a supply curve. We deduce this from the law of supply: quantity supplied rises (falls) as the price rises (falls). (98)
   c. The equilibrium price and quantity are where the demand and supply curves intersect. This is at $P = \$40, Q = 80$. At a price above \$40, such as \$45, quantity supplied exceeds quantity demanded and there is pressure for price to fall. At a price below \$40, such as \$35, quantity demanded exceeds quantity supplied and there is pressure for price to rise. (104-105)

2. a. As the price of pizza increases, the *quantity demanded* of pizza decreases. (92)

Note that a change in the price of an item will cause a change in the quantity demanded; <u>not</u> a change in demand! A change in something else other than the price may cause a change in demand–such as a change in one of the shift factors of demand discussed in the textbook.

b. Whenever the price of bicycles increases, the *quantity of bicycles supplied* also increases. (99)

Note that a change in the price will cause a change in the quantity supplied; <u>not</u> supply! A change in something else other than the price–such as a change in one of the shift factors of supply discussed in the textbook–may cause a change in supply.

c. The price of electricity is cheaper in the NW part of the U. S. and therefore the *quantity demanded* of electricity is greater in the NW. (92-93)

d. An increase in incomes of car buyers will increase the *demand* for cars. (92-93)

Notice that a change in a shift factor of demand, such as income, will change demand; <u>not</u> the quantity demanded!

e. An increase in the *demand* for lobsters means consumers are willing and able to buy more lobsters at any given price (whatever the current price is). (92-93)

In order for there to be an increase in the quantity demanded there would have to be a decrease in the price. Moreover, recall that an increase in demand is reflected as a rightward shift of the demand curve. Upon viewing a graph where the demand curve has shifted to the right you will see that more will be purchased at any given price.

f. This is a correct use of the term "supply." Notice that a decrease in supply is reflected graphically as a leftward shift of the curve and less will be provided in the market at any given price. (99-100)

3. a. The market demand table is the summation of individual quantities demanded at each price as follows (95-96):

P	Q
$7	73
10	52
13	40
16	31
19	23
22	14

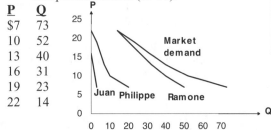

b. The individual and market demand curves are shown to the right of the demand table. (95-96)

c. At $13 a disc, total market quantity demanded is 40 discs. Total market quantity demanded falls to 23 when the price of discs rises to $19 per disc. (95-96)

d. Quantity demanded at each price rises by 25% for each individual and for the market as a whole. The new demand table is shown below. Graphically, both the individual and market demand curves shift to the right. The graph below shows the rightward shift in market demand. (95-96)

Price	Juan	Philippe	Ramone	Market
$7	3.75	25	62.50	91.25
$10	2.50	12.5	50	65
$13	1.25	8.75	40	50
$16	0	6.25	32.5	38.75
$19	0	3.75	25	28.75
$21	0	0	17.5	17.5

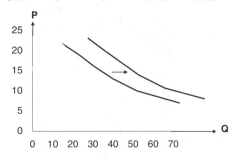

4. a. See the graph below. (See Figure 4-8 on page 105.)

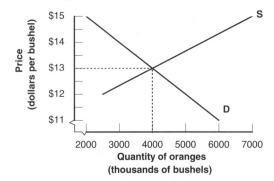

b. The equilibrium price is $13, the equilibrium quantity is 4000. This is an equilibrium because the quantity supplied equals the quantity demanded at this price. That is, there is neither a surplus (excess supply) nor a shortage (excess demand) and hence no tendency for the price to change. (104-105)

c. Because the quantity supplied exceeds the quantity demanded when the price is $14 per bushel, we would observe a surplus of 2,500 bushels (in thousands of bushels). We can expect the price of oranges per bushel to fall as sellers scramble to rid themselves of their excess supplies. (104-105)

d. Because the quantity demanded exceeds the quantity supplied at $12 per bushel, we would observe a shortage of 2,500 bushels (in thousands of bushels). We can expect the price of oranges per bushel to rise as some buyers competitively bid up the price just to get some oranges. (104-105)

5. A hypothetical market for cyber cafes shows an upward sloping supply curve, a downward sloping demand curve and an equilibrium price and quantity where the two curves intersect.

a. A technological breakthrough that lowers the cost of computers will shift the supply of cyber cafes to the right as shown in the graph below. (99)

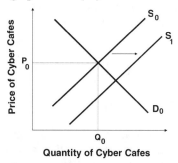

b. A rise in consumers' income will shift the demand for cyber cafes to the right as shown in the graph below. (92-93)

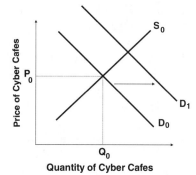

c. If a fee is charged to coffee houses to use the Internet, the supply of cyber cafes will shift to the left as shown in the accompanying graph. (99)

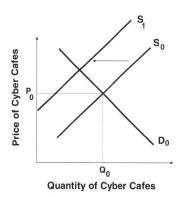

d. If the price of newspapers in print rises, the demand for cyber cafes will shift to the right as shown in the graph for answer (b). (102-103)

e. If possible suppliers expect cyber cafes to become more popular, the supply of cyber cafes will shift to the right as shown in the graph for answer (a). (99)

6. a. This will increase the demand for surfboards shifting the demand curve to the right. At the original price a temporary shortage would be observed putting upward pressure on price. We end up with a higher equilibrium price and a greater equilibrium quantity as illustrated in the graph below. (*When dealing with a change in D or S curves, just remember to go from the initial point of intersection will give you between the curves to the new point of intersection. The initial point of intersection will give you the initial equilibrium P and Q and the new point of intersection the new equilibrium P and Q. Then recall that if the price went up in the market, it was a response to a temporary shortage (excess demand). If the equilibrium price went down, then it was a response to a temporary surplus (excess supply).* (106-107)

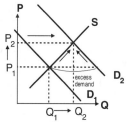

b. This would cause a decrease in the demand for surfboards shifting the demand curve to the left. At the original price a temporary surplus would be observed putting downward pressure on price. We end up with a lower equilibrium price and a lower equilibrium quantity, as illustrated in the graph below. (106-107)

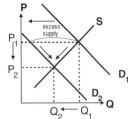

c.   This would cause an increase in the supply of surfboards, shifting the supply curve to the right. At the original price a temporary surplus would be observed, putting downward pressure on price. We end up with a lower equilibrium price and a higher equilibrium quantity, as illustrated in the graph below. (106-107)

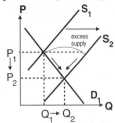

d.   This would cause a decrease in the supply of surfboards ,shifting the supply curve to the left. At the original price a temporary shortage would be observed, putting upward pressure on price. We end up with a higher equilibrium price and a lower equilibrium quantity, as illustrated in the graph below. (106-107)

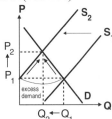

7.   a.   An increase in production technology will increase the supply of beef. The temporary surplus (excess supply) of beef at the original price will cause the market price to fall. Eventually we get a lower equilibrium price of beef and a greater amount bought and sold in the market. (106-107)

b.   Chicken and beef are substitute goods– they can be used instead of each other. Therefore, this "60 Minutes" report will likely increase the demand for beef. The temporary shortage (excess demand) at the original price will cause the price to be competitively bid up. Eventually we observe a higher equilibrium price and a greater equilibrium quantity. (106-107)

c.   The new development would increase the supply of beef while the reports of the health benefits of beef would increase the demand for beef. Quantity of beef sold would definitely rise. The impact on equilibrium price, however, depends upon the relative sizes of the shifts. (106-107)

d.   Because people will postpone their purchases of beef until the price de-creases, the demand for beef will fall today. A decrease in demand is reflected as a leftward shift of the demand curve. The temporary excess supply (surplus) that is created at the original price puts downward pressure on the market price of beef. Eventually we get a lower equilibrium price and quantity. (106-107)

ANSWERS

A BRAIN TEASER

1.   a.   This innovation will shift the supply curve to the right as shown in the graph on the left below. As a result, this creates excess supply and the equilibrium price falls while the equilibrium quantity rises. (106-107)

b.   The market demand and supply for apple juice is shown below on the right. As a result of the fall in milk prices (assuming milk and apple juice are substitutes), the demand for apple juice shifts to the left. This creates excess supply of apple juice. The equilibrium price will fall. The equilibrium quantity will also fall. (106-107)

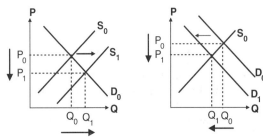

ANSWERS

MULTIPLE CHOICE

1. a   As discussed on page 91, the correct answer is a. A possible answer is d, which is a restatement of the law of demand, but since the actual law was among the choices, and is more precise, a is the correct answer.

2. d   An equal rise in price will cause individuals to switch more to other goods when there are more substitutes. See page 91.

3. c   As discussed on pages 92-93, it is important to distinguish between a change in the quantity demanded and a change in demand. Weather is a shift factor of demand, so demand, not quantity demanded, will increase. Supply will not increase; the quantity supplied will, however. Who knows what will happen to the quality demanded? We don't.

4. b   As discussed on page 92, when the price falls there is a movement along the demand curve which is expressed by saying the quantity demanded increased. Moreover, as the price falls, the quantity supplied falls.

5. a   As discussed on pages 92-93, an increase in demand is expressed as an outward (or rightward) shift of the demand curve. It is caused by something other than the price. It means people will buy more at any price or pay a higher price for a given quantity demanded.

6. c   All of these are shift factors of demand. However, only c will increase demand and shift the demand curve to the right. See pages 92-93.

7. b   As is discussed on page 92, b is the only correct response.

8. a   A flood will likely bring about a significant increase in the demand for bottled water since a flood makes most other water undrinkable. A flood would be a shift factor of demand for bottled water. See pages 92-93.

9. b   The curve slopes downward, so we can surmise that it is a demand curve; and the two points are on the demand curve, so the movement represents an increase in the quantity demanded, not an increase in demand. Moreover, as price falls, the quantity demanded rises. A shift in demand would be a shift of the entire curve. (See figures on page 94.)

10. b   This demand curve is the only demand curve that goes through all the points in the table. See page 95.

11. a   As discussed in the text on page 96 (Figure 4-4), market demand curves are determined by adding individuals' demand curves horizontally. That is, you add the quantities demanded at each price.

12. d   Since the market demand curve is derived by adding the individual demand curves horizontally, it will always be flatter. See pages 95-96 and Figure 4-4.

13. a   As discussed on pages 97-98, the law of supply is stated in a. The others either have the movement in the wrong direction or are not holding all other things constant.

14. b   It is a shift in supply because the curve is upward sloping; and it's a shift of the entire curve, so it is not a movement along. See pages 99-100 and Figure 4-6.

15. c   As discussed on page 99, technology is a shift factor of supply so it must be a shift of the supply curve. Since it is an improvement, it must be a shift rightward (or downward). (See also page 100, Figure 4-6)

16. b   When there is excess demand, demanders start searching for new suppliers, as discussed on pages 102-104.

17. d   The greater the extent to which the quantity supplied exceeds the quantity demanded, the greater the surplus (excess supply) and the greater the pressure for the price to fall. See pages 102-104.

18. a   As discussed on page 103, there is a surplus (excess supply) when the price is above equilibrium. A surplus will motivate sellers to reduce price to rid themselves of their excess supplies. As the price falls, the quantity demand rises and the quantity supplied falls; demand and supply curves do *not* shift.

19. c As discussed on pages 103-104 whenever price is below equilibrium, a shortage is observed, and price rises.

20. b Since this statement says demand increases, then the demand curve shifts rightward. There is no change in the supply curve. Assuming an upward sloping supply curve, that means that price will rise and quantity will rise. See pages 106-107.

21. d Since this statement says supply decreases, then the supply curve shifts leftward. There is no change in the demand curve. Assuming a downward sloping demand curve, that means that price will rise and quantity will fall. See pages 106-107.

22. a The demand for bikinis would rise shifting the demand curve to the right. The supply curve does not change. This creates a temporary shortage that is eliminated over time as the market moves to its new equilibrium at a higher price and a greater quantity traded. See pages 106-107.

23. c Only a decrease in demand will result in a decrease in quantity and a decrease in price. See pages 106-107.

24. a An increase in demand has a tendency to increase price and increase the quantity. An increase in supply has a tendency to *decrease* the price and increase the quantity. So, on balance, we are certain of an increase in the equilibrium quantity, but we are uncertain about the impact on the price in the market. See pages 106-107.

25. a An increase in demand causes the quantity demanded to exceed the quantity supplied, creating excess demand (a shortage). This increases the price causing movement *up* along the demand and supply curves resulting in a *greater* quantity traded in the market. See pages 106-107.

26. b The fallacy of composition is the false assumption that what is true for a part will also be true for the whole. See page 108.

ANSWERS

POTENTIAL ESSAY QUESTIONS

The following are annotated answers. They indicate the general idea behind the answer.

1. The shortage of parking spaces implies that permit prices are below equilibrium. The price of a permit should be increased. At least with the purchase of a permit you could be reasonably certain that a space would be available.

2. Suppose there is an increase in demand. The demand curve shifts out to the right, creating a temporary shortage (excess demand) at the original price. As a result, buyers competitively bid up the price. As the price rises, the quantity demanded falls (movement up along the demand curve toward the new point of intersection) and the quantity supplied rises (movement up along the supply curve toward the new point of intersection). Eventually, the price rises enough until the quantity demanded is once again equal to the quantity supplied. Because there is neither a shortage nor a surplus at this new point of intersection, the new market equilibrium price and quantity is obtained. The market equilibrium price and quantity will both increase as a result of an increase in demand. *You should be able to illustrate this graphically as well.*

USING SUPPLY AND DEMAND

● CHAPTER AT A GLANCE

This review is based upon the learning objectives that open the chapter.

1. Changes (shifts) in demand and supply are what cause changes in the price and the quantity traded in real-world markets. (114-121)

   Shifts in both demand and supply can be tricky. But remember, simply locate the new point of intersection. When both curves shift, the effect on either price or quantity depends on the relative size of the shifts. Moreover, the effect on either price or quantity (one of them) will be certain, while the effect on the other will be uncertain. Note:

$\uparrow$D and $\uparrow$S→?P;$\uparrow$Q $\uparrow$D and $\downarrow$S→$\uparrow$P;? Q

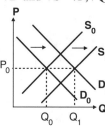

$\downarrow$D and $\uparrow$S→$\downarrow$P; ?Q $\downarrow$D and $\downarrow$S→?P;$\downarrow$ Q

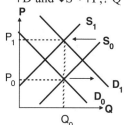

2. The determination of exchange rates—the price of currencies—can be determined by supply and demand analysis, in the same way supply and demand analysis applies to any other good. (116-117)

Exchange rates reported daily in newspapers enable us to determine the dollar price of foreign goods.

3. Price ceilings cause shortages; price floors cause surpluses. (121-125)

   A price ceiling is a legal price set by government below equilibrium. An example is rent controls. A price floor (sometimes called a price support) is a legal price set by government above equilibrium. An example is the minimum wage.

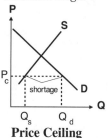

Price Ceiling   **Price Floor**

4. Excise taxes and tariffs (excise taxes paid by foreign producers on imported goods) raise price and reduce quantity. Quantity restrictions also decrease supply (shift the supply curve up, to the left) raising the price and reducing the quantity. (125-127)

   Any excise tax imposed on suppliers shifts the supply curve up by the amount of the tax. Rarely is the tax entirely passed on to consumers in the form of a higher price. Quantity restrictions also decrease supply.

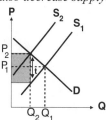

With tax t, price rises to P_2 and the government collects revenue shown by the shaded region. A quantity restriction of Q_2 has the same effect on price and quantity.

5. In a third-party payer system, the consumer and the one who pays the cost differ. In third-party payer systems quantity demanded, price, and total spending are greater than when the consumer pays. (127-128)

The graph below shows the effects of a third-party payer market. In a free market, given the supply and demand curve shown, equilibrium price is P_1 and equilibrium quantity is Q_1. If the co-payment, however, is P_0, the consumer purchases quantity Q_2. The supplier will only sell that quantity at price P_2, so the third party pays the difference $(P_2 - P_0)$. Under a third-party payer system, total expenditures are larger—shown by the larger shaded square—than a free market—shown by the smaller and darker shaded square.

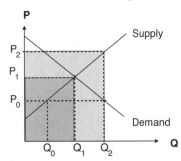

Third-party payers are typically health insurance companies, Medicare or Medicaid. Consumers have little incentive to hold down costs when someone else pays. Much of the health care system in the United States today is a third-party payer system.

See also, "Appendix A: Algebraic Representation of Supply, Demand, and Equilibrium."

● SHORT-ANSWER QUESTIONS

1. Demonstrate graphically what happens in the following situation: Income in the U.S. rose in the 1990s and more and more people began to buy luxury items such as caviar. However, about that same time, the dissolution of the Soviet Union threw suppliers of caviar from the Caspian Sea into a mire of bureaucracy, reducing their ability to export caviar. Market: Caviar sold in the United States.

2. What changes in demand or supply would increase the exchange rate value of the dollar?

3. What is a price ceiling? Demonstrate graphically the effect of a price ceiling on a market.

4. What is a price floor? Demonstrate graphically the effect of a price floor on a market.

5. Why are rent controls likely to worsen an existing shortage of housing?

6. Demonstrate graphically what happens to equilibrium price and quantity when a tariff is imposed on imports.

7. What is a third-party payer system? Name one example.

MATCHING THE TERMS
Match the terms to their definitions

___ **1.**	euro	**a.**	The lowest wage a firm can legally pay an employee.
___ **2.**	exchange rate	**b.**	Tax on an imported good.
___ **3.**	excise tax	**c.**	Tax that is levied on a specific good.
___ **4.**	minimum wage	**d.**	The person who decides how much of the good to buy differs from the person paying for the good.
___ **5.**	price ceiling		
___ **6.**	price floor	**e.**	A government-imposed limit on how high a price can be charged.
___ **7.**	rent control	**f.**	The price of one currency in terms of another currency.
___ **8.**	tariff	**g.**	Price ceiling on rents set by government.
___ **9.**	third-party payer market	**h.**	A government-imposed limit on how low a price can be charged.
		i.	The currency used by some members of the European Union.

PROBLEMS AND APPLICATIONS

1. Suppose you are told that the price of Cadillacs has increased from last year, as has the number bought and sold. Is this an exception to the law of demand, or has there been a change in demand or supply that could account for this?

2. Suppose the exchange rate is one dollar for 125 Japanese yen. How much will a $50 pair of Levi jeans cost a Japanese consumer? How much will a 4,000,000 yen Toyota cost an American consumer?

3. The following table depicts the market supply and demand for milk in the United States.

Price in dollars per gal.	Quantity of gal. supplied in 1,000s	Quantity of gal. demanded in 1,000s
$1.50	600	800
$1.75	620	720
$2.00	640	640
$2.25	660	560
$2.50	680	480

a. Graph the market supply and demand for milk.

b. What is the equilibrium market price and quantity in the market?

c. Show the effect of a government–imposed price floor of $2.25 on the quantity supplied and quantity demanded.

d. Show the effect of a government–imposed price ceiling of $1.75 on the quantity supplied and quantity demanded.

e. What would happen to equilibrium price and quantity if the government imposes a $1 per gallon tax on the sellers and as a result, at every price supply decreases by 100,000? What price would the sellers receive?

4. Suppose the U.S. government imposes stricter entry barriers on Japanese cars imported into the United States. This could be accomplished by the U.S. government either raising tariffs or imposing a quantity restriction (such as a quota).

    a. What impact would this have on the market for Japanese cars in the United States?

    b. What impact would this likely have on the market for American-made cars in the United States?

    c. What do you think could motivate the U.S. government to pursue these stricter entry barriers on Japanese cars coming into the U.S.?

    d. Would Japanese car manufacturers prefer a tariff or a quota? Why?

5. Describe what likely happens to market price and quantity for the particular goods in each of the following cases:

    a. A technological breakthrough lowers the costs of producing tractors in India while there is an increase in incomes of all citizens in India. Market: tractors.

    b. The United States imposes a ban on the sale of oil by companies that do business with Libya and Iran. At the same time, very surprisingly, a large reserve of drillable oil is discovered in Barrington, Rhode Island. Market: Oil.

    c. In the summer of 2004, many people watched the Summer Olympics on television instead of going to the movies. At the same time, thinking that summer is the peak season for movies, Hollywood released a record number of movies. Market: Movie tickets.

    d. After a promotional visit by Michael Jordan to France, a craze for Nike Air shoes develops, while workers in Nike's manufacturing plants in China go on strike, decreasing the production of these shoes. Market: Nike shoes.

A1. The supply and demand equations for strawberries are given by $Q_s = -10 + 5P$ and $Q_d = 20 - 5P$ respectively, where P is price in dollars per quart, Q_s is millions of quarts of strawberries supplied, and Q_d is millions of quarts of strawberries demanded.

    a. What is the equilibrium market price and quantity for strawberries in the market?

b. Suppose a new preservative is introduced that prevents more strawberries from rotting on their way from the farm to the store. As a result, the supply of strawberries increases by 20 million quarts at every price. What effect does this have on market price and quantity sold?

c. Suppose it has been found that the spray used on cherry trees has ill effects on those who eat the cherries. As a result, the demand for strawberries increases by 10 million quarts at every price. What effect does this have on market price for strawberries and quantity of strawberries sold?

A2. The supply and demand equations for roses are given by $Q_s = -10 + 3P$ and $Q_d = 20 - 2P$ respectively, where P is dollars per dozen roses and Q is dozens of roses in hundred thousands.

a. What is the equilibrium market price and quantity of roses sold?

b. Suppose the government decides to make it more affordable for individuals to give roses to their significant others, and sets a price ceiling for roses at $4 a dozen. What is the likely result?

c. Suppose the government decides to tax the suppliers of roses $1 per dozen roses sold. What is the equilibrium price and quantity in the market? How much do buyers pay for each dozen they buy for their significant others? How much do suppliers receive for each dozen they sell?

d. Suppose the government decides instead to impose a $1 tax on buyers for each dozen roses purchased. (Government has determined buying roses for love to be a demerit good.) What is the equilibrium price and quantity in the market? How much do the buyers pay and how much do the sellers receive?

● A BRAIN TEASER

1. Buchananland wants to restrict its number of auto imports from Zachstan. It is trying to decide whether it should impose a tariff or quantity restrictions (in this case called quotas) on Zachstani cars. With the help of a diagram, explain why auto makers in Zachstan have hired a lobbyist to persuade the government of Buchananland to set quotas instead of imposing tariffs.

● MULTIPLE CHOICE

Circle the one best answer for each of the following questions:

1. If a frost in Florida damages oranges, what will likely happen to the market for Florida oranges?
a. Demand will increase.
b. Demand will fall.
c. Supply will increase.
d. Supply will decrease.

2. Assume that the cost of shipping automobiles from the United States to Japan decreases. What will most likely happen to the selling price and quantity of cars made in the U.S. and sold in Japan?
   a. The price will rise, and quantity will fall.
   b. Both price and quantity will rise.
   c. The price will fall, and quantity will rise.
   d. The price will fall. What happens to quantity is not clear.

3. Assuming standard supply and demand curves, what will likely happen to the price and quantity of cricket bats in Trinidad as interest in cricket dwindles following the dismal performance of the national cricket team, while at the same time taxes are repealed on producing cricket bats?
   a. The price will decrease, but what happens to quantity is not clear.
   b. The price will decrease, and quantity will increase.
   c. The price will increase, but what happens to quantity is not clear.
   d. It is not clear what happens to either price or quantity.

4. A higher equilibrium price with no change in market equilibrium quantity could be caused by:
   a. supply shifting in and no change in demand.
   b. supply and demand both increasing.
   c. a decrease in supply and an increase in demand.
   d. demand and supply both shifting in.

5. A fall in the value of the euro relative to the dollar:
   a. could be caused by an increase in the demand for the euro.
   b. could be caused by an increase in the supply of the euro.
   c. will make American-made goods cheaper for Europeans.
   d. will make European-made goods more expensive for Americans.

6. An increase in the value of the dollar relative to the euro could be caused by:
   a. an increase in the supply of the dollar.
   b. an increase in the demand for the dollar.
   c. a decrease in the demand for the dollar.
   d. an increase in U.S. imports.

7. An expected decline in the value of U.S. stocks will most likely:
   a. increase the supply of the euro and increase the demand for the dollar.
   b. increase the supply of the dollar and increase the demand for the euro.
   c. decrease the demand for the dollar and the euro.
   d. increase the demand for the dollar and the euro.

8. Referring to the graph below, if there is a price ceiling imposed on this market of P_2, consumers will pay:

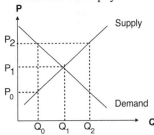

   a. P_1 and buy quantity Q_1.
   b. P_2 and buy quantity Q_2.
   c. P_0 and buy quantity Q_0.
   d. P_2 and buy quantity Q_0.

9. Referring to the graph below, if there is a price floor imposed on this market of P_2, consumers will pay:

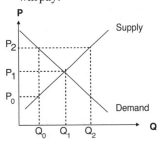

   a. P_1 and buy quantity Q_1.
   b. P_2 and buy quantity Q_2.
   c. P_0 and buy quantity Q_0.
   d. P_2 and buy quantity Q_0.

10. Effective rent controls:
   a. are examples of price floors.
   b. cause the quantity of rental occupied housing demanded to exceed the quantity supplied.
   c. create a greater amount of higher quality housing to be made available to renters.
   d. create a surplus of rental occupied housing.

11. An increase in the minimum wage can be
    expected to:
    a. cause unemployment for some workers.
    b. cause a shortage of workers.
    c. increase employment.
    d. help businesses by reducing their costs of
       production.

12. A tariff:
    a. is a tax imposed on an imported good.
    b. is a quantitative restriction on the amount
       that one country can export to another.
    c. imposed on a good will shift the supply of
       that good outward to the right.
    d. will reduce the price paid by the consumer
       of the good.

13. Quantity restrictions on supply imposed below
    equilibrium quantity on a market:
    a. increase price and reduce quantity traded.
    b. increase price and increase quantity traded.
    c. decrease price and reduce quantity traded.
    d. decrease price and increase quantity traded.

14. Referring to the graph below, suppose initial
    supply is represented by S_0. A tax T on
    suppliers will raise the price that:

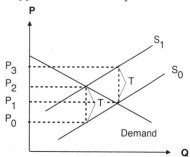

    a. suppliers receive net of the tax to P_1.
    b. suppliers receive net of the tax to P_2.
    c. consumers pay to P_2.
    d. consumers pay to P_3.

15. In a third-party payer system:
    a. the person who chooses the product pays
       the entire cost.
    b. the quantity demanded would be lower than
       it otherwise would be.
    c. the quantity demanded will be higher than it
       otherwise would be.
    d. consumers are hurt.

16. In the graph below that demonstrates a third-
    pary payer market, suppose the consumer is
    required to make a co-payment of P_0. Which of
    the following areas represents the cost of the
    program to the third party?

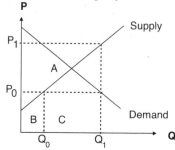

    a. rectangle A.
    b. retangle B.
    c. retangle C.
    d. the sum of rectangles A, B, and C.

17. Third-party payer markets result in:
    a. a lower equilibrium price received by the
       supplier.
    b. a smaller quantity supplied.
    c. a smaller quantity demanded
    d. increased total spending.

A1. The supply and demand equations for Nan-
    tucket Nectar's Kiwi-berry juice are given
    by $Q_s = -4 + 5P$ and $Q_d = 18 - 6P$ respec-
    tively, where price is dollars per quart and
    quantity is thousands of quarts. The equilib-
    rium market price and quantity is:
    a. P = $2, Q = 6 thousand quarts.
    b. P = $3, Q = 5 thousand quarts.
    c. P = $14, Q = 66 thousand quarts.
    d. P = $22, Q = 106 thousand quarts.

A2. The supply and demand equations for side-
    walk snow removal in a small town in
    Montana are given by $Q_s = -50 + 5P$ and Q_d
    = 100 - 5P respectively, where price is in
    dollars per removal and quantity is numbers
    of removals per week. It snows so much that
    demand for sidewalk snow removals
    increases by 30 per week. The new equilib-
    rium market price and quantity is:
    a. P = $15, Q = 6 sidewalk snow removals.
    b. P = $15, Q = 5 sidewalk snow removals.
    c. P = $18, Q = 66 sidewalk snow removals.
    d. P = $18, Q = 40 sidewalk snow removals.

A3. The supply and demand equations for Arizona
Ice Tea in Arizona is given by $Q_s = -10 + 6P$
and $Q_d = 40 - 8P$; P is the price of each bottle
in dollars; and quantity is in hundreds of
thousands of bottles per month. Suppose
the state government imposes a $1 per bottle
tax on the suppliers. The market price the
suppliers receive and the equilibrium
quantity in the market are:

   a. $3 per bottle and 8 hundred thousand bottles
per month.

   b. $3 per bottle and 16 hundred thousand
bottles per month.

   c. $4 per bottle and 8 hundred thousand bottles
per month.

   d. $4 per bottle and 16 hundred thousand
bottles per month.

● POTENTIAL ESSAY QUESTIONS

*You may also see essay questions similar to the "Problems
& Applications" and "Brain Teaser" exercises.*

1.   Discuss the impact on the relative price of
American exports and imports if the exchange
rate value of the dollar rises.

2.   Explain why a third-party payer system results
in a greater quantity demanded and increases
total spending.

ANSWERS

SHORT-ANSWER QUESTIONS

1. The demand curve for Russian caviar shifts out; supply shifts in; the price rises substantially. What happens to quantity depends upon the relative sizes of the shifts. (120-121)

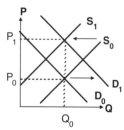

2. Either an increase in the demand or a decrease in the supply of the dollar could increase its price (exchange rate). (120-121)

3. A price ceiling is a government imposed limit on how high a price can be charged. An effective price ceiling below market equilibrium price will cause $Q_D > Q_S$ (a shortage) as shown in the graph below. (121-123)

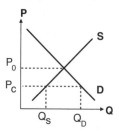

4. A price floor is a government imposed limit on how low a price can be charged. An effective price floor above market equilibrium price will cause $Q_S > Q_D$ (a surplus) as shown in the graph below. (123-125)

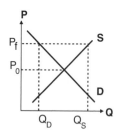

5. Rent controls are price ceilings and result in shortages in rental housing. As time passes and as the population rises, the demand for rental housing rises. On the supply side, other ventures become more lucrative relative to renting out housing. Owners have less incentive to repair existing buildings, let alone build new ones, reducing the supply of rental housing over time. The shortage becomes more acute over time (121-123)

6. A tariff is an excise tax paid by foreign producers on an imported good. As a tariff of t is imposed, the supply curve shifts upward to S_1 by the amount of the tariff. The equilibrium price goes up and quantity goes down. (125-126)

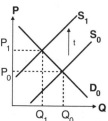

7. In a third-party payer system the person who decides how much of a good to buy differs from the person who pays for the good. One example is the health care system in the United States today. (127-128)

ANSWERS

MATCHING

1-i; 2-f; 3-c; 4-a; 5-e; 6-h; 7-g; 8-b; 9-d;

ANSWERS

PROBLEMS AND APPLICATIONS

1. This is not an exception to the law of demand (there are very few exceptions). Instead, an increase in demand could account for a higher price and a greater amount bought and sold, as is illustrated in the figure below. (120-121)

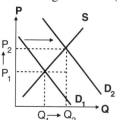

2. The Levi jeans will cost the Japanese consumer 6,250 yen (125x50). The Toyota will cost the American consumer $32,000 (4,000,000/125). (116-117)

3. a. The market supply and demand for milk is graphed below. (120-121)

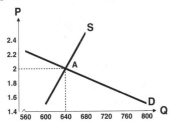

b. The equilibrium market price is $2 and equilibrium quantity in the market is 640 thousand gallons of milk because the quantity supplied equals the quantity demanded. This is point A on the graph above. (120-121)

c. A government–imposed price floor of $2.25 is shown in the figure below. Since it is a price above market price, quantity supplied (660) exceeds quantity demanded (560) by 100 thousand gallons. (123-125)

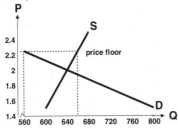

d. A government-imposed price ceiling of $1.75 is below market price. Quantity supplied (620 thousand gallons) will be less than quantity demanded (720 thousand gallons) by 100 thousand gallons, as shown below. (121-123)

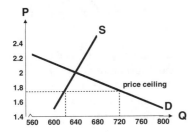

e. Because of the tax, the quantity supplied at every price level will decline by 100 thousand gallons. The supply and demand table will change as follows:

Price in dollars per gal.	Quantity of gal. supplied 1,000s	Quantity of gal. demanded 1,000s
$1.50	500	800
$1.75	520	720
$2.00	540	640
$2.25	560	560
$2.50	580	480

The market equilibrium price would be $2.25 and the equilibrium quantity would be 560 thousand gallons. Since the sellers will have to pay $1 tax on every gallon they sell, they will receive $1.25 per gallon milk. (125-126)

4. a. A higher tariff or a stricter quota imposed on Japanese cars would decrease the supply of Japanese cars in the United States. The upward (leftward) shift of the supply curve, such as from S_1 to S_2 shown in the figure below, creates a temporary shortage (excess demand) at the original price that puts upward pressure on the prices of Japanese cars. The result over time will be higher prices for Japanese cars, as well as a decrease in the amount bought and sold in the U.S. market, as shown below. (125-127)

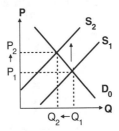

b. Because Japanese and American-made cars are substitutes for each other, some people will switch from buying the now relatively more expensive Japanese cars (law of demand in action) to buying more American-made cars. (Notice that "relative" prices are what are relevant.) This increases the demand for American-made cars, increasing their prices as well as the amount bought and sold. This is illustrated in the figure below. (125-127)

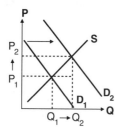

c. These trade barriers may be advocated by American car manufacturers. They could obviously benefit from the higher prices and greater sales. American automotive workers could also benefit from the greater job security that comes with more cars being produced and sold. These "special interest groups" may put political pressure on government, and the government may succumb to that pressure. (125-127)

d. The Japanese would prefer a quota over a tariff. This is because a tariff would require them to pay taxes to the U.S. government; while a quota would not. (125-127)

5. a. The supply curve will shift out from S_0 to S_1 as the new technology makes it cheaper to produce tractors. Increased incomes will shift the demand for tractors out from D_0 to D_1. Equilibrium price may go up, remain the same, or go down, depending on the relative shifts in the two curves. Equilibrium quantity, however, will definitely increase. (120-121)

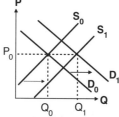

b. The ban on the companies doing business with Libya and Iran will shift the supply curve in from S_0 to S_1. The discovery of oil will, however, shift it back out to possibly S_2. Depending on the relative shifts, equilibrium price and quantity will change. In the case shown in the diagram, the shift resulting from the discovery of

the new oil source dominates the shift resulting from the ban, and the equilibrium price falls and quantity goes up. (120-121)

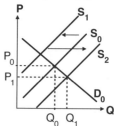

c. With more people watching the Olympics, the demand for movies shifts in from D_0 to D_1. At the same time the increased supply of movies will shift the supply curve out from S_0 to S_1. Equilibrium price will fall, while the change in equilibrium quantity will depend on the relative shifts in the curves. (120-121)

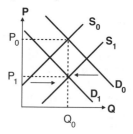

d. With more people demanding Nike Air shoes, the demand curve will shift out from D_0 to D_1. The worker strike will, however, reduce supply and shift it in from S_0 to S_1. The resulting equilibrium price will be higher, while the change in quantity depends on the relative shifts in the curves. (120-121)

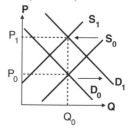

A1. a. Equating Q_s to Q_d and then solving for equilibrium price gives us $3 per quart. Substituting $3 into the demand and supply equations, we find that equilibrium quantity is 5 million quarts. (133)

b. Since supply increases by 20 million quarts, the new supply equation is $Q_s = 10 + 5P$. Equating this with the demand equation, we find the new equilibrium price to be $1 per quart. Substituting into either the new supply equation or the demand equation we find that equilibrium quantity is 15 million quarts. (134-135)

c. With demand increasing, the new demand equation is $Q_d = 30 - 5P$. Setting Q_s equal to Q_d and solving for price we find equilibrium price to be $4 per quart. Substituting this into either the new demand or the supply equation we find equilibrium quantity to be 10 million quarts. (134-135)

A2. a. Equating Q_s and Q_d, then solving gives equilibrium price $6 and quantity 8 hundred thousand dozen. (133)

b. If price ceiling is set at $4, $Q_s = 2$, and $Q_d = 12$; the resulting shortage is 10 hundred thousand dozen. (135)

c. If a $1 tax is imposed on suppliers, the new supply equation will be $Q_s = -10 + 3(P-1) = -13 + 3P$. Equating this with Q_d gives equilibrium price $6.60 and quantity 6.8 hundred thousand. Buyers pay $6.60 for each dozen they buy, and the sellers receive $1 less than that, or $5.60, for each dozen they sell. (135-136)

d. As a result of the tax, the new demand equation will be $Q_d = 20 - 2(P+1) = 18 - 2P$. Equating this with Q_s gives equilibrium price $5.60 and quantity 6.8 hundred thousand. Buyers pay $6.60 (P + 1) for each dozen they buy, and the sellers receive $5.60 for each dozen they sell. (135-136)

━━ ANSWERS ━━

A BRAIN TEASER

1. The supply and demand equilibrium are at price P_e and quality Q_e. If quotas for Zachstani cars are set at Q_2, the price received for each car sold is P_2, which is well above P_t, the price they would normally sell for at that quantity. A tariff of t $(P_2 - P_t)$ would have to be imposed to reduce imports to Q_2 reflected by the supply curve shifting in to S_1. In both cases, consumers pay Zachstan producers P_2 for each car. In the case of the quota, Zachstan producers keep P_2 for each car. In the case of the tariff, Zachstan producers must give up t to the government for each car sold. Because with quotas the price received (and therefore profits) are higher, they have the lobbyist lobbying for quotas. (125-127)

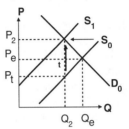

━━ ANSWERS ━━

MULTIPLE CHOICE

1. **d** A frost will reduce the quantity of oranges available for sale at every price. Supply will decrease. See page 118.

2. **c** The supply curve will shift out, market price will fall and the quantity will rise. See pages 120-121.

3. **a** Demand for cricket bats will fall, shifting the demand curve in, while the tax repeal will shift the supply curve out. Price will fall, and quantity may change depending on the relative shifts of the supply and demand curves. Related issues are discussed on page 120 of the textbook.

4. **c** When the demand curve shifts out, while the supply curve shifts in, the price rises and the quantity can remain the same. See page 120 in the text.

5. **b** The analysis of currencies is the same as the analysis for any other good. A shift of supply out and to the right will result in a lower price. A fall in the value of the euro means it will take fewer dollars to purchase one euro, making European-made goods

cheaper for Americans and American-made goods more expensive for Europeans. See pages 116-117 in the text.

6. b An increase in the price of anything would require an increase in demand or a decrease in supply. An increase in U.S. imports will increase the supply of dollars lowering the price of the dollar. See pages 116-117 in the text.

7. b Falling U.S. stock prices would encourage people to get out of the U.S. stock market and place their funds elsewhere, for example, in European financial markets. Therefore, people would sell (supply) dollars and buy (demand) more euros. See pages 116-117 in the text.

8. a As discussed on pages 121-123, a price ceiling above equilibrium price will not affect the market price or quantity. Equilibrium price and quantity, in this case will be determined by the intersection of the supply and demand curves—at price P_1 and quantity Q_1.

9. d At a price of P_2 the quantity demanded by consumers is Q_0. The quantity supplied by sellers would be Q_2 at price P_2. A surplus of $Q_2 - Q_0$ would put downward pressure on price. However, government does not allow a lower price. So, the equilibrium price and quantity of P_1 and Q_1 would not prevail when government intervenes with a price floor. See pages 123-125.

10. b Rent controls are price ceilings and therefore cause the quantity demanded to exceed the quantity supplied. Indeed, the quantity demanded rises while the quantity supplied falls creating a shortage. See pages 121-123 in the text.

11. a Because the minimum wage is a price floor it increases the quantity supplied and decreases the quantity demanded (*decreasing* employment) and creating a *surplus* of workers (causing some unemployment). The higher minimum wage would *increase* costs of production to businesses. See pages 123-125 in the textbook.

12. a The correct answer is a by definition. Also, a tariff will decrease supply, shifting the supply curve inward to the left. This causes the price consumers must pay to rise. See pages 125-126 in the text.

13. a Quantity restrictions reduce supply and create a higher price and lower quantity traded in a market. See pages 126-127 in the text.

14. c A tax shifts the supply curve up by the amount of the tax. The price consumers pay is determined by the price where the demand curve and the after-tax supply curve intersect. The after-tax price suppliers receive falls to P_0, the new equilibrium price less the tax ($P_2 - T$). See pages 125-126 in the text.

15. c In a third-party payer system the person who chooses the product pays some but not all of the cost. As a result of a lower effective price to the consumer, the quantity demanded will be higher than otherwise. See pages 127-128 in the text.

16. a At a price of P_0, the consumer demands quantity Q_1. The supplier requires a price of P_1 for that quantity. Therefore, total expenditures are P_1 times Q_1 or areas A, B, and C. Of this, consumers pay areas B and C. The third party pays area A. See pages 127-128.

17. d In third-party payer markets the quantity demanded, price, and total spending are greater than when the consumer pays. See pages 127-128.

A1. a Equating the supply and demand equations gives equilibrium P = $2. Substituting this into either the supply or demand equation tells us that Q = 6 thousand quarts. See page 133.

A2. d The new demand becomes $Q_d = 130 - 5P$. Equating the supply and demand equations gives equilibrium P = $18. Substituting this into either the supply or demand equation tells us that Q = 40 sidewalk snow removals. See pages 134-135.

A3. a   A \$1 per bottle tax on suppliers makes the
supply equation $Q_s = -10 + 6(P-1) = -16 + 6P$. Equating this with the demand
equation gives equilibrium P = \$4 and Q =
8 hundred thousand. The supplier receives
\$3 (\$4 − \$1). See pages 135-136 of the
textbook.

ANSWERS

POTENTIAL ESSAY QUESTIONS

*The following are annotated answers. They
indicate the general idea behind the answer.*

1.   An increase in the exchange rate value of the
dollar means that the dollar will buy more
units of foreign currencies. Therefore, the
relative price of foreign products imported into
the United States will decrease and Americans
will import more. Likewise, a stronger dollar
will maker American products relatively more
expensive to foreigners. Foreigners will buy
fewer American products and the United
States will export less. If U.S. imports rise and
exports fall, the U.S. trade deficit rises.

2.   Because part of the costs of obtaining a good
or service in a third-party payer system is paid
by someone other than the consumer, the
effective price to the consumer is lower and
the quantity demanded is greater. At this
higher quantity demanded the price charged by
sellers is greater. The result is greater consumption at a higher price and therefore
greater total spending on the good or service.
See Figure 5-8 on page 119 for a graphic
illustration of this.

Pretest
Chapters 1 - 5

I

Take this test in test conditions, giving yourself a limited amount of time to complete the questions. Ideally, check with your professor to see how much time he or she allows for an average multiple choice question and multiply this by 26. This is the time limit you should set for yourself for this pretest. If you do not know how much time your teacher would allow, we suggest 1 minute per question, or about 25 minutes.

1. Economic reasoning:
   a. provides a framework with which to approach questions.
   b. provides correct answers to just about every question.
   c. is only used by economists.
   d. should only be applied to economic business matters.

2. You bought stock A for $10 and stock B for $50. The price of each is currently $20. Assuming no tax issues, which should you sell if you need money?
   a. Stock A.
   b. Stock B.
   c. The price at which you bought it doesn't matter
   d. You should sell an equal amount of both.

3. The opportunity cost of reading Chapter 1 of the text:
   a. is about 1/34of the price you paid for the book because the chapter is about one twentieth of of the book.
   b. zero since you have already paid for the book
   c. has nothing to do with the price you paid for the book.
   d. is 1/34 the price of the book plus 1/34 the price of the tuition.

4. If at Female College there are significantly more females than males (and there are not a significant number of gays) economic forces:
   a. will be pushing for females to pay on dates.
   b. will be pushing for males to pay on dates.
   c. will be pushing for neither to pay on dates.
   d. are irrelevant to this issue. Everyone knows that the males always should pay.

5. The statement, "The distribution of income should be left to the market," is:
   a. a positive statement.
   b. a normative statement.
   c. an art-of-economics statement
   d. an objective statement.

6. If the opportunity cost of good X in terms of good Y is 2Y, so you'll have to give up 2Y to get one X, the production possibility curve would look like:
   a. A.
   b. B.
   c. C.
   d. A, B or C.

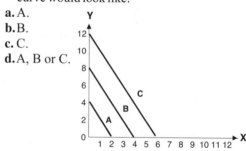

7. Given the accompanying production possibility curve, when you're moving from point C to point B the opportunity cost of butter in terms of guns is:
   a. 1/3.
   b. 1.
   c. 2.
   d. 3/2.

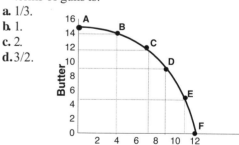

8. If countries A and B have production possibility curves A and B respectively, country A has a comparative advantage in the production of:

a. no good.
b. both goods.
c. good X only.
d. good Y only.

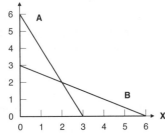

9. In the international market, government agreements tend to be related to:
a. provisions of public goods.
b. free trade.
c. environmental issues.
d. redistribution of income.

10. Outsourcing in the United States is evidence that:
a. the United States does not have any comparative advantages.
b. the U.S. dollar is valued too low.
c. the law of one price doesn't hold.
d. the law of one price is affecting global production.

11. In theory, socialism is an economic system:
a. that tries to organize society in the same ways as most families organize, striving to see that individuals get what they need.
b. based on central planning and government ownership of the means of production.
c. based on private property rights.
d. based on markets.

12. In Soviet-style socialism, the "what to produce" decision in practice was most often made by:
a. consumers.
b. the market.
c. government.
d. firms.

13. The largest percentage of business receipts are by:
a. partnerships.
b. sole proprietorships.
c. corporations.
d. nonprofit companies.

14. The largest percentage of state and local expenditures is on:
a. education.
b. health and medical care.
c. highways.
d. income security.

15. Globalization:
a. is decreasing in importance.
b. increases competition.
c. reduces the need to specialize.
d. reduces productivity.

16. There are many more substitutes for good A than for good B.
a. The demand curve for good B will likely shift out further.
b. The demand curve for good B will likely be flatter.
c. You can't say anything about the likely relative flatness of the demand curves.
d. The demand curve for good A will likely be flatter.

17. If the price of air conditioners falls, there will be:
a. an increase in demand for air conditioners.
b. an increase in the quantity of air conditioners demanded.
c. an increase in the quantity of air conditioners supplied.
d. a shift out of the demand for air conditioners.

18. The movement in the graph below from point A to point B represents:

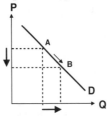

a. an increase in demand.
b. an increase in the quantity demanded.
c. an increase in the quantity supplied.
d. an increase in supply.

19. The law of supply states that:
    a. quantity supplied increases as price increases, other things constant.
    b. quantity supplied decreases as price increases, other things constant.
    c. more of a good will be supplied the higher its price, other things changing proportionately.
    d. less of a good will be supplied the higher its price, other things changing proportionately.

20. If at some price the quantity supplied exceeds the quantity demanded then:
    a. a surplus (excess supply) exists and the price will fall over time as sellers competitively bid down the price.
    b. a shortage (excess demand) exists and the price will rise over time as buyers competitively bid up the price.
    c. the price is below equilibrium.
    d. equilibrium will be reestablished as the demand curve shifts to the left.

21. An increase in demand for a good will cause:
    a. excess demand (a shortage) before price changes.
    b. movement down along the demand curve as price changes.
    c. movement down along the supply curve as price changes.
    d. a higher price and a smaller quantity traded in the market.

22. If a frost in Florida damages oranges, what will likely happen to the market for Florida oranges?
    a. Demand will increase.
    b. Demand will fall.
    c. Supply will increase.
    d. Supply will decrease.

23. A higher equilibrium price with no change in market equilibrium quantity could be caused by:
    a. supply shifting in and no change in demand.
    b. supply and demand both increasing.
    c. a decrease in supply and an increase in demand.
    d. demand and supply both shifting in.

24. Effective rent controls:
    a. are examples of price floors.
    b. cause the quantity of rental occupied housing demanded to exceed the quantity supplied.
    c. create a greater amount of higher quality housing to be made available to renters.
    d. create a surplus of rental occupied housing.

25. Referring to the graph below, suppose initially supply is represented by S_0. A tax T, on suppliers will raise the price that:

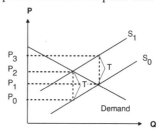

    a. suppliers receive net of the tax to P_1.
    b. suppliers receive net of the tax to P_2.
    c. consumers pay to P_2.
    d. consumers pay to P_3.

26. Third-party payer markets result in:
    a. a lower equilibrium price.
    b. a smaller quantity supplied.
    c. a smaller quantity demanded
    d. increased total spending.

ANSWERS

Key: The figures in parentheses refer to multiple choice question and chapter numbers. For example (1:2) is multiple choice question 2 from chapter 1.

1.	a	(1:1)	**14.**	a	(3:13)
2.	c	(1:5)	**15.**	b	(3:16)
3.	c	(1:10)	**16.**	d	(4:2)
4.	a	(1:12)	**17.**	b	(4:4)
5.	b	(1:16)	**18.**	b	(4:9)
6.	d	(2:3)	**19.**	a	(4:13)
7.	d	(2:6)	**20.**	a	(4:18)
8.	d	(2:12)	**21.**	a	(4:25)
9.	b	(2:19)	**22.**	d	(5:1)
10.	d	(2:15)	**23.**	c	(5:4)
11.	a	(3:2)	**24.**	b	(5:10)
12.	c	(3:5)	**25.**	c	(5:14)
13.	c	(3:9)	**26.**	d	(5:17)

DESCRIBING SUPPLY AND DEMAND: ELASTICITIES

CHAPTER AT A GLANCE

This review is based upon the learning objectives that open the chapter.

1. Elasticity is defined as percentage change in quantity divided by percentage change in some variable that affects demand or supply. The most commonly used elasticity concept is price elasticity of demand. (140-141)

   The price elasticity of <u>demand</u> measures <u>buyer</u> responsiveness to a price change. It equals the percentage change in <u>quantity demanded</u> divided by the percentage change in price.

   The price elasticity of <u>supply</u> measures <u>seller</u> responsiveness to a price change. It equals the percentage change in <u>quantity supplied</u> divided by the percentage change in price.

2. To calculate price elasticity of a price range, calculate the percentage change at the midpoint of the range. (142-144)

   $$\text{Price Elasticity} = \frac{\text{percent change in quantity}}{\text{percent change in price}}$$

   $$\text{Percentage change in quantity} = \frac{Q_2 - Q_1}{1/2\,(Q_1 + Q_2)}$$

   $$\text{Percentage change in price} = \frac{P_2 - P_1}{1/2\,(P_1 + P_2)}$$

   Elasticity is not the same as slope!

3. Five elasticity terms listed from most to least elastic are: perfectly elastic (E = infinity); elastic ($E > 1$); unit elastic ($E = 1$); inelastic ($E < 1$); and perfectly inelastic ($E = 0$). (146-147)

   Consider the price elasticity of demand for a good.

   - *A <u>perfectly elastic</u> demand curve is a horizontal line.*
   - *An <u>elastic</u> demand for a good means buyers are relatively responsive to a price change (the percentage change in the quantity demanded is greater than the percentage change in the price).*
   - *When the demand for an item is <u>unit elastic</u>, buyers are neither relatively responsive nor unresponsive—(the percentage change in the quantity demanded equals the percentage change in the price).*
   - *An <u>inelastic</u> demand for a good means buyers are relatively <u>un</u>responsive to a price change (the percentage change in the quantity demanded is less than the percentage change in the price).*
   - *A <u>perfectly inelastic</u> demand curve is a vertical line, indicating there is no change in the quantity demanded given a change in the price.*

4. The more substitutes, the more elastic the demand and the more elastic the supply. (148-150)

   The number of substitutes a good has is affected by several factors. Four of the most important determinants of substitutability that give rise to a <u>greater</u> elasticity of demand for a good are:

- *The time period being considered: the longer the time interval, the larger the elasticity.*
- *The degree to which the good is a luxury: luxuries have greater elasticities.*
- *The market definition: the more specifically the good is defined the greater the elasticity. (e.g. there are more substitutes for Swiss cheese than for dairy products in general.)*
- *The importance of the good in one's budget: the greater the price relative to one's budget, the greater the elasticity.*

As for the elasticity of supply: the greater the amount of time under consideration, the greater the elasticity of supply (this is because the greater the amount of time, the greater the ability of sellers to respond to the price change).

5. With elastic demands, a rise in price decreases total revenue. With inelastic demands, a rise in price increases total revenue. (151-153)

   Therefore, firms have a strong incentive to separate people according to their price elasticity of demand. People with a more inelastic demand are charged a higher price.

   Know the relationship between the price elasticity of demand and total revenue:

   Elastic: $\uparrow P \rightarrow \downarrow TR$; $\downarrow P \rightarrow \uparrow TR$
   Unit Elastic: $\uparrow P$ or $\downarrow P \rightarrow$ no change in TR
   Inelastic: $\uparrow P \rightarrow \uparrow TR$; $\downarrow P \rightarrow \downarrow TR$

   So $\downarrow P$ when demand is elastic and $\uparrow P$ when demand is inelastic to increase TR..

6. Income elasticity of demand shows the responsiveness of demand to changes in income. Cross-price elasticity shows the responsiveness of demand to changes in prices of other goods. (154-157)

Income elasticity of demand equals the percentage change in quantity demanded divided by the percentage change in income. Normal goods have income elasticities greater than zero while inferior goods have negative income elasticities. Moreover, luxuries have an income elasticity greater than 1 while necessities have an income elasticity less than 1 (but still positive).

Cross-price elasticity of demand equals the percentage change in quantity demanded divided by the percentage change in the price of another good. Substitutes have positive cross-price elasticities; complements have negative cross-price elasticities.

7. Figure 6-6 reviews the effect of shifts in demand and supply with various elasticities. (158-160)

   Knowledge of elasticity enables us to determine to what extent the equilibrium quantity and the equilibrium price will change given a change in demand and supply. For example, if demand is highly inelastic and supply shifts in to the left, the price rises significantly while the quantity hardly decreases at all.

   More precisely, when demand shifts:

   $\%\Delta$ in price = ($\%\Delta$ in demand) / ($E_D + E_S$)

   and when supply shifts:

   $\%\Delta$ in price = ($\%\Delta$ in supply) / ($E_D + E_S$)

● SHORT-ANSWER QUESTIONS

1. Define the concepts *price elasticity of demand* and *price elasticity of supply*.

2. If the price of a good changes by 30 percent and quantity demanded for that same good remains unchanged, what is the price elasticity of demand for that good?

3. If price elasticity of supply is 4 and price changes by 10 percent, by what percent will the quantity supplied change?

4. Define the terms *elastic*, *inelastic,* and *unit elastic* as applied to points on supply and demand curves.

5.   What are the four mail determinants of the price elasticity of demand?

6. What is the main determinant of the price elasticity of supply?

7. In each of the following cases, state what will be the effect of a rise in price on total revenue:

   a. Demand is inelastic.

   b. Demand is elastic.

   c. Demand is unit elastic.

8.   Define income elasticity of demand. How do the income elasticities of demand differ among normal goods, necessities, luxuries, and inferior goods?

9. Define cross-price elasticity of demand.

10. What is a complementary good? What is the general value of the cross-price elasticity of demand for a complementary good? What is a substitute good? What is the general value of the cross-price elasticity of demand for a substitute good?

11. Explain how using the concept *elasticity* makes supply and demand analysis more useful.

MATCHING THE TERMS
Match the terms to their definitions

____ **1.** complements
____ **2.** cross-price elasticity of demand
____ **3.** elastic
____ **4.** elasticity
____ **5.** inelastic
____ **6.** income elasticity of demand
____ **7.** inferior goods
____ **8.** luxury
____ **9.** necessity
____ **10.** normal goods
____ **11.** perfectly elastic demand curves
____ **12.** perfectly inelastic demand curves
____ **13.** price elasticity of demand
____ **14.** price elasticity of supply
____ **15.** substitutes
____ **16.** unit elastic

a. A measure of the percent change in the quantity demanded divided by the percent change in the price of that good.

b. Goods whose consumption decreases when income increases.

c. Goods that can be used in place of one another.

d. Goods that are used in conjunction with other goods.

e. Goods whose consumption increases with an increase in income.

f. Horizontal demand curves. E_d = infinity.

g. % change in quantity is greater than % change in price. $E > 1$.

h. % change in quantity is less than % change in price. $E < 1$.

i. A good that has a positive income elasticity less than one.

j. For points on curves, the case that the percentage change in quantity is equal to the percentage change in price. $E_d = 1$.

k. Vertical demand curves. $E_d = 0$.

l. The percentage change in quantity demanded divided by percentage change in income.

m. The percentage change in quantity demanded of one good divided by the percentage change in the price of a related good.

n. Refers to responsiveness.

o. A good that has an income elasticity greater than one.

p. A measure of the percent change in the quantity supplied divided by the percent change in the price of that good.

● PROBLEMS AND APPLICATIONS

1. Assume the price elasticity of demand for a good is 0.5 (after we take the absolute value—drop the negative sign). If there is a 10% decrease in the price, what would happen to the percentage change in the quantity demanded? What if the price were to rise by 15%?

2. Calculate the price elasticity for each of the following. State whether price elasticity of demand is elastic, unit elastic, or inelastic. Will revenue rise, decline, or stay the same with the given change in price?

   a. The price of pens rises 5%; the quantity demanded falls 10%.

   b. The price of a ticket to a Boston Red Sox baseball game rises from $10 to $12 a game. The quantity of tickets sold falls from 160,000 tickets to 144,000.

   c. The price of an economics textbook declines from $50 to $47.50. Quantity demanded rises from 1,000 to 1,075.

   d. The price of water beds rises from $500 to $600. Quantity demanded falls from 100,000 to 80,000.

3. Suppose that in deciding what price to set for the video *Shrek II*, Disney decided to either charge $12.95 or $15.95. It estimated the demand to be quite elastic. What price did it most likely charge and why?

4. Calculate the price elasticity of the following products. State whether elasticity of supply is elastic, unit elastic, or inelastic.

   a. Cocoa Puffs: The price of a 14-oz. box of Cocoa Puffs rises 4 percent while quantity supplied rises 15 percent.

   b. Japanese yen: The price of Japanese yen in terms of dollars rises from 100 yen per dollar to 110 yen per dollar. Its quantity supplied rises from 5,000,000 yen to 5,300,000 yen per year.

c. Jansport backpacks: The price of Jansport backpacks falls from $30 a pack to $25 a pack. The quantity supplied falls from 150,000 to 125,000 per week.

a. The price of a pizza rises from $9 to $12, and the quantity demanded of Big Macs increases from 3 million to 4 million burgers per year.

5. Calculate the income elasticity of demand for the following goods. State whether each is a luxury, a necessity, or an inferior good.

a. As average income per student rises from $10,000 to $12,000 a year, demand for ice cream cones increases from 30,000 cones to 37,500 cones per year.

b. The price of hot dogs falls from $4 a pound to $2 a pound, and the quantity demanded of mustard increases from 15 tons to 20 tons per year.

7. What will likely happen to equilibrium price and quantity in the following cases?

a. Demand is highly inelastic. The supply curve shifts out.

b. As income decreases from 120,000 to 100,000 Mexican pesos per year, demand for margarine increases from 50 to 60 pounds per year.

b. Supply is highly inelastic. The demand curve shifts out.

c. As income decreases from $20,000 to $18,000 per year, demand for summer cottages in Vermont decreases from 80 to 75.

c. Supply is highly elastic. The demand curve shifts in.

8. Suppose demand shifts out to the right by 10 percent, the elasticity of demand is 1.2, and the elasticity of supply is 0.8. How much will price change?

6. Determine the cross-price elasticity of demand for the following examples. Are they substitutes or complements? How do you know?

● A BRAIN TEASER

1. Farmers have a relatively inelastic demand for their crops. Suppose there is a bumper crop year (an unusually large harvest). Will farmers be happy or sad about the news there has been an unusually large amount of their crops produced this year? Why?

● MULTIPLE CHOICE

Circle the one best answer for each of the following questions:

1. The definition of price elasticity of demand is:
    a. the change in quantity demanded divided by the change in price.
    b. the percentage change in quantity demanded divided by the percentage change in price.
    c. the percentage change in price divided by the percentage change in quantity demanded.
    d. the percentage change in the quantity supplied divided by the percentage change in price.

2. When the price of a good was raised from $10 to $11, the quantity demanded fell from 100 to 99. The price elasticity of demand is approximately:
    a. .1.
    b. 1.
    c. 10.
    d. 100.

3. If a firm can sell 1,200 units at a price of $14 per unit and 2,000 units at a price of $10 per unit, we can conclude:
    a. the price elasticity of demand for that good is 1.5.
    b. that the demand for this good is inelastic.
    c. that a price reduction would decrease the firm's total revenue.
    d. there must be very few substitutes for this good.

4. As the manager of a hotel, you want to increase the number of occupancies by 12%. It has been determined that the price elasticity of demand for rooms in your hotel is 2. This information implies:
    a. the demand for rooms in your hotel is inelastic.
    b. if you lower your rates by 6% then you will increase the number of occupancies by 12%.
    c. if you were able to raise your rates your total revenue would rise.
    d. there must be few substitutes for your hotel services.

5. A rise in price has just increased total revenue, other things constant. One would surmise that the demand for the firm's product is:
    a. inelastic.
    b. elastic.
    c. unit elastic.
    d. none of the above.

6. As a manager, you have determined that the demand for your good is quite elastic. Therefore:
    a. increasing the price of your good will increase revenues.
    b. decreasing the price of your good will increase revenues.
    c. increasing the price of your good will have no impact on the quantity demanded.
    d. any change in your price will not impact revenues.

7. In reference to the graph below, which of the following is true?

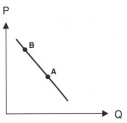

    a. Point B is more elastic than point A.
    b. Point A is more elastic than point B.
    c. Points A and B have equal elasticity.
    d. One cannot say anything about the elasticities without more information.

8.   The elasticity of the curve below is:

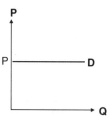

   a. perfectly elastic.
   b. perfectly inelastic.
   c. unit elastic.
   d. partially inelastic.

9.   The more a good is a necessity:
   a. the more elastic its demand curve.
   b. the more inelastic its demand curve.
   c. the more unit elastic its demand curve.
   d. the flatter the demand curve.

10.   The more specifically or narrowly a good is
   defined the:
   a. more substitutes it has and therefore the
   more elastic its demand curve.
   b. more substitutes it has and therefore the
   more inelastic its demand curve.
   c. fewer substitutes it has and therefore the
   more inelastic its demand curve.
   d. more unit elastic its demand curve.

11.   In the long run, the elasticity of demand is
   generally:
   a. greater than in the short run.
   b. smaller than in the short run.
   c. the same as in the short run.
   d. unrelated to the elasticity in the short run.

12.   When price changes from 4 to 5, output
   supplied changes from 50 to 60. The
   elasticity of supply is approximately:
   a. .5.
   b. .8.
   c. 1.25.
   d. 7.25.

13.   In the graph below, point A on the supply
   curve, S, is:

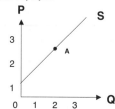

   a. elastic.
   b. inelastic.
   c. unitary elastic.
   d. unknown because one cannot say from the
   graph.

14.   In the graph below, point A on the supply
   curve, S, is:

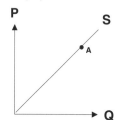

   a. elastic.
   b. inelastic.
   c. unitary elastic.
   d. unknown because one cannot say from the
   graph.

15.   The supply curve in the graph below is:

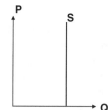

   a. perfectly inelastic.
   b. perfectly elastic.
   c. unit elastic.
   d. showing that its elasticity changes at various
   points.

16.   A good whose consumption decreases when
   income increases is generally called:
   a. a normal good.
   b. an inferior good.
   c. a substitute good.
   d. a complementary good.

17.   Two goods are substitutes when they:
   a. are goods that are used in conjunction with
   each other.
   b. have negative income elasticities.
   c. have positive income elasticities.
   d. have positive cross-price elasticities.

18. Price discrimination is most likely to occur in markets:
    a. when all individuals have equal elasticities.
    b. when some individuals have highly inelastic demands and some have highly elastic demands.
    c. in which the elasticity of demand is 1.
    d. in which the elasticity of demand is 0.

19. A significant price rise with virtually no change in quantity would most likely be caused by a highly:
    a. elastic demand and supply shifts to the right.
    b. inelastic supply and a shift in demand to the right.
    c. inelastic demand and supply shifts out.
    d. elastic supply and demand shifts in.

20. A significant quantity rise with virtually no change in price would most likely be caused by a highly:
    a. elastic demand and supply shifts to the right.
    b. inelastic supply and demand shifts to the right.
    c. inelastic demand and supply shifts to the right.
    d. elastic supply and demand shifts to the left.

21. A significant price decline with virtually no change in quantity would most likely be caused by:
    a. a highly elastic demand and supply shifts to the right.
    b. a highly inelastic supply and demand shifts to the right.
    c. a highly inelastic demand and supply shifts out.
    d. a highly elastic supply and demand shifts in.

22. If supply increases by 4 percent, the elasticity of demand is 0.5, and the elasticity of supply is 1.5. Price will:
    a. increase by 8 percent.
    b. increase by 2 percent.
    c. decrease by 8 percent.
    d. decrease by 2 percent.

POTENTIAL ESSAY QUESTIONS

You may also see essay questions similar to the "Problems & Applications" and "Brain Teaser" exercises.

1. What can cause some products to exhibit elastic demand while others have inelastic demand?

2. Why are some businesses interested in trying to determine which consumers have an elastic demand and which have an inelastic demand for the product being sold?

━━━   ANSWERS   ━━━

SHORT-ANSWER QUESTIONS

1. *Price elasticity of demand* is the percentage change in quantity demanded divided by the percentage change in price. *Price elasticity of supply* is the percentage change in quantity supplied divided by the percentage change in price. (140-141)

2. Price elasticity of demand is the percentage change in quantity demanded divided by the percentage change in price. Since the quantity demanded has not changed, the price elasticity of demand is zero. In other words, demand is perfectly inelastic. (140, 147)

3. Price elasticity of supply is the percentage change in quantity supplied divided by the percentage change in price. Thus, if the elasticity of supply is 4 and price changes by 10%, quantity supplied will change by 40%. (141)

4. For elastic points, the percentage change in quantity is greater than the percentage change in price. For inelastic points, the percentage change in quantity is less than the percentage change in price. For unit elastic points, the percentage change in quantity is equal to the percentage change in price. (140, 147)

5. The four main determinants of price elasticity of demand are (1) the time interval considered, (2) whether the good is a necessity or a luxury, (3) how specifically the good is defined, and (4) its price as a percentage of one's total expenditures. The larger the time interval, the more elastic is demand. The more a good is a luxury, the more demand is elastic. The more specifically a good is defined, the more elastic is demand. The more a good's price is a percentage of one's expenditures, the more elastic is demand. (148-149)

6. Price elasticity of supply essentially depends on the time period considered: the longer the time period, the more elastic the supply curve, because there are more options for change. Also, the easier it is to substitute production of a good, the more elastic the supply curve. (149)

7. **a.** If demand is inelastic, the percent fall in quantity demanded will be *less than* the percent rise in price. So a rise in price will increase total revenue. (151-153)
    b. If demand is elastic, the percent fall in quantity demanded will be *greater than* the percent rise in price. So a rise in price will reduce total revenue. (151-153)
    c. If demand is unit elastic, the percent fall in quantity demanded will *equal* the percent rise in price. So a rise in price will not change total revenue. (151-153)

8. Income elasticity of demand is the percentage change in demand divided by the percentage change in income. Normal goods have positive income elasticities. Luxury goods have positive income elasticities greater than one, while necessities have positive income elasticities less than one. Inferior goods have negative income elasticities. (155-156)

9. Cross-price elasticity of demand is the percentage change in quantity demanded of one good divided by the percentage change in the price of another good. (156-157)

10. A complementary good is a good whose consumption goes down when the price of the other good (for which it is a complement) goes up. Complements have negative cross-price elasticities. A substitute good is a good whose consumption goes up when the price of the other good (for which it is a substitute) goes up. Substitutes have positive cross-price elasticities. (156-157)

11. Knowledge of elasticity enables us to determine *to what extent* there will be a change in the equilibrium quantity and the equilibrium price, given a change in demand and supply. (158-160)

━━━   ANSWERS   ━━━

MATCHING

1-d; 2-m; 3-g; 4-n; 5-h; 6-l; 7-b; 8-o; 9-i; 10-e; 11-f; 12-k; 13-a; 14-p; 15-c; 16-j.

ANSWERS

PROBLEMS AND APPLICATIONS

1. Given that the $E_d = 0.5$, and the price falls by 10%, the quantity demanded will rise by 5%. [The trick is to multiply the E_d number (0.5), by the percentage change in the price (10) to get the percentage change in the quantity demanded (5). But remember, the law of demand tells us that the quantity demanded moves in the opposite direction from the change in the price.] If the price were to rise by 15%, the quantity demanded would fall by 7.5% (0.5 × 15=7.5). (140-141)

2. Price elasticity of demand is the percent change in quantity demanded divided by the percent change in price. Demand is elastic if the price elasticity is greater than one (always drop the negative sign—take the absolute value); a rise in price will lower total revenue. Demand is inelastic if the price elasticity is less than one; a rise in price will increase total revenue. Demand is unit elastic if the price elasticity is equal to one; a rise in price leaves total revenue unchanged. (140-141, 151-153)
    a. Price elasticity of demand is 10%/5%=2. Since 2 > 1, demand is elastic. Total revenue falls.
    b. Price elasticity of demand is [(144,000−160,000)/152,000]/[(12−10)/11] =0.58. Since 0.58 < 1, demand is inelastic. Total revenue rises.
    c. Price elasticity of demand is [(1,075−1,000)/1,037.5]/[(47.5−50)/48.75]= 1.41. Since 1.41 > 1, demand is elastic. Total revenue falls.
    d. Price elasticity of demand is [(80,000−100,000)/90,000]/[(600−500)/550] = 1.2. Since 1.2 > 1, demand is slightly elastic. Total revenue falls slightly.

3. It would charge the lower price, $12.95, because a lower price will increase total revenue when demand is elastic. (151-153)

4. a. Price elasticity of supply is 15%/4% = 3.75. Since 3.75 > 1, supply is elastic. (140-144)
    b. Price elasticity of supply is [(5,300,000−5,000,000)/5,150,000]/ [(110−100)/105]=0.61. Since 0.61 < 1, supply is inelastic. (140-144)
    c. Price elasticity of supply is [(125,000−150,000)/137,500]/[25−30/27.5] = 1. Since 1 = 1, supply is unit elastic. (140-144)

5. a. The income elasticity of demand is [(37,500−30,000)/33,750]/[(12,000− 10,000)/11,000]=1.22. Since 1.22>1, ice cream cones are a luxury good. (155-156)
    b. The income elasticity of demand is [(60−50)/55]/[(100,000−120,000)/110,000] = −1. Since −1 < 0, margarine is an inferior good. (155-156)
    c. The income elasticity of demand is [(75−80)/77.5]/[(18,000−20,000)/19,000]= 0.61. Since 0<0.61<1, summer cottages are a necessity. (155-156)

6. a. The cross-price elasticity of demand is [(4,000,000−3,000,000)/3,500,000]/[(12−9)/ 10.5] = 1. Since 1 > 0, pizzas and Big Macs are substitutes. (154, 156-157)
    b. The cross-price elasticity of demand is [(20−15)/17.5]/[(2−4)/3] = −0.43. Since −0.43 < 0, hot dogs and mustard are complements. (154, 156-157)

7. a. The price will fall considerably but quantity will not rise significantly, as shown below. (158-160)

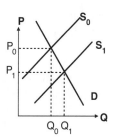

b. The price will rise considerably but quantity will not rise significantly, as shown below. (158-160)

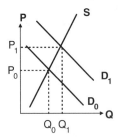

c. The quantity will fall considerably, but price will not fall significantly, as shown below. (158-160)

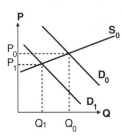

8. When demand shifts, the percent change in price = (percent change in demand)/$(E_D + E_S)$ = 10/2 = 5 percent. In this case, because demand increases, the price rises by 5 percent. (158-160)

ANSWERS

A BRAIN TEASER

1. They will be sad. The bumper crop year will increase the supply of the crop and reduce the price significantly. A fall in the price given the inelastic demand will decrease total revenues—farmers' incomes fall. (142-144, 151-153)

ANSWERS

MULTIPLE CHOICE

1. b The price elasticity of demand is the percentage change in quantity demanded divided by the percentage change in price. Option d is the definition of the price elasticity of supply. See pages 140-141.

2. a Substituting in the basic formula for elasticity gives .01/.1 = .1. See pages 140-141.

3. a Using the formula for elasticity of demand (percent change in quantity divided by percent change in price = .5/.33) gives 1.5 (out of convention we always take the absolute value). Therefore, the good is elastic because its absolute value is greater than one and it likely has many subsitutes. A price fall would increase the firm's total revenue. See pages 140-142.

4. b The price elasticity of demand of 2 means that every 1% change in the price will cause a 2% change in the quantity demanded. To obtain a 12% increase in the quantity demanded means the price must fall by 6%. See the formula for elasticity of demand on page 141.

5. a The revenue gain from the increase in price had to exceed the loss from the reduction in quantity, so the demand must be inelastic. See pages 151-153.

6. b When a good is price–elastic then a price decrease will result in a proportionately larger increase in the quantity demanded and revenues will rise. See pages 151-153.

7. a The elasticity changes along a straight line demand curve from highly elastic in upper portions of the demand curve to highly inelastic in the lower portions of the curve. See pages 143-145.

8. a A horizontal demand curve is perfectly elastic because the percentage change in quantity is infinite. See Figure 6-2 on page 146.

9. b Necessities tend to have few substitutes and the fewer the substitutes, the more inelastic the demand curve. See pages 148-149.

10. a The more specifically or narrowly a good is defined, the more substitutes it tends to have and the greater its elasticity of demand. See pages 148-149.

11. a   The greater the time period under consideration, the greater the possibility for substitution and, therefore, the greater the elasticity of demand. See pages 148-149.

12. b   Elasticity of supply is the percent change in quantity divided by the percent change in price: 20% / 25% = .8. See page 141.

13. a   You can either calculate the elasticity (percent change in quantity divided by the percent change in price) or you can use the trick in the Knowing the Tools Box (any straight line supply curve that intersects the vertical axis is elastic). See page 147.

14. c   Use the trick in the Knowing the Tools Box (any straight line supply curve going through the origin will be unit elastic.) See page 147.

15. a   For a vertical supply curve, the percent change in quantity becomes zero, so the elasticity becomes zero, making supply perfectly inelastic. See pages 141 and 147.

16. b   People buy fewer inferior goods when income rises. See pages 155-156.

17. d   When the price of a good increases and this increases the demand for its substitute, then the cross-price elasticity of demand is positive. See pages 157-158.

18. b   Price discrimination requires separating consumers by their elasticities and charging higher prices to individuals who have inelastic demands. See page 154.

19. b   Since price rose significantly while quantity remained virtually unchanged, either demand or supply is inelastic. Since price rose, either demand shifted out or supply shifted in. Only option b fits these conditions. See pages 159-160.

20. a   Since quantity rose significantly while price remained virtually unchanged either demand or supply is elastic. Since quantity rose, either demand shifted out or supply shifted out. Only option a fits these conditions. See pages 159-160.

21. c   Since price declined significantly while quantity remained virtually unchanged, either demand or supply is inelastic. Since price declined, either demand shifted in or supply shifted out. Only option c fits these conditions. See pages 159-160.

22. d   When supply shifts, the percent change in price = (percent change in supply)/(E_D+E_S) = 4/2=2. Because supply increased, the price decreases by 2 percent. See pages 159-160.

ANSWERS

POTENTIAL ESSAY QUESTIONS

The following are annotated answers. They indicate the general idea behind the answer.

1.   As a general rule, the more substitutes a good has, the more elastic is its demand. The number of substitutes is, in turn, affected by the time interval under consideration, whether the good is considered a necessity or a luxury, the specificity with which the good is defined, and the relative price of good compared to one's income.

2.   In order to maximize revenues firms will try to charge a higher price for the product to those consumers that have a more inelastic demand (because an increase in the price increases total revenue) and a lower price to those that have an elastic demand (because a decrease in the price increases total revenue).

TAXATION AND GOVERNMENT INTERVENTION

CHAPTER AT A GLANCE

This review is based upon the learning objectives that open the chapter.

1. Equilibrium maximizes consumer and producer surplus (166-167)

   Consumer surplus is the difference between the price buyers would have been willing to pay and the price they actually had to pay. Equal to Area A in the graph below.

   Producer surplus is the difference between the price sellers would have been willing to accept and the price they actually received as payment. Equal to Area B in the graph below.

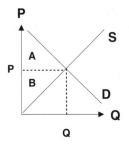

   Hint: To answer numerical problems calculating producer and consumer surplus, remember the formula for the area of a triangle is 1/2 base × height.

2. The cost of taxation to society includes the direct cost of the revenue paid to government, the loss of consumer and producer surplus caused by the tax, and the cost of administering the tax codes. (168-170)

   Total cost to consumers and producers is more than tax revenue. Refer to the graph below. Suppose a per unit tax "t" is paid by suppliers. Consumers pay rectangle B in tax revenue and lose area C in consumer surplus. Producers pay area D in tax revenue and lose area E in producer surplus. The triangular area represented by areas C (lost consumer surplus) and E (lost producer surplus) represents a cost of taxation in excess of the revenue paid to government. It is lost

consumer and producer surplus that is not gained by government. This loss of consumer and producer surplus from a tax is known as "deadweight loss." Graphically, deadweight loss is shown by the "welfare loss triangle"— area C + E.

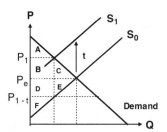

3a. The **benefit principle of taxation** states: individuals who receive the benefit of the good or service should pay the tax necessary to supply that good. (171)

   The reasoning behind the benefit principle is that if you use something, you pay for it. For example, some people pay more gas taxes because they use the roads more.

3b. The **ability-to-pay principle** states: individuals who are most able to bear the burden of the tax should pay the tax. (171)

   The reasoning behind the ability-to-pay principle is that the wealthy should pay more taxes because they can afford it. There is much debate about how a tax ought to be implemented if it is to be considered "fair."

4. The person who physically pays a tax is not necessarily the person who bears the burden of the tax. Who bears the burden of the tax (also know as tax incidence) depends upon who is best able to change his behavior in response to the tax, or who has the greater elasticity. (173-175)

The more inelastic one's relative supply and demand, the larger the burden of the tax one will bear.

The general rule about elasticities and tax burden is this: if demand is more inelastic than supply, demanders will pay a higher percentage of the tax. If supply is more inelastic than demand, suppliers will pay a higher share. More specifically:

fraction of tax borne by demander = price elasticity of supply divided by the sum of the price elasticity of demand and supply $= E_S / (E_D + E_S)$.

fraction of tax borne by supplier = price elasticity of demand divided by the sum of the price elasticity of demand and supply $= E_D / (E_D + E_S)$.

5. A price ceiling is, in essence, an implicit tax on producers and an implicit subsidy to consumers. (176-177)

Refer to the graph in the next column. With an effective price ceiling of P_1 the quantity supplied (and the amount consumed) falls from Q_e to Q_1. The welfare loss equals area C + E. This is the same effect as a tax. However, the loss of producer surplus, area D, is now transferred to consumers. It is as if government places a tax on suppliers and then gives that tax revenue to consumers when they consume the good.

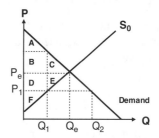

6. Rent seeking is an activity designed to transfer surplus from one group to another. If demand is inelastic, suppliers have an incentive to restrict supply to raise the price because this will raise their revenue. When the supply of a good is inelastic, consumers have an incentive to hold the price down. (179-182)

For example, the demand for food is inelastic. Farmers have an incentive to lobby government to restrict supply or to create a price floor for their commodities (sometimes called price supports) because they will be better off.

On the other hand, when the supply of a good is inelastic like that of rental-occupied housing, and demand rises, rental rates will rise significantly and consumers will scream for rent controls.

Government sometimes succumbs to political pressure for price controls (price floors and price ceilings). However, price controls create surpluses and shortages that only become more severe over time.

● SHORT-ANSWER QUESTIONS

1. What are consumer surplus and producer surplus? How are they related to demand and supply curves?

2. What happens to combined consumer and producer surplus when government sets a price floor above equilibrium price?

3. What are the costs and benefits of taxation to society?

4. What is the benefit principle of taxation?

5. What is the ability-to-pay principle of taxation?

6. What is the general rule about who bears the relative burden of a tax?

7. What is the general rule about elasticities and tax burden?

8. For whom is a price ceiling an implicit tax? For whom is a price ceiling an implicit subsidy?

9. For whom is a price floor an implicit tax? For whom is a price floor an implicit subsidy?

10. What is an important similarity and an important difference between taxes and price controls (price ceilings and price floors)?

11. What is rent seeking and how is rent seeking related to elasticity?

MATCHING THE TERMS
Match the terms to their definitions

_____ 1. ability-to-pay principle

_____ 2. benefit principle

_____ 3. consumer surplus

_____ 4. deadweight loss

_____ 5. excise tax

_____ 6. price ceiling

_____ 7. price floor

_____ 8. producer surplus

_____ 9. public choice economists

_____ 10. rent-seeking activities

_____ 11. welfare loss triangle

a. A tax that is levied on a specific good.

b. Economists who integrate an economic analysis of politics with their analysis of the economy.

c. The individuals who receive the benefit of the good or service should pay the tax necessary to supply that good.

d. A geometric representation of the welfare cost in terms of misallocated resources caused by a deviation from a supply-demand equilibrium.

e. The individuals who are most able to bear the burden of the tax should pay the tax.

f. The loss to society of consumer and producer surplus from a tax.

g. A government-set price above which price may not rise.

h. Activities designed to transfer surplus from one group to another.

i. A government-set price below which price may not fall.

j. The value the consumer gets from buying a product less its price.

k. The price the producer sells a product for less the cost of producing it.

● PROBLEMS AND APPLICATIONS

1. Refer to the graph below when answering the following questions.

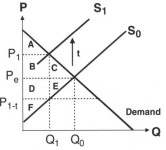

a. Given supply curve S_0, what is the area representing consumer surplus at the market equilibrium price?

b. Given supply curve S_0, what is the area representing producer surplus at the market equilibrium price?

c. Now suppose a per unit tax, t, paid by the supplier shifts the supply curve up from S_0 to S_1. Equilibrium price rises from P_e to P_1 and equilibrium quantity falls from Q_0 to Q_1. What area represents consumer surplus after the tax?

d. After the tax, what area represents what consumers pay in tax revenue to government?

e. What area represents lost consumer surplus caused by the tax and not gained by government?

f. What area represents producer surplus after the tax?

g. After the tax, what area represents what producers pay in tax revenue to government?

h. What area represents lost producer surplus caused by the tax and not gained by government?

i. What area represents deadweight loss; that is, what is the welfare loss triangle?

2. For each of the following determine whether the benefit principle or the ability-to-pay principle is being primarily relied on to raise revenues to provide public goods and services.

   a. The gas tax.

   b. Camping site overnight fees.

   c. Tolls on highways and bridges.

   d. Income taxes.

   e. Property taxes.

   f. Social Security taxes.

3. The supply and demand for foreign cars in Bangladesh is shown in the graph below. Suppose the government imposes a tax on supply of 10,000 takas per car. The new equilibrium price and quantity are shown in the graph below.

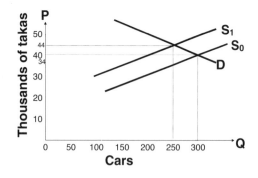

   a. What would be the tax paid by consumers? Suppliers? What price do suppliers with and without the tax receive?

   b. Demonstrate graphically the tax paid by each.

   c. From your answer to (b), what can you conclude about the relative elasticities of the supply and demand curves?

4. What is the deadweight loss of the tax equal to in question #3?

5. Suppose the price elasticity of supply is 0.5 and the price elasticity of demand is 1.5. If the government imposes a tax on the good, what percentage of the tax is borne by buyers?

6. a. If government, given its targeted revenue from a tax, wants to have as large an effect on individual actions as possible, should it tax goods with an inelastic or elastic demand? Why?

b. If government wants to raise revenues from a tax and minimize welfare loss, should it tax goods with *inelastic* demand or supply, or *elastic* demand or supply? Why?

e. How is a price ceiling equivalent to a tax on producers and a subsidy to consumers?

f. Suppose that instead of government imposing a price ceiling, it imposed a tax that reduced the quantity supplied to Q_1. What is an essential similarity between the two outcomes? What is an essential difference?

7. Refer to the graph below when answering the following questions.

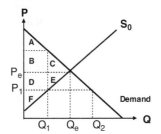

a. In market equilibrium, what area represents consumer surplus? Producer surplus?

b. Suppose government imposes a price ceiling of P_1. What happens to the quantity demanded and the quantity supplied?

c. What happens to consumer and producer surplus as a result of the price ceiling?

d. What is the welfare loss triangle as a result of the price ceiling?

8. How could the fact that farmers lobby government to restrict the supply of agricultural production or to pursue agricultural price supports (price floors) be viewed as rent-seeking activity?

9. Why will shortages that result from price ceilings, and surpluses that result from price floors, become more acute over time?

● A BRAIN TEASER

1. Who bears the larger burden of an excise tax on cigarettes: smokers or tobacco companies? If government increases the tax on cigarettes, what will happen to government's tax revenues?

MULTIPLE CHOICE

Circle the one best answer for each of the following questions:

1.　Refer to the graph below. The amount of consumer surplus at market equilibrium is:
　　a. $18.
　　b. $9.
　　c. $72.
　　d. $36.

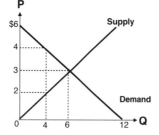

2.　Refer to the graph in Question #1. The lost combined consumer and producer surplus from a price of $4 is:
　　a. $2.
　　b. $4.
　　c. $12.
　　d. $36.

3.　Assume equilibrium in the graph below. What area represents consumer surplus?
　　a. A + B + C.
　　b. D + C + E.
　　c. E.
　　d. E + F.

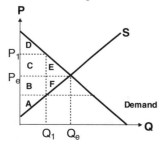

4.　Refer to the graph for Question #3. Assume equilibrium. What area represents the welfare loss from a price floor of P_1?
　　a. B + C + E + F.
　　b. C + B.
　　c. B.
　　d. E + F.

5.　Refer to the graph below. If a per unit tax, t, is paid by sellers:

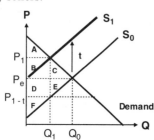

　　a. producer surplus is represented by areas A, B and C before the tax and A after the tax.
　　b. consumer surplus is represented by areas D, E and F before the tax and B after the tax.
　　c. the tax, t, imposes a deadweight loss represented by the welfare loss triangle-areas C and E.
　　d. consumers lose surplus given by area E while producers lose surplus given by area C.

6.　Refer to the graph in Question #5. If a per unit tax, t, is paid by sellers, which of the following is true?
　　a. Tax revenue paid equals the tax, t, times the equilibrium quantity, Q_1, or areas B and D.
　　b. The total cost to consumers and producers is less than tax revenue to government.
　　c. Producers pay area B in tax revenue and also lose area C in producer surplus.
　　d. Consumers pay area D in tax revenue and lose area E in consumer surplus.

7.　Deadweight loss from a tax is:
　　a. the loss of consumer surplus from a tax.
　　b. the loss of producer surplus from a tax.
　　c. the loss of consumer *and* producer surplus from a tax.
　　d. the amount of tax revenues collected by government.

8.　The welfare loss triangle is a geometric representation of the:
　　a. lost quantity traded that would have otherwise benefited both consumers and producers.
　　b. amount of tax paid by consumers and businesses.
　　c. consumer surplus after a tax.
　　d. producer surplus after a tax.

9.　With regard to taxation, it is true that:
　　a. the benefit and ability-to-pay principles of taxation are easy to apply, in part because they suggest the same taxes to raise revenue.
　　b. if government, given its targeted revenue, wants to have as little effect on individual actions as possible, then it should tax goods with elastic demand or supply.
　　c. if government wants to minimize the welfare loss, it should tax goods with inelastic supply and demand.
　　d. taxes are generally higher in the United States than in most other countries.

10. The burden of a tax is:
    a. most heavily borne by those with the more inelastic demand or supply.
    b. most heavily borne by those with the more elastic demand or supply.
    c. usually equally split between buyers and sellers.
    d. usually passed on to consumers in the form of a higher price.

11. How much of a $100 tax will consumers pay if the price elasticity of demand is 3 and the price elasticity of supply is 2?
    a. $50.
    b. $40.
    c. $30.
    d. $20

12. How much of a $100 tax will consumers pay if the price elasticity of supply is 2 and the price elasticity of demand is 4?
    a. $20.
    b. $33.
    c. $40.
    d. $60.

13. Social Security taxes are:
    a. levied by government more heavily on employees than employers, even though the burden of the tax is most heavily borne by employers.
    b. most heavily borne by employers if the demand for labor tends to be more inelastic than supply.
    c. most heavily borne by workers if the demand for labor tends to be more inelastic than the supply of labor.
    d. most heavily borne by workers if the supply of labor tends to be more inelastic than the demand for labor.

14. An effective price ceiling:
    a. is a government-set price above market equilibrium price.
    b. is in essence an implicit tax on producers and an implicit subsidy to consumers.
    c. will create a surplus.
    d. causes an increase in consumer and producer surplus.

15. Refer to the graph below. A price ceiling of P_1 will:

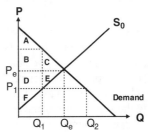

    a. create a shortage of $Q_e - Q_1$.
    b. transfer surplus D from producers to consumers.
    c. create a deadweight loss equal to areas A + B+C.
    d. increase combined producer and consumer surplus by triangles C and E.

16. Rent-seeking activity is designed to:
    a. produce additional revenue for government.
    b. minimize welfare loss.
    c. maximize welfare loss.
    d. transfer surplus from one group to another.

17. In which case will a price floor result in the greatest excess supply?
    a. When both demand and supply are highly inelastic.
    b. When both demand and supply are highly elastic.
    c. When demand is elastic and supply is inelastic.
    d. When demand is inelastic and supply is elastic.

● POTENTIAL ESSAY QUESTIONS

You may also see essay questions similar to the "Problems & Applications" and "Brain Teaser" exercises.

1. Discuss the relationship between elasticity and tax burden.

2. What are the basic similarities and differences between the effects of taxes and price controls?

ANSWERS

SHORT-ANSWER QUESTIONS

1. Consumer surplus is the difference between the price buyers are willing to pay (shown by the demand curve) and the price they actually pay. Producer surplus is the difference between what the sellers are willing to accept as payment (shown by the supply curve) and what they actually receive as payment. (166-167)

2. A price floor above equilibrium price will result in a lower quantity purchased and therefore a lower combined producer and consumer surplus. (166-167, especially Figure 7-1)

3. The costs of taxation to society includes (1) the direct cost of the revenue paid to government; (2) the loss of consumer and producer surplus caused by the tax; and (3) the cost of administering the tax codes. The benefits of taxation to society is the goods and services that government provides (when fulfilling the six roles in a market economy, as discussed in Chapter 5). (167-168)

4. The benefit principle follows the same principle as the market: *the individuals who receive the benefit of the good or service should pay the tax necessary to supply that good.* (171)

5. The ability-to-pay principle simply states: *the individuals who are most able to bear the burden of the tax should pay the tax.* (171)

6. The relative burden of a tax (also known as a tax incidence) follows the general rule: *The more inelastic one's relative supply and demand, the larger the burden of the tax one will bear.* (173-175)

7. The general rule about elasticities and tax burden is this: *if demand is more inelastic than supply, consumers pay a higher percentage of the tax. If supply is more inelastic than demand, suppliers pay a higher share.* (173-175)

8. A price ceiling (a government-set price below market equilibrium price) is in essence an implicit tax on producers and an implicit subsidy to consumers. (176-177)

9. A price floor (a government-set price above market equilibrium price) is in essence an implicit tax on consumers and an implicit subsidy to producers. (176-177)

10. An important similarity between taxes and price controls (which include price ceilings and price floors) is that they all create a loss of consumer and producer surplus shown graphically by a welfare loss triangle. An important difference between taxes and price controls is that price controls create surpluses (in the case of a price floor) and shortages (in the case of a price ceiling), while taxes do not create surpluses or shortages. (177)

11. Rent seeking is an activity designed to transfer surplus (consumer or producer surplus) from one group to another. The more inelastic the demand, the greater the incentive suppliers have to drive the price up because this will increase their revenue and lower their cost, which raises their profits. The more inelastic supply, the greater the incentive consumers have to lobby government to set a price ceiling because it will result in a larger transfer of surplus to themselves. (179-182)

ANSWERS

MATCHING

1-e; 2-c; 3-j; 4-f; 5-a; 6-g; 7-i; 8-k; 9-b; 10-h; 11-d.

ANSWERS

PROBLEMS AND APPLICATIONS

1. a. Area A + B + C represents consumer surplus at the market equilibrium price. (168-170, and Figure 7-3)
    b. Area D + E + F represents producer surplus at the market equilibrium price. (168-170, and Figure 7-3)
    c. Area A is consumer surplus after the tax. (168-170, and Figure 7-3)
    d. Area B is what consumers pay in tax revenues to government. This represents

lost consumer surplus gained by government. (168-170, and Figure 7-3)

e. Area C is lost consumer surplus not gained by government. (168-170, and Figure 7-3)

f. Area F is producer surplus after the tax. (168-170, and Figure 7-3)

g. Area D is what producers pay in tax revenues to government. This represents lost producer surplus gained by government. (168-170, and Figure 7-3)

h. Area E represents lost producer surplus not gained by government. (168-170, and Figure 7-3)

i. Area C + E is the deadweight loss from a tax. This area is the welfare loss triangle. (168-170, and Figure 7-3)

2. a. Benefit principle of taxation. Gas taxes raise revenues to provide roads to those who use them. (171)

b. Benefit principle of taxation. The fees raise revenues to provide public parks to those who use them. (171)

c. Benefit principle of taxation. The tolls raise revenues to provide roads to those who use them. (171)

d. Ability-to-pay principle. The income tax is a progressive tax (the percentage of taxes paid increases as income increases) because the wealthy can "afford" to pay more taxes. (171)

e. Ability-to-pay principle. The more property you own, the more you pay. (171)

f. Benefit principle of taxation. Although current taxes are used to pay pensions to current retirees, the expectation is that when current workers retire, a similar pension will be paid to them from social security taxes collected at that time. (171)

3. a. The consumers now have to pay 44,000 takas per car, which is 4,000 takas more than before. Their tax burden is (4,000 × 250) = 1,000,000 takas. Suppliers now receive 34,000 takas (44,000-10,000) on each car they sell, which is 6,000 takas less per car than before the tax. Their tax burden is (6,000 × 250) = 1,500,000 takas. (173-175, especially Figure 7-4)

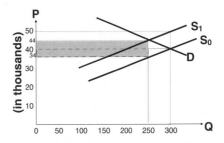

b. The graph above shows the relative taxes paid by consumers and producers. The upper shaded portion is consumers' tax burden. The lower shaded portion is suppliers' tax burden. (173-175, especially Figure 7-4)

c. Since the supplier's tax burden is greater, the supply curve is more inelastic than the demand curve. (173-175, especially Figure 7-4)

4. The deadweight loss of a tax is shown by a welfare loss triangle. In this case that triangle has a base of 10,000 takas and a height of 50 cars (when the triangle is turned on its side). The area of that triangle = ½ x base x height = ½ x 10,000 x 50 = 250,000 takas. (168-170)

5. The tax borne by buyers equals the price elasticity of supply divided by the sum of the price elasticities of supply and demand (0.5/2)= .25 or 1/4. Producers bear the other 75 percent or 3/4 of the tax. Producers pay the largest fraction (percentage) of a tax when demand is elastic and supply is inelastic. The one with the greater inelasticity bears the biggest burden of a tax. (173-175)

6. a. Government should tax goods with *elastic* demand if it wishes to have as large an effect on individual actions as possible. This is because an elastic demand means there are many substitutes buyers can turn to in response to the higher price as a result of the tax. Buyers will cut back on their consumption rather dramatically. (175-176)

b. Government should tax goods with *inelastic* demand or supply if it wishes to raise revenues and minimize welfare loss. Revenues to government will rise because an inelastic demand or supply means there are few substitutes or alternatives for buyers and sellers to turn to. Graphically, an inelastic demand or supply will minimize welfare loss because the welfare loss triangle will be smaller the steeper (the more inelastic) the demand or supply curves. (173-176, Figure 7-4, and the Apply the Tools box on page 172)

7. **a.** Market equilibrium is P_e and Q_e. Consumer surplus is area A + B + C. Producer surplus is area D + E + F. (166-167 and Figure 7-3 on page 169)

   b. As a result of the price ceiling, the quantity supplied falls from Q_e to Q_1 and the quantity demanded rises from Q_e to Q_2. This creates a shortage of $Q_2 - Q_1$. (176-177, especially Figure 7-5)

   c. Consumer surplus becomes area A + B + D. Producer surplus becomes area F. (176-177)

   d. The welfare loss triangle is area C + E. (176-177, especially Figure 7-5)

   e. A price ceiling is equivalent to a tax on producers and a subsidy to consumers because area D is transferred from producers to consumers as a result of the price ceiling. (176-177, especially Figure 7-5)

   f. The welfare loss would be the same (the welfare loss triangle would still be area C + E). However, an essential difference between the two is that a price ceiling creates a shortage, while a tax would not. Another difference is who gets the surplus. In the case of the tax, government gets areas B and D as tax revenue. (176-177, especially Figure 7-5)

8. Because the demand for agricultural goods is inelastic, farmers have an incentive to get government to restrict supply or create a price floor, thereby raising their revenue (their income). This is rent seeking because farmers are attempting to shift consumer surplus to themselves. (179-180)

9. Price ceilings and price floors create greater shortages and surpluses over time because in the long run, supply and demand tend to be more elastic than in the short run. (183)

═══ **ANSWERS** ═══

A BRAIN TEASER

1. Smokers will bear the biggest burden of the cigarette tax because the demand for cigarettes is inelastic (for those "hooked" on smoking there are few substitutes for cigarettes). If government increases the cigarette tax, this will increase the price by a greater percentage than the quantity demanded falls (because demand is inelastic). That is, few people stop smoking. Therefore, tax revenues to government rise. (173-175)

═══ **ANSWERS** ═══

MULTIPLE CHOICE

1. **b** The consumer surplus triangle has a base of 6 (the equilibrium quantity) and a height of $3 (6 - 3). Since the area of a triangle is ½ (base x height), the consumer surplus is ½(3 x 6) = $9. See pages 166-167 and Figure 7-1.

2. **a** The lost consumer and producer surplus when price rises to $4 is the triangle that has a height (looked at sideways) of 2 (6 − 4) and a base of 2 (4 - 2). Since the area of a triangle is ½ (base x height), the lost surplus is ½(2 x 2) = $2. See pages 166-167 and Figure 7-1.

3. **b** Consumer surplus is the area under the demand curve above the equilibrium price. See page 169 and Figure 7-3.

4. **d** The loss to consumers is E and C (but C is gained by producers). The loss to producers is F. So the total loss is $E + F$. See page 169 and Figure 7-3.

5. **c** The incorrect options have consumer and producer surplus confused. Deadweight loss is surplus lost by consumers and producers but not gained by anyone. It is a net loss to society because of deviation from market equilibrium. See page 169 and Figure 7-3.

6. **a** Tax revenue is the tax per unit times the units sold, area B + D. To be correct, option b should read "is *greater* than."

Options c and d would be correct if we reversed the terms consumer and producer, as well as the terms consumer surplus and producer surplus. See page 169 and Figure 7-3.

7. c   Deadweight loss is the loss of consumer and producer surplus from a tax. See pages 168-170.

8. a   The welfare loss triangle is the cost of taxation in *excess* of the revenue paid to government. Moreover, it represents the *loss* of consumer *and* producer surplus from a tax. See pages 168-170.

9. c   The benefit and ability-to-pay principles of taxation are *not* easy to apply and *are* often in conflict. With regard to b, government should tax *inelastic* goods. Taxes are generally *lower* in the U.S. than in most other countries. See pages 171.

10. a   Those with inelastic demand or supply are less able to change their behavior as a result of the tax and therefore bear a greater share of the tax. See pages 173-175.

11. b   The fraction of a tax borne by consumers equals the price elasticity of supply divided by the sum of the price elasticity of demand and supply (2/5= 0.4). 4/10 or 40 percent of $100 is $40. See page 174.

12. b   The fraction of a tax borne by consumers equals the price elasticity of supply divided by the sum of the price elasticity of demand and supply (2/6 = 1/3). One third of $100 is $33.33. See page 174.

13. d   Government divides the taxes among employees and employers equally. However, since the supply of labor is relatively more inelastic, employees bear the greater burden of Social Security taxes. See page 175.

14. b   A price ceiling is a government-set price *below* equilibrium and creates a *shortage*. A price ceiling reduces consumer and producer surplus, but a portion of the lost producer surplus is transferred to consumers. A price ceiling creates welfare loss just like taxes do. See pages 176-177.

15. b   A price ceiling creates a shortage equal to $Q_2 - Q_1$. Producer surplus D is transferred to consumers because of the lower price. Producer and consumer surplus *falls* by areas C and E (the welfare loss triangle). See pages 176-177, especially Figure 7-5.

16. d   Rent-seeking activity is designed to transfer surplus from one group to another—whether it be from producers to consumers or the other way around. See page 179.

17. b   When both parties have the greatest possibility of change, there will be the greatest surplus. This occurs in the long run when both demand and supply are more elastic. See pages 180-181.

■■■■ ANSWERS ■■■■

POTENTIAL ESSAY QUESTIONS

The following are annotated answers. They indicate the general idea behind the answer.

1.   The general rule about elasticities and tax burden is this: if demand is more inelastic than supply, consumers will pay a higher percentage of the tax. If supply is more inelastic than demand, suppliers will pay a higher share.

2.   Price controls and taxes are similar in that they both create welfare loss. They differ in that price controls create shortages (in the case of a price ceiling) and surpluses (in the case of a price floor), while taxes do not. Another difference is who gets the surplus. For a tax, government gets some of the surplus as tax revenue.

THE LOGIC OF INDIVIDUAL CHOICE

CHAPTER AT A GLANCE

This review is based upon the learning objectives that open the chapter.

1. The principle of diminishing marginal utility states that after some point, the marginal utility received from each additional unit of a good decreases with each unit consumed, other things equal. (190-191)

   Marginal means "extra."
   Utility means "satisfaction."

2. The principle of rational choice tells us to spend our money on those goods that give us the most marginal utility per dollar. (192-193)

   If $MU_x/P_x > MU_y/P_y$, choose to consume an additional unit of good x;

   If $MU_x/P_x < MU_y/P_y$, choose to consume an additional unit of good y;

   If $MU_x/P_x = MU_y/P_y$, you are maximizing utility; you cannot increase your utility by adjusting your choices.

   $MU_x/P_x = MU_y/P_y$ means the extra satisfaction per last dollar spent on x equals that for y.

3. When the ratios of the marginal utility to the price of goods are equal, you're maximizing utility; that is the utility maximizing rule. (193-196)

   The equality: $MU_x/P_x = MU_y/P_y$ implies a combination of quantities of goods x and y consumed that will maximize your satisfaction given your budget, preferences, and the prices of x and y. No other combination of goods x and y will satisfy you as much.

4a. According to the principle of rational choice, if there is diminishing marginal utility and the price of a good goes up, we consume less of that good. Hence, the principle of rational choice leads to the law of demand. (196-198)

   If $MU_x/P_x = MU_y/P_y$ and then P_x increases, we get $MU_x/P_x < MU_y/P_y$ and we buy more of y and buy less of x.

   The law of demand tells us that less will be purchased at higher prices.

4b. According to the principle of rational choice, if there is diminishing marginal utility and the price of supplying a good goes up, you supply more of that good. (198-199)

   Consider labor. As the wage rate goes up, you will be willing to work more hours. Note that the law of supply can be derived from the principle of rational choice.

5. Economists use their simple self-interest theory of choice because it cuts through many obfuscations, and, in doing, so often captures a part of reality that others miss. (203-204)

   Approaching problems by asking, "What's in it for the people making the decision?" can provide insight.

6. Three assumptions of the theory of choice are: decision making is costless, tastes are given, and individuals' maximize utility. (199-201)

   We must understand that these three assumptions don't always hold. The ultimatum game suggests that people care about fairness as well as maximizing their total utility. The status quo bias suggests that actions are based on perceived norms.

   See also, Appendix A: "Indifference Curve Analysis."

● SHORT-ANSWER QUESTIONS

1. What is marginal utility?

2. Suppose you and your friend are studying hard for an economics exam. You have a craving for double cheese pizza. You order a large. Your mouth is watering as you sink your teeth into the first slice. Oh, the pleasure! You eagerly reach for the second slice. The additional pleasure that you get from this slice is less than that from the first. The third and fourth slice each give you even less pleasure. What principle does this describe? State the principle in general terms.

3. Suppose you had $8 to spend. You like going to see Ben Affeck movies a lot, but you like to see John Turturro movies even more. If these were your only choices to spend the $8 on, which movie would you go to see? Show how your choice follows the principle of rational choice.

4. What are the formulas that embody the principle of rational choice?

5. Explain why you're maximizing utility when the ratios of the marginal utility to the price of goods are equal.

6. Suppose you are maximizing utility by consuming two Big Macs at $2 apiece and three ice cream cones at $1 apiece. What happens to the number of Big Macs and ice cream cones consumed if the price of an ice cream cone rises to $2? How does this change in consumption account for the law of demand?

7. Why can economists believe there are many explanations of individual choice, but nonetheless focus on self-interest?

8. Describe the ultimatum game. What have economists learned about people's tastes from the ultimatum game? What are the implications for the theory of rational choice?

MATCHING THE TERMS
Match the terms to their definitions

___ **1.** conspicuous consumption	**a.** As you consume more of a good, at some point, consuming another unit of the good will yield less additional pleasure compared to the preceding unit.
___ **2.** marginal utility	**b.** A rule stating that one should consume that combination of goods where the ratios of their marginal utilities to their prices are equal.
___ **3.** principle of diminishing marginal utility	**c.** A measure of the pleasure or satisfaction one gets from consuming a good or service.
___ **4.** principle of rational choice	**d.** Spend your money on those goods that give you the most marginal utility per dollar.
___ **5.** status quo bias	**e.** The satisfaction one gets from consuming one additional unit of a product above and beyond what has already been consumed up to that point.
___ **6.** total utility	**f.** The total satisfaction one gets from a product.
___ **7.** ultimatum game	**g.** Consumption of goods not for one's direct pleasure, but simply to show off.
___ **8.** utility	**h.** Individuals' actions are influenced by the current situation even when that situation is not important to the decision.
___ **9.** utility maximizing rule	**i.** An exercise that demonstrates people care about fairness as well as personal total utility.

● PROBLEMS AND APPLICATIONS

1. a. Fill in the blanks for the following table that shows how marginal utility and total utility change as more and more chocolate chip cookies are consumed. (Marginal utility refers to the marginal utility of increasing to that row; e.g., the marginal utility of going from 0 to 1 is 20.)

Number of choc. chip cookies	Total utility	Marginal utility
1	___	20
2	37	___
3	51	___
4	___	11
5	___	8
6	___	5
7	77	___
8	___	–1

b. On the axes below, graph the total utility curve of the table above.

c. Graph the marginal utility curve on the axes for b.

d. Is the principle of diminishing marginal utility operative in this case? Explain your answer.

e. At what point does the principle of diminishing marginal utility take effect? At what point does marginal utility become zero?

2. Using the principle of rational choice, choose the best option in each case:

a. A $2 slice of pizza giving you 80 units of utility and a $2 hero sandwich giving you 60 units of utility.

b. A $40,000 BMW giving you 200,000 units of utility and a $20,000 Toyota giving you 120,000 units of utility.

c. Taking an economics course that meets 3 times a week for ten weeks giving 900 units of utility or taking a history course that meets 2 times a week for ten weeks giving 800 units of utility. Both class periods last 50 minutes. There is no homework or studying.

d. Taking Tory out for a date at the Four Seasons restaurant in New York City at a cost of $120 which gives you 600 units of utility and taking Sam out at the corner pizza place at a cost of $15 which gives you 60 units of utility. (Tory is short for Victoria or Torrence and Sam is short for Samantha or Samuel — you choose which.)

3. Suppose you are taking courses from two different colleges, both on a part-time basis. One college offers only science courses. The other offers only humanities courses. Each class meets for the same amount of time and you have an unlimited number of hours you can devote to course work, but only $10,500 to devote to tuition. Science courses cost $1,500 a course and humanities courses cost $3,000 a course. You are taking the courses for enjoyment and you have estimated the utility from the consumption of these courses as presented in the following table:

Number of courses	Science Total utility	Humanities Total utility
0	0	0
1	4,500	7,500
2	7,500	12,000
3	9,750	15,750
4	11,250	18,750
5	11,750	21,000
6	12,000	22,500

a. How many science courses and how many humanities courses should you take (assuming you follow the principle of rational choice)?

b. Suppose the price of humanities courses falls to $1,000 a course, how would your answer to (a) change?

A1. Suppose you have a budget constraint of $10 to spend on pens and notebooks. Pens are 50 cents apiece and notebooks are $1 apiece. Draw the budget constraint, putting pens on the vertical axis and notebooks on the horizontal axis.

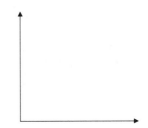

a. What is the slope of the line?

b. What happens to the budget constraint if your income available to spend falls to $8? What is the slope of the new curve? Show this graphically on the graph for (a).

c. Given the new $8 budget constraint, now suppose the price of notebooks rises to $2 apiece. What happens to the budget constraint? Show this graphically using the same axes as in the graph for (a) and (b).

A2. Suppose the following table depicts your indifference between combinations of pens and notebooks:

	Notebooks	Pens
A	12	6
B	8	7
C	6	8
D	5	10
E	4	14

a. Graph the indifference curve on the axes below, with pens on the vertical axis and notebooks on the horizontal axis.

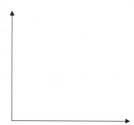

b. What is the marginal rate of substitution between combinations C and D?

c. Combine the indifference curve from question A2 with the $10 budget constraint from question A1 on the graph above. What is the combination of goods you will choose using the principle of rational choice?

A BRAIN TEASER

1. The wedding industry is a $32 billion business. Weddings tend to be a onetime expense, with lavish expenditures on first marriages per wedding and smaller expenditures on later marriages. Would you expect the profit margins on wedding supplies to be higher or lower than for grocery stores? Why?

MULTIPLE CHOICE

Circle the one best answer for each of the following questions:

1. The principle of diminishing marginal utility says that after some point the marginal utility received from each additional unit of a good:
  a. remains constant with each good consumed.
  b. increases with each unit consumed.
  c. decreases with each unit consumed.
  d. approaches infinity with each good consumed.

2. The utility gained from eating one slice of pizza is 30 and the utility gained from eating a second slice of pizza is 20. From this we know:
  a. the marginal utility of the second slice of pizza is 50.
  b. the total utility of the second slice of pizza is 50.
  c. the marginal utility of the second slice of pizza is 20.
  d. there is not enough information to compute the marginal utility.

3. With regard to utility, it is true that
  a. the total satisfaction one gets from one's consumption of a product is called marginal utility.
  b. if you buy one Big Mac that gives you marginal utility of 400 and a second one that gives you marginal utility of 250, total utility of eating two Big Macs is 650.
  c. according to the law of diminishing marginal utility, the more we consume of something, the smaller the total satisfaction received from that good.
  d. when choosing between two goods, a rational consumer will choose that product that gives the greatest total utility per dollar.

4. The principle of rational choice specifically states that you choose how to spend additional income based on what gives you:
    a. the most total utility for that dollar.
    b. the most marginal utility for that dollar.
    c. the most average utility for that dollar.
    d. the least total utility for that dollar.

5. The price of good A is $1; the price of good B is $2. The marginal utility you get from good A is 40; the marginal utility you get from good B is 60. Assuming you can make marginal changes, you should:
    a. consume more of good A and less of good B.
    b. consume more of good B and less of good A.
    c. keep consuming equal amounts of both goods.
    d. realize that you don't have enough information to answer the question.

6. The price of good A is $2; the price of good B is $2. The marginal utility you get from good A is 40; the marginal utility you get from good B is 60. Assuming you can make marginal changes, you should:
    a. consume more of good A and less of good B.
    b. consume more of good B and less of good A.
    c. keep consuming equal amounts of both goods.
    d. realize that you don't have enough information to answer the question.

7. The price of good A is $1; the price of good B is $2. The marginal utility you get from good A is 40; the marginal utility you get from good B is 80. Assuming you can make marginal changes, you should:
    a. consume more of good A and less of good B.
    b. consume more of good B and less of good A.
    c. keep consuming the amount of both goods that you are currently consuming.
    d. realize that you don't have enough information to answer the question.

8. Dennis is deciding where to spend his spring break. If he goes to Vail, Colorado, the trip will give him 10,000 units of utility (satisfaction) and will cost him $500. If, instead, he travels to Padre Island, Texas, the trip will give him 6,000 units of pleasure and will cost him $400. Dennis should go to:
    a. Vail because his total pleasure will be greater.

    b. Padre Island because it is cheaper.
    c. Vail because his pleasure per dollar spent will be greater.
    d. Padre Island because his pleasure per dollar spent will be greater.

9. Economists assume that consumers will choose to purchase and consume:
    a. those goods that cost the least.
    b. those goods with the highest total utility.
    c. that combination of goods at which marginal utilities per dollar spent are equal.
    d. that combination of goods for which total utilities per dollar spent are equal.

10. The rational consumer will buy more of good X when:
    a. $MU_X/P_X < MU_Y/P_Y$
    b. $MU_X/P_X > MU_Y/P_Y$
    c. $MU_X/P_X = MU_Y/P_Y$
    d. the price of good X increases

11. If $MU_X/P_X = MU_Y/P_Y$ and the price of Y decreases, then the rational consumer will:
    a. continue consuming the same combination of X and Y.
    b. buy more of Y.
    c. buy more of X.
    d. buy less of X and Y.

12. If your marginal utility of additional income is 60 units of utility, your opportunity cost of working is $5.00 per hour, and you are currently working 10 hours per week at $6.00 per hour, what is the minimum wage that you will require to work another hour?
    a. 60 units of utility.
    b. $5.00.
    c. $6.00.
    d. Insufficient information has been given to answer this question.

13. The theory of bounded rationality suggests that:
    a. all goods will be normal goods.
    b. all goods will be substitutes.
    c. many of our decisions are based on rules of thumb.
    d. individual tastes will be bounded and hence there will be diminishing marginal utility.

14. A focal point equilibrium is an equilibrium in which a set of goods is consumed:
   a. because the goods are subjectively preferred to all other goods.
   b. because the goods are objectively preferred to all other goods.
   c. not because the goods are necessarily preferred to all other goods, but simply because through luck, or advertising, they have become the goods to which people gravitate.
   d. through luck, or advertising, they have become focal points to which people gravitate despite the fact that other goods are definitely preferred.

15. Economists' theory of choice assumes:
   a. decision-making has costs.
   b. peoples' preferences are given, and are not shaped by society.
   c. people do not always make decisions that are rational.
   d. people maximize many things, one of which is utility.

16. Behavioral economists find that people:
   a. always give the same answer regardless of how questions are posed.
   b. care only about maximizing their own utility, not fairness.
   c. tend to make choices consistent with the perceived norm.
   d. can handle decisions with 2 choices just as easily as decisions with 5 choices.

A1. Refer to the graph below. The budget constraint reflects a relative price of chocolate (in terms of soda) of:
   a. one-fourth.
   b. one-half.
   c. one.
   d. two.

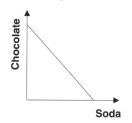

A2. Refer to the graph below. If the price of chocolate falls, the budget constraint will:

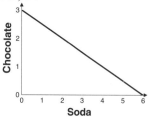

   a. rotate out and become flatter.
   b. rotate in but keep the same slope.
   c. rotate in and become steeper.
   d. rotate out and become steeper.

A3. Refer to the graph below. The absolute value of the slope of the indifference curve represents:

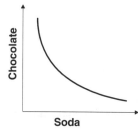

   a. the marginal utility of chocolate divided by the marginal utility of soda.
   b. the marginal utility of soda divided by the marginal utility of chocolate.
   c. the marginal utility of soda times the marginal utility of chocolate.
   d. the marginal utility of chocolate divided by the price of chocolate.

A4. Refer to the graph below. The equilibrium in the indifference curve model is at point:
   a. A.
   b. B.
   c. C.
   d. D.

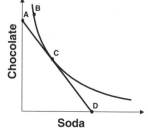

● POTENTIAL ESSAY QUESTIONS

You may also see essay questions similar to the "Problems & Applications" and "Brain Teaser" exercises.

1. Discuss the principle of diminishing marginal utility. How is this related to the principle of rational choice and the law of demand?

2. Explain how marginal utility accounts for the law of supply.

ANSWERS

SHORT-ANSWER QUESTIONS

1. Marginal utility refers to the satisfaction one gets from the consumption of an incremental or additional product above and beyond what has already been consumed up to that point. (189-190)

2. The fact that you enjoy each subsequent slice less and less follows the principle of diminishing marginal utility. It states that after some point, the marginal utility received from each additional unit of a good decreases with each unit consumed. (190-191)

3. You would choose to see the John Turturro movie because it would give more pleasure for the same amount of money. This decision follows the principle of rational choice which tells us to spend our money on those goods that give us the most marginal utility per dollar. (192-193)

4. The formulas that embody the principle of rational choice are:
    If $MU_x/P_x > MU_y/P_y$, choose to consume an additional unit of good x;
    If $MU_x/P_x < MU_y/P_y$, choose to consume an additional unit of good y;
    If $MU_x/P_x = MU_y/P_y$, you're maximizing utility. (192-194)

5. If the ratios of the marginal utility to the price of goods are equal, you cannot adjust your spending in any way to increase total utility. Changing your spending will result in additional total utility for that good you increased. But that additional utility is less than the decrease in utility for that good that you have given up. Thus, the marginal utilities per dollar are no longer equal and overall total utility has fallen. Total utility is maximized where the ratios of the marginal utility to the price of goods are equal. (195-196)

6. If you were initially maximizing utility, it must be that $MU_{Big\ Macs}/\$2 = MU_{i.c.}/\$1$. If the price of ice cream cones rises, then you are no longer maximizing utility because $MU_{Big\ Macs}/\$2 > MU_{i.c.}/\$2$. To once again maximize utility, you would raise the marginal utility of ice cream cones and lower the marginal utility of

Big Macs by choosing to consume more Big Macs and fewer ice cream cones because the marginal utility per dollar spent on Big Macs is greater than that for ice cream cones. You would adjust your consumption to the point where the marginal utilities per dollar were once again equal. The price of ice cream cones *relative to Big Macs* rose and the quantity demanded fell; and the price of Big Macs *relative to ice creams* fell and the quantity demanded rose. This is the law of demand in action. (193-196)

7. Economists believe there are many explanations of individual choice, but nonetheless they focus on self-interest because their simple self-interest theory cuts through many complications and in doing so often captures a part of reality other approaches miss. (203-204)

8. The ultimatum game is a game in which one person is given a sum of money that they can then share with another person. The person with the money can offer the other person any amount of that sum. If the offer is accepted, both people keep the money as negotiated. If the offer is rejected, all money must be returned. While economic theory suggests any offer would be accepted, offers that aren't close to half the sum are generally rejected. This suggests that people care about fairness as well as maximizing their total utility. The implications are that the assumptions of the theory of rational choice do not always hold true in reality. (202-203)

ANSWERS

MATCHING

1-g; 2-e; 3-a; 4-d; 5-h; 6-f; 7-i; 8-c; 9-b.

ANSWERS

PROBLEMS AND APPLICATIONS

1. **a.** This question tests the concepts of marginal utility, total utility, and the principle of diminishing marginal utility. Marginal utility is the satisfaction one gets from the consumption of an *incremental*

product. Total utility is the total satisfaction from all units consumed up to that point of consumption; it is the sum of all marginal utilities from consumption. (189-191)

Number of choc. chip cookies	Total utility	Marginal utility
1	20	20
2	37	17
3	51	14
4	62	11
5	70	8
6	75	5
7	77	2
8	76	−1

b.   The total utility curve is shown below. It is bowed downward because the marginal utility diminishes as more cookies are consumed. (190-191, especially Figure 8-1)

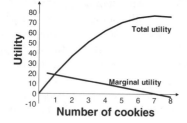

c.   The marginal utility curve is shown above. Its slope is always negative because the marginal utility of each additional cookie is always declining. (191, especially Figure 8-1)

d.   The principle of diminishing marginal utility is operative in this case. It states that as more of a good is consumed, beyond some point the additional units of consumption will yield fewer units of utility than the previous units. This is shown in the table by the third column. Its values are always declining. (189-191)

e.   The principle of diminishing marginal utility operates from the second cookie on. The second cookie gave less pleasure than the first cookie. This is true throughout, from 2 through 8. Marginal utility becomes zero between 7 and 8 cookies. The marginal utility of the 7th cookie is 2, but the marginal utility of the 8th is −1. (190-191)

2.   The principle of rational choice, discussed on page 192, states: Spend your money on those

goods that give you the most marginal utility (MU) per dollar. (192-193)

a.   Choose the $2 slice of pizza. Marginal utility per dollar of the slice of pizza is 80 units of utility/$2 = 40 units of utility per dollar. Marginal utility per dollar of a hero sandwich is 60/ $2 = 30 units of utility per dollar. 40>30.

b.   Choose the $20,000 Toyota. Marginal utility per dollar for the Toyota is 120,000 units of utility/$20,000 = 6 units of utility per dollar. Marginal utility per dollar for the BMW is 200,000/$40,000 = 5 units of utility per dollar. 6>5.

c.   Choose the history course. Here the two alternatives have a cost in time, not money. The analysis is the same. Just calculate the marginal utility per minute and choose the one with the higher marginal utility per minute. Marginal utility per minute for the economics course is 900 units of utility/1500 minutes = 0.6 units of utility per minute. Marginal utility per minute for the history course is 800 units of utility/ 1000 minutes = 0.8 units of utility per minute. 0.8 > 0.6.

d.   Take Tory out on a date to the Four Seasons. Marginal utility per dollar for taking Tory out is 600 units of utility/ $120 = 5 units of utility per dollar. Marginal utility per dollar for taking Sam out is 60 units of utility/ $15 = 4 units of utility per dollar. 5 > 4.

3.   This tests your understanding of the principle of rational choice, which states that a rational individual will adjust consumption of all goods until the marginal utilities per dollar are equal. (192-196)

a.   You should take 3 science courses and 2 humanities courses, given your budget constraint of $10,500. To determine this, first you must calculate the marginal utilities, and then the marginal utilities per dollar when you are spending all your money. We show the calculations to arrive at the answer in the table on the next page. Following the principle of rational choice, select that combination where the marginal utilities per dollar are equal. Looking only at those combinations where you are spending all your money, this is at the combination of 3 science courses and 2 humanities courses. We concluded this out by figuring out different combinations of courses beginning with 6 science courses, calculating how many humanities courses could be purchased with the remaining funds, and comparing marginal utilities per dollar. If the marginal utility per dollar of science courses is lower than that for humanities course, choose one less science course and repeat the calculation. Keep doing this until the marginal utilities per dollar are the same for both.

SCIENCE COURSES

Number of Courses	Total utility	Marginal utility	MU per $
0	0	0	0
1	4,500	4,500	3
2	7,500	3,000	2
3	9,750	2,250	1.5
4	11,250	1,500	1
5	11,750	500	0.33
6	12,000	250	0.17

HUMANITIES COURSES

Number of Courses	Total utility	Marginal utility	MU per $
0	0	0	0
1	7,500	7,500	2.5
2	12,000	4,500	1.5
3	15,750	3,750	1.25
4	18,750	3,000	1
5	21,000	2,250	0.75
6	22,500	1,500	0.5

b. Now you should take 3 science courses and 6 humanities courses, given your budget constraint of $10,500. First you must calculate the marginal utilities and then the marginal utilities per dollar. This is shown in the accompanying table. Next, following the principle of rational choice, select that combination where the marginal utilities per dollar are equal and you cannot buy any more courses. This is at the combination of 3 science courses and 6 humanities courses.

SCIENCE COURSES

Number of Courses	Total utility	Marginal utility	MU per $
0	0	0	0
1	4,500	4,500	3
2	7,500	3,000	2
3	9,750	2,250	1.5
4	11,250	1,500	1
5	11,750	500	0.33
6	12,000	250	0.17

HUMANITIES COURSES

Number of Courses	Total utility	Marginal utility	MU per $
0	0	0	0
1	7,500	7,500	7.5
2	12,000	4,500	4.5
3	15,750	3,750	3.75
4	18,750	3,000	3
5	21,000	2,250	2.25
6	22,500	1,500	1.5

A1. The budget constraint is drawn below. It was constructed by first finding out the y-intercept —how many pens could be bought with the entire $10: 20 pens—and then finding out the x-intercept—how many notebooks could be bought with the entire $10: 10 notebooks. Connect these points to get the budget constraint. (209)

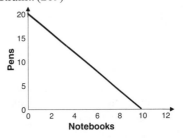

a. The slope of the budget constraint is $-P_{notebooks} / P_{pens} = -\$1/0.50 = -2$.

b. The budget constraint shifts in, intersecting the pen axis at 16 and the notebook axis at 8. To find this, use the process described above to find the initial budget constraint. Since relative prices did not change, the slope is still -2. This is shown below.

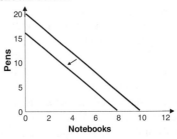

c. Since relative prices changed, the budget constraint rotates. To find the new budget constraint, find first how many notebooks can be bought at their new price: 4. The y-intercept remains at 16 since the price of pens did not change. The budget constraint rotates in along the notebook axis and intersects it at 4 notebooks. Since notebooks became more expensive, the slope became steeper. The slope of the line is $-P_{\text{notebooks}}/P_{\text{pens}} = -\$2/0.50 = -4$. This is shown below. (212)

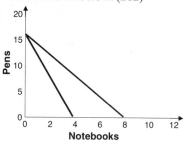

A2.a. To graph the indifference curve, plot each set of points which give the same utility. This is done below. (209-211)

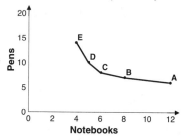

b. The marginal rate of substitution between the combinations C and D is equal to the slope between C and D, $MU_{\text{notebooks}}/MU_{\text{pens}} = -2$. (210)

c. To find where you maximize utility given the budget constraint, find that point where the slope of the budget constraint equals the marginal rate of substitution between pens and notebooks. This is at points between C and D shown in the graph below. At points between C and D, the slope of the budget constraint is equal to the marginal rate of substitution: $MU_{\text{ntbks}}/MU_{\text{pens}} = -2 = -P_{\text{ntbks}}/P_{\text{pens}}$.

The budget constraint is tangent to the indifference curve at points between C and D. This implies that any other indifference curve that intersects the budget constraint line gives you less total utility than does the current indifference curve. A rational choice maximizes your own utility. Hence, you should choose combinations represented by points between C and D. (211-212)

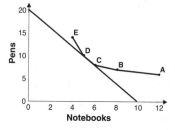

A BRAIN TEASER

1. Higher, because the marginal utility on marriages is very high–especially for the first marriage. That is, people are willing to pay dearly for a memorable event. Moreover, there is a very inelastic demand (there are few "acceptable" substitutes) for the services and supplies provided for weddings. This, too, has a tendency to result in high prices. Moreover, there's more to life than a literal application of the rational choice model. We do crazy things just for the sake of doing crazy things. We follow rules of thumb–such as, we don't want to be seen as a "cheap skate" on our child's (or our future spouse's) wedding day. Moreover, we are more apt to be conspicuous consumers when it comes to weddings. All of these elements are not nearly as strong for grocery store shopping (199-201)

MULTIPLE CHOICE

1. c The principle of diminishing marginal utility says that after some point, the additional satisfaction one gets from consuming additional units declines. See page 190.

2. c When we say that the utility of the second slice of pizza is 20, we mean we are getting an additional 20 units of utility, so the marginal utility of the second slice is 20. See page 190-191.

3. b Options a, c and d would be true statements if "total" was changed to "marginal." See pages 190-191, especially the table in Figure 8-1.

4. b You are better off by choosing to spend an additional sum of money on the good that provides you the greatest marginal utility per dollar. See pages 192-194.

5. a Applying the rational choice rule, you divide the MU by the price. Increase consumption of the good that gives the greater marginal utility per dollar. Since 40/1 is greater than 60/2 then increase consumption of A and decrease consumption of B. See pages 192-194.

6. b   Increase the consumption of that good that provides the greatest MU/P. Since 40/2 is less than 60/2 you consume more of good B. See pages 192-194.

7. c   Increase the consumption of that good that provides the greatest MU/P. Since 40/1 equals 80/2 you continue to consume the same amounts of both goods you are currently consuming. See pages 192-194.

8. c   The trip to Vail will give you the greatest marginal utility per dollar spent. See pages 192-194.

9. c   This is the rational choice. See page 193.

10. b   When $MU_X/P_X > MU_Y/P_Y$ the marginal utility for the money spent on good X exceeds that for good Y. You are getting more satisfaction for the last dollar spent on good X. Therefore, buy more of good X. See pages 195-196.

11. b   A decrease in the price of Y will cause $MU_X/P_X < MU_Y/P_Y$. Therefore, one should buy more of good Y (and less of good X). See page 199.

12. b   Only the opportunity cost is needed to determine what would be required to get you to work another hour. See pages 189-190.

13. c   The theory of bounded rationality suggests that many of our decisions are based on rules of thumb rather than on the principle of rational choice. See page 200.

14. c   A focal point equilibrium may be the preferred equilibrium but it does not necessarily have to be the preferred equilibrium if individuals had better information. See pages 190-191.

15. b   Economists' theory of choice assumes that decision-making is costless, people's preferences are given (and are not shaped by society), and individuals are rational and attempt to maximize utility. See pages 199-203.

16. c   Behavioral economists have found that people tend to make decisions consistent with the perceived norm. This is the status quo bias. They also find that decisions are not costless. The greater the number of choices, the more costly the decision. Also people care about fairness as well as maximizing utility. See pages 201-203.

A1. d   Divide the intercept on the soda axis by the intercept on the chocolate axis to find the price of chocolate in terms of soda. One can buy either 6 sodas or 3 chocolates, or, 2 sodas or 1 chocolates. See page 209.

A2. d   A fall in the price of chocolate means that the same amount of soda will give more pieces of chocolate, so the budget constraint rotates up from the intersection of the soda axis, becoming steeper. See page 209.

A3. b   A movement down the curve represents the soda needed to compensate the individual—i. e., keep her utility constant—for giving up some chocolate. See pages 209-211.

A4. c   The equilibrium is where the indifference curve is tangent to the budget constraint. See pages 211-212.

━━━━━ ANSWERS ━━━━━

POTENTIAL ESSAY QUESTIONS

The following are annotated answers. They indicate the general idea behind the answer.

1. As we consume more of any good or service the marginal utility declines. We consume combinations of goods and services for which their marginal utilities in relation to their prices are equal. If the price for good X falls, the marginal utility of good X in relation to its price will be greater than for other goods and services. We are simply getting more satisfaction for the money spent on the last unit of good X consumed. Therefore, we buy more of good X. So as the price of good X falls we find it rational to buy more of good X. This is the law of demand.

2. According to the principle of rational choice, if there is diminishing marginal utility and the price of supplying an item goes up, you supply more of that item. Consider the supply of labor. As the wage rises, the cost (opportunity cost) of not working (leisure) increases. So we are willing to work more at higher wages. This is the law of supply in action.

PRODUCTION AND COST ANALYSIS I

CHAPTER AT A GLANCE

This review is based upon the learning objectives that open the chapter.

1. Accounting profit is explicit revenue less explicit cost. Economists include implicit revenue and cost in their determination of profit. (215-217)

   Economic profit = (explicit and implicit revenue) – (explicit and implicit cost).

   Implicit revenue includes the increases in the value of assets owned by the firm.

   Implicit costs include the opportunity cost of time and capital provided by the owners of the firm. Accountants do not include these implicit revenues and costs in their calculations of profit.

2. A long-run decision is a decision in which the firm can choose among all possible production techniques. A short-run decision is a decision in which the firm is constrained in regard to what production decisions it can make. (218)

   Long run → all inputs are variable → all costs are variable.

   Short run → at least one input is fixed → some costs are fixed and some are variable (vary with the production level).

3. The law of diminishing marginal productivity states that as more and more of a variable input is added to an existing fixed input, at some point the additional output one gets from the additional input will fall. (219-220)

   Sometimes called "flowerpot law." Its existence eventually causes costs of production to rise.

   Study all tables and figures in this chapter! Marginal product is the extra output from an additional unit of an input.

   Marginal productivity declines because of the law of diminishing marginal productivity. It is because of diminishing marginal productivity that costs of production eventually rise.

4. The most important categories of costs are shown in Table 9-1. Notice total costs, marginal costs, average fixed costs, average variable costs, and average total costs can be calculated given fixed costs and variable costs at each level of output. (220-222)

   Know how to calculate all 7 short-run cost figures! (FC, VC, TC, MC, AFC, AVC, and ATC). Notice the two ways to calculate each:

   $$TC = FC + VC \; (= ATC \times Q)$$
   $$VC = TC - FC \; (= AVC \times Q)$$
   $$FC = TC - VC \; (= AFC \times Q)$$
   $$MC = \Delta TC/\Delta Q \; (= \Delta TVC/\Delta Q)$$
   $$ATC = TC/Q \; (= AFC + AVC)$$
   $$AVC = VC/Q \; (= ATC - AFC)$$
   $$AFC = FC/Q \; (= ATC - AVC)$$

5. The marginal cost curve goes through the minimum point of the average total cost curve and average variable cost curve; each of these curves is U-shaped. The average fixed cost curve slopes down continuously. (222-227)

   See Figure 9-2b. Remember that all cost curves (except FC and AFC) are shaped the way they are because of increasing and diminishing marginal productivity!

6. When marginal and average productivity are rising, marginal and average cost curves are falling. When marginal and average productivity are falling, marginal and average cost curves are rising. (223-227)

    Figure 9-3 in the textbook on page 225 shows how marginal productivity and marginal costs are mirror images of one another. The same is true for average productivity and average cost.

7. When marginal cost exceeds average cost, average cost must be rising. When marginal cost is less than average cost, average cost must be falling. This relationship explains why marginal cost curves always intersect the average cost curve at the minimum of the average cost curve. (225-227)

    If MC > ATC, then ATC is rising.
    If MC = ATC, then ATC is at its low point.
    If MC < ATC, then ATC is falling.

    If MC > AVC, then AVC is rising.
    If MC = AVC, then AVC is at its low point.
    If MC < AVC, then AVC is falling.

    Study the box, "Applying the Tools: Review of Costs."

● SHORT-ANSWER QUESTIONS

1. What is the difference between accounting profit and economic profit?

2. Suppose you are the president of a corporation who is designing a 2-year plan of operations and a 10-year plan of operations. How would those plans differ?

3. Suppose you are a novice gardener. You plant one seed in a flower pot and watch it grow into a stalk of wheat with plump wheat berries. The next year, you plant two seeds in that pot and harvest double the amount of wheat berries. You deduce that at this rate, you can provide the world's supply of wheat berries in your little pot. Why is this obviously not true? What principle is your answer based on?

4. What is the algebraic relationship between total cost, total variable cost, and total fixed cost? What is the algebraic relationship between average total cost, average variable cost, and average fixed cost? What is marginal cost equal to?

5. What does the marginal cost curve measure?

6. What does the average variable cost curve measure?

7. What does the average fixed cost curve measure?

8. What does the average total cost curve measure?

9. How does the law of diminishing marginal productivity affect the shape of short-run cost curves?

10. Where does the marginal cost curve intersect the average total cost and average variable cost curves? Explain why the relationship between marginal cost and average cost is how you have described it.

11. Draw typical *AFC*, *AVC*, *ATC,* and *MC* curves on the same graph, making sure to maintain the relationships among them.

MATCHING THE TERMS
Match the terms to their definitions

____ 1. average total cost

____ 2. average fixed cost

____ 3. average product

____ 4. average variable cost

____ 5. economic profit

____ 6. fixed costs

____ 7. law of diminishing marginal productivity

____ 8. long-run decision

____ 9. marginal cost

____ 10. marginal product

____ 11. production function

____ 12. profit

____ 13. short-run decision

____ 14. total cost

____ 15. variable costs

a. A decision in which the firm can choose among all possible production techniques.

b. Additional output forthcoming from an additional input, other inputs constant.

c. As more and more of a variable input is added to an existing fixed input, after some point the additional output one gets from the additional input will fall.

d. Total revenue minus total cost.

e. Costs that are spent and cannot be changed in the period of time under consideration.

f. Equation that describes the relationships between inputs and outputs, telling the maximum amount of output that can be derived from a given number of inputs.

g. Firm is constrained in regard to what production decisions it can make.

h. Fixed cost divided by quantity produced.

i. Sum of fixed and variable costs.

j. Variable cost divided by quantity produced.

k. The costs of variable inputs.

l. The cost of changing the level of output by one unit.

m. Total output divided by the quantity of the input.

n. Total cost divided by the quantity produced.

o. Explicit and implicit revenue minus explicit and implicit cost.

PROBLEMS AND APPLICATIONS

1. Suppose you and a friend are thinking about opening a fast food vending service at a nearby resort during your summer break. This will entail serving pizzas out of a vendor's truck. This venture is an alternative to working at a factory job where you could each earn $7,000 over the summer break. A fully equipped truck could be leased for $10,000. Insurance and other miscellaneous operating expenses total $1,000. Given your projected sales revenues of $33,000 you anticipate your variable costs to total $8,000. Together, you and your friend have just enough money in the bank to cover all of the summer's fixed and variable costs of the business. If you pull that money out of the bank, you will have to collectively forgo $500 in interest income for the summer.

a. What would be the accounting profit for your business?

b. What would be the economic profit for your business?

2. Find *TC*, *AFC*, *AVC*, *ATC,* and *MC* for the following table. Also, graph the TC curve on one graph and graph AFC, AVC, ATC, and MC on another graph.

Units	FC	VC	TC	MC	AFC	AVC	ATC
0	50	0					
1	50	90					
2	50	120					
3	50	165					
4	50	220					
5	50	290					

3. You are presented with the following table on average productivity. Labor is your only variable cost. The price of labor is $20 per hour, and the fixed cost is $50.

Labor	TP	MP	AP	TC	MC	AVC
1	2					
2	6					
3	15					
4	20					
5	23					
6	24					

a. Fill in the table above for marginal product (MP), average product (AP), total cost (TC), marginal cost (MC), and average variable costs (AVC).

b. Graph the average variable cost curve.

c. Show that the graph you drew in 3(b) is the approximate mirror image of the average productivity curve.

d. Graph the marginal cost and the marginal productivity curves. Show that they are approximate mirror images of each other.

e. What is the relationship between marginal cost (*MC*) and average cost (*AVC* and *ATC*)? What is the relationship between marginal product (*MP*) and average product (*AP*)?

4. A firm has fixed cost of $50. Variable costs are as follows:

Units	VC
1	75
2	110
3	150
4	200
5	260
6	335

a. Graph *AFC*, *ATC*, *AVC,* and *MC* curves on the axes below from the information provided in the table above (all on the same graph).

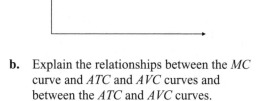

b. Explain the relationships between the *MC* curve and *ATC* and *AVC* curves and between the *ATC* and *AVC* curves.

c. Suppose fixed costs fall to $20. Graph new *AFC*, *ATC*, *AVC,* and *MC* curves.

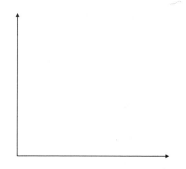

d. Which curves shifted? Why?

5. A box of Wheaties cereal with a wholesale price of $1.60 has the following costs:

Labor:	$ 0.15
Materials:	0.30
Sales cost:	0.30
Advertising:	0.15
Research and Development:	0.15
Rent on factory building and equipment:	0.15
Owner's profit:	0.40

a. Which are likely variable costs?

b. Which are likely fixed costs?

c. If output were to rise, what would likely happen to *ATC*?

A BRAIN TEASER

1. Refer to the cost curves for a firm shown below when answering the following questions. Assume the firm is currently producing 100 units of output.

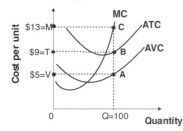

a. What is the number representing the marginal cost of producing the 100th unit of output? What geometric line segment represents that number?

b. What is ATC when output is 100? What geometric line segment represents that number?

c. What is AVC when output is 100? What geometric line segment represents that number?

d. What is AFC when output is 100? What geometric line segment represents that number?

e. What is TC when output is 100? What geometric *area* represents that number?

f. What is VC when output is 100? What geometric *area* represents that number?

g. What is FC when output is 100? What geometric *area* represents that number?

h. Why does the vertical distance between the AVC and ATC curves decrease as output expands?

MULTIPLE CHOICE

Circle the one best answer for each of the following questions:

1. Economic profit:
    a. equals explicit and implicit revenues minus explicit and implicit costs.
    b. is the same as accounting profit.
    c. will always be larger than an accounting profit.
    d. does not include the opportunity cost of the entrepreneur in the total revenue calculation.

2. The difference between the short run and the long run in the cost model is that:
    a. the short run pertains to a period of time less than one year; long run is longer than one year.
    b. in the short run at least one input (factor of production) is fixed; in the long run all inputs are variable.
    c. in the short run some costs are fixed; in the long run all costs are fixed.
    d. in the short run all costs are variable; in the long run all costs are fixed.

3. In a short-run decision:
    a. a firm has more options than in the long run.
    b. a firm has fewer options than in the long run.
    c. a firm has the same number of options as in the long run.
    d. there is no relation between the number of options a firm has and whether it is a short-run decision or a long-run decision.

4. If a firm can produce 560 units of output with 5 workers and 600 units of output with 6 workers then the:
    a. marginal product of the 6th worker is 100 units.
    b. marginal product of the 6th worker is 40 units.
    c. average product of 6 workers is 70 units.
    d. average product of 5 workers is 100 units.

5. Refer to the graph below. The range marked "A" shows:

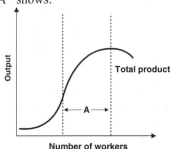

a. increasing marginal productivity.
b. diminishing marginal productivity.
c. diminishing absolute productivity.
d. diminishing absolute marginal productivity.

6. The law of diminishing marginal productivity:
   a. states that as more and more of a variable input is added to an existing fixed input, after some point the additional output one gets from the additional input will fall.
   b. states that as more and more of a variable input is added to an existing fixed input, after some point the additional output one gets from the additional input will rise.
   c. explains why marginal costs of production fall as additional units of output are produced.
   d. explains why average productivity always rises.

7. When the law of diminishing marginal productivity is operating:
   a. increasing returns to scale are realized.
   b. marginal productivity is falling and average productivity is rising.
   c. marginal productivity is falling and marginal costs are rising.
   d. marginal productivity is rising and marginal costs are rising.

8. Five workers are producing a total of 28 units of output. A worker's marginal product:
   a. is 5.
   b. is 28.
   c. is 28 divided by 5.
   d. cannot be determined from the information provided.

9. The firm is producing an output of 24 and has total costs of 260. Its marginal cost:
   a. equals 10.83.
   b. equals 8.75.
   c. equals 260.
   d. cannot be determined from the information provided.

10. Fixed costs:
    a. are costs that do not change with the output level.
    b. equal total costs plus variable costs.
    c. equal average fixed costs divided by the output level.
    d. rise at first then decline as output rises.

11. Concerning costs of production, it is true that:
    a. if a firm shuts down for a month its total costs for the month will equal its fixed costs for the month.
    b. average variable costs equal total variable costs multiplied by the output level.
    c. marginal costs equal the change in total costs divided by the change in variable costs.
    d. marginal cost equals average total cost multiplied by the output level.

12. A firm is producing 100 units of output at a total cost of $800. The firm's average variable cost is $5 per unit. The firm's:
    a. marginal cost is $8.
    b. total variable cost is $300.
    c. average fixed cost is $3.
    d. average total cost is $500.

13. The only variable input used in the production of pickles in a small factory is labor. Currently 5 workers are employed; each works 40 hours per week and is paid $15 per hour. If fixed costs are $4,000 per week and total output is 4,000 jars of pickles per week, then:
    a. average fixed cost is $16,000.
    b. total costs are $7,000.
    c. total variable costs are $4,000.
    d. average total costs are $0.75.

14. A firm's total fixed costs are $100; total variable costs are $200; and average fixed costs are $20. The firm's total output:
   a. is 1.
   b. is 5.
   c. is 10.
   d. cannot be determined from the information provided.

15. Refer to the graph below. The curves in the graph are:

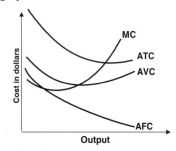

   a. correctly drawn.
   b. incorrectly drawn because the average total cost curve is above the average variable cost curve.
   c. incorrectly drawn because the marginal cost curve is positioned wrong.
   d. incorrectly drawn because marginal cost and average variable costs are confused.

16. Refer to the graph below. The curve represented is most likely:

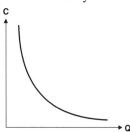

   a. an average total cost curve.
   b. an average variable cost curve.
   c. an average fixed cost curve.
   d. a total cost curve.

17. Concerning costs and cost curves for a firm, it is true that:
   a. if a firm increases its output from 100 to 101 and total costs increase from $55 to $60 then marginal cost of producing the 101st unit of output is $115.
   b. if marginal cost exceeds average total cost then average total cost is falling.
   c. the vertical distance between the average total and average variable cost curves at any given output level equals average fixed cost at that output level.
   d. the marginal cost curve intersects the average variable and average total cost curves when they are sloping downward.

18. If marginal cost exceeds average total cost then:
   a. average total cost is falling.
   b. average total cost is at its low point.
   c. average total cost is rising.
   d. marginal cost is at its low point.

19. Marginal cost reaches its minimum at a production level in which:
   a. average total cost is at its minimum.
   b. average variable cost is at its minimum.
   c. average productivity is at its maximum.
   d. marginal productivity is at its maximum.

● POTENTIAL ESSAY QUESTIONS

You may also see essay questions similar to the "Problems & Applications" and "Brain Teaser" exercises.

1. Describe the relationship between the law of diminishing marginal productivity and costs of production in the short run.

2. Distinguish the various kinds of cost curves and describe the relationship between them.

ANSWERS

SHORT-ANSWER QUESTIONS

1. Accounting profit = explicit revenue – explicit cost. Economic profit = (explicit *and* implicit revenue) – (explicit *and* implicit cost). Implicit revenue includes the increases in the value of assets owned by the firm. Implicit costs include the opportunity cost of time and capital provided by the owners of the firm. Accountants do not include these implicit revenues and costs in their calculations of profit. (215-217)

2. In a long-run planning decision, a firm chooses among all possible production techniques. In a short-run planning decision, the firm has fewer options. (218)

3. This is obviously not true because eventually each additional seed you add will produce fewer and fewer berries. At some point, the plants will choke one another out. This follows from the law of diminishing marginal productivity: as more and more of a variable input is added to an existing fixed input, after some point the additional output one gets from the additional input will fall. (219-220)

4. $TC = VC + FC$. $ATC = AVC + AFC$. $MC = \Delta TC/\Delta Q\ (= \Delta TVC/\Delta Q)$. (221-222)

5. A marginal cost curve measures the change in cost associated with a change in output. It is the extra cost of producing an additional unit of output. (222-223)

6. An average variable cost curve measures variable cost averaged over total output. (222-223)

7. An average fixed cost curve measures fixed costs averaged over total output. (222-223)

8. An average total cost curve measures total cost (variable plus fixed cost) averaged over total output. (222-223)

9. The law of diminishing marginal productivity means that eventually marginal productivity falls. When that happens, short-run costs (except fixed costs that are fixed) begin to rise. When marginal and average productivity are rising, marginal and average cost curves are falling. When marginal and average productivity are falling, marginal and average cost curves are rising. (223-225)

10. The marginal cost curve intersects the average total and average variable cost curves at their minimum points. The marginal cost curve intersects these average cost curves at their minimum points because when marginal cost exceeds average cost, average cost must be rising; when marginal cost is less than average cost, average cost must be falling. (225-227)

11. Typical *AFC*, *AVC*, *ATC*, and *MC* curves are graphed below. Since fixed costs are the same for all levels of output, the *AFC* curve is always falling as the same fixed costs are spread over larger and larger levels of output. The *MC* curve first declines because of increasing marginal productivity but then rises because decreasing marginal productivity eventually sets in. The *MC* curve intersects the *AVC* and *ATC* curves at their minimum points. This is true because if marginal cost is below average cost, average cost must be falling and if marginal cost is above average cost, average cost must be rising. (222-227, especially Figure 9-2(b) and Figure 9-4)

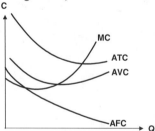

ANSWERS

MATCHING

1-n; 2-h; 3-m; 4-j; 5-o; 6-e; 7-c; 8-a; 9-l; 10-b; 11-f; 12-d; 13-g; 14-i; 15-k.

ANSWERS

PROBLEMS AND APPLICATIONS

1. **a.** Accounting profit = explicit revenue – explicit cost = $33,000 – ($10,000 + $1,000 + $8,000) = $14,000 accounting profit. (215-217)

b. Economic profit = (explicit and implicit revenue) − (explicit and implicit cost) = ($33,000) − ($7,000 + $7,000 + $10,000 + $1,000 + $8,000 + $500) = − $500; $500 economic loss. (215-217)

2. By definition, $TC = FC + VC$, $AFC = FC/Q$, $AVC = VC/Q$, $ATC = AFC + AVC$, and $MC = $ the change in TC per unit of output. Using this information, we completed the following table. (Marginal cost refers to the marginal cost of increasing output to that row, e.g., the marginal cost of going from 0 to 1 is 90.) (220-223)

Units	TC	MC	AFC	AVC	ATC
0	50	—	—	—	—
1	140	90	50.00	90	140.00
2	170	30	25.00	60	85.00
3	215	45	16.67	55	71.67
4	270	55	12.50	55	67.50
5	340	70	10.00	58	68.00

The total cost curve is shown below. The *ATC*, *AVC, MC,* and *AFC* curves are also shown below. (222-223; Figure 9-2)

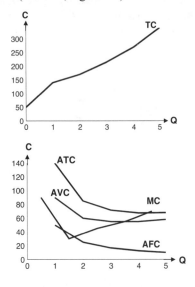

3. **a.** $AP = TP/Q$, $MP = $ change in TP, TC is (Labor $\times$ $20) + FC$, $MC = $ change in TC divided by the change in TP (or Q). AVC is VC/Q. Using these definitions, we completed the following table. (Marginal cost refers to the marginal cost of increasing to that row, e.g., the marginal cost of increasing total product from 2 to 6 is 5.00.) (219, 221; Figure 9-1 and Table 9-1)

Labor	TP	MP	AP	TC	MC	AVC
1	2	—	2.0	70	—	10.00
2	6	4	3.0	90	5.00	6.67
3	15	9	5.0	110	2.22	4.00
4	20	5	5.0	130	4.00	4.00
5	23	3	4.6	150	6.67	4.35
6	24	1	4.0	170	20.00	5.00

b. The average variable cost curve is shown below. (223; Figure 9-2)

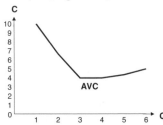

c. The *AP* and *AVC* curves are shown below. They are the mirror images of one another in that the maximum point on the *AP* curve occurs at the minimum point on the *AVC* curve. Also, when the *AP* curve is falling, *AVC* is rising, and vice versa. This is because as productivity falls, costs per unit rise, and as productivity increases, costs per unit decrease. (225; Figure 9-3)

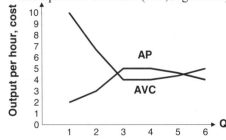

d. The marginal cost and marginal productivity curves are shown below. The maximum point on the *MP* curve occurs at the minimum point on the *MC* curve. When the *MP* curve is falling *MC* is rising, and vice versa. This is because as productivity falls, costs per unit rise and as productivity increases, costs per unit decrease. (225, Figure 9-3)

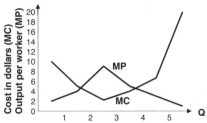

e. When the *MC* curve is below the *AVC* (or *ATC*) curve, the *AVC* (or *ATC*) curve is falling. The *MC* curve intersects with the *AVC* (or *ATC*) curve at its minimum point. When the *MC* curve is above the *AVC* (or *ATC*) curve, the *AVC* (*ATC*) curve is rising. The same goes for marginal product and average product. When marginal product is below average product, average product is falling and when marginal product is above average product, average product is rising. (224-227)

4. a. To graph the *ATC, AFC, AVC,* and *MC* curves, first determine the values of these curves for units 1 through 6. *TC = FC + VC, AFC = FC/Q, AVC = VC/Q, ATC = AFC + AVC,* and *MC =* the change in *TC.* These values are shown in the table below. The curves are also shown below. (Marginal cost refers to the marginal cost of increasing to that row, e.g., the marginal cost of going from 0 to 1 is 75.) (222-223)

Units	VC	ATC	AVC	AFC	MC
1	75	125	75	50	75
2	110	80	55	25	35
3	150	66.67	50	16.67	40
4	200	62.5	50	12.5	50
5	260	62	52	10	60
6	335	64.17	55.83	8.33	75

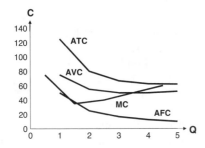

b. The *MC* curve goes through the minimum points of both the *ATC* and *AVC* curves, which are rising when they are below the *MC* curve, and falling when they are above the *MC* curve. *ATC* and *AVC* curves are both U-shaped. Because of fixed costs, the *AVC* curve is always below the *ATC* curve, but the two curves converge as output increases (because AFC equals ATC – AVC, and AFC decreases as output increases). (225-227)

c. The curves are shown below. (225-227)

Units	VC	ATC	AVC	AFC	MC
1	75	95	75	20	75
2	110	65	55	10	35
3	150	56.67	50	6.67	40
4	200	55	50	5	50
5	260	56	52	4	60
6	335	59.17	55.83	3.33	75

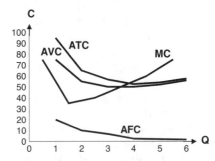

d. Only the *AFC* and *ATC* curves shifted because they are the only curves that depend on fixed costs. All the others are based only on variable costs. Because the fixed cost falls to $20, the average fixed cost must fall as well. (225-227)

5. a. Labor and material costs are variable costs since they will rise and fall as production of Wheaties rises and falls. (221)

b. Sales, advertising, R&D, and rent on factory building and equipment are fixed costs since they are most likely independent of the level of Wheaties produced. (220)

c. Because fixed cost is high in this production process, almost equal to half of the revenue, an increase in output is likely to reduce *AFC*. If *AVC* does not rise more then *ATC* would likely fall as well. (221-222)

━━━━━ ANSWERS ━━━━━

A BRAIN TEASER

1. a. MC for the 100th unit of output is equal to $13 (the extra cost of producing that 100th unit is $13), or line segment 0M. (The line segment 0M simply represents the distance or amount of $13). (222-227)

b. ATC = $9, or line segment 0T, when output is 100. (222-227)

c. AVC = $5, or line segment 0V, when output is 100. (222-227)

d. AFC = $4. Note that AFC = ATC − AVC. The line segment representing AFC is line segment AB, which is also equal to line segment VT. Recall that, at a given output level, the vertical distance between the ATC and AVC curves equals AFC at that particular output level. (222-227)

e. TC = $900. (Note that TC = ATC × Q = $9 × 100 = $900). The geometric area representing TC is area 0TBQ. (Note that the area 0TBQ is equal to a width multiplied by a length. Think of the width as line segment 0T, representing ATC. Think of the length as line segment 0Q, representing the output level, Q. 0T multiplied by 0Q equals area 0TBQ.) (222-227)

f. VC = $500 (VC = AVC × Q = $5 × 100 = $500), or area 0VAQ (0VAQ = line segment 0V multiplied by line segment 0Q). (222-227)

g. FC = $400 (FC = AFC × Q = $4 × 100 = $400; or, FC = TC − VC = $900 − $500 = $400). The area representing FC is area VTBA. (FC = TC − VC = 0TBQ − 0VAQ = VTBA). (222-227)
Note that one can obtain all seven (7) short-run cost numbers when only provided with the MC, AVC, and ATC curves! Remember how to do this. It will come in handy later.

h. Because the vertical distance between the ATC and AVC curves equals AFC, and AFC decreases as output increases, then the vertical distance between the ATC and AVC curves decreases as output increases. (222-227)

ANSWERS

MULTIPLE CHOICE

1. a Economic profit is explicit and implicit revenue minus explicit and implicit costs. Economists include opportunity costs in total cost. Since implicit revenue might be positive and greater than implicit cost, economic profit could be higher than accounting profit but that is not always the case. Indeed, economic profit is typically smaller than an accounting profit because implicit costs usually exceed implicit revenue. See pages 215-217.

2. b There is no set calendar time associated with the short run or the long run. In the short run some costs are fixed; in the long run all costs are variable costs—because nothing is fixed in the long run. See page 218.

3. b The longer the time period, the more numerous the options. See page 218.

4. b Marginal product is the change in total product. That is, 600 − 560 = 40. Average product is total product divided by the number of workers. Average product of 5 workers is 112 and the average product of 6 workers is 100. See pages 218-219, especially Figure 9-1.

5. b A bowed downward production function has marginal product decreasing as output increases. See Figure 9-1 on page 219.

6. a Because of diminishing marginal productivity, marginal costs of production rise as additional units are produced. In addition, diminishing marginal productivity causes average productivity to fall. See pages 219-220.

7. c When marginal productivity is falling, more inputs are necessary to increase production by the same amount. Thus, marginal costs are rising. See pages 219-220, and especially, page 224-225.

8. d To determine marginal product you need to know the change in total product as you add a worker. See pages 219-220.

9. d To determine marginal costs one must know the change in costs associated with a change in quantity. See page 222.

10. a Fixed costs remain constant no matter what output is. Also, fixed costs equal total costs minus variable costs. Moreover, fixed costs equal average fixed costs

multiplied by the output level. See pages 220-221.

11. a   Total costs equal fixed costs when a firm shuts down. This is because there are no variable costs when a firm shuts down. Average variable costs equal total variable costs *divided* by the output level. Marginal costs equal the change in total costs divided by the change in *the output level. Total cost* equals average total cost multiplied by the output level. See pages 221-222.

12. c   Average total cost equals total cost divided by output ($800/100 = $8). Average fixed cost equals average total cost minus average variable cost ($8–$5 = $3). See pages 221-222.

13. b   5 workers times 40 hours times $15 is $3,000. These are variable costs. Add this to fixed cost to get total cost. Average total cost is $7,000 divided by 4,000, or $1.75. Average fixed cost is $4,000 divided by 4,000, or $1. See pages 221-222.

14. b   Average fixed costs equal total fixed costs divided by output. If the firm's total fixed costs are $100 and average fixed costs are $20, the quantity must be 100/20 = 5. See pages 221-222.

15. a   The *ATC* curve is above the *AVC* curve and the *MC* curve goes through the minimum points of the *AVC* and the *ATC* curves. The *AFC* curve is always falling. See Figure 9-2 on page 222.

16. c   Only the average fixed cost curve falls continuously. See Figure 9-2 on page 223.

17. c   *AFC = ATC – AVC.* See pages 221 and 222.

18. c   If marginal cost exceeds average total cost, average total cost is rising. Marginal cost reaches a minimum well below average total cost. See page 226 and Figure 9-4.

19. d   When marginal productivity is at its maximum then the extra cost of producing

additional units (marginal cost) reaches its minimum. See page 225 and Figure 9-3.

ANSWERS

POTENTIAL ESSAY QUESTIONS

The following are annotated answers. They indicate the general idea behind the answer.

1.   When marginal productivity is increasing, costs of production (except fixed cost, which do not vary with the output level) are falling. When marginal productivity is decreasing, costs of production (except fixed cost, which do not vary with the output level) are rising.

2.   When productivity is falling, marginal cost and therefore average variable (and average total) costs must be rising.

Know how to calculate all 7 short-run costs!

PRODUCTION AND COST ANALYSIS II

● CHAPTER AT A GLANCE

This review is based upon the learning objectives that open the chapter.

1. Technical efficiency is efficiency that does not consider costs of inputs. But the least-cost technically efficient process is the economically efficient process. (233)

    Firms try to be economically efficient because they want to minimize costs to maximize profits.

2. In the long run all inputs are variable, so only economies and diseconomies of scale can influence the shape of the long-run cost curve. (233-237)

    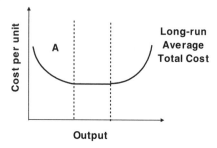

    Note that in the long run, as quantity of production increases, the firm is using ever-larger scales of operation (larger plant or factory sizes).

    If you double all inputs and per-unit costs fall (rise), the firm is experiencing economies (diseconomies) of scale.

    If per-unit (or average) costs do not change, the firm is experiencing constant returns to scale.

    Don't get short-run costs confused with long-run costs. The U-shape of short-run average variable and average total cost curves reflects increasing and diminishing marginal productivity. The U-shape of the long-run average total cost curve reflects economies and diseconomies of scale.

3. The envelope relationship is the relationship showing that, at the planned output level, short-run average total cost equals long-run average total cost, but at all other levels of output, short-run average total cost is higher than long-run average total cost. (237-239)

    See Figure 10-2 in the textbook (page 238)

    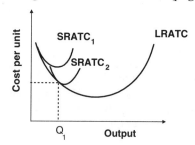

    $SRATC_2$ is the appropriate plant size to produce Q_1 because costs per unit are lower.

4. The expected price per unit must exceed the opportunity cost of supplying the good for a good to be supplied. (239)

    Potential economic profit motivates entrepreneurs to supply those goods demanded by consumers. The greater the demand, the greater the price, the greater the profit potential, and the greater the quantity supplied.

5. Some of the problems of using cost analysis in the real world include: (240-245)
    ● Economies of scope;
    ● Learning by doing and technological change;
    ● Many dimensions; and
    ● Unmeasured costs such as opportunity costs.

    See also, Appendix A: "Isocost/Isoquant Analysis."

● SHORT-ANSWER QUESTIONS

1. You are consulting for a firm. Through analysis the firm has determined that the best it can do is produce 100 tons of wheat per day with 10 workers and 1 acre of land or 100 tons of wheat per day with 10 acres of land and 1 worker. You are asked to choose the most efficient method of production. What do you advise?

2. After having read your report, the executives come running after you. They tell you that they have forgotten to tell you that an acre of land costs $40 an acre per day and workers can be hired for $100 a day. They wonder whether your answer to Question 1 changes.

3. The cost of developing a typical introductory economics textbook is well over $1 million. Once the textbook is developed and ready to print, the actual print costs for large runs are about $6 per book. What do these facts suggest about the shape of the long-run average total cost curve of producing textbooks?

4. What is the envelope relationship between short-run cost curves and long-run cost curves?

5. Why does an entrepreneur start a business? How are the decisions by the entrepreneur central to all supply decisions?

6. Suppose you are giving a talk on costs to decision-makers of firms. Without caveat, you have presented the cost curves as taught to you in this text. What are some likely problems your audience might have with your presentation?

MATCHING THE TERMS
Match the terms to their definitions

____ **1.** constant returns to scale	**a.** A decrease in per-unit costs as a result of an increase in output.
____ **2.** diseconomies of scale	**b.** An increase in per-unit costs as a result of an increase in output.
____ **3.** economically efficient	**c.** An increase in the range of production techniques that provides new ways of producing goods and the production of new goods.
____ **4.** economies of scale	
____ **5.** economies of scope	**d.** Becoming more proficient at doing something by actually doing it.
____ **6.** entrepreneur	**e.** Where long-run average total costs do not change with an increase in output.
____ **7.** indivisible setup cost	**f.** Individual who sees an opportunity to sell an item at a price higher than the average cost of producing it.
____ **8.** learning by doing	
____ **9.** minimum efficient level of production	**g.** The costs of producing products are interdependent so that producing one good lowers the cost of producing another.
____ **10.** monitoring costs	**h.** The level of production run that spreads out setup costs sufficiently for a firm to undertake production profitably.
____ **11.** team spirit	**i.** The cost of an indivisible input for which a certain minimum amount of production must be undertaken before the input becomes economically feasible to use.
____ **12.** technical efficiency	
____ **13.** technological change	**j.** Using the method of production that produces a given level of output at the lowest possible cost.
	k. A situation in which as few inputs as possible are used to produce a given output.
	l. Costs incurred by the organizer of production in seeing to it that the employees do what they're supposed to do.
	m. The feelings of friendship and being part of something that bring out people's best efforts.

● PROBLEMS AND APPLICATIONS

1. In some developing countries relatively primitive labor-intensive production processes are often used. Farming is an example. Why might a firm be economically efficient by not using the latest technology in the production process?

2. The following table represents long-run total costs:

Q	TC	LRATC
1	60	
2	66	
3	69	
4	72	
5	75	
6	90	
7	126	
8	184	
9	297	
10	600	

a. Calculate the long-run average total cost in the column provided.

b. Graph the *LRATC* curve on the graph below.

c. Label the area of economies of scale and the area of diseconomies of scale on the graph.

3. How can the extent to which economies and diseconomies of scale are present in an industry help account for the size and the number of firms in that industry? That is, if economies of scale were quite extensive in a particular industry, would you expect a large number of relatively small firms, or a small number of relatively large firms to be operating within that industry? What if diseconomies of scale set in at a relatively small output level?

4. What could help account for computer hardware manufacturers getting increasingly more involved with the development and production of computer software? Or, the airline passenger service businesses getting involved in air parcel and small package delivery service, and soft drink manufacturers buying up fast food restaurants (e.g. Pepsi-Cola company buying up Kentucky Fried Chicken and Pizza Hut—to name just a few)?

A1. Suppose the following table depicts the combinations of factors of production that result in the production of 100 units of bhindi.

	Labor	Machinery
A	25	4
B	20	5
C	10	10
D	5	20
E	4	25

a. Graph the isoquant curve for this table on the graph below, with machinery on the vertical axis and labor on the horizontal axis.

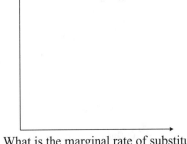

b. What is the marginal rate of substitution between combinations C and D?

A2. Suppose you had $120 available to produce the same product (bhindi) as in the previous question. Labor costs are $4 per person and machinery costs are $8 per unit. Draw the isocost line with machinery on the vertical axis and labor on the horizontal axis.

a. What is the slope of the line?

b. What happens to the isocost line if you frivolously spend $40 of your $120 on entertaining your good-for-nothing boyfriend Kyle? What is the slope of your new isocost line? Show this graphically.

c. Suppose the labor union raises labor costs to $10 per person. What happens to the isocost line? Show this graphically.

d. Combine the isoquant curve from *A1* with the original isocost line from *A2* on the graph below. What combination of labor and machinery will you choose for the economically efficient point of production?

A BRAIN TEASER

1. Explain why when long-run average total costs are decreasing, and economies of scale are experienced, it may be better for a firm to operate a larger plant with some excess capacity (not operating at that scale of operation's minimum average total costs), as opposed to using a smaller plant that is operating at peak efficiency (at that plant's

minimum average total costs). *(Hint: You may want to graph a long-run average cost curve as an envelope of short-run average cost curves and use that graph as a visual aid in helping you answer this question.)*

MULTIPLE CHOICE

Circle the one best answer for each of the following questions:

1. Which of the following concerning technical and economic efficiency is true?
  a. Many different production processes can be economically efficient, but only the method that involves the lowest possible cost is technically efficient.
  b. To achieve technical efficiency, managers must use the most up-to-date technology.
  c. The economically efficient method of production is the same in all countries.
  d. To achieve economic efficiency, managers need to use the least costly input combination.

2. The long run average total cost of production:
  a. rises as output increases when we experience economies of scale.
  b. is explained by decreasing marginal productivity.
  c. passes through the minimum point of each short-run average total cost curve.
  d. is considered to be an envelope curve because each short-run average total cost curve touches it at only one level of output.

3. Indivisible setup costs refer to:
  a. the cost of an indivisible input for which a certain minimum amount of production must be undertaken before production becomes economically feasible.
  b. the cost of an indivisible input for which a certain maximum amount of production must be undertaken before production becomes economically feasible.
  c. the cost of an indivisible input whose cost is invisible.
  d. the cost of an indivisible input whose cost of production is lower because an interdependent good is also being produced.

4. Economies of scale:
- **a.** account for the upward-sloping portion of the long-run average total cost curve.
- **b.** exist because of the difficulties in coordinating and managing a large business enterprise.
- **c.** imply an increase in per-unit costs of production associated with an increase in output.
- **d.** arise because large indivisible setup costs are spread out among a larger level of output and because of the efficiencies of greater labor and management specialization.

5. Refer to the graph below. The section of the long-run average total cost curve marked as "A" represents:

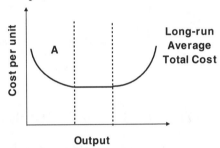

- **a.** economies of scale.
- **b.** diseconomies of scale.
- **c.** diminishing marginal productivity.
- **d.** increasing marginal productivity.

6. Explanations for diseconomies of scale include all of the following *except:*
- **a.** as firm size increases, monitoring costs generally increase.
- **b.** as firm size increases, team spirit or morale generally decreases.
- **c.** as firm size increases, monitoring costs generally decrease, thereby increasing other costs.
- **d.** All of the above are explanations.

7. Which of the following is associated with diseconomies of scale?
- **a.** Producing 1,000 lawn mowers costs $100,000 while producing 2,000 lawn mowers costs $220,000.
- **b.** 50 workers and 5 machines produces 1,000 units of output while 100 workers and 10 machines produces 2,500 units of output.

- **c.** 50 workers and 5 machines produces 1,000 units of output while 60 workers and 5 machines produces 1,200 units of output.
- **d.** Producing 1,000 lawn mowers costs $100,000 while producing 2,000 lawn mowers costs $150,000.

8. Refer to the graph below. Which of the following statements about the graph is true?

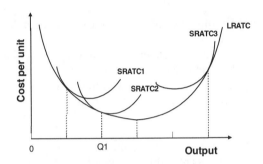

- **a.** The scale of operation associated with $SRATC_3$ is realizing some economies of scale.
- **b.** $SRATC_2$ is a smaller scale of operation than $SRATC_1$.
- **c.** The lowest-cost scale of operation to produce Q_1 is $SRATC_1$.
- **d.** The lowest-cost scale of operation to produce Q_1 is $SRATC_2$.

9. Constant returns to scale:
- **a.** refer to the upward sloping portion of the long-run ATC curve.
- **b.** refer to the downward sloping portion of the long-run ATC curve.
- **c.** means long-run average total costs do not change with an increase in output.
- **d.** are a result of rising monitoring costs and a loss of team spirit.

10. The envelope relationship refers to the fact that the:
- **a.** short-run average cost curve forms an envelope around long-run average cost curves.
- **b.** long-run average cost curve forms an envelope around short-run average cost curves.
- **c.** average cost curve forms an envelope around the marginal cost curve.
- **d.** marginal cost curve forms an envelope around the average cost curve.

11. Economies of scope occur when:
   a. firms increase production of a good, and that good's cost falls.
   b. firms increase their long-run vision and costs fall.
   c. the costs of production of one product fall when the firm increases the production of another product.
   d. technological change lowers cost of production.

12. Learning by doing and increases in technology cause the long-run:
   a. average cost curve to be downward sloping.
   b. average cost curve to be upward sloping.
   c. average cost curve to shift down.
   d. marginal cost curve to be downward sloping.

13. Total revenue is $1,000; explicit measurable costs are $500. Accounting profit:
   a. is $1,000.
   b. is $500.
   c. is $200.
   d. cannot be determined from the figures given.

14. A business owner makes 400 items by hand in 500 hours. She could have earned $20 an hour working for someone else. If the items sell for $50 each and the explicit costs total $12,000, then:
   a. total revenue equals $10,000.
   b. implicit costs equal $20,000.
   c. the accounting profits equals $10,000.
   d. the economic loss equals $2,000.

A1. Refer to the graph below. The isocost line represents a price of machinery (in terms of labor) of:
   a. one-eighth unit of labor.
   b. one-fourth unit of labor.
   c. one-half unit of labor.
   d. two units of labor.

A2. Refer to the graph for Question A1. If the price of machinery increases, the isocost line will rotate :
   a. in and become flatter
   b. in and become steeper
   c. out and become flatter.
   d. out and become steeper.

A3. The economically efficient point in the isoquant model in the graph below is at point:
   a. A.
   b. B.
   c. C.
   d. D.

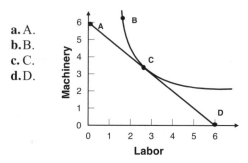

● POTENTIAL ESSAY QUESTIONS

You may also see essay questions similar to the "Problems & Applications" and "Brain Teaser" exercises.

1. What are economies and diseconomies of scale? Why do they exist?

2. Discuss some of the problems of using cost analysis in the real world.

ANSWERS

SHORT-ANSWER QUESTIONS

1. You tell them that both methods are of equal technical efficiency, but you cannot determine which is more economically efficient. To make this decision you would need to know the relative prices of each input. (233)

2. You smile and say that is exactly the information you need to tell them the most economically efficient method of production. At these prices, the first method of production costs $1,040 per 100 tons and the second method costs $500 per 100 tons. The second method is the economically efficient method. Technical efficiency means as few inputs as possible are used to produce a given output. It does not consider the costs of inputs. Economic efficiency means using that combination of inputs with the lowest possible cost for a given output. (233)

3. Because of the large indivisible setup costs, large economies of scale are possible in printing books. These economies of scale suggest that the long-run average total cost curve is steeply downward sloping. As production expands, economies of scale dominate and cost per unit declines. After some point, as output increases, however, diseconomies could set in and cost per unit could rise. This would lead to a U-shaped average total cost curve in the long run. (233-237)

4. The envelope relationship is the relationship between short-run and long-run average total costs. At the planned output level, short-run average total cost equals long-run average total cost, but at all other levels of output, short-run average total cost is higher than long-run average total cost. (237-239)

5. An entrepreneur will supply a good if the expected price of the good exceeds the cost of producing it. This difference is the entrepreneur's expected profit. It is the profit incentive that underlies production in an economy. (239)

6. Since your audience is working with the real world, they will see that actual production processes diverge from textbook analysis.

Some of the problems the audience might list are (1) economies of scope; (2) learning by doing and technological change; (3) the supply decision is multidimensional; and (4) the relevant costs are not always the ones you find in a firm's accounts. (240-245)

ANSWERS

MATCHING

1-e; 2-b; 3-j; 4-a; 5-g; 6-f; 7-i; 8-d; 9-h; 10-l; 11-m; 12-k; 13-c.

ANSWERS

PROBLEMS AND APPLICATIONS

1. Using the latest technology in combination with the required inputs may be a more costly production process than using more primitive techniques—especially when labor is cheap. What a firm wants to do is to use whatever combination of inputs that minimizes costs of production so that it can remain price competitive in the market. (233)

2. Before graphing *LRATC*, first calculate the figures. $LRATC = TC/Q$. (233-235)

    a.

Q	TC	LRATC
1	60	60
2	66	33
3	69	23
4	72	18
5	75	15
6	90	15
7	126	18
8	184	23
9	297	33
10	600	60

    b. The graph shown below plots the values from the table above to show the *LRATC* curve. (See Figure 10-1 on page 235)

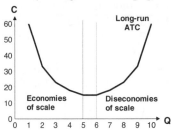

c. As shown in the figure, economies of scale is to the left of $Q = 5$, where *LRATC* is falling. Diseconomies of scale is to the right of $Q = 6$, where *LRATC* is rising. (See Figure 10-1 and page 235)

3. If economies of scale are quite extensive in an industry (i.e., larger and larger scales of operation result in lower and lower long-run average total costs of production) one would expect a relatively small number of very large firms. This is because all firms will be trying to reduce their costs by expanding, to lower their prices, and to gain a greater share of the market. You have to "get big or get out"—or be driven out of business by your competitor's lower prices. On the other hand, if diseconomies of scale set in at a relatively small output level, then you would expect a relatively large number of relatively small firms. (233-237)

4. Economies of scope can explain this. It is cheaper for these firms to produce, market, or distribute these goods or services when they are already involved in producing the other. Indeed, this concept seems to explain best why firms produce multiple rather than single products. (240-241)

A1. a. To graph the isoquant curve, plot each of the combinations of labor and machinery which generate the same (100) units of production of bhindi, as is done in the graph below. (249)

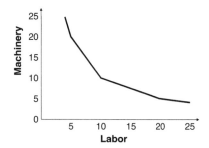

b. The marginal rate of substitution between combinations C and D is equal to the absolute value of the slope between C and D, $MP_{labor}/MP_{machinery} = 2$. (250)

A2. a. The x-axis (labor axis) intercept is 30 ($120/$4), and the y-axis (machinery axis)

intercept is 15 ($120/$8). The slope of the line is $-P_{labor}/P_{machinery} = -4/8 = -1/2$. It is shown in the graph below. (250-251).

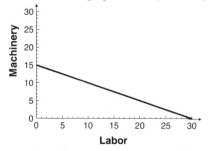

b. The isocost line shifts in to the left as money available for production is reduced to $80. Now maximum 20 units of labor or 10 units of machinery can be purchased. Since the relative price of labor and machinery doesn't change, the slope of the isocost line remains $-1/2$. This is shown in the graph below. (250-251)

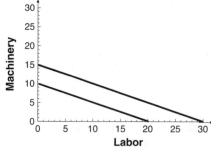

c. Now because relative prices change, the isocost line rotates. To find the new isocost line, find first how many units of labor can be purchased for $120 at the new price $10. The isocost line rotates along the labor axis and intersects it at 12 units of labor. The y intercept remains the same at 15 since the price of machinery did not change. Since labor becomes more expensive, the slope becomes steeper. The slope of the line now is $-P_{labor}/P_{machinery} = -10/8 = -1.25$. This is shown in the graph below. (250-251)

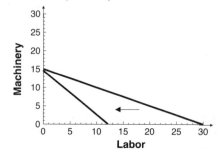

d. To find the most economically efficient combination of inputs, find that point where the slope of the isocost line equals the slope of the isoquant curve (which is the marginal rate of substitution between labor and machinery). This is at points between B and C where $-MP_{labor}/MP_{machinery} = -1/2 = -P_{labor}/P_{machinery}$. The isocost line is tangent to the isoquant curve at points between B and C. This implies that any other isoquant curve that intersects the isocost line is less economically efficient. This is shown in the graph below. (251-252)

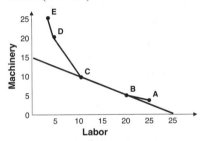

ANSWERS

A BRAIN TEASER

1. This is best explained by viewing a long-run average total cost (LRATC) curve. See the graph below. Note that the downward sloping portion of the LRATC curve indicates decreasing LRATC and therefore economies of scale. Also, one needs to keep in mind that a LRATC curve is really an envelope of short-run average total cost (SRATC) curves, and that each SRATC curve is associated with a larger scale of operation (or plant size) as the quantity increases. Also note that a firm's objective is to find that scale of operation (or plant size) that minimizes LRATC given the targeted output level it wishes to produce. This is shown as that scale of operation where its SRATC curve is just tangent to the LRATC curve at the targeted output level.

    Now suppose that a firm has determined that the profit maximizing quantity it should produce, given the market demand for its product, is Q_1—this is the targeted output level. To produce Q_1, the firm should use the plant size associated with SRATC$_2$—this curve is just tangent to the LRATC curve. No other plant size can produce Q_1 cheaper, even though this scale of operation is not operating at its minimum average total costs (we are not at the low point on SRATC$_2$). Notice that SRATC$_1$ is a smaller plant size. It could produce Q_1 at its minimum average total costs (at the low point on SRATC$_1$). But the per-unit costs associated with this smaller plant size are higher (note that SRATC$_1$ lies above SRATC$_2$).

    The idea, in the long run, is to minimize long-run average total costs (even if that means operating with a scale of operation that has some excess productive capacity—not operating at its SRATC curve's low point). (See Figure 10-2 on page 238)

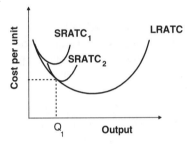

ANSWERS

MULTIPLE CHOICE

1. **d**   Economic efficiency means producing with least cost while technical efficiency means producing with the least number of inputs. Many combinations are technically efficient. Which is economically efficient depends upon the costs of each input. Because inputs to production have different costs in various countries, an economically efficient method of production in one country might not be the same method in another country. See page 233.

2. **d**   Economies of scale cause the LRATC curve to decrease (slope downward). Long run costs are *not* related to marginal productivity. The curve is not tangent to the low points of all SRATC curves. See pages 233-237.

3. a   This is the definition of indivisible setup costs found on page 234. Note that huge setup costs require high levels of production to get per-unit production costs down to a level to where production is profitable.

4. d   Economies of scale cause the LRATC curve to slope downward. Per unit production costs fall. Difficulties in coordinating and managing a large business cause *dis*economies of scale. See pages 233-235.

5. a   Economies of scale cause the LRATC curve to slope downward. The law of diminishing marginal productivity relates to short-run curves only. See Figure 10-1 on page 235.

6. c   Monitoring costs generally rise as a firm enlarges. Moreover, there is no reason to assume that decreasing monitoring costs will cause other costs to increase. See page 236.

7. a   Economies and diseconomies of scale relate to instances where all inputs are varied. That eliminates the option where only the number of workers is increased as a possibility. Diseconomies of scale exist when *average* costs rise. Average costs rise in (a) from $100 to $110. See pages 233-236.

8. d   The lowest-cost scale of operation is on the SRATC curve that is tangent to the LRATC curve at that level of output. The scale of operation represented by $SRATC_3$ suffers from diseconomies of scale. See pages 237-239, especially Figure 10-2.

9. c   Constant returns to scale refer to the flat portion of the LRATC curve where long-run average total costs remain constant when output increases. See page 236.

10. b   As discussed on pages 237-239 (including Figure 10-2), the long-run average cost curve forms an envelope around short-run average cost curves.

11. c   As discussed on page 240, c is the definition of economies of scope. Economies of scope play an important role in forms' decisions about what combinations of goods produce.

12. c   Learning by doing reduces average costs at every level of output. This is shown by a downward shift in the average cost curve. See pages 229-231.

13. b   Accounting profit is total revenue minus explicit measurable costs. See pages 242-243.

14. d   Total revenue equals $20,000 ($50 \times 400$). Implicit costs ($20 \times 500 = $10,000$) plus explicit costs ($12,000) equals $22,000. Economic loss is $2,000. Accounting profit equals $8,000. See pages 244-245.

A1. c   To get one unit of machinery one must give up one-half unit of labor. See pages 249-250.

A2. a   A rise in the price of machinery means that the same amount of funds will purchase less machinery, so the isocost line rotates down from the intersection of the labor axis, hence becoming flatter. See pages 250-251.

A3. c   The economically efficient point is where the isoquant curve is tangent to the isocost line. See pages 251-252.

◼◼◼ ⬤ANSWERS◼◼◼

POTENTIAL ESSAY QUESTIONS

The following are annotated answers. They indicate the general idea behind the answer.

1.   Economies of scale have lower average total costs of production as larger scales of operation are used. They result from greater specialization of labor and management.
Diseconomies of scale arise when larger scales of operation are used and higher average total costs of production are experienced. Diseconomies of scale arise because management loses control over operations. That is, monitoring costs rise and there is often a loss of team spirit.

2.   Some of the problems of using cost analysis in the real world include: (1) economies of scope; (2) learning by doing and technological change; (3) many dimensions; and (4) unmeasured costs such as opportunity cost.

Pretest
Chapters 6 - 10

Take this test in test conditions, giving yourself a limited amount of time to complete the questions. Ideally, check with your professor to see how much time he or she allows for an average multiple choice question and multiply this by 25. This is the time limit you should set for yourself for this pretest. If you do not know how much time your teacher would allow, we suggest 1 minute per question, or 25 minutes.

1. When the price of a good was raised from $10 to $11, the quantity demanded fell from 100 to 99. The price elasticity of demand is approximately:
   a. .1.
   b. 1.
   c. 10.
   d. 100.

2. As a manager, you have determined that the demand for your good is quite elastic. Therefore:
   a. increasing the price of your good will increase revenues.
   b. decreasing the price of your good will increase revenues.
   c. increasing the price of your good will have no impact on the quantity demanded.
   d. any change in your price will not impact revenues.

3. The more specifically or narrowly a good is defined:
   a. the more substitutes it has and therefore the more elastic its demand curve.
   b. the more substitutes it has and therefore the more inelastic its demand curve.
   c. the fewer substitutes it has and therefore the more inelastic its demand curve.
   d. the more unit elastic its demand curve.

4. In the graph below, point A on the supply curve, S_1, is:

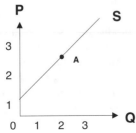

   a. elastic.
   b. inelastic.
   c. unitary elastic.
   d. unknown because one cannot say from the graph.

5. A significant price rise with virtually no change in quantity would most likely be caused by a highly:
   a. elastic demand and supply shifts to the right.
   b. inelastic supply and a shift in demand to the right.
   c. inelastic demand and supply shifts out.
   d. elastic supply and demand shifts in.

6. If supply increases by 4 percent, the elasticity of demand is 0.5, and the elasticity of supply is 1.5. Price will:
   a. increase by 8 percent.
   b. increase by 2 percent.
   c. decrease by 8 percent.
   d. decrease by 2 percent.

7. Assume equilibrium in the graph below. What area represents consumer surplus?
   a. A + B + C.
   b. D + C + E.
   c. E.
   d. E + F.

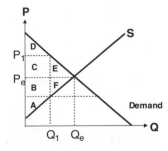

8. Refer to the graph below. If a per unit tax, t, is paid by sellers:

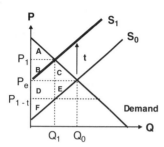

a. producer surplus is represented by areas A, B and C before the tax and A after the tax.

b. consumer surplus is represented by areas D, E and F before the tax and B after the tax.

c. the tax, t, imposes a dead weight loss represented by the welfare loss triangle-areas C and E.

d. consumers lose surplus given by area E while producers lose surplus given by area C.

9. The burden of a tax is:

a. most heavily borne by those with the more inelastic demand or supply.

b. most heavily borne by those with the more elastic demand or supply.

c. usually equally split between buyers and sellers.

d. usually passed on to consumers in the form of a higher price.

10. How much of a $100 tax will consumers pay if the price elasticity of demand is 3 and the price elasticity of supply is 2?

a. $50.

b. $40

c. $30.

d. $20

11. In which case will a price floor result in the greatest excess supply?

a. When both demand and supply are more inelastic.

b. When both demand and supply are more elastic.

c. When demand is elastic and supply is inelastic.

d. When demand is inelastic and supply is elastic.

12. The utility gained from eating one slice of pizza is 30 and the utility gained from eating a second slice of pizza is 20. From this we know:

a. the marginal utility of the second slice of pizza is 50.

b. the total utility of the second slice of pizza is 50.

c. the marginal utility of the second slice of pizza is 20.

d. there is not information to compute the marginal utility.

13. The price of good A is $1; the price of good B is $2. The marginal utility you get from good A is 40; the marginal utility you get from good B is 60. Assuming you can make marginal changes, you should:

a. consume more of good A and less of good B.

b. consume more of good B and less of good A.

c. keep consuming equal amounts of both goods.

d. realize that you don't have enough information to answer the question.

14. The rational consumer will buy more of good X when:

a. $MU_X/P_X < MU_Y/P_Y$.

b. $MU_X/P_X > MU_Y/P_Y$.

c. $MU_X/P_X = MU_Y/P_Y$.

d. the price of good X increases.

15. The theory of bounded rationality suggests that:

a. all goods will be normal goods.

b. all goods will be substitutes.

c. many of our decisions are based on rules of thumb.

d. individual tastes will be bounded and hence there will be diminishing marginal utility.

16. The difference between the short run and the long run in a cost model is that:

a. the short run pertains to a period of time less than one year; long run is longer than one year.

b. in the short run at least one input (factor of production) is fixed; in the long run all inputs are variable.

c. in the short run some costs are fixed; in the long run all costs are fixed.

d. in the short run all costs are variable; in the long run all costs are fixed.

17. Refer to the graph below. The range marked "A" shows:

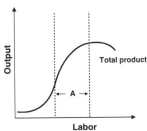

   a. increasing marginal productivity.
   b. diminishing marginal productivity.
   c. diminishing absolute productivity.
   d. diminishing absolute marginal productivity.

18. Five workers are producing a total of 28 units of output. A worker's marginal product:
   a. is 5.
   b. is 28.
   c. is 28 divided by 5.
   d. cannot be determined from the information provided.

19. A firm is producing 100 units of output at a total cost of $800. The firm's average variable cost is $5 per unit. The firm's:
   a. marginal cost is $8.
   b. total variable cost is $300.
   c. average fixed cost is $3.
   d. average total cost is $500.

20. Refer to the graph below. The curves in the graph are:

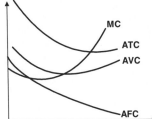

   a. correctly drawn.
   b. incorrectly drawn because the average total cost curve is above the average variable cost curve.
   c. incorrectly drawn because the marginal cost curve is positioned wrong.
   d. incorrectly drawn because marginal cost and average variable costs are confused.

21. Which of the following concerning technical and economic efficiency is true?
   a. Many different production processes can be economically efficient, but only the method that involves the lowest possible cost is technically efficient.
   b. To achieve technical efficiency, managers must use the most up-to-date technology.
   c. The economically efficient method of production is the same in all countries.
   d. To achieve economic efficiency, managers need to use the least costly input combination.

22. Economies of scale:
   a. account for the upward-sloping portion of the long-run average total cost curve.
   b. exist because of the difficulties in coordinating and managing a large business enterprise.
   c. imply an increase in per-unit costs of production associated with an increase in output.
   d. arise because large indivisible setup costs are spread out among a larger level of output and because of the efficiencies of greater labor and management specialization.

23. Constant returns to scale:
   a. refer to the upward sloping portion of the long-run ATC curve.
   b. refer to the downward sloping portion of the long-run ATC curve.
   c. means long-run average total costs do not change with an increase in output.
   d. are a result of rising monitoring costs and a loss of team spirit.

24. The envelope relationship refers to the fact that the:
   a. short-run average cost curve forms an envelope around long-run average cost curves.
   b. long-run average cost curve forms an envelope around short-run average cost curves.
   c. average cost curve forms an envelope around the marginal cost curve.
   d. marginal cost curve forms an envelope around the average cost curve.

25. Total revenue is $1,000; explicit measurable
      costs are $500. Accounting profit:

a. is $1,000.

b. is $500.

c. is $200.

d. cannot be determined from the figures given.

ANSWERS

1.	a	(6:2)	**14.**	b	(8:10)
2.	b	(6:6)	**15.**	c	(8:13)
3.	a	(6:10)	**16.**	b	(9:2)
4.	a	(6:13)	**17.**	b	(9:5)
5.	b	(6:19)	**18.**	d	(9:8)
6.	d	(6:22)	**19.**	c	(9:12)
7.	b	(7:3)	**20.**	a	(9:15)
8.	c	(7:5)	**21.**	d	(10:1)
9.	a	(7:10)	**22.**	d	(10:4)
10.	b	(7:11)	**23.**	c	(10:9)
11.	b	(7:17)	**24.**	b	(10:10)
12.	c	(8:2)	**25.**	b	(10:13)
13.	a	(8:5)			

*Key: The figures in parentheses refer to multiple
choice question and chapter numbers. For example
(1:2) is multiple choice question 2 from chapter 1.*

PERFECT COMPETITION

CHAPTER AT A GLANCE

This review is based upon the learning objectives that open the chapter.

1. Six conditions for a market to be perfectly competitive are: (253-254)

   - Both buyers and sellers are price takers.
   - Large number of firms.
   - No barriers to entry.
   - Identical product.
   - Complete information.
   - Profit-maximizing entrepreneurial firms.

   Compare these with the non-competitive markets (next 2 chapters).

2. If marginal revenue does not equal marginal cost, a firm can increase profit by changing output. Therefore, profit is maximized when MC=MR=P. (257-259)

   P = MR for a perfectly competitive firm.

   In general, for any firm, if
   MR > MC, increase Q.
   MR = MC, profit is maximized.
   MR < MC, decrease Q.

3. Because the marginal cost curve tells us how much of a produced good a firm will supply at a given price, the marginal cost curve is the firm's supply curve. (259)

   A firm's short-run supply curve is its MC curve above minimum AVC. This is because at any P greater than minimum AVC, a competitive firm will produce where P = MR = MC.

4. The profit-maximizing output can be determined in a table (as in Table 11-1 on page 261) or in a graph (as in Figure 11-5 on page 262). (261-264)

   Just find that output level at which MR = MC. This is shown graphically where the two curves intersect. (Remember: the demand curve facing the firm is also its MR curve and it is horizontal at the market price).

   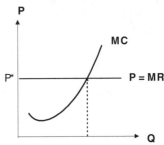

5. The market supply curve is the horizontal sum of all the firms' marginal cost curves, taking account of any changes in input prices that might occur. (265-266)

   At each price, draw a vertical line from the marginal cost curve to the quantity axis to determine the quantity supplied by each firm in the market. Then add the quantity supplied by each firm at each price to obtain the market supply curve.

6. Since profits create incentives for new firms to enter, output will increase, and the price will fall until zero profits are being made. (266-267)

Over time if economic profits are earned, the number of sellers increases, increasing market supply and decreasing market price. The lower market price decreases firms' profits until the economic profits are competed away. Note that a zero economic profit (a normal profit) is earned by competitive firms in the long run.

7. The long-run market supply curve may be upward sloping, horizontal, or downward sloping, depending on what happens to input prices as an industry expands. (267-270)

    If the demand for an industry's product increases, the industry will expand (more of the good is produced) and:

    ● *An increasing-cost industry has an upward-sloping long-run market supply curve reflecting higher input prices as the industry expands.*

    ● *A constant-cost industry has a horizontal long-run market supply curve reflecting no change in input prices as the industry expands.*

    ● *A decreasing-cost industry has a down-ward-sloping long-run market supply curve reflecting lower input prices as the industry expands.*

● SHORT-ANSWER QUESTIONS

1. How is competition as a process different from competition as a state?

2. What are six necessary conditions for perfect competition?

3. You are advising a vendor of ice cream at a beach. There are plenty of vendors on the beach and plenty more waiting to begin selling. Your client can't seem to change the market price for ice cream, but she still wants to make sure she maximizes profits. What do you advise she do? She knows all her costs of doing business.

4. You are given a competitive firm's marginal cost curve and asked to determine the supply curve for that firm. What do you say?

5. Given the following table, what is the profit-maximizing output and profit of a perfect competitor?

P=MR	Q	FC	VC
35	0	10	0
35	1	10	20
35	2	10	38
35	3	10	50
35	4	10	77
35	5	10	112
35	6	10	156

6. On the graph below, show the output and short-run profit of a perfect competitor.

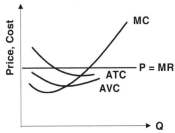

7. When should a firm shut down?

8. How are firms' marginal cost curves and the market supply curve related?

9. Given the graph below, showing a representative firm in a competitive market, what will happen in the long run? Explain, using the graph and words.

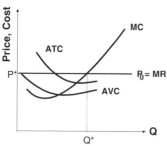

10. Suppose the owners of a small drug store decided to close their store after Wal-Mart opened a store nearby. Assuming the market was competitive before and after Wal-Mart opened its store, show graphically and explain with words the likely conditions for the small drug store before and after Wal-Mart opened.

11. What does the long-run market supply curve look like in an increasing-cost industry? Why? What about the constant-cost and decreasing-cost industries?

MATCHING THE TERMS
Match the terms to their definitions

___ 1.	barrier to entry	a.	Firm or individual who takes the market price as given.
___ 2.	marginal cost	b.	Anything that prevents other firms from entering a market.
___ 3.	marginal revenue	c.	The change in total cost associated with a change in quantity.
___ 4.	market supply curve	d.	The change in total revenue associated with a change in quantity.
___ 5.	normal profit		
___ 6.	perfectly competitive market	e.	Market in which economic forces operate unimpeded.
___ 7.	price taker	f.	Point at which the firm will gain more by temporarily shutting down than it will by staying in business.
___ 8.	profit-maximizing condition	g.	The horizontal sum of all the firms' marginal cost curves, taking account of any changes in input prices that might occur.
___ 9.	shutdown point	h.	The amount of money the owners of a business would have received in their next-best alternative.
		i.	Produce where MC = MR.

● PROBLEMS AND APPLICATIONS

1. The following table shows the total cost for a product that sells for $20 a unit.

Q	TC
0	30
1	55
2	75
3	85
4	100
5	120
6	145
7	185
8	240
9	310
10	395

   a. What is the output level for a profit-maximizing firm? Use the space to the right of the table to work out your answer.

   b. How does your answer change if price rises to $25?

   c. Calculate profit in part *a* and *b* above.

   d. Should the firm stay in business at $P = $20? At $25?

   e. Suppose $P = $15, what output level maximizes profit? What is the profit? Should the firm stay in business?

2. The following cost curves are for a representative firm in a competitive market.

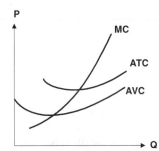

   a. Label the minimum point of the *ATC* and *AVC* curves as A and B respectively. Explain your answer.

   b. Draw a demand curve for this firm on that same graph, assuming the market is in equilibrium. Explain why you have drawn it this way.

   c. Illustrate the long-run equilibrium price and quantity for the firm on that same graph. Is the firm earning economic profit? Explain your answer.

3. Consider the market demand and supply curves below on the left and a representative firm's cost curves below on the right.

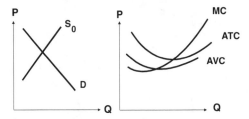

   a. Is this representative firm earning economic profit, loss, or zero profit? Shade the area for profit or loss, or label the point of zero profit.

b. In the long run, what will happen?

c. Beginning with the long-run equilibrium in *b*, show the effect of a decrease in demand on profit. What will happen in the long run to supply, price, and profit?

4. What is wrong with each of the following graphs?

a.

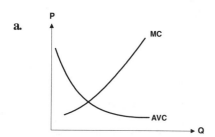

b.

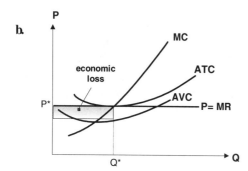

c.

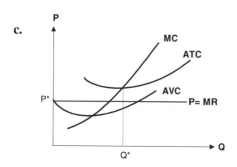

d.

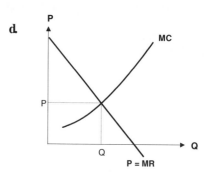

A BRAIN TEASER

1. Suppose a competitive firm experiences a sudden increase in its fixed costs. For example, suppose property taxes increase dramatically. What impact, if any, will this have on the firm's profit-maximizing quantity to produce? What will happen to the firm's profit?

MULTIPLE CHOICE

Circle the one best answer for each of the following questions:

1. Which of the following is a requirement of a perfectly competitive market?
  a. Buyers and sellers are price takers.
  b. There are barriers to entry.
  c. There are indivisible setup costs.
  d. Selling firms maximize sales.

2. In a perfectly competitive market:
  a. firms sell a differentiated product where one firm's output can be distinguished from another firm's output.
  b. there are so many firms selling output in the market that no one individual firm has the ability to control the market price.
  c. economic profits can be earned in the long run.
  d. there are very strong barriers to entry which can prevent potential competitors from entering the market.

3. Refer to the graph below. The perceived demand curve faced by an individual firm in a competitive market is best represented by which of the following?

    a. A.
    b. B.
    c. C.
    d. D.

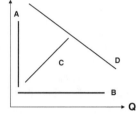

4. Refer to the graph below. The market demand curve in a competitive market is best represented by which of the following?

    a. A.
    b. B.
    c. C.
    d. D.

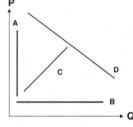

5. Refer to the graph below. A competitive firm is producing at output A.

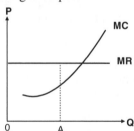

    a. It could increase profits by increasing output.
    b. It could increase profits by decreasing output.
    c. It cannot increase profits.
    d. One can say nothing about profits from the diagram.

6. Refer to the graph below. A competitive firm is producing at output A.

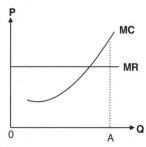

    a. It could increase profits by increasing output.
    b. It could increase profits by decreasing output.
    c. It cannot increase profits.
    d. One can say nothing about profits from the diagram.

7. In order to maximize profits (or minimize losses) a firm should produce at that output level at which:

    a. total revenue is maximized.
    b. average total costs are minimized.
    c. marginal revenue equals marginal cost.
    d. marginal revenue exceeds marginal cost by the greatest amount.

8. Price in a competitive market is $6. The firm's marginal cost is $4 and the marginal cost curve has the normal shape. What would you advise the firm to do?

    a. Raise its price.
    b. Increase its output.
    c. Decrease its output.
    d. Lower its price.

9. In a competitive market, which of the following is the firm's supply curve?

    a. The average variable cost curve.
    b. The marginal cost curve.
    c. The average total cost curve.
    d. The average revenue curve.

10. If a firm is producing at an output level at which:

    a. marginal revenue exceeds marginal cost, then the firm should reduce its output level to maximize profits.
    b. marginal revenue is less than marginal cost, then the firm should expand its output level to maximize profits.
    c. price exceeds average total costs, then the firm is earning an economic profit.
    d. price is less than minimum average total cost but greater than average variable cost, then the firm should shut down.

11. Refer to the graph below. The firm's profit in this case will be measured by:

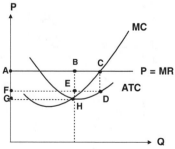

a. the rectangle ABEF.
b. the rectangle ACDF.
c. the rectangle ABHG.
d. the rectangle BCDE.

12. Refer to the graph below. How low must the price fall before the firm will decide to shut down?

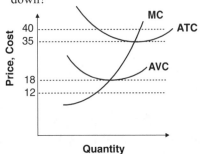

a. Approximately $40.
b. Approximately $35.
c. Approximately $18.
d. Approximately $12.

13. Refer to the graph below. This firm:

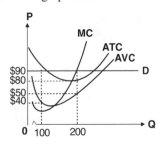

a. is earning an economic profit equal to $2,000.
b. should produce 100 units of output and charge a price of $40.
c. is incurring total costs equal to $80.
d. should shut down because price is less than minimum average variable cost.

14. In the graph below for a perfectly competitive firm:

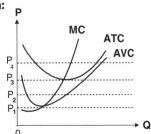

a. at P_2 the firm is incurring an economic loss but should remain in operation to minimize losses.
b. at P_3 a zero economic profit is being earned.
c. at P_4 an economic profit is earned.
d. all of the above.

15. Normal profits are:
a. approximately 6 percent of costs.
b. approximately 8 percent of costs.
c. returns to the owners of business for the opportunity cost of their implicit inputs.
d. generally larger than accounting profits.

16. In the long-run competitive equilibrium the average firm:
a. will be going out of business.
b. will be expanding.
c. will be making only a normal profit.
d. won't even be making a normal profit.

17. In a competitive market for good X, the price of a complementary good falls. If it is a constant-cost industry, we know that in the long run, equilibrium quantity will:
a. increase and equilibrium price will remain the same.
b. increase and equilibrium price will increase.
c. decrease and equilibrium price will increase.
d. decrease and equilibrium price will remain the same.

18. In an increasing-cost industry, the long-run market supply curve will be:
a. upward sloping.
b. horizontal.
c. vertical.
d. downward-sloping.

● POTENTIAL ESSAY QUESTIONS

You may also see essay questions similar to the "Problems & Applications" and "Brain Teasers" exercises.

1. Describe how to find a competitive firm's price, level of output, and profit given the firm's marginal cost curve and average total cost curve.

2. According to the textbook author, there are four major things to remember when considering a perfectly competitive industry. What are these four things?

ANSWERS

SHORT-ANSWER QUESTIONS

1. Competition as a process is a rivalry among firms, with one firm trying to take away market share from another firm. Competition as a state is the end result of the competitive process under certain conditions. (253)

2. The six conditions necessary for perfect competition are that (1) buyers and sellers are both price takers, (2) the number of firms is large, (3) there are no barriers to entry, (4) firms' products are identical, (5) there is complete information, and (6) selling firms are profit maximizing entrepreneurial firms. (253-254)

3. It is clear that she is in a competitive market. She has no control over prices—she is a price-taker. I would advise that she calculate her marginal cost at various levels of output and sell the number of ice creams where marginal cost equals price. This will maximize her profit. To see why, for a perfect competitor, producing where $MC = P$ maximizes total profit, you must first understand that $MR = P$ for a perfect competitor. By definition a competitive firm takes price as given, so the incremental revenue, marginal revenue, of selling an additional unit is that unit's price. If we prove that a perfect competitor maximizes profit when $MC = MR$, we simultaneously prove that profit is maximized at output where $MC = P$. If marginal revenue does not equal marginal cost, a firm can increase profit by changing output. If a firm produces where $MC < MR$, it is earning a profit per unit and the firm can increase total profits by producing more until MC is no longer less than MR. If $MC > MR$, the firm is incurring a loss for that last unit; it can increase profits by reducing output until MC is no longer greater than MR. Given these conditions, the firm maximizes profit where $MC = MR$ or $MC = P$. (257-259)

4. The marginal cost curve (above the AVC curve) is the supply curve for a perfectly competitive firm because the marginal cost curve tells us how much of a produced good a firm will supply at a given price. (259, especially Figure 11-3)

5. To find where the profit-maximizing competitive firm produces, we need to know MR and MC. We know MR. We need to calculate MC, the change in VC. We do this in column 5 in the table below. To calculate profit we need to know ATC. It is the sum of FC and VC divided by Q and is shown in column 7. (Marginal cost refers to the marginal cost of increasing to that row, e.g., the marginal cost of going from 0 to 1 is 20.)

P= MR	Q	FC	VC	MC	TC	ATC	TR	Profit
35	0	10	—	—	10	—	0	−10
35	1	10	20	20	30	30	35	5
35	2	10	38	18	48	24	70	22
35	3	10	50	12	60	20	105	45
35	4	10	77	27	87	21.75	140	53
35	5	10	112	35	122	24.4	175	53
35	6	10	156	44	166	27.67	210	44

Looking at the table, we see that $MC = MR$ at $Q = 5$. Profit is $(P - ATC) \times Q = 10.6 \times 5 = 53$. Alternatively, Profit = TR −TC = (P × Q) − TC = (35 × 5) − 122 = 175 − 122 = 53. Notice that when producing where MR = MC profit is as high or higher than at any other level of output. Increase output until MR = MC. This way you know you will be maximizing profits (minimizing losses). (261-262, especially Table 11-1)

6. The output of a perfect competitor is shown by the intersection of the marginal cost curve and the marginal revenue curve. On the graph below it is at Q^*. Profit for a perfect competitor is the profit per unit, the difference between the price for which each unit is sold and the average cost of each unit, times the number of units sold. Graphically, profit per unit is the vertical distance from the MR curve to the ATC curve. Multiply this by Q^* to get profit. It is the shaded region in the graph. (262-264)

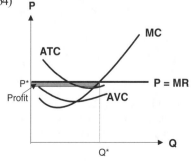

7. A firm should shut down if P ≤ minimum AVC. (Alternatively, a firm should shut down if losses are greater than total fixed costs; or, total revenue is less than total variable costs.) (264-265)

8. The market supply curve is the horizontal sum of all firms' marginal cost curves, taking account of any changes in input prices that might occur. (265-266)

9. The graph below shows a representative firm in a competitive market making an economic profit when price is P^*. Since profits create incentives for new firms to enter, output will increase and the price will fall to P_1 until zero profits are being made. (266-268)

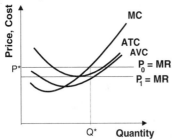

10. Before Wal-Mart opened a store, the small drug store produced Q^* at a given competitive price of P^* and earned normal profits. Since Wal-Mart is a discount drug store, opening its store in the market most likely pushed prices down to P_1. Given the new price level, the small drug store now reduced output to Q_1 and incurred a loss. Eventually, all costs are variable and the ATC curve becomes the AVC curve and prices now are below the shutdown point. This is shown in the graph below. (266-268)

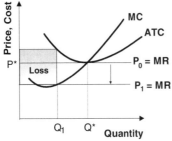

11. In an increasing-cost industry the long-run market supply curve is upward sloping because of higher input prices as the industry expands. The constant-cost industry's long-run market supply curve is horizontal because of constant input prices as the industry expands. The decreasing-cost industry's long-run market supply curve is downward sloping because of lower input prices as the industry expands. (268-270)

ANSWERS

MATCHING

1-b; 2-c; 3-d; 4-g; 5-h; 6-e; 7-a; 8-i; 9-f.

ANSWERS

PROBLEMS AND APPLICATIONS

1. To find the profit-maximizing level of output, first we determine marginal costs for the firm. We also show the values for a number of other costs. We use the formulas for these costs: MC = change in total cost, FC = $30 (costs when $Q = 0$); $VC = TC - FC$, $AVC = VC/Q$. (Marginal cost refers to the marginal cost of increasing to that row, e.g., the marginal cost of going from 0 to 1 is 25.)

Q	TC	MC	VC	FC	AVC
0	30	0	0	30	0
1	55	25	25	30	25
2	75	20	45	30	22.5
3	85	10	55	30	18.3
4	100	15	70	30	17.5
5	120	20	90	30	18
6	145	25	115	30	19.2
7	185	40	155	30	22.1
8	240	55	210	30	26.25
9	310	70	280	30	31.1
10	395	85	365	30	36.5

a. A profit-maximizing firm will produce at the output level where $MC = MR$. Since MR = market price for the competitive firm, MR =$20. MC = 20 at 2 units and 5 units. It will not choose to produce 2 units because marginal costs are declining and the firm would make additional profit by increasing output above 2. So, the profit maximizing output level is at 5 units. (257-259 and 261-262)

b. If price rises to $25, so does *MR*. *MC* = 25 at 6 units. (257-259)

c. In (a), profit = total revenue − total costs at 5 units: (5 × $20) − $120 = −$20, an economic loss. In (b), profit = total revenue − total costs at 6 units: (6 × $25) − $145 = $5. (261-262)

d. The firm will stay in business at *P* = $20 or $25, since *P* > *AVC* at both these prices. (264-265)

e. At *P* = $15, the profit-maximizing level of output is 4 units. The profit in this case is −$40 (loss of $40). Since *P* < *AVC* in this case, the firm should temporarily shut down its business. (264-265)

2. a. As shown in the graph below, points A and B are the minimum of the *ATC* and *AVC* curves. It is where they intersect the *MC* curve. From an earlier chapter, we know that the *MC* curve goes through the *ATC* and *AVC* curves at their minimum points. (See Figure 11-5 on page 263)

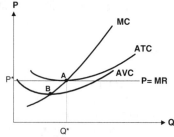

b. A demand curve for the representative firm is drawn in the graph above. It is a horizontal line because an individual firm in a competitive market is a price taker; the demand for its product is perfectly elastic. (262-264)

c. As illustrated above, the long-run equilibrium position occurs when the demand curve is tangent to the *ATC* curve because it is only at this point that economic profit for the firm is equal to zero. There is no incentive for new firms to enter the market, nor would existing firms exit the market. The long-run equilibrium is reached. (See Figure 11-6 on page 265)

3. a. As shown by the shaded region on the following graph, the representative firm is earning an economic profit. (262-264)

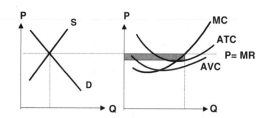

b. Refer to the graphs below. More firms will enter the market to share the profit. But as market supply increases from S_0 to S_1, the market price falls which in turn reduces the profit margin for all the firms. This process continues until price falls to P_1 where there is no more economic profit. This assumes a constant-cost industry. (266-268)

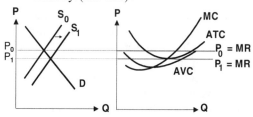

c. As shown on the graphs below, a decrease in market demand from D_0 to D_1, results in a fall of market price from P_0 to P_1 which in turn reduces the profit for each firm in the market to a loss. The losses will cause some firms to exit the market. Hence, market supply shrinks from S_0 to S_1, until prices rise from P_1 to P_0. In the long run, price returns to the original level. Each firm still has zero economic profit. This assumes a constant-cost industry. (268-270)

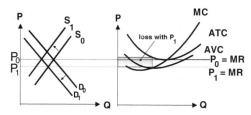

4. a. The curve labeled *AVC* is really an *AFC* curve. The correct *AVC* curve would intersect the *MC* at the minimum point of the *AVC* curve and rise thereafter. (See Figure 11-5 on page 263)

b. Loss is mis-labeled in the graph. Loss and profit are measured by the vertical difference between price and average total costs, not average variable costs. Here, economic profit is zero (there is no loss). (See Figure 11-5 on page 263)

c. Output should be where $MC = MR = P$, not where $ATC = MC$. A competitive firm will maximize profits where $MC = MR = P$. (See Figure 11-5 on page 263)

d. A competitive firm faces a horizontal demand curve since it cannot affect prices. Here it is downward-sloping. (See Figure 11-5 on page 263)

═══ ANSWERS ═══

A BRAIN TEASER

1. An increase in fixed costs (FC) will increase average total cost (ATC). Average variable cost (AVC) and marginal cost (MC) will remain unchanged. The ATC curve will shift up. Because MC has not changed (the MC curve has not shifted), and assuming the price in the competitive market (MR for the firm) has not changed, the profit- maximizing output level will not change for the firm. However, its profits will decrease because of higher costs. (261-262)

═══ ANSWERS ═══

MULTIPLE CHOICE

1. a   In a competitive market, firms are profit-maximizing, not sales-maximizing firms. Buyers and sellers are pricetakers because each one cannot affect the market. See pages 253-254.

2. b   Competitive firms sell a homogenous product, there are no barriers to entry, and they cannot earn economic profits in the long run. See pages 253-254 and 266-267.

3. b   Although the market demand curve is downward sloping, individual firms are so small in relation to the market that they perceive their demand curves as horizontal. See pages 256-257 and Figure 11-1.

4. d   The market demand curve is downward sloping. See pages 256-257 and Figure 11-1.

5. a   For the perfectly competitive firm P = MR. If P > MC, increase output to increase profits. See pages 256-257 (especially Figure 11-2).

6. b   For the perfectly competitive firm P = MR. If P < MC, decrease output to increase profits. See pages 256-257 (especially Figure 11-2).

7. c   Any firm maximizes profit by producing where marginal revenue equals marginal cost. Also note, for the perfectly competitive firm, price equals marginal revenue. See pages 257-259.

8. b   Since P > MC, increase output until MC = P = MR, the profit-maximizing level of output. See pages 257-259.

9. b   Since a perfect competitor chooses to produce where P = MC, the marginal cost curve is the firm's supply curve (above minimum average variable cost). See page 259.

10. c   Profit per unit = (P – ATC). Total profit equals profit per unit times quantity. To maximize profits (or minimize losses), firms will produce where marginal revenue equals marginal cost. Firms will shut down if price is less than average variable costs. See pages 261-264.

11. b   Output is determined where marginal cost equals price (and price equals marginal revenue for the competitive firm). To determine profit one finds the rectangle formed by ATC at the output level and price determined by where marginal cost equals price. See Figure 11-5, page 262.

12. c   The shutdown point is where the marginal cost equals minimum average variable cost. See pages 264-265.

13. a   Quantity is where P = MR = MC. Profit is (P – ATC) times quantity produced. Total cost is ATC times quantity. See pages 262-264.

14. d   If P > ATC an economic profit is earned. If P = ATC a zero economic profit (a normal profit) is earned. If P < ATC but above minimum AVC, the firm is incurring an economic loss but should remain in operation to minimize losses. See pages 262-264.

15. c   See definition of normal profit in the textbook on page 266.

16. c   The zero profit condition for long-run competitive equilibrium discussed in the text includes a normal profit. See page 266.

17. a   If the price of a complement falls, the demand for X will increase, increasing quantity and increasing price in the short run. Economic profits will induce new firms to enter the market over time and the supply curve will shift to the right. Since it is a constant-cost industry, the long-run supply curve is horizontal—price remains the same while output rises. See pages 267-270.

18. a   If an industry expands and this increases input prices then the long-run market supply curve will be upward sloping. See pages 268-270.

ANSWERS

POTENTIAL ESSAY QUESTIONS

The following are annotated answers. They indicate the general idea behind the answer.

1.   To find a competitive firm's price, level of output, and profit given the firm's marginal cost curve and average total cost curve, do the following: (See the "Knowing the Tools" box on page 266)
   1.   Determine the market price where market supply and demand curves intersect. This is the price the competitive firm accepts for its products. Draw a horizontal marginal revenue (MR) curve at this market price.
   2.   Determine the profit-maximizing level of output by finding the level of output where the MR and MC curves intersect.
   3.   Determine profit by subtracting average total costs at the profit-maximizing level of output from the price and multiplying by the firm's output.

If you are determining profit graphically, find the point at which MR = MC. Extend a line down to the ATC curve. Extend a line from that point to the vertical axis. To complete the box indicating profit, go up the vertical axis to the market price.

2.   Four things to remember when considering a perfectly competitive industry: (See "Knowing the Tools" box on page 269)
   1.   The profit-maximizing condition for perfectly competitive firms is MC = MR = P.
   2.   To determine profit or loss at the profit-maximizing level of output, subtract average total cost at that level of output from price and multiply the result by the output level.
   3.   Firms will shut down production if price is equal to or falls below the minimum of their average variable costs.
   4.   A competitive firm is in long-run equilibrium only when it is earning zero economic profit, or where price equals the minimum of long-run average total costs.

MONOPOLY

12

● CHAPTER AT A GLANCE

This review is based upon the learning objectives that open the chapter.

1. A competitive firm produces where marginal revenue equals price. A monopolist does not. The monopolist takes into account the fact that its decision can affect price. (276-277)

   The monopolist faces the market demand curve. It must reduce P to sell more. Hence, MR < P.

2. The general rule that any firm must follow to maximize profit is: Produce at an output level at which MC = MR. (277-278)

   If MR > MC then increase Q.

   If MR = MC then the firm is maximizing profit (minimizing loss).

   If MR < MC then decrease Q.

3. To find a monopolist's level of output, price and profit, follow these four steps: (277-280 and especially Figures 12-1, 12-2, and 12-3, and "Knowing the Tools" box on page 283)

   a. Draw the marginal revenue curve.

   b. Determine the output the monopolist will produce: The profit-maximizing level of output is where *MR* and *MC* curves intersect. *(See the graph in the next column.)*

   c. Determine the price the monopolist will charge: Extend a line from where *MR* = *MC* up to the demand curve. Where this line intersects the demand curve is the monopolist's price. *(See the graph at the top of the next column.)*

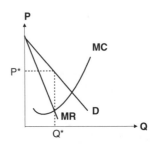

d. Determine the profit the monopolist will earn: Subtract the *ATC* from price at the profit-maximizing level of output to get profit per unit. Multiply profit per unit by quantity of output to get total profit. *(See the graph below.)*

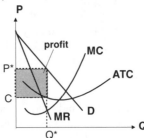

4. The welfare loss from monopoly is the triangle in the graph below. It is not the loss that most people consider. They are often interested in normative losses that the graph does not capture. (284-285)

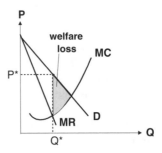

Because monopolists reduce output and charge a price that is higher than marginal cost, monopolies create a welfare loss to society.

5. When a monopolist price discriminates, it charges individuals high up on the demand curve higher prices and those low on the demand curve lower prices. (285-286)

If a monopolist can (1) identify groups of customers who have different elasticities of demand, (2) separate them in some way, and (3) limit their ability to re-sell its product between groups, it can price discriminate.

A price discriminating monopolist earns more profit than a normal monopolist because it can charge a higher price to those with less elastic demands and a lower price to those with more elastic demands. Price discrimination increases profits.

6. If there were no barriers to entry, profit-maximizing firms would always compete away monopoly profits. (286-289)

Know the different types of barriers to entry. The stronger the barriers to entry, the stronger the monopoly power (the greater the ability to charge a higher price) and the greater the ability to earn economic profits over time.

7. Normative arguments against monopoly include:
- monopolies are inconsistent with freedom,
- the distributional effects of monopoly are unfair, and
- monopolies encourage people to waste time and money trying to get monopolies. (289-291)

Possible economic profits from monopoly lead potential monopolists to spend money to get government to give them a monopoly.

*See also, **Appendix A: "The Algebra of Competitive and Monopolistic Firms."***

● SHORT-ANSWER QUESTIONS

1. What is the key difference between the decisions by monopolists and the collective decisions of competing firms with regard to setting price and production levels?

2. The president of Corning Fiberglass comes to you for advice. The firm has patented its pink fiberglass. It seems to be able to set its own price. In fact, you can say it has a monopoly on its shade of pink fiberglass. It wants you to tell it how to maximize profits. What information would you ask the president for, and what would you do with that information?

3. Calculate a monopolist's price, output, and profit using the following table:

Q	Price	Total cost
0	$36	$47
1	33	48
2	30	50
3	27	58
4	24	73
5	21	89
6	18	113
7	15	153
8	12	209
9	9	289

4. Show a monopolist's price, output, and profit using the graph below.

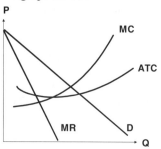

5. Show graphically the welfare loss from monopoly on the axes below.

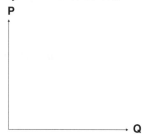

6. Why will a price discriminating monopolist earn more profit than a normal monopolist?

7. Why, without barriers to entry, would there be no monopoly?

8. After seeing your answer to question 5, a group of consumers are outraged. "Why," they say, "that doesn't come close to the harm monopolists inflict on us." Why might the welfare loss from monopoly you demonstrated underestimate their view of the loss from monopoly?

MATCHING THE TERMS
Match the terms to their definitions

___ 1. monopoly	**a.**	A legal protection of a technical innovation that gives the person holding the patent sole right to use that innovation.
___ 2. natural monopoly	**b.**	Geometric representation of the welfare cost in terms of the resource misallocation caused by monopoly.
___ 3. patent	**c.**	The condition under which a monopolist (or any firm) is maximizing profit.
___ 4. price discriminate	**d.**	Monopolies that exist because economies of scale create a barrier to entry.
___ 5. MR = MC	**e.**	To charge a different price to different individuals or groups of individuals.
___ 6. welfare loss triangle	**f.**	A market structure in which one firm makes up the entire market.

PROBLEMS AND APPLICATIONS

1. What are some real-world examples of monopolies?

2. Consider the following graph for a monopoly.

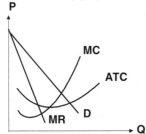

    a. Indicate on the graph the monopolist's output and price. Shade the area representing any economic profit (or loss).

    b. If this monopolist earns economic profits, then what is expected to happen over time? What if economic losses were incurred?

3. Consider the following graph for a monopoly.

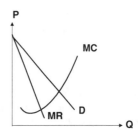

    a. Illustrate the output level and price charged by the monopoly on the graph.

    b. What would the price and output level be if this were a competitive market?

    c. Illustrate the area representing welfare loss on the graph. Explain what is meant by "welfare loss" associated with a monopoly.

4. The following table represents the market for Corning Fiberglass. Corning is the sole producer of fiberglass.

Q	Price	TC
0	—	60
1	46	65
2	42	81
3	38	111
4	34	145
5	30	189
6	24	249

a. Determine the profit-maximizing price and output.

b. What is the monopolist's profit?

c. Suppose the market is competitive, what is output and price? Would this company stay in business?

A1. Suppose the marginal costs, and therefore the market supply, for Mimi Chocolates is given by $P = Q_s/2 + 3$. The market demand is given by, $Q_d = 10 - 2P$.

a. What is the equilibrium price and quantity if the market for chocolates is perfectly competitive?

b. If Mimi Chocolates has a monopoly in the market, what will be the price and the quantity produced in the market?

● A BRAIN TEASER

1. Suppose you are in the business of staging concerts. You have just contracted to stage a concert featuring a red-hot rock group. The total cost of staging the concert is $10,000. This total cost is independent of how many people attend the concert. Your market research indicates that attendance at the concert will vary depending on the price of an admission ticket, as shown below. What ticket price should you charge to maximize profit? Briefly explain.

Ticket Price	Attendance
$20	771
$18	979
$16	1,133
$14	1,327
$12	1,559
$10	1,625
$ 8	1,803

● MULTIPLE CHOICE

Circle the one best answer for each of the following questions:

1. Monopoly is the market structure in which:
a. one firm makes up the entire market.
b. two firms make up the entire market.
c. the market is made up of a few big firms.
d. firms make a supernormal profit.

2. Which of the following is *false*?
a. A monopoly is a price-maker, whereas a competitive firm is a price-taker.
b. The monopolist produces where MR = MC while the perfect competitor does not.
c. The monopoly's marginal revenue curve lies below the demand curve whereas the

competitive firm's marginal revenue curve is horizontal at the market price.
   d. A monopolist is protected by barriers to entry whereas a competitive firm is not.

3. A profit-maximizing monopolist will:
   a. produce an output level at which MR > MC.
   b. produce an output level at which P > MC.
   c. always earn an economic profit in the short run.
   d. increase production when MR < MC.

4. Refer to the graph below. Which curve is the marginal revenue curve for the market demand curve D faced by a monopolist?
   a. Curve A.
   b. Curve B.
   c. Curve C.
   d. Curve D.

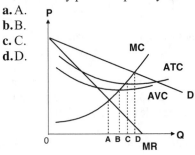

5. Refer to the graph below. A monopolist would most likely produce quantity shown by:
   a. A.
   b. B.
   c. C.
   d. D.

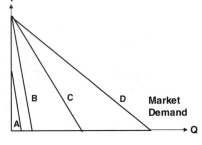

6. Refer to the graph below. Which rectangle represents the monopolist's profit?
   a. A.
   b. A + B + C.
   c. C + D.
   d. None of the above.

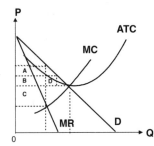

7. Refer to the graph below. The monopolist represented is:

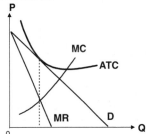

   a. making a profit.
   b. making a loss.
   c. making zero profit.
   d. unable to determine what kind of profit the monopolist is making.

8. Refer to the graph below. Which of the following statements about the market represented is true?

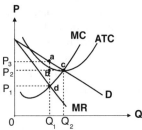

   a. A monopolist would charge price P_2 and produce output Q_2.
   b. A monopolist would charge price P_1 and produce output Q_1.
   c. A competitive market would charge price P_2 and produce output Q_2.
   d. A monopolist would earn a profit per unit equal to P_3 minus P_1.

9. Refer to the graph for Question #8. Which of the following statements about the effect of the monopolist represented is true?
   a. Triangle *bac* represents the lost producer surplus to society due to the monopoly.
   b. Triangle *dbc* represents the lost consumer surplus to society due to the monopoly.
   c. Triangle *dac* represents the welfare loss to society due to the monopoly.
   d. Lost production due to the monopoly is equal to Q_1.

10. Refer to the graph below. This monopolist is:

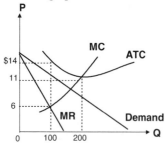

a. earning a profit of $600.
b. earning a profit of $800.
c. breaking even.
d. incurring a loss of $300.

11. A price-discriminating monopolist:
   a. charges different prices to customers with different elasticities of demand.
   b. will earn a lower profit than a non-price-discriminating monopolist.
   c. will have a marginal revenue curve that lies above its demand curve.
   d. is trying to allow some people to purchase the good who could not normally afford to do so.

12. Price discrimination requires:
   a. identifying groups of customers with different elasticities.
   b. separating customers in some way.
   c. limiting customers' ability to re-sell the product between different groups.
   d. all of the other options listed to be successful.

13. A natural monopoly is a monopoly:
   a. that exists because of economies of scale.
   b. that is created by natural law.
   c. where natural legal barriers prevent entry.
   d. in which patents exist.

14. Refer to the graph below. Which area represents the welfare loss due to a monopolist?
   a. A.
   b. A + B.
   c. B + C.
   d. A + B + C.

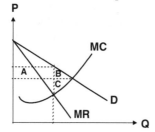

15. For a monopolist to earn an economic profit in the long run, which of the following must happen?
   a. There are barriers to entry.
   b. Average total costs must fall.
   c. Welfare loss due to monopoly must increase.
   d. Fixed costs must be eliminated.

16. Which of the following statements is *least* likely to explain public ire against monopolies?
   a. Monopolies are inconsistent with freedom.
   b. The distributional effects of monopolies are unfair.
   c. Monopolies encourage people to waste time and money trying to get monopolies.
   d. Monopolies sometimes exist because of an ability to produce superior products.

A1. Suppose the marginal costs, and therefore the market supply, for ketchup in Mexico is given by $P = Q_s/2 + 1$. The market demand is given by, $Q_d = 20 - 4P$. If there is a monopoly in the ketchup market the price and the quantity produced are:
   a. $P = 11/3$, $Q = 16/3$.
   b. $P = 11/3$, $Q = 4$.
   c. $P = 3$, $Q = 4$.
   d. $P = 4$, $Q = 4$.

● POTENTIAL ESSAY QUESTIONS

You may also see essay questions similar to the "Problems & Applications" and "Brain Teasers" exercises.

1. What is the objective of price discrimination? What conditions must be present for a firm to be able to price discriminate?

2. What are three normative arguments against monopoly?

ANSWERS

SHORT-ANSWER QUESTIONS

1. For a competitive firm, marginal revenue equals price regardless of output. But for a monopolist, price depends on output. A monopolist must take into account the fact that its output decisions can affect price. Its marginal revenue does not equal the price it charges. Instead, MR < P for the monopolist. (276-277)

2. You tell the president that the firm needs to know its marginal costs and its marginal revenues. To maximize profits, it should produce where $MR = MC$. A monopolist produces where $MC = MR$ to maximize total profit for the same reasons a perfectly competitive firm does. If $MC < MR$, it can increase total profits by producing more. If $MC > MR$, it can increase total profits by decreasing output. It is only where $MC = MR$ that it cannot increase profits by changing output. (277-278)

3. To calculate a monopolist's output, first calculate total revenue ($P \times Q$) for each output level. Then calculate marginal revenue (the change in total revenue). Find where $MR = MC$. This is at 4 units and a price of $24. Profit is calculated as total revenue minus total cost: $23. Notice that profit is maximized at an output where $MR = MC$. Profits are as high or higher here than at any other output level. (Marginal cost refers to the marginal cost of increasing to that row, e.g., the marginal cost of going from 0 to 1 is 1. The same goes for marginal revenue.) (277-278)

Q	Price	Total revenue	Marginal revenue	Total cost	Marginal cost
0	$36	0	—	$47	—
1	33	33	33	48	1
2	30	60	27	50	2
3	27	81	21	58	8
4	24	96	15	73	15
5	21	105	9	89	16
6	18	108	3	113	24
7	15	105	−3	153	40
8	12	96	−9	209	56
9	9	81	−15	289	80

4. A monopolist's output is set where $MC = MR$ (where the MC and MR curves intersect). Extend a line vertically; it sets price where that line intersects the demand curve, here at P*. Profit is determined by dropping a vertical line from the price the monopolist charges to the ATC curve and multiplying by Q*. This is the shaded region in the graph below. (279-283; especially page 283 "Knowing the Tools")

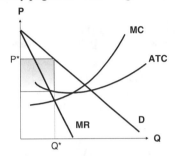

5. Welfare loss from monopoly is shown as the shaded region on the graph below. (284-285)

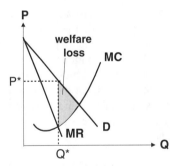

6. If a monopolist can (1) identify groups of customers who have different elasticities of demand, (2) separate them in some way, and (3) limit their ability to re-sell its product between groups, it can price discriminate. A price discriminating monopolist earns more profit than a normal monopolist because it can increase output without reducing the price it charged for previous units. It can charge a higher price to those with less elastic demands and a lower price to those with more elastic demands. Price discrimination increases profits. (285-286)

7. Without barriers to entry there would be no monopoly because profit-maximizing firms would always enter to compete away monopoly profits. (286-289)

8. You first think that they are wrong. They simply do not understand the model. Upon further reflection, you realize that your model does not include normative arguments against monopoly. These include: (1) monopolies are inconsistent with freedom, (2) the distributional effects of monopoly are unfair, and (3) monopolies encourage people to waste time and money trying to get monopolies. (289-291)

━━ ANSWERS ━━

MATCHING

1-f; 2-d; 3-a; 4-e-; 5-c; 6-b.

━━ ANSWERS ━━

PROBLEMS AND APPLICATIONS

1. Your local cable television, water, gas, and electric companies are a few examples. In some small towns the only grocery store in town will behave as a monopoly. Note that it may be helpful to think in terms of regional markets, and in terms of the number of suitable substitutes available for the good or service. The smaller the number of suitable substitutes the greater the monopoly power. (276-277)

2. a. The monopolist will produce Q* and charge price P*. Because $P > ATC$ the monopoly is earning an economic profit shown as the shaded area in the graph below. (279-280)

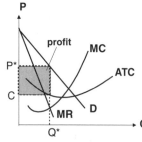

b. Economic profits always attract other businesses. However, because the barriers to entry in a monopoly are so strong, potential competitors will find it very

difficult to enter this market. Therefore, economic profits are likely to persist for some time. If losses are incurred by a monopolist, like any other firm, the monopolist will shut down if $P < AVC$ in the short run. No firm can sustain losses in the long run. (286)

3. a. See the graph below. The monopoly would produce Q_m and charge price P_m. (279-280)

 b. See the graph below. The competitive outcome would be Q_c and P_c. (As you would expect, the monopolist charges a higher price and produces less than if the market were competitive.) (See pages 280-281 and especially Figure 12-1)

 c. The shaded area in the graph below illustrates welfare loss. Welfare loss is the amount by which the marginal benefits to society (measured by the prices people are willing to pay along the demand curve) exceed the marginal costs to society (measured by points along the marginal cost curve) for those units that would be produced in a competitive market but are not produced in a non-competitive market. (284-285)

4. To answer the following questions, first calculate *MC, MR,* and *AVC. MC* is the change in *TC, AVC* is *VC/Q,* and *MR* is the change in *TR,* where *TR* is $P \times Q$. This is shown below. (Marginal cost refers to the marginal cost of increasing to that row, e.g., the marginal cost of going from 0 to 1 is 5. The same goes for marginal revenue.) (277-278)

Q	Price	TC	MC	TR	MR	AVC
0	—	60	—	0	—	0
1	46	65	5	46	46	5
2	42	81	16	84	38	10.5
3	38	111	30	114	30	17.00
4	34	145	34	136	22	21.25
5	30	189	44	150	14	25.8
6	24	249	60	144	–6	31.5

a. Monopolists maximize profits where $MR = MC$. $MR = MC$ at 3 units. Corning will charge a price of $38. (277-278)

b. Profit = total revenue minus total costs = $3. (277-278)

c. If the market were competitive, then the firm would produce where $MC = P$. So Q is 4 units and $P = \$34$. Profit = total revenue − total costs = −$9. The firm will still stay in business in the short run since $P > AVC$. (280-281)

A1. a. Rewriting the marginal cost equation with quantity supplied on the left gives: $Q_s = 2P - 6$. Setting this equal to quantity demanded gives equilibrium price at 4 and quantity at 2. (295-296)

b. Specifying the demand curve in terms of quantity demanded gives: $P = 5 - Q/2$. Multiplying this by Q gives total revenue $TR = 5Q - Q^2/2$. The marginal revenue is the first derivative of this. Thus, $MR = 5 - Q$. By setting $MR = MC$ and solving for Q we get the quantity that would be produced if the chocolate market were a monopoly. (295-296)

$$5 - Q = Q/2 + 3$$
$$3/2Q = 2$$
$$Q = 4/3, \text{ or } 1.33.$$

The monopolist charges the price that consumers are willing to pay for that quantity. Substituting $Q = 4/3$ into the demand equation gives $P = 13/3$, or 4.33. You can see that if there is a monopoly in the market, the price charged is higher than the competitive market price; also, the quantity produced is lower. (283-284)

ANSWERS

A BRAIN TEASER

1. The profit-maximizing price is $12. It generates maximum revenues of $18,708. Since all costs of staging the concert are fixed (sunk) costs, a price which maximizes revenues also maximizes profit. Profit will equal $8,708 (TR − TC = $18,708 − $10,000). (277-278)

ANSWERS

MULTIPLE CHOICE

1. **a** Monopoly means one firm; that firm may or may not make a supernormal profit. See pages 276-277.

2. **b** Both monopolies and competitive firms produce where MR = MC. Recall that P = MR for a competitive firm. So , the profit-maximizing rule for a competitive firm is sometimes written: produce where P = MC. See pages 280-281.

3. **b** A monopolist produces where MR = MC. Since MR is below the demand curve, this means the monopolist produces where P > MC. If MR > MC, it will *increase* production. If MR < MC, it will *decrease* production. See pages 277-278.

4. **c** The marginal revenue curve equals the demand curve at the vertical axis and bisects the distance between the origin and the point where the demand curve intersects the horizontal axis. See page 279, "Knowing the Tools."

5. **a** Output is determined where marginal revenue equals marginal cost. This is shown where the MR and MC curves intersect. See pages 279-280, especially Figure 12-1.

6. **a** Output is determined where marginal revenue equals marginal cost. Profit is determined by the rectangle created by the relevant price and average cost at that output. See pages 281-282, and "Knowing the Tools" on page 283.

7. **c** A monopolist produces where MC = MR and charges a price determined by the demand curve. Since P = ATC, the monopolist is earning no profit. See Figure 12-4a on page 283.

8. **c** A monopolist produces where MC = MR and charges a price determined by the demand curve. This results in a price of P_3 and output Q_1. The profit per unit is P_3 minus P_2. A perfectly competitive market produces where MC intersects the market demand curve. See Figure 12-1 on page 280.

9. c   A monopolist produces where MC = MR and charges a price determined by the demand curve. A perfectly competitive market produces where MC intersects the market demand curve. Welfare loss is lost consumer and producer surplus due to the decline in output. This is the triangle above the MC curve, below the demand curve and between Q_1 and Q_2. See pages 284-285, especially Figure 12-5.

10. d   The monopolist produces where MC = MR, or 100, and charges a price determined by the demand curve, or $11. Because ATC = $14, the monopolist is losing $3 per unit. $3 x 100 = $300 loss. See page 282 and Figure 12-3.

11. a   By segmenting the market into groups of customers with different elasticities of demand a price-discriminating monopolist can increase profits by charging higher (lower) prices to consumers with a more inelastic (elastic) demand. See pages 285-286.

12. d   By segmenting the market into groups of customers with different elasticities of demand a price-discriminating monopolist can increase profits by charging higher (lower) prices to consumers with a more inelastic (elastic) demand. This requires all the options listed. See pages 285-286.

13. a   If large fixed (setup) costs create barriers to entry for an industry and average total costs decline as output rises, it is more efficient for there to be only one producer. This industry is known as a natural monopoly. See pages 286-289.

14. c   A monopolist produces where MC = MR and charges a price determined by the demand curve. A perfectly competitive market produces where MC intersects the market demand curve. Welfare loss is lost consumer and producer surplus due to the decline in output. This is the triangle above the MC curve, below the demand curve and between the two levels of output. See pages 284-285, especially Figure 12-5.

15. a   If there were no barriers to entry, competitors would enter the market and drive down price until only normal profits were earned. See page 286.

16. d   As discussed on page 286, monopolies based on ability usually don't provoke the public's ire. Often in the public's mind such monopolies are "just monopolies."

A1. d   Specifying the demand curve in terms of quantity produced gives: $P = 5 - Q/4$. Multiplying this by Q gives total revenue $TR = 5Q - Q^2/4$. The marginal revenue is the first derivative of this. Thus, MR = $5 - Q/2$. By setting MR = MC and solving for Q we get the quantity produced: $5 - Q/2 = Q/2 + 1$; $Q = 4$. The monopolist charges the price that consumers are willing to pay for that quantity. Substituting $Q = 4$ into the demand equation gives $P = 4$. Thus, *d* is the correct answer. See pages 295-296.

ANSWERS

POTENTIAL ESSAY QUESTIONS

The following are annotated answers. They indicate the general idea behind the answer.

1. The objective of price discrimination is to increase profits. In order to price discriminate, a firm must be able to segment its markets or customers. It must also be able to determine which markets or customers have the more inelastic demand for the good or service, and then charge those people the higher price. Finally, the product cannot be easily resold.

2. Normative arguments against monopoly include (1) monopolies are inconsistent with freedom, (2) the distributional effects of monopoly are unfair, (3) monopolies encourage people to waste time and money trying to get monopolies.

MONOPOLISTIC COMPETITION, OLIGOPOLY, AND STRATEGIC PRICING

13

CHAPTER AT A GLANCE

This review is based upon the learning objectives that open the chapter.

1. To measure industry structure, economists use one of two methods: the concentration ratio or a Herfindahl index. (299)

    A concentration ratio is the value of sales by the top firms of an industry stated as a percentage of total industry sales. For example, a four-firm concentration ratio of 60% means the four largest firms account for 60% of total industry sales.

    A Herfindahl Index is a method used by economists (and the Department of Justice) to classify how competitive an industry is. A Herfindahl Index has 2 advantages over a concentration ratio: (1) it takes into account all firms in an industry, and (2) it gives extra weight to firms with especially large shares of the market.

2. Four distinguishing characteristics of monopolistic competition are: (300-302)

    1. Many sellers.
    2. Differentiated products.
    3. Multiple dimensions of competition.
    4. Easy entry of new firms in the long run.

    Know these as well as the distinguishing characteristics of all 4 market models.

3. The equilibrium of a monopolistic competitor is: (302-303)

    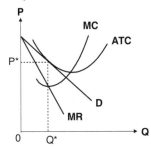

Notice the tangency between the D and ATC curves at output where MR = MC. Also note only a zero economic profit in the long run (P= ATC). But because P>MC this implies underproduction from society's perspective and hence some welfare loss.

4. The central element of oligopoly is that there are a small number of firms in an industry so that, in any decision it makes, each firm must take into account the expected reaction of other firms. (306)

    Oligopolistic firms are mutually interdependent and can be collusive or non-collusive. If they collude and form a cartel, they can increase their collective profits. Although there is a tendency for collusion (getting together to avoid competing), holding firms to an agreement is difficult because each firm has a tendency to cheat.

5. In the contestable market model of oligopoly, pricing and entry decisions are based only on barriers to entry and exit, not on market structure. Thus, even if the industry contains only one firm, it could still be a competitive market if entry is open. (306-309)

    Two extreme models of oligopoly behavior:

    - Cartel model: Firms set a monopoly price.
    - Contestable market model: An oligopoly with no barriers sets a competitive price.

    Most real-world oligopolies are between these extremes.

6. In the prisoner's dilemma, while trust gets one out of the dilemma, confessing is the rational choice. (310-314)

    When firms collude they maximize joint profits. However, the threat of cheating results in all firms cheating and we get a competitive result.

    Also notice the table on page 315, which compares the various market structures. Study this table! (It makes for "nice" exam questions.)

● SHORT-ANSWER QUESTIONS

1. What is the 4-firm concentration ratio for an industry in which 10 firms all have 10% of the market?

2. What is a Herfindahl index for an industry in which 10 firms all have 10% of the market?

3. The soap industry is characterized by monopolistic competition. There are many types of soap: Ivory, Irish Spring, Lever, and so on. When one firm lowers its price it won't calculate the reaction of the other firms. In the automobile market, which is oligopolistic, GM does worry about how Chrysler prices its cars. Based on level of competition, what distinguishes these two (monopolistically competitive vs. oligopolistic) markets?

4. Show graphically the equilibrium of a monopolistic competitor.

5. State the central element of oligopoly and the two basic types of oligopolies.

6. Major oil producers in the world have formed a tight cartel, OPEC. At times, the cartel has fallen apart. What are the reasons the major oil producers have a powerful desire to keep OPEC strong?

7. How does the contestable market theory lead to determining competitiveness by performance rather than structure?

8. How is the prisoner's dilemma related to an oligopoly?

MATCHING THE TERMS
Match the terms to their definitions

___ **1.** cartel

___ **2.** cartel model of oligopoly

___ **3.** concentration ratio

___ **4.** contestable market model

___ **5.** duopoly

___ **6.** game theory

___ **7.** Herfindahl Index

___ **8.** implicit collusion

___ **9.** market structure

___ **10.** monopolistic competition

___ **11.** North American Industry Classification System (NAICS)

___ **12.** oligopoly

___ **13.** prisoner's dilemma

___ **14.** strategic decision making

___ **15.** strategic pricing

a. A market structure in which many firms sell differentiated products.

b. A market structure with a few interdependent firms.

c. A well-known game that nicely demonstrates the difficulty of cooperative behavior in certain circumstances.

d. A combination of firms that acts like a single firm.

e. A model that bases pricing and output decisions on entry and exit conditions, not on market structure.

f. The physical characteristics of the market within which firms interact.

g. An index of market concentration calculated by adding the squared value of the individual market shares of all firms in the industry.

h. An industry classification that categorizes firms by type of economic activity and groups firms with like production processes.

i. An oligopoly with only two firms.

j. Firms set their price based upon the expected reactions of other firms.

k. Multiple firms making the same pricing decisions even though they have not consulted with one another.

l. A model that assumes that oligopolies act as if they were monopolists that have assigned output quotas to individual member firms of the oligopoly so that total output is consistent with joint profit maximization.

m. Taking explicit account of a rival's expected response to a decision you are making.

n. The application of economic principles in which players make interdependent choices.

o. The value of sales by the top firms of an industry stated as a percentage of total industry sales.

● PROBLEMS AND APPLICATIONS

1. For each of the following calculate the four-firm concentration ratio and the Herfindahl index.

   a. 20 firms in the market each having equal shares.

   b. 10 firms are in the market. One firm has 91% of market share. The remaining 9 firms share the remaining market equally.

   c. The industry's top firm has 31% of the market and the next three have 2% apiece. There are 63 remaining firms, each with a 1% share.

   d. 4 firms equally share the market.

e. Rank each of these markets by how competitive they are: from the most to least competitive, first using the concentration ratio and then the Herfindahl index. Do they differ? Why or why not?

2. Given the following demand and marginal revenue curves, add a marginal cost curve.

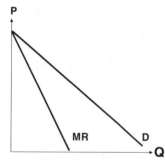

a. Label profit-maximizing price and output for a monopolist. Label profit-maximizing price and output for a monopolistically competitive firm.

b. Add an average total cost curve that is consistent with long-run equilibrium in a market characterized by monopolistic competition. What is the economic profit? Explain your answer.

3. For each of the following graphs state whether it characterizes perfect competition, monopoly, or monopolistic competition in the long run. Explain your answer.

(a)

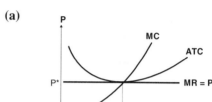

(b)

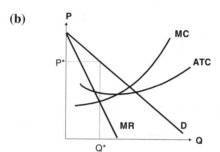

(c)

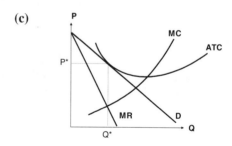

4. Suppose there are two ice-cream stands on opposite sides of the road: Ben's stand and Jerry's stand. Each has identical costs of 25 cents a cone. Each has the option of charging $1 a cone or $1.50 a cone. If Ben and Jerry collude, both charging $1.50 a cone, each will sell 50 cones each day. Ben thinks that he would sell more cones if he sells his at $1 a cone. If he does this, he will sell 80 cones and Jerry will sell 20. Jerry is considering the same strategy. If they both charge $1, each will sell 50 cones per day.

a. Construct a payoff matrix for Ben and Jerry.

c. If the stands are to be in business all summer long, what would you advise Ben?

b. If the stand is to be in business only one day, what would you advise Ben?

5. Fill in the following table, which captures the central differences among various market structures.

	Monopoly	Oligopoly	Monopolistic Competition	Perfect Competition
Number of Firms				
Pricing Decisions				
Output Decisions				
Profit				

● BRAIN TEASER

1. Advertising firms often argue, "Advertising doesn't cost, it pays!" How would you respond?

● MULTIPLE CHOICE

Circle the one best answer for each of the following questions:

1. In a market there are many firms selling differentiated products. This market is:
    a. a competitive market.
    b. a monopolistically competitive market.
    c. an oligopolistic market.
    d. a monopoly.

2. Several firms are operating in a market where they take the other firms' response to their actions into account. This market is:
    a. a competitive market.
    b. a monopolistically competitive market.
    c. an oligopolistic market.
    d. a monopoly.

3. In the NAICS classification system, the broadest classification would be:
    a. a two-digit industry.
    b. a three-digit industry.
    c. a four-digit industry.
    d. a five-digit industry.

4. The top four firms in the industry have 10 percent, 8 percent, 8 percent, and 6 percent of the market. The four-firm concentration ratio of this market is:
    a. 8.
    b. 32.
    c. 66.
    d. 264.

5. The top four firms in the industry have 10 percent, 8 percent, 8 percent, and 6 percent of the market. The Herfindahl index of this market is closest to which of the following?
    a. 8.
    b. 32.
    c. 66.
    d. 264.

6. Strategic decision making is most important in:
    a. competitive markets.
    b. monopolistically competitive markets.
    c. oligopolistic markets.
    d. monopolistic markets.

7. At the equilibrium output for a monopolistic competitor:
    a. price equals marginal cost equals marginal revenue.
    b. price equals average total cost equals marginal revenue.
    c. marginal cost equals marginal revenue equals average total costs.
    d. price equals average total cost and marginal cost equals marginal revenue.

8. Refer to the graph below. Which of the following is the output chosen by the monopolistically competitive firm?

    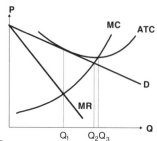

    a. Q_1.
    b. Q_2.
    c. Q_3.
    d. Output cannot be determined.

9. In long-run equilibrium, a monopolistically competitive firm:
    a. makes a loss.
    b. makes only a normal profit.
    c. makes a monopolistic profit.
    d. may make a loss or a profit.

10. Goals of advertising include shifting the firm's demand curve to the:
    a. left and making it more elastic.
    b. left and making it more inelastic.
    c. right and making it more elastic.
    d. right and making it more inelastic.

11. In the cartel model of oligopoly, the firms would decide how much to produce where:
    a. marginal cost equals marginal revenue.
    b. marginal cost equals price.
    c. marginal cost equals average total cost.
    d. the kink in the demand curve is.

12. According to the kinked demand curve theory of sticky prices, in an oligopolistic market:
    a. a price decrease by one firm will not be followed by the other firms.
    b. a price increase by one firm will be followed by the other firms.
    c. the kinked demand curve is inelastic in the upper portion and elastic in the lower portion of the curve.
    d. the kinked demand curve is elastic in the upper portion and inelastic in the lower portion of the curve.

13. In a contestable market model of oligopoly, prices are determined by:
    a. costs and barriers to exit.
    b. costs and barriers to entry.
    c. costs, barriers to entry, and barriers to exit.
    d. costs alone.

14. There is only one firm in the market. The economist analyzing that market has said she would expect the price to equal the firm's average total costs.
    a. She must be analyzing this market using a contestable market model.
    b. She must be analyzing this market using a game theory model.
    c. She must be analyzing this market using a cartel model.
    d. She must not be an economist, because that answer is clearly wrong.

15. The prisoner's dilemma is a well-known game in which:
    a. cooperation is costless.
    b. independent action is not necessarily the best joint action, but is the best independent action.
    c. firms always cheat.
    d. firms never cheat.

16. A market has the following characteristics: There is strategic pricing, output is somewhat restricted, there is interdependent decision-making, and some long-run economic profits are possible. This market is:
    a. a monopoly.
    b. an oligopoly.
    c. monopolistically competitive.
    d. perfectly competitive.

● POTENTIAL ESSAY QUESTIONS

You may also see essay questions similar to the "Problems & Applications" and "Brain Teasers" exercises.

1. What is the "monopolistic" element and the "competitive" element of monopolistic competition?

2. What is the difference between the contestable market model and the cartel model of oligopoly? How are they related?

ANSWERS

SHORT-ANSWER QUESTIONS

1. A concentration ratio is the value of sales by the top firms of an industry stated as a percentage of total industry sales. A 4-firm concentration ratio is calculated by adding together the market shares of the four firms with the largest market shares. In the case given, the 4-firm concentration ratio is 40. (299)

2. A Herfindahl index is a method used by economists to classify how competitive an industry is. It is calculated by summing the squares of the market shares of all the firms in the industry. In this case the Herfindahl index is $10 \times 10^2 = 1000$. (299)

3. The distinguishing characteristics are: (1) In the soap industry there are many sellers in a highly competitive market. In the automobile industry there are about 5 big producers. (2) In the soap industry, the different labels are distinct, but firms still act independently. In the automobile industry, the products are distinct and the firms do not act independently. (3) In the soap industry, there is easy entry of new firms in the long run so there are no long-run profits. In the auto industry entry is not easy. In both industries firms compete on more than price; they also compete on image. (300-302; 306)

4. The equilibrium of a monopolistic competitor is shown in the graph below. A monopolistic competitor earns no economic profit, so the price equals *ATC*. (302-303)

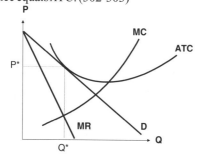

5. The central element of oligopoly is that there are a small number of firms in an industry so that, in any decision it makes, each firm must take into account the expected reaction of other firms. Oligopolistic firms are mutually interdependent and can be collusive or non-collusive. (306)

6. Since there are only a few large oil-producing nations, together they are an oligopoly. Oil-producing nations have a powerful desire to keep OPEC strong because as a cartel it can increase the profits going to the combination of oil-producing nations by reducing output. (306-308)

7. In the contestable market theory, pricing decisions are based on the threat of new entrants into the market, not market share. Thus, even if the industry has only one firm, it could still price competitively. (309)

8. When firms collude they maximize joint profits. However, the threat of cheating results in all firms cheating and we get a competitive result. (310-311)

ANSWERS

MATCHING

1-d; 2-l; 3-o; 4-e; 5-i; 6-n; 7-g; 8-k; 9-f; 10-a; 11-h; 12-b; 13-c; 14-m; 15-j.

ANSWERS

PROBLEMS AND APPLICATIONS

1. A four-firm concentration ratio is the percent of total industry sales accounted for by the top four firms. It is calculated by adding together the top four firms' market shares. The Herfindahl index is calculated by adding the squared value of the market shares of *all* the firms in the industry. (299)

   a. Four-firm concentration ratio = 5+5+5+5 = 20. Herfindahl index is $20 \times 5^2 = 500$.

   b. Four-firm concentration ratio = 91+1+1+1 = 94. Herfindahl index is $91^2+1^2+1^2+1^2+1^2+1^2+1^2+1^2+1^2+1^2 = 8,290$.

   c. Four-firm concentration ratio = 31+2+2+2 = 37. Herfindahl index is $31^2+2^2+2^2+2^2+63 \times 1^2 = 1,036$.

d. Four-firm concentration ratio =
$25+25+25+25 = 100$. Herfindahl index is
$25^2+25^2+25^2+25^2 = 2,500$.

e. A higher concentration ratio and
Herfindahl index indicates that the market
is less competitive. The ranking using the
four-firm concentration ratio is a (20), c
(37), b (94), d (100). Using the Herfindahl
index, the ranking is a (500), c (1036), d
(2500), b (8290). They differ because the
Herfindahl index takes into account *all* the
firms in the market and gives extra weight
to a single firm with an especially large
share of the market (this accounts for the
difference in the ranking of b).

2. a. The graph below shows a typical marginal
cost curve for a firm. The profit-maximizing level of output for a monopolist is
where $MC = MR$. It will set price by
extending the quantity line to the demand
curve and extending a horizontal line to
the price axis. This is the price a monopolistically competitive firm would charge.
All this is labeled as Q^* and P^* respectively. The profit maximizing price and
output procedure for a monopolistically
competitive firm is the same as for a
monopolist. (302-303)

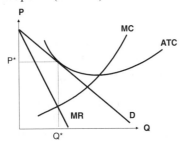

b. The average total cost curve consistent
with long-run equilibrium in a market
characterized by monopolistic competition
is drawn on the graph above. It is tangent
to the demand curve at the profit-maximizing price and quantity combination.
Economic profit is zero. It is drawn this
way because competition implies zero
economic profit in the long run. (302-303)

3. a. This graph depicts perfect competition
because the demand curve facing the firm
is horizontal and zero economic profit is
earned. (303 and especially Figure 13-2)

b. This graph depicts a monopolist because
it faces a downward-sloping demand curve
and it is earning economic profit. (305)

c. This graph depicts a monopolistic
competitor because it faces a downward-
sloping demand curve and its economic
profit is zero. (It could also depict a
monopolist if it so happens that the *ATC*
curve is drawn as given.) (305)

4. a. The payoff matrix is shown below. Ben's
strategies are listed vertically. Jerry's
strategies are listed horizontally. The first
number in each cell is Ben's profits
calculated as quantity times profit per
unit. The second number is Jerry's profit
calculated in the same way. (313-314)

		Jerry's Price	
		$1.50	$1.00
Ben's Price	$1.50	$62.50/$62.50	$25/$60
	$1.00	$60/$25	$37.50/$37.50

b. If the stand is to be in business only one
day I would tell Ben that his profit-
maximizing strategy is to charge $1.
Expected profit of charging $1.50 is
$43.75 ((62.5+25)/2), assuming it is
equally likely that Jerry will charge $1.50
or $1.00. Expected profit of charging
$1.00 is $48.75 ((60+37.5)/2), assuming it
is equally likely that Jerry will charge
$1.50 or $1.00. He should charge $1.00.
(313-314)

c. If they were going to sell ice cream all
summer long I would recommend that Ben
and Jerry develop some level of trust
between themselves and collude to charge
$1.50 each. This way, they maximize joint
profits. (313-314)

5. See the following table. (315)

	Monopoly	**Oligopoly**	**Monopolistic Competition**	**Perfect Competition**
Number of Firms	One	Few	Many	Almost Infinite
Pricing Decisions	MC=MR	Strategic pricing between monopoly and perfect competition	MC=MR	MC=MR=P
Output Decisions	Most output restricted	Output somewhat restricted	Output restricted relatively little by product differentiation	No output restriction
Profit	Possibility of long-run economic profit	Some long-run economic profit	No long-run-economic profit possible	No long-run economic profit possible

ANSWERS

A BRAIN TEASER

1. Advertising does cost money, but if advertising increases total production and if there are economies of scale, advertising could even lower long-run average total cost. In addition, advertising is designed to increase demand and to make it more inelastic. If a firm has some market control, the firm can translate this into a higher profit per unit. Advertising pays off only when additional revenues outweigh any additional costs due to advertising. (305-306)

ANSWERS

MULTIPLE CHOICE

1. b A monopolistically competitive market has many firms selling differentiated products. See page 300.

2. c An oligopoly is a market in which a few firms engage in strategic decision making. See page 306.

3. a In the North American Industry Classification System (NAICS), the more numbers, the greater the particular subdivisions, so the answer is a two-digit sector. See page 298.

4. b The concentration ratio is calculated by summing the market shares of the top four firms. See page 299.

5. d The Herfindahl index sums the squares of the market shares of all firms in the industry. Squaring these market shares and adding them gives 264, so the Herfindahl index exceeds 264 if there are more than four firms. See page 299.

6. c It is within oligopolies that firms explicitly take other firms' expected reactions into account, so it is oligopoly where strategic decision making is most important. See page 300.

7. d The equilibrium output is determined where marginal costs equal marginal revenue. At that output average total costs equal price, but that price does not equal either marginal cost or marginal revenue. See page 303 and Figure 13-1.

8. a   The equilibrium output is determined where marginal cost equals marginal revenue. See pages 302-303 and Figure 13-1.

9. b   In long-run equilibrium, a monopolistically competitive firm must make zero profit (a normal profit), so that no entry is induced. See page 303.

10. d   By shifting the firm's demand curve to the right and making it more inelastic, advertising allows the firm to charge a higher price and to earn a higher profit per unit. See pages 305-306.

11. a   The cartel model has the oligopoly acting like a monopolist. See pages 306-308.

12. d   Because a price increase is not followed by other firms and sales plummet, the demand curve is elastic in the upper portion. However, a price decrease is followed by others and revenues fall. Thus, demand is inelastic in the lower portion of the curve. See page 308.

13. c   Costs determine reference price, and barriers to both entry and exit determine the degree to which price deviates from cost. See page 309.

14. a   In a contestable market model, exit and entry conditions determine the firm's price and output decisions. Thus, if there are no barriers to entry and exit, even if there is only one firm in the industry, the firm will produce where price equals the firm's average total costs. See page 309.

15. b   In the prisoner's dilemma game, cooperation is beneficial for both prisoners, but difficult to achieve. Firms do not always get together. There may or may not be cheating, but firms expect others to cheat. See pages 310-311.

16. b   An oligopoly is a market in which a few firms operate, each taking into consideration other firms' behavior when making decisions. Because output is somewhat restricted, some long-run profit is possible. See page 306.

ANSWERS

POTENTIAL ESSAY QUESTIONS

The following are annotated answers. They indicate the general idea behind the answer.

1. The "monopolistic" element is the ability to charge a higher-than-competitive price that is directly related to the success the firm has in differentiating its product from its competitors. The "competitive" element is that there are many sellers who are able to earn only a zero economic profit in the long run because of the weak barriers to entry into the market (the only real barrier to entry is the an ability to differentiate the product from competitors).

2. The cartel model argues that oligopolists will come together to behave as a monopoly in terms of their pricing and output decisions because it is in their self-interest to do so—they'll make more money. (However, there is always a tendency for a firm to want to "cheat" and the mere rumor of cheating can cause a breakdown of the collusion.) The contestable market model argues that an industry that looks like an oligopoly (because there are a few dominant firms in the industry) could set highly competitive prices and produce a competitive output level. What is important in pricing and output decisions, according to the contestable market model, is not the number of firms in the industry, but the strength of the barriers to entry that exist in the market. If there are few, if any, barriers to entry, then a competitive price and output level will be observed. These two models are related in that the stronger the barriers to entry, usually the fewer the number of firms, and therefore the greater the probability for collusion.

REAL-WORLD COMPETITION AND TECHNOLOGY

CHAPTER AT A GLANCE

This review is based upon the learning objectives that open the chapter.

1. The monitoring problem is that employees' incentives differ from the owner's incentives. By changing employees' incentives, the efficiency of the firm can sometimes be improved. (322-324)

   Self-interest-seeking managers are interested in maximizing firm profit only if the structure of the firm requires them to do so.

   An incentive-compatible contract is needed to match the goals of managers with owners.

2. Corporate takeovers, or simply the threat of a takeover, can improve firms' efficiency. (324-325)

   Because corporate takeovers often mean a change in management, takeovers pressure managers to maintain a certain level of efficiency (to avoid X-inefficiency) so the firm does not become the target of a takeover.

3. When competitive pressures get strong, individuals often fight back through social and political pressures. Competition is a process— a fight between the forces of monopolization and the forces of competition. (326)

   Everyone applauds competition, except for themselves.

   Competitive markets will exist if producers or consumers don't collude.

4. Actions firms take to break down monopoly include (1) lobbying government to change the law underpinning that monopoly if the monopoly is a legal monopoly and (2) making slight modifications to a monopolist's patent within the limits of the law. (328-331)

   Firms protect their monopolies by (1) advertising and lobbying government, (2) producing products as nearly unique as possible, and (3) charging low prices.

   Firms will spend money and time to obtain monopoly power until the marginal cost equals the marginal benefit.

5. Oligopoly tends to be most conducive to technological change. (332-334)

   Since the typical oligopolist realizes on-going economic profit, it has the funds to carry out research and development. Moreover, the belief that its competitors are innovating also forces it to do so.

   Oligopolists are constantly searching for new ways to get an edge on competitors, so most technological advance takes place in oligopolistic industries.

● SHORT-ANSWER QUESTIONS

1. Is the high pay that top-level management receives an example of the monitoring problem?

2. What are the implications of the monitoring problem for economics?

3. How can corporate takeovers improve firms' efficiency?

4. What is meant by the phrase "Competition is a process, not a state"?

5. List two actions firms take to break down monopoly.

6. List three ways in which firms protect their monopoly.

7. Explain how technology has changed competition.

8. Which market structure is most conducive to technological advance? Why?

MATCHING THE TERMS

Match the terms to their definitions

___ **1.** corporate takeover

___ **2.** dynamic efficiency

___ **3.** incentive-compatible contract

___ **4.** lazy monopolist

___ **5.** monitoring problem

___ **6.** network externality

___ **7.** reverse engineering

___ **8.** technological development

___ **9.** technological lock-in

___ **10.** X-inefficiency

a. Problem that employees' incentives differ from the owner's incentives.

b. An agreement in which the incentives and goals of both parties match as closely as possible.

c. Firm that does not push for efficiency, but merely enjoys the position it is already in.

d. Operating less efficiently than possible, which raises costs.

e. A firm or a group of individuals issues an offer to buy up the stock of a company to gain control and to install its own managers.

f. The ability to promote cost-reducing or product-enhancing technological change.

g. Firm buying up other firms' products, disassembling them, figuring out what's special about them, and then copying them within the limits of the law.

h. When greater use of a product increases the benefit of that product to everyone.

i. When prior use of a technology makes the adoption of subsequent technologies difficult.

j. The discovery of new or improved products or methods of production.

● PROBLEMS AND APPLICATIONS

1. College Retirement Equities Fund (CREF) is a pension fund for college teachers, which has billions of dollars invested in the stock market. A few years ago fund participants voted on a proposal that would have placed strict limits on the amount of compensation paid to CREF executives. Why do you think 75 percent of the participants voted against the proposal?

2. Demonstrate, using the graph below, the net gain to producers and the net loss to consumers if suppliers are able to restrict their output to Q_R. What is the net deadweight loss to society?

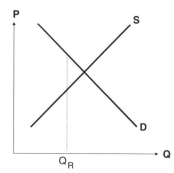

3. How can branding increase the monopoly position of a firm?

A BRAIN TEASER

1. Consider the graph below, which represents a natural monopoly.

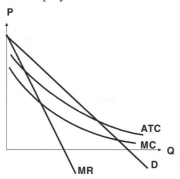

a. What price would the firm charge if it were unregulated?

b. What price would you advise to the government that the firm should be allowed to charge? Explain your answer.

c. What potential problem might your advice create over time?

MULTIPLE CHOICE

Circle the one best answer for each of the following questions:

1. The *best* definition of an incentive-compatible contract is:
a. a contract with sympathetic incentives.
b. a contract with compatible incentives.
c. a contract in which the incentive structure makes the managers' goals correspond with the firm's goals as much as possible.
d. a contract that pays bonuses.

2. A firm is making no profit. If there is X-inefficiency, what can we conclude?
a. The firm is operating at least cost.
b. The firm is operating using the fewest inputs possible.
c. The firm is operating less efficiently than economically possible.
d. We can say nothing about the efficiency of the firm.

3. The goals of managers are generally:
a. identical to the goals of owners.
b. identical to the goals of workers.
c. totally inconsistent with the goals of owners.
d. somewhat inconsistent with the goals of owners.

4. When there is little competitive pressure, large organizations have a tendency to make decisions that:
a. benefit the consumer.
b. benefit the managers.
c. benefit the government.
d. do not benefit anyone.

5. Economists would expect that generally:
a. for-profit firms operate more efficiently than nonprofit firms.
b. nonprofit firms operate more efficiently than for-profit firms.
c. for-profit firms operate equally efficiently as nonprofit firms.
d. nonprofit firms cannot exist because they operate so inefficiently.

6. Refer to the graph below. If suppliers restrict output to OL, what area represents the welfare loss to society?
   a. A + B.
   b. B + C.
   c. C + D.
   d. A + D.

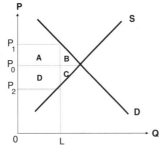

7. A patent is:
   a. a type of reverse engineering.
   b. a type of natural monopoly.
   c. a type of corporate takeover.
   d. a type of legal monopoly.

8. If average total costs are decreasing throughout the relevant range of production, the industry will be:
   a. a natural monopoly.
   b. a prime target for rent-seeking.
   c. a lazy monopolist.
   d. an example of monitoring problems.

9. When regulated monopolies are allowed to pass on all cost increases to earn a normal profit, they:
   a. have a strong incentive to operate efficiently.
   b. have little incentive to operate efficiently.
   c. become a focal point of reverse engineering.
   d. will apply for a patent.

10. Ways in which firms try to protect their monopoly include all the following *except:*
   a. advertising and lobbying.
   b. charging low prices.
   c. making their product unique.
   d. reverse engineering.

11. Many economists consider competition today to be more intense than competition ten or twenty years ago because of:
   a. technological development.
   b. greater governmental regulation and more reverse engineering.
   c. more corporate takeovers and higher trade barriers.
   d. greater political tensions among governments and lower taxes.

12. Technological advance:
   a. decreases competition.
   b. decreases specialization.
   c. increases productivity.
   d. increases costs of production.

13. The market structure most conducive to technological advance is:
   a. perfect competition.
   b. monopolistic competition.
   c. oligopoly.
   d. monopoly.

14. Technological advances are most likely for markets that:
   a. earn economic profits.
   b. have one firm supplying all the output.
   c. are protected by government regulation.
   d. produce where MR = MC.

15. Network externalities:
   a. occur when greater use of a product increases the benefit of that product to everyone.
   b. inhibit the development of industry standards.
   c. make it more likely that the most efficient standards will be adopted.
   d. reduce the likelihood that an industry becomes a "winner takes all" industry.

● POTENTIAL ESSAY QUESTIONS

You may also see essay questions similar to the "Problems & Applications" and "Brain Teasers" exercises.

1. Describe two actions firms take to break down monopoly and three they take to protect their monopoly.

2. Explain how technology has changed competition.

ANSWERS

SHORT-ANSWER QUESTIONS

1. The monitoring problem is the problem of seeing that self-seeking individuals working for an organization follow the goals of the organization rather than their own goals. The high pay that top-level management receives might be pay for performance, or it might be an example of the monitoring problem. To determine which it is, one would need to consider the specific case and determine whether there are incentive-compatible contracts (such as low base pay and high optional bonuses based on performance) that make the managers' goals consistent with the goals of the firms' owners. (322-324)

2. Economics assumes that firms and the economy operate efficiently because firms maximize profits. The monitoring problem undermines that assumption since managers, to some degree, will follow their own goals rather than the profit-maximizing goal. Firms may become lazy monopolists and exhibit X-inefficiency. So the monitoring problem has significant implications. The degree to which firms become lazy monopolists will be limited, however, by competitive pressures. (322-324)

3. Answer *2* above pointed out that when there is a monitoring problem a firm can exhibit X-inefficiency—it can have higher costs than necessary. When that happens, the firm's stock price will fall and it may be worthwhile for another firm to come in and take the inefficient firm over, eliminate the inefficiency, and develop better incentive-compatible contracts. Often, these takeovers are financed by large amounts of debt, which means that the resulting firm must make high interest payments. So even if the new firm does not establish incentive-compatible contracts, the high debt can force the firm to operate more efficiently. (325)

4. The basic idea of economics is that self-seeking individuals try to do the best they can for themselves—to make life as easy as possible for themselves. One of the important ways in which they can do that is to create a monopoly for themselves. When they do that

they create the possibility of profits for other individuals who come in and steal their market—thereby breaking down their monopoly. This process of monopolization and competition breaking down the resulting monopoly is pervasive in our economy and is what is meant by the phrase: "competition is a process, not a state." (326)

5. To acquire monopoly profits for themselves, firms will break down monopoly through political and economic means. If the monopoly is a legal monopoly, high profit will lead potential competitors to lobby to change the law underpinning that monopoly. If the law can't be changed—say, the monopolist has a patent—potential competitors will generally get around the obstacle by developing a slightly different product or by working on a new technology that avoids the monopoly but satisfies the relevant need. (328)

6. Three ways in which firms protect their monopoly are (1) advertising and lobbying; (2) producing products as nearly unique as possible; and (3) charging low prices that discourage entry. All these methods cost the firms money in the short run, but increase their monopoly rents (profits) in the long run. (330-331)

7. Technological advance is a result of specialization that allows producers to learn more about the particular aspects of production in which they specialize. As they learn more, they not only become more productive but are more likely to generate technological advances because they gain a deeper understanding of their speciality. Technology has changed competition because competitive success hinges on an ability to specialize. (332)

8. Oligopoly tends to be most conducive to technological change. Since the typical oligopolist realizes on-going economic profit, it has the funds to carry out research and development. Moreover, the belief that its competitors are innovating also forces it to do so. Oligopolists are constantly searching for new ways to get an edge on competitors, so most technological advance takes place in oligopolistic industries. (333-334)

---●ANSWERS●---

MATCHING

1-e; 2-f; 3-b; 4-c; 5-a; 6-h; 7-g; 8-j; 9-i; 10-d.

---●ANSWERS●---

PROBLEMS AND APPLICATIONS

1. The fund participants are aware of incentive-compatible contracts. Structuring CREF executive pay based on the fund's performance in the stock market increases the chances that the interests of the owners and the managers of the fund are compatible. (332)

2. As shown on the graph below, if suppliers restrict supply to Q_R, they will be able to charge a price of P_R, which is higher than competitive price, P_C. This gives suppliers supplying Q_R additional income, labeled A. Some suppliers are excluded from the market $(Q_c$-$Q_R)$. They lose area C in producer surplus. Consumers who cannot now purchase as many goods lose consumer surplus represented by area B. Those who can afford the higher-priced good pay the higher price. Higher expenditures are represented by area A (the additional income to firms). Since A is transferred from consumers to producers, this is not a loss to society as a whole. However, areas B and C are lost by consumers and producers, respectively, but not transferred to anyone. Those areas, B and C, are the deadweight loss to society. (See Figure 14-2 on page 327)

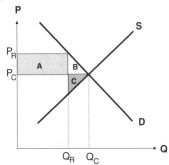

3. Branding is an important way in which firms try to differentiate their goods and services from real or potential competitors. If a firm is successful in distinguishing its product from other producers and in associating that

positive image with its brand name, then other firms will find it difficult to compete. Remember that differentiation (through branding and other means) acts as a barrier to entry, and the stronger the barriers, the greater the monopoly power. (See "Applying the Tools" box on page 331.)

---●ANSWERS●---

BRAIN TEASER

1. **a.** The natural monopolist would produce quantity where $MC = MR$ and charge the price that corresponds to that quantity from the demand curve. This combination is shown on the graph below as (Q_M, P_M). (328-329)

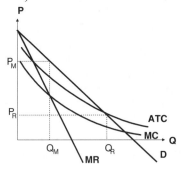

b. I would advise the government that the natural monopolist should be regulated to charge a price where average total costs intersects the demand curve. This way, the monopolist earns normal profit. You cannot require that $MC = P$ because at that price $MC < ATC$, losses would be incurred, and the monopolist would not be able to survive under these circumstances. (329)

c. The problem with this advice is that there is little incentive for the firm to keep its costs down. Why should it keep costs down if it knows it can raise its price sufficiently to cover its costs? (329)

---●ANSWERS●---

MULTIPLE CHOICE

1. c While incentive-compatible contracts could pay bonuses, they do not necessar-

ily have to, which rules out this option. The contract with compatible incentives doesn't say what it is compatible with. See the definition of incentive-compatible contract on page 322.

2. c   Whenever there is X-inefficiency, the firm is not operating at least cost. That is, it is not economically efficient. See page 324.

3. d   Managers' goals are somewhat inconsistent with the goals of the owners. However, managers do not want to get fired and competitive pressures mean managers must make sufficient profits so they don't get fired. To that degree, their goals are consistent with the goals of the owners. See pages 322-324.

4. b   When there are no competitive pressures, organizations tend to make decisions that benefit employees or the decision-makers within these organizations rather than consumers. See pages 322 and 324.

5. a   While for-profit firms can exhibit inefficiency, the market limits that inefficiency. See pages 322-324.

6. b   The welfare loss is the triangle made up of areas *B* and *C*. This area represents the producer and consumer surplus lost but not gained by the other. The other areas represent transfers. See page 327 and Figure 14-2.

7. d   A patent is the legal right to be the sole supplier of a product. It is a type of legal monopoly. See page 328.

8. a   A "natural monopoly" is the best answer. The other answers fit, but nowhere near as closely. The statement you are asked to complete is essentially the definition of a natural monopoly. See pages 328-330.

9. b   When you can pass on cost increases, why try to hold costs down? See pages 328-330.

10. d   Reverse engineering is a method firms use to try to break down other firms' monopolies. See pages 328 and 330-332.

11. a   Technological development increases competition by providing more specialized products. See page 332.

12. c   Technological advance requires specialization. Specialization increases productivity and lowers costs of production. This results in more intense competition. See page 332.

13. c   Oligopoly provides the best market structure for technological advance because firms have an incentive to innovate (they face competition) and they also have the profits to devote to research and development. See pages 333-334.

14. a   Technological advance requires large amounts of investment. Only firms that earn economic profit can afford to invest in research and development. See pages 332-335.

15. a   Network externalities promote industry standards, although those standards may not be the most efficient. They also increase the likelihood that an industry becomes a "winner takes all" industry. See page 334.

ANSWERS

POTENTIAL ESSAY QUESTIONS

The following are annotated answers. They indicate the general idea behind the answer.

1.   Actions firms take to break down monopoly include (1) lobbying government to change the law underpinning that monopoly if the monopoly is a legal monopoly and (2) making slight modifications to a monopolist's patent within the limits of the law. Firms protect their monopolies by (1) advertising and lobbying government, (2) producing products as nearly unique as possible, and (3) charging low prices.

2.   Technological advance requires specialization. Specialization increases productivity and lowers costs of production. This results in intense competition.

ANTITRUST POLICY AND REGULATION

● CHAPTER AT A GLANCE

This review is based upon the learning objectives that open the chapter.

1. Judgment by performance is the view that competitiveness of a market should be judged by the behavior of firms in that market; judgment by structure is the view that competitiveness of a market should be judged by the structure of the market. (341-342)

   Both criteria have their problems. There are no definitive criteria for judging whether a firm has violated antitrust statutes. However, since 1945, most court decisions have relied on judgment by structure for the reason of practicality.

2. Public outrage at the formation and activities of trusts such as Standard Oil led to the passage of the Sherman Act, the Clayton Act, and the Federal Trade Commission Act. (342-344)

   Know what these Acts outlaw.

3a. The IBM case was dropped by the United States, but the prosecution of the case likely led to some of IBM's problems in the 1990s. It won but it also lost. (347-349)

   Changes in technology can alter market structure (the degree of competition) rather rapidly.

3b. The AT&T case was settled by AT&T agreeing to be split up into regional companies handling local service, and AT&T itself competing in the long-distance market. (349-351)

   Up until 1982, AT&T was a regulated monopoly. Telephone services were believed to be a natural monopoly. More recent technological innovations continue to change the competitive nature of the telecommunications industry.

3c. Whether one sees Microsoft as a monopolist depends on whether one views it in a static or dynamic framework. (351-354)

   In 2000, the U.S. court ruled that Microsoft was guilty of being a monopoly and involved in anticompetitive practices. The government recommended breaking the company into two separate companies. Microsoft had the decision reversed on appeal. Instead, the case was settled through mediation between the Federal government, nine states, and Microsoft. Microsoft agreed not to undertake non-competitive practices in the future. Even though Microsoft was eventually found guilty of being a monopolist, by delaying the ultimate decision, maybe it won. More recently the European Commission has found Microsoft guilty of conspiring to monopolize the European market. Microsoft is appealing that decision.

   Note: Since the 1980s the United States has been more lenient in antitrust cases because of a change in ideology, the globalization of the U.S. economy, and the increasing complexity of technology.

4. Horizontal mergers are companies in the same industry merging together. Vertical mergers are combinations of two companies, one of which supplies inputs to the other's production. Conglomerate mergers are combinations of unrelated businesses. (355-357)

   Know the differences. Also become familiar with the various terms associated with takeovers.

   Most antitrust policy has concerned horizontal mergers.

5. Five reasons why unrelated firms merge include: (356-357)
   - To achieve economies of scope;
   - To get a good buy;
   - To diversify;
   - To ward off a takeover bid; and
   - To strengthen their political-economic influence.

   When unrelated firms merge, this constitutes a conglomerate merger.

6. Other countries have historically had more lenient antitrust laws compared to U.S. antitrust laws. Perhaps the biggest change on the international front is the emergence of a strong European antitrust policy. (358-360)

   Before the European Union (EU) was formed most now member-nations had relatively weak antitrust laws because large domestic firms needed to achieve economies of scale to be profitable; nations saw the international market as the relevant market; these countries were less populist than the United States; and saw government and business as partners, not antagonists. But, since the establishment of the EU, the European Commission, the EU's antitrust agency, has become less lenient toward non-European firms.

   Antitrust issues are by nature global, but a country's antitrust laws are not.

7. The government can also affect the competitive process by (1) regulation, (2) government ownership, and (3) industrial policy. (360-362)

   Two types of regulation are price regulation and social regulation. Price regulation is regulation directed at industries that have natural monopoly elements. Social regulation is concerned with the condition under which goods, and services are produced, the safety of those goods, and the side effects of production on society.

   Government-owned firms tend not to have an incentive to hold costs down.

   An industrial policy is a formal policy that government takes toward business.

● SHORT-ANSWER QUESTIONS

1. How does judging competition by structure differ from judging competition by performance?

2. What are the two provisions of the Sherman Antitrust Act? What year was it passed by Congress?

3. What was the resolution of the IBM antitrust case?

4. What was the resolution of the AT&T antitrust case?

5. What was the resolution of the Microsoft antitrust case?

6. What are horizontal, vertical, and conglomerate mergers?

7. What are five reasons why unrelated firms would want to merge?

8. How has U.S. antitrust enforcement changed over the last ten to twenty years? What contributed to the change?

9. What is perhaps one of the biggest changes on the international antitrust front in recent years?

10. List three alternatives to antitrust policy that government can use to affect the competitive process.

MATCHING THE TERMS
Match the terms to their definitions

___ **1.** acquisition

___ **2.** antitrust policy

___ **3.** Clayton Antitrust Act

___ **4.** conglomerate merger

___ **5.** deacquisition

___ **6.** European Commission

___ **7.** Federal Trade Commission Act

___ **8.** horizontal merger

___ **9.** hostile takeover

___ **10.** industrial policy

___ **11.** judgment by performance

___ **12.** judgment by structure

___ **13.** merger

___ **14.** natural monopoly

___ **15.** Sherman Antitrust Act

___ **16.** takeover

___ **17.** vertical merger

a. A company buys another company; the buyer has the right of direct control of the resulting venture, but does not necessarily exercise that direct control.

b. A merger of companies in the same industry.

c. A merger in which one company buys another that does not want to be bought.

d. A government's formal policy toward business.

e. The act of combining two firms.

f. A law that made it illegal for firms to use "unfair methods of competition" and to engage in "unfair or deceptive acts or practices."

g. Combination of unrelated businesses.

h. Combination of two companies, one of which supplies inputs to the other's production.

i. An industry in which significant economies of scale make the existence of more than one firm inefficient.

j. Judging the competitiveness of markets by the number of firms in the market and their market shares.

k. Judging the competitiveness of markets by the behavior of firms in that market.

l. Law passed by the U.S. Congress in 1890 to attempt to regulate the competitive process.

m. One company's sale of parts of another company it has bought.

n. Purchase of a firm by another firm that then takes direct control over its operations.

o. Government's policy toward the competitive process.

p. A law that made four specific monopolistic practices illegal.

q. The European Union's antitrust agency.

● PROBLEMS AND APPLICATIONS

1. For each of the following situations determine what type of merger activity is being undertaken.

   a. Pepsi-Cola Corporation buys Pizza Hut and Kentucky Fried Chicken.

   b. A bakery corporation buys up a grocery store chain.

   c. A steel manufacturer buys up all other steel producing factories.

2. American auto manufacturers sell their models at a lower price on the west coast in an effort to remain competitive with Japanese imports. This has upset many car dealers on the east coast who view this as price discrimination and therefore a violation of antitrust. Which antitrust law are these dealers referring to? What possible defense might the auto manufacturers claim?

3. Suppose a grocery store is interested in buying a particular brand name of canned tomato soup from a food processing vendor. However, before the vendor agrees to deliver any cans of tomato soup the grocer is required to sign a contract guaranteeing that the grocery store will buy all of its canned goods from the vendor. The grocery store objects because it argues that such a requirement is against the law. Which antitrust law would the grocer argue is being broken? What possible defense might the vendor claim?

4. You're an economist in the Antitrust Division of the Justice Department. In the personal computer market, suppose Compaq has petitioned to merge with AT&T. Compaq currently has 14% of the PC market and AT&T has 3%. The other three large firms in the market, Packard Bell, IBM, and Apple, have 11%, 9%, and 8% of the PC market respectively. In the Windows-based PC market, Compaq has 18% of the market and AT&T has 5%. The other three large firms in the Windows-based PC market, Packard Bell, IBM, and Hewlett Packard, have 14%, 12%, and 9% of the PC market respectively.

   a. Calculate the approximate Herfindahl and 4-firm concentration ratios for these firms in each industry before the merger and after the merger.

   b. If you were Compaq's economist, which industry definition would you suggest using when making your petition to the Justice Department?

c. Give an argument why the merger might decrease competition.

d. Give an argument why the merger might increase competition.

● A BRAIN TEASER

1. Suppose you are advising a regulatory agency of the Federal government to regulate the prices of a monopolist depicted by the graph below.

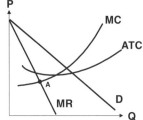

   a. Would you recommend setting prices at point A where *MC = MR*? Why or why not?

   b. What would be the minimum price you would recommend? Why?

c. Does the monopolist still enjoy economic profit at the minimum price you determined in *b*? If so, what area on the graph represents that profit?

d. What potential problem might be associated with your recommendation?

MULTIPLE CHOICE

Circle the one best answer for each of the following questions:

1. When judging the competitiveness of markets by the behavior of firms in that market, one is using the:
   a. "judgment by performance" criteria.
   b. "judgment by structure" criteria.
   c. "judgment by merger" criteria.
   d. "judgment by antitrust" criteria.

2. When judging the competitiveness of markets by the size and number of firms in that market, one is using the:
   a. "judgment by performance" criteria.
   b. "judgment by structure" criteria.
   c. "judgment by merger" criteria.
   d. "judgment by antitrust" criteria.

3. An important law in the U.S. regulation of markets is the:
   a. Standard Oil Antitrust Act of 1890.
   b. Sherman Antitrust Act of 1890.
   c. Alcoa Antitrust Act of 1890.
   d. Lincoln Antitrust Act of 1890.

4. In the Standard Oil and American Tobacco Company antitrust cases in 1911, the Court ruled that:

   a. the two companies had a monopolistic structure and therefore should be broken up.
   b. the two companies were guilty of unfair business practices and therefore should be broken up.
   c. the Sherman Antitrust Act did not apply.
   d. the two companies had to be disbanded.

5. The Clayton Antitrust Act made all of the following monopolistic practices illegal *except*:
   a. price discrimination.
   b. tie-in contracts.
   c. interlocking directorships.
   d. creation of a natural monopoly.

6. In the ALCOA antitrust case in 1945, the Court ruled that the:
   a. company had a monopolistic structure and therefore should be broken up.
   b. company was guilty of unfair business practices and therefore should be broken up.
   c. Sherman Antitrust Act did not apply.
   d. two companies had to be disbanded.

7. The resolution of the IBM antitrust case was that:
   a. IBM was broken up.
   b. IBM was combined with AT&T.
   c. the government dropped the IBM case.
   d. IBM was allowed to stay in the large-computer market but was kept out of the personal-computer market.

8. The resolution of the AT&T antitrust case of the 1980s was:
   a. AT&T agreed to split up into three operating divisions.
   b. AT&T agreed to split up and allow the Baby Bells to be independent.
   c. AT&T was combined with MCI and Sprint.
   d. MCI and Sprint were broken off from AT&T and developed as competitors to AT&T.

9. In the Microsoft antitrust case:
   a. the government ruled that Microsoft was a monopoly and was involved in anti-competitive practices.
   b. the government divided Microsoft into two companies.
   c. Microsoft agreed to government regulation of its prices.
   d. Microsoft was forced to get out of the Internet business.

10. When two merging companies are in the same industry, their merger is called a:
    a. horizontal merger.
    b. vertical merger.
    c. conglomerate merger.
    d. takeover merger.

11. When one of two merging companies supplies one or more of the inputs to the other merging company, the merger is called a:
    a. horizontal merger.
    b. vertical merger.
    c. conglomerate merger.
    d. takeover merger.

12. When two companies that are in unrelated industries merge, the merger is called a:
    a. horizontal merger.
    b. vertical merger.
    c. conglomerate merger.
    d. takeover merger.

13. Reasons firms would want to enter into a conglomerate merger include all the following *except:*
    a. to achieve economies of scope.
    b. to diversify.
    c. to strengthen their political and economic influence.
    d. to become a natural monopoly.

14. Antitrust laws in Europe:
    a. have become less lenient toward non-European firms.
    b. tend to be stronger than in the United States.
    c. tend to be approximately the same strength as antitrust laws in the United States.
    d. do not exist; there are no antitrust laws in Europe.

15. Globalization has impacted competition and antitrust in that:
    a. U.S. antitrust policymakers increasingly see the international market (as opposed to the purely domestic market) as the relevant market when determining the degree of competition in a market.
    b. U.S. antitrust policymakers are more strictly enforcing antitrust laws to ensure firms do not take advantage of consumers.
    c. U.S. antitrust policymakers are less willing to allow large domestic firms to achieve economies of scale.
    d. we can expect fewer international jurisdictional battles in antitrust.

16. Industrial policy is:
    a. a policy of government entering into competition with business.
    b. a policy of government industries entering into competition with business.
    c. a formal policy that government takes towards business.
    d. a laissez-faire policy of government towards business.

● POTENTIAL ESSAY QUESTIONS

You may also see essay questions similar to the "Problems & Applications" and "Brain Teasers" exercises.

1. Why has there been a more lenient approach in the United States to the enforcement of antitrust laws in recent years?

2. What is the difference between horizontal, vertical, and conglomerate mergers? Which merging activity has most U.S. antitrust policy been concerned with? What is the principal guideline used by the Department of Justice since 1982 with respect to mergers?

ANSWERS

SHORT-ANSWER QUESTIONS

1. Judging competition by structure is the view that competitiveness of a market should be judged by the number of firms in the market and their market shares. Judging competition by performance is the view that competitiveness of a market should be judged by the behavior of firms in that market. (341-342)

2. The two provisions of the Sherman Antitrust Act passed in 1890 are (1) every contract, combination, or conspiracy in restraint of trade is illegal and (2) every person who shall monopolize or attempt to monopolize shall be deemed guilty of a misdemeanor. (342-343)

3. The IBM case was dropped by the United States, but the prosecution likely led to IBM's problems in the 1990s. (347-349)

4. The AT&T case was settled by AT&T agreeing to be split up into regional companies handling local service and AT&T itself competing in the long-distance market. (350)

5. Whether one sees Microsoft as a monopolist depends on whether one views it in a static or dynamic framework. But the court did find Microsoft guilty. However, Microsoft may have still won by ending up only having to promise to not behave monopolistically in the future. (353-354)

6. A horizontal merger is a merger between two companies in the same industry. A vertical merger is a firm merging with the supplier of one (or more) of its inputs. A conglomerate merger is a merger between unrelated businesses. (355-357)

7. Five reasons why unrelated firms would want to merge are (1) to achieve economies of scope, (2) to get a good buy, (3) to diversify, (4) to ward off a takeover bid, and (5) to strengthen political-economic influence. (356-357)

8. Because of greater international competition, more and more, U.S. antitrust policymakers see the international market as the relevant market. The policy focus is shifting from "Is U.S. industry internally competitive so that it does not take advantage of the consumer?" to "Is U.S. industry internationally competitive so that it can compete effectively in the world economy?" (358)

9. Perhaps the biggest change on the international antitrust front is the emergence of a strong European antitrust policy. Before the European Union (EU) was established, most of the now member-countries had relatively weak antitrust laws. But now the European Commission, the EU's antitrust agency has become much less lenient toward non-European firms. Antitrust issues are by nature global, but a country's antitrust laws are not. (358-360)

10. The government can also affect the competitive process by (1) regulation, (2) government ownership, and (3) industrial policy. (360-362)

ANSWERS

MATCHING

1-a; 2-o; 3-p; 4-g; 5-m; 6-q; 7-f; 8-b; 9-c; 10-d; 11-k; 12-j; 13-e; 14-i; 15-l; 16-n; 17-h.

ANSWERS

PROBLEMS AND APPLICATIONS

1. a. Conglomerate merger (designed to achieve economies of scope). (356-357)
   b. Vertical merger. (356)
   c. Horizontal merger. (355-356)

2. The Clayton Antitrust Act prohibits price discrimination if it has the effect of lessening competition. The auto manufacturers could claim that the lower prices on the west coast do not result in less competition but are instead a consequence of the intense competition that exists on the west coast. (344)

3. The Clayton Antitrust Act prohibits tie-in contracts in which the buyer must agree to deal exclusively with one seller and not to purchase goods from competing sellers. The vendor may claim that this is not reducing competition. (344)

4. a. The Herfindahl index is calculated by adding the squared value of the market shares of all the firms in the industry. The 4-firm concentration ratio is calculated by adding the market shares of the four firms with the largest market shares.

PC Market: Before the merger, the Herfindahl index is greater than $14^2 + 11^2 + 9^2 + 8^2 + 3^2 = 196 + 121 + 81 + 64 + 9 = 471$. The exact Herfindahl index cannot be calculated since we do not know the market shares of all the firms in the market. The 4-firm concentration ratio before the merger is $14 + 11 + 9 + 8 = 42$. The Herfindahl index after the merger is at least $17^2 + 11^2 + 9^2 + 8^2 = 289 + 121 + 81 + 64 = 555$. The 4-firm concentration ratio after the merger is $17 + 11 + 9 + 8 = 45$.

Windows-based PC market: Before the merger, the Herfindahl index is at least $18^2 + 14^2 + 12^2 + 9^2 + 5^2 = 324 + 196 + 144 + 81 + 25 = 770$. The 4-firm concentration ratio before the merger is $18 + 14 + 12 + 9 = 53$. The Herfindahl index after the merger is at least $23^2 + 14^2 + 12^2 + 9^2 = 529 + 196 + 144 + 81 = 950$. The 4-firm concentration ratio after the merger is $23 + 14 + 12 + 9 = 58$. (Chapter 13)

b. I would use the broader PC-based computer industry definition because the Herfindahl indexes and concentration ratios are lower in this market, indicating more competition. (Chapter 13)

c. The merger might be expected to decrease competition because within the PC market the Herfindahl index rises from 471 to 555 and the 4-firm concentration ratio rises from 42 to 45. This suggests the merger would result in a less competitive market. The larger merged company may have more ability to set prices above marginal costs, resulting in a loss to society. (Welfare loss with a monopoly is shown graphically in the chapter on monopoly.) (341-342)

d. This merger might be expected to increase competition if Compaq and AT&T cannot compete separately against the other three firms in the market. A combined Compaq and AT&T might also be more competitive in a global market. Most likely, however, this merger will lower the level of domestic competition—especially if the merger would enable economies of scale and scope to be experienced. (341-342)

A BRAIN TEASER

1. a. I would not recommend setting prices at point A where $MC = MR$ because at that point price is less than average total costs. The monopolist would be losing money and would eventually go out of business. This is shown in the graph below. (341-342; and the chapter on monopoly)

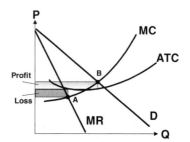

b. The minimum price I would recommend would be where the marginal cost curve intersects the demand curve at point B in the graph above. This eliminates all welfare loss to society associated with a monopoly and is the competitive price and quantity. (341-342; and the chapter on monopoly)

c. The monopolist still enjoys economic profit that is represented by the shaded area in the graph above. (341-342; and the chapter on monopoly)

d. There may be little incentive for the monopolist to hold down its costs. (341-342 and the chapter on monopoly)

MULTIPLE CHOICE

1. a "Judgment by performance" is judging the competitiveness of markets by the performance (behavior) of firms in that market. See page 342.

2. b The "judgment by structure" is judging the competitiveness of markets by their structure (the relative size and number of competitors in that market). See pages 341-342.

3. b The Sherman Antitrust Act passed in 1890 was an early law passed to regulate the competitive process. See page 342.

4. b The early cases were decided upon by the performance, or abuse, standard, not on whether the companies were monopolies. The Act applies to unfair business practices as well as to monopolistic structure. "Disbanded" would mean the companies ceased totally to exist, whereas these two companies were changed by reorganization. See page 343-344.

5. d The Clayton Antitrust Act is a law that made four specific monopolistic practices illegal. They are price discrimination, tie-in contracts, interlocking directorships, and buying a competitor's stock to reduce competition. See page 344.

6. a In the ALCOA case, the Court applied the monopolistic structure (or judgment by structure) standard. See pages 344-345.

7. c The antitrust suit was dropped since new competitors had changed the market structure. See pages 347-349.

8. b AT&T split up into the Baby Bells. These Baby Bells then consolidated in the 1990s. See page 350.

9. a The court ruled that Microsoft was a monopoly and that it had engaged in anti-competitive practices. Essentially, Microsoft just promised not to behave monopolistically in the future. See pages 353-354.

10. a A horizontal merger is when two firms that produce the same product merge. See pages 355-357.

11. b A vertical merger is when two firms involved in different parts of the same production process merge. See pages 355-357.

12. c A conglomerate merger is when two firms producing unrelated products merge. See pages 355-357.

13. d Unrelated firms would want to merge to achieve economies of scope, to get a good buy, to diversify, to ward off a takeover bid, or to strengthen their political-economic influence. See pages 356-357.

14. a Most countries have weaker antitrust laws compared to the United States. Nonetheless, the European Commission, the EU's antitrust agency, has become less lenient with non-European firms. See pages 358-360.

15. a The U.S. policy focus of government is shifting from "Is U.S. industry internally competitive so that it does not take advantage of the consumer?" to "Is U.S. industry internationally competitive so that it can compete effectively in the world economy?" See pages 358-360.

16. c Industrial policy is a formal policy government takes toward business. An example is the U.S. military-industrial complex. See page 362.

━━━━━━ ANSWERS ━━━━━━

POTENTIAL ESSAY QUESTIONS

The following are annotated answers. They indicate the general idea behind the answer.

1. In recent years antitrust law has worked mainly through its deterrent effect. First, because of a change in American ideology "big business" is no longer viewed as necessarily being bad. Second, the market structure in the U.S. has become less relevant as the United States has become more integrated into the global economy where there is generally more competition. Third, as technologies have become more complicated, the issues in antitrust enforcement also have become more complicated for the courts to handle. Moreover, the IBM, AT&T, and Microsoft cases have significantly influenced perceptions of antitrust, creating a more lenient modern approach.

2. Two companies in the same industry merging is a horizontal merger. A firm merging with the supplier of one of its inputs is a vertical merger. Two firms in unrelated industries merging is a conglomerate merger. Horizontal mergers have attracted most U.S. antitrust policy attention. The principal guideline used by the Justice Department since 1982 is to carefully consider the approval or disapproval of a merger if, after the merger, the Herfindahl index would be above 1000.

Pretest
Chapters 11 - 15

Take this test in test conditions, giving yourself a limited amount of time to complete the questions. Ideally, check with your professor to see how much time he or she allows for an average multiple choice question and multiply this by 25. This is the time limit you should set for yourself for this pretest. If you do not know how much time your teacher would allow, we suggest 1 minute per question, or 25 minutes.

1. In a perfectly competitive market:
   a. firms sell a differentiated product where one firm's output can be distinguished from another firm's output.
   b. there are so many firms selling output in the market that no one individual firm has the ability to control the market price.
   c. economic profits can be earned in the long run.
   d. there are very strong barriers to entry which can prevent potential competitors from entering the market.

2. Refer to the graph below. A competitive firm is producing at output A.

   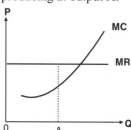

   a. It could increase profits by increasing output.
   b. It could increase profits by decreasing output.
   c. It cannot increase profits.
   d. One can say nothing about profits from the diagram.

3. In order to maximize profits (or minimize losses) a firm should produce at that output level at which:
   a. total revenue is maximized.
   b. average total cost are minimized.
   c. marginal revenue equals marginal cost.
   d. marginal revenue exceeds marginal cost by the greatest amount.

4. Refer to the graph below. The firm's profit in this case will be measured by:

   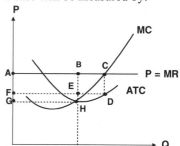

   a. the rectangle ABEF.
   b. the rectangle ACDF.
   c. the rectangle ABHG.
   d. the rectangle BCDE.

5. Normal profits are:
   a. approximately 6 percent of costs.
   b. approximately 8 percent of costs.
   c. returns to the owners of business for the opportunity cost of their implicit inputs.
   d. generally larger than accounting profits.

6. Monopoly is the market structure in which:
   a. one firm makes up the entire market.
   b. two firms make up the entire market.
   c. the market is made up of a few big firms.
   d. firms make a supernormal profit.

7. A profit-maximizing monopolist will:
   a. produce an output level at which MR > MC.
   b. produce an output level at which P > MC.
   c. always earn an economic profit in the short run.
   d. increase production when MR < MC.

8. Refer to the graph below. The monopolist represented is:

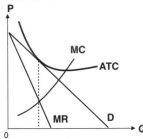

   a. making a profit.
   b. making a loss.
   c. making zero profit.
   d. unable to determine what kind of profit the monopolist is making.

9. Price discrimination requires:
   a. identifying groups of customers with different elasticities.
   b. separating customers in some way.
   c. limiting customers' ability to re-sell the product between different groups.
   d. all of the other options listed to be successful.

10. Refer to the graph below. Which area represents the welfare loss due to a monopolist?
   a. A.
   b. A + B.
   c. B + C.
   d. A + B + C.

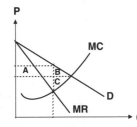

11. In a market there are many firms selling differentiated products. This market is:
   a. a competitive market.
   b. a monopolistically competitive market.
   c. an oligopoly.
   d. a monopoly.

12. The top four firms in the industry have 10 percent, 8 percent, 8 percent, and 6 percent of the market. The four-firm concentration ratio of this market is:
   a. 8.
   b. 32.
   c. 66.
   d. 264.

13. Refer to the graph below. Which of the following is the output chosen by the monopolistically competitive firm?

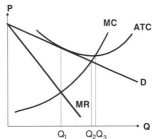

   a. Q_1.
   b. Q_2.
   c. Q_3.
   d. Output cannot be determined.

14. In a contestable market model of oligopoly, prices are determined by:
   a. costs and barriers to exit.
   b. costs and barriers to entry.
   c. costs, barriers to entry, and barriers to exit.
   d. costs alone.

15. A market has the following characteristics: There is strategic pricing, output is somewhat restricted, decision-making is interdependent, and some long-run economic profits are possible. This market is:
   a. a monopoly.
   b. an oligopoly.
   c. monopolistically competitive.
   d. perfectly competitive.

16. A firm is making no profit. If there is X-inefficiency, what can we conclude?
   a. The firm is operating at least cost.
   b. The firm is operating using the fewest inputs possible.
   c. The firm is operating less efficiently than economically possible.
   d. We can say nothing about the efficiency of the firm.

17. Economists would expect that generally:
   a. for-profit firms operate more efficiently than nonprofit firms.
   b. nonprofit firms operate more efficiently than for-profit firms.
   c. for-profit firms operate equally efficiently as nonprofit firms.
   d. nonprofit firms cannot exist because they operate so inefficiently.

18. Refer to the graph below. If suppliers restrict output to OL, what area represents the welfare loss to society?
   a. A + B.
   b. B + C.
   c. C + D.
   d. A + D.

19. When regulated monopolies are allowed to pass on all cost increases to earn a normal profit, they:
   a. have a strong incentive to operate efficiently.
   b. have little incentive to operate efficiently.
   c. become a focal point of reverse engineering.
   d. will apply for a patent.

20. Technological advances are most likely for markets that:
   a. earn economic profits.
   b. have one firm supplying all the output.
   c. are protected by government regulation.
   d. produce where MR = MC.

21. When judging the competitiveness of markets by the behavior of firms in that market, one is using the:
   a. "judgment by performance" criteria.
   b. "judgment by structure" criteria.
   c. "judgment by merger" criteria.
   d. "judgment by antitrust" criteria.

22. The resolution of the IBM antitrust case was that:
   a. IBM was broken up.
   b. IBM was combined with AT&T.
   c. the government dropped the IBM case.
   d. IBM was allowed to stay in the large-computer market but was kept out of the personal-computer market.

23. In the Microsoft antitrust case:
   a. the government ruled that Microsoft was a monopoly and involved in anti-competitive practices.
   b. the government divided Microsoft into two companies.
   c. Microsoft agreed to government regulation of its prices.
   d. Microsoft was forced to get out of the Internet business.

24. When one of two merging companies supplies one or more of the inputs to the other merging company, the merger is called a:
   a. horizontal merger.
   b. vertical merger.
   c. conglomerate merger.
   d. takeover merger.

25. Industrial policy is:
   a. a policy of government entering into competition with business.
   b. a policy of government industries entering into competition with business.
   c. a formal policy that government takes towards business.
   d. a laissez-faire policy of government towards business.

━━━━━━ ANSWERS ━━━━━━

1.	a	(11:1)	14.	c	(13:13)
2.	a	(11:5)	15.	b	(13:16)
3.	c	(11:7)	16.	c	(14:2)
4.	b	(11:11)	17.	a	(14:5)
5.	c	(11:15)	18.	b	(14:6)
6.	b	(12:2)	19.	b	(14:9)
7.	b	(12:3)	20.	a	(14:14)
8.	c	(12:7)	21.	a	(15:1)
9.	d	(12:12)	22.	c	(15:7)
10.	c	(12:14)	23.	a	(15:9)
11.	b	(13:1)	24.	b	(15:11)
12.	b	(13:4)	25.	c	(15:16)
13.	a	(13:8)			

Key: The figures in parentheses refer to multiple choice question and chapter numbers. For example (1:2) is multiple choice question 2 from chapter 1.

WORK AND THE LABOR MARKET

16

CHAPTER AT A GLANCE

This review is based upon the learning objectives that open the chapter.

1. An increase in the marginal tax rate is likely to reduce the quantity of labor supplied because it reduces the net wage of individuals and hence, through individuals' incentive effect, causes them to work less. (371)

   Higher marginal tax rates reduce the incentive to work.

2. Elasticity of market labor supply depends on: (371-372)
   - Individuals' opportunity cost of working.
   - The type of market being discussed.
   - The elasticity of individuals' supply curves.
   - Individuals entering and leaving the labor market.

   An elastic supply of labor means workers are quite responsive to a change in the wage rate. For example, an increase in the wage will result in a relatively large increase in the quantity of labor supplied (the number of people looking for work).

3. Derived demand is the demand for factors of production by firms, which depends on consumers' demands. (372-373)

   For example, if the demand for automobiles increases, the demand for automotive workers increases. It simply takes more workers to produce more cars.

4. Four factors that influence the elasticity of demand for labor are: (373-374)
   - The elasticity of demand for the firm's good.
   - The relative importance of the factor in the production process.
   - The possibility of, and cost of, substitution in production.
   - The degree to which marginal productivity falls with an increase in the labor.

An elastic demand for labor means employers are quite responsive to a change in the wage rate. For example, an increase in the wage rate will result in a rather dramatic reduction in the number of workers employed.

5. A monopsony is a market in which there is only one buyer. A bilateral monopoly is a market in which a single seller faces a single buyer. (377-378)

   A monopsony will hire fewer workers (Q_m) and pay a lower wage (W_m) compared to the competitive outcome.

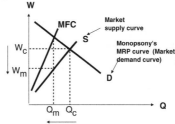

6. To understand real-world labor markets one must broaden the analysis. (379-381)

   What we see in the real world is a consequence of the interaction of market, social and political forces.

7. Three types of discrimination are: (381-384)

   - Discrimination based on individual characteristics that will affect job performance.
   - Discrimination based on correctly perceived statistical characteristics of the group.
   - Discrimination based on individual characteristics that don't affect job performance or are incorrectly perceived.

   One can think of discrimination as treating individuals whom one views as equals unequally.

See also, Appendix A: "Derived Demand."

SHORT-ANSWER QUESTIONS

1. Use the theory of rational choice and the concept of opportunity cost to explain why firms generally offer time-and-a-half for workers to work on Thanksgiving Day.

2. Suppose Congress passes an increase in the marginal income tax rate. What is the likely effect on work effort?

3. List four factors that influence the elasticity of labor supply.

4. Explain how the demand for labor is a derived demand.

5. List four factors that influence the elasticity of labor demand.

6. Define the terms *monopsonist* and *bilateral monopoly*.

7. On average, women earn about 85 cents for every $1 earned by men. Discuss this phenomenon in terms of political forces, social forces, and market forces.

8. What are three types of discrimination?

MATCHING THE TERMS
Match the terms to their definitions

___ **1.**	bilateral monopoly	**a.** A market in which only a single firm hires labor.
___ **2.**	closed shop	**b.** A firm in which all workers must join the union.
___ **3.**	comparable worth laws	**c.** A market with only a single seller and a single buyer.
___ **4.**	derived demand	**d.** A firm in which the union controls hiring.
___ **5.**	downsizing	**e.** Wage that is above the going market wage; paid to keep workers happy and productive.
___ **6.**	efficiency wages	**f.** Factor market in which individuals supply labor services for wages to other individuals and to firms that demand labor services.
___ **7.**	entrepreneurship	**g.** Labor services that involve high degrees of organizational skills, concern, oversight, responsibility, and creativity.
___ **8.**	incentive effect	**h.** How much a person will change his or her hours worked in response to a change in the wage rate.
___ **9.**	labor market	**i.** A firm shifting production from its own plants to other firms, typically offshore, where wages are lower.
___ **10.**	marginal factor cost	**j.** Laws mandating comparable pay for comparable work.
___ **11.**	monopsony	**k.** The additional cost to a firm of hiring another worker.
___ **12.**	outsourcing	**l.** A reduction in the workforce of major corporations, especially at the level of middle management.
___ **13.**	union shop	**m.** The demand for factors of production by firms, which depends on consumers' demands.

● PROBLEMS AND APPLICATIONS

1. Use the graph below to answer the following questions.

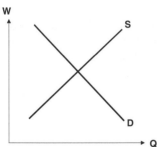

a. Label the equilibrium wage and number of workers.

b. If wages were set by the government above the equilibrium wage, what happens to the quantity supplied and the quantity demanded for labor? How do they differ?

c. Show how a technological innovation that leads to a higher demand for labor affects equilibrium wage and quantity of labor.

2. Consider again demand and supply in a labor market. For each of the following situations determine whether there would be an increase or a decrease in demand or supply of labor. Furthermore, determine the impact on the equilibrium wage rate (W) and the equilibrium quantity (Q) of labor. (You may want to use a graph of demand and supply curves for labor to help you.)

a. The demand for the product workers are

producing increases.

"open-door" immigration policy.

b. It is Christmas Day, and workers value their leisure time more highly.

h. Workers are now more productive.

c. The other factory in town is now offering a higher wage rate.

3. Answer the following questions using the graph below.

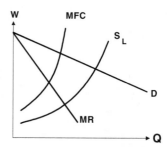

d. The fringe (nonmonetary) benefits of this job have increased substantially. Now more lucrative health and dental coverage is provided, as well as a retirement program, paid vacations, a company car, etc...

a. Label the equilibrium wage and number of workers on the graph if the market is competitive.

b. Label the equilibrium wage and number of workers on the graph under a monopsonist. Compare this with the competitive outcome.

e. The price of a machine, which is a substitute for this labor, is now less expensive and its productivity has increased substantially due to an increase in technology. Note: the new technology does not affect worker productivity.

c. If there is a worker's union, what would be the equilibrium wage and level of employment?

f. The firms in this industry have successfully convinced government to impose stricter tariffs and import quotas on a foreign good that is a substitute for the good produced by these workers.

g. The government has just adopted an

A1. Complete the table below for a perfectly

competitive firm that produces halogen light bulbs. Each light bulb sells for $1. (Marginal values refers to the marginal change of increasing to that row, i.e., the marginal physical product of going from 23 to 24 workers is 9. The same goes for marginal revenue product.)

	No. of Workers	Total Product per hour	Marginal Physical Product per hour	Average Product per hour	Marginal Revenue Product per hour
	20	200		—	
A	21	—	—	—	15
B	22	228	—	—	—
C	23	—	—	10.39	—
D	24	—	9	—	—
E	25	—	—	10.20	—
F	26	260	—	—	—

a. Draw the corresponding labor demand curve, from the values in the table.

b. Suppose the price of halogen light bulbs falls to $.50 per bulb. How does this change labor demand?

c. If halogen light bulbs sold for $1 per bulb

as in (a), how many workers would the firm hire if wages were $7 per hour? How many workers would the firm hire if wages were $11 per hour?

● A BRAIN TEASER

1. Your boss has given you three possible combinations of raw materials in addition to labor and capital (machines) to produce the desired production target at the company's new production facility. Your job is to determine the least cost combination of inputs to employ. Suppose the price per unit of raw material usage per hour is $5, the wage rate per hour is $10, and the cost per hour for machines is $20. The marginal physical product (or productivity) of raw material, labor, and capital usage associated with the three combinations of input usage is summarized in the table below. Which combination of input usage will minimize the firm's costs of production to produce the desired production target at the new facility?

	MPP of Raw Material	MPP of Labor	MPP of Capital
Comb. A:	5	10	50
Comb. B:	10	20	40
Comb. C:	20	15	30

● MULTIPLE CHOICE

Circle the one best answer for each of the following questions:

1. Generally, economists believe the higher the wage:
    a. the higher the quantity of labor supplied.
    b. the greater the supply of labor.
    c. the lesser the supply of labor.
    d. the lower the quantity of labor supplied.

2. As the wage rate increases the opportunity cost of leisure:
    a. increases.
    b. decreases.
    c. remains the same.
    d. cannot be determined given the information provided.

3. An increase in the marginal tax rate will:
    a. increase the quantity of labor supplied.
    b. increase the supply of labor.
    c. decrease the supply of labor.
    d. decrease the quantity of labor supplied.

4. The irony of any need-based program is that it:
    a. increases the number of needy.
    b. decreases the number of needy.
    c. creates other needs.
    d. destroys needs.

5. Which of the following is *not* a factor influencing the elasticity of market labor supply?
    a. Individuals' opportunity cost of working.
    b. The elasticity of individuals' supply curves.
    c. The elasticity of market labor demand.
    d. Individuals entering and leaving the labor market.

6. Which of the following is *not* a reason why the labor supply for heads of households (primary workers) is more inelastic than that for secondary workers?
    a. Institutional factors, such as hours of work, are only slightly flexible.
    b. There are many more new secondary workers who can enter the market than there are primary workers.
    c. Heads of households have responsibility for seeing that there's food and shelter for the household family members.
    d. There are more secondary workers than primary workers.

7. The term "derived demand" refers to:
    a. demand by consumers for advertised products.
    b. the demand for luxury goods that is derived from cultural phenomena such as fashion.
    c. the demand for factors of production by firms.
    d. the demand for derivatives.

8. The more elastic the demand for a firm's good:
    a. the more elastic the firm's derived demand for factors.
    b. the less elastic the firm's derived demand for factors.
    c. The elasticity of demand for a firm's good has nothing to do with the firm's derived demand.
    d. The elasticity of demand could cause the elasticity of the derived demand to be either higher or lower.

9. As a factor becomes more important in the production process, the:
    a. firm's derived demand for the factor becomes less elastic.
    b. firm's derived demand for the factor becomes more elastic.
    c. firm's derived demand will not be affected.
    d. elasticity of the derived demand could become either higher or lower.

10. Economists distinguish entrepreneurship from labor because:
    a. entrepreneurship is more like capital.
    b. entrepreneurship has nothing to do with labor.
    c. entrepreneurship is such an important part of labor that it needs a specific discussion.
    d. entrepreneurs receive only profit.

11. A firm has just changed from being a competitive firm to being a monopolist. Its derived demand for labor:
    a. will increase.
    b. will decrease.

c. might increase or might decrease.

d. is unaffected because whether the firm is a competitive firm or a monopolist has no effect on the firm's derived demand for labor.

12. A monopsony in a labor market has:
    a. only a single seller and a single buyer of labor.
    b. only a single seller of labor.
    c. only a single buyer of labor.
    d. one seller and two buyers.

13. Compared to a competitive labor market, a monopsonist hires:
    a. fewer workers and pays them a higher wage.
    b. fewer workers and pays them a lower wage.
    c. more workers and pays them a higher wage.
    d. more workers and pays them a lower wage.

14. Which of the following cases of discrimination is likely to be most easily eliminated with market forces?
    a. A warehousing firm turns down an applicant because she is physically unable to lift boxes of the weight required by the job.
    b. An Internet firm begins a younger worker at a lower pay because younger workers are more likely to leave the job shortly after being trained.
    c. A manufacturing firm decides against hiring an individual who is black (even though the candidate is the most qualified) because the person doing the hiring is white.
    d. A retail store decides against hiring an individual who is black (even though the candidate is the most qualified) because they believe their customers will be less likely to buy from blacks.

15. Discrimination that is likely the most difficult to eliminate is discrimination that has:
    a. a social motivation.
    b. a cultural motivation.
    c. a political motivation.
    d. an economic motivation.

A1. The graph below shows the marginal revenue product of workers. If the wage is $10, approximately how many workers should it hire?
    a. 4.
    b. 8.
    c. 12.
    d. 16.

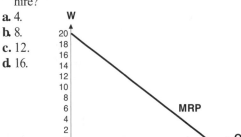

A2. The marginal product of input A is 20. The marginal product of input B is 40. The price of input A is 2. The price of input B is 3. Which of the following would be the best recommendation you could give based on this information? The firm should
    a. hire more A and less B.
    b. hire more B and less A.
    c. hire more of both A and B.
    d. not change its hiring of A and B.

● POTENTIAL ESSAY QUESTIONS

You may also see essay questions similar to the "Problems & Applications" and "Brain Teasers" exercises.

1. What is a monopsony and how does a monopsony determine the quantity of workers employed and the wage it pays? How does this compare with the competitive labor market outcome? What is a bilateral monopoly? Could a bilateral monopoly result in a competitive labor market outcome?

2. How do market, social, and political forces interact in determining the equilibrium wage and quantity of workers employed in any real-world labor market?

━━━ ● ANSWERS ● ━━━

SHORT-ANSWER QUESTIONS

1.   Work involves opportunity cost. By working one more hour, you have one less hour to devote to nonmarket activities. The theory of rational choice in the case of work means that you will supply work as long as the opportunity cost of working is less than the wage received. Since the opportunity cost of working on a holiday is greater than on other days, firms must offer workers higher wages to work on Thanksgiving Day. This demonstrates that the supply curve for labor is upward sloping: the higher the wage, the higher the quantity of labor supplied. (365-370)

2.   An increase in the marginal tax rate is likely to reduce the quantity of labor supplied because it reduces the net wage of individuals and lowers the opportunity cost of not working. (371)

3.   Factors that affect the elasticity of labor supply include (1) the individuals' opportunity costs of working, (2) the type of labor market, (3) the elasticity of the individuals' labor supplied, and (4) the individuals entering and leaving the market. (371-372)

4.   Derived demand is the demand for factors of production by firms, which depends on consumers' demands. For example, if the demand for medical care increases, the demand for nurses increases. It simply takes more nurses to deliver more medical care. (372-373)

5.   Factors that influence the elasticity of labor demand are (1) the elasticity of demand for the firm's good, (2) the relative importance of labor to production, (3) the possibility of, and costs of, substitution in production, and (4) the degree to which marginal productivity falls with an increase in labor. (373-374)

6.   A *monopsonist* is the only buyer in a market. A *bilateral monopoly* is a market in which a single seller faces a single buyer. (377-378)

7.   Real-world labor markets are complicated and must be explained through the interaction of political, social and market forces. For example, the fact that women earn about 85 percent of men's earnings must be explained by these forces. Here are some of the many ways in which these forces can explain this phenomenon: It is argued that employers discriminate against women, paying them less for the same job, because they have a distaste for hiring women. This is an example of social forces at play and would result in lower wages. Women's lower pay may also result from social forces that discourage mothers from working outside the home so that women will supply labor intermittently, lowering their wage. This is an example of social forces and market forces. Comparable worth laws, anti-discrimination laws, and affirmative action laws have been passed in an effort to counteract this pay inequality. These are examples of social, political and legal forces at play in real-world labor markets. (379-381)

8.   Three types of discrimination are (1) discrimination based on individual characteristics that affect job performance, (2) discrimination based on correctly perceived statistical characteristics of the group; and (3) discrimination on individual characteristics that do not affect job performance or that are incorrectly perceived. (381-384)

━━━ ● ANSWERS ● ━━━

MATCHING

1-c; 2-d; 3-j; 4-m; 5-l; 6-e; 7-g; 8-h; 9-f; 10-k; 11-a; 12-i; 13-b.

━━━ ● ANSWERS ● ━━━

PROBLEMS AND APPLICATIONS

1.   a.   Equilibrium wage and number of workers with demand, D_0, and supply, S, are shown on the graph below as W_E and Q_E. At this point, the quantity of labor demanded equals the quantity of labor supplied. At a wage above W_E, there will be pressure for wages to fall because the quantity of labor supplied exceeds the quantity of labor demanded. At a wage below W_E, there will be pressure for wages to rise because the

quantity of labor demanded exceeds the quantity of labor supplied. (Figure 16-2 on page 373)

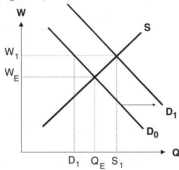

b. If wages were set by the government at W_1, the quantity of labor supplied would rise to S_1 and the quantity of labor demanded would fall to D_1. Quantity supplied would exceed quantity demanded. This is shown in the graph above. (Figure 16-3 on page 376)

c. A technological innovation that leads to a higher demand for labor will lead to a higher equilibrium wage and higher quantity of labor employed as the demand curve shifts to the right from D_0 to D_1. Equilibrium wage will rise to W_1 and equilibrium quantity of labor will rise to S_1. (374-375 and Figure 16-3 on page 376)

2. a. The demand for labor would increase, increasing W and Q. (Applying concepts introduced in the appendix to this chapter, notice that the increase in the demand for the product increases the price of the product. The higher price for the product increases workers' marginal revenue product—MRP = MPP × P—which is the competitive firms' demand for labor.) (374-375, 392-396)

b. The supply of labor would decrease on Christmas Day, which would increase W and decrease Q. (374-376)

c. Supply would decrease, increasing W and decreasing Q. (374-376)

d. Supply would increase, decreasing W and increasing Q. (374-376)

e. Demand would decrease, decreasing W and Q. (374-376)

f. Demand would increase, increasing W and Q. (374-376)

g. Supply would increase, decreasing W and increasing Q. (374-376)

h. Demand would increase (according to the appendix: workers' MRP would be greater), increasing W and Q. (374-376)

3. a. If the market is competitive, the wage and employment level will be where the demand and supply curves for labor intersect. This is at W_c and Q_c respectively on the graph below. (376-377, and Figure 16-4)

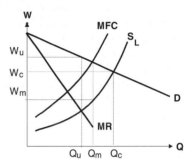

b. The monopsonist will hire workers where the marginal factor cost of labor intersects the demand for labor. A monopsonist would hire Q_m workers, less than the competitive level, and pay a wage W_m, lower than the competitive wage. (376-378, and Figure 16-4)

c. Unions would push for higher wages than a firm in a competitive market or a monopsonist would be willing to pay. The wage would be somewhere between W_u and W_m and would depend on negotiating skills and other noneconomic forces. The number of workers hired would then be somewhere between Q_u and Q_m depending upon the negotiated wage. (376-378, and Figure 16-4)

A1. Below is the completed table for a perfectly competitive firm which produces halogen light bulbs.

No. of Workers	Total Product per hour	Marginal Physical Product per hour	Average Product per hour	Marginal Revenue Product per hour
20	200		10	
A 21	215	15	10.24	15
B 22	228	13	10.36	13
C 23	239	11	10.39	11
D 24	248	9	10.33	9
E 25	255	7	10.2	7
F 26	260	5	10	5

We use the following relationships to fill in the table: Marginal physical product equals the change in the total product. Average product is the total product divided by the number of workers. Marginal revenue product equals marginal physical product times the price of the product. (392-394, especially Figure A16-1)

a. The corresponding labor demand curve is shown on the graph below. The demand curve shows the marginal revenue product at each quantity of labor. Labor demand is a derived demand. A firm is willing to pay a wage up to the marginal revenue product of the additional worker to hire that additional worker. That is, keep hiring workers for as long as MRP >W and stop hiring when MRP = W. (394-396, especially Figure A16-1)

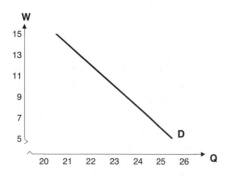

b. If the price of halogen light bulbs fell to $.50 per bulb, the marginal revenue product would be halved and the demand curve for labor would shift in as shown on the accompanying graph and table. (394-396, especially Figure A16-1)

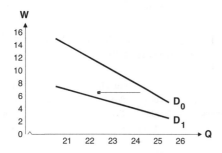

No. of Workers	Total Product per hour	Marginal Physical Product per hour	Average Product per hour	($0.50) Marginal Revenue Product per hour
	20	200		10	
A	21	215	15	10.24	7.5
B	22	228	13	10.36	6.5
C	23	239	11	10.39	5.5
D	24	248	9	10.33	4.5
E	25	255	7	10.2	3.5
F	26	260	5	10	2.5

c. At $1 per bulb and wages of $7 per hour, the firm would hire up to 25 workers; At $1 per bulb and a minimum wage of $11 per hour the firm would hire up to 23 workers. A firm in a competitive industry will hire up to the point where the wage equals *MRP* (*MPP* times *P*). (392-396)

━━━━━━━   ANSWERS   ━━━━━━━

A BRAIN TEASER

1. See the table on the next page. The cost minimizing condition exists at the combination of inputs (factors) employed for which the MPP/P for each input is equal. Therefore, Combination B should be adopted. For Combination A, the productivity for the money spent (MPP/P) is greater for capital than for the other inputs. Therefore, more capital and less labor and raw materials should be employed. By doing so, the firm will be able to produce the same amount at a lower cost. For Combination C, more raw materials should be employed in the production process while less labor and capital should be employed (because MPP/P for raw materials is higher).

   Remember: if the cost minimization condition is not met, the firm could hire more of the input with the higher marginal product-to-price ratio and less of the other inputs, and produce the same amount of output at a lower cost. (396)

	MPP of Raw Material	MPP of Labor	MPP of Capital
Comb. A:	5	10	50
	(MPP/P=5/5=1)	(MPP/P=10/10=1)	(MPP/P=50/20=2.5)
Comb. B:	10	20	40
	(MPP/P=10/5=2)	(MPP/P=20/10=2)	(MPP/P=40/20=2)
Comb. C:	20	15	30
	(MPP/P=20/5=4)	(MPP/P=15/10=1.5)	(MPP/P=30/20=1.5)

ANSWERS

MULTIPLE CHOICE

1. a　The supply curve of labor is generally considered to be upward sloping. When there is a movement along the supply curve caused by an increase in the wage, the movement is called an increase in the quantity supplied, not an increase in supply. See pages 368-369.

2. a　The opportunity cost of not working increases as the wage rate rises and that is why the labor supply curve slopes upward. See pages 369-370.

3. d　An increase in the marginal tax rate will reduce the quantity of labor supplied because it reduces the net wage of individuals and hence, through individuals' incentive effect, causes them to work less. See pages 371.

4. a　A need-based program reduces people's incentives to prevent themselves from becoming needy, and thus a need-based program increases the number of needy. See page 371.

5. c　The elasticity of demand has no impact on the elasticity of supply. See pages 373-374.

6. d　The number of primary workers compared to the number of secondary workers has nothing to do with elasticity. See pages 373-374.

7. c　Derived demand refers to the fact that the demand for factors of production is derived from the demand for a firm's goods. Because consumers demand a firm's goods, the firm demands factors of production to produce those goods. See pages 372-373.

8. a　When a rise in price will cause significant loss of revenue (which it does when demand for the good is elastic), the firm takes that into account in its decision of what to pay workers and how many workers to hire. See page 373.

9. a　As the importance of a factor to the production process rises, the less elastic is demand. This is because a more important factor has fewer substitutes. See page 373.

10. c　Entrepreneurship is a type of creative labor that is very important and needs a separate discussion. Entrepreneurs can receive more than merely profit. See page 374.

11. b　The monopolist uses marginal revenue, which is lower than the price that the competitive firm uses. Therefore, the monopolist's derived demand for labor is lower. See pages 377-378.

12. c　While a monopoly is a market with a single seller, a monopsony is a market with a single buyer. See page 377.

13. b　A profit-maximizing monopsonist will pay a lower wage and hire fewer workers than if that labor market were competitive. See pages 377-378.

14. c　Differential treatment based upon individual characteristics that do not affect job performance is costly to firms. Market forces will work toward eliminating this type of discrimination. The warehousing firm is turning down an applicant who cannot fulfill the duties of the job. The Internet firm is basing its decision on characteristics of the group to which the individual belongs. Although the particular individual may not quit the job, such statistical discrimination, using such rules of thumb do have a basis in keeping costs of a firm down. The final option is also costly to the firm. The easiest discrimination to eliminate is when economic incentives are working to eliminate it. See pages 379-381.

15. d   Discrimination that is economically motivated out of individuals pursuing their self-interest is most difficult to eliminate. People are least motivated to adopt change they believe may personally hurt them. See pages 381-384.

A1. b   The firm should hire workers until the wage equals the marginal revenue product. See pages 392-394.

A2. b   The marginal revenue per dollar is higher for input B so the firm should hire more of B and less of A. The other answers do not meet the cost minimization condition. See pages 395-396.

ANSWERS

POTENTIAL ESSAY QUESTIONS

The following are annotated answers. They indicate the general idea behind the answer.

1.   A monopsony is a market in which a single firm is the only buyer. The monopsonist's demand for labor is the market demand for labor. The monopsony also faces the market supply curve. The profit maximizing monopsony will hire fewer workers and pay a lower wage than the competitive outcome.

   A bilateral monopoly is a monopsony employing unionized workers. It's a bilateral monopoly because there is monopoly power on both sides of the labor market. It's possible that the monopoly power of the two sides will cancel out, giving rise to a competitive wage and quantity of labor employed.

2.   The economic forces of demand and supply, social forces, and legal or government forces all interact in the labor market. Social forces of "fairness," seniority, and discrimination as well as the political forces of child labor laws, comparable worth laws, equal opportunity laws, and laws governing unions etc., all affect the labor market along with the market forces of supply and demand.

WHO GETS WHAT?
THE DISTRIBUTION OF INCOME

● CHAPTER AT A GLANCE

This review is based upon the learning objectives that open the chapter.

1. A Lorenz curve is a geometric representation of the share distribution of income among families in a given country at a given time. (399-400)

   Shows the relative equality of the distribution of income. The farther below the diagonal line, the more unequal the distribution of income.

2. Poverty is defined by the U.S. government as earning income equal to or less than three times an average family's minimum food expenditures as calculated by the U.S. Department of Agriculture. The official poverty measure is an absolute measure because it is based on the minimum food budget for a family. It is a relative measure because it is adjusted for average inflation. (402)

   The poverty income threshold level is approximately $18,000 for a family of four. Poverty figures, like all statistics, should be used with care. Think about some causes of poverty and the problems it poses for society.

3. The United States has less income inequality than most developing countries but more income inequality than many developed countries. (404-406)

   There is more income inequality among countries than income inequality within a country. Worldwide, income inequality is enormous. Therefore, the Lorenz curve of world income would show much more inequality than the Lorenz curve for a particular country.

4. In the United States wealth is significantly more unequally distributed than is income. (406-407)

   The bottom fifth have no net wealth while the top fifth have 84 percent of the wealth.

5. Two alternative ways to describe income distribution are the share distribution of income inequality and the income distribution according to socioeconomic characteristics. (399, 407-410)

   Most Americans are in the middle class. However, income differs substantially by class and by other socioeconomic characteristics such as age, race, and gender.

6. Three problems in determining whether an equal income distribution is fair are:
   (1) people don't start from equivalent positions; (2) people's needs differ; and (3) people's efforts differ. (412)

   When most people talk about believing in equality of income, they usually mean an equality of opportunity to earn income.

   Fairness is a philosophical question. People must judge a program's fairness for themselves.

7. Three side effects of redistribution of income include:
   a. the labor/leisure incentive effect;
   b. the avoidance and evasion incentive effects;
   c. the incentive effect to look more needy than you are. (412-413)

   Income is difficult to redistribute because of incentive effects of taxes, avoidance and evasion effects of taxes, and incentive effects of redistribution programs.

8. Expenditure programs have been more successful than taxes in redistributing income. (413-418)

   On the whole, the U.S. tax system is roughly proportional, so it is not very effective as a means of redistributing income. Government spending programs are more effective than tax policy in reducing income inequality in the United States.

● SHORT-ANSWER QUESTIONS

1.   What does a Lorenz curve show?

2.   What is the U.S. official definition of *poverty*?

3.   How is the poverty definition both an absolute and a relative measure?

4.   How does income inequality in the United States compare with other countries?

5.   How does the Lorenz curve for household wealth compare with the Lorenz curve for family income in the United States?

6.   What are two alternative ways to describe income distribution?

7.   You and your friends are having a lunchtime discussion about fairness. A friend offers a statement that since income distribution has become more unequal in the past few decades, income distribution in the United States has become less and less fair. Assume you are a contrarian. How do you respond?

8.   "Nevertheless," your friend says, "I believe the current distribution is not fair. The government should do something to make the income distribution more equal." You agree to some extent, but warn that there are side effects of redistributing income. State your argument.

9.   Which has been more successful in the United States in redistributing income: expenditure or taxation programs? Why?

10. What are five expenditure programs that redistribute income?

MATCHING THE TERMS
Match the terms to their definitions

____ 1. income
____ 2. Lorenz curve
____ 3. Medicare
____ 4. poverty threshold
____ 5. progressive tax
____ 6. proportional tax
____ 7. public assistance
____ 8. regressive tax
____ 9. share distribution of income
____ 10. Social Security
____ 11. socioeconomic distribution of income
____ 12. Supplemental Security Income
____ 13. unemployment compensation
____ 14. wealth

a. A geometric representation of the share distribution of income among families in a given country at a given time.

b. The income below which a family is considered to live in poverty.

c. The relative division of total income among income groups.

d. Payments received plus or minus changes in value in a person's assets in a specific time period.

e. The value of the things individuals own less the value of what they owe.

f. The relative division or allocation of total income among relevant socioeconomic groups.

g. An average tax rate that increases with income.

h. A social insurance program that provides financial benefits to the elderly and disabled and to their dependents and/or survivors.

i. Means-tested social programs targeted to the poor and providing financial, nutritional, medical, and housing assistance.

j. An average tax rate that is constant regardless of income.

k. A multibillion-dollar medical insurance system.

l. Short-term financial assistance, regardless of need, to eligible individuals who are temporarily out of work.

m. An average tax rate that decreases with income.

n. A federal program that pays benefits, based on need, to the elderly, blind, and disabled.

● PROBLEMS AND APPLICATIONS

1. Use the Lorenz curve below to answer the following questions.

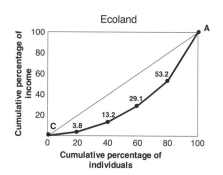

a. What percentage of total income do the top 20 percent of individuals in Ecoland receive?

b. What percentage of total income do the top 40 percent of individuals in Ecoland receive?

c. Which value, the one in (a) or the one (b), is greater? Why?

d. What does the straight line in the diagram represent? Describe points A and C. Why is the Lorenz curve always anchored at those points?

2. Use the following table to answer the questions.

Income quintile	% of Total Family Income		
	Eco-land	Fantasy-land	Text-land
Lowest 20%	5%	7%	2%
Second quintile	8	10	6
Third quintile	10	25	9
Fourth quintile	20	25	19
Highest 20%	57	33	64

a. Draw a Lorenz curve for each country.

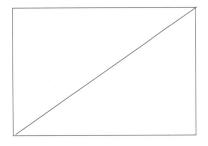

b. Rank the countries from most equal income distribution to least equal income distribution.

3. For each of the following state whether the tax is most likely proportional, regressive, or progressive with income.

a. 5 cent per gallon tax on gasoline.

b. School taxes based on assessed value of a home.

c. Sales tax of 6 percent.

d. Medical insurance taxes of 1.45% on all income.

● A BRAIN TEASER

1. You are completing your tax return. You are filing as a single taxpayer. Your income is $87,300. Deductions are $20,000. The rate is 15% for taxable income up to $22,750, 28% of income between $22,750 and $55,100, and 31% of income above $55,100.

a. Calculate your tax liability.

b. Calculate your average tax rate.

c.   Calculate your marginal tax rate.

d.   Is the tax schedule proportional, regressive, or progressive? Explain your answer.

● MULTIPLE CHOICE

Circle the one best answer for each of the following questions:

1.   The Lorenz curve is:
   a. a type of supply curve.
   b. a type of demand curve.
   c. a geometric representation of the share distribution of income.
   d. a geometric representation of the socioeconomic distribution of income.

2.   Refer to the graph below. Which of the four Lorenz curves demonstrates the most income inequality?
   a. A.
   b. B.
   c. C.
   d. D.

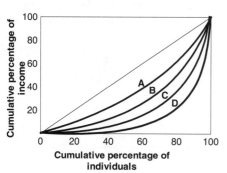

3.   A family is in poverty if its income is:
   a. above the poverty income threshold level.
   b. less than $14,280.
   c. less than three times the average food budget for that family size.
   d. less than five times the national average household income level for that family size.

4.   The official definition of poverty is:
   a. an absolute measure of poverty since it is based upon a minimum food budget determined in the 1960s.
   b. a relative measure of poverty since the poverty line is defined as the income level that exceeds the income of 15 percent of all households in the United States.
   c. both a relative and absolute measure of poverty since the minimum food budget is adjusted each year for average inflation in the economy.
   d. neither an absolute nor relative measure of poverty since the poverty threshold changes each year.

5.   If the government increases the amount of food stamps and housing assistance it gives out, the direct effect on U.S. poverty, as officially defined:
   a. will be reduced.
   b. will be increased.
   c. will remain unchanged.
   d. cannot be determined from the information.

6.   A Lorenz curve for the entire world would show:
   a. more income inequality than in the United States.
   b. less income inequality than in the United States.
   c. approximately the same level of income inequality as in the United States.
   d. no income inequality.

7.   In a Lorenz curve for the United States, household wealth would:
   a. show the same amount of inequality as does family income.
   b. show more inequality than does family income.
   c. show less inequality than does family income.
   d. would show no wealth inequality at all.

8. Refer to the graph below. The Gini coefficient is shown by which area?
   a. A/B
   b. A/(A + B).
   c. B/A.
   d. B/(A + B).

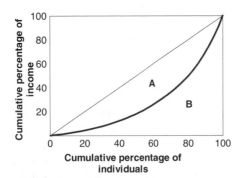

9. The U.S. class system is *best* represented by which shape?
   a. A diamond.
   b. A right-side-up pyramid with upper class on the top.
   c. An upside-down pyramid with upper class on the top.
   d. A square.

10. Imposing a tax of 40 percent on high income workers in order to give the revenue to low income workers may not be especially effective in redistributing income if the tax:
    a. has large incentive effects.
    b. has no incentive effects.
    c. is seen as a sin tax.
    d. is not seen as a sin tax.

11. The largest government program to redistribute income is the:
    a. Social Security system.
    b. Medicaid program.
    c. food stamp program.
    d. Supplemental Security Income (SSI) program.

12. On the whole, the U.S. tax system is:
    a. unfair.
    b. roughly progressive.
    c. roughly proportional.
    d. roughly regressive.

13. In the United States, government spending programs:
    a. are less effective than tax policies in redistributing income.
    b. are more effective than tax policies in redistributing income.
    c. and tax policies are equally effective in redistributing income.
    d. and tax policies have had no measurable impact in redistributing income.

14. The U.S. federal program that pays benefits, based on need, to the elderly, blind, and disabled is called:
    a. Medicare.
    b. Medicaid.
    c. Temporary Assistance to Needy Families (TANF)
    d. Supplemental Security Income (SSI).

● POTENTIAL ESSAY QUESTIONS

You may also see essay questions similar to the "Problems & Applications" and "Brain Teasers" exercises.

1. Explain three problems in determining whether an equal income distribution is fair. When people talk about believing in the equality of income, what do they usually mean?

2. What are two direct methods through which government redistributes income? Which has generally been more successful and why?

ANSWERS

SHORT-ANSWER QUESTIONS

1. A Lorenz curve is a geometric representation of the share distribution of income among families in a given country at a given time. (399-400)

2. The official definition of *poverty* is an income equal to or less than three times an average family's minimum food expenditures as calculated by the U.S. Department of Agriculture. (402)

3. The official poverty measure is earning an absolute measure because it is based on the minimum food budget for a family. It is a relative measure because it is adjusted for average inflation. (402-403)

4. The United States has less income inequality than most developing countries but more income inequality than many developed countries. (405-406)

5. The Lorenz curve for household wealth is more bowed than the Lorenz curve for family income. This means that household wealth is less equally distributed than family income. (406-407 and Figure 17-5)

6. Two alternative ways to describe income distribution are the share distribution of income inequality and income distribution according to socioeconomic characteristics. (399)

7. Determining whether an equal income distribution is fair is problematic. You tell your friend that, first of all, people do not start from equivalent positions and income depends upon those initial positions. Second, people's needs differ; some people are happy with less income, while others seem to need a higher income. Lastly, people's efforts differ; some people are willing to work harder than others. Shouldn't that effort be rewarded with higher income? Equality is not synonymous with fairness. (410-412)

8. Although some might agree that a more equal distribution is desirable, there are side effects of redistributing income. They are: (1) A tax to redistribute income may result in a switch from labor to leisure and, consequently, less production and less total income. (2) An increase in taxes to redistribute income might lead to attempts to avoid or evade taxes, leading to a decrease in measured income. (3) Government programs to redistribute money may cause people to make themselves look poorer than they really are. (410-412)

9. In the United States, expenditure programs have been more successful than tax programs for redistributing income. This is because, on the whole, the U.S. tax system is roughly proportional, so it is not very effective as a means of redistributing income. (417-418)

10. Five expenditure programs to redistribute income are (1) Social Security, (2) public assistance, (3) Supplemental Security Income, (4) unemployment compensation, and (5) housing programs. (415-417)

ANSWERS

MATCHING

1-d; 2-a; 3-k; 4-b; 5-g; 6-j; 7-i; 8-m; 9-c; 10-h; 11-f; 12-n; 13-l; 14-e.

ANSWERS

PROBLEMS AND APPLICATIONS

1. **a.** 46.8%. The top 20 percent of individuals earn 46.8 percent of the income. Calculate this by starting at 80% on the horizontal axis. Draw a vertical line to the Lorenz curve. Look at the value on the vertical axis where this line intersects the Lorenz curve. This is the percent of income that the bottom 80% of individuals earn. To get the amount that the top 20% earn, subtract this number, 53.2, from 100. (399-400)

    b. 70.9%. Going through the same exercise as in 1(a) but starting at 60%, we find that the bottom 60% earn 29.1% of total income. Subtracting this from 100, we get 70.9%, the percent of total income earned by the top 40%. (399-400)

c. (b) is greater than (a). This has to be true, because the vertical axis is the *cumulative* percentage of income. If the top 20% earn a certain percentage of the total, the top 40% includes that top 20% plus more. (399-400)

d. The straight line represents the Lorenz curve if income were equally distributed. Point A says that 100% of individuals earn 100% of the income. This is true by definition. Point C says that 0% of individuals earn 0% of the income. The Lorenz curve is anchored at those points by definition. (399-400)

2. a. First we want to calculate the cumulative percentage of income for each country. We do this below by cumulatively adding together consecutive percentages.

Income quintile	Cumulative % of Income		
	Eco-land	Fantasy-land	Text-land
Lowest 20%	5%	7%	2%
Second quintile	13	17	8
Third quintile	23	42	17
Fourth quintile	43	67	36
Highest 20%	100	100	100

The Lorenz curve is the graph of these values connected. This is shown in the graph below. (399-400)

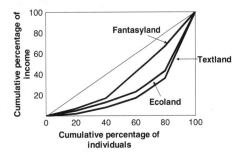

b. Fantasyland; Ecoland; Textland. The country most bowed out to the right of the diagonal line has the least equal income distribution. This is Textland. The country bowed out the least has the most equal income distribution. This is Fantasyland. Ecoland is in the middle. (399-400)

3. a. 5 cent per gallon tax on gasoline is a sales tax and sales taxes tend to be slightly regressive since poor people often spend a higher percentage of their incomes on gasoline than do rich people. (414)

b. School taxes based on assessed value of a home are considered to be roughly proportional since the value of a person's home is related to income. (414)

c. A sales tax is regressive since poor people often consume a higher percentage of their incomes than do rich people. (414)

d. Medical insurance taxes are proportional since the rate is 1.45% on all income, no matter how high or low. (414)

--- **ANSWERS** ---

A BRAIN TEASER

1. a. $16,252.50. First deduct $20,000 from $87,300 to get taxable income of $67,300. You pay 15% on the first $22,750, 28% on income from $22,751 to $55,100, and 31% on the remaining $12,200. Your taxes are $.15 \times \$22,750 + .28 \times 32,350 + .31 \times \$12,200 = \$3,412.5 + \$9,058 + \$3,782 = \$16,252.50$. (414)

b. 18.6%. Your average tax rate is total taxes divided by total income: $16,252.50/$87,300. (414)

c. 31%. Your marginal tax rate is the rate at which your last dollar earned is taxed. This is 31%. (414)

d. The tax schedule is progressive. A progressive tax is one in which the average tax rate increases with income. As can be seen by the tax schedule, the marginal tax rate is increasing. Since the marginal tax rate is increasing, and it is above the average tax rate (because of deductions), the average tax rate is increasing too. (414)

--- **ANSWERS** ---

MULTIPLE CHOICE

1. c   A Lorenz curve describes how income is distributed in a country. It has proportion of the population on the horizontal axis and proportion of income on the vertical axis. See pages 399-400.

2. d   A Lorenz curve describes how income is distributed in a country. It has proportion of the population on the horizontal axis and proportion of income on the vertical axis. The further the Lorenz curve is from the diagonal, the more unequally income is distributed. See pages 399-400.

3. c   A family is in poverty if its income is equal to or less than three times an average family's minimum food expenditures as calculated by the U.S. Department of Agriculture. See page 402.

4. c   The poverty threshold equals three times the minimum food budget. Thus, it is in part an absolute measure. But since it is adjusted for average inflation and not just inflation on food and since food prices have risen more slowly than average inflation, it is a relative measure. See page 402.

5. c   These aspects of income are not taken into account in determining U.S. poverty figures. See page 403.

6. a   Since world income is more unequally divided among countries, the world Lorenz curve would have to show more income inequality. See page 405.

7. b   In the United States wealth is considerably less equally distributed than income. See pages 406-407.

8. b   The Gini coefficient describes the degree of income inequality. It is the area between the diagonal and the Lorenz curve divided by the total area below the diagonal. See "Knowing the Tools" box on page 404.

9. a   The U.S. class system is best seen as a diamond. There is a relatively small upper class and a small lower class, and a large middle class. See pages 408-409, especially Figure 17-6.

10. a   Incentive effects can undermine attempts to redistribute income. See pages 412-413.

11. a   As stated in the text, the Social Security system is by far the largest expenditure program to supplement income. See page 415.

12. c   The overall U.S. tax system is roughly proportional. This can be deduced from the observation that the U.S. tax system does little to redistribute income. Whether it is fair or not is a matter of opinion. See pages 417-418 and Figure 17-7.

13. b   In the United States, government spending programs are more effective than tax policies in redistributing income. See pages 417-418.

14. d   Medicare is a multibillion-dollar medical assistance insurance system for the elderly. Medicaid is medical assistance to the poor. TANF provides assistance to needy families with children under age 19. See pages 415-417.

━━━━━ ANSWERS ━━━━━

POTENTIAL ESSAY QUESTIONS

The following are annotated answers. They indicate the general idea behind the answer.

1.   Three problems in determining whether an equal income distribution is fair are (1) people don't start from equal positions, (2) people's needs differ, and (3) people's efforts differ.

When people talk about believing in equality of income, they usually mean they believe in equality of opportunity for comparably endowed individuals to earn income. If equal opportunity of equals leads to inequality of income, that inequality in income is fair. Unfortunately, there's enormous latitude for debate on what constitutes equal opportunity of equals.

2.   The two methods are: taxation (policies that tax the rich more than the poor) and expenditures (programs that help the poor more than the rich). Most government redistribution of income works through expenditure programs (public assistance; social programs), not through taxes. This is because on the whole, the U.S. tax system is roughly proportional, so it is not very effective as a means of redistributing income.

GOVERNMENT POLICY AND MARKET FAILURES

18

CHAPTER AT A GLANCE

This review is based upon the learning objectives that open the chapter.

1. An externality is an effect of a decision on a third party not taken into account by the decision maker. (423-425)

   Externalities can either be negative (have undesirable social side effects in which case society would want less of the good) or positive (have desirable social side effects in which case society would want more of the good). Externalities are only one source of market failure.

   3 sources of market failure:
   - *Externalities*
   - *Public goods*
   - *Imperfect information*

   Any time a market failure exists there is a reason for possible government intervention to improve the outcome. However, government failure (government intervention in the market to improve the market failure actually making matters worse) is always a possibility. Economic policy is often a choice between market failure and government failure.

2. Ways to deal with externalities include (1) direct regulation, (2) incentive policies (tax incentive policies and market incentive policies), and (3) voluntary solutions. (425-428)

   Economists tend to like incentive policies to deal with externalities.

   The optimal policy is one in which the marginal cost of undertaking the policy equals the marginal benefit of that policy.

3. A public good is a good that is nonexclusive (no one can be excluded from its benefits) and nonrival (consumption by one does not preclude consumption by others). (429-432)

   The public/private good differentiation is seldom clear-cut since many goods are somewhat public and somewhat private in nature, with the degree of publicness in large part determined by available technology.

   It is difficult for government to decide the efficient quantity of a public good. If the public good is to be financed by a tax on citizens who benefit from it, individuals have an incentive to conceal their willingness to pay for it.

   Similarly, if citizens think they will not be the ones taxed to fund the public good, but will benefit from it, they have an incentive to exaggerate their willingness to pay. We get the free rider problem with public goods.

4. Adverse selection problems can occur when buyers and sellers have different amounts of information about the good for sale. (432-434)

   When there is a lack of information or buyers and sellers don't have equal information, markets in some goods may not work well (hence, market failure). Adverse selection problems can be partially resolved by signaling.

   2 general policies to deal with informational problems are:

   - *Regulatory approach*
   - *Market approach*

5. Should government intervene in the market? It depends. (436-437)

One needs to weigh the benefits against the costs of government intervention on a case-by-case basis and remain as objective as possible in the measurement of those benefits and costs.

Government failure may occur because sometimes:

- *Governments don't have an incentive to correct the problem*
- *Governments don't have enough information to deal with the problem*
- *Intervention is more complicated than it initially seems*
- *The bureaucratic nature of government precludes fine-tuning*
- *Government intervention often leads to more government intervention*

SHORT-ANSWER QUESTIONS

1. What are three sources of market failures?

2. Suppose a steel plant begins production near your home. The resulting smoke pollutes the air you breathe. You bring a complaint to the local town board saying, "I didn't ask for that factory to be built, but I'm having to endure polluted air." The basis of your complaint is an example of what concept in economics?

3. Briefly describe the three methods of dealing with externalities.

4. Which of the methods you stated in Question #3 do most economists prefer to use when dealing with externalities?

5. What is an optimal policy?

6. Define "public good." Why is it difficult for government to decide the efficient quantity of a public good to provide?

7. What are two ways society can deal with informational problems that lead to market failures?

8. When should the government intervene in the economy?

MATCHING THE TERMS
Match the terms to their definitions

____ **1.** adverse selection problem

____ **2.** direct regulation

____ **3.** efficient

____ **4.** effluent fees

____ **5.** externality

____ **6.** free rider problem

____ **7.** government failure

____ **8.** inefficient

____ **9.** marginal social benefit

____ **10.** marginal social cost

____ **11.** market failure

____ **12.** market incentive plan

____ **13.** negative externality

____ **14.** optimal policy

____ **15.** positive externality

____ **16.** public good

____ **17.** signaling

____ **18.** tax incentive program

a. A situation in which the invisible hand pushes in such a way that individual decisions do not lead to socially optimal outcomes.

b. Equals the marginal private costs of production plus the cost of the negative externalities associated with that production.

c. The effect of a decision on a third party that is not taken into account by the decision maker.

d. The amount of a good people are allowed to use is directly limited by the government.

e. When the effect of a decision not taken into account by the decision maker is detrimental to others.

f. Charges imposed by government on the level of pollution created.

g. When the effect of a decision not taken into account by the decision maker is beneficial to others.

h. A plan requiring market participants to certify that they have reduced total consumption—not necessarily their own individual consumption—by a specified amount.

i. A good that is nonexclusive (no one can be excluded from its benefits) and nonrival (consumption by one does not preclude consumption by others).

j. Achieving a goal at the lowest cost in total resources without consideration as to who pays that cost.

k. A problem that occurs when buyers and sellers have different amounts of information about the good for sale.

l. When government intervention in the market to improve a market failure makes the situation worse.

m. Individuals' unwillingness to share in the cost of a public good.

n. Equals the marginal private benefit of consuming a good plus the benefit of the positive externalities resulting from consuming that good.

o. Achieving a goal in a more costly manner than necessary.

p. A policy in which the marginal cost of undertaking the policy equals the marginal benefit.

q. A program using a tax to create incentives for individuals to structure their activities in a way that is consistent with the desired ends.

r. An action taken by an informed party that reveals information to an uninformed party that offsets the false signal that caused the adverse selection problem in the first place.

● PROBLEMS AND APPLICATIONS

1. Secondhand cigarette smoke is believed to have a negative effect on the health of non-smokers. These people have not chosen to smoke, but nevertheless are negatively affected by the choice of others to smoke. Draw the market for cigarettes showing the marginal cost and marginal social cost of smoking cigarettes if this belief is correct.

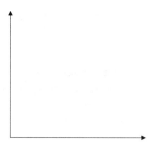

Pollution Control	Total Social Benefits	Total Social Costs
1	$200,000	$40,000
2	$275,000	$75,000
3	$330,000	$110,000
4	$375,000	$145,000
5	$410,000	$180,000
6	$435,000	$215,000

a. Demonstrate graphically the market price and quantity of cigarettes.

b. Demonstrate graphically the efficient level of cigarettes. Explain your answer.

c. Demonstrate graphically the tax the government would have to impose on cigarettes to arrive at the efficient level and price of cigarettes.

d. Demonstrate graphically the tax revenue that government would collect from such a tax.

2. A small city located by a lake has been dumping its raw sewage into the lake. This has created a public outcry by those citizens who like to fish, swim, and water-ski in the lake. The city council has surveyed the community and has estimated the social benefits associated with different levels of pollution control. These benefits, as well as the costs associated with pollution control efforts for the community, are shown in the accompanying table. What is the optimal level of pollution control? Will there still be some pollution of the lake?

3. Assume a community has decided that there are some substantial social benefits associated with after-school organized recreational activities (such as basketball or soccer) provided to kids before many of their parents arrive home from work. The graph below shows the private demand (marginal private benefit) and society's demand (marginal social benefit) and the supply (marginal private plus social cost) of these recreational activities.

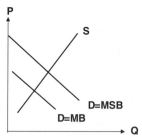

a. Demonstrate graphically the efficient output level in the graph above. Why would this be an efficient output level?

b. Assume the government is interested in a policy to increase the number of children spending time at these facilities. What policy would you recommend?

4. a. If you are willing to pay $7,000 for a used car that is a "cherry" and $2,000 for a used car that is a "lemon," how much will you be willing to offer to purchase a car if there is a 50 percent chance of purchasing a lemon?

b. If many owners of cherry cars want $4,500 for their cherries, and you are still willing to offer the same dollar amount for a used car as in part *a*, how will your estimate of the chance of getting a cherry change?

5. Suppose there are just two individuals, Bob and Susie, in a community. Bob and Susie are both interested in using a public park (a public good). Below are Bob and Susie's individual demand tables for the use of the public park per month.

Bob		Susie	
Price per month	Qty Demanded in hours per month	Price per month	Qty Demanded in hours per month
$13	4	$10	4
9	6	6	6
7	8	4	8

a. Construct a market demand table for the public park in this community.

b. Construct individual demand curves for Bob and Susie as well as the market demand curve and place them on the same graph in the space below.

A BRAIN TEASER

1. Environmentalists are concerned about the deforestation of the United States. Some of these environmentalists have advocated government regulating the number of trees that can be cut down. As an economic adviser to the Department of the Interior you are asked to evaluate this policy and provide any recommendations. What do you say?

MULTIPLE CHOICE

Circle the one best answer for each of the following questions:

1. All of the following are market failures *except:*
a. positive externalities.
b. imperfect information.
c. negative externalities.
d. the invisible hand.

2. An externality is:
a. the effect of a decision on a third party not taken into account by a decision maker.
b. another name for exports.
c. an event that is external to the economy.
d. the external effect of a government policy.

3. Refer to the graph below. The S curve represents the marginal private cost of production, and the D curve represents the marginal private benefit to consumers of the good. If there is a negative externality of production, and one wants to adjust the curves so that the equilibrium demonstrates the appropriate marginal social costs, either the:

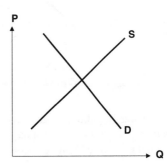

a. S curve should be shifted in to the left or the D curve should be shifted out to the right.

b. S curve should be shifted out to the right or the D curve should be shifted in to the left.

c. S curve should be shifted out to the right or the D curve should be shifted out to the right.

d. S curve should be shifted in to the left or the D curve should be shifted in to the left.

4. Refer to the graph for Question #3. The S curve represents the marginal private cost of production, and the D curve represents the marginal private benefit to consumers of the good. If there is a positive externality of consumption, and one wants to adjust the curves so that the equilibrium demonstrates the appropriate marginal social benefits, either the:

   a. S curve should be shifted in to the left or the D curve should be shifted out to the right.

   b. S curve should be shifted out to the right or the D curve should be shifted in to the left.

   c. S curve should be shifted out to the right or the D curve should be shifted out to the right.

   d. S curve should be shifted in to the left or the D curve should be shifted in to the left.

5. Which of the following is *not* one of the ways to deal with negative externalities?

   a. Regulation.

   b. Subsidizing producers.

   c. Creating a market in the externality.

   d. Voluntary solutions.

6. Refer to the graph below. If the government were attempting to set an effluent fee, the amount of that effluent fee should be:

   a. P_1.

   b. P_2.

   c. $P_1 - P_2$.

   d. $P_1 - P_3$.

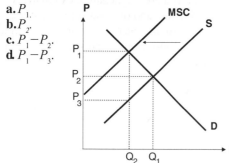

7. Mr. A is using 10 gallons of gas a day and Mr. B is using 20 gallons of gas a day. The marginal cost of reducing gas consumption

by 3 gallons a day is $8 for Mr. A and $4 for Mr. B. The government places a tax on the use of gasoline. Economists would expect:

   a. Mr. A to reduce his consumption by the same amount as Mr. B.

   b. Mr. A to reduce his consumption by more than Mr. B.

   c. Mr. B to reduce his consumption by more than Mr. A.

   d. both to reduce their consumption to zero.

8. Refer to the graph below, which shows the marginal private and social cost of fishing and the demand for fishing. The socially efficient price for consumers of fishing would be:

   a. 0.

   b. P_1.

   c. P_2.

   d. P_3.

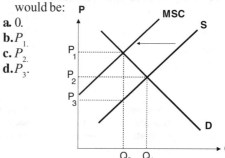

9. In addressing pollution problems, economists would most likely prefer:

   a. direct regulation.

   b. subsidies provided to suppliers.

   c. a market incentive plan.

   d. banning the production of those products that pollute.

10. Voluntary policies to resolve externalities:

   a. have historically been effective in addressing externalities.

   b. are generally favored by economists as the optimal policy to address externalities.

   c. are generally opposed by economists because of the free rider problem.

   d. are generally opposed by economists because of government failure.

11. A public good is:

   a. any good traded in markets.

   b. a good that is nonexclusive and nonrival.

   c. a good provided only to those who pay for it.

   d. rarely provided by government.

12. The optimal level of pollution control, or any other government policy, exists when the marginal benefit:
a. exceeds the marginal cost.
b. equals the marginal cost.
c. is less than the marginal cost.
d. is maximized.

13. The market demand curve for a public good is:
a. the vertical sum of the individual demand curves at every quantity.
b. the horizontal sum of the individual demand curves at every price.
c. vertical at the quantity desired.
d. always horizontal.

14. If health insurers cannot distinguish between people who have a high-risk and low-risk of medical needs, but those buying the health insurance can, the price at which insurers are willing to provide insurance to cover health care costs will be:
a. low enough so that at least one-half of all those covered are low-insurance risks.
b. set with the expectations that high-risk people will not purchase coverage.
c. at a level that insurers will be unwilling to provide health coverage.
d. at a level that many of those in good health may be unwilling to buy insurance.

15. Government failure:
a. always outweighs market failure.
b. sometimes outweighs market failure.
c. never outweighs market failure.
d. is the same as market failure.

● POTENTIAL ESSAY QUESTIONS

You may also see essay questions similar to the "Problems & Applications" and "Brain Teasers" exercises.

1. Evaluate the benefits and costs of the regulatory versus the market approach to resolving informational problems that lead to market failure.

2. Discuss five reasons why government's solution to a market failure could worsen the market failure.

ANSWERS

SHORT-ANSWER QUESTIONS

1. Three sources of market failures are: externalities, public goods, and imperfect information. (422)

2. The pollution that you endure is an example of a negative externality. An externality is an effect of a decision not taken into account by the decision maker. In this case, the air pollution is the effect of steel production not taken into account by the firm. (424-425)

3. Ways to deal with externalities include (1) direct regulation (2) incentive policies (tax incentive policies and market incentive policies), and (3) voluntary solutions. In a program of direct regulation, the government directly limits the amount of a good people are allowed to use. A tax incentive program is a program using a tax to create incentives for individuals to structure their activities in a way that is consistent with the desired ends. A market incentive program is a plan requiring market participants to certify that they have reduced total consumption—not necessarily their own individual consumption—by a specified amount. Voluntary solutions leave individuals free to choose whether to follow what is socially optimal or what is privately optimal. (425-428)

4. Economists tend to like incentive policies to deal with externalities. Direct regulation tends to be more costly to society in achieving the desired end. Voluntary policies will tend to fail because a small number of free riders often undermine the social consciousness of many in society. (426-428)

5. An optimal policy is one in which the marginal cost of undertaking the policy equals the marginal benefit of that policy. (429)

6. A public good is a good that is nonexclusive (no one can be excluded from its benefits) and nonrival (consumption by one does not preclude consumption by others). It is difficult for government to decide the efficient quantity of a public good because of the free rider problem. If the public good is to be financed by a tax on citizens who benefit from it, individuals have an incentive to conceal their willingness to pay for it. Similarly, if citizens think they will not be the ones taxed to fund the public good, but will benefit from it, they have an incentive to exaggerate their willingness to pay. (429-432)

7. Two general policies to deal with informational problems include the regulatory approach and the market approach. The regulatory approach would have government regulate the market and see that individuals provide the right information, or the government could license individuals in the market, requiring those with licenses to reveal full information about the good being sold. The market approach suggests that allowing markets for information to develop may be the best approach. (433-434)

8. The government should intervene in the economy only if the benefits outweigh the costs. One needs to weigh the benefits against the costs on a case-by-case basis and to remain as objective as possible. Government failure (government intervention only making matters worse) is always a real possibility. (436-437)

ANSWERS

MATCHING

1-k; 2-d; 3-j; 4-f; 5-c; 6-m; 7-l; 8-o; 9-n; 10-b; 11-a; 12-h; 13-e; 14-p; 15-g; 16-i; 17-r; 18-q.

ANSWERS

PROBLEMS AND APPLICATIONS

1. a. When there is a negative externality, as with the case of secondhand cigarette smoke, the supply curve which represents the marginal private cost, *S*, is lower than the marginal social cost, *MSC*. The supply curve represents the private costs of smokers who chose to smoke. The cost for society is higher, and the marginal social cost is higher, because cigarette smoke hurts those who do not smoke. The demand curve represents marginal social benefits. These curves are drawn on the next page.

Because the market does not take into account the third-party effects, equilibrium quantity is Q_e and equilibrium price is P_e. (423-425 and Figure 18-1)

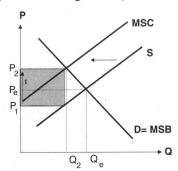

b. The efficient level of cigarettes is where marginal social costs equal marginal social benefits. This is at Q_2 and P_2. (423-425 and Figure 18-1)

c. The tax the government would have to impose on cigarettes to arrive at the efficient level of cigarettes is t equal to $P_2 - P_1$; it's the tax sufficient to shift the supply curve back to the marginal social cost curve. (427 and Figure 18-3)

d. This is t times the quantity of cigarettes in the market after the tax. This is shown by the shaded boxed region in the graph above. (427 and Figure 18-3)

2. See the table below. The optimal level of pollution control is 5 units, because this is the quantity of pollution control at which the marginal social benefit of the control just equals its marginal social cost. There will still be some pollution of the lake as evidenced by the increased marginal benefits associated with the 6th unit of pollution control—but that amount of pollution control is not worth it to the community given its marginal cost. (429)

Pollution Control	Total Benefits	Total Costs	Marginal Benefit	Marginal Cost
1	$200,000	$40,000	$200,000	$40,000
2	275,000	75,000	75,000	35,000
3	330,000	110,000	55,000	35,000
4	375,000	145,000	45,000	35,000
5	410,000	180,000	**35,000**	**35,000**
6	435,000	215,000	25,000	35,000

3. a. The efficient level of output (services provided in the community) is where the marginal social benefit equals the marginal social cost. This occurs at that output level, Q*, where the MSB curve intersects the supply curve as shown below. (It is reasonable to assume there is no difference between the private and social costs. So marginal social costs are given by the supply curve.) (425 and Figure 18-2)

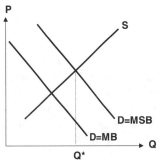

b. The private demand and/or the supply needs to be increased. This could be accomplished by subsidizing parents (increasing demand) and/or subsidizing the facilities (increasing supply). Either one of these options would increase the output level toward the efficient level where MSB = MSC. It may be much easier to administer the subsidization of the facilities. (425 and Figure 18-2)

4. a. Knowing that you have a 50 percent chance of buying a lemon, you will offer $4,500 (the average of $2,000 and $7,000). Given that offer price, individuals with cherries will be very hesitant to sell and will begin to exit the market, while individuals with lemons will be anxious to sell. (432)

b. If many owners of cherries want $4,500 and you are still willing to pay $4,500 for a used car then there will be more owners of cherries left in the market, increasing the chances you will be able to purchase a cherry used car. (432)

5. a. The market demand table for the public park is shown on the next page. Notice that to derive the market demand table for a public good one needs to add the marginal benefit each individual receives from the public good (the price they are willing to pay) at each quantity. (This is just the opposite from deriving a demand table for a private good where one would have to add the quantity demanded at each price.) (430)

Price per month	Quantity Demanded in hours per month
$23	4
$15	6
$11	8

b. The lowest curve is Susie's demand curve. The middle curve is Bob's demand curve. The highest curve is the market demand curve. Notice that we vertically sum the individual demand curves to construct the market demand curve for a public good. (430 and Figure 18-4)

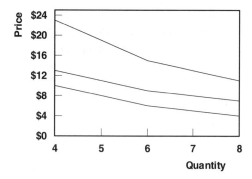

ANSWERS

A BRAIN TEASER

1. First, one must look carefully at the evidence to see if the marginal social benefit equals the marginal social cost at the current quantity of trees harvested in the timber industry. If so, then there is not a problem. After all, trees are a renewable resource. If they become scarcer, their price will rise and people will voluntarily conserve. Moreover, a higher price will increase the quantity supplied—more trees will be planted. However, if at the current market equilibrium quantity the marginal social cost exceeds the marginal social benefit, too many trees are being cut down. That is, an

external cost exists. That external cost is often cited as the reduced ability of trees to clean the air—to absorb carbon dioxide. Even if we assume the external cost is sufficiently large to warrant government action, direct regulation by government often is not the most efficient approach.

Instead, a more efficient proposal may be to continue to impose a higher and higher tax on the production of lumber until supply is restricted to that quantity at which the marginal social benefit just equals the marginal social cost. At the resulting higher market price for lumber, people will voluntarily conserve trees.

Another possibility might be to subsidize people or communities to plant more trees to absorb carbon dioxide (and continue to require the timber industry to plant a new tree to replace each one cut down). This course of action may preclude the necessity to tax the timber industry. (425-428)

ANSWERS

MULTIPLE CHOICE

1. d An outcome where individual buyers and sellers do not have any control over price (the invisible hand) is a desirable competitive market outcome. See page 422.

2. a An externality occurs when there is an effect of a trade on a third party. See page 423.

3. d A negative externality of production makes the marginal social cost higher than the marginal private cost. See pages 424-425 and Figure 18-1.

4. a A positive externality of consumption makes the marginal social benefit higher than the marginal private benefit. See page 425 and Figure 18-2.

5. b Subsidizing producers would increase the production of the product. Instead, we would want to restrict the production of a product that has a negative externality. See pages 424-425.

6. d The effluent fee should be set to equate marginal social cost with marginal social benefit (which, in absence of any information to the contrary, the marginal social benefit can be assumed to be represented by the demand curve). To achieve this equality, the effluent fee needs to be sufficient to shift the supply curve up to the marginal social cost curve. See page 427 and Figure 18-3.

7. c The amount of reduction will be based on the marginal costs of reduction. Since the marginal costs of reduction are higher for Mr. A, economists would expect Mr. B to reduce his consumption by more than Mr. A. See page 427.

8. b The socially efficient price is where the marginal social cost equals the marginal social benefit (which, in absence of any information to the contrary, can be assumed to be represented by the demand curve). See pages 424-425 and Figure 18-1.

9. c Economists prefer market incentive plans because they are more efficient. See pages 425-428.

10. c Economists believe a small number of free riders will undermine the social consciousness of many in society and that eventually a voluntary policy will fail. Generally, the results of voluntary programs have not been positive. Government failure can exist only if government intervenes. The optimal government intervention exists when the marginal benefits equal the marginal costs. See pages 428.

11. b A public good is a good that is nonexclusive and whose consumption by one does not preclude its consumption by others. See page 429.

12. b Whenever the marginal benefit exceeds the marginal cost then do more of that activity. Do less whenever the marginal benefit is less than the marginal cost. See page 429.

13. a To arrive at the market demand curve for a public good we vertically add the price that each individual is willing to pay for each unit since each receives a benefit when the good is supplied. See page 430 and Figure 18-4.

14. d With certainty, insurers would not offer to provide health insurance at a price low enough so that low-risk people would purchase insurance. The only people left looking for health insurance are high-risk people. The price will rise even further until very few will buy health insurance. This is known as adverse selection. See pages 432-433.

15. b Government failure occurs when government intervention does not improve the market failure. As with almost all economic issues, there is always an "on the other hand" so the "sometimes" is the right answer. See pages 436-437.

ANSWERS

POTENTIAL ESSAY QUESTIONS

The following are annotated answers. They indicate the general idea behind the answer.

1. The regulatory approach would have government regulate the market and see that individuals provide the right information, or the government could license individuals in the market, requiring those with licenses to reveal full information about the good being sold. Although regulatory solutions have their benefits they may also create government failure. The market approach suggests that allowing markets for information to develop may be the best approach because it may at least avoid some government failure.

2. Government intervention may worsen the problems created by market failure. Government failure may occur because (1) governments don't have an incentive to correct the problem, (2) governments don't have enough information to deal with the problem, (3) intervention is more complicated than it initially seems, (4) the bureaucratic nature of government precludes fine-tuning, and (5) government intervention often leads to more government intervention.

POLITICS AND ECONOMICS: THE CASE OF AGRICULTURAL MARKETS

CHAPTER AT A GLANCE

This review is based upon the learning objectives that open the chapter.

1. In many ways agricultural markets fit the classic picture of perfect competition. In other ways, however, agricultural markets are far from perfectly competitive. The competitiveness of many agricultural markets is influenced by government programs. (442-443)

    The study of agricultural markets shows us how powerful a tool supply and demand analysis is in helping us understand not only the workings of perfectly competitive markets, but also the effects of government intervention in a market.

2. The good/bad paradox is the phenomenon of doing poorly because you're doing well. (443)

    Because of the inelastic demand for farm goods, a good harvest (increase in supply) means the percentage decline in the price outweighs the percentage increase in the quantity demanded and therefore revenues (income) to farmers fall. This is known as the good/bad paradox in farming.

3. The general rule of political economy in a democracy states that small groups that are significantly affected by a government policy will lobby more effectively than large groups that are equally affected by that same policy. (445-446)

    The farm lobby has been successful in generating higher prices and incomes for farmers even though consumers and taxpayers are worse off.

4. In a price support system, the government maintains a higher-than-equilibrium price. (446-447)

    Because the price support (or, price floor $-P_F$) creates a surplus, which causes downward pressure on the price, government tries to offset this by various measures.

    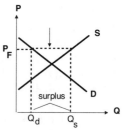

5. Four methods of price support are: (447-450)

    *   Regulatory force.
    *   Economic incentives to reduce supply.
    *   Subsidizing the sale of goods to consumers.
    *   Buying up and storing, giving away, or destroying the good.

    The distributional effects are shown in Figure 19-3 on page 448.

    Note: option #2 is sometimes implemented through an acreage control program or a land bank program and #4 is often referred to as a non-recourse loan program.

    Know these! Study Figure 19-3! For each method know who benefits the most and who is hurt the most–evaluate them.

The two prevalent farm programs in the U.S. have been the land bank program, in which government gives farmers economic incentives to reduce supply, and the nonrecourse loan program, in which government "buys" goods in the form of collateral on defaulting loans (similar to option #4 above and discussed in the textbook).

6. Politicians weigh the farm program options by attempting to balance their view of the general good with the power and preferences of the special interest groups that they represent or who contribute to their election campaigns. (451-452)

   The special interest groups involved include consumers, taxpayers and farmers. They are not distinctly separate groups.

   Always keep in mind the general law of political economy in a democracy: When small groups are helped by a government action and large groups are hurt by that same action, the small group tends to lobby far more effectively than the large group. It will likely continue to ring true.

● SHORT-ANSWER QUESTIONS

1. What is the good/bad paradox in farming?

2. What is the underlying cause of the good/bad paradox in farming?

3. What is the general rule of political economy in a democracy?

4. How does a price support system work?

5. What are the four price support options?

6. What are the distributional consequences of the four alternative methods of price support? Use supply and demand curves to support your answers.

7. What two farm programs have been the most prevalent in the United States?

8. What real-world pressures do politicians face in determining agriculture policy?

MATCHING THE TERMS
Match the terms to their definitions

____ 1. general rule of political economy

____ 2. good/bad paradox

____ 3. grandfather (clause)

____ 4. land bank program

____ 5. nonrecourse loan program

____ 6. price stabilization program

____ 7. price support program

a. Small groups that are significantly affected by a government policy will lobby more effectively than large groups that are equally affected by that same policy.

b. The phenomenon of doing poorly because you are doing well.

c. Program designed to eliminate short-run fluctuations in prices but allows prices to follow their long-term trend line.

d. Program that maintains prices at a level higher than the market price.

e. To pass a law affecting a specific group but providing that those in the group before the law was passed are exempt from some provisions of the law.

f. Program that supports prices by giving farmers economic incentives to reduce supply.

g. Program where government "buys" goods in the form of collateral on defaulting loans.

● PROBLEMS AND APPLICATIONS

1. Hog farming has become high tech. Companies, called agrifirms, now house thousands of
genetically uniform pigs in large complexes and
regulate their environment electronically. The
effect of this technological change has been to
increase the supply of pigs. The farm lobby is
trying to convince government to intervene.

   a. Why would the technological development be troublesome to pig farmers who
   have small operations? (Hint: use the
   good/bad paradox). Demonstrate this
   using supply and demand curves.

   b. Show the effect of regulation when it
   restricts the development of new agrifirms
   in order to get back to the original price.
   Who is hurt? Who is helped?

   c. Show the effect of a price support system
   in which government buys up all the
   supply that consumers don't buy at the
   support price (equal to the original price).
   Who is hurt? Who is helped?

   d. Show the effect of a price subsidy in
   which the government buys hogs at the
   original price, P_0, and then sells the hogs
   to consumers at P_2, so there is no surplus.
   Who is hurt? Who is helped?

   e. Which would the government favor if it
   wants to balance its budget without
   increasing taxes? Why?

2. Consider the following market demand and
supply schedules for peanuts in the U.S.

	Price per ton	Quantity Supplied (mil. tons)	Quantity Demanded (mil. tons)
A	$50	−1.0	4.25
B	100	−0.5	4.0
C	150	0.0	3.75
D	200	0.5	3.5
E	250	1.0	3.25
F	300	1.5	3.0
G	350	2.0	2.75
H	400	2.5	2.5
I	450	3.0	2.25
J	500	3.5	2.0
K	550	4.0	1.75
L	600	4.5	1.5

a. Graph the corresponding demand and supply curves. What is equilibrium price and quantity?

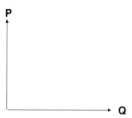

	Price per ton	Quantity Supplied
A	$50	−.25
B	100	.25
C	150	.75
D	200	1.25
E	250	1.75
F	300	2.25
G	350	2.75
H	400	3.25
I	450	3.75
J	500	4.25
K	550	4.75
L	600	5.25

Demonstrate the effect of this technological innovation on the graph in (a). What is the new equilibrium quantity and price?

b. Calculate the elasticity of supply from H to G. Calculate the elasticity of demand from H to G.

f. As a result of the efforts by the peanut lobby, the government agrees to buy up all the supply that consumers don't buy at the original equilibrium price. Show this program graphically.

c. How would you characterize the elasticity of supply and demand calculated in (b)?

d. What would happen to revenue for peanut growers if price fell from $400 to $350?

g. Calculate how much consumers benefit or are hurt from the government program in *f*. Calculate the cost to taxpayers.

e. Suppose a technological innovation in peanut growing shifts supply to the following:

● A BRAIN TEASER

1. Suppose government guarantees or supports the price of an agricultural commodity by using the nonrecourse loan program (similar to option #4 discussed in the textbook). Who is likely to benefit most: the large agrifirms, or the small family farms for which many people believe the program was designed to help? Why?

● MULTIPLE CHOICE

Circle the one best answer for each of the following questions:

1. In the absence of government involvement, agricultural markets most closely correspond to:
   a. perfect competition.
   b. monopolistic competition.
   c. oligopoly.
   d. monopoly.

2. The good/bad paradox exists because there is:
   a. an inelastic demand for agricultural goods.
   b. an inelastic supply of agricultural goods.
   c. an elastic demand for agricultural goods.
   d. an elastic supply of agricultural goods.

3. Agriculture is a highly productive industry. This enormous productivity has:
   a. caused agriculture to increase in relative importance as a percent of national output.
   b. caused agriculture to decrease in relative importance as a percent of national output.
   c. caused farmers to be rich and prosperous.
   d. increased the share of the national labor force working in agriculture.

4. Say that most apple farmers are having a bad crop, but that in your particular area the weather was great so you individually are having a great crop. You would:
   a. be unhappy because of the good/bad paradox.
   b. favor price controls.
   c. not be hurt by the good/bad paradox.
   d. receive a low price for your apple crop and not be able to sell much of it.

5. Refer to the graph below. What area represents the change in income going to farmers from an increase in supply from S_0 to S_1?
   a. A – C.
   b. A + C.
   c. A + B + C.
   d. C – A.

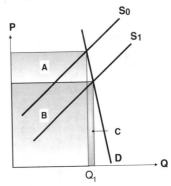

6. Refer to the graph above. What area represents the final income going to farmers after the supply shifts out from S_0 to S_1?
   a. A + B.
   b. B + C.
   c. A + C.
   d. A + B + C.

7. The general rule of political economy in a democracy states:
   a. small groups that are significantly affected by a government policy will lobby more effectively than will large groups who are equally affected by that policy.
   b. large groups that are significantly affected by a government policy will lobby more effectively than small groups who are equally affected by that policy.
   c. large groups will always win in majority rule situations.
   d. Congress will always be inefficient.

8. Refer to the graph below. If the government imposes a quantity restriction of Q_1 on suppliers, compared to the free market situation, suppliers' net income will:
   a. fall by B.
   b. rise by A.
   c. rise by A – B.
   d. be unaffected.

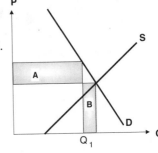

9. Refer to the graph below. The government gives enough economic incentives to suppliers to decrease output sufficiently so that the price rises from $3.50 to $5. The area *best* representing the amount that this program transfers from consumers to suppliers is:
   a. A.
   b. B.
   c. C.
   d. A + B + C.

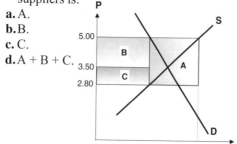

10. Refer to the graph below. If the government sets a price floor of $5 and buys up the surplus, the area *best* representing the cost to the government is:
    a. A.
    b. A + B.
    c. B + C.
    d. A + C.

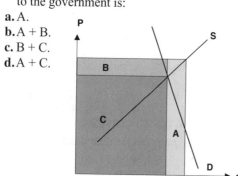

11. Refer to the graph below. If the government subsidizes the sale of wheat so that farmers get $5 but the price to consumers is brought down to $1.75, the cost to the government of doing so will be *best* represented by the area:
    a. A.
    b. C.
    c. A +B.
    d. A + B + C.

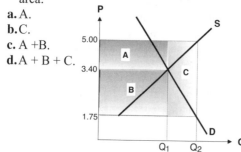

12. Which of the following four methods of price supports would taxpayers favor *least*?
    a. Regulatory methods.
    b. Economic incentives to reduce supply.
    c. Subsidizing the sale.
    d. Buying up and storing the good.

13. What two farm programs have been the most prevalent in the United States?
    a. The "land bank" and the "nonrecourse loan" programs.
    b. The "regulatory" and the "incentives to reduce supply" programs.
    c. The "regulatory" and the "subsidizing the sale" programs.
    d. The "subsidizing the sale" and the "buying up and storing the good" programs.

14. The government price support program that costs the government the *least* and benefits the farmers the *least* is:
    a. supporting the price by regulatory measures.
    b. providing economic incentives to reduce supply
    c. subsidizing the sale of the good.
    d. buying up and storing, giving away, or destroying the good.

15. The government price support program that benefits consumers the most with lower prices and benefits farmers with higher prices, and costs taxpayers the most of any program is:
    a. supporting the price by regulatory measures.
    b. providing economic incentives to reduce supply
    c. subsidizing the sale of the good.
    d. buying up and storing, giving away, or destroying the good.

⬤ POTENTIAL ESSAY QUESTIONS

You may also see essay questions similar to the "Problems & Applications" and "Brain Teasers" exercises.

1. What are some of the benefits and the costs of government involvement in agricultural markets? That is, who benefits and who is hurt?

2. Explain, using supply and demand curves, the distributional consequences of four alternative methods of price supports.

ANSWERS

SHORT-ANSWER QUESTIONS

1. The good/bad paradox in farming is the phenomenon of doing poorly because you are doing well. That is, total revenue (income for farmers) declines even though crop yields have risen. (443 and Figure 19-1)

2. The underlying cause of the good/bad paradox in farming is that demand for agricultural goods is inelastic. When supply increases, its price declines so much that total revenue to farmers also declines. (444 and Figure 19-1)

3. The general rule of political economy in a democracy is that small groups that are significantly affected by a government policy will lobby more effectively than large groups that are equally affected by that same policy. (445-446)

4. In a price support system, the government maintains a higher than equilibrium price. Referring to Figure 19-2 on page 446 of the text, at support price P_1, the quantity of goods demanded is only Q_D while the quantity supplied is Q_S. This causes downward pressure on the price, shown by arrow A, which must be offset by government measures shown by arrow B. (446-447)

5. The four price support options are (1) regulatory force, (2) economic incentives to reduce supply, (3) subsidizing the sale of goods to consumers, and (4) buying up and storing, giving away, or destroying the good. (447)

6. The distributional consequences of the four alternative methods of price support are shown in the four accompanying graphs. (447-451 and Figure 19-3)

    The following graph shows the effect of regulating price directly at P_2. Farmers are allowed to produce at Q_1. The farmers who can no longer sell their goods lose areas *B* and *C* but gain back *B* in their other pursuits. Revenue to remaining producers increases by area A. Consumers lose areas A and D in consumer surplus. Areas *C* and *D* are lost to society.

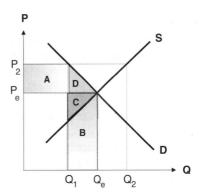

The graph below shows the effect of providing economic incentives to reduce supply by paying farmers not to produce. The government has to pay farmers area A to reduce the price to P_1, which is the price necessary to get farmers to supply quantity Q_1. Existing farmers receive payment A from the government and get rectangle B from consumers in the form of higher prices. Consumers pay a higher price for fewer goods.

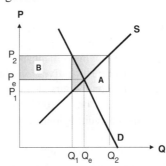

The graph below shows the effect of subsidizing the sale of the good. Suppliers supply quantity Q_2 to the government and are paid the price support P_2. Consumers purchase Q_2 at P_1 from the government. They benefit by area *A*, getting more goods at a lower price. Suppliers benefit by area *B*, getting a higher price. The taxpayers foot the bill which equals $A + B + C$.

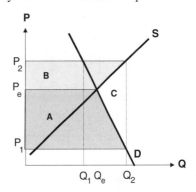

The graph below shows the effect of the government buying up the goods that consumers do not buy at the support price, P_2, and storing or otherwise disposing of the good. The government pays the farmers area $A + B$. The farmers gain area $B + C$. Taxpayers foot the bill of $A + B$. To the extent that the government can get something for the goods it bought, its expenses are lower than area $A + B$. Area C is transferred from consumers to producers.

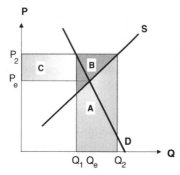

7. The two farm programs most prevalent in the United States have been the land bank program (in which government supports prices by giving economic incentives to reduce supply) and the non-recourse loan program (in which government "buys" goods in the form of collateral on defaulting loans). (451)

8. Politicians must weigh the agricultural policy options by attempting to balance their view of the general good with the power and preferences of the special interest groups that they represent (consumers, taxpayers, and farmers) or that contribute to their campaigns. (451-452)

ANSWERS

MATCHING

1-a; 2-b; 3-e; 4-f; 5-g; 6-c; 7-d.

ANSWERS

PROBLEMS AND APPLICATIONS

1. a. Farmers are upset because demand for pork is relatively inelastic. This is shown in the graph below. Before the new technology, price and quantity are P_0 and Q_0. Total income is $P_0 \times Q_0$. The supply of pigs, however, has shifted to S_1 with the development of agrifirms. Now, equilibrium price is P_1 and quantity is Q_1. Because demand is inelastic, farmers' income has fallen. The lost income, area A, is greater than the gain in income, area C. (443-444 and Figure 19-1)

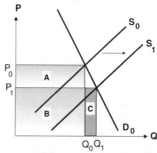

b. In this case, the government would restrict the supply of hogs to Q_0 as shown in the graph below. Farmers' total revenue increases by area A and decreases by areas C and E. There is a net gain in revenue to suppliers. Some suppliers who want to supply $Q_1 - Q_0$ must be excluded from the market. Consumers must pay a higher price, P_0 and get a lower quantity, Q_0. The triangle, areas D and E, represent deadweight loss. It represents a loss to society from the quantity restriction. (447-449 and Figure 19-3)

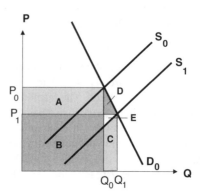

c. Consumers buy Q_0 at P_0 shown in the graph below. The government buys $Q_2 - Q_0$ at price P_0, paying rectangle A in total. Consumer surplus equal to rectangle B is transferred to hog farmers. Taxpayers are hurt because they have to pay rectangle A for goods that most likely cannot be sold elsewhere. Consumers are hurt by having to pay a higher price for fewer goods. (450 and Figure 19-3)

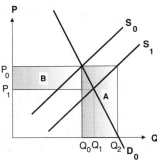

d. In this case, government spends $P_0 \times Q_2$ to buy the hogs and sells them for $P_2 \times Q_2$ shown in the graph below. Consumers benefit from enjoying the lower price P_2 and higher quantity represented by a net gain of area B. Suppliers benefit from a higher price, P_0, and higher quantity, Q_2. Their net gain is represented by area A. The cost to taxpayers, however, is areas A, B and C, so the net welfare loss is area C. (449-450 and Figure 19-3)

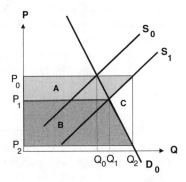

e. If government wanted to hold government expenditures down, it would favor (b) because the direct cost to government is zero, although there are enforcement and administrative costs. (450-451)

2. a. The corresponding demand and supply curves are shown in the next column.

Equilibrium exists at a price of $400 per ton where the quantity demanded equals the quantity supplied of 2.5 million tons. The equilibrium price and quantity is shown graphically where the demand and supply curves intersect. (Chapter 5)

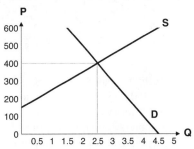

b. $E_S = 1.7$; $E_D = 0.7$. The elasticity of supply is percent change in quantity supplied divided by the percent change in price. From H to G this is $[(2.5\text{-}2)/2.25]/[(400\text{-}350)/375] = .22/.13 = 1.7$. The elasticity of demand is percent change in quantity demanded divided by the percent change in price. From H to G this is $|[(2.5\text{-}2.75)/2.625]/[(400\text{-}350)/375]| = .095/.13 = 0.7$. (Chapter 6.)

c. Supply is elastic since $E_S > 1$; demand is inelastic since the absolute value of $E_D < 1$. (Chapter 6.)

d. Since demand is inelastic between H and G, total revenue would fall. (Chapter 6.)

e. The increase in supply will shift the curve to the right as shown in the graph below. Supply shifts from S_0 to S_1. Equilibrium quantity is now 2.75 million tons. Equilibrium price is now $350 per ton. (Chapter 5)

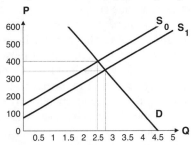

f. This program is shown in the graph on the next page. Consumers buy 2.5 million tons at $400 per ton. Government buys 0.75 million tons at $400, spending a total of area A, or $300 million. (450 and Figure 19-3)

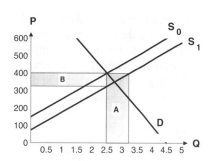

g. Consumers pay an extra $50 per ton over the $350 they would have paid if the new equilibrium were reached. This means consumers pay an additional $125 million (2.5 million x 50). This is represented by area *B*. The cost to taxpayers is area *A*, or $300 million. (450 and Figure 19-3)

ANSWERS

A BRAIN TEASER

1. The large agrifirms are likely to benefit most. These large corporate farms usually have lower average costs of production because of the economies of scale they are able to experience. Because the price received is the same for small and large farms alike, much larger profits can be earned by the agrifirms. Moreover, the agrifirms may produce most of the output. Hence, most of the government tax revenues used to buy up the surplus production ends up in the hands of those large corporate farms that least need assistance. This has caused some critics to argue that this prevalent form of government involvement in agricultural markets has resulted in an upside-down "welfare" program—it has most benefited those who need it least. Critics argue that it may be cheaper for taxpayers to simply make a cash payment to small family farms if it is their incomes which society wishes to support. (450-451)

ANSWERS

MULTIPLE CHOICE

1. **a** In the absence of government involvement, agricultural markets fit the classic picture of perfect competition. There are so many sellers and buyers that all are price-takers. Products are homogenous and interchangeable, and prices can, and do, vary considerably. See page 442.

2. **a** The inelastic demand makes the total revenue vary inversely with shifts in supply. See page 444.

3. **b** The high level of productivity has led to falling food prices, and decreasing agriculture in relative importance as a percent of the economy's output. This is an example of the long-run good/bad paradox. See pages 443-444.

4. **c** The good/bad paradox applies when you are part of a group of farmers that is having a bad year or a group of farmers that is having a good year. If you are an individual having a good year when most farmers are having a bad year, you are receiving a high price for your high level of output. See pages 443-444.

5. **d** The increased income from the higher quantity is area *C* and the lost income from the lower price is area *A,* so the net change in income going to farmers is area *C* - *A*. It is a loss because demand is inelastic. See page 444, especially Figure 19-1.

6. **b** The revenue or income going to farmers is represented by the rectangle determined by the price they receive and the quantity they sell. See page 444 especially Figure 19-1.

7. **a** Congress may always be inefficient, but this is not the general rule of political economy. See pages 445-446.

8. c   Suppliers will lose the income *B* because of the quantity restriction, but will gain the area *A* due to the higher price. See Figure 19-3, and pages 447-449.

9. b   Consumers lose the area under the demand curve at the higher price. Of that, producers gain area B in additional revenue. The triangles are welfare loss. See Figure 19-3, and page 449.

10. a   With a price floor of $5 the surplus will be Q_2-Q_1, for which the government will have to pay $5. See Figure 19-3, and page 450.

11. d   If the price to consumers is held down at $1.75, the quantity supplied will be Q_2 and the subsidy per unit supplied will have to be $3.25. See Figure 19-3 and pages 449-450.

12. c   Taxpayers will likely *least* favor the price support method of subsidizing the sale of goods to consumers because this method costs taxpayers the most. The low price paid by consumers and the high price received by farmers necessitate large subsidies. See Figure 19-3 and pages 450-451.

13. a   The land bank program, which gives farmers incentives to reduce supply, and the nonrecourse loan program, which buys up goods, have been the most prevalent U.S. farm programs. See page 451.

14. a   Regulatory price supports cost government the least, but benefit farmers the least. See pages 450-451.

15. c   Subsidizing the sale of the good costs taxpayers the most of any program as it helps consumers the most while supporting farm prices. See pages 450-451.

━━━━ ANSWERS ━━━━

POTENTIAL ESSAY QUESTIONS

The following are annotated answers. They indicate the general idea behind the answer.

1.   The benefit is more stable and higher prices and more stable and higher farm incomes. Farmers benefit. (However, it may benefit "rich" farmers most—those who need it least. It may be an upside-down "welfare" program. See the "Brain Teaser" problem.) The costs to society are the higher prices consumers must pay for food and fiber. Taxpayers are also hurt by having to pay higher taxes to support farm prices and incomes. The government also may have to deal with the surplus production in some manner. This too can be costly.

2.   Four methods of price support are:
1. Regulatory force.
2. Economic incentives to reduce supply.
3. Subsidizing the sale of goods to consumers.
4. Buying up and storing, giving away, or destroying the good.
The distributional effects are shown in Figure 19-3, on page 448.

MICROECONOMIC POLICY, ECONOMIC REASONING, AND BEYOND

20

● CHAPTER AT A GLANCE

This review is based upon the learning objectives that open the chapter.

1. Economists' views on social policy differ widely because: (459-461)

   1. they have different underlying values,
   2. they interpret empirical evidence differently, and
   3. they use different underlying models.

   Analysis should be as objective as possible. Unfortunately, in practice, social goals are seldom neat—they're generally vaguely understood and vaguely expressed.

2. Liberal and conservative economists agree on many policy prescriptions because they use the same models. These models focus on incentives and individual choice. (461)

   There is more agreement among economists than most lay people realize because they all use cost/benefit analysis. Disagreement among economists usually arises because they assess the qualitative benefits and costs (those benefits and costs that cannot be easily measured) differently.

3. Cost/benefit analysis is analysis in which one assigns a cost and benefit to alternatives, and draws a conclusion on the basis of those costs and benefits. (461-465)

   Economists argue that government should keep regulating until the marginal benefits of regulation just equal the marginal costs. Unfortunately, many costs and benefits (especially social and political) cannot be easily quantified.

4. Three separate types of failure of market outcomes include: (466-470)

   1. failures due to distributional issues,
   2. failures due to rationality problems of individuals, and
   3. failures due to violations of inalienable, or at least partially inalienable, rights of individuals.

   Failure of market outcome occurs when even though it is functioning properly the market is not achieving society's goals.

5. Government failure as well as market failure exists. For the government to correct a problem it must: (470-472)

   1. recognize the problem,
   2. have the will to deal with it, and
   3. have the ability to deal with it.

   Government can often not do all three of these well. Often the result is that government action is directed at the wrong problem at the wrong time. And sometimes the government fails to improve a situation (hence the term "government failure.")

   Economics provides the tools, not the rules, for policy. Economics involves the thoughtful use of economic insights and empirical evidence. An economist must carefully consider all views. Subjective moral value judgments can't be ignored.

SHORT-ANSWER QUESTIONS

1. List three reasons why the statement "If you laid all economists end to end, they still wouldn't reach a conclusion" is partly true with regard to social policy.

2. Although the quotation in Question #1 has some validity, nevertheless liberal and conservative economists often agree in their views on social policy. What is the basis for their agreement?

3. What is *cost/benefit analysis*?

4. When it comes to the actions of politicians regulating our economy, most economists are cynics. Why?

5. What are three types of failure of market outcomes?

6. Why are many economists doubtful that the government can correct failure of market outcomes?

7. Your friend finds you tucked away in a cozy chair in the library studying for an economics exam on policy issues. Your friend says, "Why are you wasting your time? All you have to remember is *supply and demand* and you'll be able to answer any question in economics." How do you respond?

MATCHING THE TERMS
Match the terms to their definitions

___ **1.**	cost/benefit approach	**a.**	Approach in which one assigns a cost and benefit to alternatives, and draws a conclusion on the basis of those costs and benefits.
___ **2.**	economic efficiency		
___ **3.**	failure of market outcomes	**b.**	Policies that benefit some people and hurt no one.
___ **4.**	Marxian (radical) model	**c.**	A model that focuses on equitable distribution of power, rights, and income among social classes.
___ **5.**	Pareto optimal policies	**d.**	Taxes that discourage activities society believes are harmful.
___ **6.**	public choice (conservative) model	**e.**	A model that focuses on self-interest of politicians.
		f.	What individuals do is in their own best interest.
___ **7.**	rational	**g.**	Achieving a goal at the lowest possible cost.
___ **8.**	sin taxes	**h.**	Even though the market is functioning properly, it is not achieving society's goals.

● PROBLEMS AND APPLICATIONS

1. Which of the following regulations would you recommend government implement?

    a. A regulation requiring airline mechanics to check whether all bolts are tightened. This decreases the probability of having an accident by .001. The cost of the average crash is estimated at $200 million for the plane and $400 million in lives. The cost of implementing the program is $16 million.

    b. A regulation requiring that all cars have driver-side airbags. This adds $500 to the cost of a car. Having an airbag in a car reduces the chance of dying in a car crash by 1/720. The average individual values his/her life at $500,000.

    c. A regulation stiffening government rules for workplace safety. The cost per worker is $5,000 and the regulations are expected to reduce workplace fatalities by .002. Workers value their lives at an average of $2 million.

    d. What are the problems with using the cost/benefit approach to decide (a), (b), and (c)?

2. Why does it often appear to the lay public that economists never agree on social policy?

3. Assume economists have undertaken cost/benefit analysis of a problem and are unanimously in favor of a particular policy proposal over all other proposals. Why might this policy recommendation not be enacted as policy?

● A BRAIN TEASER

1. Why did former President Harry S. Truman say in jest that he wished he could find a one-armed economist?

● MULTIPLE CHOICE

Circle the one best answer for each of the following questions:

1. Which statement follows from economic theory alone?
    a. The minimum wage should be increased.
    b. The minimum wage should be decreased.
    c. There should be no minimum wage.
    d. No policy prescription follows from economic theory alone.

2. It is important to be familiar with many economic models because:
    a. the models are objective.
    b. the models are subjective.
    c. each model captures different aspects of reality.
    d. the models are Pareto optimal.

3. When an economist states that whether baby seals should be killed depends upon the costs and benefits, according to the text they are being:
    a. coldhearted.
    b. subjective.
    c. objective.
    d. conjective.

4. In an automobile crash, people were killed because an automobile company saved $10 by placing the gas tank in the rear of the car. An economist would:
    a. determine whether this made sense with cost/benefit analysis.
    b. see this as reasonable.
    c. see this as unreasonable.
    d. argue that no amount of money should be spared to save a life.

5. Suppose that filtering your water at home reduces your chances from dying of giardia (an intestinal parasite) by 1/45,000. The filter costs you $400 to install. You have chosen to install the filter. Which dollar value best reflects the minimum value you implicitly place on your life?
    a. $400.
    b. $45,000.
    c. $1,800,000.
    d. $18,000,000.

6. The government is considering requiring auto manufacturers to reinforce the roofs of SUV vehicles to reduce their collapse in roll-over accidents. The reinforcement adds $600 to the cost of an SUV. The probability of a fatality from a collapsed roof is 1/1,000. The average individual values his/her life at $1,000,000. Economists would be:
    a. in favor of the regulation because the marginal benefit of $1,000 exceeds the marginal cost.
    b. in favor of the regulation because the marginal cost of $600 exceeds the marginal benefit.
    c. against the regulation because the marginal cost of $1,000 exceeds the marginal benefit.
    d. against the regulation because the marginal benefits of $600 exceeds the marginal cost.

7. If the equilibrium wage is below the wage necessary for survival:
    a. there is no problem because the market is in equilibrium.
    b. there is a market failure due to informational problems.
    c. there is a market failure due to an externality.
    d. there is a failure of market outcome.

8. Maximizing total producer and consumer surplus in a market means that:
    a. the economy is as well off as it can be.
    b. total market output is as large as it can be in that market.
    c. income is unfairly distributed.
    d. income is fairly distributed.

9. As economists generally use the term, in a society it is *inefficient* to supply medicine to those who do not have the income to pay for it. This statement is:
    a. correct because economists use the term efficiency as a shorthand referring only to total output.
    b. wrong because medicine is necessary for life.
    c. correct because economists do not care about the poor.
    d. wrong because economics does not take distribution into account.

10. If a person buys more of a good, that person is:
    a. better off.
    b. worse off.
    c. most likely better off.
    d. most likely worse off.

11. If society establishes a law preventing people from selling themselves into slavery:
    a. consumer surplus will be lowered.
    b. consumer surplus will be increased.
    c. economic theory will find that law incorrect.
    d. economic theory will find that law correct.

12. An economist might *not favor* undertaking a policy to correct a failure of market outcome because economists:
    a. don't recognize failures in market outcomes.
    b. see the possibility of government failure.
    c. are trained to support the market no matter what.
    d. see the possibility of market failure offsetting the failure in market outcome.

● POTENTIAL ESSAY QUESTIONS

You may also see essay questions similar to the "Problems & Applications" and "Brain Teasers" exercises.

1. What is cost/benefit analysis? How is this related to why economists often find themselves united with one another but at odds with the general public?

2. How can the presence of the economic (market), social, and political forces in all real-world economies, and economists' use of benefit/cost analysis help explain the disagreement among economists concerning what is considered "appropriate" social policy? Even if economists all agreed upon what is "appropriate" policy, why might that policy never be enacted?

━━━ ANSWERS ━━━

SHORT-ANSWER QUESTIONS

1. The statement is true to the extent that economists sometimes differ in their views on social policy. Three reasons for their differing views are that (1) they have different underlying values, (2) they interpret empirical evidence differently, and (3) they use different underlying models. (459)

2. Liberal and conservative economists often agree in their views on social policy because they use the same models, which focus on incentives and individual choice. (461)

3. *Cost/benefit analysis* is an analysis in which one assigns a cost and benefit to alternatives and draws a conclusion on the basis of those costs and benefits. The optimal amount of any activity is the level at which marginal benefit equals marginal cost. (462)

4. The typical economist views many government regulations as the result of political expediency, and not a reflection of cost/benefit considerations. Most economists believe that decisions should be made on a cost/benefit basis instead of on the basis of political pressure placed on politicians by special interest groups. (465)

5. Three separate types of failures of market outcomes include (1) failures due to distributional issues, (2) failures due to rationality problems of individuals, and (3) failures due to violations of inalienable, or at least partially inalienable, rights of individuals. (466-470)

6. For the government to correct a problem it must (1) recognize the problem, (2) have the will to deal with it, and (3) have the ability to deal with it. Government can seldom do all three of these well. (470-472)

7. You tell your friend to remember the admonition in your textbook: "Teaching a parrot the phrase *supply and demand* does not make it an economist." Elaborating, you tell her that economics involves the thoughtful use of economic insights and empirical evidence. Real-world problems are complex and cannot

be explained just with simple models. You are right in taking the time to learn the details. (472)

━━━ ANSWERS ━━━

MATCHING

1-a; 2-g; 3-h; 4-c; 5-b; 6-e; 7-f; 8-d.

━━━ ANSWERS ━━━

PROBLEMS AND APPLICATIONS

1. For each of these, you calculate the costs and benefits of the regulation. If the cost is higher than the benefit, you would recommend not implementing the program. If the cost is lower than the benefit, you would recommend implementing the program. For each you are assuming you are given all relevant information.

    a. The benefit is saving a plane worth $200 million and saving lives worth $400 million. The regulation reduces the probability of a crash by .001. The marginal benefit is .001 times $600 million = $600,000. The marginal cost is $16 million. Don't implement the program because marginal cost is more than marginal benefit. (462-463)

    b. The benefit is the value of a saved life of $500,000, times the increased probability of living, 1/720 = $694. This is greater than the marginal cost to consumers of $500. Implement the program. (462-463)

    c. The benefit is the value of a saved life of $2 million times the increased probability of not having a fatal accident, $2 million × .002 = $4,000. The marginal cost is $5,000 per worker, which is greater than the marginal benefit. Don't implement the program. (462-463)

    d. The above examples include only quantifiable costs and benefits and involve a huge amount of ambiguity and subjectivity in the calculations. Economists' subjective estimates of the benefit of lives and costs of the program can vary enormously, thus affecting the recommendation enormously. (464)

2. Economists often disagree on social policy because of their different underlying subjective value judgments, because of imprecise empirical evidence and because they focus on different aspects of a policy or problem (because their underlying models differ). (459-461)

3. Because the policymakers (e.g. politicians) may have weighed the non-quantifiable (qualitative) social and political costs and benefits of the policy recommendation differently than the economists have. Equally reasonable people disagree over non-quantifiable costs and benefits. Therefore, what makes sense from a purely economic perspective may not be deemed politically, or socially, acceptable. (465)

ANSWERS

A BRAIN TEASER

1. Economists are trained to weigh both benefits and costs associated with any policy or course of action. On the one hand, there are the benefits. On the other hand, there are the costs. Usually, like Harry Truman, politicians only want to hear the benefits. But, unfortunately, "there ain't no such thing as a free lunch." (464-462 and 471)

ANSWERS

MULTIPLE CHOICE

1. d   Economic theory must be combined with subjective value judgments and empirical evidence to arrive at policy recommendations. See pages 459-461.

2. c   Models are neither objective, subjective, nor Pareto optimal. They simply are a framework for looking at reality. See pages 459-461.

3. c   Economists are trained to look at every decision in reference to costs and benefits as a way of maintaining their objectivity and keeping their subjective views out of

policy. Conjective is not a word. While that may seem coldhearted, the text emphasizes that it seems so only in the short run. See pages 461-465.

4. a   Economists approach all issues with cost/benefit analysis. See pages 461-465.

5. d   You implicitly value your life at $(45,000 \times \$400) = \$18,000,000$. See pages 462-463.

6. a   The marginal benefit is $1,000 ($1,000,000 $\times 1/1,000$). It exceeds the marginal cost of $600. Economists would favor the regulation. See pages 462-463.

7. d   The market is working as it is supposed to but almost all would agree that the result is undesirable; there is a failure of market outcome. See pages 466-467.

8. b   Consumer and producer surplus focus on total output regardless of how it is distributed. See pages 465 and 467.

9. a   The statement is correct given the shorthand that economists use when referring to efficiency. What is efficient may not be desirable. See page 465.

10. c   While economists generally assume that people will do what is in their best interest, it is still possible that they will not do so. See page 468.

11. a   Since the law involves a restriction of trade, consumer surplus will be lowered. It still is a good law, however. Economic theory does not find laws correct or incorrect. See pages 468-470.

12. b   Economists see government failure as important and sometimes government intervention can make a problem worse, not better. See page 470.

ANSWERS

POTENTIAL ESSAY QUESTIONS

The following are annotated answers. They indicate the general idea behind the answer.

1. Cost/benefit analysis is analysis in which one assigns costs and benefits to alternatives, and draws a conclusion on the basis of those costs and benefits. Note that it is marginal costs and marginal benefits that are relevant. Economists try to quantify those costs and benefits—to use empirical evidence to help reach a conclusion. The general public often does not.

2. Economists do take into consideration the economic, social, and political consequences associated with a policy. However, not all the costs and benefits associated with a particular policy are quantifiable with respect to each of these three forces. This leaves some room for subjective value judgments with respect to what the benefits and costs of a policy are. Moreover, empirical evidence is not exact. There is also some room for focusing on different aspects of a problem. Finally, if the policy is undertaken in a political environment, as is usually the case, then political considerations by policymakers may take precedence over the social and economic considerations.

INTERNATIONAL TRADE POLICY

CHAPTER AT A GLANCE

This review is based upon the learning objectives that open the chapter.

1. The primary trading partners of the United States are Canada, Mexico, the European Union, and the Pacific Rim countries. (478-481)

   A trade balance is the difference between a country's exports and imports. When imports exceed exports, a country has a trade deficit. When exports exceed imports a country has a trade surplus. Because the United States has had large trade deficits since the 1970s, it is a net debtor nation.

   The nature of trade is continually changing. The United States is importing more and more high-tech goods and services from India and China and other East Asian countries.

   Outsourcing is a type of trade. Outsourcing is a larger phenomenon today compared to 30 years ago because countries where jobs are outsourced today—China and India—are much larger.

2. The principle of comparative advantage states that as long as the relative opportunity costs of producing goods differ among countries, there are potential gains from trade. (483-485)

   When countries specialize in the production of those goods for which each has a <u>comparative advantage</u> and then trade, all economies involved benefit.

   A country has a comparative advantage in producing good "x" if its opportunity cost of producing good "x" is lower.

3. Three determinants of the gains of trade are: (485-486)

- The more competition, the less the trader gets.
- Smaller countries get a larger proportion of the gain than larger countries.
- Countries producing goods with economies of scale get a larger gain from trade.

   Also: countries which specialize and trade along the lines of comparative advantage are able to consume more than if they did not undertake trade (they are able to escape the confines of their own production possibility curves).

4. Three reasons for differences between economists' and laypeople's views of trade are: (1) gains from trade are often stealth gains, (2) comparative advantage is determined by more than wages, and (3) nations trade more than just manufactured goods. (486-488)

   The gains from trade in the form of low consumer prices tend to be widespread and not easily recognizable, while the costs in jobs lost tend to be concentrated and readily identifiable. But, the gains outweigh the costs over time. Convincing the public of this remains a challenge, especially for policymakers.

5. Transferable comparative advantages will tend to erode over time. (489-491)

   The U.S. has comparative advantages due to its skilled workforce, institutions, and infrastructure, among other things. Some of these are inherent comparative advantages, while others are transferable comparative advantages. The law of one price and the convergence hypothesis will work to erode any transferable comparative advantages over time. The degree to which, and how quickly, the United States loses some of its comparative advantages depends on how transferable they are.

6. Three policies used to restrict trade are: (491-495)
   - <u>tariffs</u>: taxes on internationally traded goods;
   - <u>quotas</u>: quantity limits placed on imports; and
   - <u>regulatory trade restrictions</u>: government-imposed procedural rules that limit imports.

   Countries can also restrict trade through: voluntary restraint agreements, embargoes, and nationalistic appeals.

   Arguments for restricting trade include:
   - *Unequal internal distribution of the gains from trade;*
   - *Haggling by companies over the gains from trade;*
   - *Haggling by countries over trade restrictions;*
   - *Specialized production; learning by doing; and economies of scale;*
   - *Macroeconomic aspects of trade;*
   - *National security;*
   - *International politics;*
   - *Increased revenue brought in by tariffs.*

   Understand these motives for trade barriers and be able to explain why they may be fallacious.

7. Economists generally oppose trade restrictions because: (500-502)
   - from a global perspective, free trade increases total output;
   - international trade provides competition for domestic companies;
   - restrictions based on national security are often abused or evaded; and
   - trade restrictions are addictive.

   Economists generally argue that the benefits of free trade outweigh the costs—especially over time.

   Trade restrictions limit the supply of an imported good, increasing its price and decreasing quantity. Governments prefer tariffs over quotas because they generate tax revenues, while companies prefer quotas.

8. Free trade associations help trade by reducing barriers to trade among member nations. Free trade associations could hinder trade by building up barriers to trade with nations outside the association. (502-504)

   A free trade association is a group of countries that allows free trade among its members and puts up common barriers against all other countries' goods.

   The WTO and GATT are important international economic organizations designed to reduce trade barriers among <u>all</u> countries.

● SHORT-ANSWER QUESTIONS

1. Who are the primary trading partners of the United States?

2. How has U.S. trade with the rest of the world changed in recent years?

3. What is the principle of comparative advantage?

4. What are three determinants of the gains of trade?

5. What are three reasons laypeople's and economists' views of trade differ?

6. What are four sources of comparative advantages for the United States?

7. Why is the United States losing some of its comparative advantages?

8. In a talk to first-year members of Congress you are asked what they can do to restrict trade. You oblige.

9. You reveal to these first-year members of Congress that you believe in free trade. Hands fly up from people just waiting to tell you why they want to restrict trade. What are some of their reasons?

10. After listening to their remarks, you gather your thoughts and offer them reasons why you generally oppose trade restrictions. What do you say?

11. The first-year members of Congress ask you how the nation joining a free trade association could help and hinder international trade. What do you say?

MATCHING THE TERMS
Match the terms to their definitions

____ **1.** balance of trade

____ **2.** economies of scale

____ **3.** embargo

____ **4.** free trade association

____ **5.** General Agreement on Tariffs and Trade (GATT)

____ **6.** infant industry argument

____ **7.** inherent comparative advantages

____ **8.** law of one price

____ **9.** learning by doing

____ **10.** most-favored nation

____ **11.** comparative advantage

____ **12.** quotas

____ **13.** regulatory trade restrictions

____ **14.** strategic bargaining

____ **15.** strategic trade policy

____ **16.** tariff

____ **17.** trade adjustment assistance programs

____ **18.** transferable comparative advantage

____ **19.** World Trade Organization

a. A tax governments place on internationally traded goods—generally imports.

b. All-out restriction on import or export of a good.

c. As long as the relative opportunity costs of producing goods differ among countries, there are potential gains from trade, even if one country has an absolute advantage in everything.

d. Costs per unit output go down as output increases.

e. Country that will pay as low a tariff on its exports as will any other country.

f. Demanding a larger share of the gains of trade than you might get normally.

g. Government-imposed procedural rules that limit imports.

h. Group of countries that allow free trade among its members and put up common barriers against all other countries' goods.

i. Periodic international conference held in the past to reduce trade barriers.

j. Programs designed to compensate losers for reductions in trade restrictions.

k. Quantity limit placed on imports.

l. An organization whose functions are generally the same as were those of GATT—to promote free and fair trade among countries.

m. With initial protection, an industry will be able to become competitive.

n. You become better at a task the more you perform it.

o. The difference between the value of exports and the value of imports

p. Threatening to implement tariffs to bring about a reduction in tariffs or some other concessions from the other country.

q. Comparative advantages based on factors that are relatively unchangeable.

r. Comparative advantages based on factors that can change relatively easily.

s. In a competitive market there will be pressure for equal factors to be priced equally.

PROBLEMS AND APPLICATIONS

1. a. State whether there is a basis for trade in the following:

Case 1: In Country A the opportunity cost of producing one widget is two wadgets. In Country B the opportunity cost of producing two widgets is four wadgets.

Case 2: In Country C the opportunity cost of producing one widget is two wadgets. In Country D the opportunity cost of producing two widgets is one wadget.

Case 3: In Country E the opportunity cost of producing one widget is two wadgets. In Country F the opportunity cost of producing one widget is four wadgets.

b.   On what general principle did you base your reasoning?

c.   Assume that in Case 3 there are constant marginal returns and constant returns to scale. Country E is currently producing 10 widgets and 4 wadgets. Country F is currently producing 20 widgets and 20 wadgets. Can you make an offer involving trade that will make both countries better off?

d.   How would your answer differ if each country experiences economies of scale?

2.   Suppose Country A and Country B are potential trading partners. Each country produces two goods: fish and wine. If Country A devotes all of its resources to producing fish, it can produce 1,000 fish, and if it devotes all of its resources to producing wine, it can produce 2,000 bottles of wine. If Country B devotes all of its resources to producing fish, it can produce 3,000 fish, and if it devotes all of its resources to producing wine it can produce 3,000 bottles of wine. For simplicity, assume the production possibility curves of these countries are straight lines.

a.   Draw the production possibility curve for Country A on the axes below. In Country A, what is the opportunity cost of one bottle of wine in terms of fish?

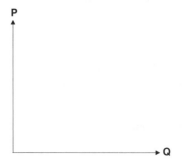

b.   Draw the production possibility curve for Country B on the axes for (a). In Country B, what is the opportunity cost of one bottle of wine in terms of fish?

c.   Does Country A have a comparative advantage in producing either wine or fish? Does Country B have a comparative advantage in producing either wine or fish?

d.   Suppose Country A specialized in that good for which it has a comparative advantage and Country B specialized in that good for which it has a comparative advantage. Each country would then trade the good it produced for the good the other country produced. What would be a fair exchange of goods?

3. Suppose two countries A and B have the following production possibility tables:

% Resources devoted to Machines	Country A Production		Country B Production	
	Machines	Food	Machines	Food
A	100	200	0	40	0
B	80	160	8	32	40
C	60	120	16	28	80
D	40	80	24	24	120
E	20	40	32	16	160
F	0	0	40	0	200

a. Draw the production possibility curves for Country A and Country B on the axes below.

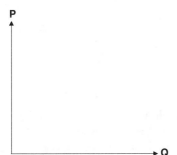

b. Which country has the comparative advantage in the production of food?

c. Suppose each country specializes in the production of one good. Explain how Country A can end up with 50 food units and 150 machines and Country B can end up with 150 food units and 50 machines. Both points are outside the production possibility curve for each country without trade.

4. State whether the trade restriction is a quota, tariff, or regulatory trade restriction.

a. The EU (European Union) requires beef to be free of growth-inducing hormones in order to be traded in EU markets.
b. Hong Kong has maintained rice import controls on quantity since 1955 in order to keep local rice importers in business and to secure a steady wartime food supply.

c. To encourage domestic production of automobile parts, Japan limits the importation of automobile parts according to a rigid schedule of numbers.

d. The United States charges French wineries 10% of the value of each case of French wine imported into the United States.

5. Suppose the U.S. is considering trade restrictions against EU-produced hams. Given the demand and supply curves drawn below, show a tariff and a quota that would result in the same exports of ham to the United States.

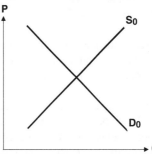

a. Would a tariff or a quota result in higher government revenue?

b. Which would the EU prefer?

c. Which would American ham producers prefer?

d. Which would American consumers prefer?

A BRAIN TEASER

1. What are the benefits and the costs to a nation of lower trade barriers? Which are greater for the nation: the benefits or the costs of free trade?

MULTIPLE CHOICE

Circle the one best answer for each of the following questions:

1. If a nation is a debtor nation it:
    a. is currently running a trade deficit.
    b. is currently running a trade surplus.
    c. has run trade deficits in the past.
    d. has run trade surpluses in the past.

2. If a country has a trade deficit, it is:
    a. consuming more than it is producing.
    b. lending to foreigners.
    c. buying financial assets.
    d. buying real assets.

3. Compared to the past, the United States is now:
    a. importing more high-tech goods and services from India and China and other East Asian countries.
    b. importing more goods and services that are lower down the technological ladder.
    c. outsourcing less to newly emerging industrialized countries like China and India.
    d. facing less competition from newly emerging industrialized countries like China and India.

4. Refer to the graph below. Given these production possibility curves, you would suggest that:

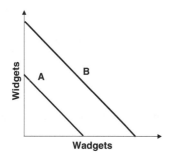

a. Country A should specialize in widgets and Country B in wadgets.
b. no trade should take place.
c. Country A should specialize in wadgets and Country B in widgets.
d. Both countries should produce an equal amount of each.

5. Refer to the graph below. The graph demonstrates Saudi Arabia's and the United States' production possibility curves for widgets and wadgets. Given these production possibility curves, you would suggest that:

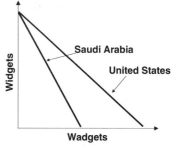

a. Saudi Arabia specialize in widgets and the United States in wadgets.
b. no trade should take place.
c. Saudi Arabia specialize in wadgets and the United States in widgets.
d. Both countries should produce an equal amount of each.

6. If a nation has a comparative advantage in the production of good X then:
    a. it can produce good X at the lowest opportunity cost.
    b. it will import good X.
    c. it can produce more of good X than any other nation.
    d. the opportunity cost of producing an additional unit of good X is greater than for any other nation.

7. A widget has an opportunity cost of 4 wadgets in Saudi Arabia and 2 wadgets in the United States. Given these opportunity costs, you would suggest that:
    a. Saudi Arabia specialize in widgets and the United States in wadgets.
    b. no trade should take place.
    c. Saudi Arabia specialize in wadgets and the United States in widgets.
    d. both countries should produce an equal amount of each.

8. Country A's cost of widgets is $4.00 and cost of wadgets is $8.00. Country B's cost of widgets is 8 euros and cost of wadgets is 16 euros. Which of the following would you suggest?
   a. Country A should specialize in widgets and Country B in wadgets.
   b. Trade of widgets for wadgets would not benefit the countries.
   c. Country A should specialize in wadgets and Country B in widgets.
   d. Both countries should produce an equal amount of each.

9. In considering the distribution of the gains from trade:
   a. smaller countries usually get a larger proportion of the gains from trade.
   b. larger countries usually get a larger proportion of the gains from trade.
   c. the gains are generally split equally between small and large countries.
   d. no statement can be made about the general nature of the split.

10. Which of the following statements correctly summarizes a difference between the layperson's and the economists' views of the net benefits of trade?
    a. Economists often argue that the gains from trade in the form of low consumer prices tend to be widespread and not easily recognizable while the costs in jobs lost tend to be concentrated and readily identifiable.
    b. Economists often argue that most U.S. jobs are at risk of outsourcing while laypeople intuitively recognize that inherent in comparative advantage is that each country has a comparative advantage in the production of some good.
    c. Economists focus on trade in manufactured goods while laypeople also focus on trade involving the services of people who manage the trade.
    d. Economists most often argue that the costs of trade outweigh the benefits while laypeople often argue that the benefits of trade outweigh the costs.

11. Transferable comparative advantages are:
    a. based on factors that are relatively unchangeable.
    b. based on factors that can change relatively easily.
    c. becoming more like inherent comparative advantages with technological innovations.
    d. rarely eroded over time.

12. Trade restrictions tend to:
    a. increase competition.
    b. increase prices to consumers.
    c. benefit consumers.
    d. have economic benefits that outweigh the economic costs.

13. A tariff is a:
    a. tax government places on internationally-traded goods.
    b. quantity limit placed on imports.
    c. total restriction on imports.
    d. government-imposed procedural rule that limits imports.

14. An embargo is a:
    a. tax government places on imports.
    b. quantity limit placed on imports.
    c. total restriction on imports.
    d. government-imposed procedural rule that limits imports.

15. For governments:
    a. tariffs are preferred over quotas because tariffs can help them collect revenues.
    b. quotas are preferred over tariffs because quotas can help them collect revenues.
    c. neither quotas nor tariffs can help collect revenues.
    d. both quotas and tariffs are sources of revenues.

16. Reasons for restricting trade include all of the following *except:*
    a. the existence of learning by doing and economies of scale.
    b. national security reasons.
    c. the increased revenue brought in from tariffs.
    d. the fact that trade decreases competitive pressures at home.

17. Economists generally oppose trade restrictions for all of the following reasons *except:*
    a. from a global perspective, free trade increases total output.
    b. the infant industry argument.
    c. trade restrictions lead to retaliation.
    d. international politics.

18. Free trade associations tend to:
    a. reduce restrictions on trade and thereby always expand free trade.
    b. lower trade barriers for all countries.
    c. replace multinational negotiations, and thereby always hurt free trade.
    d. expand, but also reduce, free trade.

POTENTIAL ESSAY QUESTIONS

You may also see essay questions similar to the "Problems & Applications" and "Brain Teasers" exercises.

1. What is the difference between a tariff and a quota? Why do governments prefer tariffs while foreign producers prefer quotas? What is the result of tariffs and quotas on the price and equilibrium quantity of the imported good?

2. What are six ways in which a country may restrict trade? Why do most economists support free trade and oppose trade restrictions?

ANSWERS

SHORT-ANSWER QUESTIONS

1. The primary trading partners of the United States are Canada, Mexico, the European Union, and Pacific Rim countries. (478-480)

2. The kinds of goods and services the U.S. imports has shifted from primarily basic manufacturing goods and raw commodities to high-tech manufacturing goods and services from developing countries such as India, China, and other East Asian countries. In addition, more and more production of more sophisticated goods and services is being outsourced to these countries because their economies are much larger. (480-481)

3. The principle of comparative advantage is that as long as the relative opportunity costs of production differ among countries, there are potential gains from trade, even if one country has an absolute advantage in everything. (483)

4. Three determinants of the gains of trade are (1) the more competition, the less the trader gets and the more will go to the countries who are trading; (2) smaller countries get a larger proportion of the gain than larger countries; and (3) countries producing goods with economies of scale get a larger gain from trade. (485-486)

5. Three reasons for differences between economists' and laypeople's views of trade are: (1) gains from trade are often stealth gains, (2) comparative advantage is determined by more than wages, and (3) nations trade more than just manufactured goods. (486-488)

6. The United States has comparative advantages due to: (1) skills of the U.S. labor force, (2) U.S. governmental institutions, (3) U.S. physical and technological infrastructure, (4) English is the international language of business, (5) wealth from past production, (6) U.S. natural resources, (7) cachet, (8) inertia, (9) U.S. intellectual property rights, and (10) a relatively open immigration policy. (488-489)

7. The United States is losing some of its transferable comparative advantages (as opposed to inherent comparative advantages) because economic forces push to spread technologies, which eliminates transferable comparative advantages. These economic forces include lower wages, a growing entrepreneurial spirit, institutions conducive to production in developing countries and exchange rate adjustments. (489-491)

8. Three policies countries use to restrict trade are (1) tariffs, (2) quotas, and (3) regulatory trade restrictions. There are others. (491-495)

9. Their answers might include: (1) although foreign competition might make society better off, some people may lose their jobs because of foreign competition (unequal internal distribution of the gains from trade); (2) some foreign companies are taking tough bargaining positions, and restricting trade is our only weapon against that (haggling by companies over trade restrictions); (3) some foreign countries are threatening us with trade restrictions (haggling by countries over the gains from trade); (4) trade restrictions will protect new U.S. industries until they learn to be competitive (learning by doing and economies of scale); (5) imports hurt U.S. domestic income in the short run, and the economy needs to grow in the short run (trade can reduce domestic output in the short run); (6) some restrictions are needed to protect our national security; (7) we do not want to trade with countries who violate our human rights standards or whose ideology conflicts with our democratic ideals (international politics may dominate trade considerations); and (8) tariffs bring in revenue for the U.S. government. (495-500)

10. I would say that I generally oppose trade restrictions because (1) from a global perspective, free trade increases total output, (2) international trade provides competition for domestic companies, (3) restrictions based on national security are often abused, and (4) trade restrictions are addictive. (500-502)

11. Free trade associations promote trade among members by reducing barriers to trade among the member nations. However, free trade associations could hinder trade by building up barriers to trade with nations outside the association. (502-504)

ANSWERS

MATCHING

1-o; 2-d; 3-b; 4-h; 5-i; 6-m; 7-q; 8-s; 9-n; 10-e;11-c; 12-k; 13-g; 14-f; 15-p; 16-a; 17-j;18-r; 19-l.

ANSWERS

PROBLEMS AND APPLICATIONS

1. **a.** There is a basis for trade in Cases 2 and 3 because opportunity costs differ. (483-485)
   b. The general principle is that there are gains from trade to be made when each country has a comparative advantage in a different good. (483-485)
   c. I would have country E specialize in widgets and country F specialize in wadgets. Since country E is currently producing 10 widgets and 4 wadgets, I would have it produce 12 widgets and no wadgets, promising that I will give it 5 wadgets for the extra two widgets it produced. I would have Country F produce 28 wadgets and 18 widgets, promising that I will give it 2 widgets in return for 7 of its wadgets. After I made this trade both countries are one wadget better off. I am two wadgets better off. (These two wadgets are the return to me for organizing the trade.) (483-485)
   d. If there were economies of scale, there would be an even stronger argument for trade. (483-485)

2. **a.** The production possibility curve for Country A is the curve labeled A in the graph below. In Country A the opportunity cost of one bottle of wine is 1/2 fish. Each fish forgone frees up resources sufficient to make two bottles of wine. (483-485)

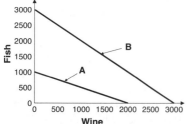

   b. The production possibility curve for Country B is the curve labeled B in the graph above. In Country B the opportu-

nity cost of one bottle of wine is one fish. Each fish forgone frees up resources sufficient to make one bottle of wine. (483-485)

   c. Country A has a comparative advantage in wine because it has to give up only 1/2 a fish for each bottle of wine while Country B has to give up 1 fish for each bottle of wine. Country B must necessarily have a comparative advantage in fish. (483-485)
   d. A fair exchange for B would be giving up one fish for one bottle of wine or better because that is its opportunity cost of producing one fish. A fair exchange for A would be giving up two bottles of wine for 1 fish or better since its opportunity cost of producing two bottles of wine is one fish. Any exchange between these two, such as 2 fish for 3 bottles of wine, would be a fair exchange. (483-485)

3. **a.** The production possibility curves for Country A and Country B are drawn below. (484)

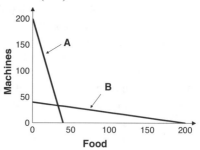

   b. Country B has the comparative advantage in the production of food since it has to give up only 1/5 machine to produce one unit of food while Country A has to give up 5 machines to produce one unit of food. (483-485)
   c. Country A would be willing to supply 5 machines for 1 unit of food. Country A would be willing to supply 5 units of foods for one machine. Let's suppose they trade 1 for 1. Country A would produce 200 machines, selling 50 to Country B for 50 units of foods. Country B would produce 200 food units, and sell 50 to Country A for 50 machines. This way they each reach their higher desired level of consumption. (483-485)

4. **a.** Regulatory trade restriction because this is a regulation that has the final effect of reducing imports without a tax or numerical limitation. (494-495)

b. Quota. It is a numerical restriction on the amount of rice entering the country. (492-494)

c. Quota because it is a numerical restriction on imports. (492-494)

d. Tariff because it is a tax on imports. (492-494)

5. A tariff would shift the supply curve up by the amount of the tariff. A quota with the same result would be at Q_1. Equilibrium quantity would fall from Q_0 to Q_1. Equilibrium price would rise from P_0 to P_1. This is shown on the graph below. (492-494 and Figure 21-5)

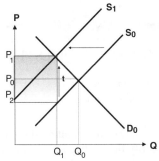

a. The government receives no revenue from the quota, but receives the shaded region as revenue from the tariff as shown on the graph above. (492-495 and Figure 21-5)

b. The EU would prefer the quota since it will receive a higher price, P_1, for the same quantity of goods, Q_1 as it would with a tariff. With a tariff it would receive P_2, for Q_1. (492-495 and Figure 21-5)

c. American ham producers prefer the quota because any increase in domestic demand would be met by domestic supply. (492-495)

d. American consumers do not prefer either since the resulting price and quantity is the same with both. If, however, the tariff revenue were to lead to lower taxes or higher government services, they might prefer the tariff over the quota. They also might prefer the tariff to the quota because any increase in domestic demand will be partially met with imports, keeping domestic producers more efficient than under a quota system. (492-494)

━━━━ **ANSWERS** ━━━━

A BRAIN TEASER

1. The benefits of lower trade barriers are a wider variety of higher quality, lower-priced products made available to consumers. This translates into an increase in the average absolute standard of living for the nation. The costs of lower trade barriers to a nation are the loss of jobs in those industries that find it difficult to compete in the global economy. The economic benefits of free trade outweigh the costs, at least over time. This is why economists generally favor free trade. (500-502)

━━━━ **ANSWERS** ━━━━

MULTIPLE CHOICE

1. c   A debtor nation may currently be running a surplus or a deficit. Debt is accumulated deficits. A debtor nation could be running a surplus if it ran deficits in the past. See pages 482-483.

2. a   If a country has a trade deficit, it is importing (consuming) more than it is exporting (producing). See pages 482-483.

3. a   The U.S. is importing more and more high-tech goods and services that are higher up the technological ladder from India and China and other East Asian countries. The U.S. is outsourcing more to these newly emerging industrialized countries and is therefore facing more competition from these nations. See pages 480-481.

4. b   Since the curves have the same slope, no country has a comparative advantage in either good and there is no basis for trade. See pages 483-485 and Figure 21-3.

5. a   The opportunity cost for Saudi Arabia of wadgets in terms of widgets is higher than the opportunity cost for the United States. So Saudi Arabia should specialize in widgets and the United States in wadgets. See pages 483-485 and Figure 21-3.

6. a   A comparative advantage in the production of X means the nation can produce that good with a lower opportunity cost. Because the nation is relatively more efficient at producing X, it will specialize in its production and export that good. Answer c may be true, but it is also possible to have a comparative advantage in X without being able to produce more of X than any other nation. See pages 483-485.

7. c The opportunity cost for the United States of wadgets in terms of widgets is higher than the opportunity cost for Saudi Arabia. So the United States should specialize in widgets and Saudi Arabia in wadgets. See pages 483-485.

8. b The opportunity cost of widgets and wadgets is equal in both countries so neither country has a comparative advantage in either good and there is no basis for trade. See pages 483-485.

9. a Smaller countries usually find that their production possibilities are changed more, and hence they benefit more. See pages 485-486.

10. a It is because the costs of trade are more visible than the benefits that many laypeople oppose free trade. Switching "economists" and "laypeople" would make options b through d correct. See pages 486-488.

11. b Transferable comparative advantages are based on factors that can change relatively easily and will tend to erode over time. Technological innovations are turning inherent comparative advantages into transferable comparative advantages. See page 489.

12. b Trade restrictions reduce competition and therefore increase prices to consumers. Thus, consumers are hurt. The benefits of trade restrictions go to the domestic producers that do not have to compete as aggressively. The economic costs of trade restrictions (in the form of higher prices consumers must pay) far outweigh their benefits (which go to the protected domestic industries in the form of higher profits and more secure jobs). See pages 491-495.

13. a A tariff is a tax placed on imported goods. See pages 492.

14. c An embargo is an all-out restriction on the trade of goods with another country. See page 494.

15. a Governments prefer tariffs because they generate revenues, quotas do not. See pages 492-494.

16. d Trade increases competitive pressures at home and increases competitiveness. See pages 495-500.

17. b The infant industry argument is an argument in favor of trade restrictions. Economists' response to the infant industry argument is that history shows that few infant industries have ever grown up. See page 499.

18. d While free trade associations may work toward lowering trade barriers among member nations, they may result in higher trade barriers for nonmember countries. See pages 502-504.

■■■■ ANSWERS ■■■■

POTENTIAL ESSAY QUESTIONS

The following are annotated answers. They indicate the general idea behind the answer.

1. A tariff is a tax on an imported item. A quota is a quantity limitation. Tariffs are preferred by governments because they raise revenues and are disliked by foreign producers because they require tax payments to the imposing government. However, notice that both tariffs and quotas raise prices and decrease the quantity of imported goods bought and sold.

2. Countries use a variety of policies to restrict trade. These include:
- Tariffs.
- Quotas.
- Voluntary restraint agreements.
- Embargoes.
- Regulatory trade restrictions.
- Nationalistic appeals.

Economists generally oppose trade restrictions because: (1) from a global perspective, free trade increases total output—it raises standards of living; (2) international trade provides competition for domestic companies; (3) restrictions based on national security are often abused or evaded, and (4) trade restrictions often become addictive for domestic firms that benefit. Free trade forces domestic firms to be efficient—to provide higher quality goods at cheaper prices. Economists argue that trade restrictions may create some short-run benefits, but the costs (or harm done, which includes higher prices domestic consumers must pay) outweigh the benefits over time.

Pretest
Chapters 16 - 21

Take this test in test conditions, giving yourself a limited amount of time to complete the questions. Ideally, check with your professor to see how much time he or she allows for an average multiple choice question and multiply this by 27. This is the time limit you should set for yourself for this pretest. If you do not know how much time your teacher would allow, we suggest 1 minute per question, or about 30 minutes.

1. The irony of any need-based program is that it:
   a. increases the number of needy.
   b. decreases the number of needy.
   c. creates other needs.
   d. destroys needs.

2. The term "derived demand" refers to:
   a. demand by consumers for advertised products.
   b. the demand for luxury goods that is derived from cultural phenomena such as fashion.
   c. the demand for factors of production by firms.
   d. the demand for derivatives.

3. As a factor becomes more important in the production process, the:
   a. firm's derived demand for the factor becomes less elastic.
   b. firm's derived demand for the factor becomes more elastic.
   c. firm's derived demand will not be affected.
   d. elasticity of the derived demand could become either higher or lower.

4. A firm has just changed from being a competitive firm to being a monopolist. Its derived demand for labor:
   a. will increase.
   b. will decrease.
   c. might increase or might decrease.
   d. is unaffected because whether the firm is a competitive firm or a monopolist has no effect on the firm's derived demand for labor.

5. Compared to a competitive labor market, a monopsonist hires:
   a. fewer workers and pays them a higher wage.
   b. fewer workers and pays them a lower wage.
   c. more workers and pays them a higher wage.
   d. more workers and pays them a lower wage.

6. The Lorenz curve is:
   a. a type of supply curve.
   b. a type of demand curve.
   c. a geometric representation of the share distribution of income.
   d. a geometric representation of the socioeconomic distribution of income.

7. If the government increases the amount of food stamps and housing assistance it gives out, the direct effect on U.S. poverty, as officially defined:
   a. will be reduced.
   b. will be increased.
   c. will remain unchanged.
   d. cannot be determined from the information.

8. Refer to the graph below. The Gini coefficient is shown by which area?
   a. A/B
   b. A/(A + B).
   c. B/A.
   d. B/(A + B).

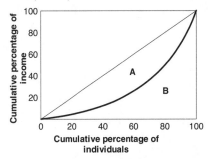

9. Imposing a tax of 40 percent on high income workers in order to give it to low income workers may not be especially effective in redistributing income if the tax:
   a. has large incentive effects.
   b. has no incentive effects.
   c. is seen as a sin tax.
   d. is not seen as a sin tax.

10. An externality is:
 a. the effect of a decision on a third party not taken into account by a decision maker.
 b. another name for exports.
 c. an event that is external to the economy.
 d. the external effect of a government policy.

11. Refer to the graph below. The S curve represents the marginal private cost of production, and the D curve represents the marginal private benefit to consumers of the good. If there is a negative externality of production, and one wants to adjust the curves so that the equilibrium demonstrates the appropriate marginal social costs, either the:

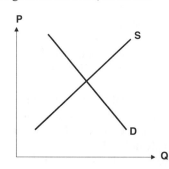

 a. S curve should be shifted in to the left or the D curve should be shifted out to the right.
 b. S curve should be shifted out to the right or the D curve should be shifted in to the left.
 c. S curve should be shifted out to the right or the D curve should be shifted out to the right.
 d. S curve should be shifted in to the left or the D curve should be shifted in to the left.

12. Refer to the graph below. If the government were attempting to set an effluent fee, the amount of that effluent fee should be:
 a. P_1.
 b. P_2.
 c. $P_1 - P_2$.
 d. $P_1 - P_3$.

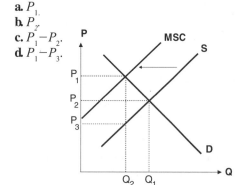

13. A public good is:
 a. any good traded in markets.
 b. a good that is nonexclusive and nonrival.
 c. a good provided only to those who pay for it.
 d. rarely provided by government.

14. Government failure:
 a. always outweighs market failure.
 b. sometimes outweighs market failure.
 c. never outweighs market failure.
 d. is the same as market failure.

15. The good/bad paradox exists because there is:
 a. an inelastic demand for agricultural goods.
 b. an inelastic supply of agricultural goods.
 c. an elastic demand for agricultural goods.
 d. an elastic supply of agricultural goods.

16. Refer to the graph below. What area represents the change in income going to farmers from an increase in supply from S_0 to S_1?
 a. A − C.
 b. A + C.
 c. A + B + C.
 d. C − A.

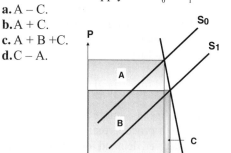

17. Refer to the graph below. If the government imposes a quantity restriction of Q_1 on suppliers, compared to the free market situation, suppliers' net income will:
 a. fall by B.
 b. rise by A.
 c. rise by A − B.
 d. be unaffected.

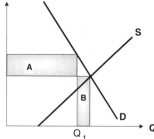

18. Which of the following four methods of price supports would taxpayers favor *least*?
    a. Regulatory methods.
    b. Economic incentives to reduce supply.
    c. Subsidizing the sale.
    d. Buying up and storing the good.

19. Which statement follows from economic theory alone?
    a. The minimum wage should be increased.
    b. The minimum wage should be decreased.
    c. There should be no minimum wage.
    d. No policy prescription follows from economic theory alone.

20. In an automobile crash, people were killed because an automobile company saved $10 by placing the gas tank in the rear of the car. An economist would:
    a. determine whether this made sense with cost/benefit analysis.
    b. see this as reasonable.
    c. see this as unreasonable.
    d. argue that no amount of money should be spared to save a life.

21. Suppose that filtering your water at home reduces your chances from dying of giardia (an intestinal parasite) by 1/45,000. The filter costs you $400 to install. You have chosen to install the filter. Which dollar value best reflects the minimum value you implicitly place on your life?
    a. $400.
    b. $45,000.
    c. $1,800,000.
    d. $18,000,000.

22. If society establishes a law preventing people from selling themselves into slavery:
    a. consumer surplus will be lowered.
    b. consumer surplus will be increased.
    c. economic theory will find that law incorrect.
    d. economic theory will find that law correct.

23. If a country has a trade deficit, it is:
    a. consuming more than it is producing.
    b. borrowing from foreigners.
    c. selling financial assets.
    d. selling real assets.

24. Refer to the graph below. The graph demonstrates Saudi Arabia's and the United States' production possibility curves for widgets and wadgets. Given these production possibility curves, you would suggest that:

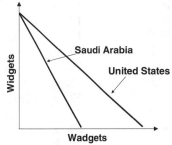

    a. Saudi Arabia specialize in widgets and the United States in wadgets.
    b. no trade should take place.
    c. Saudi Arabia specialize in wadgets and the United States in widgets.
    d. Both countries should produce an equal amount of each.

25. Country A's cost of widgets is $4.00 and cost of wadgets is $8.00. Country B's cost of widgets is 8 francs and cost of wadgets is 16 francs. Which of the following would you suggest?
    a. Country A should specialize in widgets and Country B in wadgets.
    b. Trade of widgets for wadgets would not benefit the countries.
    c. Country A should specialize in wadgets and Country B in widgets.
    d. Both countries should produce an equal amount of each.

26. Transferable comparative advantages are:
    a. based on factors that are relatively unchangeable.
    b. based on factors that can change relatively easily.
    c. becoming more like inherent comparative advantages with technological innovations.
    d. rarely eroded over time.

27. Economists generally oppose trade restrictions for all of the following reasons *except:*
    a. from a global perspective, free trade increases total output.
    b. the infant industry argument.
    c. trade restrictions lead to retaliation.
    d. international politics.

ANSWERS

1.	a	(16:4)		**15.**	a	(19:2)
2.	c	(16:7)		**16.**	d	(19:5)
3.	a	(16:9)		**17.**	c	(19:7)
4.	b	(16:11)		**18.**	c	(19:12)
5.	b	(16:13)		**19.**	d	(20:1)
6.	c	(17:1)		**20.**	a	(20:4)
7.	c	(17:5)		**21.**	d	(20:5)
8.	b	(17:8)		**22.**	a	(20:11)
9.	a	(17:10)		**23.**	a	(21:2)
10.	a	(18:2)		**24.**	a	(21:5)
11.	d	(18:3)		**25.**	b	(21:8)
12.	d	(18:6)		**26.**	b	(21:11)
13.	b	(18:11)		**27.**	b	(21:17)
14.	b	(18:15)				

Key: The figures in parentheses refer to multiple choice question and chapter numbers. For example (1:2) is multiple choice question 2 from chapter 1.

ECONOMIC GROWTH, BUSINESS CYCLES, UNEMPLOYMENT, AND INFLATION

22

● CHAPTER AT A GLANCE

This review is based upon the learning objectives that open the chapter.

1. The long-run framework focuses on supply. The short-run framework focuses on demand. (512-513)

   Issues of growth are considered in a long-run framework. Business cycles are generally considered in a short-run framework. Unemployment and inflation fall within both frameworks.

2a. Growth is usually measured by changes in real GDP. U.S. economic output has grown at an annual rate of 2.5 to 3.5 percent. (513-514)

   Today's growth rates are high by historical standards.

2b. The range of growth rates among countries is wide. (514-515)

   Economies in Africa have consistently grown at below average rates. Japan and Western Europe grew quickly in the last half of the 20th century.

2c. Since 1945 the United States has had 10 recessions. (516-517)

2d. Since the 1980s the target rate of unemployment has been between 5 percent and 6 percent. (522)

   The target rate of unemployment has been called the "natural" rate of unemployment.

2e. Since World War II, the U.S. inflation rate has remained positive and relatively stable. (529)

3. The four phases of the business cycle are: the peak, the downturn, the trough, and the upturn. (517-518)

   Note!
   - *There is an overall upward secular growth trend of 2.5-3.5% shown by the dotted line.*
   - *We want to smooth out fluctuations because of the problems associated with them.*
   - *Two problems with a downturn (recession) are (a) cyclical unemployment and (b) low growth rate.*
   - *One problem with upturn (expansion) is demand-pull inflation.*

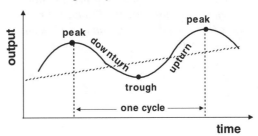

4a. Unemployment rate $= \dfrac{\text{unemployed}}{\text{labor force}} \times 100$. (520)

   Unemployment measures are imperfect but are still a good gauge of the economy's performance.

4b. Some microeconomic categories of unemployment identified by: reason for unemployment, demographic unemployment, duration of unemployment, and unemployment by industry. (528)

   Know the different types of unemployment.

5. Potential output is defined as the output that will be achieved at the target rate of unemployment and the target level of capacity utilization. It is difficult to know precisely where potential output is. (526-527)

Recession:
Actual output (income) < Potential output.

Expansion:
Actual output (income) > Potential output.

Target rate of unemployment (about 5%) is the lowest rate of unemployment that policymakers believe is achievable under existing conditions (where inflation is not accelerating). It is the rate of unemployment that exists when the economy is operating at potential.

6a. Inflation is a continual rise in the price level. (529)

Price indexes are used to measure inflation; The most often used are the Producer Price Index (PPI), GDP deflator, and the Consumer Price Index (CPI).

6b. The "real" amount is the nominal amount divided by the price index multiplied by 100. It is the nominal amount adjusted for inflation. (532-533)
Real means "inflation-adjusted."

$$\text{Real output} = \frac{\text{nominal output}}{\text{price index}} \times 100.$$

7. While inflation may not make the nation poorer, it does cause income to be redistributed and can reduce the amount of information that prices are supposed to convey. (533-534)

Inflation hurts those who cannot or do not raise their prices, but benefits those who can and do raise their prices.

● SHORT-ANSWER QUESTIONS

1. What are the two frameworks economists use to analyze unemployment, inflation, growth, and business cycles? What distinguishes the two frameworks from one another?

2. What is the average growth rate of real output in the United States since 1890 to the present? What are the costs and the benefits of growth?

3. How long has the average expansion since mid-1945 lasted?

4. Since the 1980s, what has been the target rate of unemployment?

5. What is the difference between pre-World War II and post-World War II (1945 the present) inflation in the United States?

6. Label the four phases of the business cycle in the graph below.

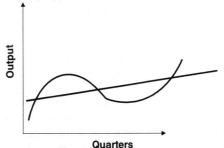

7. How is the unemployment rate calculated?

8. Who in the United States does not work and is nevertheless not counted as unemployed?

9. State two categories of unemployment for which microeconomic policies are appropriate. Why are such categories important to follow?

10. How is the target rate of unemployment related to potential output?

11. Define inflation. If there were no inflation what would happen to the distinction between a real concept and a nominal concept?

13. What is the difference between expected and unexpected inflation?

12. Suppose the price of a Maserati in 1975 was $75,000 and the price of a Maserati in 2005 was $210,000. Your parents exclaim that the prices of Maseratis have risen by 140%! Wow! You tell them that the price of a Maserati really hasn't risen that much. They are confusing real and nominal concepts. Explain what you mean.

14. What are two important costs of inflation?

MATCHING THE TERMS
Match the terms to their definitions

____ 1. business cycle

____ 2. consumer price index

____ 3. cyclical unemployment

____ 4. deflation

____ 5. frictional unemployment

____ 6. GDP deflator

____ 7. hyperinflation

____ 8. inflation

____ 9. labor force participation rate

____ 10. Okun's rule of thumb

____ 11. potential output

____ 12. real output

____ 13. recession

____ 14. structural unemployment

____ 15. target rate of unemployment

____ 16. unemployment rate

a. A downturn that persists for more than two consecutive quarters.

b. A continual rise in the price level.

c. A one percentage point change in the unemployment rate will cause income to change in the opposite direction by 2 percent.

d. Lowest sustainable rate of unemployment policymakers believe is achievable under existing conditions.

e. Index of inflation measuring prices of a fixed "basket" of consumer goods, weighted according to each component's share of an average consumer's expenditures.

f. Index of the average price of the components in GDP relative to a base year.

g. Labor force as a percentage of the total population at least 16 years old.

h. Inflation that hits triple digits (100 percent) or more per year.

i. Output that would materialize at the target rate of unemployment and the target rate of capacity utilization.

j. The total amount of goods and services produced, adjusted for price level changes.

k. The upward or downward movement of economic activity that occurs around the growth trend.

l. The percentage of people in the labor force who can't find a job.

m. Unemployment caused by new entrants to the job market and people who have left their jobs to look for and find other jobs.

n. Unemployment resulting from changes in the structure of the economy itself.

o. Unemployment resulting from fluctuations in economic activity.

p. A continual fall in the price level.

● PROBLEMS AND APPLICATIONS

1. State Okun's law. For each of the following increases in the unemployment rate, state what will likely happen to income in the United States:

    a. Unemployment rate falls 2 percentage points.

    b. Unemployment rate falls 1 percentage point.

    c. Unemployment rate increases 3 percentage points.

2. For each, state whether the unemployment is structural or cyclical.

    a. As the United States becomes a more high-tech producer, labor-intensive factories relocate to low-wage countries. Factory workers lose their jobs and the unemployment rate rises.

    b. As it becomes more acceptable for mothers to work, more women enter the labor market looking for work. The unemployment rate rises.

    c. Foreign economies slow and demand fewer U.S. exports. Unemployment rate rises.

3. Calculate the following given the information about the economy in the table:

Total population	290 million
Noninstitutional population	220 million
Incapable of working	70 million
Not in the labor force	75 million
Employed	135 million
Unemployed	10 million

    a. Labor force.

    b. Unemployment rate.

4. Create a price index for New England Patriots fans using the following basket of goods with 2005 prices as the base year.

Quantities in 2005	Prices 2005	2006
12 packs of Pepsi	$2.50/pck	$2.00/pck
12 fan T-shirts	$15/shirt	$20/shirt
16 football tickets	$25/ticket	$30/ticket

    a. What is the price of the basket of goods in each year? Show how the price index is 100 in the base year 2005.

    b. Using 2005 as the base year, what is the price index in 2006? By how much have prices risen?

    c. What are some potential flaws of this price index?

5. Calculate the following given the following information about the economy in 1985, 1995, and 2004:

	1985	1995	2004
Nominal GDP (in billions of dollars)	4,220.3	____	11,735
GDP deflator (index, 2000=100)	69.7	92.1	____
Real GDP (in billions of 2000 dollars)	____	8031.7	10,841.9
Population (in millions)	238	265	296

a. Nominal GDP in 1995.

b. Real GDP in 1985.

c. Rise in the price level from 1985 to 2004.

d. Growth in real output from 1985 to 2004.

e. Per capita real GDP in 1985, 1995, 2004. What was the growth in per capita real output from 1985 to 2004?

6. Answer each of the following questions about nominal output, real output, and inflation:
    a. Nominal output increased from $11.0 trillion in 2003 to $11.7 trillion in 2004. The GDP deflator rose over that same year by 2.2%. By how much did real output increase?

b. Real output increased from $9.19 trillion to $9.21 trillion from 2000 to 2001. The GDP deflator rose over that same year by 2.5%. By how much did nominal output increase?

c. Real output decreased from $6.70 billion in 1990 to $6.67 billion in 1991. Nominal output rose by 3.2%. By how much did the price level rise from 1990 to 1991?

● A BRAIN TEASER

1. How could output and unemployment rise in an economy at the same time?

● MULTIPLE CHOICE

Circle the one best answer for each of the following questions:

1. Inflation and unemployment:
    a. are best studied in the long-run framework.
    b. are best studied in the short-run framework.
    c. fall within both the short- and long-run frameworks.
    d. are not problems of today and therefore are not studied.

2. All of the following are long-run growth policies *except*:
    a. increasing government spending to spur consumer spending.
    b. reducing tax rates to increase incentives to work.
    c. providing funding for research.
    d. following policies to reduce interest rates and increase business investment.

3. If a country of 296 million people has a total income of $12 trillion, its per capita income is:
   a. $32.52.
   b. $35,520.
   c. $40.54.
   d. $40,541.

4. The secular trend growth rate in the United States is approximately:
   a. 1 to 1.5 percent per year.
   b. 2.5 to 3.5 percent per year.
   c. 5 to 5.5 percent per year.
   d. 7 to 7.5 percent per year.

5. Some people have argued that the two goals of (1) environmental protection and (2) economic growth that involves increased material consumption by individuals do not necessarily contradict each other because spending on the environment can create growth and jobs. This argument:
   a. offers great hope for the future.
   b. is incorrect because environmental issues are not as important as material consumption.
   c. is correct because material consumption is not as important as the environment.
   d. is incorrect because the environmental projects will use the resources generated from growth, leaving little or nothing for increased personal consumption.

6. From 1950 to 2005, which geographic area or country had the highest per capita growth rate?
   a. China.
   b. Western Europe.
   c. North America.
   d. Latin America.

7. The business cycle characterized by the Great Depression occurred in the early
   a. 1900s.
   b. 1930s.
   c. 1950s.
   d. 1960s.

8. Leading indicators include:
   a. manufacturing and trade sales volume.
   b. number of employees on non-agricultural payrolls.
   c. industrial production.
   d. new orders for goods and materials.

9. A Classical economist is most likely to support government intervention when an economy is:
   a. at a peak.
   b. at a trough.
   c. in a depression.
   d. in an upturn.

10. Under pure capitalism, the main deterrent of unemployment is:
    a. pure government intervention.
    b. pure market intervention.
    c. the fear of hunger.
    d. new immigrants entering the country.

11. Since the 1980s the target rate of unemployment generally has been:
    a. between 2 and 4 percent.
    b. between 3 and 5 percent.
    c. between 4 and 6 percent.
    d. between 7 and 9 percent.

12. Keynesians:
    a. generally favor activist government policies.
    b. generally favor laissez-faire policies.
    c. believe that frictional unemployment does not exist.
    d. believe that all unemployment is cyclical unemployment.

13. Classicals:
    a. generally favor activist government policies.
    b. generally favor laissez-faire policies.
    c. believe that frictional unemployment does not exist.
    d. believe that all unemployment is cyclical unemployment.

14. The level of output that would materialize at the target rate of unemployment and the target rate of capital utilization is called:
    a. nominal output.
    b. actual output.
    c. potential output.
    d. utilized output.

15. Okun's rule of thumb states that:
    a. a 1 percentage-point change in the unemployment rate will cause income to change in the same direction by 2 percent.
    b. a 1 percentage-point change in the unemployment rate will cause income to change in the opposite direction by 2 percent.
    c. a 2 percentage-point change in the unemployment rate will cause income to change in the same direction by 1 percent.
    d. a 2 percentage-point change in the unemployment rate will cause income to change in the opposite direction by 1 percent.

16. Using Okun's rule of thumb, if unemployment rises from 5 to 6 percent, one would expect total output of $5 trillion to:
    a. rise by $5 billion.
    b. rise by $100 billion.
    c. fall by $100 billion.
    d. fall by $5 billion.

17. A one-time rise in the price level is:
    a. inflation if that rise is above 5 percent.
    b. inflation if that rise is above 10 percent.
    c. inflation if that rise is above 15 percent.
    d. not inflation.

18. Food and beverages make up about 15 percent of total expenditures. If food and beverage prices rise by 10 percent while the other components of the price index remain constant, approximately by how much will the price index rise?
    a. 1 percent.
    b. 1.5 percent.
    c. 15 percent.
    d. 25 percent.

19. Real output is:
    a. total amount of goods and services produced.
    b. total amount of goods and services produced adjusted for price level changes.
    c. total amount of goods produced, adjusted for services that aren't real.
    d. total amount of goods and services that are really produced as opposed to ones that are resold.

20. If the price level rises by 20 percent and real output remains constant, by how much will nominal output rise?
    a. 1 percent.
    b. 5 percent.
    c. 20 percent.
    d. 40 percent.

21. A cost of inflation is that:
    a. it makes everyone poorer.
    b. it makes the poor poorer but the rich richer.
    c. There are no costs of inflation because inflation does not make the society as a whole poorer.
    d. it reduces the informational content of prices.

22. Unexpected inflation:
    a. makes everyone poorer.
    b. redistributes income from those who raised their prices to those who did not.
    c. redistributes income from those who did not raise their prices to those who did.
    d. is impossible since firms always plan price increases.

● POTENTIAL ESSAY QUESTIONS

You may also see essay questions similar to the "Problems & Applications" and "Brain Teasers" exercises.

1. Full employment, keeping inflation under control, and economic growth are among the major macroeconomic goals of all societies. Why is economic growth a major macroeconomic goal?

2. What is potential output and how is it related to the target rate of unemployment and the target level of capacity utilization? Which is greater: potential or actual output during a recession? During an economic boom?

3. What are some of the problems with the interpretation of unemployment statistics that can cause unemployment statistics to underestimate and to overestimate the true rate of unemployment? How do Classical and Keynesian economists differ in this regard?

ANSWERS

SHORT-ANSWER QUESTIONS

1. Economists use the long-run framework and the short-run framework to analyze macroeconomic problems. The long-run framework focuses on supply while the short-run framework focuses on demand. (512-513)

2. Real output has grown 2.3 - 3.5% per year since 1890. The benefits of growth are improvements in the standard of living, on average. The costs are pollution, resource exhaustion and destruction of natural habitat. (513-514)

3. The average expansion since mid-1945 has lasted 57 months. (519)

4. Since the 1980s, the target rate of unemployment has been between 5 and 6 percent. (522)

5. The inflation rate in the U.S. before World War II fluctuated and was sometimes positive and sometimes negative. Since World War II the price level has continually risen. (529)

6. The four phases of the business cycle are: the peak, the downturn, the trough, and the upturn. They are labeled in the graph below. (517-518)

7. The unemployment rate is calculated by dividing the number of unemployed individuals by the number of people in the civilian labor force, and multiplying the result by 100. (524-525)

8. Those who are not in the labor force and those incapable of working are not employed and are not counted as unemployed. They include students, retirees, homemakers, those incapable of working, and those who choose not to participate in the labor force. (525)

9. Two microeconomic subcategories of unemployment include the reason for unemployment and demographic unemployment. Others are duration of unemployment and unemployment by industry. These categories are important to follow because policies affect different types of unemployment differently and sometimes macro policies should be supplemented by micro policies. (528)

10. Potential output is that level of output that will be achieved at the target rate of unemployment. (527)

11. Inflation is a continual rise in the price level. If there were no inflation there would be no difference between real and nominal concepts. A real concept is the nominal concept adjusted for inflation. (529, 532-533)

12. Nominally Maseratis have risen by 150% from 1975 to 2005, but all other prices have risen during that time period too, including wages. You must adjust the rise in the aggregate price level to find out how much Maseratis have risen in real terms. From 1975 to 2005, the price level rose by 147%. (We used the *Economic Report of the President* to find this information.) So, the real price of the Maserati rose by only approximately 3% from 1975 to 2005. (532-533)

13. Expected inflation is the amount of inflation that people predict. Unexpected inflation is inflation that is a surprise. (533-534)

14. Two important costs of inflation are that it redistributes income from people who do not raise their price to people who do raise their price; and it can reduce the amount of information that prices are supposed to convey. (534-535)

ANSWERS

MATCHING

1-k; 2-e; 3-o; 4-p; 5-m; 6-f; 7-h; 8-b; 9-g; 10-c; 11-i; 12-j; 13-a; 14-n; 15-d; 16-l.

ANSWERS

PROBLEMS AND APPLICATIONS

1. Okun's rule of thumb states that a 1-percentage point change in the unemployment rate will cause income in the economy to change in the opposite direction by 2 percent.
    a. Income rises 4 percent. (527)
    b. Income rises 2 percent. (527)
    c. Income falls 6 percent. (527)

2. a. Structural because this is a structural change in the economy. (520)
    b. Structural because this is a change in social structure. (520)
    c. Cyclical because this is unemployment due to a change in economic activity. (520)

3. a. Labor force = employed + unemployed = 145 million. (524-525)
    b. Unemployment rate = (unemployed/labor force)×100 = 6.9%. (524-525)

4. a. The price of the basket in 2005 is $610 and in 2006 is $744. Since 2005 is the base year, the index must be 100. This is calculated as (price of the basket in 2005)/(price of the basket in 2005) = $610/$610 × 100 = 100. (530)
    b. The price index in 2006 is (price of the basket in 2006)/(price of the basket in 2005) = $744/$610 × 100 = 122. Prices rose by 22%. (530)
    c. Some potential flaws are that (1) the basket of goods is small and might not reflect the true basket of goods purchased by Patriots fans, (2) the basket of goods is fixed (since the price of Pepsi fell, fans might be buying more Pepsi and fewer football tickets), (3) the basket does not reflect quality improvements (since the Patriots won the Super Bowl in 2005, the quality of subsequent games in 2006 might

improve, but the tickets are counted as if they were the same as in 2005). (530)

5. a. Nominal GDP in 1995 is $7,397.2 billion dollars. Calculate this by multiplying real GDP in 1995 by the GDP deflator and dividing by 100. (532-533)
    b. Real GDP in 2000 dollars in 1985 is $6,055 billion. Calculate this by dividing nominal GDP by the GDP deflator and multiplying by 100. (532-533)
    c. The price level rose by 55% from 1985 to 2004. Calculate this by dividing the change in the GDP price deflator by the base year deflator and multiplying by 100: (108.2 − 69.7)/69.7 × 100. (532-533)
    d. Real output grew by 79% from 1985 to 2004. Calculate this by dividing the change in real GDP from 1985 to 2004 by the base year real GDP and multiplying by 100: (10,841.9 − 6,055)/6,055 × 100. (532-533)
    e. Per capita real GDP in 1985 was $25,441; in 1995 it was $30,308; in 2004 it was $36,628. Calculate this by dividing real GDP by the population. Per capita real GDP rose by 44% from 1985 to 2004. (532-533)

6. a. Nominal output increased by 6.4% from 2003 to 2004. Since the GDP deflator rose over that same year, we know that real output increased by less—specifically by 4.2% from 2003 to 2004. Subtract inflation from the change in nominal output to get the change in real output: 6.4% − 2.2% = 4.2%. (532-533)
    b. Real output increased 0.2% from 2000 to 2001. Since the GDP deflator rose 2.5% over that same year, we know that nominal output increased 2.7% from 2000 to 2001. Add inflation to the change in real output to find the change in nominal output: 2.5% + 0.2% = 2.7%. (532-533)
    c. Real output fell 0.45% from 1990 to 1991. Since nominal output rose by 3.2%, we know the price level rose 3.65% from 1990 to 1991. Subtract the change in real output from the change in nominal output to find the inflation rate: 3.2% − (−0.45%) = 3.65%. (532-533)

━━━ ANSWERS ━━━

A BRAIN TEASER

1. Usually one would expect unemployment to fall as output rises because it takes more workers to produce more output. However, an increase in productivity of workers can cause an increase in output without any reduction in unemployment. Another possibility is that the labor force participation rate could be rising so that the labor force is rising at a faster pace than employment. This would cause unemployment to rise even though output is expanding and the economy is growing. (520-521)

━━━ ANSWERS ━━━

MULTIPLE CHOICE

1. c   As the text states on page 512, inflation and unemployment are both short- and long-run problems.

2. a   As stated on page 513, the long run focuses on supply issues that increase the incentive to work, create new technologies, and invest in capital.

3. d   Per capita income is calculated by dividing total income by total population as stated on page 514.

4. b   The secular trend is the long-term growth trend. See pages 513-514.

5. d   As more material goods made available by growth are used for antipollution equipment, less is available for personal consumption. The added material goods have already been used. See page 516.

6. a   As seen in the table on page 514, China's per capita growth rate averaged 4.5 percent from 1950 to 2005. Western Europe's per capita growth rate was 2.2 percent, while North America's was 2.1 percent and Latin America's was 1.9 percent.

7. b   See page 518.

8. d   The others are coincident indicators. Even if you didn't remember this, you should be able to figure out that the change in inventory predicts what firms think will be happening in the future, whereas the others tell what is happening now. See pages 519-520.

9. c   Almost all economists believe government should intervene during a depression. See page 518.

10. c   As discussed on page 521, the fear of hunger was the main deterrent to unemployment. A second deterrent would have been emigration, but that would not be as good an answer. Since d says immigration (the flowing in of people), not emigration, d is definitely wrong.

11. c   See page 522.

12. a   See pages 516-517.

13. b   See pages 516-517.

14. c   As discussed on page 527, the statement that begins the question is the definition of potential output.

15. b   See page 527.

16. c   Total output moves in the opposite direction by 2% times $5 trillion, which equals a fall of $100 billion. See page 527.

17. d   As the text points out on page 529, inflation is a continual rise in the price level, so the use of the term "one-time" should have clued you that d is the answer.

18. b   To determine the price level rise you multiply each component by its price rise. Since only 15% of the total rose, you get 10% times 15% = 1.5%. See page 530.

19. b   See pages 532-533. A reminder: A service is considered just as much a good and a component of real output as is a physical good.

20. c If real output remains constant, then the nominal output must also rise by 20%, as discussed on page 533.

21. d Inflation does not make society richer or poorer, and the distributional consequences of inflation differ, eliminating answers a and b. While the second part of c is true, that doesn't mean that there are no costs of inflation and, as discussed on pages 534-535, one of those costs is the reduction in the informational content of prices.

22. c As discussed on page 533, unexpected inflation is inflation that surprises people. Those people who didn't raise their prices are surprised. Income is redistributed from those people who didn't raise their prices to those who did.

ANSWERS

POTENTIAL ESSAY QUESTIONS

The following are annotated answers. They indicate the general idea behind the answer.

1. Economic growth is a major macroeconomic goal because it provides more jobs for a growing population. If output increases more than population increases then per capita growth occurs. Assuming there is no change in the distribution of the nation's income then everybody gets a "bigger piece of the pie." In this way economic growth increases the average absolute standard of living for people. *Remember, economic growth is valued by all nations because it raises the standard of living.*

2. Potential output is the output that would materialize at the target rate of unemployment and the target level of capacity utilization. Potential output grows at the secular (long-term) trend rate of 2.5 to 3.5 percent per year. When the economy is in a recession, actual output is below potential output. When the economy is in a boom, actual output is above potential output.

3. The Bureau of Labor Statistics (BLS) estimates the rate of unemployment. Underestimation can occur because discouraged workers are not counted as unemployed. Also, many people may work part-time but would like to work full-time. This "underemployment" is not reflected in unemployment statistics and suggests that the official unemployment statistics underestimate the true problem. Alternatively, some people may be counted as being unemployed when they are working in the underground economy–working for "cash under the table." In this case, the official statistics will overestimate true unemployment. The Classicals and Keynesians differ most when it comes to the number of discouraged workers. Some Keynesians argue that the BLS underestimates unemployment significantly because a great number of discouraged workers are not counted as being unemployed.

NATIONAL INCOME ACCOUNTING

CHAPTER AT A GLANCE

This review is based upon the learning objectives that open the chapter.

1. National income accounting enables us to measure and analyze how much a nation is producing and consuming. (539-540)

    GDP is:
    - *Most common measure of a nation's output (income)*

    - *Calculated by either:*
      a) expenditures approach, or
      b) income approach

2a. Gross domestic product (GDP): Aggregate final output of residents and businesses in an economy in a one-year period. (540)

    GDP is total market ($) value of all __final__ goods and services produced in a one-year period.

    GDP is output produced within a country's borders; GNP is output produced by a country's citizens wherever they may be in the world.

    GNP = GDP + Net foreign factor income where:

    Net foreign factor income is the foreign income of a country's citizens less the income of residents who are not citizens.

2b. To avoid double counting, you must eliminate intermediate goods, either by calculating only final output (expenditures approach), or by calculating only final income (income approach) by using the value added approach. (541-542)

Know what is and what is not included when calculating GDP.

GDP does not include:
- *intermediate goods (sold for resale or further processing);*
- *second-hand sales;*
- *government transfers, housespouse production, or any other non-market activity;*
- *underground economic activity.*

3. GDP can be calculated using either the income or expenditures approach because of the national income identity. (545-546)

    The definition of profit is key to the equality of income and expenditures. Profit is total output less payments to the factors of production.

    Hint: In most "non-technical" discussions, "output" (GDP) and "income" (NI) are used interchangeably—that is, GDP is assumed to be equal to NI for purposes of simplification.

4. GDP = C + I + G + (X − M) is an accounting identity because it is defined as true. (546-547)

    The above identity is really the expenditures approach, which states:

    Total output = Total expenditures;
    Total output = GDP;
    Total expenditures=C+I+G+(X−M);
    By substitution: GDP = C + I + G + (X−M).

    Know what C, I, G, and X−M stand for!

    Also note:
    (X − M) = Net exports.
    If (X−M) is positive, then X>M→Trade surplus.
    If (X−M) is negative, then X<M→Trade deficit.
    If (X−M) is zero, then X=M→Trade balance.

5. Real GDP is nominal GDP adjusted for inflation. (552-553)

    GDP is a price times quantity (P×Q) phenom-enon. GDP can rise due to an increase in P (price level) and/or an increase in Q (real quantity of output).

    Real GDP, in essence, holds prices (P) constant. Hence, real GDP is inflation (or deflation) adjusted.

6. Limitations of national income accounting include: (553-556)

    ● Measurement problems exist.
    ● GDP measures economic activity, not welfare; and
    ● Subcategories are often interdependent.

    GDP is not and was never intended to be a measure of social well-being.

7. Using GDP to compare standards of living among countries has its problems. (551-552)

    GDP only measures market activity. In developing countries individuals often produce and trade outside the market.

    Market prices often vary considerably among countries making the value of the same income in terms of purchasing power different.

● SHORT-ANSWER QUESTIONS

1. What is the purpose of national income accounting?

2. What is GDP?

3. What is GNP? How does it differ from GDP?

4. Calculate the contribution of Chex cereal (from seeds to consumer) to GDP, using the following information:

Participants	Cost of materials	Value of Sales
Farmer	0	200
Chex factory	200	500
Distributor	500	800
Grocery store	800	1000

5. What are the four components of gross domestic product? What are the four components of national income?

6. Say the price level rises 10% from an index of 1 to an index of 1.1 and nominal GDP rises from $4 trillion to $4.6 trillion. What is nominal GDP in the second period? What is real GDP in the second period?

7. As pointed out by the quotation that begins the chapter on national income accounting, statistics can be misleading. In what way can national income statistics be misleading? Given your answer, why use them at all?

MATCHING THE TERMS
Match the terms to their definitions

___ 1. depreciation
___ 2. disposable personal income
___ 3. gross domestic product
___ 4. gross national product
___ 5. intermediate products
___ 6. national income (NI)
___ 7. national income accounting
___ 8. net domestic product
___ 9. net foreign factor income
___ 10. nominal GDP
___ 11. real GDP
___ 12. value added
___ 13. wealth accounts

a. Personal income less personal taxes.
b. GDP calculated at existing prices.
c. Aggregate final output of residents and businesses in an economy in a one-year period.
d. Total income earned by citizens and businesses of a country.
e. GDP adjusted to take account of depreciation.
f. Aggregate final output of citizens and businesses of an economy in a one-year period.
g. Income from foreign domestic factor sources minus foreign factor incomes earned domestically.
h. Nominal GDP adjusted for inflation.
i. Products of one firm used in some other firm's production of another firm's product.
j. A balance sheet of an economy's stock of assets and liabilities.
k. The increase in value that a firm contributes to a product or service.
l. A set of rules and definitions for measuring economic activity in the aggregate economy.
m. The decrease in an asset's value.

PROBLEMS AND APPLICATIONS

1. Using the value added or final sales approach to calculate GDP, state how much the action described has added to GDP:

   a. A used car dealer buys a car for $3,000 and resells it for $3,300.

   b. A company sells 1,000 disks for $500 each. Of these, it sells 600 to other companies for production and 400 to individuals.

   c. A company sells 50 computers at a retail price of $1,000 apiece and 100 software packages at a retail price of $50 apiece to consumers. The same company sells 25 computers at $800 and 50 software packages at $30 apiece to wholesalers. The wholesalers then sell the 25 computers at $1,250 apiece and the 50 software packages at $75 apiece.

   d. Fred purchases 100 stock certificates valued at $5 apiece and pays a 10% commission. When the price declines to $4.50 apiece, Fred decides to sell all 100 certificates, again at a 10% commission.

   e. Your uncle George receives $600 Social Security income each month for one year.

2. Use the following table showing the production of 500 boxes of Wheaties cereal to calculate the contribution to GDP using the value-added approach.

Participants	Cost of materials	Value of sales
Farmer	$ 0	$ 150
Mill	$ 150	$ 250
Cereal maker	$ 250	$ 600
Wholesaler	$ 600	$ 800
Grocery store	$ 800	$ 1,000

a. Calculate the value added at each stage of production.

b. What is the total value of all sales?

c. What is the total value added?

d. What is the contribution to GDP of the production of those Wheaties?

3. There are three firms in an economy: X, Y, and Z. Firm X buys $200 worth of goods from firm Y and $300 worth of goods from firm Z, and produces 250 units of output at $4 per unit. Firm Y buys $150 worth of goods from firm X, and $250 worth of goods from firm Z, and produces 300 units of output at $6 per unit. Firm Z buys $75 worth of goods from firm X, and $50 worth of goods from firm Y, and produces 300 units at $2 per unit. All other products are sold to consumers. Answer the following:

a. What is GDP?

b. How much government revenue would a value added tax of 10% generate?

c. How much government revenue would an income tax of 10% generate?

d. How much government revenue would a 10% sales tax on final output generate?

4. You have been hired as a research assistant and are given the following data about the economy:
    All figures are in billions of dollars.

Transfer payments	$70
Non-business interest income	5
Net exports	10
Indirect business taxes	44
Net foreign factor income	3
Corporate income tax	69
Social Security taxes	37
Personal income taxes	92
Corporate retained earnings	49
Gross private investment	200
Government purchases	190
Personal consumption	550
Depreciation	65

You are asked to calculate the following:

a. GDP.

b. GNP.

c. NDP.

d. NI.

e. Personal income.

f. Disposable personal income.

5. You have been hired as a research assistant and are given the following data about another economy (profits, wages, rents, and interest are measured nationally):

Corporate income tax	$200
Net non-business interest income	10
Profits	505
Employee compensation	880
Rents	30
Depreciation	20
Indirect business taxes	110
Corporate retained earnings	50
Net foreign factor income	-5
Interest	175
Social Security taxes	0
Transfer payments	0
Personal taxes	150

Calculate the following:

a. GDP.

b. GNP.

c. NDP.

d. National income.

e. Personal income.

f. Disposable personal income.

6. Use the following table to answer the questions:

	Real output bils. of 2000 $	Nominal output bils. of dollars	GDP deflator 2000=100
2000	9,817.0	9,817	_____
2001	9890.7	10,128	
2002	10,074.8	_____	104.1
2003	_____	_____	106.0
2004	_____	111,735	108.2

a. What is output for 2004 in 2000 dollars?

b. What is the output in nominal terms in 2002?

c. What is the GDP deflator in 2000?

d. Real output grew by 1.9% from 2002 to 2003. By how much did nominal output grow from 2002 to 2003?

● A BRAIN TEASER

1. Why must imports be subtracted in calculating GDP?

● MULTIPLE CHOICE

Circle the one best answer for each of the following questions:

1. GDP is:
    a. the total market value of all final goods and services produced in an economy in a one-year period.
    b. the total market value of all goods and services produced in an economy in a one-year period.
    c. the total market value of all final goods and services produced by a country's citizens in a one-year period.
    d. the sum of all final goods and services produced in an economy in a one-year period.

2. To move from GDP to GNP, one must:
    a. add net foreign factor income.
    b. subtract inflation.
    c. add depreciation.
    d. subtract depreciation.

3. If a firm's cost of materials is $100 and its sales are $500, its value added is:
    a. $100.
    b. $400.
    c. $500.
    d. $600.

4. If you, the owner, sell your old car for $600, how much does GDP increase?
    a. By $600.
    b. By the amount you bought it for, minus the $600.
    c. By zero.
    d. By the $600 you received and the $600 the person you sold it to paid, or $1,200.

5. There are two firms in an economy, Firm A and Firm B. Firm A produces 100 widgets and sells them for $2 apiece. Firm B produces 200 gadgets and sells them for $3 apiece. Firm A sells 30 of its widgets to Firm B and the remainder to consumers. Firm B sells 50 of its gadgets to Firm A and the remainder to consumers. What is GDP in this economy?
    a. $210.
    b. $590.
    c. $600.
    d. $800.

6. If a woman divorces her husband (who has been cleaning the house) and hires him to continue cleaning her house for $20,000 per year, GDP will:
    a. remain constant.
    b. increase by $20,000 per year.
    c. decrease by $20,000 per year.
    d. remain unchanged.

7. The national income identity shows that the value of:
    a. factor services is equal to the value of final goods plus investment.
    b. factor services is equal to the value of final goods plus savings.
    c. factor services is equal to the value of final goods sold.
    d. consumption goods is equal to the value of factor services.

8. Which of the following correctly lists the components of total expenditures?
    a. consumption, investment, depreciation, exports minus imports.
    b. consumption, investment, government expenditures, exports minus imports.
    c. rent, profit, interest, wages.
    d. consumption, net foreign factor income, investment, government expenditures.

9. The largest component of expenditures in GDP is:
    a. consumption.
    b. investment.
    c. net exports.
    d. government purchases of goods and services.

10. The largest component of national income is:
    a. rents.
    b. net interest.
    c. profits.
    d. compensation to employees.

11. Gross investment differs from net investment by:
    a. net exports.
    b. net imports.
    c. depreciation.
    d. transfer payments.

12. While the size of the U.S. federal government budget is approximately $2.2 trillion, the federal government's contribution in the GDP accounts is approximately:
    a. $0.5 trillion.
    b. $1.5 trillion.
    c. $2.0 trillion.
    d. $5.0 trillion.

13. Which of the following factors serves to equate income and expenditure?
    a. profit.
    b. depreciation.
    c. net foreign factor income.
    d. value added.

14. Switching from the exchange rate approach to the purchasing power parity approach for calculating GDP generally:
    a. does not make a significant difference for a developing country's GDP relative to a developed country's GDP.
    b. increases a developing country's GDP relative to a developed country's GDP.
    c. decreases a developing country's GDP relative to a developed country's GDP.
    d. changes the relative GDP of developing country's GDP, but not in a predictable fashion.

15. If inflation is 10 percent and nominal GDP goes up 20 percent, real GDP goes up approximately:
    a. 1 percent.
    b. 10 percent.
    c. 20 percent.
    d. 30 percent.

16. Which of the following is the *preferable* measure available to compare changes in standards of living among countries over time?
    a. changes in nominal income.
    b. changes in nominal per capita income.
    c. changes in real income.
    d. changes in real per capita income.

17. If nominal GDP rises, welfare:
    a. has definitely increased.
    b. has definitely decreased.
    c. may have increased or decreased.
    d. most likely has increased.

18. Estimates of the importance of the underground economy in the United States indicate that it is:
    a. very small—under 1 percent of the total economy.
    b. somewhere between 1.5 percent all the way to 20 percent of the total economy.
    c. somewhere between 1.5 percent all the way to 60 percent of the total economy.
    d. as large as the non-underground economy.

● POTENTIAL ESSAY QUESTIONS

You may also see essay questions similar to the "Problems & Applications" and "Brain Teasers" exercises.

1. Using the circular flow model, explain why any dollar value of output must give rise to an identical amount of income (at least for all practical concerns).

2. How might an economy experience an increase in nominal GDP but experience negative growth at the same time?

ANSWERS

SHORT-ANSWER QUESTIONS

1. The purpose of national income accounting is to measure and analyze how much the nation is producing and consuming. National income accounting defines the relationship among the sub-aggregates of aggregate production. (539-540)

2. GDP is the aggregate final output of *residents* and businesses *in* an economy in a one-year period. (540)

3. GNP is aggregate final output of *citizens* and businesses *of* an economy in a one-year period. GDP is output produced within a country's borders while GNP is output produced by a country's citizens anywhere in the world. Add net foreign factor income to GDP to get GNP. (540)

4. $1,000. We could use either the value added approach or the final output approach. Summing the value added at each stage of production — the difference between cost of materials and value of sales —we get $1,000. (540-541)

Participants	Cost of materials	Value of Sales	Value Added
Farmer	$0	$200	$200
Chex factory	200	500	300
Distributor	500	800	300
Grocery store	800	1000	200
Sum (total output)			1000

5. The four components of gross domestic product are consumption, investment, government expenditures, and net exports (X − M). The four components that comprise NI are compensation to employees, rents, interest, and profits. (547-548)

6. A real value is a nominal value adjusted for inflation. So, nominal GDP in the second period is $4.6 trillion, but real GDP is $4.6 trillion divided by the price index, 1.1, or $4.18 trillion. (552-553)

7. National income accounting statistics can be misleading. They are subject to measurement error; they are based on samples of data and assumptions about behavior. For example, the measurement of inflation is widely believed to overestimate true inflation. Also, GDP does not include non-market activities such as housework. It measures economic activity, not welfare; output could rise when welfare falls. Its subcategories are often interdependent; that is, arbitrary decisions were made when determining what goes in which subcategory. Nevertheless, national income accounting makes it possible to discuss the aggregate economy. It is important to be aware of the limitations of the data in those discussions. (553-556)

ANSWERS

MATCHING

1-m; 2-a; 3-c; 4-f; 5-i; 6-d; 7-l; 8-e; 9-g; 10-b; 11-h; 12-k; 13-j.

ANSWERS

PROBLEMS AND APPLICATIONS

1. **a.** $300. Only the value added by the sale would be added to GDP, which in this case is the difference between the purchase price and the sale price. (542-543)

   b. $200,000. Total output produced is $1,000 \times \$500 = \$500,000$. The intermediate goods are valued at $600 \times \$500 = \$300,000$. So, the company's contribution to GDP is $(\$500,000 - \$300,000) = \$200,000$. (542-543)

   c. Only that amount that is sold to the consumer is counted in GDP. This is $50 \times 1,000 + 100 \times 50 = \$55,000$ sold by the first company plus the sales of the wholesaler, which is $25 \times \$1250 + 50 \times \$75 = \$35,000$. Total contribution to GDP is $90,000. (542-543)

   d. Only the commissions of $50 and $45 are counted in GDP. Together they contribute $95. (542-543)

   e. Nothing has been added to GDP. Government transfers are not included in GDP. (542-543)

2.

Participants	Cost of materials	Value of sales	Value added
Farmer	$0	$150	$150
Mill	$150	$250	$100
Cereal maker	$250	$600	$350
Wholesaler	$600	$800	$200
Grocery store	$800	$1,000	$200

a. The value added at each stage of production is shown in the table above. (542-544)

b. The total value of sales is $2,800. Find this by adding the rows of the value of sales column. (542-544)

c. The total value added is $1,000. Find this by adding the value added at each stage of production. (542-544)

d. The contribution to GDP of the production of those Wheaties is $1,000. Value added at each stage of production is the contribution to GDP. This avoids double-counting. (542-544)

3.

a. $2,375: GDP is the sum of the value added by the three firms = 500 + 1400 + 475. (542-544)

b. $237.50: A 10% value added tax would generate = (.10)($2,375) = $237.50 of revenue. (542-544)

c. $237.50: A 10% income tax would generate the same revenue as a 10% value added tax. (542-544)

d. $237.50: A 10% sales tax on final output would generate = $237.50 of revenue: (.10)(775+1550+50). (542-544)

4.

a. $950: GDP = $C + I + G + (X-M)$ = 550 + 200 + 190 + 10 = 950. (546)

b. $953: GNP = GDP + net foreign factor income = 953. (547)

c. $885: NDP = GDP − depreciation = 950 − 65 = 885. (547)

d. $888: NI = GNP − depreciation = 953 − 65 = 888. (546-548)

e. $764: PI = NI + transfer payments from government + Net non-business interest income − corporate retained earnings − indirect business taxes − Social Security taxes = 888 + 70 + 5 − 49 − 44 − 69 − 37 = 764. (549)

f. $667: DPI = PI − personal income tax = 764 − 92 = 672. (550)

5.

a. $1,615: GDP = NI + depreciation − net foreign factor income = (888 + 30 + 175 + 505) + 20 − (−5) = 1505. (547-549)

b. $1,610: GNP = GDP + net foreign factor income = 1615 + (−5). (547-549)

c. $1,595: NDP = GDP − depreciation = 1615 − 20. (547)

d. $1,590: NI = Employee compensation + rent + interest + profits = 888 + 30 + 175 + 505. (548)

e. $1,440: PI = NI + transfer payments + net non-business interest income − corporate retained earnings − indirect business taxes − Social Security taxes = 1590 + 0 + 10 − 50 − 110 − 0. (548-549)

f. $1,290: DPI = PI − personal income taxes = 1440 − 150. (550)

6.

a. $10,845.7 billion in 2000 dollars: Real output = (Nominal output/deflator) × 100 = 11,735.0/108.2 × 100. (552-553)

b. $10,487.9 billion: Nominal output = (real output × deflator) / 100 = (10,074.8 × 104.1)/100. (552-553)

c. 100: Deflator = (Nominal output/real output) × 100 = (9,817/9,817) × 100. (552-553)

d. Real output grew by 1.9% and inflation rose by 2.1%, so nominal output grew by 4.0%. (552-553)

ANSWERS

A BRAIN TEASER

1. Government expenditures, consumption, investment include all expenditures in those categories regardless of where the products were produced. That is, they include products produced in foreign countries. Since GDP measures domestic production, the total value of imports must be subtracted from total expenditures. (546)

ANSWERS

MULTIPLE CHOICE

1. a   As the text emphasizes on page 540, GDP is the <u>market value</u> of all <u>final</u> goods and services produced <u>in</u> an economy in a one-year period.

2. a   Since GNP is a country's total market value of production of a country's citizens anywhere in the world, and GDP is total market value of production within a country, one must add net foreign factor income to GDP to get GNP. See page 540.

3. b   Value added equals value of sales minus cost of materials. See page 542.

4. c   As discussed on page 542, sales of used goods do not contribute to GDP except to the degree that they are sold by a second hand dealer. Then the dealer's profit would be the value added.

5. b   GDP doesn't include purchases made between businesses, only final sales to consumers. To calculate the answer, calculate total sales for Firms A and B ($600 + $200 = $800) and subtract those goods sold between the firms ($60 + $150 = $210) to get final sales ($800 − $210 = $590). See pages 541-542.

6. b   As discussed on page 544, GDP measures market transactions. The divorce-and-hire changes the housecleaning activities from non-market to market and hence increases GDP.

7. c   The national income identity shows that all income (value of factor services) equals all expenditures (value of goods sold to individuals). See pages 545-546.

8. b   GDP = C + I + G + (X − M). See pages 546-547.

9. a   Consumption makes up the majority of expenditures. See Table 23-2, page 547.

10. d   As you can see in Table 23-3 on page 548, compensation to employees is the largest percent of national income.

11. c   Net investment equals gross investment less depreciation. See page 546.

12. a   As discussed on pages 546-547 only federal government expenditures on goods and services are included as part of GDP. The federal government's entire budget also includes transfer payments.

13. a   Profit is what remains after all firms' other income is paid out. Thus, profit is the key to the income/expenditures equality. See pages 548-549.

14. b   In developing countries, living expenses are generally lower than in developed countries. Thus moving towards a purchasing power parity approach generally increases GDP in a developing country. In the example of China given on page 552, the switch increased China's GDP by more than 400 percent.

15. b   Subtract inflation from nominal GDP growth to find real GDP growth as a first approximation. See pages 552-553.

16. d   As discussed on pages 552-553 nominal GDP must be adjusted for price level increases before comparisons over time can be made. Dividing total real income by the population is a good indication of relative standards of living.

17. c   Nominal GDP must be adjusted for inflation to arrive at real GDP before one can even start to make welfare comparisons. And even if real GDP increases, it is not clear that welfare has increased, as discussed on pages 552-553.

18. b   On page 555 the text states that the underground economy in the United States is between 1.5 and 20 percent of the total economy.

ANSWERS

POTENTIAL ESSAY QUESTIONS

The following are annotated answers. They indicate the general idea behind the answer.

1.   Whenever the business community produces some $X value of output, that dollar value reflects costs of production which were incurred in producing that output level. Those costs of production are all paid out to the resource (input) owners as their income. Hence, any dollar output level (GDP) gives rise to an identical amount of national income (NI), at least for all practical purposes.

2.   The price level could have increased by a greater percentage than the decrease in the real quantity of goods and services produced. This would result in an increase in nominal GDP but a decrease in real GDP (negative growth).

GROWTH, PRODUCTIVITY AND THE WEALTH OF NATIONS

CHAPTER AT A GLANCE

This review is based upon the learning objectives that open the chapter.

1. Growth is an increase in the amount of goods and services an economy produces. (562-565)

    Growth can be measured either by increases in real GDP or increases in real GDP per person (per capita growth).

    Remember the Rule of 72: the number of years it takes for income to double equals 72 divided by the annual growth rate of income.

2. Markets create specialization and division of labor and have been empirically highly correlated with growth. The growth rate has increased as the importance of markets has increased. Five important sources of growth are: (564, 566-70)

    *   Capital accumulation–investment in productive capacity;

        Can be: (1) Privately owned by business, (2) publicly owned and provided by government–infrastructure, (3) human capital–investment in people, (4) social capital–institutions and conventions.

    *   Available resources;

        Technological advances can help overcome any lack of resources.

    *   Institutions with incentives compatible with growth;

        Government policy can help or hinder growth. Regulations have both costs and benefits, but too much regulation definitely hinders growth.

    *   Technological development;

        Technology not only causes growth, it also changes the entire social and political dimensions of society.

    *   Entrepreneurship.

        This is the ability to get things done. It involves creativity, vision, and an ability to translate that vision into reality.

3. Most growth theories center around the production function: Output = A·f(labor, capital, land). (570-571)

    Returns to scale describes what happens to output when all inputs are increased.

    *   *Constant returns to scale: output rises by* the same *proportion as the increase in all inputs. (An example: ↑all inputs 10% →↑output by 10%)*

    *   *Increasing returns to scale: output rises by a* greater *proportion than the increase in all inputs. (An example: ↑ all inputs 10% → ↑output by 15%)*

    *   *Decreasing returns to scale: output rises by a* smaller *proportion than the increase in all inputs. (An example:↑all inputs 10% → ↑output by 5%)*

    Diminishing marginal productivity involves increasing one, not all, inputs. In general, economists assume diminishing marginal productivity—which means the increase in output falls as more of one input is added.

4a. The convergence hypothesis states that per capita income in countries with similar institutional structures will converge to the income *of the country with greater income.* (573-574) *This hypothesis predicts that the U.S. economy will grow more slowly than developing economies because of technology transfers, learning by doing, and the higher marginal productivity of capital in developing countries.*

4b. Convergence hasn't occurred because of (1) lack of factor mobility, (2) differing institutional structures, (3) in-comparable factors of production, and (4) technological agglomeration effects. (573-574)

Technology accounts for 35% of U.S. growth. If technology continues to advance more quickly in developed countries, rich countries may continue to grow more quickly than developing economies.

5a. The Classical growth model focuses on the role of capital accumulation. Increases in capital lead to growth. (571-572)

Predicts that the rise in output per worker will eventually slow as additional amounts of capital are less productive. It also predicts that capital-poor countries will grow faster than capital-rich countries.

Production and diminishing marginal productivity of labor. Increases in the population beyond N* lead to starvation. Below N* the population grows because of the surplus output.

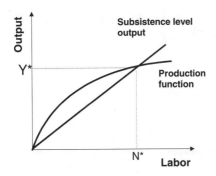

5b. New growth theory focuses on technology. Increasing returns mean growth rates can accelerate over time. (576-577)

Technology often has positive externalities that can accelerate growth.

6. Six government policies to promote growth are: (578-584)

● Policies to encourage saving and investment;

Even though new growth theorists downplay the role of capital, they agree that capital and investment are still important.

Tax laws impact saving and consequently investment. Government corruption and excessive bureaucracy hinder investment.

● Policies to control population growth;

Providing enough capital and education for a large population that is growing is difficult.

Perhaps a country needs to grow first. Then the residents will choose to have fewer children and the population growth will slow.

● Policies to increase the level of education;

Education increases the productivity of workers. Basic education is important to economic growth.

● Policies to create institutions that encourage technological innovation;

This means having institutions that provide incentives to innovate such as patents. Patents, however, also reduce the positive externalities associated with innovation.

Corporations and financial institutions reduce the risk of innovating.

● Provide funding for basic research;

The U.S. government funds 60 percent of all basic research in the United States.

● Policies to increase the economy's openness to trade.

Trade allows specialization, which leads to increases in productivity and innovation.

● SHORT-ANSWER QUESTIONS

1. What are the two ways to measure growth?

2. You've been called in by a political think tank to develop a strategy to improve growth in the U.S. What five things would you recommend they concentrate on to contribute positively to economic growth?

3. Write a production function. Use the production function to explain the difference between diminishing marginal returns and decreasing returns to scale.

4. Which economy does the convergence hypothesis predict will grow faster: Country A with per capita income of $1,000 or Country B with per capita of $10,000? Why might the prediction be wrong?

5. Why did the early Classical model predict that output would gravitate toward a subsistence level?

6. What is the focus of new growth theory?

7. How do the predictions of the Classical growth theory differ from the predictions of the new growth theory?

8. What are six types of policies to promote growth?

MATCHING THE TERMS
Match the terms to their definitions

_____ 1. Classical growth model

_____ 2. constant returns to scale

_____ 3. decreasing returns to scale

_____ 4. convergence hypothesis

_____ 5. growth

_____ 6. human capital

_____ 7. increasing returns to scale

_____ 8. law of diminishing marginal productivity

_____ 9. learning by doing

_____ 10. new growth theories

_____ 11. patents

_____ 12. per capita growth

_____ 13. positive externalities

_____ 14. productivity

_____ 15. Rule of 72

_____ 16. Say's Law

_____ 17. social capital

_____ 18. specialization

_____ 19. technological agglomeration

_____ 20. technology

a. Output rises by a greater proportionate increase in all inputs.

b. Producing more goods and services per person.

c. Legal ownership of a technological innovation that gives the owner sole rights to its use and distribution for a limited time.

d. An increase in the amount of goods and services an economy produces.

e. The habitual way of doing things that guides how people approach production.

f. Changes in the way we make goods and supply services and changes in the goods and services we buy.

g. Output will rise by the same proportionate increase as all inputs.

h. Model of growth that focuses on the role of capital accumulation in the growth process.

i. Output per unit of input.

j. Rule in which you divide 72 by the growth rate of income (or any variable) to get the number of years over which income (or any variable) will double.

k. Output rises by a smaller proportionate increase than all inputs.

l. Positive effects on others not taken into account by the decision-maker.

m. The skills that are embodied in workers through experience, education, and on-the-job training.

n. Theories that emphasize the role of technology rather than capital in the growth process.

o. Increasing one input, keeping all others constant, will lead to smaller and smaller gains in output.

p. The concentration of individuals on certain aspects of production.

q. Supply creates its own demand.

r. Improving the methods of production through experience.

s. Tendency of technological advance to spawn further technological advances.

t. Per capita income in countries with similar institutional structures will converge to the higher level.

PROBLEMS AND APPLICATIONS

1. According to the Classical growth model how will each of the following events affect a country's growth rate?

    a. An increase in the percent change in population.

    b. An increase in the saving rate.

    c. An improvement in technology.

d. The government passes a law extending the time frame in which the holder of a patent has sole ownership of a technological innovation.

2. State the Rule of 72. Answer each of the following questions:

a. How many years will it take for income to double if a country's total income grows at 2 percent? 4 percent? 6 percent?

b. If a country's income doubles in 16 years, at what rate is its income growing?

c. In 2005 per capita output in the United States was about $40,000. If real income per capita is growing at a 2% annual rate, what will per capita output be in 36 years? In 72 years?

d. If real income is rising at an annual rate of 4% per year and the population is growing at a rate of 1% per year, how many years will it take for per capita income to double?

3. Calculate per capita income for each of the following countries:

	GDP (in mils. of $)	Population (in millions)
Brazil	773,400	164
Ghana	6,600	18
Croatia	20,700	4
France	1,526,000	59

4. The inputs to an economy are labor and capital only. In each of the following state whether the production function exhibits (a) increasing returns to scale, (b) decreasing returns to scale, (c) constant returns to scale, or (d) diminishing marginal productivity.

a. Output rises by 16% when both labor and capital rise by 16%.

b. Output rises by 10% when both labor and capital rise by 16%.

c. Output rises by 10% when labor rises by 16%. (Capital doesn't change.)

5. What prediction did Thomas Malthus make about growth?

a. Draw a graph that demonstrates his predictions and explain the predictions using the graph.

b.   What law are those predictions based upon?

c.   According to Classical economists, why didn't his predictions come true?

6.   Country A has per capita income of $10,000 while Country B has per capita income of $20,000.

a.   According to the Classical growth theory, which country is predicted to grow more quickly? Why?

b.   According to the new growth theory, which country is predicted to grow more quickly? Why?

● A BRAIN TEASER

1.   How can two countries with equal population sizes have different levels of output?

● MULTIPLE CHOICE

Circle the one best answer for each of the following questions:

1.   Long-run growth analysis focuses primarily:
     a. on demand.
     b. on supply.
     c. on both supply and demand.
     d. on the distribution of output.

2.   According to Say's Law:
     a. aggregate supply will exceed aggregate demand.
     b. aggregate demand will exceed aggregate supply.
     c. there will be no relation between aggregate supply and demand.
     d. aggregate demand will equal aggregate supply.

3.   If the growth rate is 6%, how many years will it take for output to double?
     a. 4.
     b. 8.
     c. 12.
     d. 16.

4.   When earnings are adjusted for inflation, the average worker today earns:
     a. about the same as a worker in 1919.
     b. less than a worker in 1919.
     c. more than a worker in 1919.
     d. more than a worker in 1919 if he/she is unionized, but otherwise less.

5.   Suppose output grew at 2.3% in China and 2% in the United States. Based on this information alone, we can know that
     a. per capita income grew faster in China.
     b. per capita income grew faster in the U.S.
     c. per capita income could have grown faster in either country. We cannot tell which.
     d. per capita output grew faster in China.

6.   Investment relates to capital in the following way:
     a. It is the same thing as capital stock.
     b. It causes a decrease in capital over time.
     c. It causes an increase in capital over time.
     d. It is unrelated to capital.

7. Types of capital discussed in the book do *not* include:
   a. human capital.
   b. social capital.
   c. physical capital.
   d. investment capital.

8. Available resources:
   a. must always decrease.
   b. are always constant because of the entropy law.
   c. must always increase.
   d. may increase or decrease.

9. A production function:
   a. shows the relationship between inputs and outputs.
   b. is a type of technological manufacturing.
   c. is a type of manufacturing technology.
   d. is an important source of growth.

10. If there are increasing returns to scale, as:
    a. inputs rise, outputs fall.
    b. inputs rise, output rises by a smaller percentage.
    c. inputs rise, output rises by a larger percentage.
    d. one input rises, output rises by a larger percentage.

11. The law of diminishing marginal productivity states that as:
    a. inputs increase by equal percentages, output will increase by less than that percentage.
    b. inputs increase by equal percentages, output will eventually increase by less than that percentage.
    c. one input increases by a certain percentage, output will increase by less than that percentage.
    d. one input increases, output will increase by decreasing percentages.

12. The Classical growth model focuses on:
    a. technology.
    b. saving and investment.
    c. entrepreneurship.
    d. available resources.

13. Informal property rights:
    a. reflect the reality that illegal and semi-legal businesses have no assets and therefore cannot be a source of economic growth.
    b. lead to growth because business transactions are then based on trust.
    c. make it difficult for businesspeople to obtain loans and invest.
    d. make government regulation unnecessary.

14. Early predictions of the Classical model of growth were that:
    a. the economy would grow without limit.
    b. the economy will end because of pollution.
    c. wages would be driven to subsistence because of diminishing marginal productivity.
    d. wages would be driven to subsistence because of decreasing returns to scale.

15. Which of the following is *not* an explanation for why the growth rates of rich and poor countries have not converged?
    a. Human capital has increased in rich countries.
    b. Technology has increased in rich countries.
    c. The law of diminishing marginal productivity is wrong.
    d. Both human capital and technology have increased in rich countries.

16. In empirically explaining per capita growth in the United States, the increase in:
    a. physical capital is the most important element.
    b. human capital is the most important element.
    c. technology is the most important element.
    d. the quantity of labor is the most important element.

17. Convergence does not rely on:
    a. Similar institutions.
    b. Equal amounts of capital per person.
    c. Mobile technology.
    d. Comparable factors of production.

18. New growth theories are theories that emphasize:
a. technology.
b. human capital.
c. physical capital.
d. entrepreneurship.

19. In the new growth theory which of the
following may be true?
a. The law of increasing marginal productivity
overwhelms the law of diminishing marginal
productivity.
b. Learning by doing overwhelms the law of
diminishing marginal productivity.
c. The law of technology overwhelms the law
of diminishing marginal productivity.
d. The law of QWERTY overwhelms the law
of diminishing marginal productivity.

20. QWERTY is a metaphor for:
a. the invisible hand.
b. technological lock-in.
c. the law of diminishing marginal productivity.
d. the pollution caused by positive spillovers.

21. In the borrowing circle case study:
a. loans were made to large firms.
b. loans were made to an entire circle of firms.
c. guarantees of friends replaced traditional
collateral.
d. individuals were given collateral so they
could get loans.

22. Growth usually leads to decreased birth rates
because:
a. men and women are too tired to have kids.
b. the opportunity cost of having children rises.
c. pollution reduces the fertility of the population.
d. immigration crowds out endogenous
population growth.

23. Patents create:
a. incentives to innovate and hence are a good
thing.
b. barriers to entry and hence are a bad thing.
c. both barriers to entry and incentives to
innovate and hence are both a bad and good
thing.
d. common knowledge and hence are a good
thing.

24. Which of the following policies will likely *slow*
an economy's growth rate?
a. Increased trade restrictions.
b. Increasing the level of education.
c. Increasing saving.
d. Protecting property rights.

● POTENTIAL ESSAY QUESTIONS

*You may also see essay questions similar to the "Problems
& Applications" and "Brain Teasers" exercises.*

1. What does the Classical model predict about
the growth rates of poor countries relative to
rich countries? What accounts for that
prediction?

2. How can patents be both a deterrent and a
reason for growth?

━━━━━   ANSWERS   ━━━━━

SHORT-ANSWER QUESTIONS

1. Growth can be measured either as increases in the amount of goods and services an economy produces (real GDP), or as increases in the amount of goods and services an economy produces per person (per capita real GDP). Increase in per capita output is a better measure of improvements in the standard of living because it tells you how much more income an average person has. (565-566)

2. I would tell them: (1) To invest in capital. This would include not only buildings and machines, but also human and social capital. (2) To be creative in recognizing available resources. Growth requires resources and although it may seem that the resources are limited, available resources depend upon existing technology. New technology is a way of overcoming lack of resources. (3) To promote institutions with incentives compatible with growth. Institutions that encourage hard work will lead to growth. (4) To promote institutions that foster creative thinking and lead to technological development; (5) To encourage entrepreneurship. An economy deficient in the other four areas can still grow if its population can translate vision into reality. Each of these will contribute to growth. (566-569)

3. A typical production function is: Output = A· f(labor, capital, land), where labor, capital and land are the only inputs. A is a factor that is used to capture changes in technology. Decreasing returns to scale describes the situation where output rises by a smaller percentage than the increase in all inputs. For example, if labor, capital and land all increase by 20%, but output increases by only 10%, the production function exhibits decreasing returns to scale. Diminishing marginal productivity describes what happens to output when only one input is changed—output rises by a percentage that is smaller than the percentage increase in one input (while all other inputs remain the same). (570-571)

4. The convergence hypothesis predicts that, given the appropriate assumptions, Country A will grow faster because it has less capital and therefore the marginal productivity of additional capital is higher. The prediction is likely wrong because the assumptions are not met. A central assumption is that countries have similar institutional structures. Another is that the factors of production are comparable; they may not be; for example, the workers in Country B might be better educated. Another assumption is that technological advances move from country to country. They may not do so because of agglomeration effects, in which technological advances in one country accelerate growth for that country. Another assumption is that technology and capital are free to move; they may not be. (573)

5. The early Classical model predicted that output would gravitate toward a subsistence level because they focused on the law of diminishing marginal productivity of labor. As long as an additional worker could produce more than enough for him or herself, the population would grow. But land was relatively fixed. As more and more workers were added to a fixed amount of land, eventually, additional workers would not be able to produce enough additional output to survive. Workers would starve to death and the population would shrink. The equilibrium number of workers was where output was just enough to survive—no more and no less. (571-573, 576)

6. New growth theory focuses on the role of technology rather than capital in the growth process. New growth theory considers the possibility that there are positive externalities associated with technological advance so that growth rates can accelerate. It also focuses on learning by doing. Just the process of producing results in lower costs and technological innovation. (576-577)

7. Classical growth theory predicts that the growth rates of poor countries will be higher than the growth rates of rich countries because the law of diminishing marginal productivity of capital is stronger in rich countries. Eventually the incomes of rich and poor countries will converge. New growth theory, because of the positive externalities associated with technological advance, is consistent with the possibility that rich countries may grow faster than poor countries because they have more technology. Classical growth theory also predicts that growth rates will slow over time whereas the new growth theory is consistent with an acceleration in growth rates. (571-573, 576)

8. Six policies to promote growth are (1) policies to encourage saving and investment; (2) policies to control population growth; (3)

policies to increase the level of education; (4) policies to create institutions that encourage technological innovation; (5) policies to provide funding for basic research; and (6) policies to increase the economy's openness to trade. (578-784)

ANSWERS

MATCHING

1-h; 2-g; 3-k; 4-t; 5-d; 6-m; 7-a; 8-o; 9-r; 10-n; 11-c; 12-b; 13-l; 14-i; 15-j; 16-q; 17-e; 18-p; 19-s; 20-f.

ANSWERS

PROBLEMS AND APPLICATIONS

1. **a.** An increase in the percent change in population will lead to a reduction in the growth rate per capita because each worker will have less capital to produce with. (571-572)

   b. An increase in the saving rate will lead to an increase in the growth rate per capita because saving results in increased investment and more capital for each worker. Eventually, however, the law of diminishing marginal productivity of capital would set in and per capita income would cease to grow. (571-572)

   c. An improvement in technology will increase the growth rate per capita because each worker will be more productive. This will increase per capita output at the time of the technological improvement, but would not result in a lasting increase in the growth rate per capita. (571-572)

   d. Technological innovation is outside the model. Thus government policies to affect technological innovation would not affect the growth rate of an economy. (572-573)

2. The Rule of 72 is that the number of years that it takes income (or any variable) to double equals 72 divided by the annual growth rate of income (or that variable).

   a. 36 years if income grows at 2 percent per year; 18 years if income grows at 4 percent per year; 12 years if income grows at 6 percent per year. (563)

   b. Its income is growing at 4.5 percent per year. Divide 72 by 16 to find the answer. (563)

   c. If real income per capita is growing at 2 percent per year, per capita output will double in 36 years. So, real per capita output will be $80,000 in 36 years and $160,000 in 72 years. (563)

   d Per capita real income is rising at an annual rate of 3% per year (4% - 1%). At 3% per year, real per capita income will double in 24 years (72/3 = 24). (563)

3. Divide GDP by the population to find per capita income: (See page 565.)

   a. Brazil $4,716

   b. Ghana $367

   c. Croatia $5,175

   d France $25,864

4. **a.** Since output is rising by the same percentage as the increase in all inputs, the production function exhibits constant returns to scale. (570-571)

   b. Since output is rising by a smaller percentage than the increase in all inputs, the production function exhibits decreasing returns to scale. (570-571)

   c. Since capital is fixed, the correct description involves marginal productivity. Since output rises by less than the percentage increase in labor only, the production function exhibits diminishing marginal productivity. (570-571)

5. Thomas Malthus predicted that since land was relatively fixed, as the population grew, diminishing marginal productivity would set in. The growth in output would not keep pace with the growth in the population and eventually people would starve.

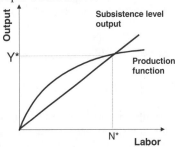

   a. The graph above demonstrates Malthus' predictions. The production function is downward bowed because of diminishing marginal productivity. Each additional worker adds less output than the individual before. At population levels below N*, there is surplus output (because output per worker exceeds the subsistence level of output). Because there is surplus output,

people have more children and the population grows. Once the population grows
beyond N*, per capita output is not
sufficient to feed the population (output per
worker is less than the subsistence level of
output) and some people starve to death.
The population declines to N*. (572)

b. The predictions of Thomas Malthus are
based upon the law of diminishing
marginal productivity. (572-573)

c. According to Classical economists, his
predictions didn't come true because some
output produced is used to increase the
amount of capital that workers have to work
with. As capital increases, even if land is
fixed, output can also increase. The economy
can still grow if capital increases at the same
rate that labor increases. (574-575)

6. a. According to the Classical growth theory,
Country A is expected to grow more
quickly because increases in capital per
worker in Country A are more productive
than in Country B due to the law of
diminishing marginal productivity. (572-573)

b. According to the new growth theory,
income doesn't need to converge. In fact,
new growth theory stresses the possibility
that countries with higher output will grow
faster than poor countries because of
positive externalities associated with
technology and learning by doing.
Increases in technology have significant
positive externalities that can accelerate the
growth rate. Further, as output increases,
the benefits from learning by doing also
increase. Therefore, greater output can lead
to faster growth rates. (573)

━━━━ **ANSWERS** ━━━━

A BRAIN TEASER

1. Total output in the long run depends upon
capital, labor, and land. It could be that the two
countries have different levels of capital or
natural resources (captured in land). For
instance, the United States has many natural
resources, but Japan does not. Japan over-
comes its lack of natural resources by investing heavily in capital and importing natural
resources. If two countries had equal amounts
of capital, land and labor, however, their
outputs could still differ if they had different
amounts of human capital (the skills that are

embodied in workers through experience,
education, and on-the-job training) and social
capital (the habitual way of doing things that
guides people in how they approach production). (570-571)

━━━━ **ANSWERS** ━━━━

MULTIPLE CHOICE

1. b On page 562 it states that in the short run
economists' analysis focuses on demand;
in the long run it focuses on supply.

2. d Say's Law states that supply creates its
own demand. See page 562.

3. c According to the rule of 72 on page 563,
divide 72 by the growth rate to determine
the number of years in which output will
double.

4. c As discussed in the text on pages 564-565
the average worker's wages buy many
more goods now than in 1919. Whether
that makes them better off is debatable,
but they definitely earn more.

5. c Per capita income (output) growth equals
output growth less population growth.
Without knowing population growth, we
do not know for which country per capita
income (output) growth is greater. See
pages 565-566.

6. c As defined in the text on page 566
investment is the increase in capital over
time.

7. d Investment is the change in capital; it is
not a description of capital. See page 567.

8. d Available resources depend on technology. That is why they can increase or
decrease. See page 567.

9. a The definition given in the text on pages
570-571 is the relationship between inputs
and outputs.

10. c As discussed in the text on page 571
increasing returns to scale refers to the
relationship between all inputs and
outputs. Increasing returns to scale exist
when output increases by a greater
percentage than the increase in all inputs.

11. d The law of diminishing marginal productivity refers to one input, not all, and to what
will happen to output as that input

continually increases, keeping other inputs constant. It is likely that c is true but it is not the law of diminishing marginal productivity. See page 571.

12. b The Classical growth focuses on increases in capital and hence on saving and investment. See page 571-572.

13. c Because illegal or semi-legal businesses often have only informal property rights, it is difficult for them to use the assets they have as collateral for loans. Informal property rights, therefore, are an impediment for investment and growth. See pages 579-580.

14. c In the early Classical model, fixed land and diminishing marginal productivity meant that wages would be driven to subsistence. See page 572.

15. c Economists continue to believe in the law of diminishing marginal productivity because there are many other explanations for the lack of convergence. See page 571.

16. c Although increases in technology and increases in the quantity of labor are of almost equal importance in explaining total growth, per capita growth decreases the importance of the quantity of labor. See pages 572-574.

17. b Convergence depends on similar institutions, mobile technology, and comparable factors of production. The initial amount of capital per person doesn't have to equal. See page 201.

18. a New growth theories center their explanation of growth on technology. See page 553.

19. b Choices a,c, and d name "laws" that aren't laws, aren't mentioned in this chapter, and can't overwhelm anything. See pages 576-577.

20. b QWERTY stands for the upper left keys on a keyboard. Placing them there is not especially efficient, but once they were placed there, they were locked in. See pages 577-578.

21. c The essence of the borrowing circle was guarantees of friends. The loans were small loans to individuals, not to firms. See page 579.

22. b In industrialized countries, people have chosen to have fewer children because the benefits of having children (such as being supported by them in your old age) are reduced. See page 580.

23. c Patents have both good and bad aspects; the policy debate is about what the optimal length of the patent should be. See pages 581-582.

24. a Economists generally believe that trade increases growth, so increasing trade restrictions would decrease growth. See pages 583-584.

◼◼◼ ANSWERS ◼◼◼

POTENTIAL ESSAY QUESTIONS

The following are annotated answers. They indicate the general idea behind the answer.

1. The Classical model predicts that poor countries with little capital will grow at faster rates than rich countries with a lot of capital. The reason for this prediction is the law of diminishing marginal productivity. Capital that is added in poor countries will be much more productive because the law of diminishing marginal productivity is weaker compared to that in rich countries.

2. Patents provide an incentive for people to innovate because the holder of a patent has the right to be the sole provider of the innovation. As a sole provider, the holder can charge more for its use by others. Based upon the law of supply a greater incentive will result in a greater quantity of innovations supplied. Alternatively, patents, because they are privately held, will have less impact on increasing total production because they cannot be used by everyone. Since the innovation is priced high, fewer existing innovations will be demanded and the innovation will have less of an impact on growth. Further, it is the common knowledge aspect of a technology that leads to positive externalities. Patents limit the common knowledge aspect of a technology and thus limit its impact on growth. Policymakers face a dilemma. Before the innovation is developed, the best strategy is to offer patents. Once the innovation is developed, the best strategy is to make it free to everyone.

AGGREGATE DEMAND, AGGREGATE SUPPLY, AND MODERN MACRO

CHAPTER AT A GLANCE

This review is based upon the learning objectives that open the chapter.

1. Keynesian economics developed as economists debated the cause of the Great Depression. (591-593)

   In the 1930s, the economy was in a Depression with 25 percent unemployment. Classical economists believed that wages would fall and eliminate the unemployment. Keynesian economists believed that the economy could remain in a Depression unless government did something to increase spending.

2a. The slope of the AD curve is determined by the wealth effect, the interest rate effect, the international effect, and repercussions of these effects. (594-596)

   As the price level falls:
   - *the cash people hold is worth more, making people richer, so they buy more. (wealth effect).*
   - *the value of money rises, inducing people to lend more money, which reduces the interest rate and increases investment expenditures (interest rate effect).*
   - *the price of U.S. goods relative to foreign goods goes down. Assuming the exchange rate doesn't change, U.S. exports increase and U.S. imports decrease. (international effect).*

   Repercussions of these effects are called multiplier effects (and make the AD curve flatter than otherwise).

2b. Five important initial shift factors of the AD curve are: (596-598)

- Changes in foreign income.
  A rise in foreign income leads to an increase in U.S. exports and an increase (outward shift to the right) of the U.S. AD curve.

- Changes in exchange rates.
  A decrease in the value of the dollar relative to other currencies shifts the AD curve outward to the right.

- Changes in expectations.
  Positive (optimistic) expectations about the future state of the economy shift the AD curve outward to the right.

- Changes in the distribution of income.
  Typically, as the real wage increases, the AD curve shifts out to the right.

- Changes in government aggregate demand policy.

  Expansionary macro policy (an increase in government spending and/or a decrease in taxes—fiscal policy; or an increase in the money supply—monetary policy) increases the AD curve, shifting it outward to the right.

  Note: Anything that affects autonomous components of aggregate expenditures (AE or "total spending") is a shift factor of AD (aggregate demand). (Recall that $AE = C + I + G + X - M$). Changes in these components of total spending are multiplied by the multiplier effect.

3a. In the short run, the SAS curve is upward sloping. (599-601)

   The SAS curve is upward sloping for two reasons: Some firms operate in auction markets where an increase in demand leads to higher prices immediately. Firms tend to increase their markup when demand increases. Along an SAS curve, input prices are constant.

3b. The SAS curve shifts in response to changes in the prices of the factors of production. (599-601)

Shift factors include changes in (1) input prices, (2) expectations of inflation, (3) excise and sales taxes, (4) productivity, and (5) import prices.

The rule of thumb economists use to predict shifts in the SAS curve is:

% change in the price level = % change in wages − % change in productivity.

4. The *LAS* curve is vertical at potential output. (601-603)

Resources are fully utilized at potential output. The LAS curve shifts when potential output rises or falls.

5a. Equilibrium in the short run is determined by the intersection of the SAS curve and the AD curve. (603-604)

Increases (decreases) in aggregate demand lead to higher (lower) output and a slightly higher (lower) price level.

To find the effect of a shift in aggregate demand, start where the AD curve and the SAS curve intersect. Given a shift of either the AD curve or SAS curve, simply find the new point of intersection. This is the new short-run equilibrium. Remember, initial shifts in the AD curve are magnified because of the multiplier effect.

5b. Equilibrium in the long run is determined by the intersection of the LAS curve and the AD curve. (604-605)

If the economy begins at a long-run equilibrium, increases in aggregate demand will lead to changes in the price level only.

If short-run equilibrium output is below long-run equilibrium output, the economy is in a recessionary gap. The price level will fall and the AS curve will shift down until output rises to potential. (See the figure below.)

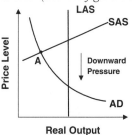

If short-run equilibrium output is above long-run equilibrium output, the economy is in an inflationary gap. The price level will rise and the SAS curve will shift up until output falls to potential. (See the figure below)

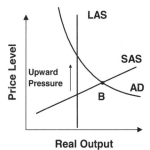

6. Macro policy is more complicated than the model makes it look. (610-611)

Fiscal policy is a slow legislative process and is often determined for political, not economic, reasons.

We have no way of precisely determining potential output, making it difficult to know what is the right policy.

● SHORT-ANSWER QUESTIONS

1. How does the Keynesian explanation of the Great Depression differ from the Classical explanation?

2. What effects determine the slope of the AD curve?

3. List some of the important shift factors of the AD curve.

4. What is the slope of the SAS curve? Why does it have this shape?

5. What will shift the SAS curve up or down?

6. What is the slope of the LAS curve? Why does it have this shape?

7. Show graphically the effect of increased government purchases on real output when (a) the economy is far below potential output and (b) the economy is at potential output.

8. Why is the AS/AD model more complicated than it looks?

MATCHING THE TERMS
Match the terms to their definitions

___1.	aggregate demand curve	a.	As the price level falls the interest rate falls, which leads to greater investment expenditures.
___2.	countercyclical fiscal policy	b.	A curve that shows the amount of goods and services an economy can produce when both labor and capital are fully employed.
___3.	fiscal policy	c.	A curve that shows how a change in the price level will change aggregate quantity of goods demanded.
___4.	equilibrium income	d.	Markets in which firms modify their supply to bring about equilibrium instead of changing prices.
___5.	short-run aggregate supply curve	e.	A curve that tells us how changes in aggregate demand will be split between real output and the price level.
___6.	inflationary gap	f.	Amount by which equilibrium output is below potential output.
___7.	interest rate effect	g.	As the price level falls, people are richer, so they buy more.
___8.	international effect	h.	As the price level in a country falls the quantity of that country's goods demanded by foreigners and residents will increase.
___9.	multiplier effect	i.	Amplification of initial changes in expenditures.
___10.	long-run aggregate supply curve	j.	Amount by which equilibrium output is above potential output.
___11.	potential income	k.	Level of income toward which the economy gravitates in the short run.
___12.	quantity-adjusting markets	l.	Level of income the economy is technically capable of producing without generating accelerating inflation.
___13.	recessionary gap	m.	Deliberate change in either government spending or taxes.
___14.	wealth effect	n.	Government policy to offset the business cycle.

PROBLEMS AND APPLICATIONS

1. What will likely happen to the shape or position of the *AD* curve in the following circumstances?

   a. A rise in the price level does not make people feel poorer.

   b. Income is redistributed from poor people to rich people.

   c. The country's currency depreciates.

   d. The exchange rate changes from fixed to flexible.

   e. Expectations of future rises in the price level develop without any current change in the price level.

2. What will happen to the position of the *SAS* curve in the following circumstances?

   a. Productivity rises by 3 percent and wages rise by 3 percent.

b. Productivity rises by 3 percent and wages rise by 5 percent.

c. Productivity rises by 3 percent and wages rise by 1 percent.

3. Graphically demonstrate the effect of each of the following on either the *SAS* curve or the *LAS* curve. Be sure to label all axes.

a. Businesses find that they are able to produce more output without having to pay more wages or increase their costs of capital.

b. A severe snow storm paralyzes most of the United States.

c. The country's currency appreciates dramatically.

4. The government of the UK wants to expand its economy through increased spending. Show the likely effects of an activist policy in the short run and in the long run in the following three cases.

a. The economy is far below potential output.

b. The economy is close to, but still below, potential output.

c. The economy is at potential output.

5. Demonstrate the following two cases using the AS/AD model. What will happen in the long run if the government does nothing?

a. Inflationary gap.

b. Recessionary gap.

c. What could government do in (a) and (b) to keep the price level constant?

A BRAIN TEASER

1. Suppose the economy has been experiencing a recession for a couple of years with no apparent relief in sight. Currently the unemployment rate is 10%. In response to political pressure "to put America back to work" government policy makers have recently reduced taxes significantly and have dramatically increased government spending on public works projects to rebuild the nation's crumbling infrastructure (roads, bridges, airports...). During a recent press conference the President of the United States remarked that the new government policy of tax cuts and spending programs will be successful in reducing unemployment and there should be no reason to fear inflation either. Because you are a student in an economics course one of your friends has asked you to evaluate the likely success of these recent policy moves. How would you respond?

● MULTIPLE CHOICE

Circle the one best answer for each of the following questions:

1. Classical economists are generally associated with:
   a. laissez faire.
   b. QWERTY.
   c. an activist policy.
   d. their support of low unemployment.

2. Keynesian economics focuses on:
   a. the long run.
   b. the short run.
   c. both the long run and the short run.
   d. neither the long run nor the short run.

3. The term *paradox of thrift* refers to the process by which individuals attempted to save:
   a. less, but in doing so spent less and caused income to decrease, ending up saving even less.
   b. less, but in doing so spent more and caused income to decrease, ending up saving even less.
   c. more, but in doing so spent less and caused income to decrease, ending up saving less.
   d. more, but in doing so spent more and caused income to decrease, ending up saving less.

4. In Keynesian economics equilibrium income:
   a. will be equal to potential income.
   b. will be below potential income.
   c. will be above potential income.
   d. may be different than potential income.

5. In the AS/AD model:
   a. price of a good is on the horizontal axis.
   b. price level is on the horizontal axis.
   c. price of a good is on the vertical axis.
   d. price level is on the vertical axis.

6. Which of the following is *not* an explanation of the downward slope of the AD curve?
   a. The wealth effect.
   b. The interest rate effect.
   c. The consumption effect.
   d. The international effect.

7. If the exchange rate becomes flexible so that changes in the price level have little effect on exports and imports, the:
   a. AD curve will become steeper.
   b. AD curve will become flatter.
   c. AD curve will be unaffected.
   d. SAS curve will become steeper.

8. If the multiplier effect is 2 rather than 3, the:
   a. AD curve will be steeper.
   b. AD curve will be flatter.
   c. AD curve will be unaffected.
   d. SAS curve will be steeper.

9. If there is a rise in foreign income the AD curve will likely:
   a. shift in to the left.
   b. shift out to the right.
   c. become steeper.
   d. become flatter.

10. If there is a rise in a country's exchange rate, the AD curve will likely:
    a. shift in to the left.
    b. shift out to the right.
    c. become steeper.
    d. become flatter.

11. Expansionary monetary policy will likely:
    a. shift the AD curve in to the left.
    b. shift the AD curve out to the right.
    c. make the AD curve steeper.
    d. make the AD curve flatter.

12. If government spending increases by 40, the AD curve will shift to the:
    a. right by 40.
    b. left by 40.
    c. right by more than 40.
    d. right by less than 40.

13. The slope of the SAS curve is determined by:
    a. opportunity cost
    b. the law of diminishing marginal returns.
    c. institutional realities.
    d. the wealth effect, the international effect and the interest rate effect.

14. If productivity rises by 2% and wages rise by 6%, the SAS curve will:
    a. likely shift up (to the left).
    b. likely shift down (to the right).
    c. become flatter.
    d. become steeper.

15. The LAS curve is:
    a. another name for the AD curve.
    b. another name for the SAS curve.
    c. a vertical line.
    d. a horizontal line.

16. Refer to the graph below. The graph demonstrates the expected short-run result if:

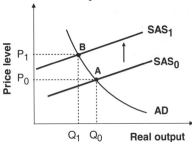

    a. productivity increases by less than wages.
    b. the government increases the money supply.
    c. the exchange rate value of a country's currency falls.
    d. there are suddenly expectations of a rising price level.

17. The graph below demonstrates the expected short-run result if:

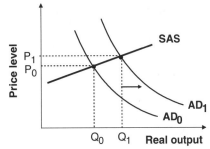

    a. productivity increases by less than wages.
    b. the government increases the money supply.
    c. a country's exchange rate appreciates (gains value).
    d. wages rise by less than the increase in productivity.

18. The graph below demonstrates the expected short-run result if:

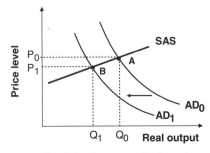

    a. productivity increases by less than wages.
    b. the government increases the money supply.
    c. a country's exchange rate appreciates (gains value).
    d. wages rise by less than the increase in productivity.

19. Assume the economy is initially at point B. The graph below correctly demonstrates an economy moving to point C if:

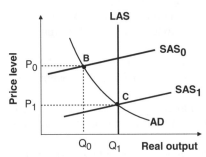

    a. productivity increases by less than the increase in wages.
    b. the government increases the money supply.
    c. a country's exchange rate appreciates (gains value).
    d. wages rise by less than the increase in productivity.

20. Assume the economy is initially at point B. The graph below correctly demonstrates an economy moving to point C if:

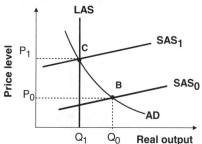

a. productivity increases by less than the increase in wages.

b. the government increases the money supply.

c. a country's exchange rate appreciates (gains value).

d. wages rise by less than the increase in productivity.

21. Which of the following distances in the graph below would represent an inflationary gap?

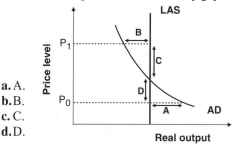

a. A.
b. B.
c. C.
d. D.

22. Expansionary fiscal policy involves:

a. increasing taxes.

b. increasing the money supply.

c. increasing government spending.

d. changing the exchange rate.

23. If the economy has an inflationary gap that it wants to eliminate, the government should use fiscal policy to shift:

a. the *LAS* curve out.

b. the *SAS* curve down (to the left).

c. the *AD* curve out to the right.

d. the *AD* curve in to the left.

24. If an economy has an inflationary gap and the government does nothing, the macro policy model predicts that:

a. the SAS curve will shift up (to the left) as input prices increase, and output will decline.

b. the SAS curve will shift down (to the right) as input prices decline, and output will rise.

c. the AD curve will shift out to the right as individuals collectively decide to increase expenditures, and output will rise.

d. the AD curve will shift in to the left as individuals collectively decide to reduce expenditures, and output will decline.

25. During World War II:

a. expansionary fiscal policy pushed the economy beyond potential and the price level rose tremendously.

b. expansionary fiscal policy pushed the economy beyond potential, but the price level was controlled by legislation.

c. contractionary monetary policy pushed the economy into a depression.

d. increased taxes to finance the war pushed the economy into recession.

26. The U.S. recession in 2001:

a. deepened because of significant increases in Social Security spending.

b. slowed accelerating inflation of the late 1990s.

c. remained mild because of tax cuts passed before the recession began.

d. provided Congress with an opportunity to respond with timely fiscal policy.

27. If the target rate of unemployment falls, potential income will:

a. first decrease, then increase.

b. increase.

c. decrease.

d. first increase, then decrease.

● POTENTIAL ESSAY QUESTIONS

You may also see essay questions similar to the "Problems & Applications" and "Brain Teasers" exercises.

1. Why is the AS/AD model more complicated than the model makes it look?

2. What was the Keynesians' main argument against the Classical view that the economy will get itself out of the Depression?

3. What is the paradox of thrift and how does it relate to the AS/AD model?

ANSWERS

SHORT-ANSWER QUESTIONS

1. Classical economists focused on the real wage. They explained that unemployment would decline if the real wage were allowed to decline. Political and social forces were keeping the real wage too high. Keynesians focused on insufficient aggregate expenditures that resulted in a downward spiral. The economy was at a below-potential-income equilibrium. (590-591)

2. The wealth effect, the interest rate effect, the international effect, and the repercussions these effects cause (the multiplier effect) determine the slope of the AD curve. (594-595)

3. Five important initial shift factors of the AD curve are changes in: (1) foreign income, (2) exchange rates, (3) expectations, (4) distribution of income, and (5) government aggregate demand policy. (596-598)

4. The SAS curve specifies how a shift in the aggregate demand curve affects the price level and real output. A standard SAS curve is upward sloping. That is, increases in aggregate demand lead to increases in output and the price level. Institutional realities about how firms set prices determine the shape of the SAS curve. Faced with an increase in demand, firms generally respond by increasing production. Some firms will take the opportunity to increase their markup over costs, which will increase the price level also. (599-601)

5. The SAS curve will shift up or down when input prices rise or fall or if productivity rises or falls. The shift in the SAS curve (the price level) is determined by the following: % change in price level = % change in wages − % change in productivity. (599-600)

6. The LAS curve is vertical. It has this shape because at potential output, all inputs are fully employed. Changes in the price level do not affect potential output. (601-602)

7. If the economy begins at point A, a well-planned increase in government expenditures (plus the multiplier) shifts the AD out to the right from AD_0 to AD_1. If the economy begins below potential output, the price level would

rise slightly to P_1 and real output would increase from Y_0 to Y_1. I've drawn it so that the AD curve shifts out enough so that the economy is in both long-run and short run equilibrium at potential output at point B. (602-603)

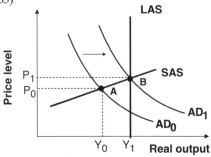

Now suppose the economy begins at point C (graph below) in both short run and long-run equilibrium. In the short-run, when the aggregate demand curve shifts from AD_0 to AD_1, real output rises from Y_0 to Y_1 and the price level rises from P_0 to P_1. Since the economy is now above potential output, however, input prices begin to rise and the SAS curve shifts up. The SAS curve continues to shift up to SAS_1 where the economy returns to a long-run equilibrium at a higher price level, P_2, but the same output level as before, Y_0. (602-603)

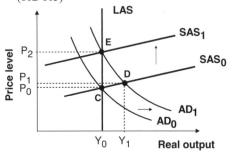

8. The AS/AD model is more complicated than it looks because fiscal policy is a slow legislative process and frequently determined by political, not economic, considerations. In addition, we do not know the level of potential output, which is the key to knowing whether contractionary or expansionary policy is needed. Economists have no sure way of estimating potential output. One method is to estimate the unemployment rate where inflation begins to rise. Unfortunately, this is also difficult to predict. Another way is to add a historical growth factor of 3% to previous levels of real output. This can be problematic if the economy is moving to a lower or higher growth rate. (610-611)

ANSWERS

MATCHING

1-c; 2-n; 3-m; 4-k; 5-e; 6-j; 7-a; 8-h; 9-i; 10-b; 11-l; 12-d; 13-f; 14-g.

ANSWERS

PROBLEMS AND APPLICATIONS

1. **a.** This would cause the wealth effect to become inoperative and the AD curve will become steeper. (594)
   b. Assuming rich people spend less of an increase in income compared to poor people, the AD curve will shift in to the left. (597)
   c. As the exchange rate depreciates, exports will rise and imports will fall. This shifts the AD curve out to the right. (596)
   d. If the exchange rate was originally fixed and became flexible, increases in the price level will be offset by changes in the exchange rate and the international effect becomes inoperative. The *AD* curve will be steeper. (596)
   e. Expectations of future price increases without changes in the current price level will tend to cause the *AD* curve to shift out to the right. (597)

2. **a.** The SAS doesn't shift at all because rises in input prices are completely offset by increases in productivity. (599-600)
   b. The SAS curve shifts up because the rise in input prices exceeds the rise in productivity. (599-600)
   c. The SAS curve shifts down because the rise in input prices is less than the rise in productivity. (599-600)

3. **a.** The LAS curve shifts to the right as shown below because business people are finding that their productive capacity is larger than they had thought. (602-603)

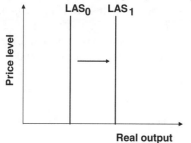

b. The potential output curve shifts to the left as shown below because bad weather will hinder production. Because the storm is temporary, however, the shift in the potential output curve is also temporary. (602-603)

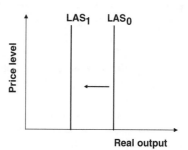

c. The short-run aggregate supply curve shown below shifts down from SAS_0 to SAS_1, because businesses will benefit from the declining import prices to the extent that imports are used in production. The fall in input prices is passed through to the goods market. (599-600)

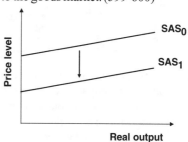

4. **a.** The economy is far below potential output at point A in the graph below. As the AD curve shifts out, the economy moves to point B—the price level rises slightly to P_1, and output increases to Y_1. As I have drawn the LAS curve, Y_1 is potential output, and point B is both a short-run and a long-run equilibrium. (606-610)

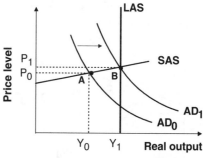

b. The economy is close to potential output at point A in the graph below. The AD curve shifts to AD_1. Real output rises to Y_1 and the price level rises to P_1. Because output is beyond potential, point B is a short-run equilibrium. Input prices begin to rise which shifts the SAS curve up. As the SAS curve shifts up, real output declines and the price level rises even further. The SAS curve will continue to shift up until the economy is at potential output Y_2 and a new price level P_2—point C. Expansionary fiscal policy will be less effective in increasing output when the economy is close to potential. Real output rises by less than in (a) and the economy experiences much more inflation. (606-610)

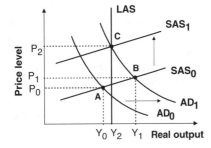

c. The economy is at potential output at point A in the graph below. As the AD curve shifts out, real output rises to Y_1 in the short run and the price level rises to P_1—point B. Since the economy is above potential however, eventually input prices will rise and the SAS curve will shift up. The SAS curve shifts up until real output falls back to potential output—Y_0—and the price level rises even further to P_2 (point C). In the long run, real output remains unchanged at Y_0 and only the price level increases from P_0 to P_2. When the economy is at or above potential, government activism is ineffective in the long run. (606-610)

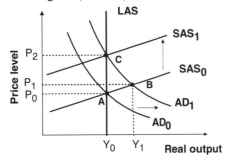

5. a. The graph below demonstrates an inflationary gap—short-run equilibrium output is above potential—point A. If government does nothing, wages will be bid up because there is a shortage of workers. This will shift the SAS curve up to SAS_1. Real output will fall to potential and the price level will rise—to point B. (606)

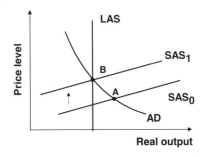

b. The graph below demonstrates a recessionary gap—short-run equilibrium output is below potential—point A. Given the excess supply in the labor market firms will be able to offer workers lower wages. Input prices will fall and the SAS curve will shift down to SAS_1. Real output will rise to potential and the price level will fall—to point B. Generally, government intervenes to increase expenditures (shifting the AD curve) before the price level declines. (605-606)

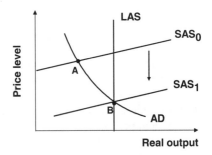

c. To avoid changes in the price level, if the economy is in an inflationary gap, the government can reduce government spending (or raise taxes) to shift the AD curve in to the left. If the economy is in a recessionary gap, it can increase government spending (or lower taxes) to shift the AD curve out to the right. (606)

━━━━━ ● **ANSWERS** ━━━━━

A BRAIN TEASER

1. My response depends on where I believe the economy is relative to potential output. If we are far below potential output then the President is right—the policy moves will increase the AD curve and the real output (employment) level will rise without creating much inflation. However, if we are close to potential output and the policy pushes the economy beyond potential, then wages will rise pushing the SAS curve up and the price level may rise more. The extent to which wages rise depends on the size of the effect on aggregate demand. It is difficult to predict. Moreover, it is also very difficult to determine how far from potential the economy actually is. (610-611)

━━━━━ ● **ANSWERS** ━━━━━

MULTIPLE CHOICE

1. a   Laissez faire is the non-activist policy that Classical economists generally support. See page 590.

2. b   The essence of Keynesian economics was its focus on the short run. See page 590.

3. c   The paradox of thrift is that if individuals increase saving, total income will decline, resulting in lower saving. See page 592.

4. d   Because of coordination problems equilibrium income could be different than potential income in Keynesian economics; it could be higher, lower, or equal to it. See page 592.

5. d   The AS/AD model is different than the micro supply/demand model. It has price *level* on the vertical axis and *total* output on the horizontal axis. See page 593.

6. c   No consumption effect is discussed in the book. See pages 594-596.

7. a   This question refers to the international effect; if the international effect is reduced, the change in the price level will have less effect on AD and the AD curve will be steeper. See page 595.

8. a   The multiplier effect increases the effect of the other effects and hence a smaller multiplier makes the AD curve steeper. See pages 595-596.

9. b   The rise in foreign income will increase demand for exports, shifting the AD curve to the right. See page 596.

10. a   The rise in the country's exchange rate will decrease demand for its exports, shifting the AD curve in to the left. See page 596.

11. b   Expansionary monetary policy will increase aggregate demand, shifting the AD curve out to the right. See page 598.

12. c   The multiplier effect would increase the effect, so the rightward shift would be more than 40. See page 598.

13. c   The SAS curve is not a derived curve; it is an empirical curve determined by institutional realities. See page 599.

14. a   Because wages are rising by more than productivity, the SAS curve will shift up. See pages 599-601.

15. c   The LAS curve shows the amount of goods and services an economy can produce when both labor and capital are fully employed. It is a vertical line since the price level does not affect potential output. See pages 601-602.

16. a   The SAS curve shifts upward when wages rise by more than increases in productivity. Real output will decline and the price level will rise. See pages 599-601.

17. b   An increase in the money supply will shift the AD curve to the right. In the short run, real output and the price level will rise. See page 603.

18. c   Demand for domestic goods will decline if one's currency appreciates because foreign goods will be less expensive compared to domestic goods. Real output will decline and the price level falls slightly. See pages 596-597.

19. d   Since at point B, the economy is below potential, there will be downward pressure on wages. Or at least wages will rise by less than the increase in productivity.

The SAS curve will shift down until the economy reaches point C. See pages 599-601.

20. a   Since at point B, the economy is above potential, there will be upward pressure on wages. Wages will rise by more than the increase in productivity. The SAS curve will shift up until the economy reaches point C. See pages 599-601.

21. a   The inflationary gap occurs when the price level is such that the quantity of aggregate demand exceeds the quantity of potential income. See page 606.

22. c   Expansionary fiscal policy is the deliberate increase in government expenditures or reduction in taxes. See page 607.

23. d   Aggregate demand management policies do not affect SAS, so a and b are out. With an inflationary gap you want to decrease output, so the answer is d. See Figure 25-8 on page 607.

24. a   Inflation results in higher input prices, which shifts the SAS curve up. See page 606.

25. b   During WW II, taxes rose, but spending rose even more so that the net result was expansionary. Although the economy exceeded potential, inflation was avoided by price controls. See pages 608-609.

26. c   The tax cuts were passed for supply-side reasons, but they became unintentionally timely when the recession began and kept the recession mild. See page 610.

27. b   Potential income varies inversely with unemployment. See page 610-611.

ANSWERS

POTENTIAL ESSAY QUESTIONS

The following are annotated answers. They indicate the general idea behind the answer.

1.   The macro model is more complicated than it appears because we do not know for sure where potential output is and because fiscal policy is more difficult to implement than is portrayed. Because we have no way of precisely determining how close the economy is to potential output, we don't know precisely by how much we should shift the AD curve.

2.   The Classical prescription for the Great Depression was to do nothing (except remove the obstacles that they argued kept wages and prices artificially high) and wait for the market to work its magic over time.

    Keynes believed that equilibrium income was not the same as potential income. He disagreed with Say's Law. Supply does *not* create its own demand. That is, there is no guaranteed equality between savings and investment. Savings could exceed investment so that aggregate expenditures would not purchase all that is produced. Inventories will rise, and output, employment, and incomes would fall creating a further decline in total spending. Keynes doubted whether falling prices could stop this downward spiral. So, we get stuck in a rut.

    The policy implications are that insufficient total spending in the economy could result in *an equilibrium* level of output, employment, and income *below potential* output. Therefore, the Keynesian recommendation for a recession: expansionary macro policy. That is, increase government spending, reduce taxes (fiscal policy), and increase the money supply (monetary policy) to stimulate aggregate expenditures. (This would shift the AD curve to the right and increase real output.)

3.   The paradox of thrift is that when people collectively decide to save more and consume less, consumption expenditures fall. If that saving is not immediately transferred into investment, total expenditures falls. Faced with excess supply, firms cut production and income falls. As people's income falls, consumption and saving both fall. It is the paradox of thrift that leads to the multiplier effect. This multiplier effect makes the AD curve flatter than it otherwise would have been and accounts for the multiplied effect of shift factors of aggregate demand.

THE MULTIPLIER MODEL

26

CHAPTER AT A GLANCE

This review is based upon the learning objectives that open the chapter.

1. Autonomous expenditures are unrelated to income; induced expenditures are directly related to income. (618-619)

   AE_0 (autonomous expenditures) can change (shift the AE curve) if there is an autonomous change in any component of aggregate expenditures (AE).

   Note: $AE_0 = C_0 + I_0 + G_0 + (X_0 - M_0)$.

   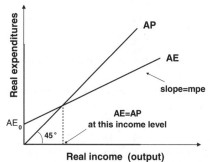

2. To determine income graphically in the multiplier model, you find the income level at which aggregate expenditures equal aggregate production. (623-624)

   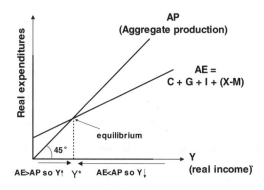

3. To determine income using the multiplier equation, determine the multiplier and multiply it by the level of autonomous expenditures (624-625)

   multiplier = 1/(1 −mpe).

   Y = (multiplier)(Autonomous expenditures)

   ΔY = (multiplier)(ΔAutonomous expenditures)

   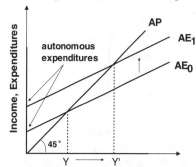

4. The multiplier process works because when expenditures don't equal production, businesspeople change planned production, which changes income, which changes expenditures, which.... (625-626)

   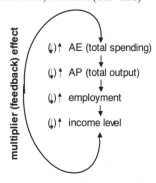

   This is the income adjustment process—the multiplier effect on income given a change in spending.

5. Expansionary fiscal policy can eliminate a recessionary gap. It shifts the AE curve up , increasing equilibrium income by a multiple of the shift. (630-633)

If the economy is below potential, at Y_0, in the graph below, expansionary fiscal policy can get the economy out of its recessionary gap by increasing government purchases or decreasing taxes. The AE/AP model assumes the price level is constant, so real output rises by the full amount of the multiplier times the change in autonomous expenditures.

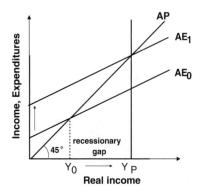

In the model, government knows by how much to increase (decrease) expenditures by dividing the recessionary (inflationary) gap by the multiplier.

6. While the multiplier model is a mechanistic multiplier model, it should be used as a guide to one's common sense. The multiplier model has limitations: (633-635)

● The multiplier is not a complete model of the economy.
The multiplier is best used as a guide for the direction and rough sizes of shifts in aggregate demand on income.

● Shifts are not as great as intuition suggests.
Because some saving is brought back into the expenditures flow, a change in autonomous expenditures has less of an effect than the model suggests.

● The price level will often change in response to shifts in demand.
The multiplier model assumes prices are fixed.

● People's forward-looking expectations make the adjustment process much more complicated.
Business decisions are forward-looking.

● Shifts in expenditures might reflect desired shifts in supply and demand.

● Expenditures depend on much more than current income.
People also base their expenditure decisions on future income.

See also, Appendix A: "An Algebraic Presentation of the Expanded Multiplier Model" and Appendix B: "The Multiplier Model and the AS/AD Model"

● SHORT-ANSWER QUESTIONS

1. What is the difference between induced and autonomous expenditures?

2. Draw an AP and an AE curve and show how the level of income is graphically determined in the multiplier model. Describe the forces that are set in motion when income levels are above and below equilibrium.

3. In the multiplier model, if autonomous expenditures are $200 and the *mpe* is 0.75, what is equilibrium income?

4. Explain the process by which the economy reaches a new equilibrium income if autonomous expenditures increase by $100. The marginal propensity to expend is 0.5.

5. How does fiscal policy affect the economy? Demonstrate the appropriate fiscal policy for an economy that has an inflationary gap.

6. True or false: The multiplier model is a complete model of the economy. Explain your answer.

MATCHING THE TERMS
Match the terms to their definitions

____1. aggregate expenditures
____2. aggregate production curve
____3. autonomous expenditures
____4. expenditures multiplier
____5. induced expenditures
____6. marginal propensity to expend
____7. multiplier equation
____8. permanent income hypothesis
____9. rational expectations model
____10. real business cycle theory

a. The hypothesis that expenditures are determined by permanent or lifetime income.
b. Expenditures that change as income changes.
c. The theory that fluctuations in the economy reflect real phenomena—simultaneous shifts in supply and demand, not simply supply responses to demand shifts.
d. A number that tells us how much income will change in response to a change in autonomous expenditures.
e. $AE = C + I + G + (X-M)$.
f. In the multiplier model, the 45° line on a graph with real income measured on the horizontal axis and real production on the vertical axis. Alternatively called the aggregate income curve.
g. The ratio of a change in expenditures to a change in income.
h. Expenditures that are unaffected by changes in income.
i. Equation that tells us how much income will change in response to a change in autonomous expenditures..
j. Model of the economy in which all decisions are based upon expected equilibrium in the economy.

● PROBLEMS AND APPLICATIONS

1. Answer the following questions about the aggregate production curve.

    a. Draw an aggregate production curve. Label all axes.

    b. What is the slope of the aggregate production function?

    c. Why is the slope as you have drawn it?

2. You are given the following information about the economy:

Income	Expenditures
0	100
500	500
1,000	900
2,000	1,700
3,000	2,500
4,000	3,300

    a. What is the level of autonomous expenditures?

b. What is the marginal propensity to expend? Explain why it is important.

c. What expenditures function (an equation) corresponds to the table?

3. Putting expenditures and production together:

a. Graph the expenditures function from question 2 on the aggregate production curve from question 1.

b. What is the slope of the expenditures function?

4. Given the following equation, answer the questions: $AE = C_0 + .6Y + I_0 + G_0 + (X_0 - M_0)$ where $C_0 = 1000$, $I_0 = 500$, $G_0 = 300$, $X_0 = 300$, $M_0 = 400$.

a. Draw the aggregate expenditures curve.

b. What is the slope of the curve?

c. What is the vertical axis intercept?

d. Add the aggregate production curve to the graph.

e. What is the multiplier?

f. What is equilibrium income? Label that point A on the graph.

g. What is the effect of an increase in autonomous consumption of $200 on equilibrium income? Demonstrate your answer graphically.

h. What is the effect on equilibrium income of a change in the *mpe* from .6 to .8? Demonstrate your answer graphically. How does your answer to (g) change with the new *mpe*?

5. Calculate the multiplier in each case.

   a. *mpe* = .7

   b. *mpe* = .6

6. For each of the following, state what will happen to equilibrium income.

   a. The *mpe* is 0.9 and autonomous government expenditures just rose $200 billion. Graph your analysis.

   b. The *mpe* is 0.65 and autonomous investment just fell $70 billion. Graph your analysis.

7. You are hired by the president who believes that the economy is operating at a level $300 billion beyond potential output. You are told that the marginal propensity to consume is 0.5. (Note: assume that the *mpe* = *mpc*.)

   a. The president wants to use taxes to close the gap. What do you advise? Show your answer using the AP/AE model. (Read the box on page 610 for a hint).

   b. The president wants to compare your plan in (a) to a plan using spending to close the inflationary gap. What do you advise? Show your answer graphically using the AP/AE model.

   c. The president's advisers from the council realize that the marginal propensity to consume is 0.75. Recalculate your answer to (b) and show your answer graphically using the AP/AE model.

A1. You've just been appointed chairman of the Council of Economic Advisers in Textland. The *mpc* is .8, and all non-consumption expenditures and taxes are exogenous.

   a. How can the government increase output by $400 through a change in expenditures?

b. Oops! There's been a mistake. Your research assistant tells you that taxes are actually not exogenous, and that there is a marginal tax rate of .1. How can the government change expenditures to increase income by $400?

c. There's more new news which your research assistant just found out. She tells you that not only is there a marginal tax rate of .1; there's also a marginal propensity to import of .2. You have to change your solutions now. How can the government change expenditures to increase income by $400?

B1. What happens to output in the AP/AE model when the AE curve shifts up due to a shift in autonomous expenditures if the economy is at potential output and the price level is flexible?

● A BRAIN TEASER

1. We have all heard about the extent to which local communities go to in attracting and recruiting new businesses, conventions, trade shows, professional meetings, etc., to their area. Sometimes they seem to "give away the farm." They may offer a commitment not to impose property taxes for a particular number of years or offer land at no charge if a company will build a production facility in the area. Why do local governments offer lucrative tax incentives, etc., to attract new businesses to their area–especially considering that there are only a relatively few number of modestly higher paying jobs created?

● MULTIPLE CHOICE

Circle the one best answer for each of the following questions:

1. In the multiplier model:
   a. production is assumed to be fixed.
   b. planned expenditures are assumed to equal actual production.
   c. the price level is assumed to be fixed.
   d. the price level is assumed to be flexible.

2. Autonomous expenditures are expenditures that:
   a. are automatically created by income.
   b. are unrelated to income.
   c. change as income changes.
   d. automatically change as income changes.

3. The marginal propensity to expend is:
   a. the change in expenditures times the change in income.
   b. the change in expenditures divided by the change in income.
   c. the change in expenditures divided by income.
   d. expenditures divided by the change in income.

4. If the mpe is .8, what is the size of the multiplier in the multiplier model?
   a. .5.
   b. 5.
   c. 1.
   d. 10.

5. As the *mpe* rises, the multiplier:
   a. increases.
   b. decreases.
   c. remains the same.
   d. sometimes rises and sometimes falls.

6. Which of the following is the expenditures function depicted in the graph below?

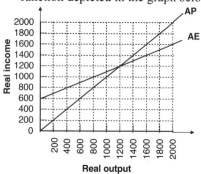

   a. AE = $600 + .5Y.
   b. AE = .5Y.
   c. AE = $600.
   d. AE = $600Y/.5.

7. Refer to the graph for Question #6. Planned expenditures exceed production at:
   a. income levels above $1,200.
   b. income levels below $1,200.
   c. income level of $1,200.
   d. no income level since planned expenditures equals production.

8. If consumer confidence suddenly falls, you would expect:
   a. the aggregate production curve to shift down.
   b. the aggregate expenditures curve to rotate to the right and equilibrium income to fall.
   c. the aggregate expenditures curve to shift up and equilibrium income to rise.
   d. the aggregate expenditures curve to shift down and equilibrium income to fall.

9. In the multiplier model, if autonomous expenditures are $5,000 and the *mpe* equals .9, what is the level of income in the economy?
   a. $5,000.
   b. $10,000.
   c. $20,000.
   d. $50,000.

10. In the multiplier model if autonomous exports fall by 40 and the *mpe* is .5, what happens to equilibrium income?
    a. Income rises by 20.
    b. Income falls by 20.
    c. Income rises by 80.
    d. Income falls by 80.

11. In the multiplier model if autonomous expenditures increase by 100, income:
    a. will rise by 100.
    b. will rise by more than 100.
    c. will fall by 100.
    d. may rise or fall. We cannot tell without more information.

12. In the multiplier model if autonomous expenditures increase by 10 and the *mpe* is .8, what happens to income?
    a. Income rises by 8.
    b. Income falls by 8.
    c. Income rises by 50.
    d. Income falls by 50.

13. In the multiplier model if autonomous exports fall by 40 and government spending increases by 20, and the *mpe* is .8, what happens to income?
    a. Income rises by 300.
    b. Income falls by 300.
    c. Income rises by 100.
    d. Income falls by 100.

14. In the multiplier model, if people begin to spend less of the increases in their income:
    a. leakages out of the circular flow will rise and equilibrium income will fall.
    b. because leakages from the circular flow will still equal injections into the circular flow, equilibrium income will not change.
    c. injections into the circular flow will rise and equilibrium income will rise.
    d. the flow of income and expenditures will no longer be circular.

15. In the graph on the next page, actual income is below potential income. The government is planning to use expansionary fiscal policy. This will:

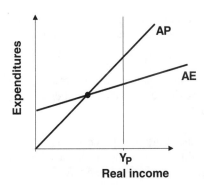

a. shift the *AP* curve up.
b. shift the *AE* curve up.
c. shift the *AP* curve down.
d. shift the *AE* curve down.

16. The economy has an *mpe* of .5, and a recessionary gap of 240. Using the Keynesian *multiplier model*, an economist would advise government to increase autonomous expenditures by:
    a. 120.
    b. 240.
    c. 480.
    d. 620.

17. The hypothesis that expenditures are determined by permanent or lifetime income (making the *mpe* close to zero) implies that the AE curve will be close to:
    a. a flat line.
    b. a vertical line.
    c. an upward sloping 45^0 line.
    d. something economists cannot determine.

18. The interpretative Keynesian macro model differs from the mechanistic Keynesian model in that:
    a. the interpretative multiplier model is essentially a Classical model.
    b. the interpretative model sees the Keynesian model as a guide, not a definitive result.
    c. the interpretative multiplier model integrates the quantity theory into the *AE/AP* model.
    d. the interpretative multiplier model integrates the quantity theory into both the Keynesian *AS/AD* and the *AE/AP* models.

19. If there is some price level flexibility:
    a. the multiplier model is no longer relevant.
    b. the results of the multiplier model will be reversed.
    c. the results of the multiplier model will be modified but the central point will remain the same.
    d. the multiplier model will turn into a Classical model.

20. In the real business cycle theory, business cycles occur because of:
    a. changes in the real price level.
    b. changes in real income.
    c. technological and other natural shocks.
    d. changes in the money supply.

A1. If the marginal tax rate increases, what would happen to the general expenditures multiplier?
    a. It would increase.
    b. It would decrease.
    c. It would remain the same.
    d. One cannot say.

A2. In the multiplier model, if a country has a very large marginal propensity to import:
    a. expansionary fiscal policy would be extremely effective in expanding domestic income.
    b. expansionary fiscal policy would not be very effective in expanding domestic income.
    c. The size of the marginal propensity to import has no effect on the effectiveness of expansionary fiscal policy.
    d. The multiplier model is not relevant to a country with a very large marginal propensity to import.

A3. Assuming the marginal propensity to import is .1, the tax rate is .2, and the marginal propensity to consume is .6, the multiplier will be approximately:
    a. 0.
    b. 1.2.
    c. 1.6.
    d. 2.6.

A4. Assume the marginal propensity to import is .1, the tax rate is .25, the marginal propensity to consume is .8, and that the government wants to increase income by 100. In the multiplier model you would suggest increasing government spending by:
  a. 10.
  b. 35.7.
  c. 50.
  d. 100.

A5. Assume the marginal propensity to import is .3, the tax rate is .2, the marginal propensity to consume is .5, and that the government wants to increase income by 200. In the multiplier model you would suggest increasing government spending by:
  a. 87.5.
  b. 100.
  c. 180.
  d. 200.

B1. When the price level falls:
  a. the aggregate expenditures curve remains constant.
  b. the aggregate expenditures curve shifts down.
  c. the aggregate expenditures curve shifts up.
  d. the slope of the aggregate expenditures curve changes.

B2. To derive the aggregate demand curve from the multiplier model, one must:
  a. relate the initial autonomous shifts caused by price level changes on the *AE* curve to the *AD* curve.
  b. relate the *AE/AP* equilibria at different price levels to the *AD* curve.
  c. relate the *AE/AP* equilibria at different quantity levels to the *AD* curve.
  d. relate the initial autonomous shifts caused by price level changes on the *AP* curve to the *AD* curve.

POTENTIAL ESSAY QUESTIONS

You may also see essay questions similar to the "Problems & Applications" and "Brain Teasers" exercises.

1. In the multiplier model, can macroeconomic equilibrium exist below full employment? Why, or why not?

2. Why does the multiplier process exist? What does the multiplier do to the income level given any change in aggregate expenditures?

3. What is the major contribution of the multiplier model to the AS/AD model?

ANSWERS

SHORT-ANSWER QUESTIONS

1. Induced expenditures depend upon the level of income. Autonomous expenditures are independent of income. (618-619)

2. The *AP* curve is a 45-degree line through the origin. At all points on the *AP* curve, output equals income. The *AE* curve is an upward-sloping line with a slope less than one that intersects the expenditures axis at the level of autonomous expenditures. These curves are shown in the graph below. Equilibrium income is where the two curves intersect. At points to the left, aggregate expenditures exceed aggregate production and businesses find their inventories are being depleted. They increase production, which increases income and expenditures, moving income up toward equilibrium. At points to the right, aggregate expenditures are less than aggregate production and businesses see their inventories accumulating. They cut production, which reduces income and expenditures, moving income down toward equilibrium. (623-624)

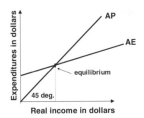

3. To determine equilibrium income, multiply the sum of all autonomous expenditures by the multiplier. In this case the multiplier is $1/(1-.75)=4$, so equilibrium income is $800. (624-625)

4. The initial shock is $100. This increase in expenditures causes aggregate production to increase also by $100, which creates an additional $100 in income. Consumers spend $50 of this additional income on additional goods. Once again aggregate production rises by the same amount as aggregate expenditures rose—$50 increase in this case. Subsequent increases in aggregate expenditures and aggregate production are determined in a similar fashion, each time getting smaller and smaller. Equilibrium income is $200 higher at the end of this multiplier process. This is determined by calculating the multiplier, $1/(1-mpe)=2$ and multiplying it by the initial

rise in aggregate expenditures of $100. (625-626)

5. Fiscal policy affects the economy by changing aggregate expenditures, which changes people's incomes, which changes people's spending even more. Expansionary fiscal policy shifts the aggregate expenditures curve up. Equilibrium income rises by a multiple of the increase in government spending. An economy in an inflationary gap is shown below. To avoid inflation, government can reduce government spending by the inflationary gap divided by the multiplier. A decline in government spending shifts the AE curve down and equilibrium income declines by a multiple of that shift. (630-632)

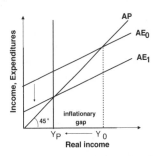

6. False. The multiplier model is not a complete model of the economy. Although it purports to determine equilibrium from scratch, it doesn't because it does not tell us where those autonomous expenditures come from. The multiplier model is best used as a guide for the direction and rough size of the effects of changes in autonomous expenditures on income. (633-635)

ANSWERS

MATCHING

1-e; 2-f; 3-h; 4-d; 5-b; 6-g; 7-i; 8-a; 9-j; 10-c.

ANSWERS

PROBLEMS AND APPLICATIONS

1. **a.** The aggregate production curve is a 45-degree line as shown below. Production is on the vertical axis and real income is on the horizontal axis. (617-618)

b. The slope is 1. (617-618)

c. The slope is one because the aggregate production curve represents the identity that aggregate production must equal aggregate income. That can only be represented by a straight line through the origin with a slope of one. (617-618)

2. a. Autonomous expenditures are $100. It is expenditures that are independent of income. (618-619)

b. The marginal propensity to expend is 0.8: This is calculated as the change in expenditures/change in income = 400/500. It is important because it tells us how much of any additional income is re-spent as the economy expands. It is because of the *mpe* that income changes by a multiple of a change in autonomous expenditures. (620)

c. The expenditures function that corresponds to the table is $AE = 100 + .8Y$. The 100 comes from the level of expenditures when income is zero and the .8 is the *mpe*. (621-622)

3. a. The graphs of the expenditures function from question 2 and the aggregate production from question 1 are shown together on the following graph. (623)

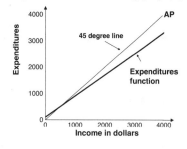

b. The slope of the expenditure function is the *mpe,* or 0.8. (621-622)

4. a. The aggregate expenditures curve is drawn below. The slope of the *AE* curve is the *mpe* and the vertical intercept is autonomous expenditures. (621-622)

b. The slope of the curve is .6. It is the *mpe*. (621-622)

c. The vertical axis intercept is $1000+500+300+(300-400) = 1700$. The vertical axis intercept is the level of autonomous expenditures. (621-622)

d. The aggregate production curve is shown in the graph below. It is a 45-degree line through the origin. (617-618)

e. The multiplier is 2.5. It is $1/(1-mpe)$. (624-625)

f. Equilibrium income is $4,250: autonomous expenditures $\times$ multiplier, $1,700 \times 2.5$. This is shown as point A on the graph below. (624-625)

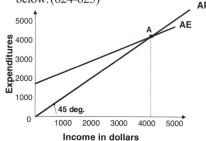

g. An increase in autonomous expenditures of $200 will increase equilibrium income by $500. This is calculated by multiplying $200 by the multiplier, 2.5. The new equilibrium income is $4,750. This is shown on the next page as an upward shift in the AE curve by 200. The new equilibrium income is point B on the graph on the next page. (627-628)

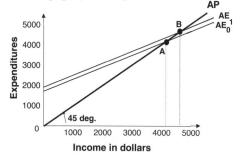

h. The *AE* curve becomes steeper with a slope of .8. The multiplier is now 5 and equilibrium income is now $8,500. This is shown as point C in the graph below. Equilibrium income is calculated by multiplying autonomous expenditures, $1,700, by the multiplier. Since the multiplier is larger, an increase of $200 in autonomous expenditures now increases equilibrium income by $1,000, up to $9,500. (624-625)

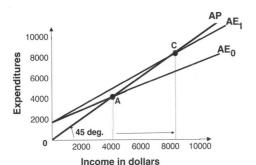

5. a. The multiplier is 3.33: $1/(1-.7)$. (625)
   b. The multiplier is 2.5: $1/(1-.6)$. (625)

6. a. Income rises by $2 trillion: $200/(1-0.9)$. In this case, the aggregate expenditures curve has a slope of 0.9 as shown in the graph below. The increase in government expenditures shifts the AE curve up from AE_0 to AE_1 and income increases by a multiple of that amount, in this case by a multiple of 10. (628-629)

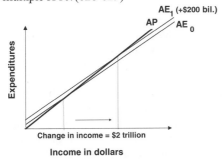

   b. Income falls by $200 billion: $70/.35$. In this case the aggregate expenditures curve has a slope of .65 as shown in the graph below. The decrease in investment shifts the AE curve down from AE_0 to AE_1 and income decreases by a multiple of that amount, in this case by a multiple of 2.86. (628-629)

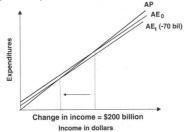

7. a. The spending multiplier is 2, $1/(1-.5)$, but only a fraction of the increase in taxes reduces spending. Taxes must be increased by $300 billion to reduce income by $300 billion. We calculate this by solving the following for change in taxes:

change in taxes $\times mpc \times [1/(1-mpe)] = \$300$ billion. The AE curve shifts down by the decrease in consumption spending ($150 billion) as shown below. (630-633)

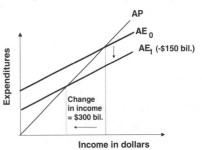

   b. The spending multiplier is 2. Spending must be decreased by $150 billion to reduce income by $300 billion. We calculate this by solving the following for change in government spending: change in government spending $\times (1/(1-mpe)) = \$300$ billion. Graphically, the analysis is the same as in part a. (630-633)

   c. The spending multiplier is now 4, $1/(1-.75)$. Government spending must be decreased by $75 billion to reduce income by $300 billion. We calculate this by solving the following for change in government spending: change in government spending $\times 4 = \$300$ billion. This is shown in the graph below. The AE curve is steeper than the AE curve in part b. (630-633)

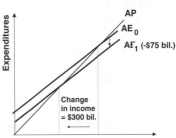

A1. Given an mpc of .8:
   a. Increase expenditures by $80. The multiplier is $1/(1-mpc) = 1/(1-.8) = 5$. Therefore, to increase GDP by $400, government spending has to increase $80. (639-642)
   b. Increase expenditures by $112. The multiplier is $1/(1-mpc+t \times mpc) = 1/(1-.8+(.1 \times .8)) = 3.57$. Therefore, to increase GDP by $400, government spending has to increase by $112. (639-648)

c. Increase expenditures by $193. The multiplier is $1/(1 - mpc + t \times mpc + mpm) = 1/(1 - .8 + .1 \times .8 + .2) = 2.08$. Therefore, to increase GDP by $400, government spending has to increase by $193. (639-642)

B1. In the multiplier model, a change in autonomous expenditures will be offset entirely by a change in the price level that shifts the AE curve in a direction opposite to the initial shift. If the initial shift causes the AE curve to shift up, prices will rise sufficiently to shift the AE curve back to its initial position. (642-644)

ANSWERS

A BRAIN TEASER

1. It may appear that the benefits do not outweigh the costs to the community of "giving away the farm"–especially when one considers that the tax breaks offered to new businesses will likely result in higher property tax rates imposed on other members of the community if the same quantity and quality of local government services are to be provided. However, even though a relatively few number of modestly higher paying jobs are created, because of the multiplier effect, this *can* translate into still more jobs and even more income, etc.–creating "significant growth and opportunities within the community." Next time you read headlines indicating the amount of jobs (or income) created in the city by having the "Pigs are Beautiful" convention in town, you'll know what they mean. (625-629)

ANSWERS

MULTIPLE CHOICE

1. c The multiplier model assumes that the price level remains constant and asks how much aggregate equilibrium income will change when aggregate expenditures change. During the adjustment to equilibrium, planned expenditures will not equal actual production. See page 616.

2. b Autonomous expenditures are expenditures that exist even when income is zero. They do not change as income changes. See pages 618-619.

3. b The marginal propensity to expend is the fraction of additional income that is spent. It can be calculated by dividing the change in expenditures by the change in income. See page 620.

4. b The multiplier equals $1/(1 - .8) = 1/.2 = 5$. See page 624.

5. a You can determine this by substituting into the formula. See page 601.

6. a The graph shows that the y-axis intercept is $600 and the slope is .5. Calculate the slope as rise over run. For example, beginning at the y-intercept, increasing expenditures by 600 means income rises by 1200 (600/1200 = .5). Substitute these values in the equation for a straight line: y = (slope)x + (intercept). See pages 618-619.

7. b Planned expenditures exceed production where the AE curve is above the AP curve. This occurs at income levels below $1,200. See page 623.

8. d A drop in consumer confidence would be expected to reduce consumption expenditures. This shifts the AE curve down and leads to a reduction in equilibrium income (output). See pages 623-624.

9. d The multiplier is 10 so the answer is 10 times $5,000. See pages 624-625.

10. d The multiplier is 2 so the answer is $2 \times (-40)$. See pages 624-625.

11. b In the multiplier model, a change in autonomous expenditures will lead to a change in income in the same direction that is a multiple of the change in expenditures. See pages 624-625.

12. c The multiplier is 5 so the answer is 5 times 10. See pages 624-625.

13. d The multiplier is 5 so the answer is 5 times $(-40 + 20)$ or minus 100. See pages 624-625.

14. a If people spend less of their income, the *mpe* will fall. Because more income leaks from the circular flow, less returns in the form of expenditures and equilibrium income falls. See pages 624-625.

15. b　Expansionary fiscal policy increases aggregate expenditures, which is shown by a shift up in the AE curve. See Figure 26-10(a) on page 631.

16. a　To determine how much to increase expenditures in the *multiplier model* to reach potential income, you divide the recessionary gap of 240 by the multiplier of 2. See pages 631-632.

17. a　The permanent income hypothesis suggests that the *mpe* out of current income would be small so, the AE curve would be quite flat. See page 635.

18. b　The interpretative multiplier model views the multiplier model as an aid in understanding. It might integrate the multiplier model with other models but that is not what is distinctive about it. See page 635.

19. c　The multiplier model assumes that the price level is constant. If, however, the price level is not constant, the multiplier model is modified. The central point, however, that an increase in expenditures has a multiplied effect on equilibrium output is still relevant. See page 634.

20. c　Real business cycle theory suggests that fluctuations in output are the result of shifting aggregate supply resulting from changes in technology. See page 635.

A1. b　This is a hard question since it requires some deduction. The marginal tax rate is one of the components of the marginal propensity to consume. It is a leakage from the circular flow, so it makes the multiplier smaller. See pages 639-642.

A2. b　A large marginal propensity to import reduces the size of the multiplier since the marginal propensity to import is one of the components of the marginal propensity to consume. See pages 639-642.

A3. c　The multiplier for the full model is $1/(1-c+ct+m)$. Substituting in gives $1/(1-.6+(.6)(.2)+.1)$ or $1/.62$ or a multiplier of about 1.6. See pages 639-642.

A4. c　First you determine the multiplier. The multiplier for the full model is $1/(1-c+ct+m)$. Substituting in gives $1/$

$(1-.8+(.8)(.25)+.1)$ or $1/.5$ or a multiplier of 2. Dividing 100 by 2 gives an increase of government spending of 50. See pages 639-642.

A5. c　First you determine the multiplier. The multiplier for the full model is $1/(1-c+ct+m)$. Substituting in gives $1/(1-.5+(.5)(.2)+.3)$ or $1/.9$ or a multiplier of about 1.11. Dividing 200 by 1.11 gives an increase of government spending of about 180. The multiplier is very small because the *mpc* is low and the *mpm* is high. See pages 639-642.

B1. c　Since a lower price level makes the cash people hold worth more, people feel wealthier, spend more, and the *AE* curve shifts up. See pages 642-644.

B2. b　As discussed on pages 642-644, especially Figure B26-1, one considers the effect of different price levels on the *AE* curve to derive an *AD* curve.

ANSWERS

POTENTIAL ESSAY QUESTIONS

The following are annotated answers. They indicate the general idea behind the answer.

1.　Yes, because equilibrium exists *wherever* AE = AP. That is, planned expenditures need not equal production at full employment. If there is inadequate spending then the income adjustment process moves the economy to an equilibrium below full employment.

2.　A change in spending changes people's incomes, which changes their spending, which changes people's incomes… Because of the induced effects within the income adjustment process, the multiplier magnifies any changes in spending into much larger changes in income. However, given an increase in expenditures, real income increases by a smaller amount when prices are flexible.

3.　The major contribution of the multiplier model to the AS/AD model is that it provides an exact number for the shift in the AD curve when autonomous expenditures change and provides the reasoning behind the multiplier effects needed to derive an AD curve.

Pretest
Chapters 22-26

Take this test in test conditions, giving yourself a limited amount of time to complete the questions. Ideally, check with your professor to see how much time he or she allows for an average multiple choice question and multiply this by 30. This is the time limit you should set for yourself for this pretest. If you do not know how much time your teacher would allow, we suggest 1 minute per question, or 30 minutes.

1. All of the following are long-run growth policies *except*:
   a. increasing government spending to spur consumer spending.
   b. reducing tax rates to increase incentives to work.
   c. providing funding for research.
   d. following policies to reduce interest rates and increase business investment.

2. The secular trend growth rate in the United States is approximately:
   a. 1 to 1.5 percent per year.
   b. 2.5 to 3.5 percent per year.
   c. 5 to 5.5 percent per year.
   d. 7 to 7.5 percent per year.

3. Leading indicators include:
   a. manufacturing and trade sales volume.
   b. number of employees on non-agricultural payrolls.
   c. industrial production.
   d. new orders for goods and materials.

4. Keynesians:
   a. generally favor activist government policies.
   b. generally favor laissez-faire policies.
   c. believe that frictional unemployment does not exist.
   d. believe that all unemployment is cyclical unemployment.

5. The level of output that would materialize at the target rate of unemployment and the target rate of capital utilization is called
   a. nominal output.
   b. actual output.
   c. potential output.
   d. utilized output.

6. To move from GDP to GNP, one must:
   a. add net foreign factor income.
   b. subtract inflation.
   c. add depreciation.
   d. subtract depreciation.

7. If you, the owner, sell your old car for $600, how much does GDP increase?
   a. By $600.
   b. By the amount you bought it for, minus the $600.
   c. By zero.
   d. By the $600 you received and the $600 the person you sold it to paid, or $1,200.

8. There are two firms in an economy, Firm A and Firm B. Firm A produces 100 widgets and sells them for $2 apiece. Firm B produces 200 gadgets and sells them for $3 apiece. Firm A sells 30 of its widgets to Firm B and the remainder to consumers. Firm B sells 50 of its gadgets to Firm A and the remainder to consumers. What is GDP in this economy?
   a. $210.
   b. $590.
   c. $600.
   d. $800.

9. Gross investment differs from net investment by:
   a. net exports.
   b. net imports.
   c. depreciation.
   d. transfer payments.

10. If inflation is 10 percent and nominal GDP goes up 20 percent, real GDP goes up approximately:
    a. 1 percent.
    b. 10 percent.
    c. 20 percent.
    d. 30 percent.

11. According to Say's Law:
    a. aggregate supply will exceed aggregate demand.
    b. aggregate demand will exceed aggregate supply.
    c. there will be no relation between aggregate supply and demand.
    d. aggregate demand will equal aggregate supply.

12. Suppose output grew at 4% in China and 2% in the United States.
    a. Per capita income grew faster in China
    b. Per capita income grew faster in the U.S.
    c. We cannot say in which country per capita income grew faster.
    d. Per capita output grew faster in China.

13. If there are increasing returns to scale, as:
    a. inputs rise, outputs fall.
    b. inputs rise, output rises by a smaller percentage.
    c. inputs rise, output rises by a larger percentage.
    d. one input rises, output rises by a larger percentage.

14. QWERTY is a metaphor for:
    a. the invisible hand.
    b. technological lock-in.
    c. the law of diminishing marginal productivity.
    d. the pollution caused by positive spillovers.

15. Which of the following policies will likely *slow* an economy's growth rate?
    a. Increased trade restrictions.
    b. Increasing the level of education.
    c. Increasing saving.
    d. Protecting property rights.

16. Classical economists are generally associated with:
    a. laissez faire.
    b. QWERTY.
    c. an activist policy.
    d. their support of low unemployment.

17. In Keynesian economics equilibrium income:
    a. will be equal to potential income.
    b. will be below potential income.
    c. will be above potential income.
    d. may be different than potential income.

18. If the multiplier effect is 2 rather than 3, the:
    a. AD curve will be steeper.
    b. AD curve will be flatter.
    c. AD curve will be unaffected.
    d. SAS curve will be steeper.

19. The slope of the SAS curve is determined by:
    a. opportunity cost
    b. the law of diminishing marginal returns.
    c. institutional realities.
    d. the wealth effect, the international effect and the interest rate effect.

20. Refer to the graph below. The graph demonstrates the expected short-run result if:

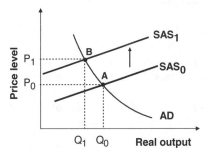

    a. productivity increases by less than wages.
    b. the government increases the money supply.
    c. the exchange rate value of a country's currency falls.
    d. there are suddenly expectations of a rising price level.

21. Assume the economy is initially at point B. The graph below correctly demonstrates an economy moving to point C if:

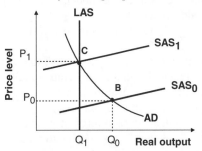

    a. productivity increases by less than the increase in wages.
    b. the government increases the money supply.
    c. a country's exchange rate appreciates (gains value).
    d. wages rise by less than the increase in productivity.

22. If the economy has an inflationary gap that it wants to eliminate, the government should use fiscal policy to shift:
   a. the *LAS* curve out.
   b. the *AS* curve down (to the left).
   c. the *AD* curve out to the right.
   d. the *AD* curve in to the left.

23. If the target rate of unemployment falls, potential income will:
   a. first decrease, then increase.
   b. increase.
   c. decrease.
   d. first increase, then decrease.

24. In the multiplier model:
   a. production is assumed to be fixed.
   b. planned expenditures are assumed to equal actual production.
   c. the price level is assumed to be fixed.
   d. the price level is assumed to be flexible.

25. If the mpe is .8, what is the size of the multiplier in the multiplier model?
   a. .5.
   b. 5.
   c. 1.
   d. 10.

26. As the *mpe* rises, the multiplier:
   a. increases.
   b. decreases.
   c. remains the same.
   d. sometimes rises and sometimes falls.

27. If consumer confidence suddenly falls, you would expect:
   a. the aggregate production curve to shift down.
   b. the aggregate expenditures curve to rotate to the right and equilibrium income to fall.
   c. the aggregate expenditures curve to shift up and equilibrium income to rise.
   d. the aggregate expenditures curve to shift down and equilibrium income to fall.

28. In the multiplier model if autonomous expenditures increases by 10 and the *mpe* is .8, what happens to the income?
   a. Income rises by 8.
   b. Income falls by 8.
   c. Income rises by 50.
   d. Income falls by 50.

29. The economy has an *mpe* of .5, and a recessionary gap of 240. Using the Keynesian *multiplier model*, an economist would advise government to increase autonomous expenditures by:
   a. 120.
   b. 240.
   c. 480.
   d. 620.

30. If there is some price level flexibility:
   a. the multiplier model is no longer relevant.
   b. the results of the multiplier model will be reversed.
   c. the results of the multiplier model will be modified but the central point will remain the same.
   d. the multiplier model will turn into a Classical model.

━━━━ ● ANSWERS ━━━━

1.	a	(22:2)	16.	a	(25:1)
2.	b	(22:4)	17.	d	(25:4)
3.	d	(22:8)	18.	a	(25:8)
4.	a	(22:12)	19.	c	(25:13)
5.	c	(22:14)	20.	a	(25:16)
6.	a	(23:2)	21.	a	(25:20)
7.	c	(23:4)	22.	d	(25:23)
8.	b	(23:5)	23.	b	(25:27)
9.	c	(23:11)	24.	c	(26:1)
10.	b	(23:15)	25.	b	(26:4)
11.	d	(24:2)	26.	a	(26:5)
12.	c	(24:5)	27.	d	(26:8)
13.	c	(24:10)	28.	c	(26:12)
14.	b	(24:20)	29.	a	(26:16)
15.	a	(24:24)	30.	c	(26:19)

Key: The figures in parentheses refer to multiple choice question and chapter numbers. For example (1:2) is multiple choice question 2 from chapter 1.

MONEY, BANKING, AND THE FINANCIAL SECTOR

● CHAPTER AT A GLANCE

This review is based upon the learning objectives that open the chapter.

1. The financial sector is central to almost all macroeconomic debates because behind every real transaction, there is a financial transaction that mirrors it. (645-646)

    If the interest rate does not perfectly translate saving (flows out of the spending stream) into investment (flows into the spending stream), then the economy will either expand or contract.

2. Money is a highly liquid, financial asset that is generally accepted in exchange for goods and services, is used as a reference in valuing other goods, and can be stored as wealth. (648-649)

    Money is any financial asset that serves the functions of money.

3. The three functions of money are: (649-651)

    ● Medium of exchange;
    As long as people are confident that the purchasing power of the dollar will remain relatively stable over time (by the Fed controlling the money supply) then people will continue to swap real goods, services, and resources for money and vice versa.

    ● Unit of account;
    Money acts as a measuring stick of the relative value (relative prices) of things. Therefore, the value of money itself must remain relatively stable over time.

    ● Store of wealth.
    Money's usefulness as a store of wealth also depends upon how well it maintains its value. The key is for the Fed to keep the purchasing power of money (and therefore prices) relatively stable over time. Inflation can be a problem!

4a. M1 is the component of the money supply that consists of cash in the hands of the public plus checking accounts and traveler's checks. (652)

    M1 is the narrowest measure of the money supply. It is also the most liquid.

4b. M2 is the component of the money supply that consists of M1 plus savings deposits, small-denomination time deposits, and money market mutual funds. (652-653)

    M2 is the measure of the money supply most used by the Fed to measure the money supply in circulation. This is because M2 is most closely correlated with the price level and economic activity.

    Anything that changes M2 changes the money supply!

4c. The broadest measure of the money supply is L (which stands for liquidity). It consists of almost all short-term financial assets. (653)

5. Banks "create" money because a bank's liabilities are defined as money. So when a bank incurs liabilities it creates money. (654-655)

    Banks "create" money (increase the money supply) whenever they make loans. Whenever a person borrows from a bank he/she is swapping a promissory note to repay the loan (the loan is really an IOU; and an individual's IOU is not money because it doesn't meet the criteria of serving the functions of money) in exchange for cash or funds put in his/her checking account. Cash and checking account balances are money! Therefore, the money supply increases. Also Note: When a loan is repaid, the money supply (M2) decreases.

6a. The money multiplier is the measure of the amount of money ultimately created by the banking system per dollar deposited. When people hold no cash it equals 1/r, where r is the reserve ratio. (657-659)

A single bank is limited in the amount of money it may create. The limit is equal to its excess reserves–the maximum amount of funds that it can legally loan out. However, when considering an entire banking system, where any bank's loans, when spent, may end up being deposited back into that bank or another bank, then the entire banking system ends up being able to increase the money supply by a multiple of its initial excess reserves (the initial maximum amount of funds that can legally be loaned out) because of the money multiplier.

Simple money multiplier = 1/r.

(Initial change in money supply)×(money multiplier) = change in the money supply

6b. When people hold cash the approximate money multiplier is 1/(r+c). (658-659)

Approximate real-world money multiplier = 1/(r+c) , where c is the ratio of money people hold in currency to the money held as deposits.

The approximate real-world money multiplier is less than the simple money multiplier because some of the funds loaned out are held as cash and therefore do not return to the banks as deposits.

7. Financial systems are based on trust that expectations will be fulfilled. Banks borrow short and lend long, which means that if people lose faith in banks, the banks cannot keep their promises. (660-661)

It is important to maintain the public's confidence in the banking system. Government guarantees of financial institu-tions can have 2 effects:
- *They can prevent unwarranted fear that causes financial crises.*
- *They can also eliminate warranted fears and hence eliminate a market control of bank loans.*

See also, Appendix A: "A Closer Look at Financial Institutions and Financial Mar-kets." Appendix B: "Creation of Money Using T-Accounts."

SHORT-ANSWER QUESTIONS

1. At lunch you and your friends are arguing about the financial sector. One friend says that real fluctuations are measured by real economic activity in the goods market and therefore the financial sector has nothing to do with the business cycle. You know better and set him straight.

2. You are having another stimulating lunchtime conversation, this time about money. Your friend says "I know what money is; it's cash, the dollar bills I carry around." What is your response?

3. You continue the conversation and begin to discuss why we have money. Your friend states that the function of money is to buy things like the lunch he has just bought. Another friend says that because she has money she is able to compare the cost of two types of slacks. Still another offers that she holds money to make sure she can buy lunch next week. What is the function of money that each has described? Are there any others?

4. What are the two most liquid measures of money? What are the primary components of each?

5. What is the broadest measure of money? What does it consist of?

6. Your friends are curious about money. At another lunchtime discussion, they ask each other two questions: Is all the money deposited in the bank in the bank's vaults? Can banks create money? Since they are stumped, you answer the questions for them.

7. Using the simple money multiplier, what will happen to the money supply if the reserve ratio is 0.2 and the Fed gives a bank $100 in reserves?

8. Using the equation for the approximate real-world money multiplier, what will happen to the money supply if the reserve ratio is 0.2, cash to deposit ratio is 0.3, and the Fed gives a bank $100 in reserves?

9. How does the interest rate regulate the flow of saving into the flow of expenditures during normal times?

10. What would happen if everyone simultaneously lost trust in their banks and ran to withdraw their deposits?

11. What is the potential problem with government guarantees to prevent bank-withdrawal panics?

MATCHING THE TERMS
Match the terms to their definitions

___ 1.	approximate real-world money multiplier	a.	Broad definition of "money" that includes almost all short-term assets.
___ 2.	asset management	b.	Cash that a bank keeps on hand that is sufficient to manage the normal cash inflows and outflows.
___ 3.	bond	c.	Component of the money supply that consists of M_1 plus savings deposits, small-denomination time deposits, and money market mutual fund shares, along with some esoteric relatively liquid assets.
___ 4.	excess reserves		
___ 5.	Federal Reserve Bank (the Fed)		
___ 6.	financial assets	d.	Component of the money supply that consists of cash in the hands of the public, checking account balances, and traveler's checks.
___ 7.	interest rate	e.	Assets whose benefit to the owner depends on the issuer of the asset meeting certain obligations.
___ 8.	L	f.	How a bank attracts deposits and what it pays for them.
___ 9.	liability management	g.	How a bank handles its loans and other assets.
___ 10.	M_1	h.	Measure of the amount of money ultimately created by the banking system, per dollar deposited, when cash holdings of individuals and firms are treated the same as reserves of banks. The mathematical expression is $1/(r+c)$.
___ 11.	M_2		
___ 12.	money	i.	Measure of the amount of money ultimately created by the banking system per dollar deposited, when people hold no cash. The mathematical expression is $1/r$.
___ 13.	nominal interest rate		
___ 14.	real interest rate	j.	Ratio of cash or deposits a bank holds at the central bank to deposits a bank keeps as a reserve against withdrawals of cash.
___ 15.	reserve ratio	k.	Reserves above what banks are required to hold.
___ 16.	reserves	l.	The U.S. central bank. Its liabilities serve as cash in the United States.
___ 17.	simple money multiplier	m.	A highly liquid financial asset that is generally accepted in exchange for other goods and is used as a reference in valuing other goods and as a store of wealth.
		n.	A promise to pay a certain amount of money plus interest in the future.
		o.	Price paid for the use of a financial asset.
		p.	The interest rate you see and pay adjusted for expected inflation.
		q.	The interest rate you see and pay.

● PROBLEMS AND APPLICATIONS

1. Complete the following table:

Nominal interest rate	Expected inflation	Real interest rate
6	3	
9		2
	−2	3

2. For each, state whether it is a component of M_1, M_2, both, or neither:

a. Money market mutual funds.

b. Savings deposits.

c. Traveler's checks.

d.   Stocks.

e.   Twenty-dollar bills.

3.   Assuming individuals hold no cash, calculate the simple money multiplier for each of the following reserve requirements:

   a.   15%

   b.   30%

   c.   60%

   d.   80%

   e.   100%

4.   Assuming individuals hold 10% of their deposits in the form of cash, recalculate the *approximate* real-world money multipliers from question 2.

   a.   15%

   b.   30%

   c.   60%

   d.   80%

   e.   100%

5.   While Jon is walking to school one morning, a helicopter flying overhead drops $300. Not knowing how to return it, Jon keeps the money and deposits it in his bank. (No one in this economy holds cash.) If the bank keeps only 10 percent of its money in reserves and is fully loaned out, calculate the following:

   a.   How much money can the bank now lend out?

   b.   After this initial transaction, by how much has the money in the economy changed?

   c.   What's the money multiplier?

   d.   How much money will eventually be created by the banking system from Jon's $300?

A1. Choose which of the following offerings you would prefer having. (Refer to the present value table on page 669)

   a. $1,500 today or $2,000 in 5 years. The interest rate is 4%.

   b. $1,500 today or $2,000 in 5 years. The interest rate is 9%.

   c. $2,000 today or $10,000 in 10 years. The interest rate is 15%

   d. $3,000 today or $10,000 in 15 years. The interest rate is 9%.

A2. A bond has a face value of $5,000 and a coupon rate of 10 percent. (A 10 percent coupon rate means that it pays annual interest of 10 percent of its face value.) It is issued in 2004 and matures in 2009. Using this information, calculate the following:

  a. What is the annual payment for that bond?

  b. If the bond is currently selling for $6,000, is its yield greater or less than 10 percent?

  c. If the bond is currently selling for $4,000, is its yield greater or less than 10 percent?

  d. What do your answers to (b) and (c) tell you about what the bond must sell for, relative to its face value, if the interest rate is 10%? Rises above 10%? Falls below 10%?

A3. For each, state whether a financial asset has been created. What gives each financial asset created its value?

  a. Your friend promises to pay you $5 tomorrow and expects nothing in return.

  b. You buy an apple at the grocery store.

c. The government sells a new bond with a face value of $5,000, a coupon rate of 8%, and a maturity date of 2016.

d. A firm issues stock.

e. An existing stock is sold to another person on the stock market.

A4. For each of the following financial instruments, state for whom it is a liability and for whom it is an asset. Also state, if appropriate, whether the transaction occurred on the capital or money market and whether a financial asset was created.

  a. First Bank grants a mortgage to David.

  b. First Bank sells David's mortgage to Financial Services, Inc.

  c. Broker McGuill sells existing stocks to client Debreu.

  d. An investment broker sells 100 shares of new-issue stock to client Debreu.

  e. U.S. government sells a new three-month T-bill to Corporation X.

  f. Corporation X sells a 30-year government bond to Sally Quinn.

B1. Assume that Textland Bank Balance Sheet looks like this:

Assets		Liabilities	
Cash	30,000	Demand Deposits	150,000
Loans	300,000	Net Worth	350,000
Phys. Assets	170,000		
Total Assets	500,000	Total Liabilities and Net Worth	500,000

a. If the bank is not holding any excess reserves, what is the reserve ratio?

b. Show the first three steps in money creation using a balance sheet if Jane Foundit finds $20,000 in cash and deposits it at Textland.

Step #1

Step #2

Step #3

c. After the first three steps, how much in excess reserves is the bank holding?

d. Show Textland's balance sheet at the end of the money creation process.

◉ A BRAIN TEASER

1. Whenever new loans are made the money supply expands. Whenever loans are repaid the money supply decreases. During any given period of time new loans are being made and old loans are being repaid. On balance, what happens to the money supply depends upon the magnitude of these conflicting forces. We also know that making loans is the principle source of profits to banks. Having said this, how can bankers' collective lending decisions (whether to give loans or not to give loans in order to maximize their profits, or to avoid losses) destabilize the business cycle, that is, cause recessions to get worse and upturns to become more pronounced?

◉ MULTIPLE CHOICE

Circle the one best answer for each of the following questions:

1. For every financial asset there is a:
   a. corresponding financial liability.
   b. corresponding financial liability if the financial asset is financed.
   c. real liability.
   d. corresponding real asset.

2. Using economic terminology, when an individual buys a bond, that individual
   a. is investing.
   b. is saving.
   c. is buying a financial liability.
   d. is increasing that individual's equities.

3. If the nominal interest rate is 2 percent and expected inflation is 1 percent, the real interest rate is:
   a. 3 percent.
   b. 2 percent
   c. 1 percent
   d. 0 percent.

4. Which of the following is not a function of
   money?
   a. Medium of exchange.
   b. Unit of account.
   c. Store of wealth.
   d. Equity instrument.

5. Which of the following is not included in the
   M_1 definition of money?
   a. checking accounts.
   b. currency.
   c. traveler's checks.
   d. savings accounts.

6. Which of the following components is not
   included in the M_2 definition of money?
   a. M_1.
   b. savings deposits.
   c. small-denomination time deposits.
   d. bonds.

7. In an advertisement for credit cards, the
   statement is made, "Think of a credit card as
   smart money." An economist's reaction to
   this would be that a credit card is:
   a. not money.
   b. dumb money.
   c. simply money.
   d. actually better than money.

8. Using a credit card creates a financial:
   a. liability for the holder and a financial asset
      for the issuer.
   b. asset for the holder and a financial liability
      for the issuer.
   c. liability for both the holder and issuer.
   d. asset for both the holder and issuer.

9. Modern bankers:
   a. focus on asset management.
   b. focus on liability management.
   c. focus on both asset management and
      liability management.
   d. are unconcerned with asset and liability
      management and instead are concerned with
      how to make money.

10. Assuming individuals hold no cash, the
    reserve requirement is 20 percent, and banks
    keep no excess reserves, an increase in an

initial inflow of $100 into the banking system
will cause an increase in the money supply of:
a. $20.
b. $50.
c. $100.
d. $500.

11. Assuming individuals hold no cash, the
    reserve requirement is 10 percent, and banks
    keep no excess reserves, an increase in an
    initial $300 into the banking system will
    cause an increase in total money of:
    a. $30.
    b. $300.
    c. $3,000.
    d. $30,000.

12. Assuming the ratio of money people hold in
    cash to the money they hold in deposits is
    .3, the reserve requirement is 20 percent, and
    that banks keep no excess reserves, an
    increase of an initial $100 into the banking
    system will cause an increase in total money
    of approximately:
    a. $50.
    b. $100.
    c. $200.
    d. $500.

13. If banks hold excess reserves whereas before
    they did not, the money multiplier:
    a. will become larger.
    b. will become smaller.
    c. will be unaffected.
    d. might increase or might decrease.

14. A sound bank will:
    a. always have enough cash on hand to pay all
       depositors in full.
    b. never borrow short and lend long.
    c. never borrow long and lend short.
    d. keep enough cash on hand to cover normal
       cash inflows and outflows.

15. FDIC is an acronym for:
    a. major banks in the United States.
    b. major banks in the world.
    c. U.S. government program that guarantees
       deposits.
    d. types of financial instruments.

16. The textbook author's view of government guarantees of deposits is:
   a. they don't make sense.
   b. stronger ones are needed.
   c. it depends.
   d. it should be a private guarantee program.

A1. If the interest rate falls, the value of a fixed rate bond:
   a. rises.
   b. falls.
   c. remains the same.
   d. cannot be determined as to whether it rises or falls.

A2. Two bonds, one a 30-year bond and the other a 1-year bond, have the same interest rate. If the interest rate in the economy falls, the value of the:
   a. long-term bond rises by more than the value of the short-term bond rises.
   b. short-term bond rises by more than the value of the long-term bond rises.
   c. long-term bond falls by more than the value of the short-term bond falls.
   d. short-term bond falls by more than the value of the long-term bond falls.

A3. A secondary financial market is a market in which:
   a. minor stocks are sold.
   b. minor stocks and bonds are sold.
   c. previously issued financial assets can be bought and sold.
   d. small secondary mergers take place.

A4. If you are depositing money at a bank, the bank is likely:
   a. an investment bank
   b. a commercial bank.
   c. a municipal bank.
   d. a government bank.

A5. Liquidity is:
   a. a property of water stocks.
   b. the ability to turn an asset into cash quickly.
   c. the ability to turn an asset into liquid quickly.
   d. a property of over-the-counter markets.

A6. A financial market in which financial assets having a maturity of more than one year are bought and sold is called a:
   a. money market.
   b. capital market.
   c. commercial paper market.
   d. commercial bank market.

B1. The demand deposits in a bank would go on:
   a. the asset side of its balance sheet.
   b. the liabilities side of its balance sheet.
   c. the net worth part of its balance sheet.
   d. on both sides of its balance sheet.

B2. The cash that a bank holds would go on:
   a. the asset side of its balance sheet.
   b. the liabilities side of its balance sheet.
   c. the net worth part of its balance sheet.
   d. on both sides of its balance sheet.

● POTENTIAL ESSAY QUESTIONS

You may also see essay questions similar to the "Problems & Applications" and "Brain Teasers" exercises.

1. Why is it important for the macroeconomy that the financial sector operate efficiently?

2. Why aren't credit cards money? What is the difference between money and credit?

3. What is the major benefit and problem of government guarantees associated with financial institutions?

ANSWERS

SHORT-ANSWER QUESTIONS

1. The financial sector is important to the business cycle because the financial sector channels the flow of savings out of the circular flow back into the circular flow either as consumer loans, business loans, or government loans. If the financial sector did not translate enough of the savings out of the spending stream back into the spending stream, output would decline and a recession might result. Likewise, if the financial sector increased flows into the spending stream (loans) that exceeded flows out of the spending stream (savings), an upturn or boom might result and inflation might rise. It is this role of the financial sector that Keynesians focused on to explain why production and expenditures might not be equal, resulting in fluctuations in output. (646-647).

2. In one sense your friend is right; cash is money. But money is more than just cash. Money is a highly liquid financial asset that is accepted in exchange for other goods and is used as a reference in valuing other goods. It includes such things as CDs and traveler's checks. (648-649)

3. The first friend has described money as a medium of exchange. The second has described money as a unit of account. And the third has described money as a store of wealth. These are the three functions of money. There are no others. (649, 651)

4. The two most liquid measures of money are M_1 and M_2. M_1 consists of currency, checking accounts, and traveler's checks. M_2 consists of M_1 plus savings deposits, small-denomination time deposits, and money market mutual funds. (652-653)

5. The broadest measure of money is L. L consists of almost all short-term financial assets. (653)

6. No, banks do not hold all their deposits in their vaults. They keep a small percentage of it for normal withdrawal needs and lend the remainder out. Banks' maintenance of checking accounts is the essence of how banks create money. You count your deposits as money since you can write checks against them and the money that is lent out from bank deposits is counted as money. Aha! The bank has created money. (655-657)

7. The equation for the simple money multiplier is $(1/r)$ where r is the reserve ratio. Plugging the values into the equation, we see that the money multiplier is 5, so the money supply increases by \$500. (658)

8. The equation for the approximate real-world money multiplier is $1/(r+c)$ where r is the reserve ratio and c is the ratio of cash to deposits. Plugging the values into the equation, we see that the money multiplier is 2, so the money supply increases by \$200. (659)

9. Just as price equilibrates quantity supplied and demanded in the real sector, interest rates equilibrate quantity supplied and demanded for saving. The supply of saving comes out of the spending stream. The financial sector transforms those savings back into the spending stream in the form of loans that are then used to purchase consumer or capital goods. (647)

10. If everyone lost their trust in banks, a financial panic could occur. The bank holds only a small portion of total deposits as reserves so that if everyone withdraws their money, the bank cannot meet its promises. (660-661)

11. The potential problem with government guarantees to prevent bank-withdrawal panics is that guarantees might lead to unsound lending and investment practices by banks. Also, depositors have less reason to monitor the practices of their banks. (662-663)

ANSWERS

MATCHING

1-h; 2-g; 3-n; 4-k; 5-l; 6-e; 7-o; 8-a; 9-f; 10-d; 11-c; 12-m; 13-q; 14-p; 15-j; 16-b; 17-i.

ANSWERS

PROBLEMS AND APPLICATIONS

1.

Nominal interest rate	Expected inflation	Real interest rate
6	3	3
9	7	2
1	−2	3

2. **a.** M_2. (652-653)
    b. M_2. (652-653)
    c. Both. (652-653)
    d. Neither. (652-653)
    e. Both. (652-653)

3. **a.** 6.67. multiplier = (1/.15). (658)
    b. 3.33. multiplier = (1/.30). (658)
    c. 1.67. multiplier = (1/.6). (658)
    d. 1.25. multiplier = (1/.8). (658)
    e. 1. multiplier = (1/1). (658)

4. **a.** 4 = 1/(.10+.15). (659)
    b. 2.5 = 1/(.1+.3). (659)
    c. 1.43 = 1/(.1+.6). (659)
    d. 1.11 = 1/(.1+.8). (659)
    e. 0.91. In reality a multiplier less than one would be highly unlikely. Recall that this is the approximate real-world multiplier. See pages 661, especially footnote 4 for the precise money multiplier. (659)

5. **a.** $270. (657-659)
    b. $270: the increase in loans that are then deposited (.9 × 300) represents the change in money. (657-659)
    c. 10: 1/r = 1/.1. (658)
    d. $3,000: money multiplier × initial deposit = 10×300. (657-659)

A1. Using the table to calculate the present value of $1 to be received in the future, we find that the better value is
    a. $2,000 in 5 years when the interest rate is 4% is valued today at $1,640. (669)
    b. $1,500 today. $2,000 in 5 years when the interest rate is 9% is worth only $1,300 today. (669)
    c. $10,000 in 10 years. $10,000 in 10 years is valued at $2,500 when the interest rate is 15%. (669)

    d. $3,000 today. $10,000 in 15 years when interest rate is 9% is worth only $2,700 today. (669)

A2. **a.** The annual payment for that bond is $500. (669)
    b. If the bond is currently selling for $6000, its yield is less than 10 percent. (669)
    c. If the bond is currently selling for $4,000, its yield is greater than 10 percent. (669)
    d. My answer to (b) and (c) tell me that the bond must sell for its face value if the interest rate is 10%, less than face value if it rises above 10%, and more than face value if it falls below 10%. (669)

A3. **a.** A financial asset has been created. Your friend's promise to pay you $5 is what gives that asset its value. (667)
    b. No, a financial asset has not been created, although a financial transaction did occur. (667)
    c. Yes, a financial asset has been created. The government's promises to pay you $5,000 at maturity and $400 each year until then are what give that asset its value. (667)
    d. Yes, a financial asset has been created. A claim to future profits is what gives that asset its value. (667)
    e. No, a financial asset has not been created. The financial asset sold already existed. (667)

A4. **a.** The mortgage is an asset for First Bank and a liability for David. The transaction occurred on the capital market. A financial asset was created. (667, 676)
    b. The mortgage is an asset for Financial Services, Inc., and a liability for David. The transaction occurred on the capital market. A financial asset was not created. (667, 676)
    c. The stocks are an asset for client Debreu and a liability for the broker's firm. The transaction occurred on the capital market. A financial asset was not created. (667, 676)
    d. The stocks are an asset for client Debreu and a liability for the firm. The transaction occurred on the capital market. A financial asset was created. (667, 676)
    e. The T-bill is a liability for the U.S. government and an asset for Corporation X. The transaction occurred on the money market. A financial asset was created. (667, 767)

f. The bond is a liability for the U.S. government and an asset for Sally Quinn. The transaction occurred on the capital market. A financial asset was not created. (667, 676)

B1. a. .2: cash/deposits = 30,000/150,000. (680-682)

b. Step 1: Increase of $20,000 in demand deposits and cash: (680-682)

Assets		Liabilities	
Cash	30,000	Demand Deposits	150,000
Cash from Jane	20,000	Jane's deposit	20,000
Total cash	50,000	Total deposits	170,000
Loans	300,000	Net Worth	350,000
Phys. Assets	170,000		
Total Assets	520,000	Total Liabilities and net worth	520,000

Step 2: Assuming the reserve ratio is .2 as calculated in (a), the bank can now lend out 80% of the $20,000 received in cash. It lends $16,000 to another person, Sherry: (680-682)

Assets		Liabilities	
Cash	50,000	Demand Deposits	170,000
Cash to Sherry	−16,000		
Total cash	34,000		
Begin. Loans	300,000	Net Worth	350,000
Loan to Sherry	16,000		
Total loans	316,000		
Phys. Assets	170,000		
Total Assets	520,000	Total Liabilities and net worth	520,000

Step 3: Sherry uses the loan to purchase a car from John. John deposits the cash in the bank (680-682):

Assets		Liabilities	
Cash	34,000	Demand Deposits	170,000
Cash from John	16,000	Deposit from John	16,000
Total cash	50,000	Total Deposits	186,000
Begin. Loans	316,000	Net Worth	350,000
Phys. Assets	170,000		
Total Assets	536,000	Total Liabilities and net worth	536,000

c. The bank is holding $12,800 in excess reserves. Required reserves for $186,000 in deposits is .2 × 186,000 = $37,200. The bank has $50,000 in reserves, $12,800 higher than required. (680-682)

d. The ending balance sheet will look like this (680-682):

Assets		Liabilities	
Cash	50,000	Demand Deposits	250,000
Loans	380,000	Net Worth	350,000
Phys. Assets	170,000		
Total Assets	600,000	Total Liabilities and net worth	600,000

ANSWERS

A BRAIN TEASER

1. An uncontrolled private banking system (where government is not involved in trying to control the money supply) is destabilizing to the business cycle. Why? Because during recessions, bankers are reluctant to grant loans due to the greater probability of default on loans (bankers are simply wishing to avoid losses). Fewer loans made during a recession coupled with the concurrent repayment of old loans (most likely given during the previous upturn in the economy) means that, on balance, the money supply decreases. Less money means less spending. Less spending means the recession gets worse–unemployment rises further and the economy grows even more slowly. Conversely, during an economic expansion, banks make more loans than old loans are being repaid (bankers are happy to make loans when there is a low probability of default–after all, workers are not likely to lose their jobs and businesses' markets and profits are expanding). Therefore, the money supply expands and total spending increases–people spend their loans. The economy expands even more. (654-660)

ANSWERS

MULTIPLE CHOICE

1. a   The very fact that it is a financial asset means that it has a financial liability, so the qualifier in b is unnecessary. See page 645.

2. b   In economic terminology, buying a financial asset, which is what buying a bond is, is a form of saving. Investing occurs when a firm or an individual buys a real asset. See pages 646-647.

3. c   The real interest rate = nominal interest rate less inflation. In this case 1 percent (2-1). See page 648.

4. d.   Money is not a type of stock so it is not an equity instrument. See page 649.

5. d M_2 includes savings accounts. M_1 does not. See pages 652-653 and Figure 27-2 on page 653.

6. d   Bonds are not part of M_2. See pages 652-653 and Figure 27-2 on page 653.

7. a   A credit card is not money and thus *a* would be the best answer. A credit card replaces money, making the same amount of money able to handle many more transactions. See pages 653-654.

8. a   One is borrowing money when one uses a credit card, thereby incurring a financial liability. See pages 653-654.

9. c   As discussed on pages 654-655, banks are concerned with both asset management and liability management. The second part of answer d is obviously true, but it's through management of assets and liabilities that they make money, so the first part is wrong.

10. d   The simple money multiplier is $1/r=1/.2=5$, which gives an increase in total money of $500. See pages 657-658.

11. c   The simple money multiplier is $1/r=1/.1=10$ which gives an increase of total money of $3,000. See pages 657-658.

12. c   The approximate real-world money multiplier is $1/(r+c)=1/.5=2$, which gives an increase in total money of $200. See pages 659-660.

13. b   Holding excess reserves would be the equivalent to increasing the reserve requirement, which would decrease the multiplier. See pages 659-660.

14. d   Banks earn income by managing their assets and liabilities. To follow any policy other than d would cost them income. See pages 659-660.

15. c.   FDIC stands for Federal Deposit Insurance Corporation. See page 662.

16. c   For this textbook author, just about everything depends; you can't get him to take a firm position on anything. See pages 662-663.

A1. a   The present value formula tells us that the value on any fixed interest rate bond varies inversely with the interest rate in the economy. See page 668.

A2. a   Since bond values vary inversely with interest rate changes, the answer must be a or b. Judging between a and b will be hard for you at this point unless you have studied present value in another course. However, based on the discussion in the text on pages 668-670, you can deduce that since a long-term bond is not paid back for a long time, it will be much more strongly affected by interest rate changes.

A3. c   Secondary markets trade previously issued assets. See pages 664-665.

A4. b   Investment banks don't take deposits, and who knows what the last two types of banks are; we certainly don't. See pages 671-672.

A5. b   Answers a and c are total gifts to you — water stocks; give us a break — and it's unclear what d means. The b option is the definition given on page 675.

A6. b Capital (money) markets trade financial assets with maturity greater (less) than one year. See page 676.

B1. b Demand deposits at banks are liabilities for those banks and hence go on the liability side. See pages 681-682.

B2. a The cash that banks hold is an asset for them; hence it goes on the asset side. See pages 681-682.

ANSWERS

POTENTIAL ESSAY QUESTIONS

The following are annotated answers. They indicate the general idea behind the answer.

1. Recall that for every real transaction there is a financial transaction that mirrors it. The financial sector's role is to ensure the smooth flow of savings out of the spending stream back into the economy. Whenever the financial sector is not operating efficiently then it is quite possible that the flow of savings out of the spending stream could be greater than the amount of money going through the financial sector and back into the economy. If this happens, we will experience a recession. The opposite would create inflationary (demand-pull inflation) problems.

2. Money is a financial asset of individuals and a financial liability of banks. Credit card balances cannot be money since they are assets of a bank and a liability of the nonbanking public. In a sense, credit card balances are the opposite of money. Credit is savings made available to be borrowed. Credit is not an asset for the holder of the card. However, ready availability of credit through the use of credit cards does reduce the amount of money people need or wish to hold.

3. The benefit is that they prevent unwarranted fears that causes financial crises. People are less likely to create a run on a bank when they know they will be able to get all of their money back even if the bank fails. The problem is that these guarantees can eliminate warranted fears. A bank manager may be more reckless when depositors are less concerned about the financial well-being of the bank.

MONETARY POLICY AND THE DEBATE ABOUT MACRO POLICY

28

● CHAPTER AT A GLANCE

This review is based upon the learning objectives that open the chapter.

1a. Monetary policy is a policy that influences the economy through changes in the money supply and available credit. (684)

Monetary policy is undertaken by the Fed. Expansionary (contractionary) monetary policy shifts the AD curve to the right (left). The effect on real income depends upon the range of the AS curve the economy is operating in.

1b. The Fed is a semiautonomous organization composed of 12 regional banks. It is run by the Board of Governors. (685-686)

The Fed (Federal Reserve Bank) is in charge of monetary policy (changing the money supply, credit availability, and interest rates).

1c. Congress gave the Fed six explicit duties. The most important is conducting monetary policy. (686)

Six functions of the Fed:

1. *Conducting monetary policy (influencing the supply of money and credit in the economy).*
2. *Supervising and regulating financial institutions.*
3. *Serving as a lender of last resort to financial institutions.*
4. *Providing banking services to the U.S. government.*
5. *Issuing coin and currency.*
6. *Providing financial services (such as check clearing) to commercial banks, savings and loan associations, savings banks, and credit unions.*

2. The three tools of monetary policy are: (690-693)

1. Changing the reserve requirement;
   This is the least-used tool. It is a potentially very powerful tool (could be a case of overkill) because it changes (1) banks' excess reserves and (2) the money multiplier.

2. Changing the discount rate;
   The discount rate is the interest rate the Fed charges banks for loans. It is the least powerful tool.
   Banks don't usually like to borrow from the Fed any more than we do from our parents.

3. Executing open market operations.
   Open market operations are the Fed's buying and selling of U.S. government securities. This is the most frequently used and most important tool to change the money supply.

   If the economy is in a recession, the Fed should increase the money supply (pursue an expansionary monetary policy) by doing any one or more of the following:
   - *Decrease the reserve requirement.*
   - *Decrease the discount rate.*
   - *Buy government securities.*

3. The Federal funds rate is the interest rate banks charge one another for overnight bank reserve loans. The Fed determines whether monetary policy is loose or tight depending upon what's happening to the Fed funds rate. The Fed funds rate is an important intermediate target. (695-696)

The Fed targets a range for the Fed funds rate. If the Fed funds rate goes above (below) that target range, the Fed buys (sells) bonds. These are "defensive" actions by the Fed.

4. The Taylor rule states: (696-697)
Set the Fed funds rate at 2 percent plus current inflation if the economy is at desired output and desired inflation and

if inflation is higher (lower) than desired, increase (reduce) the Fed funds rate by .5 times the difference between desired and actual inflation.

if output is higher (lower) than desired, increase (decrease) the Fed funds rate by .5 times the percentage deviation from potential.

Formally, the Taylor rule is:

Fed funds rate = 2 percent + current inflation + 0.5 × (actual inflation - desired inflation) + 0.5 × (percent deviation of aggregate output from potential)

This rule described Fed policy in the late 1990s and early 2000s.

5. In the AS/AD model, monetary policy works as follows: (697-699)

Contractionary monetary policy shifts the AD curve to the left:
M↓→ i↑→I↓→Y↓

Used during an upturn in the economy to close an inflationary gap.

Expansionary monetary policy shifts the AD curve to the right:
M↑→ i↓→I↑→Y↑

Used during a downturn in the economy to close a recessionary gap.

To increase the money supply (M2), the Fed must first increase banks' excess reserves and therefore bank loans.

6. Six problems of monetary policy: (701-703)

- Knowing what policy to use.
Need to know the potential income level first.

- Understanding what policy you're using.
Fed only indirectly controls M.

- Lags in monetary policy.
It takes time to work.

- Liquidity trap.
Increasing reserves doesn't always increase the money supply. Sometimes it just increases excess reserves.

- Political pressure.
Fed is not totally insulated from political pressures.

- Conflicting international goals.
We live in a global economy. The desired domestic policy may adversely affect the exchange rate value of the dollar and our trade balance.

See also, Appendix A: "The Effect of Monetary Policy Using T-Accounts."

● SHORT-ANSWER QUESTIONS

1. You have been asked to speak to the first-year Congresspeople. Your talk is about the Fed. They want to know what monetary policy is. You tell them.

2. To clarify your answer to question 1 you tell them when the Fed was created and what its specific duties are.

3. Another Congressperson asks what monetary policy actions the Fed can take. You answer.

4. You are asked to elaborate on your answer to question 3. Now that you have listed each of the tools of monetary policy, how does each work?

5. One Congressperson realizes that the Fed does not have complete control over the money supply. She states that people could demand more cash, which will reduce the money supply. How does the Fed know whether its buying and selling of bonds is having the desired effect? You answer by explaining the Fed's intermediate target.

6. Another Congressperson asks whether there are any rules that they could use to predict what the Fed will do to the Fed's intermediate target. You explain the rule that has described Fed policy in the 1990s and early 2000s.

7. Another Congressperson asks how monetary policy can keep the economy from overheating. You reply from the perspective of the AS/AD model.

8. Suppose the economy is below potential output. Now how can monetary policy boost output? You reply again from the perspective of the AS/AD model.

9. You take one final question at the conference and it is a difficult one: "It doesn't seem that the Fed is doing a good job. I read in the paper that the Fed has followed too contractionary a policy and has caused a recession or that it is not even sure what policy it is following." How do you respond to those concerns?

MATCHING THE TERMS

Match the terms to their definitions

___ 1.	central bank	**a.** Interest rate you actually see and pay.
___ 2.	contractionary monetary policy	**b.** Interest rate adjusted for expected inflation.
		c. Rate of interest the Fed charges on loans it makes to banks.
___ 3.	discount rate	**d.** The Fed's day-to-day buying and selling of government securities.
___ 4.	expansionary monetary policy	**e.** The percentage the Federal Reserve System sets as the minimum amount of reserves a bank must have.
___ 5.	Federal Open Market Committee (FOMC)	**f.** A banker's bank; it conducts monetary policy and supervises the financial system.
___ 6.	Federal funds rate	**g.** Currency in circulation, vault cash plus reserves that banks have at the Fed.
___ 7.	liquidity trap	**h.** Monetary policy aimed at raising the money supply and raising the level of aggregate demand.
___ 8.	monetary base	**i.** Monetary policy aimed at reducing the money supply and reducing the level of aggregate demand.
___ 9.	monetary regime	**j.** The Fed's chief policy making body.
___ 10.	nominal interest rate	**k.** The interest rate banks charge one another for Fed funds.
___ 11.	open market operations	**l.** Set the Fed funds rate at 2 plus current inflation plus ½ the difference between actual and target inflation and ½ the deviation of actual output from potential.
___ 12.	real interest rate	**m.** A predetermined statement of the monetary policy that will be followed in various situations.
___ 13.	reserve requirement	**n.** Situation in which increasing reserves does not increase the money supply.
___ 14.	Taylor rule	

● PROBLEMS AND APPLICATIONS

1. The Fed wants to change the reserve requirement in order to change the money supply (which is currently $3,000). For each situation below, calculate the current reserve requirement and the amount by which the Fed must change the reserve requirement to achieve the desired change in the money supply. Assume no cash holdings.

   a. Money multiplier is 3 and the Fed wants to increase the money supply by $300.

   b. Money multiplier is 2.5 and the Fed wants to increase the money supply by $300.

   c. Money multiplier is 4 and the Fed wants to decrease the money supply by $500.

   d. Money multiplier is 4 and the Fed wants to increase the money supply by $1,000.

2. How do your answers change for 1 (a) - (d) if instead of changing the reserve requirement, the Fed wants to use an open market operation to change the money supply? Assume the reserve requirement remains unchanged. What should the Fed do to achieve the desired change? (The multiplier and desired change in money supply for each are listed.)

    a. Money multiplier is 3 and the Fed wants to increase the money supply by $300.

    b. Money multiplier is 2.5 and the Fed wants to increase the money supply by $300.

    c. Money multiplier is 4 and the Fed wants to decrease the money supply by $500.

    d. Money multiplier is 4 and the Fed wants to increase the money supply by $1000.

3. Instead of changing the reserve requirement or using open market operations, the Fed wants to change the discount rate to achieve the desired change in the money supply. Assume that for each 1 percentage-point fall in the discount rate, banks borrow an additional $20. How do your answers to questions 1 (a) - (d) change? (The multiplier and desired change in money supply for each are listed below.)

    a. Money multiplier is 3 and the Fed wants to increase money supply by $300.

    b. Money multiplier is 2.5 and the Fed wants to increase the money supply by $300.

    c. Money multiplier is 4 and the Fed wants to decrease the money supply by $500.

    d. Money multiplier is 4 and the Fed wants to increase the money supply by $1,000.

4. Using the Taylor rule, what do you predict will be the Fed's target for the Fed funds rate in the following situations?

    a. Inflation is at the Fed's target of 2 percent, but output is 1 percent below potential.

    b. Output is at potential, but inflation is 5 percent, 2 percentage points above the Fed's target.

    c. Inflation is 4 percent, 1 percentage point above the Fed's target and output is 1 percent above potential.

    d. Inflation is 4 percent, 2 percentage points above the Fed's target and output is 2 percent below potential.

5. Fill in the blanks in the following table:

	Inflation rate	Nominal Interest rate	Real Interest rate
a.	5%	10%	____
b.	____	15%	7%
c.	−3%	____	9%
d	4%	____	10%

6. Suppose the Fed decides to pursue an expansionary monetary policy. The money supply is currently $1 billion. Assume people hold no cash, the reserve requirement is 10 percent, and there are no excess reserves.

a. By how much must the Fed change the reserve requirement to increase the money supply by $100 million?

b. What would the Fed do to increase the money supply by $100,000 through open market operations?

7. The money supply is currently $1 billion. Assume people hold 25 percent of their money in the form of cash balances, the reserve requirement is 25 percent, and there are no excess reserves.

a. By how much must the Fed change the reserve requirement to increase the money supply by $200 million?

b. What would the Fed do to increase the money supply by $200 million through open market operations?

A1. Suppose the money multiplier is 2.5 and there are no cash holdings. Textland Bank is the only bank in the country. The Fed wants to decrease the money supply by $10,000. The initial balance sheet is shown below.

Initial Balance Sheet

Assets		Liabilities	
Cash	20,000	Demand Deposits	50,000
Loans	120,000	Net Worth	100,000
Phys. Assets	10,000		
Total Assets	150,000	Total Liabilities and net worth	150,000

a. What open market operations must the Fed execute to reduce the money supply by $10,000?

b. Using T-accounts, show the first two steps of the effects of the Fed open market operation reducing the money supply by $10,000.

Step #1

Assets	Liabilities

Step #2

Assets	Liabilities

c. Show the final balance sheet for Textland bank.

Final Position

Assets	Liabilities

A2. Using T-accounts, show the effect of a decrease in the reserve ratio from .2 to .1 given the following initial position of Textland. Again, Textland is the only bank, no one holds cash, and there are no excess reserves. Show the first two steps and then the final position.

Initial Position

Assets		Liabilities	
Cash	40,000	Demand Deposits	200,000
Loans	230,000	Net Worth	100,000
Phys. Assets	30,000		
Total Assets	300,000	Total Liabilities and net worth	300,000

Step #1

Assets	Liabilities

Step #2

Assets	Liabilities

Final Position

Assets	Liabilities

A BRAIN TEASER

1. Assume the economy is currently experiencing a recessionary gap of $1,000. Also assume that the expenditures multiplier is 4, the reserve ratio is 0.1, and the ratio of people's cash-to-deposits is 0.4. Investment changes by $100 for every 1% change in the interest rate. The interest rate changes by 1% for every $50 change in the money supply. Generally, what should the Fed do with its three monetary policy tools? By how much would the Fed have to change banks' excess reserves if it wished to close the recessionary gap? (Assume all excess reserves are loaned out.)

MULTIPLE CHOICE

Circle the one best answer for each of the following questions:

1. The central bank of the United States is:
   a. the Treasury.
   b. the Fed.
   c. the Bank of the United States.
   d. Old Lady of Threadneedle Street.

2. Monetary policy is:
   a. a variation of fiscal policy.
   b. undertaken by the Treasury.
   c. undertaken by the Fed.
   d. the regulation of monetary institutions.

3. There are seven Governors of the Federal Reserve, who are appointed for terms of:
   a. 5 years.
   b. 10 years.
   c. 14 years.
   d. 17 years.

4. Explicit functions of the Fed include all the following *except:*
   a. conducting monetary policy.
   b. conducting fiscal policy.
   c. providing banking services to the U.S. government.
   d. serving as a lender of last resort to financial institutions.

5. FOMC stands for:
   a. Federal Open Money Committee.
   b. Federal Open Market Committee.
   c. Fixed Open Market Commitments.
   d. Federation of Open Monies Committee.

6. Tools of monetary policy include all the
   following *except:*
   a. changing the reserve requirement.
   b. changing the discount rate.
   c. executing open market operations.
   d. running deficits.

7. If expansionary monetary policy increases real
   income by 4 percent and nominal income by
   6 percent, the price level will rise by:
   a. 2 percent.
   b. 4 percent.
   c. 6 percent.
   d. 10 percent.

8. Assuming $c = .2$ and $r = .1$, the approximate
   real-world money multiplier would be:
   a. 1.33.
   b. 2.33.
   c. 3.33.
   d. 4.33.

9. The discount rate refers to the:
   a. lower price large institutions pay for
      government bonds.
   b. rate of interest the Fed charges for loans to
      banks.
   c. rate of interest the Fed charges for loans to
      individuals.
   d. rate of interest the Fed charges for loans to
      government.

10. The primary tool of monetary policy is:
    a. open market operations.
    b. changing the discount rate.
    c. changing the reserve requirement.
    d. imposing credit controls.

11. If the Fed wants to increase the money supply,
    it should:
    a. buy bonds.
    b. sell bonds.
    c. pass a law that interest rates rise.
    d. pass a law that interest rates fall.

12. When the Fed sells bonds, the money supply:
    a. expands.
    b. contracts.
    c. Selling bonds does not have any effect on
       the money supply.
    d. sometimes rises and sometimes falls.

13. An open market purchase:
    a. raises bond prices and reduces interest rates.
    b. raises both bond prices and interest rates.
    c. reduces bond prices and raises interest rates.
    d. reduces both bond prices and interest rates.

14. The Federal funds rate is the interest rate:
    a. the government charges banks for Fed
       funds.
    b. the Fed charges banks for Fed funds.
    c. the banks charge individual investors for
       Fed funds.
    d. the banks charge each other for Fed funds.

15. Assuming the Fed is following the Taylor
    Rule, if inflation is 3 percent, target inflation
    is 2 percent, and output is 1 percent above
    potential, what would you predict would be
    the Fed funds rate target?
    a. 4 percent.
    b. 5 percent.
    c. 5.5 percent.
    d. 6 percent.

16. In the short run if the Fed undertakes expan-
    sionary monetary policy, the effect will be to
    shift the:
    a. AD curve out to the right.
    b. AD curve in to the left.
    c. SAS curve up.
    d. SAS curve down.

17. In the short run if the Fed undertakes
    contractionary monetary policy, the effect
    will be to shift the:
    a. AD curve out to the right.
    b. AD curve in to the left.
    c. SAS curve up.
    d. SAS curve down.

18. Which of the following is the path through which contractionary monetary policy works?
    a. Money down implies interest rate up implies investment down implies income down.
    b. Money down implies interest rate down implies investment down implies income down.
    c. Money down implies interest rate up implies investment up implies income down.
    d. Money down implies interest rate down implies investment up implies income down.

19. A monetary regime is preferred to a monetary policy because:
    a. a monetary policy is too closely related to fiscal policy.
    b. a monetary regime takes into account feedback effects.
    c. a monetary policy takes into account feedback effects.
    d. One is not preferred to the other; the two are essentially the same thing.

20. Expected inflation is 4 percent; nominal interest rates are 7 percent; the real interest rate is
    a. 1 percent.
    b. 2 percent.
    c. 3 percent.
    d. 7 percent.

21. The real interest rate is 3 percent; the nominal interest rate is 7 percent. It is likely that one could deduce an expected inflation rate of
    a. 1 percent.
    b. 2 percent.
    c. 3 percent.
    d. 4 percent.

22. The Fed most directly controls
    a. M_1.
    b. M_2.
    c. the monetary base.
    d. the amount of credit in the economy.

POTENTIAL ESSAY QUESTIONS

You may also see essay questions similar to the "Problems & Applications" and "Brain Teasers" exercises.

1. According to the AS/AD model, what is considered to be appropriate monetary policy during different phases of the business cycle? What is the cause-effect chain relationship through which a change in the money supply will effect the level of economic activity? How would this cause-effect relationship be reflected graphically?

2. What are some general problems associated with the implementation of monetary policy?

3. Why do economists keep an eye on the Fed funds rate in determining the state of monetary policy?

4. How do open market operations affect interest rates through the bond market?

ANSWERS

SHORT-ANSWER QUESTIONS

1. Monetary policy is a policy that influences the economy through changes in the money supply and available credit. The Fed conducts U.S. monetary policy. (684)

2. The Fed was created in 1913. Its six explicit duties are (1) conducting monetary policy, (2) regulating financial institutions, (3) serving as a lender of last resort, (4) providing banking services to the U.S. government, (5) issuing coin and currency, and (6) providing financial services to financial institutions. (686)

3. The three tools of monetary policy at the disposal of the Fed are (1) changing the reserve requirement, (2) changing the discount rate, and (3) executing open market operations (buying and selling bonds). (690)

4. Changing the reserve requirement changes the amount of reserves the banks must hold and thus changes the amount of loans they can make. This changes the money supply. Changing the discount rate changes the willingness of banks to borrow from the Fed to meet reserve requirements, thus changing the amount of loans they are willing to make. This changes the money supply. Open market operations change the reserves banks hold by directly increasing or decreasing cash held by banks and simultaneously decreasing or increasing their holdings of government bonds. This changes the amount of loans banks can make and changes the money supply. (690-691)

5. Economists and policymakers keep a close eye on the Fed funds rate, the rate banks charge one another for loans of reserves, as an intermediate target to determine the effect of an open market operation—whether it indeed was expansionary or contractionary. An expansionary action will lower the Fed funds rate and contractionary action will raise the Fed funds rate. In effect, the Fed chooses a range for the Fed funds rate and buys and sells bonds to keep the Fed funds rate within that range. If the Fed funds rate is below (above) the target, the Fed sells (buys) bonds. (695-696)

6. The Taylor rule described recent Fed policy relatively well. It states: Set the Fed funds rate at 2% plus the rate of inflation plus one-half the difference between actual and desired inflation and one-half the deviation of actual output from desired output. (696-697)

7. The Fed should decrease the money supply by increasing the reserve requirement, increasing the discount rate, and/or selling U.S. government bonds. This contractionary monetary policy in the AS/AD model increases interest rates, and lowers investment. This shifts the AD curve to the left and reduces income. (697-699)

8. The Fed should increase the money supply by decreasing the reserve requirement, decreasing the discount rate, and/or buying U.S. government bonds. This expansionary monetary policy in the AS/AD model decreases interest rates, and raises investment. This shifts the AD curve to the right and increases income. (697-699)

9. You tell the Congressperson that conducting monetary policy is difficult. Six problems often encountered in conducting monetary policy are: (1) Knowing what potential income is. No one has the magic number. It must be estimated. (2) Knowing whether the policy you are using is contractionary or expansionary. The Fed does not directly control the money supply. (3) There are significant lags in the effect of monetary policy in the economy. (4) The liquidity trap. Sometimes increasing reserves does not increase the money supply. (5) The Fed is subject to political pressure. And (6) often domestic goals differ from international goals when deciding which policy to follow. (701-702)

ANSWERS

MATCHING

1-f; 2-i; 3-c; 4-h; 5-j; 6-k; 7-n; 8-g; 9-m; 10-a; 11-d; 12-b; 13-e; 14-l.

ANSWERS

PROBLEMS AND APPLICATIONS

1. **a.** To find the reserve requirement solve $1/r = 3$ for r. $r = 1/3$. These calculations are based on the formula $M = (1/r) \times MB$, where M is the money supply, r is the reserve ratio, and MB is the monetary base (here it equals reserves). We first find out the cash (monetary base) that supports $3,000 money supply with a money multiplier of 3. It is $1,000. We want the money supply to be $3,300. So the multiplier we want is $3,300/1,000 = 3.3$. Again solving $1/r = 3.3$ we find r must be 0.3. (690-691)

    b. To find the reserve requirement solve $1/r = 2.5$ for r. $r = .4$. Cash must be $1,200 to support money supply of $3,000. The Fed must reduce the reserve requirement to .3636 to increase the money supply by $300. Use the method described in (a) to find the answer. (690-691)

    c. To find the reserve requirement solve $1/r = 4$ for r. $r = .25$. Cash must be $750 to support money supply of $3,000. The Fed must increase the reserve requirement to .3 to decrease the money supply by $500. Use the method described in (a) to find the answer. (690-691)

    d. To find the reserve requirement solve $1/r = 4$ for r. $r = .25$. Cash must be $750 to support money supply of $3,000. The Fed must reduce the reserve requirement to .1875 to increase the money supply by $1,000. Use the method described in (a) to find the answer. (690-691)

2. These calculations are based on the formula $M = (1/r) \times MB$, where M is the money supply, r is the reserve ratio, and MB is the monetary base (here it equals reserves).

    a. The Fed should buy bonds to increase reserves in the system by $100. We find this by dividing the desired increase in the money supply by the money multiplier. (692-693)

    b. The Fed should buy bonds to increase reserves in the system by $120. We find this by dividing the desired increase in the money supply by the money multiplier. (692-693)

    c. The Fed should sell bonds to decrease reserves in the system by $125. We find this by dividing the desired decrease in the money supply by the money multiplier. (692-693)

    d. The Fed should buy bonds to increase reserves in the system by $250. We find this by dividing the desired increase in the money supply by the money multiplier. (692-693)

3. These calculations are based on the formula $M = (1/r) \times MB$, where M is the money supply, r is the reserve ratio, and MB is the monetary base (here it equals reserves). Find out how much reserves must be changed and divide by 20 to find how much the discount rate must be lowered (if reserves are to be raised) or increased (if reserves are to lowered).

    a. To increase reserves in the system by $100, the discount rate should be reduced by 5 percentage points. We find how much reserves must be increased by dividing the desired increase in the money supply by the money multiplier. We find how much the discount rate must be lowered by dividing the desired increase in reserves by 20 (the amount reserves will increase with each percentage point decline in the discount rate). (691-692)

    b. To increase reserves in the system by $120, the discount rate should be reduced by 6 percentage points. See introduction to answer number 3 for how to calculate this. (691-692)

    c. To decrease reserves in the system by $125, the discount rate should be increased by 6.25 percentage points. See introduction to answer number 3 for how to calculate this. (691-692)

    d. To increase reserves in the system by $250, the discount rate should be reduced by 12.5 percentage points. See introduction to answer number 3 for how to calculate this. (691-692)

4. **a.** Begin with 2 + rate of inflation, or 4. Since output is 1 percent below potential, subtract 0.5 to get to 3.5%. (696-697)

    b. Begin with 2 + inflation, or 7. Because inflation is 2 percentage points above target, add 1 percent to get to 8%. (696-697)

    c. Begin with 2 + inflation, or 6. Since inflation is 1 percentage point above its target add 0.5 and since output is 1 percent above potential, add another 0.5 to get 7%. (696-697)

d. Begin with 2 + inflation, or 6. Since inflation is 2 percentage points above its target, add 1 but since output is 2 percent below potential subtract 1 to get 6%. (696-997)

5.

	Inflation rate	Nominal Interest rate	Real Interest rate
a.	5%	10%	5%

Real rate = nominal - inflation. (700)

b.	8%	15%	7%

Inflation = nominal - real rate. (700)

c.	-3%	6%	9%

Nominal = inflation + real rate. (700)

d.	4%	14%	10%

Nominal = inflation + real rate. (700)

6. These calculations are based on the formula $M = (1/r) \times MB$, where M is the money supply, r is the reserve ratio, and MB is the monetary base (here it equals reserves).

a. The money multiplier is $1/r = 10$. Reserves must be $100 million to support a money supply of $1 billion. The reserve ratio to support $1.1 billion money supply with $100 million reserves is about 9.1%. We find this by dividing reserves by the desired money supply. (690-692)

b. The Fed would buy $10,000 worth of bonds to increase the money supply by $100,000. Calculate this by dividing the desired increase in the money supply by the money multiplier. (692-694)

7. In this case, the approximate real-world money multiplier is $1/(r + c) = 1/(.25+.33) = 1.72$. The cash-to-deposit ratio is .33 since people hold 25% of their money in cash and the remainder, 75%, in deposits.

a. The reserve requirement must be lowered to about 15%. We find this by first calculating the monetary base: $1 billion / 1.72 = $580 million (money supply/ multiplier). For the money supply to increase to $1.2 billion, the money multiplier must be $1.2/.580 = 2.07. To find the new reserve ratio solve $1/(r+c) = 2.07$ for r. We find that $r = .15$. (690-692)

b. The Fed must buy $116,279,000 in bonds to increase the money supply by $200 million. Calculate this by dividing the desired increase in the money supply by the money multiplier: $200 million / 1.72. (692-694)

A1. These calculations are based on the formula $M = (1/r) \times MB$, where M is the money supply, r is the reserve ratio, and MB is the monetary base (here it equals reserves).

a. The Fed must sell bonds worth $4,000 to reduce reserves by $4,000. We calculate this by dividing the desired reduction in the money supply by the money multiplier. (707-708)

b. Step 1: An individual or group of individuals buy $4,000 in Treasury bonds from the Fed. Individuals withdraw the funds from the bank. (707-708)

Assets		Liabilities	
Cash	20,000	Demand Deposits	50,000
Payment to		Withdrawals	(4,000)
individuals	(4,000)		
Total cash	16,000	Total demand deposits	46,000
Loans	120,000	Net Worth	100,000
Phys. Assets	10,000		
Total Assets	146,000	Total Liabilities and net worth	146,000

Step 2: Reserves are now too low to meet the reserve requirement of .4. (We calculated the reserve requirement by solving the equation $1/r = 2.5$ for r.) The bank must call in $2,400 in loans ($46,000 \times .4 - 16,000$). This shows up as loans repaid. But the individuals repaying the loans must get the money from somewhere. Since no one holds cash and Textland bank is the only bank, the individuals must withdraw the $2,400 from the bank. This is shown as a withdrawal on the liability side and a payment to individuals on the asset side. Again reserves are too low, this time by $1,440. (707-708)

Assets		Liabilities	
Cash	16,000	Demand Deposits	46,000
Loans repaid	$2,400	Withdrawals	(2,400)
Payment			
to individuals	(2,400)	Total demand deposits	43,600
Total Cash	16,000		
Loans	120,000	Net Worth	100,000
Loans called in	(2,400)		
Total Loans	117,600		
Phys. Assets	10,000		
Total Assets	143,600	Total Liabilities and net worth	143,600

c.   Final balance sheet: The banks continue to call in loans to meet reserve requirements until the multiplier process is finished. The money supply is now $10,000 less. At last, the balance sheet is as shown: (707-708)

Assets		Liabilities	
Cash	16,000	Demand Deposits	40,000
Loans	114,000	Net Worth	100,000
Phys. Assets	10,000		
Total Assets	140,000	Total Liabilities and net worth	140,000

A2.   Step 1: The bank makes $20,000 in new loans. This money is spent and deposited into Textland by other individuals. (707-708)

Assets		Liabilities	
Cash	40,000	Demand Deposits	200,000
Payments out	(20,000)	New deposits	20,000
Payments in	20,000	Total deposits	220,000
Total cash	40,000		
Loans	230,000	Net Worth	100,000
New loans	20,000		
Total loans	250,000		
Phys. Assets	30,000		
Total Assets	320,000	Total Liabilities and net worth	320,000

Step 2: Textland still has excess reserves (40,000/220,000 > .1) of $18,000 so it makes $18,000 in new loans. Calculate excess reserves by reserves - total deposits×reserve ratio. (707-708)

Assets		Liabilities	
Cash	40,000	Demand Deposits	220,000
Payments out	(18,000)	New deposits	18,000
Payments in	18,000	Total deposits	238,000
Total cash	40,000		
Loans	250,000	Net Worth	100,000
New loans	18,000		
Total loans	268,000		
Phys. Assets	30,000		
Total Assets	338,000	Total Liabilities and net worth	338,000

Final position: The previous steps continue until the money creation process ends as shown below. (707-708)

Assets		Liabilities	
Cash	40,000	Demand Deposits	400,000
Loans	430,000	Net Worth	100,000
Phys. Assets	30,000		
Total Assets	500,000	Total Liabilities and net worth	500,000

━━━━━   ANSWERS   ━━━━━

A BRAIN TEASER

1.   The Fed should undertake expansionary monetary policy: 1) Buy government securities on the open market, 2) decrease the discount rate, and/or 3) decrease required reserves. It should do any one or more of these things to increase banks' excess reserves by $62.50. This is because to close a recessionary gap of $1,000 when the expenditure multiplier is 4 will require an increase in aggregate expenditures of $250. To accomplish this, investment spending will have to increase by $250. This will require the interest rate to decrease by 2.5%. That will require an increase in the money supply of $125. When the money multiplier equals 2, or [1/(.1 + .4)], excess reserves will only have to increase by $62.50. (697-699)

━━━━━   ANSWERS   ━━━━━

MULTIPLE CHOICE

1.   b   See page 684.

2.   c   The correct answer is "policy undertaken by the Fed." The last answer, d, involves regulation, which is also done by the Fed, but such regulation generally does not go under the name "monetary policy." Given the accuracy of answer c, answer d should be avoided. See page 684.

3.   c   See page 685.

4.   b   Fiscal policy is definitely not a function of the Fed. See page 686.

5.   b   See the text and Figure 28-2, pages 686-689.

6.   d   Deficits are a tool of fiscal policy. See page 690.

7.   a   The price level rise is the difference between the change in nominal income (6 percent) and real income (4 percent). 6-4=2 percent. See page 684.

8. c   The approximate real-world money multiplier is $1/(r+c) = 1/.3 = 3.33$. See page 691.

9. b.   The Fed makes loans only to other banks, and the discount rate is the rate of interest the Fed charges for these loans. See page 692.

10. a   Open market operations is the tool most used and relied on to change the money supply. See page 692.

11. a   The last two answers, c and d, cannot be right, because the Fed does not pass laws. When the Fed buys bonds, it lowers the interest rate but it does not lower interest rates by law. Therefore, only a is correct. See pages 692-693.

12. b   People pay the Fed for those bonds with money—Fed IOUs-—so the money supply in private hands is reduced. See page 693.

13. a   As the Fed buys bonds this increases their demand and their prices rise. Since bond prices and interest rates are inversely related, interest rates will fall. See pages 693-694.

14. d   See page 695.

15. d   The Taylor rule states that the Fed targets the Fed funds rate with this formula: 2 + rate of inflation + one-half the difference between actual and desired inflation plus one-half the deviation of output over its target. Thus, it will set a Fed funds target of 6%, (2+3+.5+.5). See pages 696-697.

16. a   Expansionary monetary policy reduces interest rates and investment increases. Hence, AD shifts out to the right by a multiple of the increase in investment. See pages 697-699.

17. b   Contractionary monetary policy increases interest rates which reduces investment, a component of aggregate expenditures. The AD curve shifts in to the left by a multiple of the decline in investment. See pages 697-699.

18. a   Contractionary monetary policy increases interest rates which decreases investment, thereby decreasing income by a multiple of that amount. See page 698.

19. b   Monetary regimes are predetermined rules of what the Fed will do in certain situations. These regimes take feedback effects into account and a regime presets monetary policy. See page 701.

20. c   To determine the real interest rates, you subtract expected inflation from nominal interest rates. $7-4=3$. See page 700.

21. d   To determine expected inflation you subtract the real interest rate from nominal interest rate. $7-3=4$. See page 700.

22. c   The monetary base is the cash in circulation, vault cash and the reserves banks have at the Fed. It is the one variable the Fed can directly control. See pages 701-702.

ANSWERS

POTENTIAL ESSAY QUESTIONS

The following are annotated answers. They indicate the general idea behind the answer.

1.   Use expansionary monetary policy (Fed reduces reserve requirements, reduces the discount rate, and/or buys government securities.) during a recession; use contractionary policy during an upturn in the business cycle. Expansionary monetary policy will increase the money supply, which will reduce the interest rate and increase investment spending. This shifts the AD curve out to the right by a multiple of the initial increase in investment spending and brings about a multiple increase in the income level. (See Figure 28-5, page 673.)

2.   See the list and the discussion that begins on page 676 of the text.

3.   When the Fed funds rate is above its targeted range many banks have shortages of reserves and therefore money must be tight (credit is tight); and vice versa. The Fed will buy (sell) bonds when the Fed funds rate is above (below) its target and monetary policy is too tight (loose).

4.   If the Fed buys (sells) bonds this increases the demand for (supply of) bonds and thereby increases (decreases) their price. As the price of bonds goes up (down), the interest rate goes down (up). Hence, the Fed buying (selling) bonds decreases (increases) interest rates.

INFLATION AND ITS RELATIONSHIP TO UNEMPLOYMENT AND GROWTH

CHAPTER AT A GLANCE

This review is based upon the learning objectives that open the chapter.

1. Inflation redistributes income from those who cannot raise their prices or wages to those who can raise their prices or wages. (709-710)

    For example, if inflation is unexpected, income is redistributed from:

    - *workers to firms if workers have fixed wage contracts but firms raise their prices.*
    - *lenders to borrowers since the real interest rate declines when the nominal interest rate is fixed.*

    On average the winners and losers in an inflation balance out; inflation does not make a nation richer or poorer.

2. Three ways expectations of inflation are formed are: (710-711)

    1. *Rational expectations → expectations that the economists' model predicts.*

    2. *Adaptive expectations → expectations based in some way on the past.*

    3. *Extrapolative expectations → expectations that a trend will continue.*

    Expectations can change the way an economy operates. Expectations play a key role in policy.

    Policymakers use the following equation to determine whether inflation may be coming:

    Inflation = Nominal wage increase – productivity growth.

3. The quantity theory of money basically states that inflation is directly related to the rise in the money supply. It is based upon the equation of exchange: $MV = PQ$. (712-713)

    Three assumptions made in the quantity theory of money:

    1. *Velocity (V) is constant.*
    2. *Real output (Q) is independent of the money supply (M).*
    3. *Causation goes from money (M) to prices (P). That is, an increase (decrease) in M causes an increase (decrease) in P.*
    Note: The price level rises because the money supply rises.

    In the 1990s, the close relationship between money and inflation broke down. Economists debate whether this is temporary or permanent. For large inflations, the connection between money and inflation is still evident.

4. The institutional theory holds that institutional and structural aspects of inflation, as well as increases in the money supply, are important causes of inflation. It sees the causation in the equation of exchange going from right to left. That is, changes in the price level result in changes in the money supply. (717-718)

    Firms find it easier to raise wages, profits, and rents to keep the peace with employees and other owners of the factors of production. To pay for those increases, firms raise prices. Government then raises the money supply to make sure there is sufficient demand to buy the goods at those higher prices.

The "insider" versus "outsider" situation creates imperfect markets. Imperfect markets provide an opportunity for "insiders" to increase their wages and prices even when unemployment and excess capacity exist in the overall economy, thereby creating inflation.

In a nutshell: According to the quantity theory, $MV \rightarrow PQ$

According to the institutionalist theory, $PQ \rightarrow MV$

5a. The long-run Phillips curve is vertical; it takes into account the feedback of inflation on expectations of inflation. (720-724)

In the long run when expectations of inflation are met, changes in the rates of inflation have no effect on the level of unemployment. This is shown as LR in the accompanying graph.

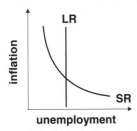

5b. The short-run Phillips curve is downward sloping. Expectations of inflation are constant along the short-run Phillips curve. (720-724)

The short-run Phillips curve reflects the empirically observed trade-off between inflation and unemployment. It is shown as SR in the graph above. Expectations of inflation are constant along the short-run (SR) Phillips curve. Increases (decreases) in inflationary expectations shift the short-run Phillips curve to the right (left).

In the long run we have more time to adjust our expectations to actual inflation. In the short run we may be fooled—we may expect less (more) inflation than actually occurs when inflation is accelerating (decelerating).

6. Quantity theorists believe that inflation

undermines long-run growth. Institutionalists are less sure of a negative relationship between inflation and growth. (726-727)

According to the quantity theory, the best policy is a policy that leads to price stability.

Institutionalists believe that low unemployment is an important goal that must be balanced with the risk of inflation.

SHORT-ANSWER QUESTIONS

1. Your study partner states that inflation is bad because it makes a nation poorer. How do you respond?

2. What are three ways people form expectations of future inflation?

3. If there is a high inflation, most economists are willing to accept that a rough approximation of the quantity theory holds true. Why?

4. What is the quantity theory of money and how does it relate to long-run growth?

5. How does the institutionalist theory of inflation differ from the quantity theory of inflation?

6. Who is more likely to favor a monetary rule: economists who support the quantity theory or economists who support the institutional theory of inflation? Why?

7. Which of the two curves in the graph below is a short-run Phillips curve, and why?

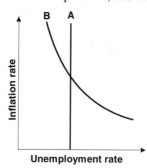

8. Would an economist who supports the quantity theory or one who supports the institutionalist theory of inflation be more likely to see a long-run trade-off between inflation and unemployment? Why?

9. Why would an institutionalist be more likely to support the introduction of an incomes policy than a quantity theorist would be?

MATCHING THE TERMS
Match the terms to their definitions

___ 1. adaptive expectations

___ 2. cost-push inflation

___ 3. deflation

___ 4. demand-pull inflation

___ 5. extrapolative expectations

___ 6. incomes policy

___ 7. inflation tax

___ 8. insider/outsider model

___ 9. long-run Phillips curve

___ 10. quantity theory of money

___ 11. rational expectations

___ 12. short-run Phillips curve

___ 13. stagflation

___ 14. velocity of money

a. Expectations based in some way on the past.

b. An institutionalist story of inflation where insiders bid up wages and outsiders are unemployed.

c. A policy placing direct pressure on individuals to hold down their nominal wages and prices.

d. A curve showing the trade-off between inflation and unemployment when expectations of inflation are constant.

e. A curve showing the trade-off (or complete lack thereof) between inflation and unemployment when expectations of inflation equal actual inflation.

f. The price level varies in response to changes in the quantity of money.

g. Combination of high and accelerating inflation and high unemployment.

h. Expectations that a trend will continue.

i. Inflation that occurs when the economy is at or above potential output.

j. The number of times per year, on average, a dollar goes around to generate a dollar's worth of income.

k. Expectations that the economists' model predicts.

l. An implicit tax on the holders of cash and the holders of any obligations specified in nominal terms.

m. Inflation that occurs when the economy is below potential.

n. Continuous decline in the price level

PROBLEMS AND APPLICATIONS

1. a. What are the three assumptions that translate the equation of exchange into the quantity theory of money?

    b. State the equation of exchange and show how the three assumptions lead to the conclusion that inflation is always and everywhere a monetary phenomenon.

2. With the equation of exchange, answer the following questions:

    a. Nominal GDP is $2,000, the money supply is 200. What is the velocity of money?

    b. The velocity of money is 5.60, the money supply is $1,100 billion. What is nominal output?

    c. Assuming velocity is constant and the money supply increases by 6%, by how much does nominal output rise?

3. Suppose the economy is operating at potential output. Inflation is 3% and expected inflation is 3%. Unemployment is 5.5%.

   a. Draw a long-run Phillips curve and a short-run Phillips curve consistent with these conditions.

   b. The government implements an expansionary monetary policy. As a result, unemployment falls to 4.5% and inflation rises to 6%. Expectations do not adjust. Show where the economy is on the graph you drew for 3(a). What happens to the short-run Phillips curve? Inflation? Unemployment?

   c. Expectations now fully adjust. Show this on the graph drawn for 3(a). What happens to the short-run Phillips curve?

4. Redraw the long-run Phillips curve and the short-run Phillips curve consistent with the conditions of the economy described in question #3 above and explain the effect of the following on inflation and unemployment using the curves you have drawn.

   a. The government implements a contractionary monetary policy. As a result, unemployment rises to 6.5% and inflation falls to 0%. Expectations do not adjust.

   b. Expectations now fully adjust.

5. For each of the following points that represents the economy on the Phillips curve, make a prediction for unemployment and inflation.

   a.

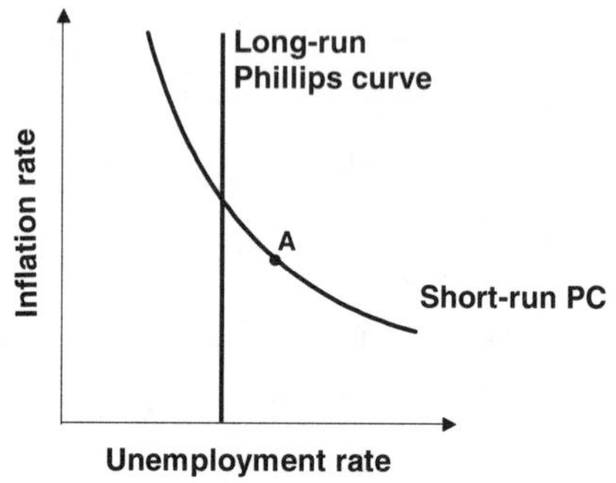

   b.

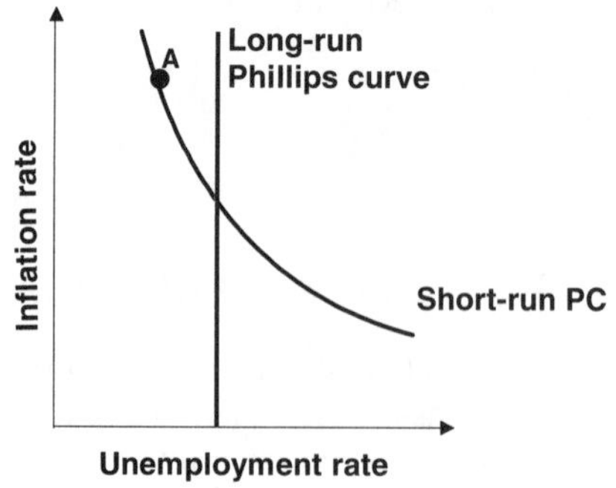

   c.

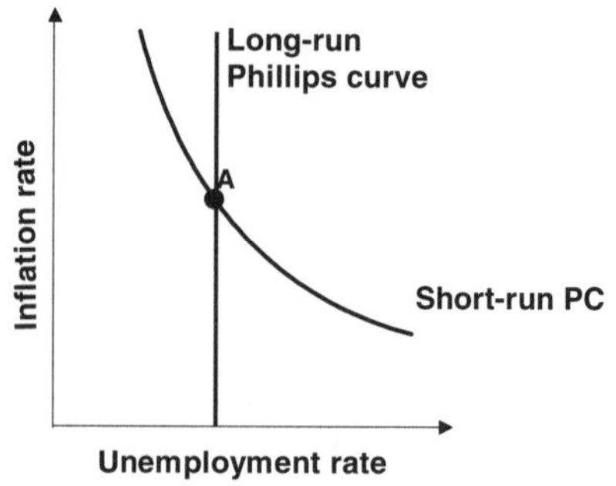

6. Suppose inflation is 12%, unemployment is 5.5%, and the natural rate of unemployment is 5.5%. The president believes inflation and unemployment are both too high.

    a. Assume you are a quantity theorist. What policy would you recommend to improve the situation?

    b. Show the short-run effect of this policy on unemployment and inflation using the Phillips curve analysis. Will the president be satisfied? What is your response?

    c. Show the long-run effect of this policy on unemployment and inflation using the Phillips curve analysis. Will the president be satisfied? What is your response? (In that response, discuss the issue of long-run growth.)

● A BRAIN TEASER

1. Why do countries increase the money supply enormously even though they know that doing so will lead to high inflation?

● MULTIPLE CHOICE

Circle the one best answer for each of the following questions:

1. In an expected inflation, lenders will generally:
    a. gain relative to borrowers.
    b. lose relative to borrowers.
    c. neither gain nor lose relative to borrowers.
    d. The effect will be totally random.

2. In an unexpected inflation, lenders will generally:
    a. gain relative to borrowers.
    b. lose relative to borrowers.
    c. neither gain nor lose relative to borrowers.
    d. The effect will be totally random.

3. According to the text if individuals base their expectations on the past we say that their expectations are:
    a. rational.
    b. historical.
    c. adaptive.
    d. extrapolative.

4. If productivity growth is 2 percent and inflation is 5 percent, on average nominal wage increases will be:
    a. 2 percent.
    b. 3 percent.
    c. 5 percent.
    d. 7 percent.

5. If the nominal interest rate is 1 percent and the economy is experiencing deflation of 2 percent, the Fed cannot lower the real interest rate below:
    a. 0 percent.
    b. 1 percent.
    c. 2 percent.
    d. 3 percent.

6. Assuming velocity is relatively constant and real income is relatively stable, an increase in the money supply of 40 percent will be associated with an approximate change in the price level of:
    a. 4 percent.
    b. 40 percent.
    c. 80 percent.
    d. zero percent.

7. According to the quantity theory:
   a. unemployment is everywhere and always a monetary phenomenon.
   b. inflation is everywhere and always a monetary phenomenon.
   c. the equation of exchange does not hold true.
   d. real output is everywhere and always a monetary phenomenon.

8. The quantity theory is most applicable to:
   a. U.S. type economies.
   b. West European type economies.
   c. developing economies.
   d. Japanese type economies.

9. The inflation tax is:
   a. a tax placed by government on inflators.
   b. a tax placed on inflators.
   c. a tax on the holders of cash.
   d. a tax on holders of goods whose price is inflating.

10. Which central bank(s) have a strict monetary rule against inflation?
    a. The U.S. and the European central banks.
    b. The European and Russian central banks.
    c. The U.S. and New Zealand central banks.
    d. The European and New Zealand central banks.

11. Individuals who hold an institutional theory of inflation argue:
    a. the equation of exchange is incorrect.
    b. the equation of exchange should be read from right to left.
    c. the equation of exchange should be read from left to right.
    d. both the quantity theory and the equation of exchange are incorrect.

12. If an economist focuses on social pressures in his or her discussion of inflation, that economist is likely an advocate of a(n):
    a. quantity theory of inflation.
    b. institutionalist theory of inflation.
    c. insider theory of inflation.
    d. outsider theory of inflation.

13. An individual has said that she favors an incomes policy. She:
    a. is likely an institutional theory of inflation advocate.
    b. is likely a quantity theory of inflation advocate.
    c. could be either a quantity theory or institutionalist theory advocate.
    d. is not an economist, because no economist could ever support an incomes policy.

14. When there is cost/push inflation, price increases:
    a. tend to lead money supply increases.
    b. tend to lag money supply increases.
    c. tend to have no relationship to money supply increases.
    d. sometimes lead and sometimes lag money supply increases.

15. The Phillips curve represents a relationship between:
    a. inflation and unemployment.
    b. inflation and real income.
    c. money supply and interest rates.
    d. money supply and unemployment.

16. The short-run Phillips curve shifts around because of changes in:
    a. the money supply.
    b. expectations of employment.
    c. expectations of inflation.
    d. expectations of real income.

17. The slope of the long-run Phillips curve is thought by many economists to be:
    a. horizontal.
    b. vertical.
    c. downward sloping.
    d. backward bending.

18. If the economy is at point A in the Phillips curve graph below, what prediction would you make for inflation?

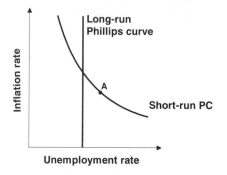

a. It will increase.
b. It will decrease.
c. It will remain constant.
d. It will explode.

19. If the economy is at Point A in the Phillips curve graph below, what prediction would you make for inflation?

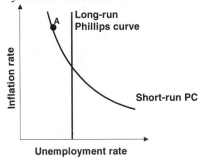

a. It will increase.
b. It will decrease.
c. It will remain constant.
d. It will immediately fall to zero.

20. Stagflation is:
   a. a combination of low and decelerating inflation and low unemployment.
   b. a combination of low and decelerating inflation and high unemployment.
   c. a combination of high and accelerating inflation and low unemployment.
   d. a combination of high and accelerating inflation and high unemployment.

21. Economists explain the "New Economy" in the last half of the 1990s and early 2000s as:
   a. an example of the stagflation.
   b. an example of the movement from the long-run to the short-run Phillips curve.
   c. an example of the movement from the short-run to the long-run Phillips curve.
   d. a case when productivity grew much faster than expected, negating the standard Phillips curve story.

22. Advocates of the quantity theory are likely to emphasize a trade-off between inflation and:
a. unemployment.
b. distribution.
c. growth.
d. money.

● POTENTIAL ESSAY QUESTIONS

You may also see essay questions similar to the "Problems & Applications" and "Brain Teasers" exercises.

1. In what way is inflation a tax? Who pays it?

2. What are the differences between the quantity theorists and the institutionalists with respect to unemployment?

3. What role does government play in the Insider/Outsider model?

ANSWERS

SHORT-ANSWER QUESTIONS

1. Inflation does not make a nation poorer. It redistributes income from those who cannot and do not raise their prices to those who can and do raise their prices. On average, the winners and losers average out. An example is lenders and borrowers. (709-710)

2. People formulate expectations in a variety of ways. Three types of expectations are adaptive expectations (expectations based in some way on the past), rational expectations (the expectations that the economists' model predicts), and extrapolative expectations (expectations that a trend will continue). (710-711)

3. The quantity theory is based on the equation of exchange, *MV=PQ*. The quantity theory adds the following assumptions: (1) that velocity is relatively constant; (2) that real output is relatively constant; and (3) that changes in money supply cause changes in prices. In reality, velocity and real output can change sufficiently to make it questionable whether this theory is useful. However, when there is significant inflation—say 100% or more—the relative changes in velocity and real output that are reasonable to assume possible are much smaller than that 100%, leaving a rough correlation between changes in the money supply and changes in the price level.

    The debate between economists does not concern the relationships between money growth and inflation; it concerns the direction of causation. Quantity theorists tend to believe that the causation goes from money to prices, and hence they are willing to accept the existence of a long-run vertical Phillips curve. Institutionalists tend to believe that the causation goes from changes in prices and expectations of prices to changes in the money supply—the government is accommodating the higher prices. Thus they favor more institutionally-oriented theories of inflation. (712-715)

4. The quantity theory of money is best summarized by the phrase "Inflation is everywhere and always a monetary phenomenon." Essentially, it is that increases in the money supply are the cause of inflation, and all other sup-

posed causes are simply diversions from the key monetary cause. According to the quantity theory there is a long-run inverse relationship between inflation and growth. (712-716)

5. The institutionalist theory of inflation differs from the quantity theory in that it is more likely to include institutional and social aspects as part of the theory. The insider/outsider model is an institutionalist model of inflation. Another way of stating the difference is that the institutional theory of inflation sees the equation of exchange as being read from right to left, rather than from left to right. (716-718)

6. Economists who support the quantity theory of money are more likely to favor a monetary rule, because they see the economy gravitating toward a natural (or target) rate of unemployment regardless of monetary policy. Thus expansionary monetary policy can lead only to inflation. A monetary rule will limit the government's attempt to expand the economy with monetary policy and hence will achieve the target rate of unemployment and low inflation. Institutional economists are less likely to see the economy gravitating toward the target rate of unemployment, so they would favor some discretionary policy to improve the operation of the macroeconomy. (712-716,719)

7. Curve B is the short-run Phillips curve. The short-run Phillips curve represents a trade-off between inflation and unemployment. It is an empirically determined phenomenon, and based on that empirical evidence, economists generally believe that whenever unemployment decreases, inflation increases, and vice versa. They explain that this empirical occurrence is due to slowly adjusting expectations and institutions. In the long run, expectations and institutions can change and hence the reason for the trade-off is eliminated, making the vertical line represent the long-run Phillips curve—it represents the lack of a trade-off between inflation and unemployment in the long run. (720-724)

8. Institutional economists see institutional and social aspects of the price setting process as more important than do quantity theorists.

They also see individuals as having a cost of rationality, so individuals may not notice small amounts of inflation. These aspects of the institutional theory make it more likely that there is a long-run trade-off between inflation and unemployment since, in their absence, we would expect that money is essentially a veil and real forces predominate. (726-727)

9. An incomes policy is a policy designed to put direct downward pressure on the nominal price setting process. Institutional economists see institutional and social aspects of the price setting process as more important than do quantity theorists. It is these social aspects of the price setting process, which place a direct upward pressure on the price level that will require an incomes policy to offset. Therefore, institutionalists are more likely to support an incomes policy. (719)

ANSWERS

MATCHING

1-a; 2-m; 3-n; 4-i; 5-h; 6-c; 7-l; 8-b; 9-e; 10-f; 11-k; 12-d; 13-g; 14-j.

ANSWERS

PROBLEMS AND APPLICATIONS

1. **a.** 1. Velocity is constant, 2. Real output is independent of the money supply, 3. Causation goes from money supply to prices. (712-713)
   b. $MV = PQ$ is the equation of exchange. Since V is constant and Q exogenous, the only remaining variables that change within the system are M and P. Since the causation runs from M to P, to keep the equation balanced, a rise in M must lead to a rise in P (and only P since Q is exogenous). (712-713)

2. **a.** $V = 10$: $MV = PQ$; $200V = \$2,000$; $V = 10$. (712-713)
   b. $6,160$ billion: $MV = PQ$; $(5.6)(1,100) = \$6,160$ billion. (712-713)
   c. By 6%. (712-713)

3. **a.** The long-run Phillips curve is vertical at the rate of unemployment consistent with potential output, here at 5.5%. The short-run Phillips curve is the downward sloping curve shown in the graph below as PC_1. In this case, we drew a short-run Phillips curve where expected inflation equals the 3% actual inflation. It intersects the long-run Phillips curve at 5.5% unemployment and 3% inflation. The economy is at point A. (720-724)

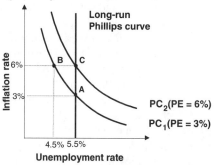

   b. The economy moves along the short-run Phillips curve up and to the left to point B. The short-run Phillips curve does not shift since inflation expectations have not changed. At point B, inflation is 6% and unemployment rate is 4.5%. (720-724)
   c. Now that expectations fully adjust, the short-run Phillips curve shifts to the right to PC_2 so that it intersects the long-run Phillips curve at an inflation rate of 6%. The unemployment rate returns to 5.5% and inflation remains at the higher 6%. (720-724)

4. **a.** The economy moves along the short-run Phillips curve down and to the right to point B in the graph below. The short-run Phillips curve does not shift since inflation expectations have not changed. At point B, inflation is 0% and unemployment rate is 6.5%. (720-724)

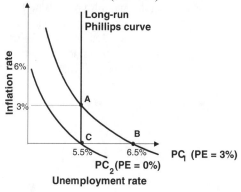

b. Now that expectations fully adjust, the short-run Phillips curve shifts to the left to PC_2 so that it intersects the long-run Phillips curve at inflation rate of 0%. The unemployment rate returns to 5.5% and inflation remains at the lower 0%. (720-724)

5. **a.** Inflation is below expected inflation and unemployment is higher than the natural rate of unemployment. As expectations adjust, the short-run Phillips curve shifts to the left and both unemployment and inflation fall. (720-724)

b. Inflation is above expected inflation and unemployment is lower than the natural rate of unemployment. As expectations adjust, the short-run Phillips curve shifts to the right and both unemployment and inflation rise. (720-724)

c. Inflation equals expected inflation and unemployment equals the target rate of unemployment. Inflation and unemployment will not change. (720-724)

6. **a.** I would assume that in the long run, only inflation can be improved, so I ignore the rate of unemployment and focus on fighting inflation. A contractionary monetary policy will improve the inflation rate. (716)

b. The economy begins at point *A* in the accompanying graph, where unemployment is 5.5% and inflation is 12%. Inflation expectations equal actual inflation. With contractionary monetary policy, the economy moves along the short-run Phillips curve down and to the right to point *B*. The short-run Phillips curve does not shift since inflation expectations have not changed. At point B, inflation is lower than 12% and the unemployment rate is higher than 5.5%. The president will be happy that inflation is lower, but disappointed that unemployment is higher. I tell him that in the short run there is a trade-off between the two. Just wait for expectations of inflation to adjust and we will return to 5.5% unemployment. (720-724)

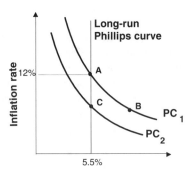

c. Now that expectations fully adjust, the short-run Phillips curve shifts to the left to PC_2 so that it intersects the long-run Phillips curve at inflation rate of below 12% at point *C*. The unemployment rate returns to 5.5%. The president is now pleased because inflation is lower and unemployment returned to 5.5%. But he wanted the unemployment rate to be below 5.5%. I tell him that 5.5% is the natural rate. If he were to follow an expansionary policy, unemployment would fall in the short run, but would return to 5.5% in the long run and inflation would be higher than it currently is. The higher inflation would undermine the economy's long-term growth. (720-724)

ANSWERS

A BRAIN TEASER

1. The reasons are complicated. If a government does not have the capability of either taxing or borrowing to finance expenditures (and if the central bank is not independent) the government may rely on its ability to print money to finance government expenditures. For some countries the choice is between inflation and allowing an economy and its government to fall apart. (715-716)

ANSWERS

MULTIPLE CHOICE

1. c   In an unexpected inflation borrowers gain and lenders lose because the money they

are paying back will buy less because of the inflation. In an expected inflation the interest rate will have adjusted to compensate lenders for the decrease in the value of money. See pages 709-710.

2. b In an unexpected inflation borrowers gain and lenders lose because the money borrowers are paying back will buy less because of the inflation. See pages 709-710.

3. c Rational expectations are based on models; extrapolative expectations are based on expectations that a trend will continue. Historical expectations are not mentioned in the text. See pages 710-711.

4. d Inflation is the difference between nominal wage increases and productivity growth. See page 711.

5. c One of the problems of deflation is that it sets a floor for the real interest rate. In this case, the real interest rate is 3 percent since the nominal interest rate is 1%. The Real interest rate cannot fall below 2 percent. See page 711.

6. b Using the equation of exchange, $MV=PQ$, given these assumptions there is a close relationship between changes in M and changes in P. See page 712.

7. b The quantity theory directly relates money and inflation. See pages 712-713.

8. c The quantity theory is most applicable when there are large increases in the money supply and significant inflation. This is most likely to be the case in developing countries. See pages 713-714.

9. c The inflation tax is a tax on the holders of cash because inflation makes their cash worth less. See pages 715-716.

10. d As discussed in the text, the European and New Zealand central banks have strict rules against inflation. The U.S. does not; Russia is not mentioned in the text. See pages 716-717.

11. b The equation of exchange is a tautology; it cannot be incorrect; Institutionalists see price changes causing money and velocity changes so MV=PQ should be read from right to left. See pages 717-718.

12. b The book describes two general theories of inflation; social pressures definitely fit with the institutionalist theory. One type of institutionalist theory of inflation is the insider/outsider model, but that is not presented as a choice. See pages 717-719.

13. a As discussed in the text an incomes policy would most likely be favored by an advocate of an institutional theory of inflation. See page 719.

14. a As the text discusses on page 720, in most cost/push inflation, price increases cause money supply increases, and therefore they lead them. The other answers are possible, but a is clearly the best.

15. a The Phillips curve is drawn with inflation on the vertical axis and unemployment on the horizontal axis. See pages 720-721.

16. c The short-run Phillips curve holds expectations of inflation constant. Therefore, it shifts because changes in expectations of inflation cause everybody to build those expectations into their nominal price requests. See page 722.

17. b As discussed in the text, the long-run Phillips curve is vertical. Actually, there is some debate about whether it is downward sloping, but the text focuses on the vertical nature of the curve so that b is the answer that should be given. Remember, one is choosing the best answer relative to what is presented in the text. See pages 722-723.

18. b Since Point A is to the right of the long-run Phillips curve, actual unemployment exceeds the natural rate of unemployment. Therefore we would expect inflationary expectations to be decreasing, and hence inflation to be decreasing. See pages 723-724.

19. a   Since Point A is to the left of the long-run Phillips curve, actual unemployment is below the natural rate of unemployment. Therefore we would expect inflationary expectations to be increasing, and hence inflation to be increasing. See pages 723-725.

20. d   Stagflation is defined as a combination of high and accelerating inflation and high unemployment. See page 724.

21. d   The last half of the 1990s and early 2000s was a period of low inflation and low unemployment, which is not consistent with the traditional Phillips curve story. Economists' explanation of this period centered on the higher than expected increases in productivity. See pages 724-725.

22. c   Quantity theory advocates argue that in the long run a noninflationary environment is conducive to growth and thus there is a long run trade-off between inflation and growth. See pages 726-727.

ANSWERS

POTENTIAL ESSAY QUESTIONS

The following are annotated answers. They indicate the general idea behind the answer.

1.   Inflation can be viewed as a tax because it reduces the value of obligations specified in nominal terms. A simple way to see this is if prices rose at a rate of 5 percent a day, a dollar today will buy only 95 cents worth of goods tomorrow. The holder of the dollar (or any obligation specified in nominal terms) pays the tax.

2.   Quantity theorists see a competitive labor market guaranteeing full employment. Institutionalists see an imperfectly competitive labor market. Institutionalists also envision a potential lack of demand for workers because of a lack of aggregate demand for the goods they produce. To institutionalists, this can create some unemployment at any wage.

3.   Inflation is a result of *im*perfectly competitive markets. This allows workers and firms (especially "insiders") to raise their nominal wages and prices even during periods of high unemployment and excess production. Other groups, feeling relatively worse off, will push for higher wages and prices too. The government can either ratify this inflation by increasing the money supply or it can refuse to ratify it, causing unemployment (especially for the "outsiders").

AGGREGATE DEMAND POLICY
IN PERSPECTIVE

CHAPTER AT A GLANCE

This review is based upon the learning objectives that open the chapter.

1a. Policies are often characterized as either demand-side or supply-side policies. (732-734)

Demand-side policies shift the AD *curve. Examples are monetary policy and fiscal policy.*

Supply-side policies shift the LAS *curve. Examples are tax subsidies for investment, policies to promote research and development, and policies to encourage trade.*

1b. Fiscal policy isn't without problems. Six assumptions of the model that could lead to problems with fiscal policy are: (734-739)

1. Financing the deficit doesn't have any offsetting effects.

   In reality, it often does. A particular problem is crowding out, which is the offsetting effect on private expenditures caused by the government's sale of bonds to finance expansionary fiscal policy.

2. The government knows what the situation is.

   In reality the government must estimate what the situation is.

3. The government knows the economy's potential income.

   In reality the government may not know what this level is.

4. The government has flexibility in terms of spending and taxes.

   In reality, the government cannot change them quickly.

5. The size of the government debt doesn't matter.

   In reality, the size of the debt often does matter.

6. Fiscal policy doesn't negatively affect other government goals.

   In reality, it often does.

2. An automatic stabilizer is any government program or policy that will counteract the business cycle without any new government action. (739-741)

Automatic stabilizers include:
- *welfare payments*
- *unemployment insurance, and*
- *income tax system.*

In a recession, government expenditures automatically rise (because of increased welfare payments and unemployment claims). Taxes automatically decrease (because fewer people are earning income). The budget deficit increases and AE (total spending) increases. The opposite occurs during an upturn in the business cycle. <u>*Automatic stabilizers help smooth out the business cycle.*</u>

3. Conventional wisdom about monetary and fiscal policy is that they are not tools to fine-tune the economy. But they can be useful in guiding it toward achieving goals of high growth, low inflation, and low unemployment. (741-742)

The advantages and disadvantages of various policies are summarized in Figure 30-4. Often the economy is in a range where there is some chance that both inflation and unemployment will be problems, which means that these trade-offs must be dealt with. Figure 30-4 on page 716 summarizes conventional wisdom about policy.

4. Three alternatives to fiscal policy are directed investment policies, trade policies, and autonomous consumption policies. (743-745)

Anything that government can do to alter components of AE (C, I, G, and X−M) will have a multiple impact on Y (the income-output level in the macro economy) because of the multiplier. For example, rosy scenarios, bank guarantees, reduction in interest rates, export-led growth policies, and increases in consumer credit availability could increase AE and stimulate the economy.

5. Policy is a process, not a one-time event and policy regimes are often more important than any particular policy. (745-747)

People form expectations about future policy. Policy regimes help establish credibility of policymakers, which enhances the effectiveness of the policy.

The trade-off is that policy regimes give policymakers less discretion when responding to an unforeseen event.

● SHORT-ANSWER QUESTIONS

1. How do the six problems of fiscal policy limit its usefulness?

2. You are speaking at the Congressional conference. A Congressperson wonders how financing deficit spending will change the direct effect of fiscal policy. You tell her.

3. Some economists argue that crowding out totally undermines the activist view of fiscal policy. Explain their argument.

4. A country has just removed its unemployment insurance program and is experiencing a recession. How will this recession differ from earlier recessions?

5. In the short-run model, you want to lower interest rates and increase income. Would you propose expansionary monetary or fiscal policy? What concerns would you voice about this policy?

6. Suppose you are the featured speaker at a primer for the first-year Congresspeople. You have been asked to speak about fiscal policy. A Congressperson asks what fiscal policy tools Congress has to affect the economy, and what effect they have on the level of output. You tell her.

7. The first-year Congresspeople are worried about your answer to question 6. They feel they are politically unable to implement those policies. What three alternatives to fiscal policy can you offer?

8. Why do economists generally talk about policy regimes and credibility rather than just policy?

MATCHING THE TERMS
Match the terms to their definitions

___ **1.** automatic stabilizer

___ **2.** crowding out

___ **3.** exchange rate policy

___ **4.** export-led growth policy

___ **5.** policy

___ **6.** policy regime

___ **7.** procyclical fiscal policy

___ **8.** rosy scenario policy

autonomous exports thereby increasing autonomous expenditures.

b. Any government program or policy that will counteract the business cycle without any new government action.

c. Deliberately affecting a country's exchange rate in order to affects its trade balance.

d. Government policy of making optimistic predictions and never making gloomy predictions.

e. The offsetting effect on private expenditures caused by the government's sale of bonds to finance expansionary fiscal policy.

f. A predetermined statement of the policy that will be followed in various circumstances.

g. A one-time reaction to a problem.

h. Changes in government spending and taxes that increase the cyclical fluctuations in the economy instead of reducing them.

a. A policy that increases

PROBLEMS AND APPLICATIONS

1. You are called by the president to raise equilibrium income by $1,000. You are told that the *mpe* is 0 and the SAS curve is horizontal.

a. You estimate that the economy has a recessionary gap of $1,000. Make a proposal to increase short-run equilibrium income as desired by the president. What will happen to the economy in the long run?

b. How will your answer to *a* change if the *SAS* curve is upward sloping?

c. You've re-estimated potential output. The economy has a recessionary gap of only $500. The president still wants to raise equilibrium income by $1,000. Make a proposal to increase short-run equilibrium income as desired by the president. What will happen to the economy in the long run?

2. Suppose the government wants to increase income by $250 billion. The *mpe* is .6.

a. Assuming the economy is far below potential output, by how much must government increase spending to reach its goal? Show the effect of this action, using the AS/AD model. (Assume the price level is fixed.)

b. How will your answer to *a* change if the *SAS* curve is upward sloping?

c. Suppose government finances this increase in spending with the sale of bonds. As a result, interest rates increase. How does this affect the analysis in *a*? Demonstrate using the multiplier model.

● A BRAIN TEASER

1. How does formula flexibility reduce the difficulties of implementing activist fiscal policy? Is formula flexibility a politically appealing policy?

● MULTIPLE CHOICE

Circle the one best answer for each of the following questions:

1. A tax subsidy for investment is best characterized as:
   a. a demand-side policy.
   b. a supply-side policy.
   c. monetary policy
   d. export-led policy.

2. Crowding out is caused by:
   a. government running a deficit and selling bonds to finance that deficit.
   b. government printing money.
   c. the government running a surplus and selling bonds and the people who buy those bonds selling their older bonds to the government.
   d. the tendency for new workers to replace more expensive older workers.

3. If potential output is revised upwardly by 2 percent, the target rate of unemployment probably should be revised:
   a. downward 1 percentage point.
   b. upward 1 percentage point.
   c. downward 2 percentage points.
   d. upward 2 percentage points.

4. Fiscal policy is difficult to implement because:
   a. data about the economy are released after the fact and are subject to revision.
   b. it is difficult to estimate potential income.
   c. fiscal policy is often determined by political considerations.
   d. All of the above.

5. Automatic stabilizers:
   a. are government programs to employ workers during recessions.
   b. create government budget surpluses during economic recessions.
   c. are designed to reduce the price level directly.
   d. counteract both recessions and expansions through changes in spending without government action.

6. A state constitutional provision to maintain a balanced budget is an example of:
   a. an automatic stabilizer.
   b. monetary policy.
   c. procyclical policy.
   d. countercyclical policy.

7. You have been appointed adviser to the president. He comes in and says he wants very low unemployment, zero inflation, and very high growth. You should:
   a. advise him to use expansionary monetary policy.
   b. advise him to use contractionary monetary policy.
   c. tell him it is likely impossible using traditional tools.
   d. advise him to use a combination of expansionary monetary policy and contractionary fiscal policy.

8. You've been appointed adviser to the President. She wants interest rates to rise and unemployment to fall. You would suggest :
    a. expansionary monetary policy.
    b. contractionary monetary policy.
    c. expansionary fiscal policy.
    d. contractionary fiscal policy.

9. You've been appointed adviser to the President. She wants interest rates and inflation to fall. You would suggest:
    a. expansionary monetary policy.
    b. contractionary monetary policy.
    c. expansionary fiscal policy.
    d. contractionary fiscal policy.

10. Economists generally agree on all the following except:
    a. expansionary monetary and fiscal policies have short-run stimulative effects on income.
    b. expansionary monetary and fiscal policies have potentially long-run stimulative effects on inflation.
    c. monetary policy is politically easier to use than fiscal policy.
    d. expansionary monetary and fiscal policies tend to decrease the trade deficit.

11. Exchange rate policy is:
    a. increasing the size of the government deficit.
    b. deliberately affecting the country's exchange rate in order to affect its trade balance.
    c. deliberately affecting the country's money supply in order to affect its trade balance.
    d. deliberately affecting the country's tax rate in order to affect its trade balance.

12. Which of the following would not be a likely alternative to expansionary fiscal policy?
    a. Government officials talking positively about the economic outlook.
    b. A policy intended to raise the value of the dollar.
    c. A financial guarantee to bail out failing banks.
    d. Changes to bank regulation that resulted in greater access to credit by consumers.

13. Rational expectations:
    a. are forward-looking based on available information.
    b. are easy to predict because they follow economists' models.
    c. make policymaking easier because they create more certainty.
    d. are one reason the Fed does not reveal its actions to the public.

14. Policy regimes are preferred to discretionary policy because:
    a. discretionary policies are more likely to affect people's expectations.
    b. regimes are more likely to be adopted by Congress.
    c. regimes provide government with more flexibility.
    d. the impact of policies is significantly affected by expectations.

● POTENTIAL ESSAY QUESTIONS

You may also see essay questions similar to the "Problems & Applications" and "Brain Teasers" exercises.

1. How do the automatic stabilizers add stability to the business cycle? Are there any time lag (delay) problems associated with the use of the automatic stabilizers?

2. What is the crowding-out effect? What impact does this have on the effectiveness of fiscal policy in stimulating the economy during a recession? How large is the crowding-out effect according to activist economists? Laissez-faire economists? What does the empirical evidence suggest about the size of the crowding-out effect?

3. Say you are a policy adviser to the government of a country that is growing at 6%, has inflation of 1%, and unemployment of 2%. You are hired by the government to advise them how they can improve the economy. What advice would you give?

━━ ANSWERS ━━

SHORT-ANSWER QUESTIONS

1. The six problems with fiscal policy limit its usefulness in the following ways: (1) Financing the deficit might have offsetting effects, reducing the net effect. (2) The government doesn't always know the current state of the economy and where it is headed, meaning these must be forecast; if you don't know the state of the economy you don't know what fiscal policy to use. (3) The government doesn't know what potential income is, meaning it must be estimated; if you estimated it wrong, you get the wrong fiscal policy. (4) The government cannot implement policy easily; if you can't implement it you can't use it. (5) The size of the debt might matter and since deficits create debt, you might not want to use it. Finally, (6) fiscal policy often negatively affects other government goals; if it does you might not use the policy even though it would change the economy in the direction you want. The bottom line is: In extreme cases, the appropriate fiscal policy is clear, but in most cases, the situation is not extreme. (734-739)

2. This first-year Congressperson is sharp! What she has described is crowding out. Crowding out is the offsetting effect on private expenditures caused by the government's sale of bonds to finance expansionary fiscal policy. If the government finances expansionary fiscal policy through the sale of bonds, interest rates will tend to rise. This will cause investment to decline, offsetting the initial stimulus. (734-736)

3. If crowding out is so strong that the reduced investment totally offsets the expansionary effect of fiscal spending, the net effect of fiscal policy can be zero. (734-736)

4. Unemployment insurance is an automatic stabilizer, a government program that counteracts the business cycle without any new government action. If income falls, automatic stabilizers will increase aggregate expenditures to counteract that decline. Likewise with increases in income: when income increases, automatic stabilizers decrease the size of the deficit. Eliminating unemployment insurance will eliminate this stabilization aspect of the policy and will contribute to making the recession more severe than it otherwise would have been. However, it would also make people more likely to accept lower wages and search harder for a job, thereby reducing the amount of unemployment. As usual, the answer depends. (739-741)

5. I would propose expansionary monetary policy. Expansionary fiscal policy would raise interest rates. I would emphasize that while the effect on income may be expansionary in the short run, in the long run, the expansionary monetary policy may simply lead to inflation. (741-742)

6. The tools of fiscal policy are changing taxes and changing government spending. Increasing taxes and lowering spending contract the economy; decreasing taxes and increasing spending expand the economy. (740)

7. Three alternatives to fiscal policy are directed investment policies, trade policies, and autonomous consumption policies. Directed investment policies include talking up the economy so that businesses will invest in expectation of better days and protecting the financial system by guarantees. Trade policies include government assistance to promote exports. Autonomous consumption policies include creating institutions conducive to easy credit. (743-745)

8. Policy is a process. Policies undertaken now influence expectations and actions in the future. Policy regimes take this into account whereas policies do not. Policy regimes involve rules. Those rules must be credible if they are to influence actions in the desired way. (745-747)

━━ ANSWERS ━━

MATCHING

1-b; 2-e; 3-c; 4-a; 5-g; 6-f; 7-h; 8-d.

ANSWERS

PROBLEMS AND APPLICATIONS

1. a. To close the recessionary gap, government expenditures need to rise by the full amount of the gap because the multiplier is 1. This is shown as a shifting from AD_0 to AD_1. In the short run, output rises by $1,000 and the price level remains constant. This is also a long-run equilibrium since short-run equilibrium output equals potential output. (732-734)

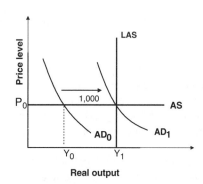

b. If the *SAS* curve is upward sloping, and one wants to increase real income by 1,000, one would have to run more expansionary fiscal policy. The more the SAS curve is upward sloping, the more expansionary the fiscal policy would have to be. (732-734)

c. An increase in expenditures of $1,000 shifts the AD curve to the right by $1,000. If the SAS curve is horizontal in the short run, output rises by $1,000 and the price level remains constant. This time, how-ever, short-run equilibrium output exceeds potential output. As long as output exceeds potential, wages will continue to rise, the AS curve will continue to shift up. In the long run, the SAS curve will shift up to SAS_1 and real output will decline by $500, to potential output. This is shown in the accompanying graph. (732-734)

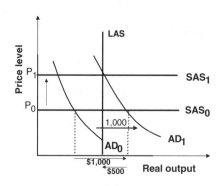

2. The spending multiplier is 2.5 ($1/(1-.6)$).

a. Assuming the economy is far below potential output (and the *SAS* curve is flat) the government must increase spending on goods and services by $100 billion to increase income by $250 billion. This is shown below as a rightward shift in the *AD* curve of $250 billion from AD_0 to AD_1 because the initial shift is multiplied by 2.5. Income increases by $250 billion. (732-734)

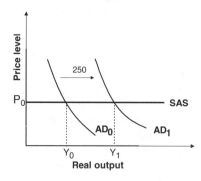

b. If the SAS curve is upward sloping, and one wants to increase real income by $250 billion, one would have to run more expansionary fiscal policy. The more the SAS curve is upward sloping, the more expansionary the fiscal policy would have to be. (732-734)

c. Since interest rates have risen, investment declines and the *AE* curve shifts down, partially offsetting the initial increase in aggregate expenditures. The net effect of the spending increase is smaller than $250 billion. This is shown by a shift down in the *AE* curve from AE_1 to AE_2 resulting in income Y_2, lower than Y_1. This is shown in the graph on the next page. (734-736)

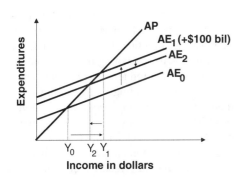

ANSWERS

A BRAIN TEASER

1. Formula flexibility is a policy in which tax rates are tied to the deviation of actual output from potential output. Formula flexibility would automatically adjust spending and taxes in a countercyclical way, thereby allowing fiscal policy to respond more quickly to economic conditions. While the idea behind formula flexibility seems to make sense, the initial problems of establishing formula flexibility are likely to be great. The formulas calling for decreases in taxes or increases in spending in a recession are likely to be politically popular, but the formulas calling for increases in taxes or decreases in spending are likely to be unappealing. (739-740)

ANSWERS

MULTIPLE CHOICE

1. b   Tax subsidies for investment provide an incentive to invest in capital, which will increase the productive capacity of an economy. Therefore, it is best seen as a supply-side policy. See pages 732-734.

2. a   As discussed on page 735 crowding out is the offsetting of a change in government expenditures by a change in private expenditures in the opposite direction. Answer c, if you could follow it, is nonsensical.

3. a   Okun's law says that a 1 percentage point fall in the unemployment rate is associated with a 2 percent rise in income. An economist who underpredicts potential output by 2 percent is overpredicting the target rate of unemployment rate by 1 percentage point. See page 736.

4. d   The text discusses six problems with fiscal policy: crowding out, knowing what the situation is, knowing potential output, flexibility of changing policy, impact of the debt, and other government goals. See pages 743-739.

5. d   Automatic stabilizers are welfare payments, unemployment insurance and taxes that raise income during recessions and lower income during expansions. See pages 739-741.

6. c   State balanced budget provisions mean that states cut spending and increase taxes during recessions and raise spending and reduce taxes during expansions. These actions exacerbate the business cycle and are therefore procyclical. See page 740.

7. c   This combination of goals, for the most part, is unattainable. See page 741.

8. c   Only expansionary fiscal policy will work since the President also wants interest rates to rise. See pages 741-742.

9. d   Only contractionary fiscal policy will work since the President also wants interest rates to fall. See page 742.

10. d   Expansionary monetary and fiscal policy increase the trade deficit. See page 742.

11. b   By changing the value of one's currency, government can affect the level of exports and imports and thus affect aggregate output. See page 745.

12. b   A higher value of the dollar will make U.S. goods more expensive for foreigners and reduce exports. This will have a contractionary effect on the economy. See pages 743-745.

13. a Rational expectations are forward-looking expectations that use available information. They are difficult to predict because how people form expectations can shift quickly. See page 746.

14. d Policy regimes are preferred because regimes are better able to affect people's expectations and the effects of a policy are more predictable. See page 747.

ANSWERS

POTENTIAL ESSAY QUESTIONS

The following are annotated answers. They indicate the general idea behind the answer.

1. When the economy is in a recession and total spending is too low then government spending automatically rises while tax collections automatically fall (the government automatically incurs a deficit). This helps to stimulate total spending and cushion the downturn in the economy. The opposite is true when the economy is expanding. Note that these changes take place while the income level falls and expands. Therefore, there are no time lag problems accompanying the automatic stabilizers.

2. The crowding-out effect states that deficit spending financed by borrowing will increase interest rates and therefore crowd out private spending. Any "crowding out" associated with deficit spending renders fiscal policy less effective in stimulating total spending and therefore the economy during a recession. Activist economists argue that the crowding out effect is relatively small. Committed laissez-faire economists argue that there is a total crowding out effect, which renders fiscal policy impotent in stimulating total spending. Some laissez-faire economists have argued that the effect of deficit spending may even be negative on the economy if private spending is more productive than government spending. The empirical evidence on the size of the crowding-out effect is mixed and has not resolved the debate. However, everyone agrees that the closer the economy comes to its potential income level, the greater is the crowding-out effect.

3. I would start by pointing out that by most western economy standards the economy is going quite well, and that perhaps they should be satisfied with what they have. If they insist on policy actions, I would try to find out more information about the economy. For example, I would be worried that with high growth and low unemployment, that inflation may soon become a problem. Thus I would be very hesitant to use any demand-based policy. With growth of 6%, I would assume that supply incentives are working, but I would consider them carefully to see if a technology or pro-savings policy may make sense.

Pretest
Chapters 27-30

Take this test in test conditions, giving yourself a limited amount of time to complete the questions. Ideally, check with your professor to see how much time he or she allows for an average multiple choice question and multiply this by 24. This is the time limit you should set for yourself for this pretest. If you do not know how much time your teacher would allow, we suggest 1 minute per question, or about 25 minutes.

1. For every financial asset there is:
   a. corresponding financial liability.
   b. corresponding financial liability if the financial asset is financed.
   c. a real liability.
   d. a corresponding real asset.

2. Which of the following is not a function of money?
   a. Medium of exchange.
   b. Unit of account.
   c. Store of wealth.
   d. Equity instrument.

3. Which of the following is not included in the M_1 definition of money?
   a. checking accounts.
   b. currency.
   c. traveler's checks.
   d. savings accounts.

4. Assuming individuals hold no cash, the reserve requirement is 20 percent, and banks keep no excess reserves, an increase in an initial inflow of $100 into the banking system will cause an increase in the money supply of:
   a. $20.
   b. $50.
   c. $100.
   d. $500.

5. If banks hold excess reserves whereas before they did not, the relative money multiplier:
   a. will become larger.
   b. will become smaller.
   c. will be unaffected.
   d. might increase or might decrease.

6. Monetary policy is:
   a. a variation of fiscal policy.
   b. undertaken by the Treasury.
   c. undertaken by the Fed.
   d. the regulation of monetary institutions.

7. Tools of monetary policy include all the following *except:*
   a. changing the reserve requirement.
   b. changing the discount rate.
   c. executing open market operations.
   d. running deficits.

8. Assuming $c = .2$ and $r = .1$, the approximate real-world money multiplier would be:
   a. 1.33.
   b. 2.33.
   c. 3.33.
   d. 4.33.

9. If the Fed wants to increase the money supply, it should:
   a. buy bonds.
   b. sell bonds.
   c. pass a law that interest rates rise.
   d. pass a law that interest rates fall.

10. Assuming the Fed is following the Taylor Rule, if inflation is 3 percent, target inflation is 2 percent, and output is 1 percent above potential, what would you predict would be the Fed funds rate target?
    a. 4 percent
    b. 5 percent
    c. 5.5 percent
    d. 6 percent

11. Which of the following is the path through which contractionary monetary policy works?
    a. Money down implies interest up implies investment down implies income down.
    b. Money down implies interest down implies investment down implies income down.
    c. Money down implies interest up implies investment up implies income down.
    d. Money down implies interest down implies investment up implies income down.

12. The real interest rate is 3 percent; the nominal interest rate is 7 percent. It is likely that one could deduce an expected inflation rate of:
    a. 1 percent.
    b. 2 percent.
    c. 3 percent.
    d. 4 percent.

13. In an expected inflation, lenders will generally:
    a. gain relative to borrowers.
    b. lose relative to borrowers.
    c. neither gain nor lose relative to borrowers.
    d. The effect will be totally random.

14. If productivity growth is 2 percent and inflation is 5 percent, on average nominal wage increases will be:
    a. 2 percent.
    b. 3 percent.
    c. 5 percent.
    d. 7 percent.

15. Assuming velocity is relatively constant and real income is relatively stable, an increase in the money supply of 40 percent will br associated with an approximate change in the price level of:
    a. 4 percent.
    b. 40 percent.
    c. 80 percent.
    d. zero percent.

16. The inflation tax is :
    a. a tax placed by government on inflators.
    b. a tax placed by god on inflators.
    c. a tax on the holders of cash.
    d. a tax on holders of goods whose price is inflating.

17. An individual has said that she favors an incomes policy. She:
    a. is likely an institutional theory of inflation advocate.
    b. is likely a quantity theory of inflation advocate economist.
    c. could be either a quantity theory or institutionalist theory advocate.
    d. is not an economist, because no economist could ever support an incomes policy.

18. The short-run Phillips curve shifts around because of changes in:
    a. the money supply.
    b. expectations of employment.
    c. expectations of inflation.
    d. expectations of real income.

19. If the economy is at Point A in the Phillips curve graph below, what prediction would you make for inflation?

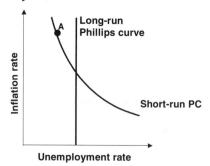

    a. It will increase
    b. It will decrease.
    c. It will remain constant.
    d. It will immediately fall to zero.

20. Crowding out is caused by:
    a. the government running a deficit and selling bonds to finance that deficit.
    b. the government printing money.
    c. the government running a surplus and selling bonds and the people who buy those bonds selling their older bonds to the government.
    d. the tendency for new workers to replace more expensive older workers..

21. Automatic stabilizers:
   a. are government programs to employ workers during recessions.
   b. create government budget surpluses during economic recessions.
   c. are designed to reduce the price level directly.
   d. counteract both recessions and expansions through changes in spending without government action.

22. You've been appointed adviser to the President. She wants interest rates and inflation to fall. You would suggest
   a. expansionary monetary policy.
   b. contractionary monetary policy.
   c. expansionary fiscal policy.
   d. contractionary fiscal policy.

23. Exchange rate policy is:
   a. increasing the size of the government deficit.
   b. deliberately affecting the country's exchange rate in order to affect its trade balance.
   c. deliberately affecting the country's money supply in order to affect its trade balance.
   d. deliberately affecting the country's tax rate in order to affect its trade balance.

24. Policy regimes are preferred to discretionary policy because:
   a. discretionary policies are more likely to affect people's expectations.
   b. regimes are more likely to be adopted by Congress.
   c. regimes provide government with more flexibility.
   d. the impact of policies are significantly affected by expectations.

ANSWERS

1.	a	(27:1)	**13.**	c	(29:1)
2.	d	(27:4)	**14.**	d	(29:4)
3.	d	(27:5)	**15.**	b	(29:6)
4.	d	(27:10)	**16.**	c	(29:9)
5.	b	(27:13)	**17.**	a	(29:13)
6.	c	(28:2)	**18.**	c	(29:16)
7.	d	(28:6)	**19.**	a	(29:19)
8.	c	(28:8)	**20.**	a	(30:2)
9.	a	(28:11)	**21.**	d	(30:5)
10.	d	(28:15)	**22.**	d	(30:9)
11.	a	(28:18)	**23.**	b	(30:11)
12.	d	(28:21)	**24.**	d	(30:14)

Key: The figures in parentheses refer to multiple choice question and chapter numbers. For example (1:2) is multiple choice question 2 from chapter 1.

POLITICS, DEFICITS, AND DEBT

31

CHAPTER AT A GLANCE

This review is based upon the learning objectives that open the chapter.

1a. A deficit is a shortfall of revenues under payments. A surplus is an excess of revenues over payments. (Surpluses are negative deficits and vice versa.) (753-754, 756)

Surpluses and deficits are flow concepts; all deficits must be financed.

1b. Surpluses and deficits are simply summary measures of the financial health of the economy. To understand that summary you must understand the methods that were used to calculate it. (754)

Different accounting procedures yield different figures for surpluses and deficits.

2. A structural deficit or surplus is that part of a budget deficit or surplus that would exist even if the economy were at its potential level of income. A passive (also called cyclical) surplus or deficit is that part that exists because the economy is operating below or above its potential income. (754-756)

Passive (cyclical) deficits or surpluses are largely due to the automatic stabilizers.

3. The real deficit is the nominal deficit adjusted for inflation.

Real deficit = Nominal deficit − (Inflation × Total debt.) (756-757)

Inflation wipes out debt. Inflation also causes the real deficit to be less than the nominal deficit. However, inflation means a higher percentage of the deficit (or spending) will be devoted to debt service (paying interest on the debt). Moreover, creditors who do not anticipate the inflation pay the cost of eliminating the debt through inflation.

4a. Debt is accumulated deficits minus accumulated surpluses. It is a <u>stock</u> concept. (758-762)

Debt is a summary measure of a country's financial situation.

GDP serves the same function for government as income does for an individual. The greater the GDP (income) the greater the ability to handle debt. However, government debt is different from an individual's debt. Government is ongoing; it can pay off the debt by printing money; and much of its is internal— owed to its citizens.

4b. Since in a growing economy a continual deficit is consistent with a constant ratio of debt to GDP, and since GDP serves as a measure of the government's ability to pay off the debt, a country can run a continual deficit. (762)

The more you earn, the more debt you can handle.

5. Since World War II, until recently, the U.S. government ran almost continual deficits. From 1998 to 2001, the government ran surpluses, but returned to deficits in 2002. (762-763)

But we still have debt.

6. The Social Security Trust Fund surplus makes the budget deficit look smaller than it really is. Regardless of whether there is, or is not, a trust fund, real output must match real expenditures when the baby boomers retire. (766)

Always watch out for political spin when discussing the government budget.

● SHORT-ANSWER QUESTIONS

1. How much importance do most economists give to the budget deficit or surplus?

2. If the U.S. economy is below potential and the surplus is $40 billion, is the structural surplus greater or less than $40 billion?

3. If the nominal interest rate is 6%, the inflation rate is 4%, the nominal deficit is $100 billion, and the debt of the country is $2 trillion, what is the real deficit?

4. If the nominal interest rate is 5%, the inflation rate is 5%, the real deficit is $100 billion, and the debt of the country is $1 trillion, what is the nominal deficit?

5. In an expanding economy a government should run a continual deficit. True or false? Why?

6. If a politician presents you with a plan that will reduce the nominal budget deficit by $40 billion, but will not hurt anyone, how would you in your capacity as an economist likely respond?

7. Are current budget deficits likely to persist?

8. In what way is the trust fund not a real solution to the Social Security problem?

MATCHING THE TERMS
Match the terms to their definitions

___ **1.**	Budget Enforcement Act of 1990	**a.**	An accounting system entering expenses and revenues only when cash is received or paid out.
___ **2.**	cash flow accounting system	**b.**	A partially unfunded pension system of the U.S.
		c.	A shortfall per year of incoming revenue under outgoing payments.
___ **3.**	deficit	**d.**	A federal law establishing a pay-as-you-go test for new spending and tax cuts, along with additional spending limits for government.
___ **4.**	external debt		
___ **5.**	internal debt		
___ **6.**	nominal deficit or surplus	**e.**	An excess of revenues over payments.
		f.	Government debt owed to individuals in foreign countries.
___ **7.**	passive deficit or surplus	**g.**	Pension system in which pensions are paid from current revenues.
___ **8.**	pay-as-you-go system	**h.**	That portion of the deficit or surplus that results from fluctuations in the economy.
___ **9.**	real deficit	**i.**	The deficit or surplus determined by looking at the difference between expenditures and receipts.
___ **10.**	Social Security system	**j.**	Government debt owed to its own citizens.
___ **11.**	structural deficit	**k.**	The deficit that would remain when the cyclical or passive elements have been netted out.
___ **12.**	surplus	**l.**	The nominal deficit adjusted for inflation's effect on the debt.

⬤ PROBLEMS AND APPLICATIONS

1. Calculate the debt and deficit in each of the following:

   a. Your income has been $30,000 per year for the last five years. Your expenditures, including interest payments, have been $35,000 per year for the last five years.

   b. This year your income is $50,000; $15,000 of your $65,000 expenditures are for the purchase of the rights to an invention.

   c. Your wage income is $20,000 per year. You have a bond valued at $100,000, which pays $10,000 per year. The market value of that bond rises to $110,000. Expenses are $35,000 per year. Use the opportunity cost approach in your calculations.

2. For each of the following calculate the real deficit:

   a. Inflation is 5%. Debt is $2 trillion. Nominal deficit is $100 billion.

   b. Inflation is -3%. Debt is $500 billion. Nominal deficit is $20 billion.

c. Inflation is 10%. Debt is $3 trillion. Nominal deficit is $100 billion.

d. Inflation is 8%. Debt is $20 billion. Nominal deficit is $5 billion.

3. Assume a country's nominal GDP is $7 trillion, government expenditures less debt service are $1.5 trillion, and revenue is $1.3 trillion. The nominal debt is $4.9 trillion. Inflation is 2% and real interest rates are 5%. Expected inflation is fully adjusted.

a. Calculate debt service payments.

b. Calculate the nominal deficit.

c. Calculate the real deficit.

d. Suppose inflation rose to 4%. Again, expected inflation is fully adjusted. Recalculate (a) - (c).

4. Potential income is $8 billion. The income in the economy is $7.2 billion. Revenues do not vary with income, but taxes do; they increase by 20% of the change in income. The current deficit is $400 million.

a. What is the economy's structural deficit?

b. What is the economy's passive deficit?

A BRAIN TEASER

1. How could deficit spending actually reduce the debt burden of future generations?

MULTIPLE CHOICE

Circle the one best answer for each of the following questions:

1. A deficit is:
a. the total amount of money that a country owes.
b. the shortfall of payments under revenues in a particular time period.
c. the shortfall of revenues under payments in a particular time period.
d. accumulated debt.

2. If the U.S. government raised the retirement age to 72 starting in 2017, the current budget deficit would be:
a. reduced.
b. increased.
c. unaffected.
d. eliminated.

3. The nominal deficit is $100 billion; inflation is 4 percent; total debt is $2 trillion. The real deficit is:
a. zero.
b. $20 billion.
c. $80 billion.
d. $100 billion.

4. If the nominal surplus is $200 billion, inflation is 10 percent, and total debt is $2 trillion:
a. the real surplus is zero.
b. the real deficit is $100 billion.
c. the real surplus is $400 billion.
d. the real surplus is $2.2 trillion.

5. The real deficit is $100 billion; inflation is 4
    percent; total debt is $2 trillion. The nominal
    deficit is:
    a. zero.
    b. $120 billion.
    c. $180 billion.
    d. $200 billion.

6. If creditors are able to forecast inflation
    perfectly and there are no institutional
    constraints on interest rates:
    a. the government will not have to make
       interest payments.
    b. interest payments will rise by the amount
       that the real debt is reduced by inflation.
    c. the real deficit will equal the nominal
       deficit.
    d. the government will be unable to finance the
       debt.

7. Country A has a debt of $10 trillion. Country
    B has a debt of $5 trillion.
    a. Country A is in a better position than
       Country B.
    b. Country B is in a better position than
       Country A.
    c. One cannot say what relative position the
       countries are in.
    d. Countries A and B are in equal positions.

8. As a percentage of GDP, since World War II:
    a. debt in the United States has been rising.
    b. debt in the United States has been falling.
    c. debt in the United States has been some-
       times rising and sometimes falling.
    d. the U.S. government has had no debt.

9. The portion of the budget deficit or surplus
    that would exist even if the economy were at
    its potential level of income is called the:
    a. structural deficit or surplus.
    b. passive deficit or surplus.
    c. primary deficit or surplus.
    d. secondary deficit or surplus.

10. If an economy is $100 billion below potential,
    the tax rate is 20 percent, and the deficit is
    $180 billion, the passive deficit is:
    a. $20 billion.
    b. $160 billion.
    c. $180 billion.
    d. $200 billion.

11. One of the reasons government debt is
    different from individual debt is:
    a. government does not pay interest on its debt.
    b. government never really needs to pay back
       its debt.
    c. all government debt is owed to other
       government agencies or to its own citizens.
    d. the ability of a government to pay off its
       debt is unrelated to income.

12. If there is growth and a country with a debt of
    $1 trillion has decided it wants to keep its
    ratio of debt-to-GDP constant:
    a. it should run a deficit.
    b. it should run a surplus.
    c. it should run a balanced budget.
    d. the deficit has no effect on debt.

13. Payroll taxes for Social Security:
    a. reduce the reported deficit and increase the
       reported surplus.
    b. increase the reported deficit and reduce the
       reported surplus.
    c. do not affect the budget since it is an off-
       budget item.
    d. are offset by future obligations in the
       budget.

14. The "real" problem of Social Security in 2017
    could be solved by:
    a. locking up the Social Security Trust Fund to
       pay for Social Security benefits only.
    b. raising the eligibility age for Social Security
       so fewer people are collecting Social Security
       in 2017, raising taxes on workers in 2017,
       increasing taxes on Social Security benefits
       in 2017, or a combination of all three.
    c. allowing current workers to divert some of
       their payroll taxes into private savings
       accounts to be withdrawn at retirement.
    d. a rise in the value of the stock market that
       would raise the value of the Social Security
       Trust fund so that it remains solvent for
       longer.

● POTENTIAL ESSAY QUESTIONS

*You may also see essay questions similar to the "Problems
& Applications" and "Brain Teasers" exercises.*

1. What are three reasons why government debt
    is different from individual debt?

2. How can a growing economy reduce the
    concern over deficits and the debt?

ANSWERS

SHORT-ANSWER QUESTIONS

1. While there are differences of opinion, most economists are hesitant to attach too much importance to a deficit or a surplus. The reason is that the deficit or surplus depends on the accounting procedures used, and these can vary widely. Only with much more additional information will an economist attribute importance to a surplus or deficit. It is financial health—the ability to cover costs over the long term—of the economy that concerns most economists. (752-753)

2. Since the economy is below potential, the structural surplus is larger than the nominal surplus. (754-756)

3. To calculate the real deficit you multiply inflation times the total debt (4% $\times$ $2 trillion), giving $80 billion; then subtract that from the nominal deficit of $100 billion. So in this example the real deficit equals $20 billion. The interest rate does not enter into the calculations. (756-757)

4. To calculate the nominal deficit you multiply inflation times the total debt (5% $\times$ $1 trillion), giving $50 billion, and add that to the real deficit of $100 billion. So in this example the nominal deficit equals $150 billion. The interest rate does not enter into the calculation. (756-757)

5. It depends. In an expanding economy with no deficits the ratio of debt to GDP will be falling; if the government wants to hold the debt-to-GDP constant it will need to run a continual deficit. If it wants to reduce that ratio, then it need not run a continual deficit. (761-762)

6. TANSTAAFL. I would check to see what accounting gimmick the politician was proposing and what the plan would do to the long-run financial health of the country. (756-757)

7. The Congressional Budget Office predicted in 2005 that the federal government budget will return to surplus in 2012. This projection, however, was based on the expiration of tax cuts implemented in 2001 and does not include expenditures related to U.S. military activity in Iraq. It is highly unlikely that these tax cuts will be allowed to expire. Current deficits are likely to persist into the indefinite future. (764)

8. Ultimately, real expenditures must equal real output in each period. The trust fund provides a financial solution to the Social Security problem, but it does not directly see to it that real expenditures will equal real output in the future. (766-769)

ANSWERS

MATCHING

1-d; 2-a; 3-c; 4-f; 5-j; 6-i; 7-h; 8-g; 9-l; 10-b; 11-k; 12-e.

ANSWERS

PROBLEMS AND APPLICATIONS

1. a. Deficit is $5,000 per year; Debt is $25,000. On page 753, deficit is defined as income less expenditures and on page 756 debt is defined as accumulated deficits minus accumulated surpluses. For each of the past 5 years, you have incurred an annual deficit of $5,000. Total debt is $5,000 times five years, or $25,000. (753-754, 756)

    b. Deficit is $15,000; Debt is $15,000. Page 754 tells you that what is included as expenses is ambiguous. If you count the purchase of the rights to the invention as a current expenditure, the deficit is $15,000. If you had no previous debt, debt is also $15,000. If, however, you count the purchase of the invention as an investment and include it in your capital budget, then your expenses are only $50,000 and your budget will be in balance. (754, 756-757)

    c. Surplus of $5,000. Using an opportunity cost approach, a person holding bonds should count the rise in the bonds' market value as revenue. Here, wage income is $20,000 per year, interest income is 10,000, and the bond's value has increased by $10,000. Total income is $40,000. Income of $40,000 less expenses of $35,000 per year yields a budget surplus of $5,000. Unless there was a previous debt, there is no debt. (754)

2. As discussed on pages 756-757, the real deficit is the nominal deficit adjusted for inflation's effect on the debt. The definition of real deficit states: Real deficit = Nominal deficit − (Inflation × Total debt).
   a. $0: $100 billion − .05 × $2 trillion. (757)
   b. $35 billion: $20 billion − (−.03) × $500. (757)
   c. Surplus of $200 billion: $100 billion − .10 × $3 trillion. (757)
   d. $3.4 billion: $5 billion − .08 × $20 billion. (757)

3. a. $343 billion: Debt service payment = nominal interest rate × nominal debt. The nominal interest rate when expected inflation is fully adjusted is the real interest rate plus inflation (5+2). Debt service payment = .07 × $4.9 trillion. (756-757)
   b. $543 billion deficit: The nominal deficit is revenues less government expenditures (including debt service), $1.3 trillion − ($1.5 trillion + $.343 trillion). (756-757)
   c. $445 billion deficit: The real deficit = Nominal deficit − (Inflation × Total debt) = $.543 trillion − .02 × $4.9 trillion). (756-757)
   d. Since bondholders must be compensated for the loss in the value of their bonds, they demand a nominal interest rate of 9% (5 + 4). Debt service payment is now $441 billion (.09 × $4.9 trillion). The nominal deficit is higher at $641 billion. ($1.3 trillion − ($1.5 trillion + $.441 trillion)). The real deficit has not changed. It is still $445 billion (The real deficit = Nominal deficit − (Inflation × Total debt) = $.641 trillion − (.04 × $4.9 trillion)). (756-757)

4. a. If the economy were at potential, government would collect $160 million more in taxes, reducing the deficit by that amount. There would a structural deficit of $400 − $160 = $240 million. (754-755)

   b. The passive deficit is the deficit that occurs because the economy is below potential. The passive deficit is $800 million × 20 percent, or $160 million. (754-755)

--------- ANSWERS ---------

A BRAIN TEASER

1. If the deficit spending is used to increase the productivity of the nation, enabling the nation to experience much higher rates of economic growth, the income of the nation could expand faster than its debt. If this happens, the debt-to-GDP ratio gets smaller, the interest expense is less burdensome, and the debt will be easier to pay off. (762)

--------- ANSWERS ---------

MULTIPLE CHOICE

1. c A country has a budget deficit if it does not collect sufficient revenue to cover expenditures during the year. See page 753.

2. c The U.S. uses a cash flow accounting method, so changes affecting the future are not seen in the current budget. See page 754.

3. b Real deficit = nominal deficit − (inflation × total debt). See page 757.

4. c Real surplus = nominal surplus + (inflation × total debt). See page 757.

5. c Real deficit = nominal deficit − (inflation × total debt). See page 757.

6. b If creditors can forecast inflation perfectly, the interest rate will rise when inflation rises and the subsequent increase in interest payments will match the decline in the real debt due to higher inflation. See page 757.

7. c   Debt must be judged relative to assets and to total GDP. See page 758.

8. c   See Figure 31-2 on page 761.

9. a   The passive deficit or surplus is the deficit or surplus that exists because the economy is below or above potential. The structural deficit or surplus is the deficit or surplus that exists even when the economy is at potential. The text doesn't define primary or secondary deficits or surpluses. See page 755.

10. a   The passive deficit is the deficit that exists because the economy is below potential. The government would collect $20 billion more in revenue if the economy were at potential, so the passive deficit is $20 billion. See page 755.

11. b   Because government goes on forever it doesn't ever need to pay back its debt. Only about 75 percent of government debt is owed to other government agencies or to its own citizens. The other government debt is owed to foreign individuals. Government is better able to pay off debt when income rises. Both government and individuals pay interest on debt. See pages 759-760.

12. a   Real growth will reduce the ratio of existing debt to GDP so to hold the ratio constant a continual deficit is necessary. See pages 761-762.

13. a   While payroll taxes for Social Security represent future obligations by government to pay social security, they are counted as current revenue today and reduce the reported deficit (increase the reported surplus). See page 765.

14. b   The real problem is the mismatch between real demand and real supply of goods as the baby boomers retire and the demand for goods and services by retirees outstrips the supply produced by workers in 2017. Real solutions must address this problem and must either reduce benefits

to seniors or reduce consumption by workers in 2017. The other solutions address the financial problem only. See pages 767-769.

ANSWERS

POTENTIAL ESSAY QUESTIONS

The following are annotated answers. They indicate the general idea behind the answer.

1. First, the government's life is unlimited and therefore it never has to settle its accounts. Second, it can pay off debt by creating money (which is not recommended, however). Third, much of the government's debt is internally held and therefore, on average as a group, people are neither richer nor poorer because of the debt (even though it may redistribute income to upper-income individuals).

2. When a society experiences real growth (growth adjusted for inflation), it becomes richer, and, being richer, it can handle more debt. Moreover, since in a growing economy a continual deficit is consistent with a constant ratio of debt to GDP, and since GDP serves as a measure of the government's ability to pay off debt, a country can run a continual deficit. Deficits should be viewed relative to GDP to determine their importance.

MACRO POLICIES IN DEVELOPING COUNTRIES

32

● CHAPTER AT A GLANCE

This review is based upon the learning objectives that open the chapter.

1. Seventy-five percent of the world's population lives in developing countries, with average per capita income of under $500 per year. (773-774)

    Be careful in judging a society by its income alone. Some developing countries may have cultures preferable to ours. Ideally, growth would occur without destroying the culture.

2. There are differences in normative goals between developing and developed countries because their wealth differs. Developing countries face basic economic needs whereas developed countries' economic needs are considered by most people to be normatively less pressing. (774-775)

    The main focus of macro policy in developing countries is on how to increase growth through development to fulfill people's basic needs.

3. Economies at different stages of development have different institutional needs because the problems they face are different. Institutions that can be assumed in developed countries cannot necessarily be assumed to exist in developing countries. (776-777)

    Developed nations have stable governments and market structures, which are often lacking in developing countries.

4. "The dual economy" refers to the existence of the two sectors in most developing countries: a traditional sector and an internationally-oriented modern market sector. (778)

    Often, the largest percentage of the population participates in the traditional sector. Tradition often resists change.

5. A régime change is a change in the entire atmosphere within which the government and the economy interrelate; a policy change is a change in one aspect of government's actions. (779)

    A régime change and macro institutional policies designed to fit the cultural and social dimensions of developing economics are what developing economies need.

6. Central banks recognize that printing too much money causes inflation, but often feel compelled to do so for political reasons. Debate about inflation in developing countries generally concerns those political reasons, not the relationship between money and inflation. (780-781)

    Governments in developing economies risk being thrown out of office unless they run deficits and issue too much money.

7. Full convertibility means one can exchange one's currency for whatever legal purpose one wants. Convertibility on the current account limits those exchanges for the purpose of buying goods and services. (782)

    Very few developing countries allow full convertibility.

8. Seven obstacles facing developing countries are: (783-792)
    1. Political instability.
    2. Corruption.
    3. Lack of appropriate institutions.
    4. Lack of investment.
    5. Inappropriate education.
    6. Overpopulation.
    7. Health and disease

    Know why these are problems!
    The opposite constitutes the ingredients for growth. Remember them!

● SHORT-ANSWER QUESTIONS

1. What percentage of the population of the world lives in developing countries?

2. What is the average per capita income in developing nations?

3. Why is there often a difference in the normative goals of developed and developing countries?

4. Why do economies at different stages of development often have different institutional needs? Explain.

5. What is the dual economy?

6. What is the difference between a regime change and a policy change?

7. Inflation is simply a problem of central banks in developing countries issuing too much money. Is this true or false? Why?

8. What are two types of convertibility?

9. Economists can't tell developing countries, "Here's what you have to do to grow." But they can identify seven obstacles facing developing countries. What are they?

MATCHING THE TERMS
Match the terms to their definitions

___ **1.**	balance of payments constraint	**a.**	A change in one aspect of a government's actions.
___ **2.**	brain drain	**b.**	A change in the entire atmosphere within which the government and economy interrelate.
___ **3.**	conditionality	**c.**	A stage when the development process becomes self-sustaining.
___ **4.**	convertibility on the current account	**d.**	A system that allows people to exchange currencies for whatever legal purpose they want.
___ **5.**	credentialism	**e.**	A system that allows people to exchange currencies for the purpose of buying goods and services only.
___ **6.**	dual economy	**f.**	A system that places some limitation on people's ability to exchange currencies to buy assets.
___ **7.**	economic takeoff	**g.**	Changing the underlying economic institutions.
___ **8.**	foreign aid	**h.**	Funds that developed countries lend or give to developing countries.
___ **9.**	full convertibility	**i.**	Investment in the underlying structure of the economy.
___ **10.**	infrastructure investment	**j.**	Limitations on expansionary domestic macroeconomic policy due to a shortage of international reserves.
___ **11.**	limited capital account convertibility	**k.**	Method of comparing income by looking at the domestic purchasing power of money in different countries.
___ **12.**	policy change	**l.**	Outflow of the best and brightest students from developing countries to developed countries.
___ **13.**	purchasing power parity	**m.**	The degrees become more important than the knowledge learned.
___ **14.**	regime change	**n.**	The existence of two sectors: a traditional sector and an internationally oriented modern market sector.
___ **15.**	restructuring	**o.**	The making of loans that are subject to specific conditions.

A BRAIN TEASER

1. You are the chief economic adviser to a developing country that is politically stable and possesses a culture you believe to be conducive to growth. What economic policies would you recommend to the developing country to enhance its growth and development?

MULTIPLE CHOICE

Circle the one best answer for each of the following questions:

1. Annual GDP per capita is about ____in developing countries and ____ in developed countries.
   a. $50; $20,000.
   b. $500; $30,000.
   c. $50; $10,000.
   d. $4,000; $20,000.

2. Two methods of comparing income among countries are the purchasing power parity method and the exchange rate method. Of these:
   a. the exchange rate method generally gives a higher relative measure of the income in developing countries.
   b. the purchasing power parity method generally gives a higher relative measure of the income in developing countries.
   c. the purchasing power parity and exchange rate methods generally give approximately equal measures of the income in developing countries.
   d. sometimes one gives a higher relative measure of income in developing countries, and sometimes the other gives a higher relative measure.

3. The concept "dual economy" refers to:
   a. the tendency of developed countries to have a traditional sector and an internationally-oriented sector.
   b. the tendency of both developed and developing countries to have a traditional sector and an internationally-oriented sector.
   c. the tendency of developing countries to have a traditional sector and an internationally-oriented sector.
   d. the fight, or dual, between developed and undeveloped countries.

4. If a country changes its entire approach to policy, that is called:
   a. a major policy change.
   b. a policy change.
   c. a régime change.
   d. a constitutional change.

5. The inflation tax is:
   a. a tax on those individuals who cause inflation.
   b. a tax on firms who cause inflation.
   c. a tax on both individuals and firms who cause inflation.
   d. a tax on holders of cash and any obligations specified in nominal terms.

6. The "revenue" of an inflation tax:
   a. goes only to government.
   b. goes only to private individuals.
   c. goes to both private individuals and government.
   d. is a meaningless term because there is no revenue from an inflation tax.

7. If you hold a fixed interest rate debt denominated in domestic currency and there is a high rate of inflation, you will:
   a. likely lose.
   b. likely gain.
   c. likely experience no effect from the large inflation.
   d. find that the large inflation could cause you either to gain or to lose.

8. If you hold a fixed interest rate debt denominated in a foreign currency and the exchange rate remains constant, and there is a large domestic inflation, you will:
   a. likely lose some.
   b. likely gain some.
   c. likely lose all your debt.
   d. likely experience little direct effect from the large inflation.

9. Conditionality refers to:
   a. the U.S. government's policy of only making loans to countries who will repay loans.
   b. the IMF's policy of making loans to countries subject to specific conditions.
   c. central banks' policies of making loans to firms only under certain conditions.
   d. the conditions under which inter-firm credit is allowed in transitional economies.

10. Foreign aid is:
    a. the primary source of income of the poorest developing countries.
    b. one of the top three sources of income of the poorest developing countries.
    c. one of the top three sources of income of developing countries who have ties to the United States.
    d. a minor source of income for developing countries.

11. The nickname for economics as "the dismal
    science" caught on because
    a. the law of diminishing marginal productivity
       predicted famine.
    b. the law of diseconomies of scale predicted
       famine.
    c. learning supply and demand economic
       models is dismal.
    d. it predicted that economic takeoff would
       seldom be reached.

12. If population grows geometrically, the amount
    of land is fixed, and there is diminishing
    marginal productivity, then
    a. famine is in the future.
    b. income per person will decrease but there
       will not necessarily be famine.
    c. famine is not in the future if there is
       technological development.
    d. famine may or may not be in the future.

13. Which of the following best represents the
    textbook author's view of development?
    a. Optimal strategies for growth are country-
       specific.
    b. A country's development strategy should
       include as much education as possible.
    c. Countries should focus on infrastructure
       investment.
    d. Countries should follow a policy of laissez-
       faire.

POTENTIAL ESSAY QUESTIONS

*You may also see essay questions similar to the
"Problems & Applications" and "Brain Teaser"
exercises.*

1.   What is the difference between economic
     development and economic growth?

2.   What are some institutional differences
     between developed and developing coun-
     tries that make it difficult for developing
     countries to develop?

3.   Why is it that no developing country allows
     full convertibility?

■ ANSWERS ■

SHORT-ANSWER QUESTIONS

1. 75 percent of the population of the world lives in developing countries. (773)

2. The average per capita income in developing countries is about $500 per year. (773)

3. Developing countries face true economic needs. Their concern is with basic needs such as adequate clothing, food, and shelter. Developed countries' needs are considered less pressing. For example, will everyone have access to a DVD player? (774-775)

4. Economies at different stages of development have different institutional needs because the problems they face are different. Institutions that can be assumed in developed countries cannot necessarily be assumed to exist in developing countries. For example, developing countries often lack the institutional structure that markets require. (777)

5. Dual economy refers to the existence of the two distinct sectors in most developing countries: a traditional sector and an internationally-oriented modern market sector. (778)

6. A régime change is a change in the entire atmosphere within which the government and the economy interrelate; a policy change is a change in one aspect of government's actions. A régime change affects underlying expectations about what the government will do in the future; a policy change does not. (779)

7. Any simple statement is generally false, and this one is no exception. The reason why this one is false is that while it is true that inflation is closely tied to the developing country's central bank issuing too much money, the underlying problem behind the central bank's actions is often large government deficits that cannot be financed unless the central bank issues debt and then buys the bonds, which requires an increase in the money supply (printing money to pay for the bonds). (780-781)

8. Two types of convertibility are full convertibility and current account convertibility. Full convertibility means you can change your money into another currency with no restrictions. Current account convertibility allows exchange of currency to buy goods but not to invest outside the country. Many developing countries have current account convertibility, but not full convertibility. (782)

9. Seven problems facing developing countries are (1) governments in developing countries are often unstable, (2) governments in developing countries are often corrupt, (3) developing countries often lack appropriate institutions to promote growth, (4) developing countries often lack the domestic savings to fund investment for growth, (5) developing countries tend to have too much of the wrong education, (6) developing countries are often overpopulated so that raising per capita income is difficult, and (7) people in developing countries have limited access to healthcare and face greater incidence of disease. (783-792)

■ ANSWERS ■

MATCHING

1-j; 2-l; 3-o; 4-e; 5-m; 6-n; 7-c; 8-h; 9-d; 10-i; 11-f; 12-a; 13-k; 14-b; 15-g.

■ ANSWERS ■

A BRAIN TEASER

1. Macro institutional policies, those designed to change the underlying macro institutions, and thereby increase output, are what is necessary for development. Although there is some debate about exactly what constitutes the right set of policies for development, all economists agree that developing countries need to get the infrastructure right. That is, they must create a climate within which individual initiative is directed toward production. This requires macro institutional policies and a regime change. (783-792)

■ ANSWERS ■

MULTIPLE CHOICE

1. b   As stated on page 773, b is the closest.

2. b   As discussed on page 775, the purchasing power parity method of comparing income cuts income differences among countries in half.

3. c   See page 778 for the definition of dual economy. Choice d was put in to throw you off. When the word means "a fight" it is, of course, spelled "duel".

4. c   See page 779.

5. d.   The answer has to be d, as discussed on page 781. The individuals and firms who cause the inflation are gaining from the inflation; they pay no inflation tax.

6. c   The only answer that makes any sense is c. The "revenue" goes from holders of fixed nominal interest rate debt to those who owe that debt. Those who owe the debt include both private individuals and government. See page 781.

7. a   Inflation wipes out the value of fixed interest rate debt. See page 781.

8. d   Because the debt is denominated in a foreign currency and exchange rates remain constant, what happens to the domestic price level does not directly affect you. There could be indirect effects, but d specifies direct effects. See pages 781-783.

9. b   See page 783.

10. d   Total foreign aid comes to less than $11 per person for developing countries. While this does not preclude b or c, it makes it very difficult for them to be true, and in fact, they are not true. See page 787.

11. a   The nickname "the dismal science" was used by Carlyle in an attack on economists for their views against slavery. It became a popular description of economics however largely because of the writings of Thomas Malthus, whose model of population focused on the law of diminishing marginal productivity and led to the prediction that society's prospects were dismal because population tends to outrun the means of subsistence. See page 791.

12. d   As discussed on pages 790-791, the Malthusian doctrine predicted famine based on the elements of this question. That doctrine did not, however, take into account technological development. Technological growth can offset the tendencies for famine. But technological growth does not necessarily have to offset those tendencies; thus c is wrong, and d is the only correct answer.

13. a   As discussed on page 792, the author believes the problems of economic development are intertwined with cultural and social issues and hence are country-specific. The other answers do not necessarily fail to reflect the author's viewpoint, but he presented arguments on both sides when discussing them. Thus, a is the best answer.

ANSWERS

POTENTIAL ESSAY QUESTIONS

The following are annotated answers. They indicate the general idea behind the answer.

1.   Growth occurs because of an increase in inputs, given a production function. Development occurs through a change in the production function. Development involves more fundamental changes in the institutional structure than does growth.

2.   First, developing nations often lack stable, socially-minded governments with which to undertake policy. Second, developing economies often have a dual economy, a traditional and an international sector. This can create some policy dilemmas. A third difference is the way in which fiscal policy is run. Collecting taxes can be very difficult in developing countries. Expenditures are often mandated by political survival.

3.   One reason is that they want to force their residents to keep their savings, and to do their investing, in their home country, not abroad. (Remember that saving is necessary for investment, and investment is necessary for growth.) These citizens usually don't want to do this because of the risks of leaving their money in their own countries; a new government takeover could possibly take it all away.

INTERNATIONAL FINANCIAL POLICY

33

CHAPTER AT A GLANCE

This review is based upon the learning objectives that open the chapter.

1a. The balance of payments is a country's record of all transactions between its residents and the residents of all foreign countries. (796-797)
It is broken down into the:
- *current account*
- *capital account*
- *official transactions account.*

Remember: If it is a minus (plus) sign, money is going out (coming in). Moreover, if foreigners are buying our goods, services, or assets, that represents a demand for the dollar (an inflow) in international exchange rate markets. If we buy foreign goods, services, or assets, that represents a supply of dollars (an outflow).

1b. The balance of trade is the difference between the value of goods and services a nation exports and the value of goods and services it imports. (798)

The balance of merchandise trade is often discussed in the popular press as a summary of how the U.S. is doing in international markets. However, it only includes goods exported and imported—not services. Trade in services is just as important as trade in merchandise, so economists pay more attention to the combined balance on goods and services.

1c. Since the balance of payments consists of both the capital account and the current account, if the capital account is in surplus and the current account is in deficit, there can still be a balance of payments surplus. (798-800)

The capital account measures the flows of payments between countries for assets such as stocks, bonds, and real estate. The current (or trade) account measures the flows of payments for goods and services.

1d. A deficit in the balance of payments means that the private quantity supplied of a currency exceeds the private quantity demanded. A surplus in the balance of payments means the opposite. (801-802)

Whenever the exchange rate is <u>above equilibrium</u> (below equilibrium), the country will experience a balance of payments <u>deficit</u> (surplus).

2. Four important fundamental determinants of exchange rates are prices, interest rates, income, and trade policy. (802)

A decrease in the value of a currency can be caused by:

- *An increase in the nation's inflation rate.*
- *A decrease in the nation's interest rates.*
- *An increase in the nation's income.*
- *A decrease in the nation's import restrictions.*

3a. Monetary policy affects exchange rates through the interest rate path, the income path, and the price-level path, as shown in the diagram on page 804. (803-804)

<u>Expansionary</u> monetary policy (increasing the money supply) lowers exchange rates. It decreases the relative price of a country's currency. Contractionary monetary policy has the opposite effect.

3b. Fiscal policy affects exchange rates through the interest rate path, the income path, and the price-level path, as shown in the diagram on page 806. (805-806)

The net effect of fiscal policy on exchange rates is ambiguous.

Be able to explain why!

4. A country fixes the exchange rate by standing ready to buy and sell its currency any time at the fixed exchange rate. (807-808)

It is easier for a country to maintain a fixed exchange rate below equilibrium. All it has to do is print and sell enough domestic currency to hold the value down.

However, if a country wants to maintain a fixed exchange rate <u>above long-run equilibrium,</u> it can do so only as long as it has the foreign currency (official) reserves to buy up its currency. Once it runs out of official reserves, it will be unable to intervene, and must either borrow, use indirect methods (domestic fiscal and monetary policies), ask other countries to buy its currency (to sell their currency), or devalue its currency.

In reality, because a country has a limited amount of official reserves, it only uses strategic currency stabilization (not a fixed exchange rate policy).

5a. Purchasing power parity is a method of calculating exchange rates so that various currencies will each buy an equal basket of goods and services. (809-811)

The PPP (Purchasing Power Parity) is one method of estimating long-run exchange rates.

5b. A real exchange rate is an exchange rate adjusted for differential inflation in countries. (811)

%Δ real exchange rate = %Δ nominal exchange rate + (domestic inflation − foreign inflation)

6a. Three exchange rate régimes are:
- <u>Fixed exchange rate:</u> The government chooses an exchange rate and offers to buy and sell currencies at that rate.
- <u>Flexible exchange rate:</u> Determination of exchange rates is left totally up to the market.
- <u>Partially flexible exchange rate:</u> The government sometimes affects the exchange rate and sometimes leaves it to the market. (811-814)

Which at best is debatable.

6b. Fixed exchange rates provide international monetary stability and force governments to make adjustments to meet their international problems. (This is *also* a disadvantage.) If they become unfixed, they create monetary instability. (812)

Know these advantages and disadvantages!

6c. Flexible exchange rate régimes provide for orderly incremental adjustment of exchange rates rather than large sudden jumps, and allow governments to be flexible in conducting domestic monetary and fiscal policy. (This is *also* a disadvantage.) They are, however, susceptible to private speculation. (813)

Know these advantages and disadvantages!

6d. Partially flexible exchange rate régimes combine the advantages and disadvantages of fixed and flexible exchange rates. (813-814)

Most countries have opted for this policy. However, if the market exchange rate is below the rate the government desires, and the government does not have sufficient official reserves (to buy and increase the demand for its currency), then it must undertake policies that will either increase the private demand for its currency or decrease the private supply. Doing so either involves using traditional macro policy—fiscal and monetary policy—to influence the economy, or using trade policy to affect the level of exports and imports.

7. The advantages of a common currency:
- creates strong political ties
- reduces the cost of trade
- facilitates price comparisons
- creates a larger single market.

The disadvantages of a common currency:
- eliminates independent monetary policy.
- loss of a national currency. (814-816)

Know the advantages and disadvantages of a common currency.

The most important disadvantage is loss of independent monetary policy. A country loses the ability to increase the money supply by itself to fight a recession.

See also, Appendix A: "History of Exchange Rate Systems."

● SHORT-ANSWER QUESTIONS

1. Distinguish between the balance of payments and the balance of trade.

2. How can a country simultaneously have a balance of payments deficit and a balance of trade surplus?

3. How does each part of the balance of payments relate to the supply and demand for currencies?

4. What are the four fundamental determinants of exchange rates?

5. If a county runs expansionary monetary policy, what will likely happen to the exchange rate?

6. If a country runs expansionary fiscal policy, what will likely happen to the exchange rate?

7. If the demand and supply for a country's currency depends upon demand for imports and exports, and demand for foreign and domestic assets, how can a country fix its exchange rate?

8. How do market exchange rates differ from exchange rates using the purchasing power parity concept?

9. How do inflation rate differentials affect the real exchange rate?

10. Differentiate among fixed, flexible, and partially flexible exchange rates.

12. You are advising Great Britain about whether it should join the European Monetary Union. What arguments can you give in support of joining? What arguments can you give against joining?

11. Which are preferable, fixed or flexible exchange rates?

MATCHING THE TERMS
Match the terms to their definitions

____ **1.** balance of merchandise trade

____ **2.** balance of payments

____ **3.** balance of trade

____ **4.** currency stabilization

____ **5.** currency support

____ **6.** current account

____ **7.** financial and capital account

____ **8.** fixed exchange rate

____ **9.** flexible exchange rate

____ **10.** forex market

____ **11.** official reserves

____ **12.** partially flexible exchange rate

____ **13.** purchasing power parity

____ **14.** real exchange rate

a. A method of calculating exchange rates that attempts to value currencies at a rate so that each will buy an equal basket of goods.

b. A country's record of all transactions between its residents and the residents of all foreign countries.

c. A regime in which government sometimes affects the exchange rate and sometimes leaves it to the market.

d. A regime in which a government chooses an exchange rate and offers to buy and sell currencies at that rate.

e. A regime in which the determination of the value of a currency is left up to the market.

f. The buying of a currency by a government to maintain its value above its long-run equilibrium.

g. The difference between the value of goods and services a nation exports and the value of goods and services it imports.

h. Government holdings of foreign currencies.

i. The part of the balance of payments account that lists all long-term flows of payments.

j. The part of the balance of payments account that lists all short-term flows of payments.

k. The difference between the value of the goods exported and the value of the goods imported.

l. Foreign exchange market.

m. Buying and selling of a currency by the government to offset temporary fluctuations.

n. Exchange rate adjusted for inflation differentials.

● PROBLEMS AND APPLICATIONS

1. State for each whether the transaction shows up on the balance of payments current account, the balance of payments capital account or neither.

    a. An American buys 100 stocks of Mercedes Benz, a German company.

    b. A Japanese businessperson buys Ameritec, an American bank.

    c. An American auto manufacturer buys $20 million in auto parts from a Japanese company.

    d. An American buys 100 shares of IBM stock.

    e. Saturn exports 10,000 cars to Germany.

    f. Toyota Motor Corporation, a Japanese firm, makes a $1 million profit from its plant in Kentucky, USA.

2. For each of the following, state who is demanding and who is supplying what currency:

    a. A French person buys a set of china from a U.S. firm.

    b. A U.S. tourist in Japan buys a Japanese kimono from a department store.

    c. An Italian exchange rate trader believes that the exchange rate value of the dollar will rise.

    d. A Swiss investor invests in Germany.

3. Draw supply and demand curves for British pounds, showing equilibrium quantity and price. Price is shown by price of pounds in dollars.

    a. What is the demand for dollars in this case?

    b. Explain a movement up along the supply curve.

    c. Explain a movement down along the demand curve.

    d. What would be the effect on the price of pounds of an increase in demand for pounds by the British? Show this graphically.

    e. What would be the effect on the price of pounds of an increase in demand for dollars by the British? Show this graphically.

4. For each of the following, show graphically what would happen to the market for British pounds. Assume there are only two countries, the United States and Britain.

    a. Income in Britain rises.

b. Income in the United States rises.

c. The prices of goods in the United States increase.

d. Interest rates rise in Britain.

e. The value of the pound is expected to fall.

5. State what will happen to the real exchange rate of the dollar in the following instances:

a. U.S. inflation is 2 percent, Japan's inflation is 5 percent, the U.S. dollar rises 3 percent.

b. U.S. inflation is 4 percent, Japan's inflation is 1 percent, the U.S. dollar rises 2 percent.

c. U.S. deflation is 1 percent, Japan's inflation is 1 percent, the U.S. dollar falls 4 percent.

d. U.S. inflation is 5 percent, Japan's inflation is 2 percent, the U.S. dollar falls 1 percent.

● A BRAIN TEASER

1. What could cause the U.S. to temporarily experience an increase in its balance of payments deficit even though there is downward movement in the exchange rate value of the dollar? (Hint: Think in terms of demand and supply analysis.)

● MULTIPLE CHOICE

Circle the one best answer for each of the following questions:

1. An exchange rate is the:
   a. rate the Fed charges commercial banks for loans.
   b. rate the Fed charges individuals for loans.
   c. rate at which one country's currency can be exchanged for another country's currency.
   d. speed at which exchange occurs.

2. If a country has perfectly flexible exchange rates and is running a current account deficit, it is running:
   a. a financial and capital account surplus.
   b. a financial and capital account deficit.
   c. an official transactions surplus.
   d. an official transactions deficit.

3. In the balance of payments accounts, net investment income shows up in:
   a. the current account.
   b. the financial and capital account.
   c. the government financial account.
   d. Net investment income is not an entry in the balance of payments.

4. If the government financial account is significantly in surplus, the country is likely:
   a. trying to hold up its exchange rate.
   b. trying to push down its exchange rate.
   c. trying to have no effect on its exchange rate.
   d. sometimes trying to increase and sometimes trying to decrease its exchange rate.

5. In recent years, the United States has:
   a. generally run a balance of trade surplus.
   b. generally run a balance of trade deficit.
   c. sometimes run a balance of trade surplus and sometimes run a balance of trade deficit.
   d. generally run a balance of trade equality.

6. In recent years, the United States has:
   a. generally run a financial and capital account surplus.
   b. generally run a financial and capital account deficit.
   c. sometimes run a financial and capital account surplus and sometimes run a financial and capital account deficit.
   d. generally run a financial and capital account equality.

7. If there is a black market for a currency, the country probably has:
   a. nonconvertible currency.
   b. a fixed exchange rate currency.
   c. a flexible exchange rate currency.
   d. a partially flexible exchange rate currency.

8. Assuming flexible exchange rates, if the European demand for U.S. imports increases, one would expect the price of euros in terms of dollars to:
   a. rise.
   b. fall.
   c. remain unchanged.
   d. sometimes rise and sometimes fall.

9. Assuming flexible exchange rates, if the U.S. demand for European imports increases, one would expect the price of euros in terms of dollars to:
   a. rise.
   b. fall.
   c. remain unchanged.
   d. sometimes rise and sometimes fall.

   Use the following graph to answer Questions 10 – 12:

   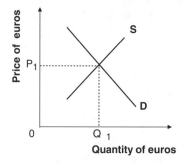

10. If U.S. income increases the:
    a. supply curve will shift out to the right.
    b. supply curve will shift in to the left.
    c. demand curve will shift out to the right.
    d. demand curve will shift in to the left.

11. If European interest rates increase relative to world interest rates:
    a. only the supply curve will shift out to the right.
    b. only the demand curve will shift in to the left.
    c. the supply curve will shift in to the left and the demand curve will shift out to the right.
    d. the supply curve will shift out to the right and the demand curve will shift in to the left.

12. If European inflation increases relative to world inflation:
    a. only the supply curve will shift out to the right.
    b. only the demand curve will shift in to the left.
    c. the supply curve will shift in to the left and the demand curve will shift out to the right.
    d. the supply curve will shift out to the right and the demand curve will shift in to the left.

13. If a country with flexible exchange rates runs expansionary monetary policy, in the short run one would expect the value of its exchange rate to:
    a. rise.
    b. fall.
    c. be unaffected.
    d. sometimes rise and sometimes fall.

14. Expansionary monetary policy has a tendency to:
    a. push interest rates up and exchange rates down.
    b. push interest rates down and exchange rates down.
    c. push income down and exchange rates down.
    d. push imports down and exchange rates down.

15. Contractionary monetary policy has a tendency to:
    a. push interest rates up and exchange rates down.
    b. push interest rates down and exchange rates down.
    c. push income down and imports down.
    d. push imports down and exchange rates down.

16. Refer to the graph below. If the U.S. government wants to fix its convertible currency at exchange rate P_1, it will have to:

    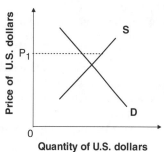

a. supply official reserves in exchange for dollars.

b. supply dollars in exchange for official reserves.

c. disallow currency conversion except at the official rate P_1.

d. supply both official reserves and dollars because excess supply of dollars is so large.

17. Say the Bangladeshi taka is valued at 42 taka to $1. Also say that you can buy the same basket of goods for 10 taka that you can buy for $1. In terms of dollars the purchasing power parity of the taka is:

a. overvalued.

b. undervalued.

c. not distorted.

d. non convertible.

18. Suppose inflation in the United States is 3 percent and inflation in Europe is 4 percent. If the U.S. dollar exchange rate falls by 5 percent relative to the euro, the real exchange rate of the dollar relative to the euro has:

a. risen 2 percent.

b. risen 6 percent.

c. fallen 2 percent.

d. fallen 6 percent.

19. If a country has fixed exchange rates:

a. the government need not worry about the exchange rate.

b. governments are committed to buying and selling currencies at a fixed rate.

c. the exchange rate is set by law.

d. the exchange rate has a fixed component and a flexible component.

20. If a country has a flexible exchange rate, the exchange rate:

a. is determined by flexible government policy.

b. is determined by market forces.

c. fluctuates continually, changing by at least 1 percent per year.

d. fluctuates continually, changing by at least 10 percent per year.

21. Compared to a fixed exchange rate system, a flexible exchange rate system:

a. allows countries more flexibility in their monetary policies.

b. allows countries less flexibility in their monetary policies.

c. has no effect on monetary policies.

d. allows countries more flexibility in their industrial policies.

22. A reason why a country might choose to join a currency union is:

a. so that its central bank can monetize the country's debt.

b. to broaden the marketplace by reducing costs of trade.

c. to reduce the demand for the common currency as a reserve currency.

d. to increase its sense of nationalism.

A1. The gold standard is a type of:

a. fixed exchange rate.

b. partially flexible exchange rate.

c. flexible exchange rate.

d. nonconvertible exchange rate.

A2. The gold specie flow mechanism works primarily by flows of:

a. money from one country to another.

b. services from one country to another.

c. merchandise from one country to another.

d. exchange rates from one country to another.

A3. Under the gold standard, if a country has a balance of payments deficit:

a. gold would flow out of the country.

b. gold would flow into the country.

c. the country's exchange rate would rise.

d. the country's exchange rate would fall.

A4. SDRs refers to:

a. Specie Draft Rights.

b. Specie Drawing Rights.

c. Special Drawing Rights.

d. Special Draft Rights.

● POTENTIAL ESSAY QUESTIONS

You may also see essay questions similar to the "Problems & Applications" and "Brain Teasers" exercises.

1. How are a government's exchange rate policy and the government financial account in the balance of payments related? Is it easier for a government to push the value of its currency up or down? Why?

2. Explain how fixed, flexible (or floating), and partially flexible exchange rates are determined. What are the advantages and the disadvantages of each? Why do most nations have a partially flexible exchange rate policy?

ANSWERS

SHORT-ANSWER QUESTIONS

1. The balance of payments is a country's record of all transactions between its residents and the residents of all foreign nations. It is divided into the current account, the capital account, and the official transactions account. The balance of trade is one part of the balance of payments—specifically that part dealing with goods. It is not all that satisfactory a measure of the country's position in international markets since it does not include services. Generally, economists pay more attention to the combined balance on goods and services account. (796-798)

2. As discussed in question 1, the balance of trade is one part of the balance of payments. Thus, if other parts of the international payments —for example, the capital account— are in deficit, the balance of trade could still be in surplus. (798-800)

3. The balance of payments records the flow of a currency in and out of a country (1) in order to buy and sell goods and services in the current account, (2) in order to buy and sell assets along with payments resulting from previous purchases of assets in the capital account, and (3) in order to affect the value of a country's currency in the official transactions account. To buy foreign goods and assets one must supply domestic currency and demand foreign currency. Therefore, the balance of payments records the demand and supply of a country's currency during a given period of time. (801-802)

4. Four fundamental determinants of the value of a country's exchange rate are (1) domestic income, (2) domestic price level, (3) domestic interest rates, and (4) trade restrictions. (802)

5. Expansionary monetary policy tends to push income and prices up and interest rates down. All these phenomena tend to push the exchange rate down. (803-804)

6. Expansionary fiscal policy tends to push income, prices, and interest rates up. Higher income and higher prices increase imports and put downward pressure on exchange rates.

Higher interest rates push exchange rates in the opposite direction, so the net effect of expansionary fiscal policy on exchange rates is unclear. (803-804)

7. The current account and capital account reflect private demand and supply of a country's currency. If the official transactions account were zero, then the currency's value is market-determined. If a country wants to fix the value of its currency to maintain its value at the fixed value, the government must buy and sell its currency using official reserves. Buying (selling) one's own currency shows up as a positive (negative) in the official transactions account. (806-807)

8. Market exchange rates are determined by the demand and supply of a country's currency. Since not all goods, services, and assets produced in a country can be traded internationally, the value of an exchange rate may not reflect the relative prices in each country. The purchasing power parity concept adjusts the value of a country's currency by determining the rate at which equivalent baskets of goods can be purchased in each country. (809-811)

9. If inflation is higher in a foreign country compared to the domestic country, and the nominal exchange rate doesn't change, the real exchange rate for the domestic country will fall. This is because the domestic currency will not be able to purchase as many foreign goods as before the foreign inflation. (811)

10. A fixed exchange rate is an exchange rate that the government chooses and then holds, by standing ready to buy and sell at that rate. Flexible exchange rates are exchange rates that are determined by the market without any government intervention. Partially flexible exchange rates are exchange rates that are determined by the market but are sometimes also affected by government intervention. (812)

11. It depends. Each has its advantages and disadvantages. Flexible exchange rates give a country more control over domestic policy, but can also cause large fluctuations in the value of the countries currency, hurting trade. With fixed exchange rates, such fluctuations can be avoided. (812-814)

12. The disadvantages of joining the European Monetary Union are that Great Britain would have to give up the pound as its currency, a source of national pride and it would have to give up independent monetary policy. The advantages are that if the euro becomes an important reserve currency, Britain will enjoy lower interest rates and its producers and consumers will have greater access to a larger market. (814-816)

━━━ **ANSWERS** ━━━

MATCHING

1-k; 2-b; 3-g; 4-m; 5-f; 6-j; 7-i; 8-d; 9-e; 10-l; 11-h; 12-c; 13-a; 14-n.

━━━ **ANSWERS** ━━━

PROBLEMS AND APPLICATIONS

1.
  a. Capital account. This is a long-term outflow. (797-800)
  b. Capital account. This is a long-term inflow. (797-800)
  c. Current account. These are merchandise imports, a short-term flow. (797-800)
  d. Neither. It is a domestic transaction. (797-800)
  e. Current account. These are merchandise exports, a short-term flow. (797-800)
  f. Current account. This is net investment income. (797-800)

2.
  a. The French person supplies euros and demands dollars because the French person must sells euros to get U.S. dollars to purchase the china. (800-802)
  b. The U.S. tourist supplies dollars and demands Japanese yen because the tourist has to sell dollars to get yen. (800-802)
  c. The Italian trader will supply euros and demand U.S. dollars because he/she wants to purchase the currency that is believed to rise, the dollar. The trader must sell euros to get the dollars. (800-802)
  d. The Swiss investor will supply Swiss francs and demand euros because the

Swiss investor needs euros to invest in Germany. (800-802)

3. A market for British pounds is shown below. Price of pounds in U.S. dollars is on the vertical axis and quantity of pounds is on the horizontal axis. Equilibrium price and quantity is determined by where they intersect. (See Figure 33-1 on page 801)

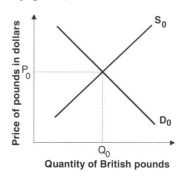

  a. If only two countries exist, the United States and Britain, the demand for dollars is the supply of pounds. (800-802)
  b. As the dollar value of the pound rises, individuals will supply more pounds. (800-802)
  c. As the dollar value of the pound declines, individuals will demand more pounds. (800-802)
  d. An increase in the demand for pounds by the British would shift the demand for pounds as shown in the graph below. The price of pounds in dollars would rise. (800-802)

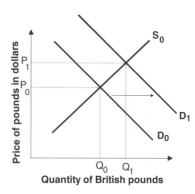

  e. An increase in the demand for dollars by the British is equivalent to an increase in the supply of pounds. The supply curve for pounds would shift to the right as shown in the graph below. The price of pounds in dollars would fall. (800-802)

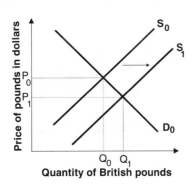

4. **a.** Demand for imports by the British rises; hence demand for dollars (supply of pounds) rises. This is shown in the graph below. (802-803)

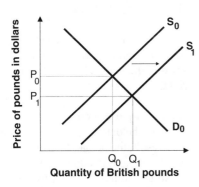

b. Demand for imports by Americans rises; hence demand for pounds rises. This is shown in the graph below. (802-803)

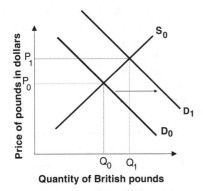

c. Demand for imports by the British falls; hence demand for dollars (supply of pounds) falls. This is shown in the graph below. (802-803)

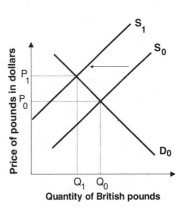

d. Demand for British assets will rise; hence the demand for the pound rises. This is shown in the graph below. (802-803)

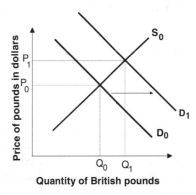

e. The demand for the pound falls. This is shown in the graph below. (802-803)

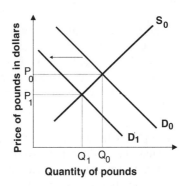

5. **a.** Remains the same. $[3+(2-5)]$. (811)
   b. Rises 5 percent $[2+(4-1)]$. (811)
   c. Falls 6 percent. $[-4+(-1-1)]$. (811)
   d. Rises 2 percent $[-1+(5-2)]$. (811)

ANSWERS

A BRAIN TEASER

1. A decrease in the demand for the dollar and/or an increase in the supply of the dollar in international exchange rate markets will create a temporary balance of payments deficit (because the quantity of dollars supplied will exceed the quantity demanded—imports will exceed exports). The balance of payments deficit will also put downward pressure on the exchange rate value of the dollar. (800-802)

ANSWERS

MULTIPLE CHOICE

1. c   An exchange rate is the rate at which one country's currency can be exchanged for another country's currency. See pages 800-801.

2. a   With perfectly flexible exchange rates the balance of payments must sum to zero; thus the financial and capital account must be in surplus if the current account is in deficit. The official transactions account could not be negative because if there are perfectly flexible exchange rates, there are no official transactions. See pages 797-798, 813-814.

3. a   Although net investment income might seem to many people as if it goes in the financial and capital account, it is a return for a service and is considered part of the current account, as is discussed on page 798.

4. a   A surplus in the government financial account means the balance of payments would otherwise be in deficit. The country is buying up its own currency. This means it is trying to hold up its exchange rate. See pages 801-802.

5. b   See page 799.

6. a   Running a financial and capital account

surplus is the other side of the balance sheet from the trade deficit. See pages 798-800.

7. a   All the others allow free exchange of currency and hence would not generate a black market. See page 811.

8. b   To purchase greater amounts of U.S. products, the European Union must increase the supply of euros, pushing down its value relative to the dollar. See pages 803-805.

9. a   To purchase greater amounts of European products, U.S. citizens must increase the supply of their currency, pushing down its value relative to the euro. That means that the value of the euro rises relative to the dollar. See pages 803-805.

10. c   If U.S. income increases, the U.S. demand for European imports will increase, shifting the demand for euros out to the right. See pages 803-805.

11. c   An increase in European interest rates will increase the demand for European assets. As a result, the demand for euros will shift out to the right. In addition, Europeans will substitute domestic assets for foreign assets shifting the supply of euros to the left. See pages 803-805.

12. d   An increase in European inflation will reduce the demand for European goods. Foreigners will demand fewer euros with which to buy European goods and Europeans will supply more euros as they exchange euros for other currencies to buy cheaper goods abroad. See pages 803-805.

13. b   This is a review question from the previous chapter. Expansionary monetary policy decreases interest rates and thereby tends to decrease the exchange rate in the short run. See pages 803-805.

14. b   See the diagram on page 804.

15. c   See the diagram on page 806.

16. a   At P_1, there is an excess supply of dollars. To keep the value of the dollar from falling, the U.S. will have to buy up that excess using official reserves of foreign currencies. Disallowing conversion except at an official rate would make the dollar a nonconvertible currency. See pages 807-808.

17. b   Since the purchasing power parity exchange rate is lower than the actual exchange rate, the taka is undervalued. See pages 809-811.

18. d   The real exchange rate has fallen 6 percent: $[-5+(3-4)]$. See page 811.

19. b   To keep the exchange rate at the stated amount governments must be willing to buy and sell currencies so that the quantity supplied and quantity demanded are always equal at the fixed rate. See page 812.

20. b   There are no predetermined levels of change with a flexible exchange rate. See pages 813-814.

21. a   Under a fixed exchange rate system, countries must use their monetary policies to meet international commitments. Thus flexible exchange rate policies allow them more flexibility in their monetary policies. Flexible exchange rates *may* allow them more flexibility in their industrial policies, but flexible exchange rates *definitely* do allow them more flexibility in their monetary policy, so a is the preferred answer. See pages 811-814.

22. b   A common currency reduces barriers to trade among member nations, thereby broadening the potential marketplace for domestic producers. See pages 814-816.

A1. a.   See page 821.

A2. a.   When there is an imbalance of trade in the gold system, gold—which is money—flows from the deficit country to the surplus country, pushing the price level down in the deficit country and up in the surplus country. This process brings about a trade balance equilibrium, eventually. See page 821.

A3. a   See page 821 about the flow of gold. The last two answers could be eliminated since the gold standard involves fixed exchange rates.

A4. c   As discussed on page 822, SDRs refers to Special Drawing Rights.

ANSWERS

POTENTIAL ESSAY QUESTIONS

The following are annotated answers. They indicate the general idea behind the answer.

1.   If a country is experiencing a balance of payments deficit (the quantity supplied of its currency exceeds the quantity demanded at the current exchange rate) then its currency will fall in value over time. A country's government could prevent its currency from falling (depreciating) by buying its own currency in exchange rate markets. If it does, then this shows up in the government financial account as a plus sign and we say that the government is supporting the value of its currency. The opposite is also true. Because a country can create and then sell its own currency, it is easier for a country to push the value of its currency down than up.

2.   See pages 811-814. Also, notice the "margin list" on page 811. Most nations have opted for a partially flexible exchange rate policy in order to try to get the advantages of both a fixed and a flexible exchange rate.

MACRO POLICY IN A GLOBAL SETTING

34

● CHAPTER AT A GLANCE

This review is based upon the learning objectives that open the chapter.

1a. There is significant debate about what U.S. international goals should be because exchange rates have conflicting effects and, depending on the state of the economy, there are arguments for high and low exchange rates. (824-825)

A high exchange rate (strong value of the $) helps hold down the prices of imports and therefore inflation. However, it creates a trade deficit that has a depressing effect on aggregate demand and therefore the income level.

1b. Running a trade deficit is good in the short run but presents problems in the long run; thus there is debate about whether we should worry about a trade deficit or not. (825-826)

Trade deficit→ imports > exports.

Short-run benefit: We are able to consume more than we would otherwise be able to.

Long-run cost: We have to sell off U.S. assets because we are consuming more than we are producing. All the future interest and profits on those assets will thus go to foreigners, not U.S. citizens.

A country with fixed exchange rates must give up any attempt to target domestic interest rates to achieve domestic goals.

2. Monetary policy affects the trade balance primarily through the income path as shown in the diagram on page 828. (827-828)

Expansionary monetary policy makes a trade deficit larger.

Contractionary monetary policy makes a trade deficit smaller.

Be able to explain why!

3. Fiscal policy affects the trade deficit primarily though the income path as shown in the diagram on page 829. (828-829)

Expansionary fiscal policy increases a trade deficit.

Contractionary fiscal policy decreases a trade deficit.

Be able to explain why!

4. Governments try to coordinate their monetary and fiscal policies because their economies are interdependent. (829-830)

Each country will likely do what's best for the world economy as long as it is also best for itself.

5. While internationalizing a country's debt may help in the short run, in the long run it presents potential problems, since foreign ownership of a country's debts means the country must pay interest to those foreign countries and that debt may come due. (831-832)

The U.S. has been internationalizing its debt since the early 1980s, which means that it must, at some point in the future, export more than it imports (consume less than it produces) to pay for this.

6. Macro policy must be conducted within the setting of a country's overall competitiveness. (832-833)

    In recent years the U.S. comparative advantage has been in assets, not produced goods. When foreigners cease wanting to purchase dollars or U.S. assets, the U.S. dollar will depreciate.

SHORT-ANSWER QUESTIONS

1. What should U.S. international goals be?

2. Why can a country achieve an interest rate target or an exchange rate target, but generally cannot achieve both at the same time?

3. Which dominates for a country: domestic or international goals? Why?

4. If a country runs contractionary monetary policy, what will likely happen to the trade balance?

5. If a country runs contractionary fiscal policy, what will likely happen to the trade balance?

6. Given the difficulty of doing so, why do countries try to coordinate their monetary and fiscal policies with other countries?

7. The United States in recent years has run a large current account deficit and has become the world's largest debtor nation. What are some of the potential problems that this presents?

8. If foreigners began to demand fewer U.S. assets, why might U.S. policymakers be forced to consider contractionary monetary and fiscal policy?

9. What would happen to U.S. comparative advantage in production of goods (as compared to assets) if the U.S. dollar fell?

PROBLEMS AND APPLICATIONS

1. You observe that over the past decade, a country's competitiveness has improved, reducing its trade deficit.

   a. What monetary or fiscal policies might have led to such results? Why?

b. You also observe that interest rates have steadily fallen along with a fall in the exchange rate. What monetary or fiscal policies might have led to such results?

2. You have been hired as an adviser to Fantasyland, a country with perfectly flexible exchange rates. State what monetary and fiscal policies you might suggest in each of the following situations. Explain your answers.

a. You want to increase domestic income and to reduce the exchange rate.

b. You want to reduce interest rates, reduce inflation, and reduce the trade deficit.

c. You want lower unemployment, lower interest rates, a lower exchange rate, and a lower trade deficit.

A BRAIN TEASER

1. Suppose a country has been running a significant expansionary fiscal policy for many years. Monetary policy has been neutral. What can you expect to have happened to this country's trade balance? What are the benefits and costs of this trade imbalance? If this country wishes to correct for its trade imbalance, what fiscal and monetary policies would you suggest this country pursue now? Will your recommended polices coincide or conflict with any of the country's domestic goals? If so, which goals?

MULTIPLE CHOICE

Circle the one best answer for each of the following questions:

1. Countries prefer:
   a. a high exchange rate.
   b. a low exchange rate.
   c. sometimes a low and sometimes a high exchange rate.
   d. a fixed exchange rate.

2. Countries prefer:
   a. a trade deficit.
   b. a trade surplus.
   c. sometimes a trade deficit and sometimes a trade surplus.
   d. a trade equilibrium.

3. If a country wants to maintain a fixed exchange rate above equilibrium, but does not have the necessary official reserves, it can:
   a. increase demand for its currency by running contractionary monetary policy.
   b. reduce the supply of its currency by running expansionary monetary policy.
   c. increase demand for its currency by running contractionary fiscal policy.
   d. increase supply of its currency by running expansionary fiscal policy.

4. If the trade deficit has gone up, it is most likely that the government ran:
   a. an expansionary monetary policy.
   b. a contractionary monetary policy.
   c. a contractionary fiscal policy.
   d. an expansionary monetary policy and a contractionary fiscal policy.

5. Expansionary monetary policy tends to push income:
   a. down and the trade deficit down.
   b. down and the trade deficit up.
   c. up and the trade deficit down.
   d. up and the trade deficit up.

6. Contractionary fiscal policy tends to push
   a. income down and imports up.
   b. income down and the trade deficit up.
   c. income down and the trade deficit down.
   d. prices down and imports up.

7. Assume the United States would like to raise its exchange rate and lower its trade deficit. It would pressure Japan to run:
   a. contractionary monetary policy.
   b. contractionary fiscal policy.
   c. expansionary monetary policy
   d. expansionary fiscal policy.

8. According to the textbook, generally, when international goals and domestic goals conflict:
   a. the international goals win out.
   b. the domestic goals win out.
   c. sometimes it's a toss-up which will win out.
   d. international monetary goals win out but international fiscal goals lose out.

9. When a country runs a large trade deficit, the amount of crowding out that occurs because of fiscal policy is:
   a. increased.
   b. decreased.
   c. unaffected.
   d. sometimes increased and sometimes decreased.

10. A country has the greatest domestic policy flexibility with:
    a. fixed exchange rates.
    b. flexible exchange rates.
    c. a trade deficit.
    d. a trade surplus.

11. A sudden fall in the price of the dollar in terms of other countries' currencies will most likely make policy makers face the possibility of implementing:
    a. capital inflow controls.
    b. import subsidies.
    c. contractionary macro policy.
    d. expansionary macro policy.

POTENTIAL ESSAY QUESTIONS

You may also see essay questions similar to the "Problems & Applications" and "Brain Teasers" exercises.

1. If there was initially a trade balance, what kind of trade imbalance would be created by an increase in the exchange rate value of the dollar (a stronger dollar)? Why?

2. What are the benefits and costs to the U.S. of having a strong dollar–a high exchange rate value of the dollar?

3. Why do domestic economic goals usually dominate international economic goals?

ANSWERS

SHORT-ANSWER QUESTIONS

1. By "international goals" economists usually mean the exchange rate and the trade balance that policymakers should shoot for. There is significant debate in the United States about what our international goals should be, and there are arguments for both high and low exchange rates, and for both trade deficits and trade surpluses. The argument for a high exchange rate is that it lowers the cost of imports; the argument against it is that it raises the price of exports, making U.S. goods less competitive. The argument in favor of a trade deficit is that it allows a country to consume more than it produces; the argument against is that a trade deficit will have to be paid off at some point. (824-826)

2. Because monetary policy affects the value of one's currency, a country cannot target both interest rates and exchange rates simultaneously. Suppose one's currency is at its desired level, but interest rates are too high. Expansionary monetary policy would lower the interest rate, but a lower interest rate reduces foreign demand for the country's interest-bearing assets. The demand for one's currency will shift in to the left and its exchange rate will fall. Likewise, citizens of the country will invest elsewhere and the supply of one's currency will shift out to the right. The value of one's currency will be lower than its target. (824-826)

3. Generally, domestic goals dominate for two reasons. (1) International goals are often ambiguous, as discussed in answer 1 above and (2) international goals affect a country's population indirectly and, in politics, indirect effects take a back seat. (826-827)

4. Contractionary monetary policy tends to push income down. Lower income means lower imports, lowering the trade deficit. (828-829)

5. Contractionary fiscal policy pushes income down. This tends to decrease imports and decrease a trade deficit. (831-832)

6. The policies of one country affect the economy of another. So it is only natural that the two countries try to coordinate their policies. It is also only natural that since voters are concerned with their own countries, coordination is difficult to achieve unless it is in the interest of both countries. (832-833)

7. While internationalizing a country's debt may help in the short run, in the long run it presents potential problems, since foreign ownership of a country's debts means the debtor country must pay interest to the foreign countries, and also, that debt may come due. (833-834)

8. If foreigners begin to demand fewer U.S. assets, the financial and capital account surplus would fall and there would be downward pressure on the price of the U.S dollar. A dramatic decline in the price of the dollar would cause inflation to rise. If that happened policymakers would likely consider contractionary monetary policy to stem the decline in the dollar and the acceleration of inflation. (832-833)

9. If the U.S. dollar fell, U.S. goods would be less expensive to foreigners, improving the U.S. comparative advantage in a number of produced goods. (832-833)

ANSWERS

PROBLEMS AND APPLICATIONS

1. a. An increase in competitiveness and a decrease in the trade deficit are probably due to contractionary fiscal policy. Contractionary fiscal policy reduces inflation, improves competitiveness, and decreases income, which reduces imports. Improved competitiveness and decreased income both work to reduce the trade deficit. Contractionary monetary policy would also reduce the trade deficit, but its effect on competitiveness is ambiguous. (828-832)
    b. If interest rates have also fallen, it is likely that fiscal policy has been very contractionary because contractionary monetary policy would have led to higher interest rates and a higher exchange rate value of the dollar. (828-832)

2. **a.** Expansionary monetary policy will reduce the exchange rate through its effect on interest rates and will increase domestic income. Expansionary fiscal policy will increase domestic income. The increase in income will increase imports, which will tend to decrease the exchange rate, but higher interest rates will tend to lead to a higher exchange rate. The effect of expansionary fiscal policy on exchange rates is therefore ambiguous. (828-832)

   b. Contractionary fiscal policy will tend to reduce inflation and interest rates. The reduction in inflation will improve competitiveness and a reduction in income will reduce imports. Both work to reduce the trade deficit. (828-832)

   c. Expansionary monetary policy will reduce unemployment and reduce interest rates. Lower interest rates will tend to make exchange rates fall. Expansionary monetary policy, however, will make the trade deficit higher. Expansionary fiscal policy will also reduce unemployment. Interest rates, however, will rise and so will the trade deficit. This mix of goals is difficult to attain. (828-832)

ANSWERS

A BRAIN TEASER

1. Because of the expansionary fiscal policy, this country will have moved in the direction of a trade deficit. The benefit of the trade deficit is that the country has been able to consume more than it has produced. The cost, however, is that it has had to sell off some of its assets. All the future interest and profits on these assets will now go to foreigners, not the country's citizens.

   To reduce the trade deficit the country should pursue contractionary fiscal and monetary policies. This will reduce imports and increase exports and increase the country's competitiveness in the global economy. That's good. However, even though fewer imports and greater exports should help stimulate aggregate expenditures, the effects of the contractionary fiscal and monetary policies are also simultaneously at play. Aggregate demand may fall on balance. If it does, then you may have created a recession. That's bad. Sometimes, countries can find themselves "in a pickle." (There could be other effects associated with the prescribed contractionary policies.) (826-832)

ANSWERS

MULTIPLE CHOICE

1. **c** The answer is "sometimes a low and sometimes a high exchange rate" because, as discussed on pages 824-825, there are rationales for both.

2. **c** The domestic economy's needs change over time and as they do, so does the country's preferred trade situation. Both a deficit and a surplus have their advantages and disadvantages. See pages 825-826.

3. **a** Contractionary monetary policy will increase the demand for one's currency and increase its value. Contractionary fiscal policy will reduce the supply of one's currency and increase its value. Contractionary monetary and fiscal policy are two ways to fix one's exchange rate without intervening in the exchange market. See page 828.

4. **a** Both expansionary monetary policy and expansionary fiscal policy increase the trade deficit. Thus, only a fits. See the discussion and charts on pages 828-829.

5. **d** See the discussion on pages 828-830 and the diagram on page 828.

6. **c** See diagram on page 829 and the discussion on pages 828-830.

7. **c** The effect of fiscal policy on the exchange rate is ambiguous, so the only sure option is c. See the box on page 830.

8.   b   As discussed in the text on pages 829-830, usually, because of political considerations, domestic goals win out.

9.   b   Since the trade deficit means capital is flowing into the country, the capital usually ends up buying some government debt, which reduces crowding out, as discussed on pages 831-832.

10.   b   When exchange rates are left to the market (flexible), the government does not have to change its domestic policy to meet its international goal for its exchange rate. Therefore, it is freer to follow domestic policy when exchange rates are flexible. See page 832.

11.   c   If the price of the dollar falls significantly in the forex market, policy makers will likely be under pressure to slow the fall and prevent inflation, which means that they will have to face the possibility of implementing contractionary policy to keep the dollar from falling too much. The other options are not ones associated with a falling price of the dollar. See pages 833-834.

━━ ANSWERS ━━

POTENTIAL ESSAY QUESTIONS

The following are annotated answers. They indicate the general idea behind the answer.

1. A stronger dollar means that a single dollar will now buy more units of a foreign currency. This makes foreign products cheaper to Americans. The U.S. would import more. At the same time, a stronger dollar means it will now take more units of a foreign currency to buy a single dollar. This will cause U.S. goods to become more expensive to foreigners. The U.S. would export less. The combined effects of more U.S. imports and fewer U.S. exports means a trade deficit will be created or will get larger in the U.S.

2. A strong dollar holds down the price of imports and therefore inflation. However, the cost is a trade deficit that would have a depressing effect on total spending and therefore on the nation's income level (there would be an especially depressing effect on the nation's exporting industries).

3. First, there is more agreement on domestic goals. Second, domestic goals affect people within one's country more directly. Finally, pursuing domestic goals is politically more appealing.

Pretest
Chapters 31-34

Take this test in test conditions, giving yourself a limited amount of time to complete the questions. Ideally, check with your professor to see how much time he or she allows for an average multiple choice question and multiply this by 20. This is the time limit you should set for yourself for this pretest. If you do not know how much time your teacher would allow, we suggest 1 minute per question, or 20 minutes.

1. A deficit is:
   a. the total amount of money that a country owes.
   b. the shortfall of payments under revenues in a particular time period.
   c. the shortfall of revenues under payments in a particular time period.
   d. accumulated debt.

2. If the nominal surplus is $200 billion, inflation is 10 percent, and total debt is $2 trillion:
   a. the real surplus is zero.
   b. the real deficit is $100 billion
   c. the real surplus is $400 billion.
   d. the real surplus is $2.2 trillion.

3. The portion of the budget deficit or surplus that would exist even if the economy were at its potential level of income is called the:
   a. structural deficit or surplus.
   b. passive deficit or surplus.
   c. primary deficit or surplus.
   d. secondary deficit or surplus.

4. One of the reasons government debt is different from individual debt is:
   a. government does not pay interest on its debt.
   b. government never really needs to pay back its debt.
   c. all government debt is owed to other government agencies or to its own citizens.
   d. the ability of a government to pay off is debt is unrelated to income.

5. The "real" problem of Social Security in 2017 could be solved by:
   a. locking up the Social Security Trust Fund to pay for Social Security benefits only.
   b. raising the eligibility age for Social Security so fewer people are collecting Social Security in 2017, raising taxes on workers in 2017, increasing taxes on Social Security benefits in 2017, or a combination of all three.
   c. allowing current workers to divert some of their payroll taxes into private savings accounts to be withdrawn at retirement.
   d. a rise in the value of the stock market that would raise the value of the Social Security Trust fund so that it remains solvent for longer.

6. Two methods of comparing income among countries are the purchasing power parity method and the exchange rate method. Of these:
   a. the exchange rate method generally gives a higher relative measure to the income in developing countries.
   b. the purchasing power parity method generally gives a higher relative measure to the income in developing countries.
   c. the purchasing power parity and exchange rate methods generally give approximately equal measures of the income in developing countries.
   d. sometimes one gives a higher relative measure to income in developing countries, and sometimes the other gives a higher relative measure.

7. The revenue of an inflation tax:
   a. goes only to government.
   b. goes only to private individuals.
   c. goes to both private individuals and government.
   d. is a meaningless term because there is no revenue from an inflation tax.

8. Conditionality refers to:
a. the U.S. government's policy of only making loans to countries subject to specific conditions.
b. the IMF's policy of making loans to countries who will repay loans.
c. central banks' policies of making loans to firms only under certain conditions.
d. the conditions under which inter-firm credit is allowed in transitional economies.

9. If population grows geometrically, the amount of land is fixed, and there is diminishing marginal productivity, then:
a. famine is in the future.
b. income per person will decrease but there will not necessarily be famine.
c. famine is not in the future if there is technological development.
d. famine may or may not be in the future.

10. If a country has perfectly flexible exchange rates and is running a current account deficit, it is running:
a. a financial and capital account surplus.
b. a financial and capital account deficit.
c. an official transactions surplus.
d. an official transactions deficit.

11. In recent years, the United States has:
a. generally run a balance of trade surplus.
b. generally run a balance of trade deficit.
c. sometimes run a balance of trade surplus and sometimes run a balance of trade deficit.
d. generally run a balance of trade equality.

12. Assuming flexible exchange rates, if the European demand for U.S. imports increases, one would expect the price of euros in terms of dollars to:
a. rise.
b. fall.
c. remain unchanged.
d. sometimes rise and sometimes fall.

13. Refer to the graph following. If U.S. income increases the:
a. supply curve will shift out to the right.
b. supply curve will shift in to the left.
c. demand curve will shift out to the right.
d. demand curve will shift in to the left.

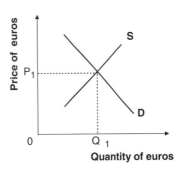

14. If a country with flexible exchange rates runs expansionary monetary policy, in the short run one would expect the value of its exchange rate to:
a. rise.
b. fall.
c. be unaffected.
d. sometimes rise and sometimes fall.

15. Suppose inflation in the United States is 3 percent and inflation in Europe is 4 percent. If the U.S. dollar exchange rate falls by 5 percent relative to the euro, the real exchange rate of the dollar relative to the euro has:
a. risen 2 percent.
b. risen 6 percent.
c. fallen 2 percent.
d. fallen 6 percent.

16. If a country has a flexible exchange rate, the exchange rate:
a. is determined by flexible government policy.
b. is determined by market forces.
c. fluctuates continually, changing by at least 1 percent per year.
d. fluctuates continually, changing by at least 10 percent per year.

17. Compared to a fixed exchange rate system, a flexible exchange rate system:
a. allows countries more flexibility in their monetary policies.
b. allows countries less flexibility in their monetary policies.
c. has no effect on monetary policies.
d. allows countries more flexibility in their industrial policies.

18. If a country wants to maintain a fixed exchange rate above equilibrium, but does not have the necessary official reserves, it can:
  a. increase demand for its currency by running contractionary monetary policy.
  b. reduce the supply of its currency by running expansionary monetary policy.
  c. increase demand for its currency by running contractionary fiscal policy.
  d. increase supply of its currency by running expansionary fiscal policy.

19. If the trade deficit has gone up, it is most likely that the government ran:
  a. an expansionary monetary policy.
  b. a contractionary monetary policy.
  c. an expansionary fiscal policy.
  d. a contractionary fiscal policy.

20. Expansionary fiscal policy tends to push income:
  a. down and the trade deficit down.
  b. down and the trade deficit up.
  c. up and the trade deficit down.
  d. up and the trade deficit up.

21. Assume the United States would like to raise its exchange rate and lower its trade deficit. It would pressure Japan to run:
  a. contractionary monetary policy.
  b. contractionary fiscal policy.
  c. expansionary monetary policy
  d. expansionary fiscal policy.

22. A country has the greatest domestic policy flexibility with:
  a. fixed exchange rates.
  b. flexible exchange rates.
  c. a trade deficit.
  d. a trade surplus.

ANSWERS

1.	c	(31:1)	**12.**	b	(33:8)
2.	c	(31:4)	**13.**	c	(33:10)
3.	a	(31:9)	**14.**	b	(33:13)
4.	b	(31:11)	**15.**	d	(33:18)
5.	b	(31:14)	**16.**	b	(33:20)
6.	b	(32:2)	**17.**	a	(33:21)
7.	c	(32:6)	**18.**	a	(34:3)
8.	b	(32:9)	**19.**	a	(34:4)
9.	d	(32:12)	**20.**	d	(34:5)
10.	a	(33:2)	**21.**	c	(34:7)
11.	b	(33:5)	**22.**	b	(34:10)

Key: The figures in parentheses refer to multiple choice question and chapter numbers. For example (1:2) is multiple choice question 2 from chapter 1.

ANSWERS TO EVEN-NUMBERED END-OF-CHAPTER QUESTIONS

The following answers are meant as guides to answering the end-of-chapter questions, not as definitive answers. The same questions often have many answers; this is especially true of policy-oriented questions. Although we have tried hard to see that mistakes are eliminated, the reality is that, as in any human endeavor, mistakes are inevitable. If you have checked and double-checked your answer and it is substantially different from that found here, assume that our answer is wrong, not yours. If you do come to a different answer, or think an answer misses an important aspect of the question, please check for corrections at my website to see if the answer has changed. If you don't find it there, please e-mail me at Colander@Middlebury.edu with your answer and an explanation of why you think it is better. I will get back to you and if I think you are right, I will post the change on the Web page marked "Corrections," together with your name and a thank-you.

⬤ CHAPTER 1 Questions for Thought and Review

2. The responses will be varied since this question asks individual students about choices they have made. In these responses students should be encouraged to consider all the costs and benefits, and to be clear about the concept of the marginal costs and marginal benefits; sunk costs should not be included in the decision-making process.

4. The opportunity cost of buying a $20,000 car is the benefit we would have gained by using that $20,000 for the next-best alternative, which could be spending it on other goods or saving it.

6. I would spend the $5 million on those projects that provide the highest marginal benefit per dollar spent. The opportunity cost of spending the money on one project is the lost benefit that the college would have received by spending it on some other project. Thus, another way to restate the decision rule is to spend the money on the project that minimizes opportunity cost per dollar.

8. Three ways (among many) that dormitory rooms could be rationed include: administrative decree, lottery, and a market system. In the first, individual behavior would be forced to fit the will of the administrator. Individuals would likely complain and try to influence the administrator's decision. In the second, individual behavior would be forced to fit the luck of the draw; individuals would likely attempt to trade rooms after the draw. In the final example, individual behavior would have already been subject to economic forces, and thus, there will be no tendency to trade after one has "bought" the room one can afford. Because administrative decree is not necessarily an efficient system, some people would likely attempt to trade rooms after the allocation.

10. It suggests that policy should be willing to give up more in possible gains to avoid losses than otherwise would be the case. Economic policies should be risk averse—more committed to maintaining the current standard of living than in risking economic losses by trying to improve it.

12. Two examples of political or legal forces are rent control laws and restrictions on immigration. They both prevent the invisible hand from working. The rent control laws place a price ceiling on rent, causing shortages of apartments, and the immigration restrictions cause the number of immigrants seeking entry to exceed those allowed to enter, which tends to cause wage rates to differ among countries.

14. No; economic theory proves nothing about what system is best. It simply gives ways to look at systems, and what the advantages and disadvantages of various systems will likely be. Normative decisions about what is best can only follow from one's value judgments.

16. Banks are economic institutions. They take a cost-benefit approach to deciding to whom to give loans and influence decision making by allowing individuals to spend more money than they either earn or have as wealth.

Problems and Exercises

2. **a.** The opportunity cost of attending college is the sacrifice one must make by attending college. It can be estimated by figuring out the benefit of the next-best alternative. If that alternative is working, one would guess the likely wage that could be earned at a job that does not require a college degree (minimum wage? more?) and then multiply by 40 hours for each week in college.

   b. The opportunity cost of taking this course could also be estimated using the same technique as in a if you otherwise would be working for these hours. If you had taken another course instead, the opportunity cost would be the benefit you would have received from taking that course.

   c. The opportunity cost of attending yesterday's lecture again would depend on what you otherwise could have done with the time (sleep? eat lunch with an interesting person?). Although this is no longer a choice to you, past activities do have opportunity costs.

4. **a.** It depends on the perspectives used to answer the question. From a pure economic perspective, we would conclude that it is reasonable to execute hackers based on cost benefit analysis. However, since this decision by no means can be simplified to pure economics, we need to take into consideration social, political, and religious factors. Therefore, Landsburg's argument should be evaluated in a more complete context.

   b. Cost benefit analysis can be extended to many areas, such as social welfare programs and almost all the policy discussions. (Source: "Feed the Worms Who Write the Worms to the Worms," http://slate.msn.com/id/2101297#ContinueArticle), *Slate Magazine*, May 26, 2004.)

6. **a.** Greater willingness to pay. Sponsorship of a stadium is a way of advertising a company and its products. Teams that are new to a city are expected to receive above-average media exposure and therefore greater benefits.

b. Greater willingness to pay. Corporations are willing to pay more at stadiums that are in more populated areas because their advertising will reach a larger number of people.

c. Lower willingness to pay. Stadiums with already well-established names are worth less because the current name is so highly recognized that it will take longer for people to adopt the new name. (Source: "What's in a Name? Price Variation in Sport Facility Naming Rights," Eastern Economic Journal, Fall 2003.)

8. The person who gains the kidney benefits if it works when transplanted into his or her body, and will no longer have the emotional and financial burden of dialysis. The person selling the kidney gains the $30,000. Their gains will also have impacts on others (their families, for example). Both parties must undergo surgery and face all of the attendant risks and costs. The seller also faces the potential cost of a future illness or injury harming his or her only remaining kidney causing a need for the seller to need dialysis. As to whether a society should allow this transaction, we must recognize that this is a question of value judgments and cultural norms. In our society we have chosen not to allow such transactions because (among other reasons) those with more money would have increased access to organs and would therefore have advantages over those of limited means, and the poor could be exploited in such transactions.

10. **a.** Micro with macro implications.
    b. Micro.
    c. Micro with macro implications.
    d. Micro.
    e. Micro.
    f. Macro with micro implications

12. **a.** Positive statement since it is a statement of fact.
    b. Normative.
    c. This could be seen as a positive statement since it is a statement of fact, although since it deals with normative issues, it could also be interpreted as a normative statement.
    d. Since this is relating a normative goal with a decision, this could be a statement in the art of economics. It could also be seen as a normative statement if one interprets it as a normative imperative.
    e. Positive statement since it is a statement of fact.

Web Questions

2. On www.movingideas.com we found an article about a case heard by the Supreme Court on April 1, 2003 to review University of Michigan's policy to promote a diverse student body. Whether their policy is legal depends on affirmative action laws, or legal forces. Another example of a political force is the United States-led war on Iraq in 2003. All major news organizations covered this event. We found an article on The American Prospect at www.prospect.org. The war affects business domestically and abroad.

● CHAPTER 2 Questions for Thought and Review

2. If there were decreasing marginal opportunity costs, the production possibility curve would be convex with respect to the origin instead of concave. This means that (in terms of the example on page 26 of the text) we would gain more and more guns for every pound of butter we give up. An example of this is found in a situation in which a practice makes perfect; i.e., smaller and smaller numbers of hours devoted to a task, or sport, will result in bigger and bigger gains in performance.

4. If a society became equally more productive in the production of both widgets and wadgets, the production possibility curve would shift out to the right as shown in the accompanying graph.

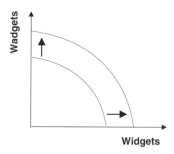

6. This statement can be true or false depending on the implicit assumptions made in the analysis. It is true since individuals will eliminate all inefficiencies they see through trading. It might be false if not everyone knows all the benefits and the inefficiencies, or does not have the opportunity to correct the inefficiencies, or if the costs of eliminating the inefficiency is too high.

8. There are no gains to trade when neither of two countries has a comparative advantage in either of two goods.

10. The fact that the production possibilities model tells us that trade is good does not mean that in the real world, free trade is the best policy. The production possibilities model does not take into account the importance of institutions and government in trade. For example, the model does not take into account externalities associated with some trades, the provision of public goods, or the need for a stable set of institutions of rules. The production possibility model shows maximum total output, but that is not the only societal goal to take into account when formulating policy.

12. Outsourcing is a product of the law of one price as it relates to the prices of factors. Because wages of workers in India and China are lower than in the United States, aspects of production that currently are done in the United States but can be done in China and India will tend to be outsourced as long as their workforce has the skills, their plants have the technology, and their countries have the necessary infrastructure. Net outsourcing will continue as long as the relative wage differential between the United States and China and India is such that it is more cost effective for firms to shift production. A fall in the U.S. exchange rate or a rise in Chinese wages are likely to slow and eventually stop outsourcing.

14. The six roles of government in a market economy are (1) providing a stable set of institutions and rules, (2) promoting effective and workable competition, (3) correcting for externalities, (4) ensuring economic stability and growth, (5) providing public goods, and (6) adjusting for undesired market results. Which of the six is the most controversial is open to debate. One possibility is the sixth role, adjusting for undesired market results. The problem is determining what results are "undersireable" and what rules should guide government in deciding on the desired result. Intervening in the market might create more problems than it solves.

16. Pollution permits require firms pay the cost of pollution they create. By making these permits tradable, firms that face the lowest cost of reducing pollution will reduce pollution emissions the most. Permits assign rights, thereby correcting for the externality.

Problems and Exercises

2. a. From the numbers alone, one would choose not to work because the opportunity cost of working is giving up an $80,000 increase in lifetime income while the benefit is $32,000 of income now. Although there is a correlation between working time and GPA, we cannot conclude that working an after-school job causes the decrease in GPA. Therefore one might be able to maintain a decent GPA while working. Moreover, earning money might be the priority for a particular student for a particular period of time, due to certain circumstances, such as saving for college that will lead to even greater lifetime earnings.

b. It depends on the particular student. Working takes time from study and thus might be a reason for the decrease in GPA. But the situation varies from student to student.

4. a. A Toyota in the U.S. costs 4/3 Chevrolets, while in Japan a Toyota costs 2 Chevrolets.

b. Japan has the comparative advantage in producing Chevrolets.

c. Since Japan has the comparative advantage in producing Chevrolets, it should produce Chevrolets and the U.S. should produce Toyotas, regardless of the fact that the U.S. demands more Chevrolets than Toyotas.

6. Following the hint that society's production possibility curve reflects more than just technical relationships, we realize that trust is an input to production to the extent that it is necessary for transactions. If everyone could fake honesty, the production possibility curve would shift inward since no one could trust anyone else leading to the disintegration of markets. If some could fake honesty, those few will gain at the expense of others. This is an example of the tragedy of the commons.

8. A merit good is a good that government believes is good for you even if you choose not to buy it. An example might be operas. A demerit good is a good that government believes is bad for you even if you choose to buy it. An example is alcohol or drugs. A public good is a good that if

supplied to one person must be supplied to all and whose consumption by one does not preclude the consumption by another. An example is national defense. An externality is the effect of a trade on a person not involved in the trade. An example is cigarette smoke.

a. Individuals might disagree as to the categorization of a good as a merit, demerit or public good or a good that involves an externality. In the case of an externality, they may believe that given sufficient property rights, the externality will be solved most efficiently by the market, not government.

b. We discuss the issues of market failure and government failure in the case of operas. There is market failure only if people do not value operas as much as they should. This normative statement is valid only if the "should" can be measured against some absolute truth as to the value of operas, otherwise how would one decide who decides the value of operas? Because it is only through the market that value is revealed, we'd argue that government intervention in this case will likely lead to government failure—the failure of government to accurately value operas. With government intervention, the value will likely reflect the preferences of those with political power, not necessarily those of the general population.

Web Questions

2. a. The defining belief of libertarians is that everyone should be free to do as they choose, so long as they don't infringe upon the equal freedom of others.

b. We were scored as centrists. We'd agree with this result. Government intervention can improve market results in certain cases. Government involvement in the market economy needs to be assessed on a case-by-case basis.

c. Libertarian's main objections to government regulation is that regulations limit an individual's choices, especially their choices about what to do with their property.

Appendix

2. See the accompanying graph.

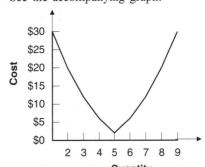

a. The relationship is nonlinear because it is not straight; it is curved.

b. From 0 to 5, cost declines as quantity rises (inverse). From 5 to 10, cost rises as quantity rises (direct).

c. From 0 to 5, the slope is negative (slopes down). From 5 to 10, the slope is positive (slopes up).

d. The slope between 1 and 2 units is the change in cost (30-20) divided by the change in quantity (1 - 2), or -10.

4. **a.** 1   **b.** −3   **c.** 1/3   **d.** −3/4   **e.** 0

6. **a.** See line a in the accompanying graph.
    b. See line b in the accompanying graph.
    c. See line c in the accompanying graph.

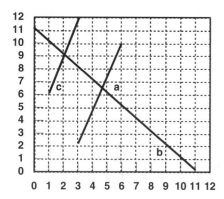

8. **a.** line graph.
    b. bar graph.
    c. pie chart.
    d. line graph.

● CHAPTER 3 Questions for Thought and Review

2. The central coordinating mechanism in Soviet-style socialism is the central planners.

4. Soviet-style socialism solves the three problems by using administrative control. Central planners decide what to produce according to what they believe is socially beneficial. Central planners decide how to produce guided by what they believe is good for the country. Central planners decide distribution based on their perception of individuals' needs.

6. Markets have little role in most families. In most families decisions about who gets what are usually made by benevolent parents. Because families are small and social bonds strong, this benevolence can work. Thus, a socialist organization seems more appropriate to a family and a market-based organization to a large economy where social bonds don't hold the social unit together. The propensity to look after the common good is much stronger in a family than in an entire economy.

8. An economy depends on coordination, and the mechanisms of coordination depend on the people who choose which goods to supply and what to demand. People supply the labor that makes the economy run. Economic growth, and what is considered a resource depend on technology, and people develop new technologies. Even the institutions that oversee the economy are governed by that economy's people. It follows that the economy's ultimate strength resides in its people.

0. Business is dynamic; it involves meeting new problems constantly, recognizing needs, and meeting those needs in a timely fashion. These are precisely the skills of entrepreneurship.

12. The two largest categories of federal expenditures are income security and health and education.

14. The Internet has added competition by increasing the amount of information available to consumers and reducing the importance of geographic location to production and sales. Increasing the amount of information to consumers lowers the cost of comparison shopping, which gives consumers more negotiating power with sellers. Because location doesn't matter, the Internet broadens the potential marketplace for both inputs and outputs, increasing competitive pressures in both factor and goods markets by increasing the number of suppliers.

16. Convergence is more likely to occur for four reasons: (1) India and China have adopted more market-based economic systems in the past decade, making them stronger competitors; (2) these countries have large numbers of well-educated workers, (3) they have increasing access to capital and technology, and (4) they are developing the infrastructure needed to increase their economic competitiveness.

Problems and Exercises

2. **a.** The fact that more money is spent on adults than on children in the family does not imply that the children are deprived or that the distribution is unfair. Children and adults have different needs. Moreover, it is the parents who earn the money, so it is only through their beneficence, and requirements of law, that they provide for their children at all.
    b. Yes, these percentages probably change with income. The lower the income, the larger the percent of total expenditures spent on children. The reason is that most families want to provide a basic level of needs for their children. Many families feel that luxuries should not be given to children until the children have learned how to work for them themselves.
    c. Our suspicion is that the allocation would not be significantly different in Soviet-style socialist countries as compared to capitalist countries. If, however, the average income in socialist countries were lower, the percentage of total expenditure spent on children might be higher, as described in b.

4. **a.** Innovation requires a certain level of freedom of thought and a possibility of profit-making from the innovation. Neither was the case with Soviet-style socialism. Government planners directed production with income based on need, so workers had neither the freedom nor the incentive to innovate.
    b. Both freedom and the possibility of making profits provide the means and incentives for innovation in capitalist countries.
    c. Schumpeter's argument was based on the idea that profit-making by innovators was necessary for innovation to occur. As firms become larger, however, the individual ceases to become the direct beneficiary of his or her innovations.
    d. Since his predictions did not materialize, one must believe either that firms have been able to create

incentive structures to foster innovation or that some other venue for innovation has arisen. Firms have large research and development departments designed to promote innovation. In addition, individual innovators have been able to raise enough capital to start their own companies to profit directly from their innovations. In the United States there has been enormous growth in the number of such firms. The U.S. government has been a large motivator of innovation through its strong patent and copyright system, as well as providing subsidies for research at universities and support of military innovations, both of which have large spillovers into private industry.

Web Questions

2. In the 1930s, government intervened very little in the market. During the Depression, however, as many people became unemployed and needed assistance, the role of government expanded and capitalism's evolution away from a pure market economy began. The Social Security Act was signed into law in 1935. The Act established two programs–a pension program for retired workers and an income support program for the unemployed. Both are administered by the federal government. In the late 1990s and early 2000s, there have been proposals to privatize portions of the Social Security system, giving workers more say about where their money is invested. This would move the pendulum back toward a market economy.

● CHAPTER 4 Questions for Thought and Review

2. The law of supply states that quantity supplied rises as price increases or, alternatively, that quantity supplied falls as price decreases. Price is directly related to quantity supplied because, as price rises, people and firms rearrange their activities to supply more of that good in order to take advantage of the higher price.

4. A change in the price causes a movement along the demand curve, a movement to a new point on the same curve. A shift in the demand curve means that the quantities will be different at all prices; the entire curve shifts.

6. Shift factors of supply include the price of inputs, technological advances, changes in expectations, and taxes and subsidies. As the price of inputs increase, the supply curve shifts to the left. As technological advances are made that reduce the cost of production, the supply curve shifts to the right. If a supplier expects the price of her good to rise, she may decrease supply now to save and sell later. Other expectational effects are also possible. Taxes paid by suppliers shift the supply curve to the left. Subsidies given to producers shift the supply curve to the right.

8. In the accompanying graph, the demand curve has shifted to the left, causing a decrease in the market price and the market quantity.

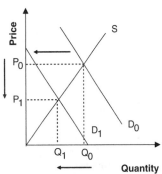

10. Sales volume increases (equilibrium quantity rises) when the government suspends the tax on sales by retailers because the price to demanders falls and hence equilibrium quantity demanded rises. This occurs because the supply curve shifts to the right because they do not have to pay taxes on their sales (cost of production declines).

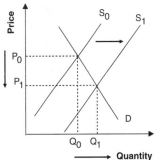

12. Customers will flock to stores demanding that funky "economics professor" look, creating excess demand. This excess demand will soon catch the attention of suppliers, and prices will be pushed upward.

14. Because the price of gas rose significantly, we'd expect people to purchase fewer gas-guzzlers and more fuel-efficient cars such as diesel cars. Demand for diesel cars rose 10-15 percent.

16. It suggests that the job is being rationed, which means that the wage is above the equilibrium wage.

18. The fallacy of composition is the false assumption that what is true for a part will also be true for the whole. It affects the supply/demand model by drawing our attention to the possibility that supply and demand are interdependent. Feedback effects must be taken into account to made the analysis complete.

20. The greatest feedback effects are likely to occur in the markets that are the largest. This is most likely to be true for housing and manufactured-goods markets.

Problems and Exercises

2. **a.** The market demand and market supply curves are shown in the accompanying graph.

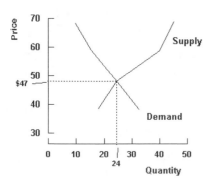

b. At a price of $37, quantity demanded is 32 and quantity supplied is 18. Excess demand is 14. At a price of $67, quantity demanded is 10 and quantity supplied is 46. Excess supply is 36.

c. Equilibrium price is $47. Equilibrium quantity is 24.

4. a. I would expect wheat prices to decline since the supply of wheat is greater than expected. Wheat commodity markets are very competitive, so the initial 35 percent increase in output was already reflected in the current price of wheat. It is only the additional 9 percent increase that will push down the price of wheat.

b. This is graphically represented by a shift to the right in the supply of wheat, as shown in the accompanying graph. Equilibrium price falls from P0 to P1 while equilibrium quantity rises from Q0 to Q1.

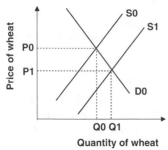

6. a. The tax shifts the supply curve to the left because it increases the cost of supplying the natural gas abroad. Equilibrium price rises and quantity declines.

b. The tax will likely reduce the price of natural gas in Argentina as more gas is diverted to domestic markets.

c. It depends; it will have a tendency to push it up, but probably since Argentina is such a small percentage of the world market, the effect would be difficult to distinguish.

8. a. It would likely raise the value significantly – it was estimated that it would raise it to 50,000 a sheet. See the accompanying graph.

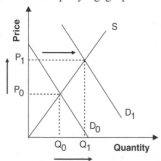

b. It would probably lower the value of the stamps – it was estimated that it would lower the price of the sheet to 100 a sheet. See the accompanying graph.

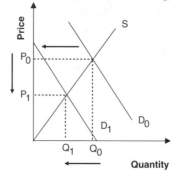

c. They would likely sue; they did and they lost.

10. a. Because the market for pencils is relatively small, supply/demand analysis would be appropriate without modification.

b. Because the labor market is very large, supply/demand analysis would not be appropriate without modification. For example, an increase in labor supply will likely lead to greater income and greater demand for goods, which will lead to an increase in quantity of goods produced and therefore an increase in the demand for labor. In this case there are significant feedback effects.

c. Aggregate markets such as savings and expenditures include feedback effects, so supply/demand analysis would not be appropriate without modification.

d. The CD market is relatively small. Supply/demand analysis would be appropriate without modification.

Web Questions

2. The answers to these questions will depend upon the current "Short-Term Energy Outlook." The answer given here should be used as a guide.

a. The Persian Gulf War is the most significant factor that is affecting supply. Iraq is unable to contribute to world oil supply. This shifts the supply of oil to the left. In addition, oil strikes in Venezuela are also limiting oil supply. No demand factors were mentioned specifically, but the end of the heating season would be expected to reduce demand for oil. The reductions in supply will lead to higher prices while the reduction in demand will mediate those price increases.

b. World oil prices are forecast to remain high and volatile while the U.S. is at war with Iraq. The effect of the supply and demand factors on price and quantity are shown in the accompanying graph.

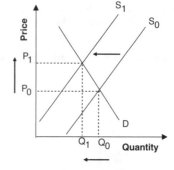

c. Higher crude oil, an input to the production of gasoline, will reduce the supply of gasoline and increase its price. As summer ends, the demand for gasoline will decline and put downward pressure on gas prices. The net effect is a decline in the near term, but a rise in the future. Higher crude oil will reduce the supply of home heating oil and a colder winter will increase demand. Both will work to increase the price of home heating oil. Gas is a substitute for oil. As the price of oil increases, the demand for gas will increase. This will lead to higher natural gas prices in the near term.

● CHAPTER 5 Questions for Thought and Review

2. If price fell and quantity remained constant, a possible cause would be a shift out of the supply curve and a shift of the demand curve in to the left. Another possibility would be a shift of the demand curve in to the left with a vertical supply curve.

4. As you can see in the accompanying graph, the rent controls create a situation in which demanders are willing to pay much more than the controlled price and much more than the equilibrium price. These payments are sometimes known as key money. In this graph, landlords are willing to supply Q_S at the current controlled rent, P_C. Consumers are willing to pay up to P_B for the quantity Q_S. Key money can be an amount up to the difference between P_B and P_C.

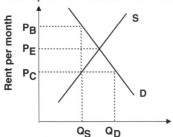

Quantity of apartments

6. A minimum wage, W_{min}, above the equilibrium wage W_E will result in the quantity of laborers looking for work to increase to Q_S and the quantity of employers looking to hire to decrease to Q_D. The difference between the two is a measure of the number of unemployed.

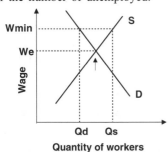

Quantity of workers

8. Political turmoil in South Africa likely led both foreign and domestic investors to question the economic stability of the country. Foreign investors reduced their demand for South African investments, and therefore their demand for the rand. This shifted the demand for the rand to the left.

Domestic investors did likewise, shifting their investments to those outside South Africa, shifting the supply of rand to the right. The combination led to a lower price for the rand in terms of other currencies.

10. Excess supply in U.S. agricultural markets is caused by the government's policy of agricultural price supports, or price floors on agricultural products. Political forces prevent the invisible hand from working.

12. Import disruptions shifted the supply curve for rice to the left. Equilibrium price rose and quantity fell as the accompanying graph shows.

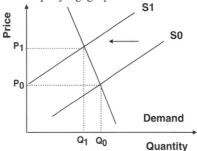

14. Public post-secondary education is an example of a third-party payer market because it is heavily subsidized by state government and in most cases, a student's parents. Those consuming the good, students, do not pay the entire cost of the education they receive. This likely leads to greater expenditures on post-secondary education than if students had to pay the entire cost of their education.

Problems and Exercises

2. **a.** A weakly enforced anti-scalping law would add an additional cost to those selling scalped tickets and push up the resale cost of tickets to include the expected cost of being caught, which would be fairly small given weak enforcement. In the accompanying graph, this shifts the supply curve from S_0 to S_1, raising equilibrium price slightly from P_0 to P_1. (Note: This assumes that only selling, not buying, is illegal.)

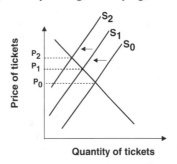

Quantity of tickets

b. A strongly enforced anti-scalping law (against suppliers) would push up prices far more as the cost of supply rose and the supply curve shifted to the left. If enforcement were sufficiently strong, a two-tier price system would emerge with a low legal resale price at P_0 and another very high price, P_2.

4. a. The government subsidy of mohair provided an enormous incentive, for those who were allowed to sell mohair, to sell large quantities at lower price than otherwise. The elimination of this subsidy shifted the supply curve to the left (shown below as a shift from S0 to S1, increasing the market price for mohair from P0 to P1 and decreasing the quantity demanded and supplied from Q0 to Q1.

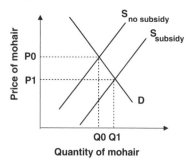

   b. This program was likely kept in existence because not many people knew about it (mohair is a relatively small market), and ranchers had no incentive to broadcast the subsidy.

   c. A law that requires that suppliers receive $3.60 more than the market price is the same as a tax, but the revenue goes to the supplier. The demand curve would shift to the left (down) to include this tax. The quantity demanded would fall dramatically. Consumers would not support this law because they would have to pay an enormously high price. Suppliers would support this law only if they were guaranteed that they could sell at that high price.

6. a. Boards often exist to benefit the consumer, but also to benefit those who currently produce. Often those who are currently certified attempt to limit the number of new certifications to limit the supply and thus boost the price.

   b. Possible changes include eliminating the board of certification, limiting its regulation to only those skills that it addresses directly, or requiring continual recertification so that skills of those already certified reflect the current demand for skills in that market.

   c. A political difficulty with implementing these changes is that a relatively small group of those currently certified will be hurt and will lobby hard for the status quo. Those currently certified may have more "clout" with the board if the board is comprised of certified hairdressers. The benefits of the changes are also large, but they are spread out over large groups of consumers, with each consumer benefiting very little. Therefore, it will be easier for the small group, whose benefit per individual is large, to organize.

8. a. Frequent-flyer programs allow companies to lower their effective prices without lowering their reported prices. Companies also use them to get business travelers to choose their airline. Such programs are an example of a third-party-payer system: The business traveler gets the benefit (frequent-flyer miles), while the business pays for the current flight.

   b. Other examples include points that hotels give to travelers and bonus checks based on charges that Discover gives those who use its credit card.

   c. Firms likely do not monitor these programs because it would be too costly to do so.

10. a. This would represent a shift in demand to the left assuming the decline in Cookie Monster's popularity represents a decline in the popularity of cookies. The price and quantity of cookies would likely fall as shown in the graph below.

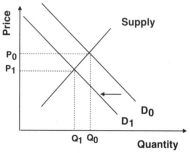

   b. This is represented by a shift in demand for bread (high in carbohydrates) to the left. Equilibrium price and quantity falls as the accompanying graph shows.

12. a. Both the shift in demand to the right and the shift of supply to the left lead to a higher equilibrium price of oil, in this case over $40 a barrel. The effect on equilibrium quantity is indeterminate. While the shift in demand to the right would lead to a rise in equilibrium quantity, the shift in supply to the left would reduce it. Whether equilibrium quantity rises or falls depends on the relative size of the shifts. The graph below shows no effect on equilibrium quantity and a significant increase in price.

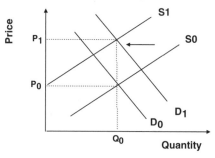

   b. The increase in the oil quota shifted supply to the right, reducing the price of oil from $42 a barrel to $38 a barrel. Equilibrium quantity increased.

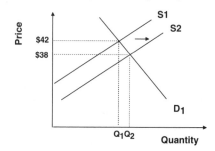

14. a. They would likely fall. In fact, they fell by 13 percent.
   b. They also would likely fall. In fact, they fell by 22 percent.
   c. The graphs below show the effect of increasing co-payments. The graph on the left has a co-payment of $15. Consumers demand Q1 and the shaded region shows the medical claim costs. In the accompanying graph, consumers must pay the first $1,500 of medical costs, demonstrated by the lower-shaded region. (For simplicity, we assume that consumers end up purchasing 50 units at a cost of $30 per unit.) As you can see, however, the medical cost to the firm (upper shaded area) is much smaller. In addition, the units of medical services demanded are lower, illustrating the second question – hospital admissions declined.

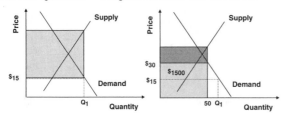

16. a. This represents a shift of the supply curve to the left because the offended decide not to supply organs, increasing the legal price significantly and perhaps reducing the equilibrium quantity to a quantity that is below the amount currently provided at zero cost.
   b. How responsive quantity supplied is to price affects the slope of the supply curve. If quantity supplied is very responsive to price, the equilibrium price might be quite low and legalizing organ sales would have significant benefits to society. In fact, the authors of the study estimate the equilibrium price of kidneys to be less than $1000.

Web Questions

2. a. The minimum wage, adjusted for inflation, has fallen nearly consistently since 1979. If the inflation-adjusted minimum wage is on the vertical axis, this will reduce the shortage of jobs (number of unemployed) that results from the minimum wage.
   b. According to the article, minorities are disproportionately represented among minimum wage earners. Compare column 1 to column 4 for each subcategory. If column 1 is greater than column 4, that category is over-represented among minimum-wage earners.
   c. The author says that the job-loss effect is small or minimal. He cites the observation that the 90-cent increase in 1996/97 did not lead to lower employment levels among minorities. The minimum wage did not prevent economic growth during the mid-1990s from raising employment levels among low-wage earners.

Appendix

2. a. The following are the demand and supply tables after the hormone is introduced:

Price ($/gal.)	Quantity Demanded (gal./yr.)	Quantity Supplied (gal./yr.)
0.00	600	225
1.00	500	125
2.00	400	275
2.50	350	350
3.00	300	425
4.00	200	575
5.00	100	725
6.00	0	875

The hormone (a technological advance) shifts the supply curve to the right by 125,000 gallons, The demand curve is unchanged.

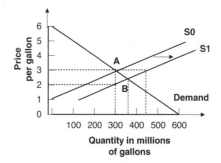

   b. The original supply curve is S0. The growth hormone shifts the supply curve to S1 (to the right by 125). Equilibrium price falls to $2.50 a gallon, and equilibrium quantity rises to 350 million gallons (point B).
   c. The demand curve remains the same at QD = 600 - 100P. The supply curve becomes QS = -25 + 150P. To solve the two equations, set them equal to one another: $600 - 100P = -25 - 150P$ and solve for P. Doing so, we get P = 2.5. Substituting this value for P into either the demand or supply equation gives us equilibrium quantity of 350.
   d. Quantity supplied would be 425 ($-25 + 150 \times 3$) and quantity demanded would be 300 (600 - 100 $\times$ 3). There would be excess supply of 125. The price floor is shown in the accompanying graph.

4. a. A demand curve follows the formula $Q_D = a - bP$, where a is the price-axis intercept and b is the slope of the curve. A shift in demand is reflected in a change in a. An increase in demand increases a and a decrease in demand reduces a.
   b. A supply curve follows the formula, $Q_S = a + bP$, where a is the price-axis intercept and b is the slope of the curve. A shift in supply is reflected in a change in a. An increase in supply increases a and a decrease in supply decreases a.

c. A movement in supply or demand is reflected in the effect of a change in P on either Q_S or Q_D.

6. a. The new supply equation is $Q_S = -150 + 150(P - 1)$ where P is the equilibrium price, or $Q_S = -300 + 150P$.
   b. $P = 3.60$; $Q = 240$.
   c. Farmers receive $2.60 per gallon, while demanders pay $3.60 per gallon.

8. a. The new supply equation is $Q_S = -150 + 150(P + 1)$ where P is the equilibrium price, or $Q_S = 150P$.
   b. $P = 2.40$; $Q = 360$.
   c. Farmers receive $3.40 per gallon.

● CHAPTER 6 Questions for Thought and Review

2. I would check to see if other things remained equal, suspecting that they did not, since the rise in price did not have the expected effect. If all other things did indeed remain equal, the elasticity would be zero.

4. Price elasticity of demand is equal to the percentage change in quantity divided by the percentage change in price. Pizzas went from $8 to $2 and quantity from 1 to 100. The price elasticity of demand is $(1.96/1.2) = 1.60$.

6. They are both the same. Any supply curve that goes through the origin has an elasticity of 1.

8. To the degree that colleges are trying to get as much revenue as possible, they will keep raising tuition until the demand is no longer inelastic. Colleges don't raise their tuition by more than what they currently do because they are not profit maximizers, and because social pressures such as student protests would result if they raised tuition too much.

10. More eager students will agree to go to a school even if they don't get much financial aid. That is, they have less elastic demands and thus will tend to get less financial aid. Whether this practice is justified is a difficult normative issue, with many alternative views.

12. a. Vodka: normal, luxury (except in Russia). Individuals tend to drink more hard liquor as their income rises. (It depends on the type: Absolut vodka is more of a luxury than store brands.)
    b. Table salt: normal, necessity. It is a small portion of people's income, and its consumption doesn't increase with income.
    c. Furniture: normal, luxury (depends on the type). While we all need some furniture, the wealthy spend large sums on furniture. The rest of us get by with cheap stuff.
    d. Perfume: normal, luxury (depends on the type). The rich blow money on perfume; the rest of us get by with toilet water, or we smell a bit.
    e. Beer: normal, inferior. Beer, the cheapest type of alcohol, tends to be the poor person's drink. As income increases, beer drinkers will choose to drink less beer and more expensive alcohol such as wine and liquor. However, new micro breweries are trying to change beer's image, and to make certain types of beer be seen as a luxury.

f. Sugar: normal, necessity. It is not used significantly more by rich than by poor.

14. If there were only two (assuming no saving) the goods must be substitutes because if a person doesn't consume one, he or she would have to consume the other.

16. To answer this question, use the formula from the chapter: percentage change in price = percentage change in supply divided by sum of demand and supply elasticities. Here, percentage change in price = $5/(1 + .2) = 4.17$ percent. The pre-terrorism price was $1.75, so the new price is $1.04 \times 1.75 = 1.82.

Problems and Exercises

2. a. Using standard reasoning, we would answer that firms decreased the size of the coffee cans to hide price increases from consumers. However, in reality people often react differently to changes in the size of packages compared to the equivalent change in price.
   b. Examples include candy bars, soap, and canned tuna fish.

4. a. A price rise of 10 percent will reduce fuel consumption anywhere from 4 to 8.5 percent. Quantity demanded would range from 9.15 to 9.6 million gallons.
   b. This suggests that there are other forces besides price at work here; making adjustments to higher prices is much easier than making adjustments to lower prices. This may be due to learning the true cost of substitutes when those substitutes are consumed. One can imagine a scenario in which a price hike significantly changes driving behavior—commuters may switch to ride sharing or public transportation, to which there may be perceived social barriers (costs). Once those barriers are overcome and the perceived costs are lowered after those alternatives are used, a larger decline in the price of gasoline is required to induce those who switched to return to driving their own cars.

6. Point A: 3; point B: 1/3; point C: 3/2; point D: 7/6.

8. a. 0.5   b. 0.60

10. a. Neither state is maximizing revenue. Maximum revenue is collected when elasticity is one. Both are collecting less than the maximum revenue: in California elasticity is less than one and in Massachusetts elasticity is greater than one.
    b. I would recommend that Massachusetts lower its price and California raise its price.
    c. Massachusetts, because not only is it not collecting maximum revenue, it could simultaneously lower price and increase revenues, making both those who buy vanity plates and the treasury happy.
    d. Elasticity of demand equals one at price P* in the accompanying graph. California is below at a price such as P_1, where demand is inelastic. So, you can see that raising the price from prices below P_1 will result in greater revenue gained (BC) than lost (F). Massachusetts is at a price above P*, such as P_0, where demand is elastic. So you can see that lowering the price to P* will result in greater revenue gained (CE) than lost (A).

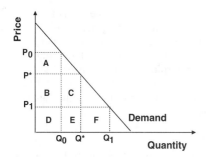

12. **a.** Peak hour travelers are likely to be commuters who have little choice but to go to work and therefore have lower demand elasticity than those who ride busses during off-peak hours, and are more likely using buses for errands or other more discretionary activities.

    b. Demand tends to be less elastic in the short run because there are few substitutes. If fares rose enough, in the long run people could find alternative modes of transportation – purchase a car, find someone to share rides with, etc.

    c. Tolls are likely a much smaller portion of high income commuter's total income, contributing to a less-elastic demand.

14. **a.** Liquor producers would not support a tax on beer because the cross-price elasticity between beer and hard liquor is negative. The beer tax would also reduce liquor consumption.

    b. Wine producers would support a tax on beer because the cross-price elasticity between beer and wine is positive. The beer tax would increase wine consumption.

16. **a.** 0.31 (40,000/260,000)/(20/40).

    b. Since the demand is inelastic, it doesn't make sense to lower the price because it reduces the total revenue.

    c. Then it makes sense to lower the price in order to increase the circulation for more advertising revenue.

Web Questions

2. **a.** $5.50 to $8.50 by 2003 and $10.50 by 2007 which is about a 55 percent increase initially and a 91 percent increase by 2007. The estimate of labor demand elasticity used is 0.22. Inelastic.

Labor costs will be raised $6.6 million per year. Since demand is inelastic, a rise in the minimum wage will raise total labor costs. The two are consistent. If elasticity of demand were greater than one, one would expect labor costs to fall when the minimum wage is raised.

In the long-run firms can keep labor costs down by hiring fewer workers and by finding substitutes for labor, such as outsourcing or automation. What accounts for the difference is that in the long run, all factors of production are variable. In the short run, firms have fewer substitutes in production and will have to accept the higher labor costs. Source: *The Effects of the Proposed Santa Fe Minimum Wage Increase*, by David McPherson.

● CHAPTER 7 Questions for Thought and Review

2. Decision making based on costs and benefits means you make purchases if the marginal benefits are greater than the price. Thus, when you decide to make a purchase, you are likely receiving something worth more to you than what you had to spend to buy it, or else you wouldn't have bought it. That net benefit is consumer surplus.

4. If demand is inelastic, raising a tax increases revenue paid by consumers; similarly with supply. Thus, what happens to total tax revenue depends on the elasticity of both supply and demand.

6. If suppliers were strong lobbyists, the government would prefer demand to be more inelastic, because then consumers will bear the largest portion of the tax. If the suppliers had to bear the greatest burden they would have an incentive to lobby against the tax.

8. The demander. The more inelastic the demand curve, the larger percentage of the burden is borne by the demander.

10. The demander will pay 30 percent of the tax [.3/(.7+.3)×100) and the supplier will pay the remaining 70 percent.

12. No. Tenants shouldn't worry too much. In the short run the supply of apartments is highly inelastic so the owner will bear the majority of the tax burden; it will not be passed on to tenants. In the long run supply is more elastic so the renter will pay some of the tax. So in the long run, tenants should worry more.

14. For an equivalent percentage rise in price, the more elastic and demand and supply, the greater the shortage that will be created. The reason is that the response in quantity supplied and demanded is greater when price elasticity is greater.

Problems and Exercises

2. **a.** Because income above a certain level are not taxed, payroll taxes are regressive. Because low-income workers receive greater benefits at retirement than they contributed and high-income workers receive less, considering the Social Security system as a whole, it is likely progressive.

    b. The benefit principle is that individuals who receive the benefit should pay the tax. A system that follows this principle exactly would mean that workers would receive all that they paid into the system plus any returns the funds earned while in trust by the government. That is not the case. So, considering this principle only, the system is not fair.

    c. The ability-to-pay principle says that individuals who are most able to bear the burden of the tax should pay. A system that follows this principle would have high-income workers subsidizing the benefits of the low-income workers, which to some degree describes the current Social Security system. So, considering this principle only, the system is fair.

4. **a.** It depends on one's view. If one sees cigarette smoking as harmful, anything that decreases smoking is good. If one uses the consumer-surplus model, assuming individuals know what they want, then it hurts smokers.

   b. It shows a loss of consumer and producer surplus (deadweight loss to society).

   c. The large majority of the money was spent on general budget items, not anti-smoking campaigns. A typical example is Erie County in New York State; it has already spent 99 percent of its money, and less than 1 percent went toward anti-smoking campaigns. This is because once they had the money, they had little incentive to actually spend it on anti-smoking campaigns.

6. **a.** Because the elasticity of demand among the top students was greater than one, lowering tuition would lead to a proportionally greater percentage increase in enrollment. Total tuition would rise.

   b. The program distinguished among top students because their elasticities likely differed. The top 10 percent were likely being offered scholarships at other academic institutions, giving them greater choices, which made their elasticities greater.

   c. It could be that the President did not reduce tuition for all students because the elasticity of demand for all students was less than one. This scheme allowed them to price discriminate – and take advantage of differing elasticities. Another reason is that price is sometimes an indicator for quality. By lowering tuition across the board, they could be sending a signal that their college has lost relative academic standing. Using this scheme they are sending a signal that they desire to increase their relative standing.

8. **a.** A poll tax would have no incentive effect, since there is no way to avoid paying it. A tax on property, where supply is somewhat elastic, will reduce the quantity of property supplied (negative incentive effect), resulting in a loss of consumer and producer surplus.

   b. Margaret Thatcher was almost thrown out of office because of this tax, and her successor, John Major, returned to a property tax. Citizens were far more concerned with the distributional consequences associated with a poll tax than they were with the loss of efficiency associated with a property tax.

10. **a.** With time the job searchers will get discouraged and drop out of the labor force, disguising the unemployment. Another possibility is that firms invest in machinery to replace labor, increasing the long term job shortage.

    b. It is likely to decrease.

12. **a.** Before the tax, equilibrium price is $6 and equilibrium quantity is 200. After the tax, equilibrium price is $8 and equilibrium quantity is 100.

    b. Producer surplus before the tax is the area above the supply curve and below price. This is a triangle with base 200 and height 4. So, producer surplus is 1/2 (200)(4) = 400. After the tax, the triangle representing producer surplus has a height of 2 and base of 100. So producer surplus is 1/2 (100)(2) = 100.

    c. Consumer surplus before the tax is the area below the demand curve and above price. This is a triangle with base 200 and height 4. So consumer surplus is 1/2 (200)(4) = 400. After the tax, the triangle representing consumer surplus has a height of 2 and base of 100. So consumer surplus is 1/2 (100)(2) = 100.

    d. Total tax revenue is $4 times equilibrium quantity, 100, or $400.

Web Questions

2. **a.** 1) Taxation should bear as lightly as possible on production. 2) It should be easy and cheap to collect, and fall directly on the ultimate payer. 3) It should be certain. 4) It should bear equally so as to give no individual an advantage.

   b. The broad based taxes burden production, but they are relatively easy and cheap to collect at least compared to other taxes and the burden is shared relatively equally. They do not necessarily fall on the ultimate payer.

   c. A land value tax best fits the criteria.

   d. The tax falls directly on the owner; tax on land does not affect cost of production or its supply, so price is not increased. Because quantity sold doesn't change, the welfare loss is zero.

⬤ CHAPTER 8 Questions for Thought and Review

2. According to the principle of diminishing marginal utility, marginal utility falls as one consumes more of a good. Marginal utility of the last unit consumed rises as one consumes less of the good.

4. Economists' theory of value depends on the underlying assumptions. Given those assumptions, price and value are related. If those assumptions (such as assumed rationality and freedom of choice) don't hold, the statement is true; if they do hold, the statement is false.

6. There are many psychological explanations for people's actions, but economists use an easy underlying psychological foundation: rational self-interest.

8. The law of demand states that quantity demanded falls as price rises and quantity demanded rises as price falls. If you are already in equilibrium and the price of a good rises, you will no longer be in equilibrium. The marginal utility per dollar of the good whose price has risen is too low. To raise it, you must reduce your consumption of that good. Therefore, as the price of the good rises, you consume less of it—the law of demand.

10. If the supply curve is perfectly inelastic, the supplier has no alternative; thus, the opportunity cost is zero.

12. For Americans, a large part of utility (happiness) is relative to others. As everyone gets more relative happiness does not increase.

14. Most people buy goods without a lot of thinking. An example of ours is when we buy meat at the store. We have a general idea of what the price should be, and if the price

is lower than that (and a sign or sticker says sale) we buy it. It follows the principle of rational choice only if that principle takes into account the costs of deciding.

Problems and Exercises

2. Given the information in the table, the best combination to purchase will be where the (MU/P) is equal for all three goods. Doing the calculations, we have:

Number	(MU/P) for A	(MU/P) for B	(MP/P) for C
1	20	10	8.33
2	18	7	1.67
3	15	6	1.67
4	10	5	1.67
5	5	4	1.67
6	2	4	1.67
7	27	3	21.67
8	220	2	21.67

(Note that marginal utility should be interpreted between units of consumption.) We start by buying that good with the highest util per dollar. With $20 to spend we would buy 1 of A, for 20 utils per dollar, leaving me with $10 to spend. We would then buy 1 more of A, getting 18 utils to the dollar. This would exhaust our money.

4. You should continue your present pattern of consumption. One more widget will give you 2 more units of utility for $2, and one more wadget will give you 3 more units of utility for $3, and since (MU1/P1) = (MU2/P2), your present consumption pattern gives you as much total utility considering your income and prices, as any variation.

6. **a.** If he or she is not a 100 percent rational economist, it is likely that you will lose your spouse or significant other—or at least lose his or her love or fondness.

   b. The utility gained from a diamond is not just its brilliance or perfection but also the knowledge that it is real (and thus expensive) and that some sacrifice (driven by affection) was made for its purchase. A fake diamond suggests that there was little sacrifice and thus the giver's love was cheap as well.

   c. Who is to say that the utility from the consumption of a product is not just?

8. **a.** Since the "rational" move now suggests that the first person should keep all the money, one would expect that the offers would be smaller, which is what economists have found. See: R. Forshthe, J. Horowitz, N. E. Savin and M. Sefton, "Fairness in Simple Bargaining Experiments," *Games and Economic Behavior*, 1994.

   b. Since the second person can impose no penalty on the first for making less than a 50-50 offer, he should accept any amount that he gets. That is what economics researchers have found.

Web Questions

2. **a.** iwon.com is a full search engine.
   The site gives out prizes to increase use, and thereby increase their advertising revenue since that is tied to usage.
   Advertisements are in the links, they include webMD, Sprint and DVD Express.
   If advertising works it likely means that preferences can be influenced.

Appendix

2. With budget constraint in a, Zach will be on utility curve II. With budget constraint in b, Zach will be on utility curve III. With budget constraint in c, Zach will be on a utility curve that is to the right of III.

   a. Zachary prefers the budget constraint that is the furthest to the right, c.

   b. The marginal rate of substitution for a is -2, for b is -1 and for c is -1. The marginal rate of substitution equals the slope of the budget constraint at the optimal combination of goods. Even though we do not know the optimal combination with budget constraint c, we can still figure out the marginal rate of substitution for that combination.

4. It would be bowed away from the origin if there were increasing marginal utility.

● CHAPTER 9 Questions for Thought and Review

2. The terms long run and short run do not necessarily refer to specific periods of time independent of the production process. The long run, by definition, is a period in which the firm can vary the inputs as much as it wants; in the long run, all inputs are variable. The question is whether a firm ever really gets to this degree of flexibility. It may be true that firms are always constrained in regard to what production decisions they can make, so in reality this statement is probably true.

4. If average productivity is falling, short-run average variable cost is rising; to say that productivity falls is equivalent to saying that cost rises.

6. If average productivity is falling, average costs must be rising; if marginal productivity is falling, marginal cost must be rising. But there is no necessary relationship between average productivity and marginal costs.

8. The shapes of the short-run average cost curve and marginal cost curve would be the same as in the more usual case where machines are the fixed factor. Either way you are still adding more and more of a variable factor to a fixed factor and encountering diminishing marginal productivity as a result. The marginal cost and average cost curves would be U-shaped.

10. These statements are true. Labor does not need to be produced (at least in the time periods that microeconomic

analysis usually considers) and hence the choice for individuals is how to divide up that labor among various activities such as work, play, and studying (opportunity costs). Goods that need to be produced ultimately depend on the opportunity costs of the factors producing them, but in the standard economic model, those costs are assumed fixed; thus, the opportunity costs are assumed fixed. This leaves the analysis of production free to focus on technical aspects of production such as diminishing marginal productivity as the determinant of costs, and hence supply.

12. Productivity gains can reduce the percentage of labor costs per vehicle, allowing GM either to lower its price (thereby increasing the quantity of its cars sold) or to increase its profits (making its shareholders happy).

Problems and Exercises

2. Rent is $4,000; labor is $40,000; utilities are $5,000; total revenue is $100,000; the opportunity cost of the entrepreneur is $50,000; and that of the funds invested is $4,000. By the accounting definition of cost and profit, Economan is making a profit equal to $100,000−($4,000 + $40,000 + $5,000) = $51,000. From an economist's point of view, where explicit and implicit costs are considered, Economan now has a loss of $100,000−($4,000 + $40,000 + $5,000 + $50,000 + $4,000)=−$3,000.

4. a. Given the price of labor at $15 per hour, and the data in the total product table; the following table represents the average variable costs:

Labor	TP	VC	AVC	AP	MP	MC
1	5	15	3.00	5.0	5	3.00
2	15	30	2.00	7.5	10	1.50
3	30	45	1.50	10.0	15	1.00
4	36	60	1.67	9.0	6	2.50
5	40	75	1.88	8.0	4	3.75

b. This is done in the next column. The AVC curve is shown in the accompanying graph, and the AP curve is shown below it. You can see that the AVC curve and AP curve are mirror images of each other.

c. The MP curve is shown below it.

d. As you can see from the graphs, the MC curve and the MP curve are approximate mirror images of each other.

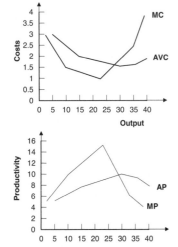

6. a. The AFC, ATC, AVC, and MC curves are shown on the graph below.

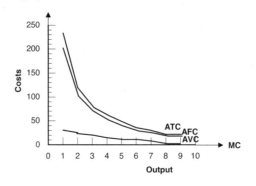

b. The AFC curve has its normal shape. Because average variable costs do not change, the marginal cost curve is coincident with the average variable cost as shown. The ATC curve is always falling since the costs are always above the MC curve. They asymptotically approach $25.

c. The law of diminishing marginal productivity is not operative.

d. The new AFC, ATC, AVC, and MC curves are shown in the graph below. The AFC curve remains the same. The MC curve is now upward-sloping, with a slope of 10. The AVC curve is also upward-sloping, with a slope of 5. The ATC curve now has a more normal shape, with a minimum where it intersects the MC curve.

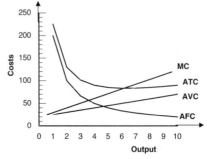

e. Marginal costs would have to decline at first and then rise for the curves to have their "normal" shapes.

8. a. The marginal cost is zero initially and 35 cents if you are over. See accompanying graph

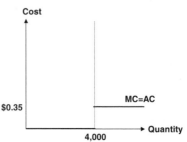

b. Since the marginal cost curve is horizontal, the average cost curve is coincident with the marginal cost curve. See graph for a.

c. You wouldn't. It is too difficult. You would guess at it. Companies are expecting that, which is why they offer such plans.

d. They are relying on people's gullibility and bringing them in as customers on the expectation of lower prices than they are getting, then relying on the difficult cost of changing phones to keep them customers.

e. They were against the portability of phone numbers because portability reduces the cost of change, and thus discourages the practice of offering confusing plans.

● Web Questions

2. This answer is based on 2001 data.

a. The operating cost of producing an acre of corn is $170.83. The total cost of producing an acre of corn is $390.59.

b. Two major components of the variable costs are seed and fertilizer.

c. Two major components of fixed costs are land and equipment.

d. Each acre yielded an average 139 bushels. Dividing operating cost per acre by 139, we calculate the price of corn needed to cover operating costs to be $1.23 per bushel.

e. Dividing total cost per acre by 139, we calculate the price of corn needed to cover total costs to be $2.81 per bushel.

● CHAPTER 10 Questions for Thought and Review

2. It is incorrect because in the long run firms can change any input they want. In the long run there would be no fixed cost—all costs would be variable. The shape of the long-run average total cost curve is determined by economies of scale.

4. If production relationships were only technical relationships, diseconomies of scale would never occur because the same technical process could be used over and over again at the same cost. In reality, however, the social dimensions of production relationships introduce the potential for diseconomies of scale because, as the firm size increases, monitoring costs increase and team spirit or morale generally decreases.

6. An entrepreneur is an individual who sees an opportunity to sell an item at a price higher than the average cost of producing it. The entrepreneur then looks at the cost of production to see if a profit can be made. If so, he or she will create supply by organizing production.

8. Cost curves are defined within a period of time. In the short run, technology is assumed constant. In the long run, technological change shifts the cost curves down. It does not explain the downward-sloping portion of cost curves.

10. Producing steel in this fashion involves an enormous fixed cost. These fixed costs must be spread out over sufficient production to lower average total costs and make the average total production costs (which includes fixed costs) less than the price.

Problems and Exercises

2. a. Variable costs would likely include: Manufacturing labor and materials and possibly sales costs to the extent that they are for the sale of additional production. Certain other costs have a variable component to them, but they will unlikely vary directly with production.

b. Fixed costs would likely include: Factor overhead, operating expenses and profit, R&D, interest, and to some extent advertising. In the real world, the division between fixed and variable costs is not as clear-cut as in the texts.

c. If output were to rise, average total cost would likely fall because fixed costs seem relatively important. This is the case for many real-world firms.

4. a. The long-run cost curve is shown in the accompanying graph. Initially it will fall because of economies of scale.

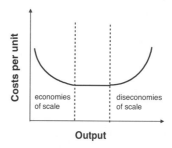

b. It will later rise due to diseconomies of scale.

c. The average cost curves in the short run are also U-shaped. Their shape is due initially to increasing marginal productivity and eventually decreasing marginal productivity.

d. There is no fixed component.

e. A straight line.

6. a. It is possible that both methods are technically efficient because neither dressmaker is using more of both inputs to produce the same number of garments.

b. The economically efficient method is the least-cost method. The cost of 800 garments for the first dressmaker is $46,000 [(160 3 $100) + (3,000× $10)]. The cost of the same number of garments for the second dressmaker is $40,000 [(200× $100) + (2,000× $10)]. Therefore, the second method is economically efficient. The first method is not.

Web Questions

2. a. Glaxo and SmighKline likely merged to create economies of scope—efficiencies in production and research that would lead to greater productivity.

b. The article mentions difficulty of monitoring a business with many offices, bureaucratic hassles associated with layers of management, and loss of "spark" in leadership.

c. These problems are associated with diseconomies of scale—increasing long-run cost as production rises. Perhaps long-run costs are higher for a combined firm GlaxoSmithKline than for separate Glaxo and SmithKline companies.

Appendix A

2. See the graph below. The dotted line is the original isocost curve. Each of the following is shown with respect to the dotted line.

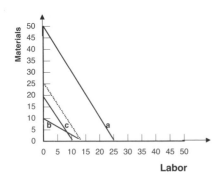

a. This is line a in the graph.
b. The isocost curve rotates in along the machinery axis as shown in the graph to line b.
c. The isocost curve shifts in along both axes as shown to line c.

4. Technical efficiency in production means that as few inputs as possible are used to produce a given output. On the accompanying graph, this would be anywhere on the isoquant curve, including points A and B. Economic efficiency means using that method that produces a given level of output at the lowest possible cost. Given the cost of inputs, the efficient point to produce that level of output corresponding to the isoquant curve is point B.

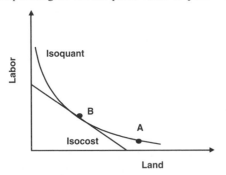

6. If the price of labor falls to $3, the isocost curve shifts out along the labor axis, intersecting at 20 units of labor. Producing 60 earrings with the new labor costs is now inefficient. The firm can now produce more than 60 earrings, shown by point D and the new isoquant curve, I2, to the right of the one corresponding to 60 earrings, I1.

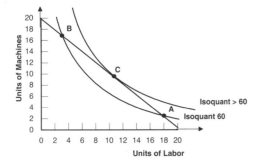

CHAPTER 11 Questions for Thought and Review

2. Typical marginal cost, marginal revenue, and average total cost curves are shown in the accompanying graph. The profit-maximizing level of output is Q*. The total profit is shown by the shaded rectangle. As we have drawn it, the firm is not in long-run equilibrium since it is earning a profit.

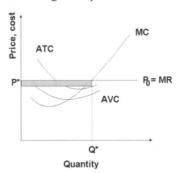

4. The firm's supply curve is that portion of the firm's marginal cost curve that lies above the minimum of the average variable cost curve. The sum of all individual firms' marginal cost curves (above the minimum AVC curve) is the market supply curve.

6. The shutdown point is the same as the point at which a firm exits a market in the long run when there are no fixed costs. That is, when AVC are the same as ATC.

8. A technological development that shifts the MC curve down will shift the market supply curve to the right. Market price will fall and output will rise. Profit for each firm will still be zero because the price will decline sufficiently so that each firm earns zero profit.

10. If both firms are producing where MR = MC and we could buy either for the same amount, I'd buy the one with the highest total profit. Remember, it is total profit, not profit per unit that is maximized by a firm. If there are perfectly competitive firms, however, eventually both will earn 0 economic profits regardless of which we bought.

12. This question requires students to find current articles in newspapers and apply supply/demand analysis to them.

14. If the older retail stores had higher costs than the new stores, they would be forced to cut prices below their costs. If that happened, they might stay in business in the short run, assuming they were covering their average variable costs, but they wouldn't stay in business in the long run. If the market remains perfectly competitive, equilibrium price will fall.

Problems and Exercises

2. a. With the information given, the clear answer is to change output in an attempt to lower costs and achieve an economic profit. We are not told whether MR = MC at the level of output at which ATC = $4. If it is, then it is maximizing profit, even though at a loss. If the firm is perfectly competitive, in the long run it should close.

b. If we now know that AVC = $3.50, we know that price is less than the average variable cost but not whether we are at the quantity where MR = MC. If AVC cannot be reduced, the firm should stop producing since it loses more by producing than it would if it shut down.

4. a. Zapateria will produce 500 pairs of shoes if the market price is $70 because at 500 pairs, the market price of equals marginal costs of $70.

b. The total profit that Zapateria will earn is $20 times 500 pairs of shoes, or $10,000.

c. Since Zapateria is making an economic profit, it should expect other shoe stores to enter the market.

d. The long-run equilibrium price is $40 a pair because at $40 a pair, zero profit is made.

6. a. As demand decreases, price will decrease in the short run. As price declines, some firms will exit the market. As firms exit, market supply will decrease, which will cause price to rise. Because it is a decreasing cost industry, however, marginal costs will be lower than with the original equilibrium and the price at which zero profit is made falls. Market equilibrium price falls in the long run.

b. The market equilibrium quantity falls.

c. The number of firms also falls because the decrease in demand decreased economic profits, making firms exit the market.

d. Profit per firm returns to zero for all firms, and for the industry in the long run.

8. a. Once the new tomato is generally available, it will likely reduce the price of equal-quality tomatoes in the off-season. However, the new, higher-quality tomato may well sell for more than the cardboard-tasting ones normally bought in winter.

b. Its effects on farmers depend on what the biotechnology firm charges for its seeds. If the prices for the seeds are high enough to extract the benefit of the better tomato, farmers will be no better off. Further, since the demand for tomatoes is fairly inelastic, the increased supply of good tomatoes (reducing their price) in the off-season will reduce revenues of farmers.

c. Tomatoes will be grown in areas much farther from their point of sale.

d. To the degree that the price of tomatoes falls, tomatoes in the winter will more likely be moved from the rear to the front of the salad bar.

10. a. Reconstituted milk can be shipped from low-cost production areas to high-cost production areas, threatening local dairy monopolies with competition.

b. This probably resulted from strong regional lobbies to protect regional markets from other lower-cost regions.

c. He is most likely incorrect economically, but correct politically. Price supports cause overproduction of milk and its elimination most likely will cut production. He made this statement because he wanted to get reelected and his supporters are dairy farmers who benefit from the price supports.

12. a. He receives $26.14 million in rent.

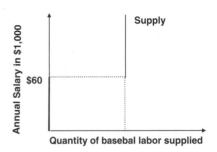

b. He will supply no baseball services at a salary below $60,000 since he could be a stockbroker for $60,000. It is vertical at $60,000 as shown in the accompanying graph because he is willing to supply the maximum number of hours that can be worked no matter what a baseball team pays him above $60,000. (This assumes he can have only one job at a time.)

c. His salary will decline, but as long as the cap is above $60,000 the amount he will play baseball will not.

14. a. Price is at the minimum of the average variable cost curve as shown in the accompanying graph.

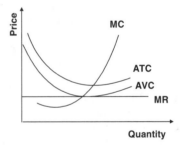

Assuming the market is perfectly competitive, Zany Brainy stores close, the supply curve shifts to the left, raising the market equilibrium price to a level at which firms in the market no longer earn losses but normal profit (zero economic profit). The market supply and demand curves are in the accompanying graph.

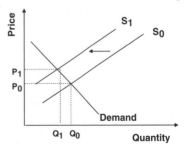

Web Questions

2. One possible answer is, Vermont 7.5%; New Jersey 7.5%; California 6.64%; South Dakota 8.1%; Alabama 7.25%.

    a. 6.64%-8.1%, a wide range.

b. Both buyers and sellers are price takers, there is a large number of firms, there is a homogeneous product, there are profit-maximizing entrepreneurial firms. It may appear that sellers are price takers because they are posting their rates, but they face many competitors. Their posted prices are set by the market. There is a lack of complete information and some barriers to entry (cost to establishing a lending institution).

c. Very few markets are perfectly competitive. Since the auto loan market doesn't meet all six conditions, it isn't surprising that there is a spread of loan rates.

CHAPTER 12 Questions for Thought and Review

2. This is not necessarily true. Monopolists may or may not make pure economic profit. In long-run equilibrium perfectly competitive firms tend to break even, which means they make only a normal profit. So profit is not the distinguishing factor. Instead, the distinguishing characteristic is that the monopolist can restrict output to hold up the market price; a perfect competitor cannot affect the market price.

4. The development of such a machine would probably reduce the demand for college education to the extent that it would be a lower-priced substitute. (But remember, gaining knowledge is not the only aspect of college—what about the social experiences, the sports, etc.?) If one college could monopolize the production of this machine, it could probably charge close to the current price of college and hire professors to do pure research with the proceeds.

6. A monopolist will tend to sell at a point on the demand curve where demand is elastic, but as the fish gets older (and smelly) the monopolist will wish to lower its price. The price will not be likely be in the inelastic range, but it may if the fish are rotting and the monopolist needs to sell all its inventory.

8. One cost is the lost profit by Bayer, which will likely lead to lower investment in drug research. If drug makers believe that government will ignore patents on future drugs, thereby lowering future profits, they will spend less on developing new drugs. So the cost to society of a policy of disregarding a patent is having fewer drugs to fight disease in the future.

10. The first thing to note is that publishers have pricing power. Therefore, they are able to price discriminate—charge buyers with different elasticities of demand different prices. The publisher charges a higher price to those who are eagerly awaiting the next book in a series and buy the book upon first release; their demand is less elastic. The publisher prints the book in hard cover to give the customer the feeling that they are buying a higher quality book. Publishers charge a lower price to those who are willing to wait a year (have more elastic demand.

12. A perfectly elastic marginal cost curve is shown in the accompanying graph as the horizontal straight line MC0. Because the opportunity cost of providing additional units does not increase, welfare loss is greatest with constant marginal costs—shown below as the shaded triangle. One can see that welfare loss falls with increasing marginal costs by rotating the marginal cost curve up. An example, MC1, is

shown. Welfare loss is bounded by the MC curve, the demand curve, and the quantity line.

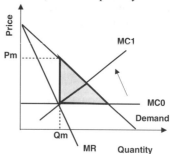

14. Removing copyrights would remove the monopoly to a text and cause the price of textbooks to fall and output to rise. The argument for copyrights (and patents) is that without some guarantee of profits from their ideas, people would be unlikely to engage in the effort (and incur the costs) associated with generating new ideas, products, etc. If that is the case, then copyrights may be justified. If people would write good books anyway, then probably society would be better off without copyrights because more books would be sold at a lower price.

Problems and Exercises

2. This is what is wrong in the graphs shown:
    a. The marginal revenue curve is too steep. It should cut the x-axis at Q. In addition, quantity should be determined where MR = MC.
    b. The curve labeled ATC is really the MC curve. Correctly labeled, the profit-maximizing level of output is determined where MC = MR.
    c. Quantity should be determined MR = MC, not MC = demand. Also, the MC curve should intersect the ATC curve at the minimum point of the ATC curve. Lastly, profit is drawn incorrectly. The rectangle cannot extend past the quantity sold.
    d. Quantity should be determined where MR = MC.

4.

Q	P	TR	MR	TC	MC	ATC
0	4.20	0.00		3.20		
1	3.80	3.80	3.80	4.20	1.00	4.20
2	3.40	6.80	3.00	5.60	1.40	2.80
3	3.00	9.00	2.20	7.80	2.20	2.60
4	2.60	10.40	1.40	10.40	2.60	2.60
5	2.20	11.00	0.60	13.40	3.00	2.68
6	1.90	11.40	0.40	16.80	3.40	2.80

a. Fixed cost is $3.20 per month per resident.
b. MC = MR at 3 collections per month. The price charged is $3 per pickup. Profit is 40 cents per pickup per person.
c. P = MC at 4 collections per month. The price charged would be $2.60 per pickup. There would be only normal profits. Economic profit would be zero.
d. The city government should prefer competitive bidding unless there is a natural monopoly. The quality of the pickup would be expected to be greater for the competitive industry because monopolists do not face competitors.

6. a. The most likely reason is price discrimination; individuals in Palo Alto have a less elastic demand than individuals in Pleasanton, and people with inelastic demands (short on time or about to run out of gas) cannot afford to look for a lower price.

    b. One possible policy is the following: They might suggest ruling that firms must charge the same price at all stations. The problem with this policy is one of enforcement. It would require enormous amounts of data and a large bureaucracy to enforce, as does any type of price control. Also, gas stations in places with higher real estate prices and wages have higher costs to cover and therefore may need to charge higher prices.

    c. Probably not; what the policy suggested in *b* would do is to equalize it, which would tend to help richer communities where gas prices now tend to be higher, and hurt poorer communities where gas prices tend now to be lower.

Web Questions

2. a. A patent is "a property right granted by the Government of the United States of America to an inventor "to exclude others from making, using, offering for sale, or selling the invention throughout the United States or importing the invention into the United States" for a limited time in exchange for public disclosure of the invention when the patent is granted." Inventors can produce and sell their inventions without a patent. An example is Coca-cola.

    b. The cost of a patent has been estimated by some to be between $5,000 and $10,000 over the life of the patent. The basic filing fee is $750 and maintenance fees are $890 at 3.5 years, $2,050 at 7.5 years, and $3,150 and 11.5 years. However, cost will also include a patent search, the patent application process, amendments to the patent application.

    c. The term of a new patent is 20 years from the date on which the application for the patent was filed in the United States. The government probably sets expiration dates for patents both to help consumers through lower prices and to stimulate further innovation.

Appendix A

2.   **a.** Q = 2, P = $39.50   **b.** ATC = $52
        c. Profit = -$25

4.   **a.** Q = 6, P = $18   **b.** Q = 12, P = 0

⬤ CHAPTER 13 Questions for Thought and Review

2. Firms differentiate products through advertising. The overriding objective of product differentiation is to maintain or increase market share by creating its own small monopolistic niche.

4. Product differentiation makes us better off to the degree that we prefer having choices of different varieties of the same product. However, in some cases, the differences may be imagined rather than real. Firms reinforce product differentiation with advertising, and so there is a question

whether devoting resources to advertising is a benefit (due to increased information) or a waste.

6. The monopolistic competitor does not earn economic profits because of free entry into the market.

8. Strategic pricing is the central characteristic of oligopoly. Monopolistic competitors face too many competitors to price strategically.

10. A cartel model is probably more likely to be judged based on performance, since a cartel is recognizable in that it acts like a monopolist, restricting output to raise price. Under the contestable market level, an oligopoly could perform exactly the same way that a perfectly competitive market does as long as there are no entry/exit barriers.

12. (In answering this question students may be aware of media coverage in the 1990s that suggested colleges colluded in establishing financial aid packages for students and in setting tuition.) Since colleges are not profit maximizers, it is difficult to characterize them as a cartel type of oligopoly. There certainly has been implicit and even explicit collusion; the goals of that collusion are complicated and not simply profit maximization.

14. The breakfast cereal market is definitely oligopolistic; the firms made interdependent strategic pricing decisions.

Problems and Exercises

2. a. The demand curve is kinked at $8 and the MR curve is discontinuous at $4. There are two places where MC = MR, at quantities 4 and 8, as shown.

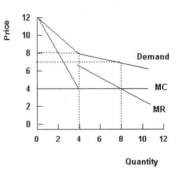

    b. The firm would prefer the equilibrium with the lower output, higher price, and higher profit. This is where output is 4 and price is about $7 a unit.

    c. If marginal cost falls, the level of output rises by a lot while the price falls by just a little.

    d. If marginal cost rises, the level of output falls by a little while the price rises by a lot.

    e. This part asks students to survey firms in their area about pricing strategies. The kinked demand model presented in the book is more likely.

4. a. This market is most likely characterized by oligopoly or possibly monopolistic competition. We say oligopoly because the largest firm will consider the response of its rivals in its decisions. We say monopolistic competition because there are many firms but their products are differentiated. There is some label recognition and loyalty.

b. The Herfindahl index is $428.49 + 289 + 44.9 + 4.84 + 4 + 51.4 = 822.63$.

c. The four-firm concentration ratio is $46.6\% = 20.7 + 17 + 6.7 + 2.2$.

6. a. See the following table.

	A: Tweedledee Does not cheat	A: Tweedledee Cheats
B: Tweedledum **Does not cheat**	A $2 mil B $2 mil	A $3 mil B $1 mil
B: Tweedledum **Cheats**	A less than $1 mil B $3 mil	A less than $2 mil B less than $2 mil

b. If the game is played only once, we would advise that Mr. Notsonice's profit-maximizing strategy is to cheat to maximize expected profit. What his "best" strategy is depends on how much he values being honest.

c. If the game were played over and over, we would advise that his profit-maximizing policy would be to develop some level of trust between the two players and agree not to cheat, avoiding the prisoner's dilemma.

d. The benefit of colluding would have to be greater than the expected benefit of cheating. It would have to be more than $3 million.

8. a. The hypothetical payoff matrix is shown in the accompanying graph. If neither offers free shipping each earns $1,000 profit. If only Amazon.com offers free shipping its profits are $2,000 while Buy.com loses $300. If both offer free shipping each earns profit of $200.

	Amazon.com	
	No Free **Shipping**	**Free** **Shipping**
Buy.com **No Free** **Shipping**	$1,000 $1,000	$2,000 -$300
Free **Shipping**	-$300 $2,000	$200 $200

b. Amazon.com is best off when it offers free shipping and Buy.com does not. It makes a profit of $2,000.

c. Buy.com is best off when it offers free shipping and Amazon.com does not. It makes a profit of $2,000.

d. Joint profits are maximized when neither offers free shipping. Combined profits are $2,000, instead of $1,700 in the case when one offers free shipping and the other does not.

e. Answers to this question will vary. At the time we answered the question, Amazon.com offered free shipping on purchases of $25 or more and Buy.com offered free shipping with no minimum purchase.

Web Questions

2. a. Answers will vary. I tried to under-price my competitor by 10 percent. I'd shut down if the price went below $500, which is the per unit variable cost.

b. My cumulative loss was about $125 million and market share was 50 percent. My competitor's cumulative loss was $26 million.

c. My competitor used a similar pricing strategy—to under-price me.

d. The other firm was likely to gain all the market because its unit variable costs were lower than mine.

● CHAPTER 14 Questions for Thought and Review

2. False. While profits are important to business, because of internal monitoring problems it is not clear that managers maximize profit. They may waste profit potential in high-priced benefits for themselves and in inefficiency generally. The market, however, provides a limit on inefficiency, and firms that exceed the limit and have losses go out of business.

4. X-inefficiency is the result of firms operating far less efficiently than they could technically. The economic forces of a market would knock a firm out of business if it operates less efficiently than the rest of the market. Only a monopolist can produce inefficiently and remain in the game.

6. This is not true because even if existing colleges are inefficient, competition from for-profit colleges would not necessarily force them out of business. The political and social forces can keep such colleges from developing. Moreover, some colleges receive state assistance or have endowments that allow them to hold their costs down even if they are inefficient.

8. This is true. By the same reasoning used in the answer to question 7, the price could decrease below the competitive equilibrium level. At that below-equilibrium price, some consumers could not get goods, but the consumers who could get goods would be able to hold the prices low nonetheless; it would be in their interest to do so.

10. Natural monopolies, by definition, are the result of a process in which market conditions dictate that monopoly is the most efficient way to produce in that industry. To break up such firms would likely result in higher costs, and thus while it would be true that there could be more competitors, the benefits associated with more competition (principally, lower prices) would not be achieved.

12. It launched a marketing campaign to retain brand recognition and loyalty to round up before the year 2000. In the year 2000 it also began to lower price to further cement its position in the market and discourage entry.

14. It needs to be dynamically efficient and able to promote cost-reducing or product-enhancing technological change. For this it needs funds to carry on research or new technologies and an ability to earn profits from that research. Oligopoly best meets these criteria.

16. Network externalities lower costs as more people use a product. As network externalities broaden the use of a product, the need for a single standard becomes more important and eventually wins out. The firm with the standard is the big winner and will dominate the market. Even better technology will have a hard time competing with the standard.

18. An advantage is that the prize will not limit future use of the idea, and thus will provide more efficiency. The disadvantage is that to achieve the same level of economic reward, the prize will have to be large, which means that it would have to be funded by taxes, which would have negative incentive effects. Also, directing prizes at specific invention goals may discourage the development of technologies whose discovery has not yet been foreseen; many of the most important technologies today have been invented in that way.

Problems and Exercises

2. If suppliers were able to restrict their output to Qr, price would rise to Pr. Suppliers kept out of the market lose area E in producer surplus. The consumers, on the other hand, lose both areas D and B. Area B is transferred to suppliers as additional revenue leaving D and E as deadweight loss.

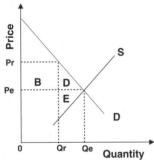

4. See the accompanying graph. The monopolist would be willing to spend any of its profit. This is depicted as the rectangle A.

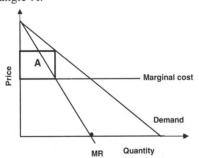

6. a. It would likely decrease the importance of art museums that exist to show "originals."
  b. It would reduce the rents of individuals—if not the holders of the art, who would gain from the royalties of selling the reproductions, but the museums and museum curators that exist to show current art. Also there are other large social resistance to this sort of innovation that makes museums irrelevant.

  c. These are allowed, but are owned by either the symphony or music label who sells them. Listeners are often barred from recording concerts.
  d. It would likely increase the demand for symphonies and for musicians to play in them because there would be no alternative ways to listen to the music.
  e. The most likely explanation is historical circumstance.

8. a. It is essentially buying a monopoly on the campus.
  b. There would be more competition, and lower prices for soda.
  c. It depends. It is a transfer of consumer surplus from students to the college; whether it is a gain depends on what the college does with the money that it receives.

Web Questions

2. We chose Laurence Ellison, CEO of Oracle.
  a. The 6-year average annual return for Oracle was 19 percent, above the industry average by 7 percent.
  b. The average over the past 5 years is about $139,524.
  c. What's fair is difficult to say. Forbes gave him a B rating. We would need to know how his compensation is determined—whether it was based on performance and what risks he took to receive that salary. Also, what are his opportunity costs?

⬤ CHAPTER 15 Questions for Thought and Review

Questions for Thought and Review

2. In the Standard Oil case the Court determined that the company was a structural monopoly (it controlled 90 percent of its market), but that alone was not a violation of the Sherman Act. Rather, it was the firm's behavior that brought it into violation. Thus, the firm was found guilty of unfair business practices. In the ALCOA case the key issue was the determination of the firm's market, and hence its share of that market. Determining that ALCOA had 90 percent of the aluminum market, the Court declared it a monopoly, and ALCOA was broken up.

4. The Clayton Antitrust Act gave specific guidelines and provided for more vigorous enforcement than the vague Sherman Act. It made four specific monopolistic practices illegal when their effect was to lessen competition.

6. Financial aid is often need-based, and so in some sense is an attempt to equalize the price as a proportion of income for students. Again, the test is the impact, and for many students financial aid is the key to access to the college of their choice. It may be more discriminatory not to have it. Moreover, the fact that something is discriminatory does not necessarily make it bad.

8. As an economist for the firm, I would want the broader definition of the market to make the firm's share a smaller proportion. Thus, I would argue for the three-digit industry as the definition of the market.

10. In some ways the service has improved, but in other ways it has worsened. What would have happened in the absence of the breakup is difficult to say. What this tells us is that making judgments about policy is enormously difficult and requires intricate knowledge of the industry affected.

12. Microsoft was charged with having a monopoly in the personal computer operating systems market. In a dynamic view of the market, technological advances, such as open-source operating systems and the merging of software and hardware, will see the market open to more competition in the future.

14. Conglomerate mergers occur when two relatively unrelated businesses merge. They tend to be approved under our antitrust laws on the assumption that they do not significantly restrict competition. These mergers should be considered like other mergers in terms of their effect, and approved or not on that basis. A blanket policy against such mergers might eliminate some mergers that would benefit firms, consumers, and the economy.

16. The two methods government may use to deal with natural monopolies are regulation and government ownership. Price regulation usually takes the form of requiring the firm to charge its average total cost plus a profit margin; this gives the firm no incentive to hold down costs, and cost increases lead directly to price increases. Another problem is that once regulation is established it may extend far beyond the natural monopolies and be introduced into industries where competition could work. Government ownership of natural monopolies is used most often in countries outside the United States, and also has the problem of no incentive to hold costs down or to introduce new technologies. Government-owned firms guarantee jobs and offer high wages, but they pass higher costs on to the consumers.

Problems and Exercises

2. In a monopolistic competition model the firms have only a small share of the market and make no profit, so antitrust would have little effect. In a cartel market, firms get together and allocate market share. Antitrust would prevent that, holding prices down and increasing quantity supplied. The graph of monopoly is the relevant graph. In a contestable market model, potential competition, not market structure, determines equilibrium, so antitrust would have little effect unless it influenced barriers to entry and exit.

4. a. The likely basis of this suit was predatory pricing to keep price so low that American Airlines' competitors would go out of business and so that the company would enjoy a monopoly position and raise prices.
   b. Knowledge of their financial instability only strengthens the argument. It suggests that American Airlines would not have to hold prices down for too long before its competitors folded.

Web Questions

2. a. "FTC Seeks Court Order to Force Blockbuster to Comply with Premerger Rules" (3/4/05) and "NHL gets $3 billion offer for entire league" (3/4/05).
   b. The FTC claims that Blockbuster has not provided adequate pricing data, a condition of its merger with Hollywood Video. The NHL article discusses how the purchase of the entire league might stifle competition and make it difficult for union negotiations.

c. Both are horizontal mergers because both Blockbuster and Hollywood videos rent videos. Also independent owners of the NHL all provide the same product—teams, space and equipment. Combining them would result in one owner of all teams, space and equipment.

CHAPTER 16 Questions for Thought and Review

2. This chapter opens with a quotation from Voltaire: "Work banishes those three great evils: boredom, vice, and poverty." Welfare laws, to the degree that they discourage work, therefore, can be said to harm the people they are meant to help. While they help people in the short run, they establish a dependency relationship, which can hurt people in the long run.

4. As argued by University of Chicago economist, Sherwin Rosen, assuming that individuals want to see the best, the new technology would give a greater premium for the best performers of each genre, and thus would increase inequality.

6. The elasticity of the labor supply is measured by the percent change in the quantity supplied divided by the percent change in the wage. In this case, 5 divided by 20 is less than 1 (it is 0.25), so the supply is said to be inelastic.

8. Supply/demand analysis is partial equilibrium analysis; immigration policy often affects the general economy and thus requires an analysis of spillover effects and changes that partial equilibrium analysis cannot capture.

10. If the labor market were monopsonistic, so that the pay were less than the competitive wage, the minimum wage could change the effective supply facing the monopsonist and could raise the wage and increase employment simultaneously, as in the accompanying graph. In the graph, the monopsonist would hire Qm workers, paying Wm. With a minimum wage We, higher than Wm, the monopsonist would hire Qf workers, higher than Qm, paying Wf, a wage higher than Wm.

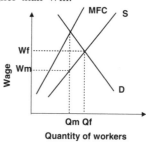

12. The fact that unemployment among blacks is nearly twice as high as it is among whites can be explained by many factors, including discrimination. There are also differences in existing income levels, with the result that many blacks reside in poorer neighborhoods and thus do not have equal access to education and other services that would lead to higher employment. The choices available in terms of opportunities may also lead young people to choose nonmarket activities over participation in the labor force. Possible solutions will vary, but could include stronger antidiscrimination enforcement, better educational programs and law enforcement to decrease the payoffs to illegal, non-market activities.

Problems and Exercises

2. a. Based on standard economic theory, one would expect the number of teens employed to rise and the employment of nonteens to decline as the relative wage of teens declines. This assumes that the minimum wage is above the market-clearing wage. Further, one would expect that a large number of employees would lose their jobs at the end of their training period (six months) for "just" reasons, such as not learning the job adequately.

   b. It is likely that the administrative costs of participating in the program were higher than the benefits of hiring teens at the lower training wage. It could also be that market clearing wage in teen labor market was already higher than the subminimum wage. A third possibility is the focal point phenomenon: teens may focus on the mandated minimum wage as their reservation wage and refuse to accept a job at the subminimum training wage.

4. a. Since they will have to pay 20 percent of what they save in added tuition in addition to the 20 percent income tax rate, the implicit marginal tax rate they face on income they save will be 36 percent. The tax on assets is a tax on savings after income taxes have been subtracted, so the tuition tax has to be adjusted to make it a tax on pre-income-tax income. So the relevant tax on tuition as a percent of pretax income is $(1 - t_i)\ 3\ t_t$ = $[(1 - 0.2) \times 0.2 = 0.16]$ where t_i is income tax and t_t is the tuition tax. Add this to the 20 percent income tax to get 36 percent.

   b. The second child will raise it to 48.8% = $[(1 - 0.36) \times 0.2 + 0.36] \times 100$. The third child will raise it to 59.04% = $[(1 - 0.488) \times 0.2 + 0.488] \times 100$.

   c. This is a complicated question, but one could argue that divorced parents share in the obligation to pay for college equally and therefore the relative incomes and asset shares of combined incomes and assets should be used to determine contributions. In reality one parent might alone bear the burden of the cost, having to shoulder contributions by both. The second part to this question is for the student to research.

   d. An ability-based scholarship program would attract students of significantly higher caliber if their elasticity of demand is high, but it would most likely compromise the diversity of the student body with respect to income. It would also promote retaliation by other schools, and the long-run benefit in having brighter students might be very small.

6. a. Firms hire children because children's marginal productivity relative to their wage is higher than it is for alternative workers. Children's marginal product/wage ratio could be higher because the child wage is lower or because the marginal product is higher. Children are often energetic, pliable, and dexterous. For certain jobs these traits could make the children's productivity high. Children may also be more trainable than older employees.

   b. Children work for the same reasons that others work—they need money, work is what is expected of them, and so on.

   c. In deciding whether there should be an international ban on child labor, one must look at the effects of that ban. What are the children's opportunity costs of working? If the ban will lead to children starving, the ban does them no good; if it allows them to go to school while the firm hires their parents instead, the ban may help the children. One must also look at the ease with which some firms may get around the ban. If it can be easily avoided in some countries, then the ban will likely hurt industries in those countries where it is effective. Also, one should consider whether the work gives children anything useful (such as education) besides pay.

8. a. Assuming that both markets are perfectly competitive (and we know how competitive campaigns are), Derek Jeter contributes much more to society than does the President of the United States.

   b. First of all, neither market is perfectly competitive. Neither Jeter nor U.S. Presidents are easily replaceable. In addition, institutional factors enter into the decision about what to pay. Being a U.S. President is considered to be a service to one's country and presidents get many non-wage perks, such as Air Force One and the White House. And after leaving office, past Presidents can sell their biographies for many millions of dollars. The adjustments suggest that calculating marginal productivity is difficult and perhaps ultimately impossible.

10. a. I would expect the test scores to increase.

   b. It would have to give them low test scores, otherwise the teachers would have an incentive to have only good students to take the test.

   c. It would make them much more likely to teach to the test, and conduct more test preparation sessions.

   d. In this case, the test scores returned to what they were before the program was implemented. No lasting changes in structure resulted.

12. a. No, one would expect that drivers would work more on busy days when their effective wage rate is higher, and less on slow days, because their marginal return is higher on busy days.

   b. It can do so because failing to achieve the daily income target feels like incurring a loss, so drivers put in longer hours to avoid it. Beating their target feels like a win, so once they have achieved it, there is less incentive to keep working.

14. a. Increases in marginal tax rates for large changes in income were significantly higher in the 1970s than in the early 2000s. Therefore, in the early 2000s, families could take home a larger percentage of their increase in wages than in the 1970s. France has very high tax rates. In fact, Edward Prescott estimates that for every 100 euros worth of goods produced, Europeans as a whole are taxed 60 euros.

   b. Other possible explanations are institutional changes in France and the U.S. that occurred at the same time. For example, in the U.S. unions are much less powerful today than 30 they were years ago.

Web Questions

1. **a.** Pay equity, according to NCPE, means the elimination of sex and race based discrimination in the wage setting system; that is, the criteria employers use to set wages must be sex and race neutral.

   b. The Equal Pay Act of 1963 and Title VII of the Civil Rights Act of 1962 are the two laws that are designed to protect workers from wage discrimination.

   c. The NCPE believes women are still segregated into a few low-paying occupations. Anti-discrimination laws cover pay equity within occupations.

2. **a.** Stephen Moore in his commentary states that he believes immigration should be increased for highly skill workers.

   b. Externalities; every additional high-tech worker brings to the United States about $110,000 of free human capital.

   c. In 1998, the unemployment rate in the high-tech field was less than 2%, the high tech fields were growing rapidly.

   d. No, Stephen Moore would not argue that the number of visas for unskilled labor should increase. Unskilled labor does not have the externalities of additional jobs for the U.S.

Appendix

2. They would likely hire fewer workers since they would take into account the fall in the marginal revenue product that hiring more workers would cause.

4. Yes. Widespread introduction of such programs would likely reduce the demand for teachers and lower their pay.

6. If the firm was a monopolist, the marginal revenue would be less than $3.00, and thus the amount it would be willing to pay would fall.

8. **a.** The proposal that should be adopted is the one that minimizes costs. Using the cost minimization condition, proposal A is the one that minimizes costs (30/5 = 42/7 = 36/6).

   b. If the price of labor rises to $14, none of the proposals meets the cost minimization condition. There are other combinations that would meet the cost minimization condition.

● CHAPTER 17 Questions for Thought and Review

2. The top 20 percent of individuals in Bangladesh earn 38 percent of the income.

4. Arguments could be made for both approaches. Poverty could be defined relatively since one of our concerns is the distribution of income and the gap between the rich and poor. Poverty could also be defined absolutely since another of our concerns is that people have enough to eat, which is an absolute concept.

6. The observed difference may be due to supply and demand factors. If many people wish to be English teachers and few wish to be garbage collectors, then market factors will result in a higher wage for the garbage collectors—and if one

believes in the market mechanism, this is right. That question raises other, more complicated questions about fairness of compensation and the social value of different occupations; it has no right answers.

8. The answer to this question will depend in part on the individual student's circumstances. In general, the incentive effects of a tax may result in a switch from labor to leisure.

10. On the surface the democratic system of one person/one vote would seem to suggest that the politics of redistribution would favor the poor, but it doesn't. One would expect that the poor would use their power to make sure that income was redistributed to them from the rich, but they don't. The reasons for this include the fact that many of the poor don't vote, and so consequently they are not seen as a voting bloc by politicians. Another reason is that when poor people do vote, they vote with other issues in mind. Also, campaigns require financing, which is often supplied by the rich, and so their interests may be more represented than those of the poor.

Problems and Exercises

2. **a.** Taking into account in-kind benefits and unreported income would reduce the number of people seen in poverty. Taking account of the fact that food makes up only a quarter of the family's budget would increase the number of people in poverty. Taking account of home ownership and cost-of-living differences would involve distributional consequences. It would raise the level of poverty for some groups and lower it for others.

   b. What is fair involves normative judgments. Even if the adjustments were made, one could still argue that the current definition of poverty is too low and that benefits should be increased.

4. Four conditions that you might list before you would favor equality of income are (1) that individuals have essentially the same needs, (2) that they work the same amount, (3) that they have essentially the same health, and (4) that they have put in the same effort up to this point.

   a. Depending on what conditions you listed, it could change your views on welfare in a number of different ways.

   b. Again, it depends on what conditions you chose. If the condition does not include differences in ability, then you would likely favor a progressive income tax.

   c. If the tax were progressive in wage rates, rather than income, hard work would be encouraged and raw ability (if represented by wage level) would be taxed more. If you did not list ability, then you should say that the conditions would be better met.

6. **a.** This would increase the incentive to work since working longer hours will not push one up into the higher tax bracket.

   b. To the extent that the wage rate measures taxability better than income does, this tax system is fair.

   c. Making the tax system regressive in hours worked would further increase the incentive to work longer hours, likely increasing the average number of hours worked.

d. Instituting such a tax system faces enormous difficulties. Wage rates for each individual would have to be measured, and many positions have no explicit wage rate. Some method for calculating wage rates of salaried positions would have to be designed. Also, measuring and verifying the hours each employee works would be difficult, especially for the self-employed.

Web Questions

2. a. Social Security earnings credits are based on wages an employee earns and these credits are used later to determine eligibility for Social Security benefits. In 2005, one credit is earned for each $920 in earnings up to a max of 4 credits a year.

b. Most people need 40 credits (10 years of work) to qualify for Social Security benefits.

c. There is no charge for a social security number.

d. Medicare is automatic age 65 or with the start of Social Security or Railroad Retirement benefits. Someone who is on Social Security disability for more than 24 months or someone with permanent kidney failure is also automatically eligible.

e. Part A Medicare is hospital insurance and carries no fee, Part B is medical insurance and at present carries a fee of $78.20 a month.

● CHAPTER 18 Questions for Thought and Review

2. The marginal social benefit of a good that exhibits positive externalities is greater than the private social benefit because the trade results in a benefit to people outside the trade.

4. An economist might argue about the word acceptable. While not many people would argue that any pollution is good, an economist who realizes that eliminating pollution completely is probably an impossible goal would find pollution acceptable if it could be reduced to a cost-efficient level.

6. The tax on oil will probably affect the pollution coming from oil, but it is possible that users could switch to other fuel sources that actually result in other and greater forms of pollution. Moreover, some types of pollution would be unaffected. Thus, the net impact on the environment is difficult to predict.

8. The public aspect of safety is that if safety provides a safe environment, it is provided for all people and one person enjoying safety does not preclude others from benefiting from that safety. Naming streets allows people to orient themselves in towns and facilitates communication. Once a street is named, it benefits all people. No one can be excluded from referring to that name. In addition, one person using that street name does not preclude others from referring to that street with its name. Before the street is named, however, if a particular name is used to refer to more than one street, the value of that name in providing geographic orientation will be diminished. The public good aspect of the lighthouse and newspaper is that once it is produced it can be consumed over and over again and benefit those who use it. Though in the case of the newspaper, the owner can keep others from benefiting by keeping it to himself. A steak dinner has no public good aspects, since it is both rival and excludable.

10. You might offer the average, $600. If sellers of cherries want $700, your $600 would buy you only lemons, since only the seller knows whether they are selling a chance on a lemon; thus you would likely lower your asking price to reflect the fact that there are now only lemons in the market.

12. In a market, when buyers and sellers have different amounts of information about the good for sale, a problem occurs called the adverse selection problem. The problem is that the market for quality products disappears. In commercial dating services, the seller certainly has more information about the negative (and positive) aspects of the product than the buyer. We suspect that the market has fewer "acceptable" dates than the general population.

14. To keep rates to a minimum, insurance companies estimate information about individuals by categorizing them. If everyone paid the same amount, low-cost customers would be paying for high-cost customers and eventually change companies, leaving only high-cost customers. One would expect that, statistically, married drivers are safer drivers.

16. Many answers are possible, beginning with (1) the label on their breakfast cereal, (2) the roads they use to get to school, (3) either the school they go to (if it is public) or the federal funds their school receives (if it is private), (4) the tax they pay on the snack at the snack bar, and (5) the laws that are enforced on the roadways. The benefits of labeling are that consumers can better plan nutritional balance and are better informed about the product they are buying. Whether this is justified is unclear. If consumers wanted such labeling, there would be market pressure to include that information on cereal boxes. Some labeling, such as whether the product contains genetically modified food, could unnecessarily alarm consumers. This would hurt those companies that use genetically modified food and help others that don't. Whether genetically modified food is harmful is still up for debate.

18. The advanced degree serves the same purpose as a license. It reduces the supply and increases the wage.

20. Three market failures that possibly justify national parks are (1) National parks are possibly public goods. Use by one does not deplete their use by others, and it is difficult to exclude to exclude people from using them. National parks are not pure public goods because they can be gated with toll booths at their entrances, requiring fees to enter. However, one aspect of national parks – existence value – is not be excludable. Existence value is the value a citizen of a country derives from the knowledge that the country has national parks. National parks create national pride and identity. This value is both nonrival and nonexcludable, leading to underproduction of national parks by the private market. (2) National parks create positive externalities. People who visit national parks learn about taking care of the environment, our national heritage, the complexity of nature – education that can be brought into other parts of economic life. Another positive externality is that they provide resources for a variety of research that themselves provide benefits to society. (3) National parks may experience increasing returns to scale. That is, the market is small relative to the size of the technically efficient firm. Thus, national parks can be seen as a natural monopoly of sorts, justifying government intervention. Source: "Market

Failures and the Rationale for National Parks," *Journal of Economic Education*, Fall 2002.

22. Pro People should undergo testing before getting life insurance because the person who is more likely to seek thrills is a greater risk to the insurance company, and should bear these higher costs themselves, rather than having them passed on to non-risk seekers.

Con People should not undergo testing before getting life insurance because whether a person is a greater risk depends on revealed behavior not the proclivity toward a particular behavior. We, not our genes, decide our behavior. Undergoing such testing would end up with people who have the gene but who avoid such behavior to unnecessarily pay a higher premium.

Problems and Exercises

2. a. Proposal A would force a downward shift in each demand curve, while Proposal B would raise the price at each quantity, also shifting the demand curves down.

   b. The consumers in group 1 have a more elastic demand, so a small increase in price results in a large decrease in quantity; these consumers can more easily adjust their usage and would therefore favor Proposal A. The members of group 2 would be more likely to favor the tax because changing their usage is more difficult. Their inelasticity can be interpreted to mean that they are more willing to pay a higher price than to use less.

4. a. The price of getting rid of garbage rose while the price of getting rid of recyclables did not. People substituted recycling for disposing.

   b. The weight of garbage fell by less than volume because the fee was based on volume; people stuffed the bags fuller, placing more garbage into a 32-gallon bag.

   c. With a flat fee, the marginal cost of placing out more garbage was essentially zero, so in the graph below, Q0 garbage pick-up was demanded. With volume pricing, the price rose to P1, and quantity demanded fell to Q1.

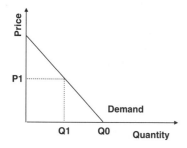

6. a. Most likely the price of all cars in California rose, and air quality rose as well.

   b. This law could possibly have increased pollution if consumers held on to their older, less efficient but lower-cost, higher-performance gas cars and delayed purchase of an electric car. This would have increased the average age of cars on the road, increasing pollution. Furthermore, if electric cars (the most likely candidates)

were designed to meet the no-pollution requirement, it could be that the process of generating sufficient electricity to run the cars would produce even more pollution, at which point even more regulation might be imposed. (The law was modified and never went fully into effect.)

   c. Economists generally favor market incentive programs over direct regulation. A market incentive program to reduce pollution by a certain percent might be to tax drivers of older, high-pollution cars and use the tax revenue to subsidize those who purchase the new, no-pollution cars. This approach will more likely equate marginal cost with marginal benefit. Another market incentive program would be to increase taxes on gasoline, causing demand for gasoline to decrease as people switch to more efficient vehicles.

8. a. Some dairy farmers would probably argue that labeling is unnecessary since the drugs they administer have been certified by the FDA. Dairy farmers who do not use BST would support BST labeling.

   b. If BST were to be listed on milk containers, one could argue that all drugs and antibiotics should be listed. However, such listing (without more information) may cause consumer concern. To support BST labeling but not other labeling, one must argue that BST is different.

   c. One would suspect that dairy farmers who support BST labeling would not support the broader law that might include drugs that they do use. Only those few farmers who use wholly organic farming would support full labeling.

Web Questions

2. a. OSHA was established in 1970 to assure safe and healthy working conditions by assisting states and providing research, information, education, and training in the field of occupational safety and health.

   b. The market failure was lack of information. Workers were not being compensated for the hazard of unsafe, unhealthy workplaces because they were unaware of the hazards or lacked the ability to ask for safer environments.

   c. Most workers come under OSHA's jurisdiction, a few examples of exceptions are miners, transportation workers and the self employed.

   e. OSHA conducts inspections to point out problems, to educate and train workers, and to enforce safety and health codes with the help of the individual states and the Department of Labor.

● CHAPTER 19 Questions for Thought and Review

2. A price support system achieved through acreage restriction is illustrated in the accompanying graph. The graph shows that, under this system, the farmers gain rectangle A as income from the government in the form of payments not to grow wheat, and rectangle B from consumers who pay more for the wheat the farmers do grow.

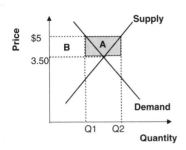

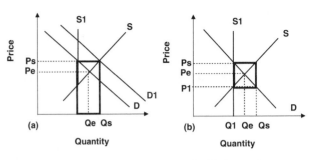

4. As shown in the accompanying graph, the method of price support that is most costly to the taxpayer is the subsidies on sales to keep prices down; taxpayers must finance the subsidy payments on all subsidized farm products, represented by areas A, B, and C.

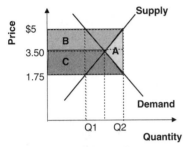

6. Tariffs and quotas generally accompany price support systems in order to prevent lower-priced foreign products from competing in the domestic market.

8. Governments find grandfathering a good option when they institute price supports because it is the easiest way of restricting supply. Existing suppliers retain their level of output, added or new entry is denied or limited, and the policy is easy to enact because there is no group lobbying against it, and easy to enforce.

10. The nonrecourse loan is a price support system in which government buys goods in the form of collateral on defaulting loans. The land bank program is an incentive-based price support in which the government supports prices by giving farmers economic incentives to reduce supply.

Problems and Exercises

2. The graph below shows an increase in demand sufficient to raise the market price to Ps. The market quantity is also increased to Qs. The cost to the government is the shaded rectangle. If instead supply is restricted (shown in the far right graph), the government must pay the farmers (Ps - P1) for every unit not grown at price Ps, resulting in a cost equal to the area of the bolded rectangle. Therefore, assuming that you cannot use the corn, the second policy is preferred.

4. a. Consumers of peanuts pay more in higher prices— estimated at between $190 and $369 million a year— and suffer from reduced consumption.

b. See the accompanying graph. Area B represents additional costs to consumers, while areas D and E represent deadweight loss of the program.

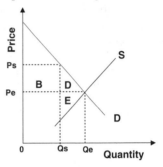

c. The land with peanut quotas is a government license to sell millions of pounds of peanuts and thus is priced higher to include the present value of the future returns to that license.

d. The government's costs would likely rise enormously in the attempt to keep supply constrained to maintain the 50 percent above competitive equilibrium price.

e. If the United States limited the guaranteed high price to U.S. producers only, administrative procedures would have to be set up to see that imported peanuts are not passed off as U.S.-produced peanuts.

6. a. The reason the difference exists is mostly political. A small group of ranchers benefits greatly from the reduced fee and is a strong lobby for the cause.

b. An advantage to getting a lower fee could be that the U.S. government could require more from ranchers in their care of the land. Also, it helps ranchers who have a difficult time competing, and allows for wider use of public lands.

c. One would expect excess demand because at the price below equilibrium, the quantity of land supplied is lower than the quantity demanded.

Web Questions

2. **a.** Genetically engineered crops are crops that are the result of seeds that have been genetically altered to borrow desirable traits from another crop that currently do not exist in that particular crop. They benefit farmers because they are pest-resistant, poor weather-tolerant, and can be shipped and stored better.

    b. Genetic engineering has led to stronger crops resistant to a greater number of pests. This has lowered operating costs and boosted yield for those farmers using genetically engineered seeds. In the short run this has increased farm profits.

    c. In the long run, because demand for crops is inelastic, this is likely to lead to greater farm production, but lower farm income and lower profits.

CHAPTER 20 Questions for Thought and Review

2. The problem with proposing only Pareto optimal policies would lie in developing them. As the text points out, there are no examples of real-world policies that benefit some people without hurting anyone. If economists seek to propose only Pareto optimal policies, they may end up proposing no policies. Focusing only on Pareto optimality condemns them to irrelevancy in real-world affairs.

4. The usual arguments against the buying and selling of body organs include the concern that people might seek to make such sales for the money involved and exploit the poor, and that those with the ability to pay would get needed organs sooner than those without means, again favoring the well-off over the poor. Some may believe that it is immoral to sell body parts. Arguments for selling body parts include that both parties freely enter the transaction, and that both sellers (since they decided they preferred the money to the body part) and buyers benefit. Economic theory provides no answers to such questions.

6. The textbook suggests a method for valuing one's life. Your answer should consider what you would pay to reduce their chance of dying by a certain amount. The value of life is that amount times the inverse of the reduced probability of dying.

8. An economist might propose a policy that has little chance of adoption because he or she might be removed from the concerns that make policies unadoptable (i.e., political concerns). In so doing, economists put ideas into the real world and may influence the way people think. The goal behind policy proposals is not always to get them implemented.

10. Most politicians say that they are out to do the public good, but in practice they often do things that just sound good in their quest to be reelected.

12. Any decision about prisons involves complicated ethical and moral as well as economic considerations. In reference to the economic issues alone, it would seem that it does make sense to build more prisons since, assuming prisons are currently full, the marginal benefits of additional prisons are greater than the marginal costs.

Problems and Exercises

2. **a.** A higher percentage of births by C-section are done at for-profit hospitals, most likely because the profit margin for C-sections is higher than that for vaginal births.

    b. The implication that can be drawn is that goodwill cannot be relied on to lead to low-cost health programs. Other mechanisms must be instituted to ensure efficiency.

    c. In the case of fixed payment, the for-profit hospital would probably do more vaginal births, which cost less than C-sections. The C-section rate would most likely rise at nonprofit institutions as necessary C-sections are limited at for-profit hospitals and shift toward nonprofit hospitals.

4. **a.** Since the supply of teenage baby-sitters shifted to the left just as the demand for them shifted to the right, the equilibrium wage probably rose dramatically, reducing the number of times parents go out without their children.

    b. The price of baby-sitters probably rose as described in a.

    c. The average age of baby-sitters probably fell as parents loosened their requirements of babysitters in an attempt to find substitutes for the reduced number of 14- to 17-year-olds.

6. **a.** According to standard economic reasoning, the value of an additional dollar spent in preventing death is (assuming the journal's figures are correct) more valuable in the United States than in Sweden and in Portugal, and thus more money should go to saving lives in the United States. However, there are moral issues that complicate matters and make the answer unclear.

    b. This is a complicated question. First, many Americans fly in Portugal and, second, it would be bad publicity for an airline to value lives of people differently by national origin or to even acknowledge making such a marginal cost/marginal benefit analysis with regard to safety precautions at all. Moreover, there are those sticky moral issues, which lead one to value all life equally.

    c. To the degree that the cost of the standard is the same, the standard economic answer is yes. If noneconomic factors are included, the answer is not so clear-cut.

8. **a.** The likely effect of that proposal would be a flood of criticism. Certain human rights such as the sanctity of the human body are held in high regard regardless of societal status. A proposal that, on its face, seems economically sound is not acceptable if it does not include issues of human rights.

    b. That was the effect because the economic model did not account for all issues. Morality issues provoke strong political reactions.

10. **a.** The study is based on the cost benefit analysis that states that a consumer will purchase a helmet if the value of the reduced risk of head injury is greater than

the cost of the helmet. So the value of life is greater than or equal to the annualized cost of helmet divided by the change in the probability of death due to the purchase of the helmet.

b. $1.6 million.

c. Because the helmet will be less effective in saving life, the probability of reducing the risk of death falls, so that the value of life increases.

d. Firstly, this measures how much the parents value their children's life, not the value children place on their own lives because parents make the buying decision. Another difficulty is addressed in part c. This calculation also places no value on reducing the risk of injury.

Web Questions

2. a. According to the New Party, a living wage at an absolute minimum means that someone working full time should never fall below the poverty line, the exact amount varies from state to state but at this time generally between $6.50 and $7.50 an hour with health benefits.

b. At this time minimum wage is $5.15 per hour.

c. The New Party's arguments for a living wage include: an honest day's work should be rewarded with an honest day's pay; the economy is moving in the wrong direction, too many working Americans still cannot make ends meet; and tax dollars do not fix problems but often make them worse—subsidies are not the answer.

● CHAPTER 21 Questions for Thought and Review

2. If Widgetland produces only widgets, it can make 240 of them and the opportunity cost is 1/1. If Wadgetland makes only wadgets could produce 720 of them at an opportunity cost of .25/1 (widgets to wadgets). Since the opportunity costs differ, there is a basis for trade in production. Widgetland should produce 240 widgets, and trade 60 of the widgets for 120 wadgets. Wadgetland should produce only 720 wadgets and trade 120 wadgets for 60 widgets. Both countries will be better off.

4. Traders get big gains from trade in newly opened markets. The more competition that exists in international trade, the more the traders' gains will be reduced and the more gains are.

6. Countries producing goods with economies of scale get a larger gain from trade. Trade allows an increase in production and if there are economies of scale, the increase can lower the average cost of production, and lower the price of the good in the producing country.

8. Any three of the following ten would be correct: (1) Skills of the U.S. labor force, (2) U.S. governmental institutions, (3) U.S. physical and technological infrastructure, (4) English as the international language of business, (5) wealth from past production, (6) U.S. natural resources, (7) cachet, (8) inertia, (9) U.S. intellectual property rights, and (10) relatively open immigration policy.

10. The law of one price is that in a competitive market there will be pressure for equal factors to be priced equally. It is important to any discussion of the future of the U.S. economy because relative wages are higher in the United States than in most other countries. The U.S. faces forces that will adjust these wages until the relative prices are equal. This will likely happen by a combination of the following: (1) faster wage growth in other countries, (2) slower wage growth in the United States, and (3) a decline in the value of the dollar.

12. An equitable method might be to tax those who gain from the trade liberalization and give the proceeds to those who are hurt by it. Assuming the original distribution is equitable and the government is not trying to redistribute income, this method is equitable because the combined policies make everyone better off. The political problems with implementation includes: (1) Everyone will try to exaggerate the amount they are hurt and minimize the amount they are helped. Thus actually finding a tax that accomplishes the goal will be difficult. (2) Once the taxes and subsidies are in place, they may not be removed after the adjustment of displaced workers is complete. Losers will be overcompensated and gainers will be taxed too much. (3) Those who have big gains (big business) may have more political power and be able to prevent the implementation of this policy.

14. Economists support free trade because it forces domestic producers to operate efficiently and it increases consumer welfare.

15. Tariffs and quotas have similar effects on limiting trade (both shift the supply curve to the left). The big difference is who gets the revenue from the resulting increase in the price of imports. With a tariff the government gets the revenue. With a quota, the revenues accrue to the foreign producers. You can see this graphically in the margin graph on page 493 of the text.

16. Both increase the price of the import, helping the domestic producers. In the case of the voluntary restraint, increases in price result in increased revenue to foreign firms and increased demand is met entirely by the domestic market. In the case of the tariff, the revenue raised goes to the domestic government.

18. With a price floor, there is a loss of consumer surplus, higher prices and lower quantities.

20. The WTO is the successor to GATT. Both work toward agreements to reduce trade. WTO includes enforcement mechanisms that GATT did not have.

Problems and Exercises

2. a. No. Both countries' opportunity cost of producing pickles is 2/1 (they must give up 2 olives to get 1 pickle). Neither has a comparative advantage, so there is no basis for trade.

b. If there are economies of scale, it definitely pays for both countries to specialize since doing so would lower total costs. Which one should specialize is an open question since neither has a comparative advantage.

4. **a.** Firms may produce in Germany, because (1) transportation costs in the other countries may be very high, so that if these costs are included, it would not be efficient to produce there; (2) there might be tariffs or quotas for imports into Germany that will prevent producing elsewhere; (3) the productivity of German labor may be so much higher that unit labor costs in Germany are the lowest; and (4) historical circumstances may have led to production in Germany and the cost of moving production may exceed potential gains.

b. One would expect some short-run movement from Greece and Italy into Germany, but only in the long run will there be substantial movement. Social restrictions such as language and culture will limit labor mobility. With such high unemployment in Germany already, one would not expect much short-run movement.

c. I would need to know how stable the political system is, what the worker productivity rates are, how sound the infrastructure (such as roads) is, and what the tax differences are between the two countries.

6. **a.** The production possibility curve is shown in the accompanying graph.

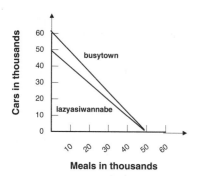

b. Since Busytown can produce more cars when all of its resources are devoted to producing cars, Busytown has an absolute advantage in producing cars. Neither has an absolute advantage in producing gourmet meals since if each devotes all of its resources to producing meals, each can produce 50, but Lazyasiwannabe has a comparative advantage in gourmet meals. It must give up 1 cars for each gourmet meal while Busytown must give up 1.2 cars for each gourmet meal.

c. Busytown should produce 60,000 cars and Lazyasiwannabe should produce 50,000 meals. Lazyasiwannabe then offers Busytown 22,000 meals for 24,000 cars. Since Busytown must give up only 24,000 cars for 22,000 meals (instead of the 26,4,00 cars it would have to if it made 22,000 meals itself) it accepts this offer. Lazyasiwannabe ends up with 28,000 meals and 24,000 cars while Busytown ends up with 22,000 meals and 36,000 cars.

8. **a.** With the quota, the quantity of clothes sold was fixed. Suppliers charged the price (P0) consumers were willing to pay for that quantity. With the removal of the quota,

as the accompanying graph demonstrates, equilibrium quantity rose (to Q1) and equilibrium price fell (to P1).

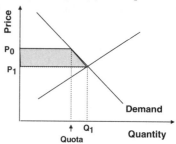

b. Consumers benefited because they were able to buy a greater quantity at a lower price. Graphically this is shown by an increase in consumer surplus shown by the shaded region in the accompanying graph.

c. The short-run effect of the removal of the quota is that profits declined because the equilibrium price declined. If economies of scale lower average total costs by more than the decline in equilibrium price, in the long run profits might increase with the removal of the quotas.

10. **a.** Economists opposed the tariff because it creates dead weight loss and hurts the welfare of the whole society.

b. The tariff shifts the supply of imports up, increasing equilibrium price to P_1 and lowering equilibrium quantity to Q_1 as shown in the accompanying graph.

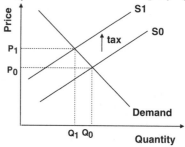

c. The tariff would help the economy by increasing the price of imported goods, making domestic goods relatively more competitive and allowing domestic producers to raise their prices if they chose to do so. It would also provide revenue for government that it could spend on consumption or investment goods, further stimulating the domestic economy.

d. The macro economy would be worsened because a retaliatory tariff reduces the trade between countries, thereby hurting both of them. They do not benefit from the full extent of their comparative advantages.

Web Questions

2. **a.** Three trade barriers listed are biotechnology bans, quotas on lumber, and export control licensing.

b. The biotechnology bans are implemented because of perceived health risks to genetically modified food. The lumber quotas are to save American jobs in the timber industry. Export control licensing of satellites has shifted from the Commerce Department for security reasons.

   c. The ban on genetically modified food is hurting the U.S. agriculture market. The import quota on lumber has led to a 35 percent increase in the price of U.S. lumber. We are losing business from China due to the change in license control.

4. The answer to this question depends on the country chosen.

Appendix A

2.   **a.** The opportunity cost for Greece of making 1 million olives is 1,000 pounds of cheese. The opportunity cost for France of making 1 million olives is 250 pounds of cheese. The opportunity cost for Greece of making 1,000 pounds of cheese is 1 million olives. The opportunity cost for France of making 1,000 pounds of cheese is 4 million olives.

    b. They are worse off since France has a comparative advantage in producing olives and Greece has a comparative advantage in producing cheese. Under the new law France produces 50,000 pounds of cheese and Greece produces 500 million olives—point A. They could have had a greater combination: 100,000 pounds of cheese produced by Greece and 600 million olives (200 million by France and 400 million by Greece)—point B. Their combined possibility curve if they were able to trade is the outermost production possibility curve shown.

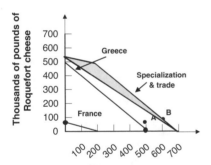

    c. See the accompanying graph. All the points in the shaded area were unattainable without specialization and trade.

● CHAPTER 22 Questions for Thought and Review

2. The U.S. per capita growth rate of 1.5 to 2.0 percent per year is lower than those of Japan (4.8 percent per year) and China (3.4 percent per year), close to those of Western Europe (2.5 percent per year) and Latin America (1.4 percent per year), and higher than those of Eastern Europe (1.0 percent per year) and Africa (0.8 percent per year).

4. A representative business cycle is shown in the accompanying graph. Each of the four phases—peak, downturn, trough, and upturn—is clearly labeled.

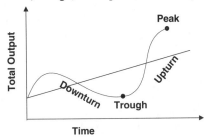

6. Reducing unemployment to 1.2 percent today is not likely for several reasons. One is that a low inflation rate seems to be incompatible with low unemployment. Another is that today's economy differs from that of the World War II period, when there was an enormous ideological commitment to the war effort and acceptance of strong wage and price controls.

8. Structural unemployment, because it results from changes in the structure of the economy, is best studied in the long-run framework. Cyclical unemployment, which results from fluctuations in economic activity, is best studied in the short-run framework.

10. Okun's rule of thumb states that a 1 percentage point change in the unemployment rate will cause income to change in the opposite direction by 2 percent. Thus, a 2 percentage point rise in unemployment will likely cause income to decrease by 4 percent.

12. Real output rose 13 percent (15 − 2).

14. False. While inflation doesn't make the nation any poorer on average, it does have costs. Its costs include 'shoe-leather' costs, capricious distributional effects, the destruction of the informational value of prices, and the breaking down of the institutional structure within which markets work.

● 22- Problems and Exercises

2. a. The index in 2005 is 68/64×100 = 106.25.
   b. Real output is Nominal output/Price index ×100 = $300 billion/115×100 = $260.9 billion.
   c. Percent change in nominal output = Percent change in real output + Percent change in the price level. Thus, rise in nominal output = 5 percent + 2 percent = 7 percent.
   d. Percent change in nominal output = Percent change in real output + Percent change in the price level. Thus, inflation = percent change in nominal output − percent change in real output = 7 percent −3 percent = 4 percent.

4. a. Possible explanations include Japanese cultural emphases on tradition, honor, and loyalty. In Japan, firms are less willing to lay off workers in times of excess supply and workers are less likely to change employers in search of higher compensation. Another explanation is the nature of Japanese production. One could suggest that Japanese production does not rely on a changing base of skills so that the skills of workers always match the skills demanded by a particular firm.
   b. It is impossible to say which is better. Each needs to be judged within the broader system of the economy.
   c. The answer to this question depends on the distribution of layoffs and hires in each of the economies. If layoffs in Japan were unavoidable and occurred among mid to-low ranking employees, the average tenure of Japanese employees would decline. If instead the elderly were asked to retire earlier, the average tenure would decline much less. In the United States firms would have to lay off fewer workers than usual due to the booming economy, and average tenure would rise.

Web Questions

2. a. The answers to this question will depend upon the current state of the economy. See the accompanying graph. The copy of the Economic Report of the President for Spring 2003 did not include quarterly data back to 1989, so we looked on BEA's web site at www.bea.doc.gov to find it. The peak and trough are marked.

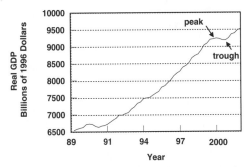

   b. The economy is currently in an expansion.
   c. It has been in an expansion for just a few quarters.
   d. The last recession was in 2001.

● CHAPTER 23 Questions for Thought and Review

2. If you add up all transactions, you will include intermediate goods—so the amount will far exceed both GDP and GNP, which are measures of final output of an economy.

4. The aggregate value added at each stage of production is, by definition, precisely equal to the value of final sales. Thus, the value-added rate should also be 15 percent. (Technical note: This is assuming the value-added tax is an income-based rather than consumption-based.)

6. NDP is actually preferable to GDP as the expression of a country's domestic output because NDP takes depreciation into account. Depreciation is a cost of producing goods. However, measuring true depreciation is difficult because asset values fluctuate, and so GDP rather than NDP is generally used in discussions of economic activity.

8. Transfer payments are not included in national income, so nothing directly would happen to it.

10. The difference between domestic personal income and national personal income is the addition of net foreign factor income to domestic personal income.

Problems and Exercises

2. **a.** GDP should fall as nonmarket transactions increase. An example is a person who cleans his partner's house for a fee cannot receive that fee as a married partner.
   b. GDP would not change.
   c. GDP would rise by the broker's commission.
   d. GDP would not change.
   e. GDP would not change.
   f. GDP would rise.

4. $GDP = C + I + G + (X - M) = 500 + 185 + 195 + 4 = 884$.
   $GNP = GDP + \text{Net foreign factor income} = 884 + 2 = 886$.
   $NDP = GDP - \text{Depreciation} = 884 - 59 = 825$.
   $NI = GNP - \text{Depreciation} = 886 - 59 = 827$.
   $PI = NI + \text{Transfers from government} + \text{Non-business interest income} - \text{Corporate retained earnings} - \text{Social Security taxes} = 780 + 72 + 10 - 51 - 47 - 35 = 619$.
   $DPI = PI - \text{Personal taxes} = 702 - 91 = 611$.

6. **a.** $GDP = C + I + G + (X - M) = 485$.
      $GNP = GDP + \text{Net foreign factor income} = 488$.
      $NI = \text{Compensation} + \text{Rent} + \text{Profits} + \text{Net interest} = 475$.
      $NNP = NI = 475$.
      $NNP = NDP + \text{Net foreign factor income: } NDP = 472$.
   b. Depreciation = GDP - NDP = 13.
   c. $GDP = C + I + G + (X - M) = 480$.
      $GNP = GDP + \text{Net foreign factor income} = 483$.
      $NI = \text{Compensation} + \text{Rent} + \text{Profits} + \text{Net interest} = 486$.
      $NNP = NI = 486$.
      $NNP = NDP + \text{Net foreign factor income: } NDP = 483$.
      Depreciation $= GDP - NDP = 23$.

Web Questions

2. **a.** The economic contributions of household and volunteer work.
   b. Crime, depletion of nonrenewable resources, family breakdown and loss of leisure time. The depletion of nonrenewable resources is the largest of these categories.
   c. The GDP has been rising faster than has the GPI in recent years.

● CHAPTER 24 Questions for Thought and Review

2. A person living in 1910 is most likely to work more to buy a dozen eggs than the person living in 2005. The reason is that, since 1910, the United States real income has been rising, on average, by more than the growth in the population. This means that real income per person has gone up since 1910. Thus, the person living in 2005 has a

higher real income than the person living in 1910 and so is likely to work less to buy the dozen eggs.

4. Through free trade, countries can produce the goods in which they have a comparative advantage and trade for those in which they do not, allowing for greater specialization and division of labor, which can result in higher productivity and greater economic growth for the involved countries.

6. The three types of capital are physical capital, human capital, and social capital. Physical capital includes the buildings and machines that are available for the production process. Human capital includes the workers' skills that are embodied in them through education, experience, and on-the-job training (i.e., through people's knowledge). Social capital includes the habitual way of doing things that guides people in how they approach production in the economy.

8. Two ways in which growth through technology differs from growth through the accumulation of physical capital are: (1) Accumulation of physical capital increases output by simply increasing the amount of the capital available for production whereas technology increases output by making the existing capital more efficient and thereby increasing the marginal return to available capital. (2) Technology can also change the types of goods people buy in an economy by introducing new types of products; accumulation of physical capital does not make such a change.

10. Thomas Malthus based his prediction that population growth would exceed the growth in goods and services on the law of diminishing marginal productivity of labor. But his prediction did not come true because labor has become more efficient as a result of education and technological progress, which has increased the output per worker.

12. Convergence might not occur because (1) factors of production are not entirely mobile, (2) countries have different institutional structures, (3) factors of production in one country are not always comparable to those in other countries, and (4) technology tends to remain concentrated in particular geographic areas.

14. The following are three ways in which growth can be undesirable: (1) Growth may contribute to increased pollution. (2) Growth changes traditional cultures with beautiful handiwork, music, and dance into cultures of modern gadgets. (3) Some argue that the number of average working hours has increased because of growth in the economy.

16. To compete with the others, the producer has an incentive to innovate (i.e., to invest in technological advance so that he can increase his efficiency and so take a lead among his competitors). But technological innovation is usually associated with a high cost initially, and the producer who has advanced his production process cannot afford to impose a high price on his product due to competition in the industry and so he cannot sustain his technological improvement. Also, competition prevents the sharing of information among firms, which can stifle further innovation.

18. Communities are willing to give tax relief to new-technology firms to help them survive during the initial stages, when the start-up costs are very high. If these companies survive, they will be able to provide employment opportunities to

the community members and thereby play a role in increasing the community's total income and standard of living.

Problems and Exercises

2. Constant returns to scale refers to the relationship between increases in *all* inputs and output. In this case, only one input rose, so we cannot make any conclusion about returns to scale.

4. **a.** −4.8%
   b. 4.6%
   c. 4%
   d. 2.0%

6. **a.** The borrowing circle probably would not work in the United States, because the strong social forces in Bangladesh that eliminate the need for collateral do not exist in the United States. Perhaps there are some minority groups that do not have the necessary collateral to get loans in the traditional way but whose culture could provide the social forces to make repayment of loans more certain.

   b. A possible modification of the program would be to require proof that the "traditional" methods of financing are not open. This would limit the program to those who have few options but do have a good business plan and intention to repay. Another modification would be to require that the business be maintained in the neighborhood where the cosigners live. This would maintain the social forces that ensure repayment.

   c. Minorities often face the same problems because they do not have adequate assets for collateral necessary to gain traditional financing. They also may face discrimination by banks and venture capitalists, or they may not be as trusting of the financial system as their majority counterparts. Nevertheless, they may have good business plans and an intention to repay.

8. Political structure can be viewed as a type of capital if it contributes to production. The longer a country is a democracy, the stronger and more well-developed are the institutions that protect civil liberties and provide secure property and contract rights. These provide the necessary incentives to innovate and produce. A stable political environment also fosters investment in technology because it makes it more likely that the firm will be around in the long term. However, although all the empirical evidence shows a correlation, the causal effects may be from development to democracy. (Source: "Democracy and Growth: A Relationship Revisited," *Eastern Economic Journal*, Winter 2003.)

Web Questions

2. This question was answered according to the Index of Economic Freedom, 2005. The ratings for the top two are Hong Kong = 1.35; Singapore = 1.6. The ratings for the bottom two are North Korea = 5.0 and Burma = 4.6.

   a. The top two are countries where there is the greatest absence of government coercion or constraint in the following spheres beyond what is necessary for the citizens' protection: production, consumption and distribution.

   b. GDP per capita growth rates published in the report were as follows: Singapore = 6.5%; Hong Kong = 7.2% ; North Korea = 0.1% ; Burma = −1.8. The two do seem to be related, but we would caution that economic upturns and downturns will mask the long-term trends in these economies, which is affected more greatly by economic freedom.

CHAPTER 25 Questions for Thought and Review

2. Classicals felt that if the wage was lowered, the Depression would end. They saw unions as preventing the fall in wages, and they saw the government lacking the political will to break up unions.

4. Say there is a rise in the price level. That would make the holders of money poorer (the wealth effect). It would also reduce the real money supply, increasing the interest rate (the interest rate effect). Assuming fixed exchange rates, it would also make goods less internationally competitive (the international effect). All three account for the quantity of aggregate demand decreasing—decreasing spending as the price level rises. These initial increases are then multiplied by the multiplier effect as the initial spending reverberates through the economy.

6. If the economy is in short-run equilibrium below potential output, input prices will fall, causing the short-run aggregate supply curve to shift down and the price level to fall. This will set the wealth, interest rate, and international effects in motion, increasing the quantity of aggregate demand and thereby bringing the economy into long-run equilibrium at potential output.

8. Yes, they would emphasize the inherent value of the program rather than discussing the program's effect on aggregate demand. This is because programs that increase aggregate demand when the economy is close to potential will ultimately lead to inflation and little increase in real output.

10. To design an appropriate fiscal policy, it is important to know the level of potential output because where the economy is relative to potential tells you whether to implement expansionary or contractionary policy. Conducting fiscal policy without having an estimate of potential output would be like driving without being able to see the road.

12. The simple model abstracts from a number of important issues such as the problem of estimating potential income. Without knowing potential income, we cannot know whether expansionary or contractionary policy is called for. Also, the model does not take into account the difficulties in implementing fiscal policies and the uncertain effectiveness of those policies.

Problems and Exercises

2. **a.** Keynes used models not in a mechanistic way, but in an interpretive way. He was a Marshallian who saw economic models as an engine of analysis, not an end in themselves.

   b. It fits in nicely with the "other things constant" assumption since the policy relevance follows only when one has eliminated that assumption and taken into account all the things held at the back of one's mind.

c. It definitely was primarily in the art of economics since the above method is the method used in the art of economics.

4. a. An increase in the availability of inputs will shift the LAS curve to the right.

b. A civil war will presumably destroy productive capacity or otherwise halt production and cause a shift in the LAS curve to the left. In the short run, it will also increase the prices of inputs and increase inflationary expectations shifting the SAS up.

c. To the degree that the rise in oil prices results in an overall rise in the price level, this will shift the SAS curve up. Otherwise, other relative prices will decline to offset the rise in oil prices and the SAS curve will not shift at all.

d. If wages that were fixed become flexible and aggregate demand increases, the SAS curve will shift up as wages rise.

6. a. The slowing of foreign economies will reduce exports, shifting the AD curve to the left by a multiple of the initial decline in exports (from AD_0 to AD_1 in the graph below). I would recommend that the government increase expenditures by an amount equal to the initial decline in exports. This will shift the AD curve back to its initial position, as shown in the graph.

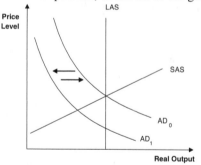

b. An economy operating above potential is shown by point A in the accompanying graph. To keep the inflation from rising (the SAS curve from shifting up), the government should reduce expenditures enough (shifting the AD curve from AD_0 to AD_1) to bring the economy back to long-run equilibrium at potential output, Y_P, and the price level, P_1, in the following graph.

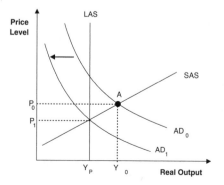

c. A new technology that increases potential output will shift the LAS curve (from LAS_0 to LAS_1), creating excess capacity and downward pressure on factor prices. If left alone, the price level will fall and real output will rise. If the government wants to keep the price level constant, it can increase expenditures enough to increase output to the new potential (shifting the AD curve from AD_0 to AD_1).

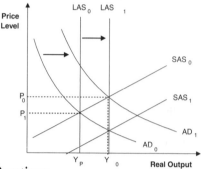

Web Questions

2. a-b. The level of output and price level is shown in the accompanying graph.

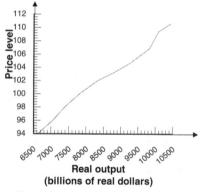

c. Since the curve involves shifts in both the SAS curve and AD curves, all we can say is that these are points of equilibrium given certain assumptions. It is neither an AD nor an SAS curve. In order to draw one or the other, simplifying assumptions must be made regarding what is held constant.

⬤ CHAPTER 26 Questions for Thought and Review

2. At levels of output above equilibrium inventories are building up because planned expenditures are below actual production. People are not buying all that is produced.

4. The AE curve becomes steeper when the marginal propensity to expend increases. Equilibrium income rises.

6. Shocks to aggregate expenditures are any sudden changes in factors that affect C, I, G, X, or M. This includes consumer sentiment, business optimism, foreign income, and government policy. It is possible that people could change their marginal propensities to consume and save, and this could also have an effect on the economy.

8. If the mpe is 0.5, the multiplier is 2. Every $1 increase in autonomous expenditures will raise income by $2. To close a recessionary gap of $200 the government needs to generate $100 of additional autonomous spending. It can accomplish this by increasing government expenditures by $100, or by cutting taxes by somewhat more than that (about $200).

10. The effects of this invention on the economy would be manifold and in many ways unpredictable because such major shocks have social, institutional, and political effects, as well as economic effects. The obvious effect is that the demand for the pill would likely be tremendous (after people were sure it was safe), and so production of the pill would gear up to meet the demand. Market structure and pricing decisions will play a big role in determining the new effect of the change. Alternative forms of transportation would suffer decreases in demand (cars, mass transit, airplanes, etc.), and levels of production of those goods and services would adjust, as would employment in those industries and elated industries. Measured GDP might actually fall.

12. A mechanistic model states the equilibrium independent of where the economy has been or where people want it to be. A mechanistic model is used as a direct guide for policy prescriptions. An interpretive model is used as a guide that highlights dynamic interdependencies and suggests the possible response of aggregate output to various policy initiatives.

Problems and Exercises

2. **a.** If the mpe is .66, the value of the multiplier is 3. A decrease in autonomous expenditures of $20 will likely result in a decrease in income of $60.
   b. This is demonstrated in the accompanying graph.

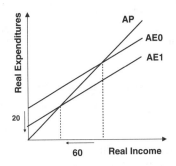

4. Given that the mpe is .6, I0 = 1,000; G0 = 8,000; C0 = 10,000; and (X0 − M0) = 1,000, then:
   a. Y = 10,000 + .6Y + 1,000 + 8,000 + 1,000.
   Y − .6Y = 20,000; 0.4Y = 20,000; Y = 50,000.
   Thus, the level of income in the country is $50,000.
   b. If net exports increase by $2,000, income will increase by $5,000 (the multiplier is 2.5, or 1/.4).
   c. According to Okun's law, a one-percentage-point change in unemployment will cause a 2 percent change in income in the opposite direction. Thus, if income has increased by $5,000, which is a 10 percent increase, then unemployment should drop by 5 percentage points.
   d. If the mpe falls from 0.6 to 0.5, the multiplier decreases from 2.5 to 2. The answer to part a would now be $40,000;

the answer to part b would be $4,000; and the answer to part c is that unemployment should fall by 5 percentage points.

6. Given that income is $50,000, the mpe is .75:
   a. To reduce unemployment by 2 percentage points (again, by Okun's rule of thumb) requires a 4 percent increase in income, which in this case is $2,000. The multiplier is 4.0, calculated as [1/(1 − mpe)]. To generate a $2,000 increase in income, increase government spending by $500 or decrease taxes by about $650.
   b. If the mpe is .67, the multiplier is about 3, which means that to generate a $2,000 increase in income, government spending would have to increase by $666.66.
   c. If the mpe is .5, then the multiplier is 2.0, which means that to generate a $2,000 increase in income, government spending would have to increase by $1,000.

8. **a.** If the mpe is .5, the multiplier is 2. To eliminate the inflationary gap, the government should undertake a contractionary fiscal policy. Since the economy is $36,000 above potential, we would advise decreasing government spending by $18,000.
   b. Using Okun's rule of thumb, since income falls by 6 percent, we would expect unemployment to rise by 3 percentage points to 8 percent.
   c. The multiplier now becomes 5, so we would advise decreasing spending by $7,200. We would not change our answer to b.

Web Questions

2. **a.** Inventories were up 0.9 percent in January 2005 from the previous month. Inventories are 8 percent above levels a year ago.
   b. Rising inventories either mean that consumer expenditures, and therefore aggregate demand, are falling, or that production is rising faster than aggregate demand is rising (or a combination of the two). Either way, production is outpacing expenditures. Unless expenditures pick up, eventually producers will want to cut production. In terms of the multiplier model, it is possible that the economy is going to slow or experience a recession.

Appendix A

2. We would recommend increasing expenditures by 80.

4. This makes the multiplier 2.08. This means that we would increase expenditures by about 192 or cut taxes by about 213.

6. This would make the multiplier = 1/(1 − c + ct + m − mt). It would be a slightly higher multiplier. (The difference between the two assumptions is whether we are assuming government imports.)

Appendix B

2. **a.** The AD curve will become steeper.
   b. An increase in the size of the multiplier makes the AD curve flatter because the effect of changes in the price level on aggregate demand will be augmented even more by the multiplier.

c. An increase of $20 in autonomous expenditures has no effect on the slope of the AD curve; it only affects its position.

d. A decline in the price level disrupting the financial market will make the AD curve steeper because it decreases the price-level interest rate effect.

● CHAPTER 27 Questions for Thought and Review

2. 6 percent.

4. Because the inflation rate was lower than expected, the demand for existing higher-interest rate bonds would rise (they would require a lower interest rate premium). Interest rates fell; in this case from 4.87 to 4.68 percent.

6. The three functions of money are: (1) it serves as a medium of exchange; (2) it serves as a unit of account; and (3) it serves as a store of wealth.

8. Two components of M2 that are not components of M1 are savings deposits and small-denomination time deposits.

10. The equation for the simple money multiplier is 1/r; the equation for the approximate real-world multiplier is 1/(r + c). Since c is positive, the simple multiplier is larger.

12 If the U.S. government were to raise the reserve requirement to 100 percent, the interest rates banks pay to depositors would decrease and possibly even become negative (you'd have to pay to have the bank handle your money), because significant opportunities for profitable loans would be lost.

14. What brought the S&Ls down were bad loans, particularly in real estate. The reasons that S&Ls made those bad loans are complex. Government deregulation in the 1980s expanded the kinds of loans S&Ls could make and the ways they could compete for deposits. Due to moral hazard and perverse incentives (government, not the bank managers, would have to pay if the S&L went down), S&Ls made risky loans and paid high interest on their deposits. When the real estate market soured, the S&Ls' net worth crumbled and the government had to step in to bail out the S&Ls and pay back depositors.

16. To be considered money, the currencies would have to fulfill the functions of money. They only partially fulfill those functions since they have only limited acceptability as a medium of exchange, store of value, and unit of -account. Thus, while they are partial moneys, we would not consider them full moneys.

Problems and Exercises

2. For a deposit of $100 and a reserve ratio of 5 percent,
   a. The bank can lend out $95.
   b. There is now an additional $195 in the economy.
   c. The multiplier is 20.
   d. John's $100 will ultimately turn into $2,000.

4. a. money   b. not money
   c. not money   d. not money
   e. money   f. not money
   g. not money

6. a. As more counterfeit money is printed and not identified as counterfeit, the value of money circulated will decline.

   b. As businesses become suspect of currency that is circulated, they will favor cashless transactions such as check cash cards and likely offer benefits for using such cards. In this case, the volume of cashless transactions will increase.

   c. As counterfeiting increases, the U.S. Treasury will likely spend more to introduce additional security measures. The cost of not doing so will be the loss in the purchasing power of circulating money and the loss to businesses that accept identified counterfeit currency.

Web Questions

2. a. There is about $575 billion of U.S. currency in circulation today but most of it resides outside of the U.S. Assuming that the world population is about 6 billion, this means that there is approximately $95 per person in the world.

   b. People typically withdraw cash at ATMs over the weekend, so there is more cash in circulation on Monday than on Friday.

   c. 1.5 years.

   d. Most of this is in the form of U.S. Government Securities owned by the Federal Reserve System. Some of it also consists of gold certificates, special drawing rights, and "eligible" paper such as bills of exchange or promissory notes.

   e. Bureau of Engraving and Printing.

Appendix A

2. It is a financial asset because it has value due to an offsetting liability of the Federal Reserve Bank.

4. No, she is not correct. While a loan is a loan, that loan is a financial asset to the one issuing the loan because it has value just as a bond does.

6. $0.50

8. a. Market rates are above 10 percent because its price is below face value.
   b. Its yield is 12.24 percent.
   c. Its price will rise.

10. Substituting into the present value formula PV = $1,060/1.1, we find that the bond is worth $964 now.

12. Using the present-value table, we see that at a 3 percent interest rate, $1 30 years from now would be worth $0.41 now, so $200 in 30 years would be worth $82 now.

14. If the interest rate is still 9 percent, the value of a lump sum of $20,000 in 10 years can be calculated using the annuity table in Table A27-1. You should be willing to pay $20,000 × 0.42, or about $8,400 for this offer.

16. An investment bank facilitates borrowing. It does not take in deposits and often does not make loans. A commercial bank takes in deposits and makes loans.

18. The prospects must not be very good, or the interest rate must be extremely high. Generally, stocks sell for a minimum of multiples of 10 or 12 times earnings. This multiple can be roughly determined by dividing the expected earnings (the

annuity) by the interest rate. More recently, the average price/earnings ratio has been 30, a historically high figure.

20. Money market assets usually pay lower interest rates than do longer-term capital assets because they offer the buyer more liquidity and less risk of asset value fluctuation.

22. **a.** Agree/Disagree. Technically, a rise in stock prices does not imply a richer economy. If, however, the rise in stock prices reflects underlying real economic improvement such as finding the cure for cancer or a technological advance, society will be richer not because of the rise in stock prices, but because of the underlying cause of their rise.

   b. Disagree. If both the real and financial asset are worth $1 million, then they have the same value as long as they are valued at market prices. Just as financial assets bear a risk of no repayment, real assets bear a risk of a fluctuation in prices.

   c. Disagree. Although financial assets have a corresponding liability, they facilitate trades that could not otherwise have taken place and thus have enormous value to society.

   d. Disagree. The value of an asset depends not only on the quantity but also on its price per unit. The price of land per acre in Japan exceeds that in the United States by so much that the total value of land in Japan also exceeds that in the United States.

   e. Disagree. The stock market valuation depends on the supply and demand for existing stock. There is, however, a relationship between relative growth in GDP and the rise in stock prices to the extent that growth in stock prices and GDP growth both reflect economic well-being in a country. Also, many of the companies are multinational companies, and where the company is based may not reflect where its value added is generated.

Appendix B

2. **a.** The effect on the balance sheet is shown below:

Assets		Liabilities	
Cash	$ 10,000	Demand deposits	50,000
	−1,000		−1,000
	9,000		49,000
Loans	100,000	Net worth	10,000
Physical assets	50,000		
Total assets	$159,000	Total liabilities and net worth	$159,000

   b. The reserve ratio is now 18 percent. This is less than the required 20 percent. The bank must decrease loans by $800 to meet the reserve requirement. But this shows up as $800 less in demand deposits and $800 less in cash. The bank must again reduce loans, but this time by $640. Demand deposits once again decline. This continues until the final position indicated by the following T-account:

Assets		Liabilities	
Cash	$ 9,000	Demand deposits	$45,000
Loans	96,000	Net worth	110,000
Physical assets	50,000		
Total assets	$155,000	Total liabilities and net worth	$155,000

   c. The money multiplier is 5.
   d. Total money supply declined by $5,000.

CHAPTER 28 Questions for Thought and Review

2. There are few regional Fed banks in the western part of the United States because in 1913, when the Fed was established, the West and South were less populated and less important economically than the rest of the country. As these regions grew, the original structure remained because no one wanted to go through the political wrangling that restructuring would bring about.

4. Three tools by which the Fed can affect the money supply are: (1) changing the reserve requirement, which changes the amount of reserves banks keep and thereby changes the money supply; (2) changing the discount rate, which changes the cost of borrowing by banks from the Fed and thereby changes the money supply (actually, it works more as a signal); and (3) open market operations, which change reserves as the Fed buys and sells bonds, and thereby changes the money supply.

6. The Federal funds rate is the interest rate that banks charge one another for Fed funds or reserves. As the Fed buys and sells bonds, it changes reserves, thereby changing the price (interest rate) banks charge for loaning reserves overnight—the Federal funds rate. Other, longer-term interest rates, such as the Treasury bill rate, are only indirectly affected.

8. When the Fed takes money out of the economy, banks are in violation of Fed regulations and have no choice but to contract their loans in order to meet their reserve requirements. When the Fed puts money into the economy, banks have excess reserves but there is no regulation that they are violating. Although they may have a financial incentive to make loans, they are not required to do so. Since they are not required to make loans, and thus will not necessarily reduce interest rates, increasing investment and expanding the economy, the saying "You can lead a horse to water, but you can't make it drink" is relevant.

10. The nominal interest rate is equal to the real interest rate plus the expected inflation rate. If the nominal interest rate is 6 percent and the expected inflation rate is 5 percent, the real interest rate is 1 percent.

2. Treasury bills pay interest; cash does not.

14. The Taylor rule suggests that the Fed will target a Fed funds rate of 5.5 percent [2 + 3 + .5(1) + .5(0)].

Problems and Exercises

2. a. If people hold no cash, the money multiplier is 1/r. If this is equal to 3, then the current reserve requirement is 33 percent. To increase the money supply by 200, the Fed should lower the reserve requirement to 32 percent.

b. Lowering the discount rate will encourage banks to borrow. This will increase the amount of reserves in the system so that the money supply increases. If the Fed wishes to increase the money supply by 200, and the multiplier is 3, reserves must be increased by 66.67. If banks will borrow an additional 20 for every point the discount rate is lowered, the Fed should lower the rate by 3.33 percentage points.

c. To increase the money supply by using open market operations, the Fed should buy bonds, thus increasing the level of reserves in the banking system. To achieve an increase of 200 (if the multiplier is 3) the Fed should buy 66.67 worth of bonds.

4. a. Increasing the reserve requirement would lower the multiplier, calculated as [1/(r + c)]. To calculate exactly how much, we would need to know the current money supply.

b. The money multiplier is [1/(r + c)] = 2.5. If the Fed sold $800,000 worth of bonds it would decrease reserves by $800,000 and so decrease the money supply by $2 million.

c. This part of the question requires information from a local bank. Reevaluate a and b in view of this information.

6. a. This would increase excess reserves enormously.

b. Banks would most likely favor this proposal because they would now earn interest on their assets held at the Fed.

c. Central banks would likely oppose this because it would reduce their superiority and may require that they ask Congress for appropriation to pay the interest, reducing their political independence.

d. This would increase the interest rate paid by banks because the additional interest would increase their profit margin. The initial increased profit margin would shift the demand for depositors out as new banks entered the market and as existing banks competed for more deposits. This would increase the interest paid to depositors until the normal profits are once again earned.

8. a. Since the money multiplier is 2.5, we would issue a directive for the Fed open market window to buy 24 worth of government bonds.

b. We could have also reduced the discount rate and lowered the reserve requirement, although by how much cannot be determined with the information given.

c. Using the quantity theory, we would predict that the price level would rise because of the increase in the money supply.

Web Questions

2. a. According to the Beige Book of March 2005, consumer spending was moderate, labor markets strengthened with some wage pressure, retail prices were flat to modestly up, and manufacturing was growing solidly.

b. The most recent FOMC action was an increase in the Fed funds rate by 25 basis points on March 22, 2005.

c. Because the economy shows signs of moderate growth with little price pressures, it should not change monetary policy.

Appendix A

2. Let's assume the following initial bank balance sheet:

Initial Bank Balance Sheet

Assets		Liabilities	
Reserves	$100,000,000	Demand deposits	$1,000,000,000
T-bill holdings	0	Net worth	5,000,000
Loans	905,000,000		
Total assets	1,005,000,000	Total Liabilites	1,005,000,000

First, individuals sell $2 million in T-bills to the Fed, and deposit the $2 million in the bank. The bank now has more reserves than is required:

Assets		Liabilities	
Reserves	$102,000,000	Demand deposits	1,002,000,000
T-bill holdings	0		
Loans	905,000,000	Net worth	5,000,000
Total assets	$1,007,000,000	Total Liabilities	$1,007,000,000

It has excess reserves of $1.8 million, which it lends out. These loans are redeposited at the bank as demand deposits:

Assets		Liabilities	
Reserves	$102,000,000	Demand deposits	$1,002,000,000
Loans	−1,800,000	New deposits	+1,800,000
New deposits	+1,800,000		
T-bill holdings	0	Net worth	5,000,000
Loans	906,800,000		
Total assets	1,008,800,000	Total Liabilites	1,008,800,000

It still has excess reserves of 1.62 million, which it lends out. Each round, the amount called in gets smaller and smaller until the bank arrives at its final position with money supply having risen by $20 million.

Assets		Liabilities	
Reserves	$102,000,000	Demand deposits	$1,020,000,000
T-bill holdings	0	Net worth	5,000,000
Loans	923,000,000		
Total assets	1,025,000,000	Total Liabilites	1,025,000,000

CHAPTER 29 Questions for Thought and Review

2. Adaptive expectations.

4. The real interest rate is 5 percent: Real interest rate = Nominal interest rate −Inflation.

6. The three assumptions are that velocity is constant, real income is independent of the money supply, and the direction of causation is from money to prices.

8. Financial institutions have changed enormously and financial markets have become increasingly connected internationally, increasing the flow of money among countries.

10. Governments and central banks sometimes increase money supply even when they know the consequences because sometimes the political ramifications of not increasing the money supply (which can include a collapse of government) are thought to be worse.

12. Quantity theorists are more likely to support rules -because they have less trust in government undertaking beneficial actions and believe that the long-run effects of monetary policy are on the price level while the short run effects cannot be predicted.

14. The insider/outsider theory of inflation divides workers into insiders and outsiders. It is an example of an insti-tutionalist theory of inflation, which says that social-pressures prevent economic pressures from working. In it, insiders push up wages and outsiders find themselves experiencing unemployment; because the costs of raising wages are not borne by those who make the decision, there is little pressure on insiders not to raise wages

16. Alfred Marshall would say that it is impossible to separate the roles of supply and demand in influencing price and that therefore we cannot distinguish between cost-push and demand-pull inflation.

18. No, as long as expectations of inflation are constant, the economy will stay on the same short-run Phillips curve.

20. Economists see a trade-off between inflation and growth because low inflation reduces price uncertainty and thereby encourages investment that increases the efficiency of the market system, allows businesses to enter into long-term contracts more easily and reduces the costs of using money.

Problems and Exercises

2. **a.** The economy is at point A on short-run and long-run Phillips curve on the accompanying graph.

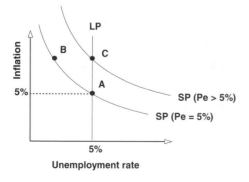

b. The answer to this question really hinges on what kind of change would be popular. Should you try to cut unemployment further? If so, then we would recommend increasing government expenditures, moving the economy to a point such as B in the accompanying graph. Or would a better strategy be cutting inflation? If so, then we would recommend reducing government expenditures, which will increase -unemployment while reducing inflation.

c. We have chosen the "lower unemployment" option. An increase in aggregate expenditures will cause a movement up along the short-run Phillips curve. Unemployment will fall, but inflation will rise. In the long run, as expectations of inflation adjust to actual inflation, the short-run Phillips curve shifts up. Unemployment returns to its target rate of 5 percent, but inflation is higher than before, as shown as point C on the graph.

4. The advantage of indexing grades is that it provides a benchmark with which to measure a student's performance in his or her class. It would distinguish between an A received in a difficult class in which many did not receive A's and an A earned in an easy class in which A's were plenty. It allows for comparisons across different schools with different grading standards. But it also does not allow for the self-selection of intelligent students into upper-level classes, where all may be deserving of A's and that of less intelligent (or at least less diligent) students into 'slacker classes' where no one deserves an A. It might result in professors making distinctions among students whose abilities are virtually the same just to make a given distribution of grades.

6. **a.** He would likely be a quantity theorist since quantity theorists see inflation most connected to long-term growth because low inflation means that the informational job of prices is working better and more investment will take place.

b. Inflation can affect household decisions in a number of ways. It can add uncertainty about the future, leading them to save less and make fewer major purchases. Alternatively, it could lead them to temporarily supply more labor than they would otherwise, causing a temporary spurt in growth and then a fall in growth once they recognize their mistakes.

8. **a.** Increases in productivity shift the long-run AS curve to the right. This allows policy makers to increase aggregate demand (perhaps through expansionary policy which would keep interest rates low, as desired) without increasing the price level. In this example, the economy moves from point A to point B.

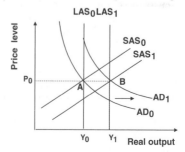

b. Increase in productivity shifts the long-run Philips curve to the left because it allows a lower unemployment rate at every rate of inflation. Policymakers, therefore are able to increase aggregate demand, shifting the short-run Phillips curve to the left, resulting in lower unemployment and the same inflation rate. In this example, the economy moves from point A to point B.

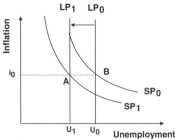

Web Questions

2. a. The article suggests that there is an inverse relationship between the two (i.e. as interest rates rise, inflation falls).

b. The article emphasizes the quantity theory viewpoint since it says that changes in interest rates (due to changes in money supply) will lead to changes in the inflation rate.

c. The Fed has to estimate the state of the economy and then make decisions regarding interest rates.

d. The terrain could include variables like production, employment, consumer expenditures and their expectations etc.

CHAPTER 30 Questions for Thought and Review

2. If the economy has a recessionary gap, the following trade policies can be adopted: (1) An export-led growth policy in which the country lobbies to remove other countries' restrictions on its exports. (2) Allowing its currency to depreciate, which means that the exchange rate of its currency relative to other currencies should fall, making its goods more competitive in the international market.

4. The budget process begins a year and a half before the budget is implemented, making it difficult to know what type of fiscal policy will be needed. In addition, many budget decisions are made for political reasons (few politicians would vote for a tax increase in an election year even if such an increase were needed). Finally, nearly two-thirds of the budget is mandated by federal programs and cannot be easily changed.

6. Automatic stabilizers reduce taxes and raise expenditures during contractions without additional government action. They therefore act to offset contractions. Likewise during recoveries, automatic stabilizers -increase taxes and reduce expenditures, which act to slow the recovery.

8. If interest rates have no effect on investment, there would be no crowding out. Crowding out occurs when the government's sale of bonds to finance expansionary fiscal policy causes interest rates to rise, choking off private investment.

10. Increasing taxes shifts the aggregate demand curve in to the left, decreasing income, increasing unemployment and making people less likely to vote for those in office. The maxim holds because people tend to have short memories.

12. Policies followed now affect expectations of future -policies, and those expectations can affect how the economy operates. By thinking about policy as a process, not a one-time event, policymakers can take these effects into account.

Problems and Exercises

2. a. In the standard AS/AD model, a tax cut will shift the AD curve to the right, leading to an increase in the price level and real output, as shown in the accompanying graph. Congressman Stable's views fit this model well.

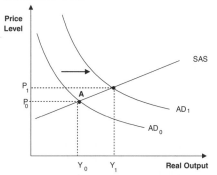

b. If Congressman Growth is correct, the tax cut will shift the LAS curve to the right. If the economy had previously been in long-run equilibrium, the economy will now be below potential and there will be pressures for factor prices to decline. Assuming nothing else happens in the meantime, the SAS curve will shift down, leading to a lower price level and higher real output, as shown in the accompanying graph.

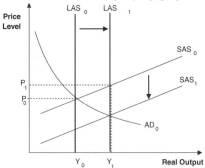

c. In the short run, Congressman Stable is likely to be correct.

d. The tax cut will require government to finance a higher budget deficit. This would lead to higher interest rates and lower investment. If there is perfect crowding out, the decline in investment will completely offset the -xpansionary effect of the tax cut. In this case, the tax cut will have no effect on either the price level or real output.

4. a. In 1995 the unemployment rate fell below the target rate of 6 percent without generating inflationary pressures. He was probably changing his estimates to reflect that reality.

c. A boom in the UK economy means an increase in its income, causing an increased demand for imports and an increase in the demand for the foreign currency to buy those imports, thus resulting in an increase in the supply of pounds. (This may also set off an expectations effect.) Thus, the supply of pounds shifts outward from S0 to S1. If demand is at D0, the exchange rate value of the pound falls from P0 to P2.

d. If interest rates in the UK rise, there will be an increased demand for its assets, so the demand for pounds will increase from D0 to D1 and the supply of pounds will decrease from S1 to S0 as fewer British investors sell their pounds to buy foreign assets. The exchange rate value of the pound rises from P2 to P1.

a. Supplier; **b.** Supplier; **c.** Supplier;
d. Demander; **e.** Demander; **f.** Demander.

a. Current account
b. Current account
c. Current and capital and financial accounts
d. Current account
e. Capital and financial account

a. If foreigners start believing that there is an increased risk of default, they will require a higher premium to buy U.S. bonds. That is, they will offer a lower price to buy them (demand for U.S. bonds will shift to the left). As this happens, bond prices will fall and interest rates, which move in the opposite direction from their prices, will rise. The value of the dollar will fall as a result of the lower demand for bonds (foreigners will not be purchasing as many dollars). That is, the demand for dollars will also decline, lowering the value of the dollar.

b. Higher interest rates increase the cost of borrowing. This hurts in the short run by reducing aggregate spending and crowding out private investment, a source of long-term growth for the U.S. economy. A lower value of the dollar may increase the competitiveness of U.S. goods in the global economy, but it also makes imports to the United States more expensive, which, in addition to hurting individuals, may hurt businesses who use imports as intermediate goods in their production processes.

Web Questions

The answer to this question depends on the country chosen. We chose Brazil.
a. The Brazilian currency is the real.
b. The currency remained virtually unchanged from 2004 to 2005.
c. Brazil has gotten inflation under control. Unemployment is expected to decline as the economy continues to grow. Fiscal spending is under control. The economy appears to be in good health, which may be contributing to a stable currency.

CHAPTER 34 Questions for Thought and Review

2. At the time that this was written, the U.S. trade deficit had risen to record highs. Still, it is unclear whether we should want to lower the U.S. trade deficit. The trade deficit was in part due to the fact that the economy has been growing for nine consecutive years. As long as the United States can borrow or sell assets, it can have a trade deficit. On the other hand, the more the United States borrows, the more U.S. assets foreigners own. Eventually, the United States will have to run a trade surplus.

4. A contractionary monetary policy by Japan and China would decrease Japanese and Chinese importation of US goods and would make the U.S. trade deficit worse.

6. If the recession was caused by a fall in domestic expenditures, we would expect that its trade balance was moving toward surplus. If, however, the recession was caused by a fall in exports, we would expect that its trade balance was moving toward deficit. The G-8 countries were trying to get Japan to boost its economy by increasing aggregate expenditures with expansionary monetary policy.

8. To finance the debt the U.S. government has to sell more bonds. Because foreign also demand these bonds (demand is greater), the government doesn't have to pay as high interest rates as it would if only U.S. investors demanded government bonds. Thus, the interest rate doesn't rise as much and crowding out is reduced.

10. The costs of internationalizing the debt are that interest and profits must be paid on the capital owned by foreigners. Future consumption must be reduced to pay that amount.

Problems and Exercises

2. a. I'd rather be holding other currencies because their price is expected to rise. I could buy them low and sell them high for a profit.

b. The same argument doesn't hold for China because it has greater concerns than personal profit, such as the effect of a falling dollar on its economy.

c. It might want to buy dollars to keep up the dollar's value. In fact, since the government can print yuan, it could theoretically buy as many dollars as it desires. It would want to buy dollars if it feels that the declining dollar would harm its exports. A declining dollar makes Chinese exports more expensive for Americans to buy and falling exports would slow the Chinese economy.

4. a. We would suggest that the IMF require a contractionary policy for both monetary and fiscal policy. I would, however, suggest a relatively more contractionary fiscal policy so that the exchange rate would also fall while inflation falls, boosting -exports.

b. This would tend to slow inflation, after an initial burst due to a fall in the exchange rate. The policy, however, would hinder growth and push the economy into a-recession.

b. It would shift the LAS curve out.

c. Using Okun's rule of thumb—which says that for every 1 percentage point rise in the unemployment rate, income falls by 2 percent—a 0.5 percentage point decline in the target unemployment rate would imply a rise in potential income of 1 percent, or $100 billion.

Web Questions

2. a. The process starts off by the formulation of the President's budget for a fiscal year. The budget documents are then prepared and transmitted to the Congress. The Congress, after reviewing this budget, develops its own budget and accepts the expenditure and revenue bills. The agency managers then execute the budget in the fiscal year after which information for the actual spending and receipts becomes available.

b. It takes about two years. For example, for Fiscal Year 2001 (begins October 1, 2000) the President formulated the budget between February-December 1999, and the data on the expenditures and receipts became available in October-November 2001.

c. The President and the Congress have to decide upon the discretionary spending, which accounts for one-third of all federal spending. The remaining two-thirds of all federal spending, called mandatory spending, is authorized by permanent laws.

CHAPTER 31 Questions for Thought and Review

2. The government can finance a deficit in either of two ways: by selling bonds or by printing money.

4. There are technical aspects of the deficit that must be understood in order to undertake a meaningful discussion of the problems deficits and debts pose for society. Since a deficit is defined as a shortfall of revenues compared to expenditures, these technical aspects include what you define as revenue and what you define as expenditure.

6. A structural deficit would exist even if the economy were at its potential level of income, which would be at full employment, or at where the unemployment rate is equal to the normal rate of unemployment. If an economist believed that the normal rate of unemployment was 4 percent instead of 6 percent, then the difference between the economy's current state and the potential income level would be larger, leading to a greater passive deficit and therefore a smaller structural deficit. Thus, it is Mr. A who should also say that the structural deficit is $20 billion.

8. It would not differ; expected inflation does not enter into the determination of the real deficit.

10. Three ways individual debt can be said to differ from government debt are: (a) government is ongoing and therefore never needs to pay back the debt; (b) government can pay off the debt by creating money; and (c) much of the government debt is internal debt owed to its own citizens and agencies.

12. Deficits are only a summary measure of the economy. A government can undertake significant future obligations and therefore get itself into trouble even if it is not running a deficit.

14. Because of the baby boom, there were many people working and relatively few collecting Social Security in the late 1990s. This caused a surplus in the Social Security Trust Fund. Since that Trust Fund is part of the government budget, the Social Security system is a primary reason for the surpluses.

16. It depends. Clearly, there is some tendency for the deficit to raise the interest rate, thereby decreasing investment and hence future growth. However, to the degree that the government spending is itself productive, not having the deficit could also decrease future growth. The ultimate effect depends on the relative size of the two effects.

Problems and Exercises

2. a. The passive deficit must be zero since it is defined as zero at potential output.

b. The structural deficit is $200 billion.

c. Now $60 billion of that deficit is passive and $140 is structural since revenue would increase by $60 billion if output rose to potential.

d. Now there is a passive surplus of $30 billion, and a structural deficit of $230 billion because revenue would decline by $30 billion if output declined to -potential.

e. The structural deficit is likely of more concern to - policymakers because normal stabilization policies will not remove it.

4. a. Debt service payments are 0.06 times $360 billion = $21.6 billion.

b. The nominal deficit is $160 - (\$21.6 + 145) = \$6.6$ billion.

c. The real deficit equals the nominal deficit ($\$6.6$ billion) $- 0.03 \times \$360$ billion = $4.2 billion surplus.

6. To make the deficit look as small as possible, we would do the following:

a. Enter government pensions when they become payable, not on an accrual basis.

b. Treat the sale of land as current income rather than spreading it out with the sale of an asset.

c. Include Social Security taxes as a current revenue because at this time revenue from Social Security exceeds payment.

d. Count prepayment of taxes as current income instead of reserves for future taxes.

e. Count expenditures on F-52 bombers as capital - xpenditures do not include their depreciation in the government accounts.

Web Questions

2. a. 28 percent is held as bills, 49 percent as notes, and 19 percent as bonds, 3 percent is held as inflation-indexed notes and an additional 1 percent as inflation-indexed bonds.

b. Intragovernmental holdings are securities held by government trust funds, revolving funds, and special funds.

c. The debt will decline during a year in which there is a budget surplus.

CHAPTER 32 Questions for Thought and Review

2. You can't just judge an economy; you must judge the entire culture. Some developing countries have cultures that, in some people's view, are preferable to ours.

4. The exchange rate method uses current exchange rates to compare relative incomes while the purchasing power parity method compares incomes by looking at the domestic purchasing power of money in different countries. Because many developing countries' currencies are undervalued, the current exchange rate overstates the income disparity between developed and developing countries.

6. Three ways in which institutions differ in developing countries are that (a) basic market institutions with well-defined property rights do not, in many cases, exist; (b) there is often a dual nature to the economy; and (c) fiscal structures with which to adequately implement fiscal policy often do not exist.

8. An economist might favor activist policies in developed countries and laissez-faire policies in developing countries because the policies one favors depends on the desire and the ability of government to work for and achieve the goals of its policies. Different views of government can lead to different views of policy. Since many economists have a serious concern about the political structure in developing countries, but less concern about it in developed countries, they can favor one set of policies for developing countries and another set for developed countries.

10. A regime change is a change in the entire structure within which the government and economy interact, whereas a policy change is a change in one aspect of government action.

12. Governments act to maintain their positions in power, and often feel that in order to do so, they have no choice but to print more money; central banks in developing countries often do not enjoy full independence, and thus cannot resist these pressures (and may not want to, since they also desire to keep the government in power.) For those making the decisions, the short-term benefits of the 'inflation solution,' keeping regimes in power, outweigh any long-term hyperinflationary consequences.

14. Investment and savings are low in developing countries because income is low, and poor people don't have a whole lot left over to save. The rich often put their savings abroad due to the fear of political instability. As for the middle class, which is usually small in developing countries, the underdeveloped financial sector leaves them with few opportunities to invest their savings.

16. An investor thinking of making an investment in a developing country should be concerned about the country's political stability and its economic condition (inflation, etc.). The existing amount of debt may also be a matter of concern.

18. Corruption limits investment and growth because knowing that payments of graft must be made prevents many people from undertaking actions that might lead to growth. Tax revenues are often diverted to those in power instead of going into legitimate productive investment, and the same

is sometimes true of foreign aid money from abroad. But that does not answer the issue, since one must deal with the political reasons why the government increases the money supply.

20. The UN could encourage the development of microcredit banks, like the Grameen Bank, which provide a low-cost alternative to money lenders. There are also significant social and cultural limitations in many areas that limit women entrepreneurs, as well as the lack of day-care alternatives to being a full-time mother.

Problems and Exercises

2. This exercise asks you to spend a day living like someone in a developing country, and then to read this chapter and contemplate the degree to which someone in such a situation can pull himself or herself up by the bootstraps.

4. a. I would want to emphasize those skills which have the highest per-dollar return—those that would lead to development. These would probably be the basic reading, writing, and problem-solving skills that fit the indigenous culture, as well as technological and computer training.

     b. This differs from the ideal educational system in the United States because the U.S. culture is different and U.S. economic problems are different. Thus, in the United States the focus would be more abstract analysis and becoming generally educated and cultured, while in developing countries the focus would be agricultural science and basic skills.

     c. This is an open-ended question. The relevant question would be: How much would individuals be willing to pay for courses that do not result in a credential compared to how much they would be willing to pay for a credential without the coursework?

6. a. I agree with this statement because of the differing importance of institutions. A detailed knowledge of a country's institutions and culture is necessary to make prescriptions for development. I disagree with this statement to the degree that the lessons learned from a general theory say that development requires stability of political structures and of economic environment and the need for savings applies across countries. The solutions are specific to the countries but fall within a general framework.

     b. This argument is made for developing countries because culture and traditional institutions play a larger role in the growth in these economies.

Web Questions

2. a. From their website: "The Bretton Woods Project works as a networker, information-provider, media informant and watchdog to scrutinise and influence the World Bank and International Monetary Fund. It monitors projects, policy reforms and the overall management of the Bretton Woods institutions with special emphasis on environmental and social concerns."

     b. Criticisms about the World Bank and IMF focus on conditions placed on borrowing countries for access to funding (which may include loss of local economic authority), its dominance by industrialized nations as

well as projects that it has funded that may harm the environment. One recent criticism is the disregard for indigenous people's right to self determination. See http://forestpeoples.gn.apc.org/index.htm. Another criticism is of human rights violation at a World Bank supported gold mine. http://www.leat.or.tz/active/buly.

CHAPTER 33 Questions for Thought and Review

2. When someone sends 100 British pounds to a friend in the United States, the transaction will show up in the component of the current account called net transfers, which include foreign aid, gifts, and other payments to individuals not exchanged for goods or services. It will also appear on the capital account as a receipt of foreign currency just like the purchase of a British stock or bond.

4. A capital and financial account deficit means that financial outflows are more than financial inflows. The excess supply of dollars is balanced by a current account surplus, which means Americans are producing more than they are consuming. In the long run, capital account deficits are nice because you are building up holdings of foreign assets, which will provide a future stream of income.

6. In the early 1980s the U.S. government was pursuing tight monetary policy and expansionary fiscal policy. The high interest rate resulted in a strong dollar. Expansionary fiscal policy failed to stimulate domestic demand as export demand fell sharply due to the high dollar. This, accompanied by the high interest rate that had cut investment, drove the economy into a recession with twin deficits, but a strong dollar.

8. It was likely increasing because imports are positively correlated with national income.

10. If Japan ran an expansionary monetary policy, it would increase Japanese imports of U.S. goods and make American goods comparatively more competitive, and thereby decrease the U.S. trade deficit. The U.S. dollar would rise relative to the Japanese yen.

12. Since the effect of monetary policy is to push the exchange rate down in all effects, this will not change the effect presented in the chapter, other than to eliminate the effect through income and replace it with the effect through prices.

14. We would use a combination of purchasing power parity, current exchange rates, and estimates of foreign exchange traders to determine the long-run exchange rate of the Neverback. This combination approach can be justified only by the "that's all we have to go on" defense. Since no one really knows what the long-run equilibrium exchange rate is, and since that exchange rate can be significantly influenced by other countries' policies, the result we arrive at could well be wrong.

16. Both fixed and flexible exchange rate systems have advantages and disadvantages. While fixed exchange rates provide international monetary stability and force governments to make adjustments to meet their international problems, they have some disadvantages as well: they can become unfixed, creating enormous instability; and their

effect of forcing governments to make ad their international problems can be a disa as an advantage. Flexible rates prov incremental adjustment of exchange governments to be flexible in conducting d and fiscal policies, but also allow speculati jumps in exchange rates (and, as before, flexibility may be a disadvantage too). Giv minuses of both systems, most policyma for a policy in between-partially flexible ex

18. They will sell that currency, which will force to use reserves to protect the currer government runs out of reserves, it may be f the currency, making the speculator's pr fulfilling.

20. He was advocating significant trade rest trade restrictions would have likely provoke our trading partners, hurting international c hurting the world economy.

22. The U.S. would want to hold up the value c help prevent the surge in import prices tha from the fall in exchange rates, and to keep f buying our assets cheaply. Other countries higher value of the dollar in order to kee competitive with U.S. goods.

24. Two disadvantages is loss of independent mo for those countries that adopt the euro and lo identity because the country must give up its c

Problems and Exercises

4.

6.

8.

2. The graph below shows the fundamental an supply and demand for British pounds sterling dollars, and the effect of the following change

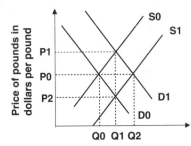

Quantity of pounds

     a. A rise in the UK price level causes foreign become cheaper. British demand for foreign will tend to increase, and foreign demand fo will tend to decrease. Thus supply of poun outward from S0 to S1 and the demand for th shifts inward from D1 to D0. The exchange r of the pound falls from P1 to P2.

     b. A reduction in U.S. tariffs would tend to s demand for pounds to the right from D0 to Americans buy more imports from the UK. If s at S1, the exchange rate value of the pound ris P2 to P0.

   c. We suspect that the country would not be happy about the proposal because its adoption might lead to a deep recession, which is politically unpopular.

6. **a.** One would expect less stabilization, because when income falls, foreign incomes will likely fall too, and thus decrease exports, which will further decrease income.

   b. This would increase the possibility of a global recession.

   c. Answers on this can differ; an expected answer is that one will need coordinated counter cyclical policy organized through G-8, World Bank, or some other international organization.

Web Questions

2. **a.** Conditionality is the requirement by the IMF that its aid recipients follow certain policies, or conditions, in order to receive aid.

   b. Typical IMF financing preconditions include reducing government spending, budget deficits, and foreign (external) debt, reducing the rate of money growth to control inflation, raising real interest rates to market levels and removing barriers to export growth. When implemented, these conditions lead in the short term to (a) a devaluation of local currency, (b) a lower trade deficit and (c) domestic problems including slower growth and unemployment.

   c. Mexico, Russia, Pakistan, Thailand and South Korea are examples of countries that have received IMF financing over the past five years.

   d. Mission creep is the term used to describe the increasing influence of the IMF on domestic policies of its aid recipients. In addition to the enforcement of financial reform in exchange for aid, the IMF has been accused of advocating an agenda in relation to geopolitics and international security, social safety nets, government corruption, the environment and human rights.

b. It would shift the LAS curve out.

c. Using Okun's rule of thumb—which says that for every 1 percentage point rise in the unemployment rate, income falls by 2 percent—a 0.5 percentage point decline in the target unemployment rate would imply a rise in potential income of 1 percent, or $100 billion.

Web Questions

2. a. The process starts off by the formulation of the President's budget for a fiscal year. The budget documents are then prepared and transmitted to the Congress. The Congress, after reviewing this budget, develops its own budget and accepts the expenditure and revenue bills. The agency managers then execute the budget in the fiscal year after which information for the actual spending and receipts becomes available.

b. It takes about two years. For example, for Fiscal Year 2001 (begins October 1, 2000) the President formulated the budget between February-December 1999, and the data on the expenditures and receipts became available in October-November 2001.

c. The President and the Congress have to decide upon the discretionary spending, which accounts for one-third of all federal spending. The remaining two-thirds of all federal spending, called mandatory spending, is authorized by permanent laws.

● CHAPTER 31 Questions for Thought and Review

2. The government can finance a deficit in either of two ways: by selling bonds or by printing money.

4. There are technical aspects of the deficit that must be understood in order to undertake a meaningful discussion of the problems deficits and debts pose for society. Since a deficit is defined as a shortfall of revenues compared to expenditures, these technical aspects include what you define as revenue and what you define as expenditure.

6. A structural deficit would exist even if the economy were at its potential level of income, which would be at full employment, or at where the unemployment rate is equal to the normal rate of unemployment. If an economist believed that the normal rate of unemployment was 4 percent instead of 6 percent, then the difference between the economy's current state and the potential income level would be larger, leading to a greater passive deficit and therefore a smaller structural deficit. Thus, it is Mr. A who should also say that the structural deficit is $20 billion.

8. It would not differ; expected inflation does not enter into the determination of the real deficit.

10. Three ways individual debt can be said to differ from government debt are: (a) government is ongoing and therefore never needs to pay back the debt; (b) government can pay off the debt by creating money; and (c) much of the government debt is internal debt owed to its own citizens and agencies.

12. Deficits are only a summary measure of the economy. A government can undertake significant future obligations and therefore get itself into trouble even if it is not running a deficit.

14. Because of the baby boom, there were many people working and relatively few collecting Social Security in the late 1990s. This caused a surplus in the Social Security Trust Fund. Since that Trust Fund is part of the government budget, the Social Security system is a primary reason for the surpluses.

16. It depends. Clearly, there is some tendency for the deficit to raise the interest rate, thereby decreasing investment and hence future growth. However, to the degree that the government spending is itself productive, not having the deficit could also decrease future growth. The ultimate effect depends on the relative size of the two effects.

Problems and Exercises

2. a. The passive deficit must be zero since it is defined as zero at potential output.

b. The structural deficit is $200 billion.

c. Now $60 billion of that deficit is passive and $140 is structural since revenue would increase by $60 billion if output rose to potential.

d. Now there is a passive surplus of $30 billion, and a structural deficit of $230 billion because revenue would decline by $30 billion if output declined to -potential.

e. The structural deficit is likely of more concern to -policymakers because normal stabilization policies will not remove it.

4. a. Debt service payments are 0.06 times $360 billion = $21.6 billion.

b. The nominal deficit is $160 - (\$21.6 + 145) = \$6.6$ billion.

c. The real deficit equals the nominal deficit ($6.6 billion) $- 0.03 \times \$360$ billion $= \$4.2$ billion surplus.

6. To make the deficit look as small as possible, we would do the following:

a. Enter government pensions when they become payable, not on an accrual basis.

b. Treat the sale of land as current income rather than spreading it out with the sale of an asset.

c. Include Social Security taxes as a current revenue because at this time revenue from Social Security exceeds payment.

d. Count prepayment of taxes as current income instead of reserves for future taxes.

e. Count expenditures on F-52 bombers as capital -xpenditures do not include their depreciation in the government accounts.

Web Questions

2. a. 28 percent is held as bills, 49 percent as notes, and 19 percent as bonds, 3 percent is held as inflation-indexed notes and an additional 1 percent as inflation-indexed bonds.

b. Intragovernmental holdings are securities held by government trust funds, revolving funds, and special funds.

c. The debt will decline during a year in which there is a budget surplus.

CHAPTER 32 Questions for Thought and Review

2. You can't just judge an economy; you must judge the entire culture. Some developing countries have cultures that, in some people's view, are preferable to ours.

4. The exchange rate method uses current exchange rates to compare relative incomes while the purchasing power parity method compares incomes by looking at the domestic purchasing power of money in different countries. Because many developing countries' currencies are undervalued, the current exchange rate overstates the income disparity between developed and developing countries.

6. Three ways in which institutions differ in developing countries are that (a) basic market institutions with well-defined property rights do not, in many cases, exist; (b) there is often a dual nature to the economy; and (c) fiscal structures with which to adequately implement fiscal policy often do not exist.

8. An economist might favor activist policies in developed countries and laissez-faire policies in developing countries because the policies one favors depends on the desire and the ability of government to work for and achieve the goals of its policies. Different views of government can lead to different views of policy. Since many economists have a serious concern about the political structure in developing countries, but less concern about it in developed countries, they can favor one set of policies for developing countries and another set for developed countries.

10. A regime change is a change in the entire structure within which the government and economy interact, whereas a policy change is a change in one aspect of government action.

12. Governments act to maintain their positions in power, and often feel that in order to do so, they have no choice but to print more money; central banks in developing countries often do not enjoy full independence, and thus cannot resist these pressures (and may not want to, since they also desire to keep the government in power.) For those making the decisions, the short-term benefits of the 'inflation solution,' keeping regimes in power, outweigh any long-term hyperinflationary consequences.

14. Investment and savings are low in developing countries because income is low, and poor people don't have a whole lot left over to save. The rich often put their savings abroad due to the fear of political instability. As for the middle class, which is usually small in developing countries, the underdeveloped financial -sector leaves them with few opportunities to invest their savings.

16. An investor thinking of making an investment in a developing country should be concerned about the country's political stability and its economic condition (inflation, etc.). The existing amount of debt may also be a matter of concern.

18. Corruption limits investment and growth because knowing that payments of graft must be made prevents many people from undertaking actions that might lead to growth. Tax revenues are often diverted to those in power instead of going into legitimate productive investment, and the same is sometimes true of foreign aid money from abroad. But that does not answer the issue, since one must deal with the political reasons why the government increases the money supply.

20. The UN could encourage the development of microcredit banks, like the Grameen Bank, which provide a low-cost alternative to money lenders. There are also significant social and cultural limitations in many areas that limit women entrepreneurs, as well as the lack of day-care alternatives to being a full-time mother.

Problems and Exercises

2. This exercise asks you to spend a day living like someone in a developing country, and then to read this chapter and contemplate the degree to which someone in such a situation can pull himself or herself up by the bootstraps.

4. a. I would want to emphasize those skills which have the highest per-dollar return—those that would lead to development. These would probably be the basic reading, writing, and problem-solving skills that fit the indigenous culture, as well as technological and computer training.

   b. This differs from the ideal educational system in the United States because the U.S. culture is different and U.S. economic problems are different. Thus, in the United States the focus would be more abstract analysis and becoming generally educated and cultured, while in developing countries the focus would be agricultural science and basic skills.

   c. This is an open-ended question. The relevant -question would be: How much would individuals be willing to pay for courses that do not result in a credential compared to how much they would be willing to pay for a credential without the-coursework?

6. a. I agree with this statement because of the differing importance of institutions. A detailed knowledge of a country's institutions and culture is necessary to make prescriptions for development. I disagree with this statement to the degree that the lessons learned from a general theory say that development requires stability of political structures and of economic -environment and the need for savings applies across countries. The solutions are specific to the countries but fall within a general framework.

   b. This argument is made for developing countries because culture and traditional institutions play a larger role in the growth in these economies.

Web Questions

2. a. From their website: "The Bretton Woods Project works as a networker, information-provider, media informant and watchdog to scrutinise and influence the World Bank and International Monetary Fund. It monitors projects, policy reforms and the overall management of the Bretton Woods institutions with special emphasis on environmental and social concerns."

   b. Criticisms about the World Bank and IMF focus on conditions placed on borrowing countries for access to funding (which may include loss of local economic authority), its dominance by industrialized nations as well as projects that it has funded that may harm the environment. One recent criticism is the disregard for indigenous people's right to self determination. See http://forestpeoples.gn.apc.org/index.htm. Another criticism is of human rights violation at a World Bank supported gold mine. http://www.leat.or.tz/active/buly.

CHAPTER 33 Questions for Thought and Review

2. When someone sends 100 British pounds to a friend in the United States, the transaction will show up in the component of the current account called net transfers, which include foreign aid, gifts, and other payments to individuals not exchanged for goods or services. It will also appear on the capital account as a receipt of foreign currency just like the purchase of a British stock or bond.

4. A capital and financial account deficit means that financial outflows are more than financial inflows. The excess supply of dollars is balanced by a current account surplus, which means Americans are producing more than they are consuming. In the long run, capital account deficits are nice because you are building up holdings of foreign assets, which will provide a future stream of income.

6. In the early 1980s the U.S. government was pursuing tight monetary policy and expansionary fiscal policy. The high interest rate resulted in a strong dollar. Expansionary fiscal policy failed to stimulate domestic demand as export demand fell sharply due to the high dollar. This, accompanied by the high interest rate that had cut investment, drove the economy into a recession with twin deficits, but a strong dollar.

8. It was likely increasing because imports are positively correlated with national income.

10. If Japan ran an expansionary monetary policy, it would increase Japanese imports of U.S. goods and make American goods comparatively more competitive, and thereby decrease the U.S. trade deficit. The U.S. dollar would rise relative to the Japanese yen.

12. Since the effect of monetary policy is to push the exchange rate down in all effects, this will not change the effect presented in the chapter, other than to eliminate the effect through income and replace it with the effect through prices.

14. We would use a combination of purchasing power parity, current exchange rates, and estimates of foreign exchange traders to determine the long-run exchange rate of the Neverback. This combination approach can be justified only by the "that's all we have to go on" defense. Since no one really knows what the long-run equilibrium exchange rate is, and since that exchange rate can be significantly influenced by other countries' policies, the result we arrive at could well be wrong.

16. Both fixed and flexible exchange rate systems have advantages and disadvantages. While fixed exchange rates provide international monetary stability and force governments to make adjustments to meet their international problems, they have some disadvantages as well: they can become unfixed, creating enormous instability; and their

effect of forcing governments to make adjustments to meet their international problems can be a disadvantage as well as an advantage. Flexible rates provide for orderly incremental adjustment of exchange rates and allow governments to be flexible in conducting domestic monetary and fiscal policies, but also allow speculation to cause large jumps in exchange rates (and, as before, the government flexibility may be a disadvantage too). Given the pluses and minuses of both systems, most policymakers have opted for a policy in between-partially flexible exchange rates.

18. They will sell that currency, which will force the government to use reserves to protect the currency. Once the government runs out of reserves, it may be forced to devalue the currency, making the speculator's predictions self-fulfilling.

20. He was advocating significant trade restrictions. These trade restrictions would have likely provoked retaliation by our trading partners, hurting international cooperation, and hurting the world economy.

22. The U.S. would want to hold up the value of the dollar to help prevent the surge in import prices that would result from the fall in exchange rates, and to keep foreigners from buying our assets cheaply. Other countries would want a higher value of the dollar in order to keep their goods competitive with U.S. goods.

24. Two disadvantages is loss of independent monetary policy for those countries that adopt the euro and loss of national identity because the country must give up its own currency.

Problems and Exercises

2. The graph below shows the fundamental analysis of the supply and demand for British pounds sterling in terms of dollars, and the effect of the following changes:

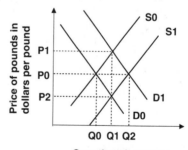

a. A rise in the UK price level causes foreign goods to become cheaper. British demand for foreign currencies will tend to increase, and foreign demand for pounds will tend to decrease. Thus supply of pounds shifts outward from S0 to S1 and the demand for the pound shifts inward from D1 to D0. The exchange rate value of the pound falls from P1 to P2.

b. A reduction in U.S. tariffs would tend to shift the demand for pounds to the right from D0 to D1 as Americans buy more imports from the UK. If supply is at S1, the exchange rate value of the pound rises from P2 to P0.

c. A boom in the UK economy means an increase in its income, causing an increased demand for imports and an increase in the demand for the foreign currency to buy those imports, thus resulting in an increase in the supply of pounds. (This may also set off an expectations effect.) Thus, the supply of pounds shifts outward from S0 to S1. If demand is at D0, the exchange rate value of the pound falls from P0 to P2.

d. If interest rates in the UK rise, there will be an increased demand for its assets, so the demand for pounds will increase from D0 to D1 and the supply of pounds will decrease from S1 to S0 as fewer British investors sell their pounds to buy foreign assets. The exchange rate value of the pound rises from P2 to P1.

4. a. Supplier; b. Supplier; c. Supplier;
   d. Demander; e. Demander; f. Demander.

6. a. Current account
   b. Current account
   c. Current and capital and financial accounts
   d. Current account
   e. Capital and financial account

8. a. If foreigners start believing that there is an increased risk of default, they will require a higher premium to buy U.S. bonds. That is, they will offer a lower price to buy them (demand for U.S. bonds will shift to the left). As this happens, bond prices will fall and interest rates, which move in the opposite direction from their prices, will rise. The value of the dollar will fall as a result of the lower demand for bonds (foreigners will not be purchasing as many dollars). That is, the demand for dollars will also decline, lowering the value of the dollar.

   b. Higher interest rates increase the cost of borrowing. This hurts in the short run by reducing aggregate spending and crowding out private investment, a source of long-term growth for the U.S. economy. A lower value of the dollar may increase the competitiveness of U.S. goods in the global economy, but it also makes imports to the United States more expensive, which, in addition to hurting individuals, may hurt businesses who use imports as intermediate goods in their production processes.

Web Questions

2. The answer to this question depends on the country chosen. We chose Brazil.
   a. The Brazilian currency is the real.
   b. The currency remained virtually unchanged from 2004 to 2005.
   c. Brazil has gotten inflation under control. Unemployment is expected to decline as the economy continues to grow. Fiscal spending is under control. The economy appears to be in good health, which may be contributing to a stable currency.

CHAPTER 34 Questions for Thought and Review

2. At the time that this was written, the U.S. trade deficit had risen to record highs. Still, it is unclear whether we should want to lower the U.S. trade deficit. The trade deficit was in part due to the fact that the economy has been growing for nine consecutive years. As long as the United States can borrow or sell assets, it can have a trade deficit. On the other hand, the more the United States borrows, the more U.S. assets foreigners own. Eventually, the United States will have to run a trade surplus.

4. A contractionary monetary policy by Japan and China would decrease Japanese and Chinese importation of US goods and would make the U.S. trade deficit worse.

6. If the recession was caused by a fall in domestic expenditures, we would expect that its trade balance was moving toward surplus. If, however, the recession was caused by a fall in exports, we would expect that its trade balance was moving toward deficit. The G-8 countries were trying to get Japan to boost its economy by increasing aggregate expenditures with expansionary monetary policy.

8. To finance the debt the U.S. government has to sell more bonds. Because foreign also demand these bonds (demand is greater), the government doesn't have to pay as high interest rates as it would if only U.S. investors demanded government bonds. Thus, the interest rate doesn't rise as much and crowding out is reduced.

10. The costs of internationalizing the debt are that interest and profits must be paid on the capital owned by foreigners. Future consumption must be reduced to pay that amount.

Problems and Exercises

2. a. I'd rather be holding other currencies because their price is expected to rise. I could buy them low and sell them high for a profit.
   b. The same argument doesn't hold for China because it has greater concerns than personal profit, such as the effect of a falling dollar on its economy.
   c. It might want to buy dollars to keep up the dollar's value. In fact, since the government can print yuan, it could theoretically buy as many dollars as it desires. It would want to buy dollars if it feels that the declining dollar would harm its exports. A declining dollar makes Chinese exports more expensive for Americans to buy and falling exports would slow the Chinese economy.

4. a. We would suggest that the IMF require a contractionary policy for both monetary and fiscal policy. I would, however, suggest a relatively more contractionary fiscal policy so that the exchange rate would also fall while inflation falls, boosting -exports.
   b. This would tend to slow inflation, after an initial burst due to a fall in the exchange rate. The policy, however, would hinder growth and push the economy into a recession.